Henry O.

Bari

Germany 1984.

THE IRISH CRIMINAL PROCESS

The Irish Criminal Process

Edward F. Ryan, M.A. (Cantab.)
of the Middle Temple,
a Bencher of King's Inns,
Barrister-at-Law,
Professor of Common Law,
University College, Cork

and

Philip P. Magee, LL.B. (Q.U.B.), LL.M. (Exon.)
of the Inn of Court of Northern Ireland
and King's Inns,
Barrister-at-Law,
One time Lecturer in Law,
The Queen's University of Belfast
and University College, Cork

THE MERCIER PRESS
DUBLIN and CORK

The Mercier Press Limited
4 Bridge Street, Cork
24 Lower Abbey Street, Dublin 1

ISBN 0 85342 700 3

Printed in Ireland by the Leinster Leader Limited.

PREFACE

This book is an attempt to satisfy the needs of law students and of practitioners with some degree of academic and comparative treatment. The result may be to satisfy none, the student finding too much citation, the practitioner irritated by what is to him trite explanation, both practitioners and academics sometimes regretting the acknowledged imbalance. We hope that the needs of the practitioner and the student may to some extent be balanced by the relegation to Appendices of the details of some statutes and rules, reproduced by kind permission of the Comptroller of Government Publications.

The book is not offered as an Irish reproduction of Archbold's *Pleading Evidence and Practice in Criminal Cases,* the practitioner's bible, first published in 1822 and now in its forty-first edition, nor as an up-dated version of Sandes' *Criminal Law and Procedure in the Republic of Ireland,* of which the last edition appeared in 1951, although we acknowledge our indebtedness to both those invaluable works, and constant reference is made to Archbold (41st Edition, unless otherwise stated) for particulars of the English authorities. We hope, however, that nearly all modern Irish cases of which reports and unreported judgments of the superior courts, circulated by permission of the Department of Justice, are available and which are still of significance have been cited. We are grateful to Geoffrey L. Frewen, Registrar of the High Court, and Neville Lloyd Blood, Secretary of the Incorporated Council of Law Reporting in Ireland, for the opportunity to read the manuscript of the former's recently published collection of unreported and reported decisions of the Court of Criminal Appeal and for advance page references, and to the latter for pre-publication sight of the most recent Irish Reports.

Whilst we have divided the labour we accept joint responsibility for the text, insofar as it tries to state the law in the light of reports and material available on 17th March, 1983, occasionally later, and for the most part agree on the comments and submissions, surprisingly perhaps in that the practical experience of one has been as prosecutor in the Republic and of the other for the defence in Northern Ireland.

We apologise for somewhat illogical sequences of footnotes and are conscious that we have been guilty of omission. We will welcome any constructive criticism. Up to three references only have been included in the Table of Cases.

We are particularly grateful to Leonard Wrigley, Professor of Management for procuring a grant from the University College Cork Management Fund.

Our thanks are also due to Dermot O'Connell, Chief Probation and Welfare Officer, Cork, for going to considerable trouble in helping with matters of sentence, particularly in relation to young persons; to T. C. Stokes in the Department of Justice; M. Donovan, Exchange Control Manager of the Central Bank; to our successive secretaries in the Department of Law and Maire Collins and the staff of the Typing Pool in University College, Cork, and to Margaret O'Riordan and Betty Conway for most of the early typing; to various colleagues for suggestions and encouragement; and especially to our publishers for their confidence, co-operation and courage in a comparatively untilled field.

We thank the President of the High Court for his gracious foreword.

Last as always, but never least, we thank our wives, Dodette and Mary, for their help and for concealing their impatience.

E.F.R.
P. P.M.
September 1983

FOREWORD

Any textbook on Irish Law from distinguished and experienced authorship, as this volume is, must be welcomed.

A particular want is filled by the publication now of a book on Criminal Practice and Procedure.

The last ten years has seen both as the result of judicial decision and legislation wide ranging changes in this field of law. It has also unfortunately been a period with an explosive increase in instances of serious crime which in turn has led to much public debate concerning our criminal law and its procedures.

This volume has with economy and an impressive accuracy analysed and brought up to date these topics.

I have no doubt that it will become an essential part of the equipment of the criminal lawyer and will make a significant contribution to the administration of justice in criminal cases.

The format and clarity of its contents allied to the academic qualifications of both the authors make this book not only a great assistance to students of criminal law but also a sound base for the initiation of discussion on reforms of our Criminal Code.

I confidently trust that its publication will be met with the success which it clearly deserves.

T. A. Finlay
President of the High Court
Four Courts
Dublin 7

Table of Contents

ARTICLES OF THE CONSTITUTION OF IRELAND

TABLE OF STATUTES

PART I

STATUTES APPLICABLE TO IRELAND

1861

1955

1956

1957

1958

1959

1977

1981

PART II

STATUTES NOT APPLICABLE TO IRELAND

TABLE OF STATUTORY ORDERS AND INSTRUMENTS

PART I

ORDERS etc. APPLICABLE TO IRELAND

PART II

INSTRUMENTS NOT APPLICABLE TO IRELAND

TABLE OF CASES

TABLE OF ABBREVIATIONS

Archbold	Archbold's *Pleading Evidence and Practice in Criminal Cases* (41st Edition, 1982, unless otherwise stated).
C.A.	Court of Appeal.
C.C.A.	Court of Criminal Appeal.
C.C.C.	Central Criminal Court.
Frewen	*Judgments of the Court of Criminal Appeal, 1924-1978*, edited by G. C. Frewen.
H.C.	High Court.
H.L.	House of Lords.
K.B.D.	King's Bench Division.
O.	Order.
Q.B.D.	Queen's Bench Division.
R., r.	Rule, Regulation.
S., s.	Section.
Sandes	*Criminal Law and Procedure in the Republic of Ireland* by R. L. Sandes (3rd Edition, 1951).
S.C.	Supreme Court.
S.I.	Statutory Instrument.
S.R. & O.	Statutory Rules & Orders.
Unrep.	Unreported.

For students of all ages

Aut lego vel scribo, doceo scrutorve sophiam;
obsecro celsithronum nocte dieque meum.
vescor, poto libens, rithmizans invoco Musas,
dormisco stertens. . .

Sedulius Scotus, Scholasticus, *at Liège*

CHAPTER 1

INTRODUCTION

Classification of offences

This work is concerned primarily with indictable criminal offences, from the time the offence is committed until the offender has been finally dealt with by process of law in the Republic of Ireland. It is not concerned with what constitutes a criminal offence, still less with substantive law governing particular offences. We are concerned in the main with procedures and are content to accept the exceedingly broad definition of a criminal offence as something which offends the social system to the extent of deserving punishment at the suit, or instance, of the State, whether it be murder or parking a motor car in a place where the appropriate authorities consider it should not be parked.

An indictable offence is one in which the guilt or innocence of the alleged offender, the accused or defendant, may only be determined, or must, if the accused so elects, be determined by a jury, directed on matters of law by a judge, on foot of an indictment, or formal charge, preferred by the People of Ireland, represented by the Director of Public Prosecutions or, in rare cases, by the Attorney General. Any offence which is not so triable is described as a summary offence, one which may be disposed of by a judge or justice without a jury.

It must, however, be remembered that summary proceedings, whilst they may be dealt with more quickly (and in that sense summarily) than the more formal proceedings before a judge and jury are nevertheless legal proceedings in every sense. Fundamental principles such as the presumption of innocence, rules of procedure and evidence, and principles of punishment apply equally to summary proceedings and to proceedings on indictment. That will become apparent by reference to cases in which similar principles have been applied.

In addition, in an attempt to deal with the whole jurisdiction of the superior courts in criminal matters, a chapter has been included relating to the protection of the liberty of the individual by way of habeas corpus applications[1] and the supervision by those courts of inferior courts, dealing for the most part with summary charges on what are commonly called State Side applications by way of certiorari, mandamus and prohibition.[2]

Indictable offences

The common law distinguished between three kinds of indictable offence: treason, felony and misdemeanour. The penalty for treason and (except in the cases of petty larceny and mayhem) for felony was death; the penalty for a misdemeanour might be imprisonment or a fine. For our purposes any distinction between treason and felony may now be disregarded and the other distinctions between felony and misdemeanour, save as regards powers of arrest and some consequences of conviction for felony, have become virtually obsolete.[3] The concept that felony was more serious than misdemeanour was frequently overlooked by the legislature even in the nineteenth century, when, for example, it provided that the penalty for simple larceny, or stealing, which is a felony, should be 5 years penal servitude, but the penalty for fraudulent conversion, a misdemeanour, should be 7 years.[4] In England the distinction was abolished by the Criminal Law Act, 1967; in Ireland the Criminal Justice Bill, 1967, sought to do the same, as well as to get rid of many other relics of the past which had ceased to serve any useful purpose, but a couple of controversial sections led to the Bill being dropped. The last Irish statutes to declare an offence to be a felony or misdemeanour were the Infanticide Act, 1949, and the Registration of Title Act, 1964, save that section 11 (1) of the

1. See Chapter 17, infra.
2. Id.
3. See Chapters 5 and 15, infra.
4. Larceny Act, 1861, ss. 4, 75; re-enacted, Larceny Act, 1916, ss. 2, 20.

Criminal Law Act, 1976, and section 20 (8) of the Criminal Law (Jurisdiction) Act, 1976, declared the common law misdemeanours of kidnapping and false imprisonment and the new offences relating to explosives and seizure of vehicles and new forms of robbery and burglary introduced by the latter Act to be felonies; otherwise modern statutes refer simply to 'offences', which may be made punishable on conviction on indictment, or punishable on summary conviction. Many such statutes create specific offences, with alternative penalties depending on whether the accused is convicted on indictment or summarily and in such hybrid cases it appears that the prosecution may elect how to proceed, although as will be seen the severity of the penalty is not the sole test as to whether an offence is a 'minor' offence.

The approach of the Constitution of Ireland enacted in 1937 is somewhat different. Article 38, so far as material to the present purpose, provides that no person shall be tried on any criminal charge without a jury, save that minor offences may be tried by courts of summary jurisdiction. If an offence is conceded to be a minor offence,[5] the accused has no right, unless there is some statutory provision to the contrary, to trial by jury.[6] The term 'minor offence' may lead to some confusion since any offence must vary in degree; to steal one pound is normally less serious than to steal a million, and stealing, if only because of the penalty it may incur, cannot be described as a minor offence, so that a person accused of that crime is always entitled to trial by jury; but, as will be seen, if the particular instance of the crime is a minor one, it may be dealt with summarily, if the accused consents, in which case the full penalty cannot be imposed.[7] What at present concerns us is the meaning to be attributed to the word 'minor' in Article 38 of the Constitution, rather than what might perhaps be more aptly described as 'trivial' examples of indictable offences, fit to be tried summarily.[8]

Before dealing with the general question of the right to trial by

5. *The State (McEvitt) v. Delap* [1981] I.R. 125 (S.C.).
6. Id.
7. Infra, pp. 227-228.
8. 'A trivial offence is quite a different thing from a minor offence.' *per* Lavery J. *Melling v. Ó Mathghamhna* [1962] I.R. 1, 12.

jury, it may be convenient to refer to certain cases in which it has been considered in relation to contempt of court, bearing in mind that, as will be seen, the most important matter determining whether an offence is minor or not is the severity of the penalty which may be imposed. A distinction is drawn for some purposes between what is called criminal contempt and civil contempt of Court. Criminal contempt is a contempt of the Court itself being calculated to prejudice the due course of justice, such as misbehaviour in Court or refusing to answer a question when required by the Court to do so, or commenting improperly on the conduct of the proceedings, described as scandalising the Court and punishable at common law as a misdemeanour, by imprisonment for an indefinite term. Civil contempt is the failure to obey an order of the Court made in civil proceedings. It is also punishable by imprisonment for an indefinite period.[9] To that extent every contempt involves the commission of a criminal offence. The right of the Court to deal summarily with either form of contempt is however part of the inherent jurisdiction of the Court and is not altered or diminished by Article 38 of the Constitution.[10]

Minor offences

Apart from the special case of contempt, the question of what constitutes a minor offence triable summarily was considered by the Supreme Court in *Melling v. Ó Mathghamhna.*[11] The accused was charged in the District Court with, in effect, smuggling butter, contrary to section 186 of the Customs (Consolidation) Act, 1876, which provided that the penalty was to be £100 or three times the value of the goods at the election of the Revenue Commissioners and that the offence was triable summarily; in addition section 132 of the Act of 1876 and section 12 of the Customs and Inland Revenue Act, 1879, provided that in default of payment of a fine the Justice might commit the offender to prison for a period (if the penalty was for £100 or more) of not

9. See the judgment of Ó Dálaigh C.J. in *Keegan v. de Búrca* [1973] I.R. 223, 227.
10. *The State (Commins) v. McRann* [1977] I.R. 78 (H.C.), not following *McEnroe v. Leonard* unrep., 9th December, 1975 (H.C.).
11. [1962] I.R. 1.

less than 6 nor more than 9 months and that for a second offence the penalty might be 12 months imprisonment.

The purported right of the Revenue Commissioners to elect which penalty the Court is to impose was held by the Supreme Court to be unconstitutional in *Deaton v. Attorney General,*[12] but this issue was not dealt with in *Melling*'s case in which the Revenue Commissioners elected for a penalty of £100 on each of 15 charges.[13] The accused obtained an adjournment of the District Court charges and instituted proceedings in the High Court claiming that the offences with which he was charged were criminal offences triable before a judge and jury, and not 'minor' offences within the meaning of the Constitution. Whilst the Supreme Court appears to have agreed that the offences were criminal offences[14] and on the appropriate criteria to determine whether an offence is to be regarded as a minor offence, the Court was divided on the application of these criteria to the particular offences in question.

Lavery J. (with whom Maguire C.J. and Maguire J. concurred) took the view that although the most important consideration was the severity of the penalty involved and that a penalty of even 11 months imprisonment was undoubtedly a serious penalty, some offences so punishable were triable summarily at the time the Constitution of 1922 was enacted and an offence carrying such a penalty could not be removed from the category of minor offences. He limited his decision, however, to cases in which the Revenue Commissioners elected to claim a penalty of £100 or treble the value of the goods being less than £100, and suggested that if they claimed substantially more the Justice might decline jurisdiction on the ground that the offence was not a minor offence. He also indicated that the moral quality of the act was something to be considered but merely suggested that an element of moral blame should be imputed to those who, on a commercial scale, violated the Revenue Acts. He held that the particular

12. [1963] I.R. 170.
13. The law has now been changed by the Finance Act, 1963, s. 34, as amended by the Finance Act, 1976, s. 44 which provide that the penalty is to be £500 or three times the value of the goods which ever is greater and that if it exceeds £500 the offence is to be triable on indictment.
14. See *The State (Gettins) v. Fawsitt* [1945] I.R. 183 (S.C.).

offences were, in the circumstances, properly to be regarded as minor offences which might be tried summarily.

Kingsmill-Moore J. took the opposite view, although with considerable doubt. He indicated that the intention of the Constitution was to safeguard the citizen so that the question of what is a 'minor' offence was to be considered primarily from the point of view of the person to be safeguarded and not that of executive convenience, although the general interest of the State was not to be ignored. He continued:[15]

> 'Regarded from the point of view of the citizen offender the difference between a minor offence and a major offence depends chiefly on the punishment which is meted out to the convicted criminal. It is this which stamps an offence as serious or not serious in his eyes. From a moral point of view the offence of smuggling varies enormously. The importation of a pair of silk stockings for personal use would not be too sternly reprobated even by strict moralists: but large-scale smuggling of valuable articles, organised and conducted as a profitable business, has not only been reprobated in severe terms by judges but would be regarded by most people as involving moral delinquency. If, however, the introduction of a pair of silk stockings is made punishable by a fine of £100 and imprisonment for six months certain if the offender cannot find the money, the offender, looking at the matter objectively, could say with reason that the offence had been stamped as major by the extent of the penalty and that, before being convicted of an offence involving such consequences, he should be able to claim that his guilt should be established before and by a jury.'

He adverted to the amounts which might be demanded and consequences, depending on the value of the goods and the ability of the offender to pay in a particular case, and stated that the Court must take into consideration the value of money when the Saorstát Éireann Constitution was enacted in 1922.

Ó Dálaigh J. (as he then was) also held that the offences in question were not 'minor' offences. He adverted to the question of when, in 1922, a fine reached such a point that it should be regarded as indicating that the offence was no longer to be looked on as minor taking into consideration the effect of the fine on the ordinary or average citizen with, if anything, a leaning in the

15. [1962] I.R. 1, 34.

direction of the people of humbler circumstances, stressing the fact that default would result in imprisonment for more than six months and taking the view that save in special cases six months imprisonment was recognised as the maximum term for minor offences.

The question again came before the Supreme Court in *Conroy v. Attorney General*[16] in which it was held that what may shortly be described as 'drunken driving' was properly treated as a minor offence triable summarily, notwithstanding that the offender could be imprisoned in default of payment of a fine, that conviction would entail a mandatory disqualification from holding a driving licence for not less than twelve months, and that it was not open to the Court to apply the Probation of Offenders Act, 1907.

Walsh J. summed up the result of the earlier case as establishing that the distinction between a minor offence and offences which should be regarded as non-minor depended on (1) the punishment prescribed for the offence, (2) the moral guilt involved, (3) the state of the law when the Constitution was enacted and (4) public opinion at the time of that enactment; he observed that the moral guilt attaching to an offence is a question of degree, depending on the circumstances of that offence. He took the view that imprisonment in default of payment of a fine was not primarily a method of punishment and the fact that the Probation of Offenders Act might not be applied meant that the legislature regarded the offence as not trivial, but not necessarily as not *minor*. Dealing with the question of disqualification he said:[17]

> 'In the opinion of this Court, so far as punishment is concerned, the punishment which must be examined for the purpose of gauging the seriousness of an offence is what may be referred to as "primary punishment". That is the type of punishment which is regarded as punishment in the ordinary sense and, where crime is concerned, is either the loss of liberty or the intentional penal deprivation of property whether by means of fine or other direct method of deprivation. Any conviction may result in many other unpleasant and

16. [1965] I.R. 411.
17. Id. 441.

even punitive consequences for the convicted person. By the rules of his professional association or organisation or trade association or any other body of which he is a member he may become liable to expulsion or suspension by reason of his conviction on some particular offence or perhaps on any offence. His very livelihood may depend upon the absence of a conviction in his record. These unfortunate consequences are too remote in character to be taken into account in weighing the seriousness of an offence by the punishment it may attract.'

He added:[18]

> 'Undoubtedly disqualification may have a deterrent quality but that does not make it a punishment.'

In *The State (Sheerin) v. Kennedy*[19] the Court again observed that the most important factor in determining whether an offence was a minor offence was the punishment which might be imposed, and that an offence committed by a young person and punishable by detention from two to three years in St Patrick's Institution could not be a minor offence.

In *Re Haughey*[20] Mr Haughey had been called upon to show cause why he should not be committed for contempt of Court in refusing to answer questions before the Committee of Public Accounts of Dáil Éireann. Failure to do so was declared to be an offence and punishable by the High Court *in like manner as if* the person concerned had been guilty of contempt of the High Court. In *The State (Commins) v. McRann*[21] Finlay P. distinguished the case of contempt involved in *Re Haughey* from other cases of contempt proper, emphasising the words 'as if' and observing that the relevant provision of the Committee of Public Accounts of Dáil Éireann (Privilege and Procedure) Act, 1970, created a distinct criminal offence. This was in fact stated by Ó Dálaigh C.J. in *Re Haughey,* when he said, 'the present case is not a case of contempt of Court but an ordinary criminal prosecution.'[22] In *Re Haughey* the Supreme Court held that in so far as that offence

18. Id. 442; see also *The State (Pheasantry Ltd) v. Donnelly* [1982] I.L.R.M. 512 (H.C.) (forfeiture of liquor licence).
19. [1966] I.R. 379 (S.C.).
20. [1971] I.R. 217 (S.C.).
21. [1977] I.R. 78 (H.C.).
22. [1971] I.R. 217, 248.

entailed punishment as if it was contempt of the High Court, namely imprisonment for an indefinite term, it could not be described as a minor offence and that a person charged with the offence was entitled to trial by jury, apart from the fact that if it were minor it would not be tried summarily by the High Court, not being a court of summary jurisdiction. Ó Dálaigh C.J. also accepted that: 'in ordinary criminal prosecutions, the severity of the penalty actually imposed, is the relevant criterion.'[23]

Section 56 of the Road Traffic Act, 1961 made it an offence, triable summarily and punishable by a fine of £100 and/or six months imprisonment, to drive a motor vehicle without insurance. Section 57 of the same Act empowered the Justice to inflict a further fine not exceeding the amount of the damages which might be recoverable in civil proceedings by a person injured on the occasion of the offence. In *Cullen v. Attorney General,*[24] Hamilton J. held that whilst the punishment imposed by section 56 was not of itself sufficient to exclude the offence from the category of a minor offence, the provisions of section 57, purporting to impose an additional fine which would take it out of that category, were unconstitutional.

In *Kostan v. Ireland*[25] McWilliam J. held that unlawful entry by a foreign sea fishing boat within the exclusive fishing limits of the State entailing forfeiture of fish and gear, which might be worth anything up to £100,000, was not a minor offence triable summarily.[26] In *The State (Rollinson) v. Kelly*[27] it was held by Gannon J. that a fine of £500 imposed under the Finance Act, 1926, for failure by a bookmaker to forward returns of bets took the case out of the category of minor offences, having regard *inter alia* to judicial salaries at the time of the enactment.

Finally in *O'Sullivan v. Hartnett*[28] the accused had been charged with having in his possession 900 salmon contrary to

23. Adopting Marshall J. in *Frank v. United States* 395 U.S. 147 (1969).
24. Unrep. 7th July, 1977 (H.C.); see also *Charlton v. Ireland*, unrep., 7th February, 1983.
25. Unrep. 10th February, 1978 (H.C.).
26. The offence has now been made indictable, and the penalties increased by sections 2 and 5 of the Fisheries (Amendment) Act, 1978.
27. [1982] I.L.R.M. 249 (H.C.).
28. [1981] I.L.R.M. 469 (H.C.).

section 182 of the Fisheries Consolidation Act, 1959,[29] and the offence carried a fine of £25 with a further £2 for each fish and forfeiture of the fish. McWilliam J. observed that whilst the moral guilt of catching one salmon when fishing for trout with a trout rod was negligible, most people would agree that the moral guilt in catching 900 salmon illegally by means of a net or engine constructed for the purpose of catching a large number was considerable. The decision was upheld by the Supreme Court[30] in which Henchy J. indicated that the criteria for deciding whether an offence is minor or not might need to be reviewed but that an offence entailing a possible penalty of several thousand pounds could not be described as minor; he suggested that the line of demarcation between minor and non-minor must depend on the circumstances of each case, having distinguished between larceny of one pound and of a million pounds – although it is submitted that this distinction goes not so much to the nature of the offence as to whether it is trivial or not.

It would thus appear that the longest term of imprisonment which may be imposed by the District Court if an offence is to fall into the category of minor offences is twelve months. As regards maximum fines the Courts, in determining what was meant by 'minor' in the successive Constitutions, have combined consideration of money values at the time of enactment of the relevant Constitution and at the time of enactment of the relevant statute. The overall view seems to have been that any offence which might incur a fine (apart from ancillary payments) in excess of £100 in 1922 or even in 1937 could not be regarded as minor but the power of the legislature to prescribe higher fines in subsequent statutes in order to keep pace with inflation has not been questioned. In a great many cases the question is, in a sense, academic since the accused must consent to disposal of the case summarily as a 'minor' offence in so far as it is liable to be treated as a trivial example of the offence in question. At the same time there are an increasing number of cases in which no right to trial by jury is given to the accused and in which substantially higher

29. The offence has now been made indictable, and the penalties increased by section 46 (1) of the Fisheries Act, 1980.
30. [1983] I.L.R.M. 79.

fines have been prescribed, although there seems to be some measure of inconsistency in the amount of fines and other penalties which may be imposed. Thus even in the case of purely summary offences, (for random examples) section 15 and the Schedule to the Companies Act, 1982, increases fines which may be imposed for purely summary offences against the Companies Act, 1963, to £500, while the Litter Act, 1982, Section 14, prescribes a fine of up to £800 for an offence under that Act. Similarly in the case of offences punishable on indictment, section 20 of the Transport (Tour Operators and Travel Agents) Act, 1982, prescribes maximum penalties on indictment of 5 years imprisonment and/or a fine of £100,000, for carrying on a tourist agency business without a licence, whereas section 15 and the Schedule to the Companies (Amendment) Act, 1982, increases the fine for making a false statement in a prospectus contrary to section 50 (1) (a) of the Companies Act, 1963, from £500 to a mere £2,500, without increasing the maximum term of imprisonment from 2 years, whilst the penalty for breaches of fire regulations under section 5 (2) of the Fire Service Act, 1981, is 2 years imprisonment and/or £10,000.

CHAPTER 2

THE CRIMINAL COURTS

Generally

The jurisdiction of the Irish courts is derived from the Constitution of Ireland – adopted and enacted by the people of Éire in 1937. Article 34 provides that justice is to be administered in courts established by law by judges appointed in the manner provided by the Constitution. Such courts are to comprise Courts of First Instance and a Court of Final Appeal. The Courts of First Instance are to include a High Court invested with full original jurisdiction in and power to determine all matters and questions whether of law or fact, civil or criminal, but may also include Courts of local and limited jurisdiction with a right of appeal as determined by law. The Court of Final Appeal is to be called the Supreme Court, and its decision in all cases is declared to be final and conclusive.

To these domestic courts must now be added the Court of Justice of the European Communities.[1]

Article 38 of the Constitution provides that no person shall be tried on any criminal charge save in due course of law and that except in three cases no person shall be tried on any criminal charge without a jury.

The exceptions are:

(a) that minor offences[2] may be tried by courts of summary jurisdiction,

(b) that special courts[3] may be established for the trial of offences in cases where it may be determined that the ordinary courts are inadequate to secure the administration of

1. Infra, pp. 22 sqq.
2. Supra, pp. 4 sqq.
3. Infra, pp. 18 sqq.

justice and the preservation of public peace and order and
(c) that military tribunals[4] may be established for the trial of offences against military law alleged to have been committed by persons while subject to military law and also to deal with a state of war or armed rebellion.

The ordinary courts

The present ordinary courts are the Supreme Court, the Court of Criminal Appeal, the High Court, the Circuit Court and the District Court and were established by the Courts (Establishment and Constitution) Act, 1961.[5] Between 1937 and 1961 the former courts retained their old jurisdiction by virtue of Article 58 of the Constitution.[6]

The Supreme Court and Court of Criminal Appeal have only appellate jurisdiction in criminal matters. The High Court has both original and quasi-appellate jurisdiction in such matters. The Circuit Court has both original jurisdiction and appellate jurisdiction and the District Court original jurisdiction only. To the extent that it is not conferred by the Constitution itself, the jurisdiction of these courts is regulated by the Courts (Supplemental Provisions) Act, 1961.

It is, however, to be remembered that whilst a court may have unlimited (or limited) jurisdiction as regards the type of case with which it may deal, that jurisdiction is only exercisable if the case is properly before the court. Thus the Central Criminal Court has jurisdiction to deal with any case of murder, *provided* that the accused has been properly returned for trial,[7] and the exercise of jurisdiction may be restricted according to where or when an offence is alleged to have been committed. As a general rule the courts are concerned only with offences committed within the State,[8] and local courts with offences committed within their

4. Infra, pp. 21-22.
5. Brought into force on 29th September 1961, S.I.217 of 1961.
6. *Sullivan v. Robinson* [1954] I.R. 161 (S.C.); see generally Kelly, *Irish Constitutional Law*, 577 sqq.
7. See however *The People v. Hannigan* [1958] I.R. 378 (C.C.A.), and *The State (Attorney General) v. Binchy* [1964] I.R. 395 (S.C.) as to the *prima facie* presumption of validity of the return.
8. Infra, Chapter 3.

respective areas[9] whilst in some cases criminal proceedings may not be instituted after a certain lapse of time.[10]

Apart from Special Criminal Courts and military courts the judiciary must be drawn from barristers and solicitors of a certain standing.

The Supreme Court

Article 34 of the Constitution confers on the Supreme Court appellate jurisdiction from all decisions of the High Court with such exceptions and subject to such regulations as may be prescribed by law; save, therefore, to the extent that its jurisdiction is restricted by Act of the Oireachtas an appeal lies to the Supreme Court from the High Court in every case. In criminal cases,[1] however, such appeals may be restricted.[2]

The Court consists of the Chief Justice, the President of the High Court and four ordinary judges.[3] Five members of the Court must sit to determine any question as to the incapacity of the President or the constitutionality of any Bill referred to the Court by the President; otherwise three members suffice.[4]

The Court of Criminal Appeal

Under section 3 of the Courts (Establishment and Constitution) Act, 1961, this Court is summoned in accordance with directions given from time to time by the Chief Justice. In practice it is convened once or more each term, according to the amount of business to be done.

It is duly constituted if it consists of not less than three judges – normally it does not consist of more – but the Chief Justice or a single judge of the Supreme Court may deal with interlocutory

9. Infra, pp. 61-62.
10. Infra, pp. 62 sqq.
1. *The State (Browne) v. Feran* [1967] I.R. 147 (S.C.) approving *Warner v. Minister for Industry and Commerce* [1929] I.R. 582 (S.C.) and *Attorney General (Fahy) v. Bruen* [1936] I.R. 750 (S.C.) and disapproving *The State (Burke) v. Lennon* [1940] I.R. 136 (S.C.); cf. *The People v. Lynch* [1982] I.R. 64.
2. Infra, Chapter 16.
3. Courts (Establishment and Constitution) Act, 1961. The number may be increased to five if a member of the Court is a member of the Law Reform Commission; Law Reform Commission Act, 1975, s. 14 (1).
4. Constitution of Ireland, Articles 12.3, 26.2; Courts (Supplemental Provisions) Act, 1961, s. 7 (4).

applications,[5] such as an application by an appellant for a free copy of the transcript, or shorthand note, of the evidence given before the court of trial. One of the three judges must be the Chief Justice or an ordinary judge of the Supreme Court nominated by him. The other two must be any two judges of the High Court (including the President of the High Court, if willing to act) nominated by the Chief Justice, but any other available judge or judges of the Supreme Court or the High Court may, at the request of the Chief Justice, attend as a member or members of the Court; this appears to mean that there must invariably be one member of the Supreme Court (other than the President of the High Court) and two judges from the High Court (of whom one may be the President) but that other judges from either Court may attend as additional members. The Court of Criminal Appeal has jurisdiction to hear appeals from the Central Criminal Court, the Circuit Court and the Special Criminal Court (when constituted).[6] The constitutionality of the Court has been challenged but upheld by the Supreme Court.[7]

The High Court

Apart from its original criminal jurisdiction, when sitting as the Central Criminal Court, which is considered below, the High Court has exclusive jurisdiction over applications for orders of habeas corpus, when a person claims that he is illegally detained, and orders of certiorari, mandamus and prohibition, where a person complains that the order of an inferior court or tribunal ought to be quashed or that such a court or tribunal should be directed to deal or not to deal with some particular matter.[8] It also has jurisdiction on appeals by way of the case stated from the District Court.

The Court consists of its President, of the President of the Circuit Court, *ex officio,* and not more than fourteen ordinary judges.[9] Normally cases are heard by a single judge, but the

5. Rules of the Superior Courts, 1961, O.86, r. 1.
6. Infra, Chapter 14.
7. *The State (Woods) v. Attorney General* [1969] I.R. 385; *The People v. Conmey* [1975] I.R. 341.
8. Infra Chapter 17.
9. Courts (Establishment and Constitution) Act, 1961, Courts (No. 2) Act, 1981,

President of the High Court may direct that any cause or matter or part of a matter be listed for hearing before two or more judges.[10] Under the former practice a Court consisting of more than one judge was termed a Divisional Court.[11]

The Central Criminal Court

This is the name given to the High Court when exercising its original criminal jurisdiction[12] and any references to the Central Criminal Court in any other enactment are to be construed as references to the High Court exercising such jurisdiction.[13] Since the High Court is vested with full original jurisdiction in all criminal matters by Article 34 of the Constitution the vesting in it by statute of any derivative original jurisdiction would appear to be unnecessary, and it is submitted that the derivative jurisdictions vested in it[14] are conferred either in relation to appellate[15] or quasi-appellate[16] jurisdictions or are conferred *ex majori cautela*. The Central Criminal Court's jurisdiction, which is original only, is exercised by a judge or judges of the High Court (including the President) nominated from time to time by the President of the High Court.[17] Thus two or more 'Central Criminal Courts' may, and often do, sit at the same time. The President may direct that two or more judges should sit together for the purpose of a particular case[18] but in practice a single judge invariably presides over the Court.

The Central Criminal Court has exclusive jurisdiction[19] in cases of treason, treason-felony and conspiracy to commit treason,[20] the major offences created by the Offences Against the

s. 1. The number may be increased to 15 if a member of a Court is a member of the Law Reform Commission; Law Reform Commission Act, 1975, s. 14 (1) as amended by the Courts (No. 2) Act, 1981, s. 2.

10. Rules of the Superior Courts, 1961, O.49 r. 1.
11. Judicature Act (Ireland), 1877, s. 45.
12. Courts (Supplemental Provisions) Act, 1961, s. 11 (1).
13. Id. s. 11 (4).
14. Id. s. 8 (2).
15. By way of appeal from the Circuit Court in civil cases only.
16. E.g. in its power to review decisions of inferior courts by way of certiorari.
17. Courts (Supplemental Provisions) Act, 1961, s. 11 (2) (a).
18. Id. s. 11 (2) (b).
19. Id. s. 25 (2), as extended by the Genocide Act, 1973, s. 2 (4).
20. Treason Act, 1939, ss. 2, 3.

State Act, 1939,[21] murder, attempt to murder, conspiracy to murder, piracy and genocide, including an offence by an accessory before or after the fact of any such crime.

The Circuit Court

The country is divided into 7 circuits[22] each of which, except Dublin and Cork, includes several counties. The Court consists of its President and not more than 12 ordinary judges, most of whom are assigned to particular Circuits.[23] The Court has the same original jurisdiction in relation to indictable offences as the Central Criminal Court, except in those cases mentioned above in which the latter Court has exclusive jurisdiction.[24] The Circuit Court also has appellate jurisdiction from the District Court.[25]

The District Court

The country is divided into a number of District Court Areas[26] and District Justices may be appointed and assigned to different areas.[27] The Court is a court of summary jurisdiction, in which a single Justice sits without a jury. It has in general no jurisdiction to dispose of indictable offences, although, as will be seen, it may in certain cases dispose of such offences if they are of a minor nature or if the accused pleads guilty, and it must investigate every other case if it is to be sent forward for trial to the Central Criminal Court or the Circuit Court.[28] The jurisdiction of the District Court is derivative in the sense that it has vested in it and transferred to it all criminal jurisdiction which was vested in the former District Court by virtue of a number of earlier enactments.[29]

21. Ss. 6, 7 and 8.
22. Dublin, Cork, Northern, Western, Midland, South Western and South Eastern: see Courts of Justice Act, 1953, s. 16 and Courts (Establishment and Constitution) Act, 1961, s. 4; Courts (Supplemental Provisions) Act, 1961, s. 20 (2).
23. Courts Act, 1977, s. 1 (2) as amended by the Courts Act, 1981, s. 30 (a).
24. Courts (Supplemental Provisions) Act, 1961, s. 25.
25. Courts of Justice Act, 1928, s. 18; Courts of Justice Act, 1953, s. 33, applied by Courts (Supplemental Provisions) Act, 1961, s. 22 (3) (a) (ii).
26. Courts (Supplemental Provisions) Act, 1961, s. 32.
27. Id. s. 32 (3).
28. Infra pp. 229 sqq.
29. Courts (Supplemental Provisions) Act, 1961, s. 33. The principal earlier enactments relating to criminal jurisdiction were the Courts of Justice Act, 1924, s. 78

Special Criminal Courts[1]

Provision for the establishment of special criminal courts was made by Part V of the Offences Against the State Act, 1939. That part of the Act is only in force so long as is provided by section 35 of the Act. It may be brought into force whenever the Government is satisfied that the ordinary courts are inadequate to secure the effective administration of justice and the preservation of public peace and order and that it is therefore necessary for it to come into force. In order to bring it into force the Government must make and publish a proclamation declaring that it is so satisfied and ordering that Part V of the Act should come into force. Any such proclamation may be annulled at any time by resolution of Dáil Éireann, without prejudice to the validity of anything done whilst the proclamation was in force. If at any time while Part V is in force the Government is satisfied that the ordinary courts are adequate to secure the administration of justice and the preservation of public peace and order it may make and publish a proclamation declaring that Part V should cease to be in force. Part V of the Act comes into force or ceases to be in force as the case may be at the date of publication of the relevant proclamation. A copy of such proclamation must be published in Iris Oifigiúil, the Official Gazette, and the Government may also publish a copy in any other manner it thinks proper.[2]

Once Part V of the Act has been brought into force the Government may by order declare any offence of a particular class or under any particular enactment to be a 'scheduled offence' for the purposes of that Part, if satisfied that the ordinary courts are inadequate to secure the effective administration of justice and the preservation of public peace and order in relation to such offence, and it may also, in effect, revoke any such order in relation to any offence of a particular class or kind or under any

and Criminal Justice Act, 1951. Section 78 of the Act of 1924 related to jurisdiction vested in the Dublin Metropolitan Divisional Justices and in Justices under the District Justices (Temporary Provisions) Act, 1923, and that Act had transferred to those Justices jurisdictions formerly exercised by Justices of the Peace and Resident Magistrates.

1. For a fuller treatment of the subject, see Robinson, *The Special Criminal Court* (1974).
2. See generally, Offences Against the State Act, 1939, s. 35.

particular enactment.[3]

Attempting or conspiring or inciting any other person to commit, or aiding or abetting the commission of any such 'scheduled offence' is itself a scheduled offence.[4]

As soon as may be after Part V of the Act of 1939 has been brought into force the Government must establish one or more courts, to be styled and known as Special Criminal Courts, for the purposes of that Part of the Act; and the Government may, if it thinks fit, reduce the number of Special Criminal Courts, if more than two, and abolish such as appear redundant.[5] Although in spite of its verbosity in other respects the Act of 1939 does not specifically so provide, every Special Criminal Court would appear to be *functus officio* once Part V ceases to be in force, since it is only established for the purposes of that Part.

The constitutionality of the Court was challenged but upheld by the Court of Criminal Appeal in *The People v. Doyle*[6] and by the Supreme Court in *Re MacCurtain.*[7]

Every Special Criminal Court must consist of an uneven number but there must be at least three members; subject to that the number of members of any such Court is determined by the Government and every member is appointed and is removable at will by the Government. No person may be appointed to be a member of a Special Criminal Court unless he is a judge of the High Court or Circuit Court, a Justice of the District Court, a barrister or solicitor of not less than seven years standing or an officer of the Defence Forces not below the rank of commandant.[8]

Part V of the Act of 1939 was first brought into force in 1939 and ceased to be in force in 1962, although apart from a few cases dealt with in 1961 and 1962 it did not operate since 1946. At that time the Special Courts consisted of members of the Defence Forces. It was again brought into force by proclamation

3. Id. s. 36 (3).
4. Id. s. 37.
5. Id. s. 38.
6. 77 I.L.T.R. 108.
7. [1941] I.R. 83; see also the judgment of the Supreme Court in *Re The Criminal Law (Jurisdiction) Bill* [1977] I.R. 129.
8. Offences Against the State Act, 1939, s. 39 (3).

on 26th May, 1972, and the present Special Criminal Court was established on 30th May, 1972.[9] The members at the present are all judges of the High Court or Circuit Court or District Justices, drawn from time to time from a panel of appointees. There is at present only one Special Criminal Court.

The offences declared to be scheduled offences when Part V of the Act of 1939 was last brought into force were any offence under the Malicious Damage Act, 1861, any offence under the Explosive Substances Act, 1883, any offence under the Firearms Acts, 1925 to 1971[10] and any offence under the Offences Against the State Act, 1939. To these was added[11] any offence under section 7 of the Conspiracy and Protection of Property Act, 1875 (intimidation, etc. with a view to compelling a person to do or abstain from doing what he has a legal right to do or abstain from doing).

The Court sits without a jury and the determination of any question is that of the majority.[12]

The object of the Act was evidently to provide a means of dealing with subversive activities of a political or allegedly political character, and in practice it is normally so used. At the same time it is to be noted that, for example, murder and bank robbery, however politically motivated, are not 'scheduled offences', whilst a great many charges of arson and malicious damage which have no political motivation whatever are scheduled.

The Special Criminal Court is given jurisdiction under sections 45 to 48 of the Offences Against the State Act, 1939, as adapted by section 3 of the Prosecution of Offences Act, 1974, not only in respect of any 'scheduled offence', (although the ordinary courts may in certain circumstances also have jurisdiction) but also in respect of other offences when the Director of Public Prosecutions certifies that in his opinion the ordinary courts are not adequate to secure the effective administration of justice and the preservation of public peace and order. This question is dealt

9. S.I. 142 of 1972.
10. This extends to an offence inserted by statute subsequent to the order in a statute referred to in the order, *The State (Daly) v. Delap,* unrep. 30th June, 1980.
11. S.I. 282 of 1972.
12. Offences Against the State Act, 1939, s. 40.

with more fully elsewhere as is the procedure before the Court.[13]

Military Courts

Chapter V of Part V of the Defence Act, 1954, provides for the convening of military courts, called courts-martial. Such courts have jurisdiction to try and punish any person for an offence against military law committed by such person while subject to military law as an officer or man.[1]

Liability to military law is imposed on officers and men of the Permanent Defence Force, in certain circumstances (e.g. when in training or in uniform) on officers and men of the Reserve Defence Force, and also on civilians attached to or accompanying any portion of the Defence Forces which is on active service.[2] A portion of the Defence Forces is deemed to be on active service if engaged in operations against an enemy or engaged in military operations in a place wholly or mainly occupied by an enemy;[3] 'enemy' includes armed mutineers, rebels, rioters and pirates.[4] More important in practice is that a portion of the Defence Forces is deemed to be on active service during any period in respect of which an order has been made declaring the Forces to be on active service, and such an order may be made by the Government during any period of emergency or whenever it considers the circumstances are of such a nature as to warrant its so doing.[5]

Chapter II of Part V of the Act of 1954 enumerates the offences which are offences against military law. Many of these are peculiar to military law (e.g. desertion, conduct to the prejudice of good order and military discipline) but in addition any person who, when subject to military law, commits an offence against the civil law is deemed to be guilty of an offence against military law.[6]

13. Infra, Chapter 14.
1. Defence Act, 1954, s. 192 (1).
2. Id. ss. 118, 119.
3. Id. s. 118 (2).
4. Id. s. 2.
5. Id. s. 5. Such orders have from time to time been made in respect of portions of the Defence Forces engaged on peace-keeping operations with the United Nations.
6. Id. s. 169.

Courts-martial are of two kinds, general and limited.[7] Membership of courts-martial is confined to officers of the Defence Forces, not less than five in the case of a general court-martial and three in the case of a limited court-martial; the lowest rank to be held by the president and members of the court depends on whether it is a general or a limited court-martial.[8] No such court may try a person for treason, murder, manslaughter or rape unless such a person is on active service.[9] A limited court-martial has no jurisdiction to try any person who is for the time being an officer or for any offence committed by such person while subject to military law as an officer; nor may it try any person for treason or murder or award any sentence greater than imprisonment.[10]

Further discussion of courts-martial is considered outside the scope of this work.[11]

The Court of Justice of the European Communities

Ireland's accession to the European Communities has resulted *inter alia* in the addition of the Court of Justice of the European Communities to the hierarchy of courts already involved in the exercise of criminal jurisdiction. In order to ensure that the founding Treaties of the Communities and the secondary legislation emanating therefrom[1] are interpreted in a uniform fashion and in a manner most conducive to the aims of the Communities, the Treaties themselves have made provision for a system of preliminary references from national courts to the European Court of Justice at Luxembourg.[2]

Article 177 (1) of the Treaty of Rome provides that the Court shall have jurisdiction to give preliminary rulings concerning:

7. Id. s. 186.
8. Id. ss. 189, 190.
9. s. 192 (3).
10. s. 192 (2).
11. See generally Defence Act, 1954, Part V; Courts-Martial Appeals Act, 1983; Rules of Procedure (Defence Forces), 1954, 1955 and 1983; Courts-Martial Appeals Court Rules, 1983; *Manual of Military Law* (12th ed. 1972) published by the British Ministry of Defence.
1. Given the effect of law by the European Communities Act, 1972, s. 2.
2. Treaty of Rome, Art. 177, Euratom Treaty, Art. 150 and European Coal and Steel Community Treaty, Art. 41.

(a) the interpretation of the Treaty;
(b) the validity and interpretation of acts of the institutions of the Community;
(c) the interpretation of the statutes of bodies established by an act of the Council, where those statutes so provide.

The Court of Justice sits in Luxembourg. It is currently composed of eleven judges with one from each member state and an extra judge who ensures that the court will not be evenly split on any issue when it sits *in pleno*.[3] The eleventh judge was added by a Council decision of 30th March, 1981. The ever-increasing workload of the Court may require more judges to be appointed and the Council of Ministers acting unanimously is empowered by the Treaty to make such an increase if so requested by the Court.[4]

In order to be qualified for appointment to the Court judges must either be eligible for appointment to the highest judicial offices in their respective Member States or alternatively be jurisconsults of recognised competence.[5] Ireland's representatives have both been members of the Supreme Court.[6]

The judges of the Court are appointed by common accord between the Governments of Member States for a term of six years[7] and it is quite common for these appointments to be renewed. The Treaty of Rome provides for the partial replacement of judges every three years and this policy of 'staggering' appointments ensures that some continuity in personnel is achieved.[8]

The judges are obliged by the Treaty to elect a President for a term of three years which may be renewed.[9] If the office of President falls vacant within this period the Court must appoint a successor. The President co-ordinates the business and administration of the Court and presides both at the hearing of cases by

3. Treaty of Rome, Art. 165 (as amended).
4. Id. Art. 165.
5. Id. Art. 167.
6. The first Irish judge, Ó Dálaigh C.J., resigned his appointment to the Court of Justice in 1974 to become President of Ireland and was replaced by O'Keeffe J. then President of the High Court and, *ex officio*, a member of the Supreme Court.
7. Treaty of Rome, Art. 167 (as amended).
8. Id. Art. 167 as amended by Act of Accession, Art. 19.
9. Treaty of Rome, Art. 167 (3).

the Plenary Court and at judicial deliberations.[10] The Court invariably sits in Plenary session to hear references under Article 177.[11]

The Court is subdivided into three chambers[12] and Presidents of the Chambers are elected by a secret ballot of the judges for one year renewable terms.

The appointment of Advocates General is specifically provided for.[13] The office of Advocate General is similar to that of the *Commissaire du Gouvernement* in the French *Conseil d'État.*[14] Although there is no counterpart of the Advocate General in the Irish adversary system the office has been likened to that of an 'institutionalised *amicus curiae*'.[15] There are currently five Advocates General[16] in the Court and this number may be increased. Advocates General enjoy the same seniority as judges of the Court and sit at the same level when the Court is hearing a case. It is the task of the Advocate General, when the written phase and the oral hearing of the parties have been completed, to collate and present to the Court a synthesis of the relevant law and to offer his views thereon. The judges are entirely free to accept or reject the conclusions and reasoning of the Advocate General.

The Court delivers a single collegiate judgment which it decides upon after private deliberations.[17] Whether a judgment has been arrived at by the judges on the basis of unanimity or by a majority is never disclosed. When a vote is taken by the judges in the deliberation room it is carried out in reverse order of seniority which is supposed to prevent the less experienced judges from being unduly influenced by their more experienced colleagues.[18].

10. Rules of Procedure of the Court of Justice, Art. 8.
11. See Treaty of Rome, Art. 165, but also Art. 95 of the Rules of Procedure of the Court of Justice which allows *certain* such referrals of an essentially technical nature to be heard by a Chamber.
12. Rules of Procedure of the Court of Justice, Art. 9 (as amended).
13. Treaty of Rome, Art. 166.
14. See Plender and Usher, *Cases and Materials on the Law of the European Communities,* 36; also Lasok and Bridge, *Law and Institutions of the European Communities,* 158.
15. See Brown and Jacobs, *The Court of Justice of the European Communities,* 58.
16. Council Decision, 30th March, 1981, increased the number from four.
17. See generally Brown and Jacobs, op. cit., 31-33.
18. Id. 168-169.

CHAPTER 3

LIMITATIONS ON JURISDICTION

I. TERRITORIAL LIMITATIONS

Whilst the High Court has full original jurisdiction under the Constitution, that jurisdiction is limited with certain exceptions to offences committed within the State, and the jurisdictions of the Circuit Court and District Court are for the most part further limited to particular areas. In addition, the jurisdiction of any court may be excluded by reference to the date of commission of an alleged offence.

Four primary principles may be stated as governing the jurisdiction enjoyed or claimed by municipal or domestic courts in criminal matters, namely the territorial principle, determining jurisdiction by reference to the place where the offence is committed; the universality principle, determining jurisdiction by reference to the custody of the person committing the offence, wherever it may have been committed; the nationality principle, determining jurisdiction by reference to the nationality or national character or place of residence of the offender; and the protective principle, providing for the peace, order and good government of the State.[1]

1. The Territorial Principle

The Irish courts exercise jurisdiction in respect of every criminal offence committed within the Republic of Ireland, regardless of the nationality[2] or domicile of the accused, but they do not in general claim jurisdiction in respect of offences committed elsewhere. It is, however, conceived that, as has been held in England, it is sufficient for some essential element of the offence to

1. O'Connell, *International Law* (2nd Edn. 1970) Vol. 2, 602-603, 826-836.
2. Aliens Act, 1935, s. 4; see also the Criminal Law (Jurisdiction) Act, 1976, s. 20 (3).

have been effected within the State, even though the accused may have organised it elsewhere.[3]

Thus, any person, whether an Irish citizen or not may be prosecuted in the State for robbing a bank in Dublin but not for robbing a bank in New York, although he might be liable for planning the Dublin robbery in New York. Certain statutory provisions which might seem at a casual glance to extend this jurisdiction appear in fact not to do so.

Thus, whilst it is an offence under section 33 (4) of the Larceny Act, 1916, as adapted,[4] for a person to receive or have in his possession within the State property known to have been stolen or unlawfully obtained elsewhere, the substantive offence is the *receiving or possession of the property* within the State. Again section 20 of the Misuse of Drugs Act, 1977, which relates to aiding and abetting the commission outside the State of an offence in relation to dangerous or otherwise harmful drugs, appears to apply only where the *aiding and abetting* takes place within the State.

The territorial jurisdiction of the Crown Court was, however, assumed to extend to the territorial waters of the United Kingdom[5] and this was confirmed by the Territorial Waters Jurisdiction Act, 1878. How far that Act applied since the establishment of the State, in view of its reference to 'Her Majesty's dominions', (an expression which has not been generally adapted) may have been doubtful, but the Act of 1878 was repealed by the Maritime Jurisdiction Act, 1959, in so far as it ever was in force in the State. The Act of 1959 provides that every offence committed within the territorial seas or internal waters of the State is an offence within the jurisdiction of the State and may be dealt with by a Court of competent jurisdiction even if com-

3. *R. v. Baxter* [1972] Q.B. 1; Archbold §2-28.
4. See Adaptation of Enactments Act, 1922, s. 3, Constitution (Consequential Provisions) Act, 1937, s. 2; *Attorney General v. Finegan* [1933] I.R. 292, (C.C.A.), *The People v. Ruttledge,* [1978] I.R. 376 (C.C.A.), *The State (Gilsenan) v. McMorrow* [1978] I.R. 360 (S.C.). It is submitted that s. 39 of the Larceny Act, 1916, which relates to the indictment of a person in one part of the United Kingdom for stealing property in another part is no longer material, since under the Acts of 1922 and 1937 the reference to the United Kingdom or Britain must be taken as a reference to the State.
5. O'Connell, op. cit., Vol. 1, 470 sqq.

mitted on board or by means of a foreign ship; and a person who commits such an offence may be arrested, tried and punished accordingly.[6] The territorial seas of the State are that portion of the sea which lies between the 'baseline' and the 'outer limit' of the territorial seas.[7] The 'outer limit' is the line every point of which is at a distance of three nautical miles from the nearest point of the baseline.[8] The 'baseline' (save as otherwise provided) is low watermark (a) on the coast of the mainland or of any island or (b) on any low-tide elevation situated wholly or partly at a distance not exceeding three nautical miles from the mainland or an island;[9] such a low tide elevation would appear to include a rock which might be exposed at low tide only. The Government may, however, prescribe straight baselines in relation to any part of the national territory and the closing line on any bay or mouth of a river and may revoke any such order.[10] The internal or inland waters of the State extend to all sea areas which lie on the landward side of the baseline, and all such sea areas are declared to be subject to the jurisdiction of the State to the same extent as its ports, harbours, bays, lakes and rivers, subject to the innocent right of passage for foreign ships in those sea areas which previously had been considered as part of the territorial seas or of the high seas.[11] Proceedings (other than the taking of depositions) for the prosecution of an alien for an offence alleged to have been committed on board or by means of a foreign ship may not in general be instituted without a certificate of the Minister for Foreign Affairs that the institution of the proceedings is, in his opinion, expedient;[12] an important exception is that of offences under Part XIII of the Fisheries (Consolidation) Act, 1959, relating to offences by sea fishing boats; another relates to

6. Maritime Jurisdiction Act, 1959, s. 10 (1); section 15 of the Larceny Act, 1916, which relates to stealing from any haven, etc. appears not to be a statutory assumption of any extra-territorial jurisdiction but merely prescribes the penalty for this particular form of larceny; *The State (Foley) v. Director of Public Prosecutions*, unrep. 23rd June, 1979 (H.C.).
7. Maritime Jurisdiction Act, 1959, s. 2.
8. Id. s. 3.
9. Id. s. 4 (1).
10. Id. s. 4 (2).
11. Id. s. 5.
12. Id. s. 11, as adapted by the External Affairs (Alteration of Name of Department and Title of Minister) Order, 1971 (S.I. 158 of 1971).

contravention of orders designed to conserve the living resources of the sea. In effect therefore, whilst the Irish courts have jurisdiction in both cases, the Minister's certificate would be required in the case of a Spaniard charged with larceny from a fellow crew-member on a Spanish trawler a mile off-shore although not for a fishery offence. In 1959 'depositions' would have been taken to mean depositions taken on the investigation of an indictable offence in the District Court; it is submitted that the reference should now be taken to mean the investigation to be conducted, normally without depositions, under the Criminal Procedure Act, 1967,[13] so that in effect no consent may be required until the accused has been sent forward for trial. The relevant provison, however, does not take into consideration the power of a District Justice, without any preliminary examination or depositions, to treat a case, such as larceny, as a minor offence and deal with it himself;[14] presumably the consent of the Minister is required before the Justice can deal with it in this way.

For the purpose of arresting any person charged with such an offence, the territorial waters and internal seas are deemed to be within the jurisdiction of any court, judge, justice or peace commissioner having power to issue warrants for the arrest of persons charged with an offence committed within its or his jurisdiction so that apparently a District Justice whose area is in Donegal may issue a warrant for the arrest of a person charged with an offence committed off the coast of County Cork.

In the Fisheries Acts, 1959 to 1980, reference is made in relation to fishery offences to 'the exclusive fishery limits of the State'. These were defined in the Maritime Jurisdiction Act, 1959, as amended by the Maritime Jurisdiction (Amendment) Act, 1964, as all sea areas which lie within the line every point of which is at a distance of twelve nautical miles from the nearest point of the baseline.[15] The Maritime Jurisdiction Acts, 1959 and

13. Infra, Chapter 9; see Criminal Procedure Act, 1967, s. 5 (2).
14. Infra pp. 227-228.
15. Maritime Jurisdiction Act, 1959, s. 6 (1), Maritime Jurisdiction (Amendment) Act, 1964, s. 2; the first of these Acts repealed the earlier definition in s. 219 of the Fisheries (Consolidation) Act, 1959.

1964, enable the Government by order to extend the fishery limits and to make special provision for citizens and ships of other States, but further consideration of this specialised and technical area is considered beyond the scope of this work.

Under the Broadcasting (Offences) Act, 1968, it is an offence for any person to broadcast from any ship or aircraft registered in the State which is in or over waters adjacent to the State within the territorial waters of the State as defined in the Maritime Jurisdiction Act, 1959, or from any ship or aircraft registered in the State which is outside such waters.[16]

2. The Universality Principle

Jurisdiction is claimed on this principle in relation to piracy, analogous offences relating to aircraft, breaches of certain international conventions and to a limited extent – if universality can be limited – to perjury.

Piracy

Whilst no Irish authority can be found it is probably safe to assume that the Irish courts, like the English courts, would claim jurisdiction, derived from that of the former Court of Admiralty, in all cases of piracy *jure gentium,* contrary to the law of nations, committed upon the high seas.[17]

Geneva Conventions

The Irish courts are given jurisdiction in respect of major breaches of the Geneva Conventions relating to sick and wounded in the field and civilians in time of war and prisoners of war and internees, wherever the offence is committed;[18] Irish citizens may be prosecuted for minor breaches, wherever committed.[19]

16. Broadcasting (Offences) Act, 1968, s. 2.
17. O'Connell, op. cit. Vol. 2, pp. 657-658; the State is not a signatory to the Geneva Convention on the High Seas, 1958, as to which reference may be made to Archbold, §§21-37.
18. Geneva Conventions Act, 1962, s. 3 (1).
19. Id. s. 4 (2).

Aircraft

Any person who, on board any civil aircraft anywhere, 'hijacks' an aircraft or is concerned in 'hijacking' it, or commits an act of violence which if committed in the State would be an indictable offence, is declared to be guilty of an offence and so triable in the State, unless the place of take-off and the place of actual landing are both situated in the territory of the State of registration of the aircraft or of some State designated in an order made pursuant to a notice communicated to the State under Article 5 of the Hague Convention for the Suppression of Unlawful Seizure of Aircraft, 1970.[20] The effect of this appears to be that if a person on a British registered aircraft on a domestic flight in England usurps control of the aircraft or assaults a passenger or member of the crew while the aircraft is in flight, he is liable to prosecution in the State, *unless* the aircraft has taken off and landed in Great Britain; he will, however, be liable to prosecution in the State if, on the same flight, he usurps control over England, forces the pilot to fly to Paris, refuels and finally lands at Dublin, or lands in Paris and comes to Dublin.

Similar provisions, but without the limitation as to places of take-off and actual landing, apply to the commission on board any civil aircraft in flight of any act of violence endangering the safety of the aircraft, or to any person who destroys or damages any civil aircraft in service, or places any destructive device on board, or interferes with navigation facilities or communicates false information so as to endanger an aircraft in flight.[21] Thus a person who places a bomb on a plane of any nationality at London Airport, or who communicates false information to the Air Traffic Controllers in Paris, appears to be liable, if arrested in Dublin, to be prosecuted in the State.

Perjury

Any person, whatever his nationality, is liable to be prosecuted in the State for the equivalent of perjury before the Court of Justice of the European Communities.[22]

20. Air Navigation and Transport Act, 1973, s. 11; no such order has been made.
21. Air Navigation and Transport Act, 1975, s. 3.
22. Court of Justice of the European Communities (Perjury) Act, 1975, s. 1.

3. The Nationality Principle

The general rule is that offences committed by Irish citizens outside the State are not punishable by the Irish courts; but this rule is subject to statutory exceptions.[23] By statute not only Irish citizens but persons who by ordinary residence have, for this purpose, put themselves in a similar position, have been made amenable to the jurisdiction of the Irish courts for crimes committed abroad. In the case of statutes enacted before 1922, however, the extent to which they still apply may be doubtful in so far as particular expressions may have lost their meaning. The Adaptation of Enactments Acts, 1922 and 1931, adapted certain expressions in Statutes of the United Kingdom and pre-Union Irish Statutes and a few other statutes dealing with particular areas of the law have done the same;[24] adaptation of Statutes of Saorstát Éireann was effected by the Constitution (Consequential Provisions) Act, 1937. In addition, the Acts referred to empower the Government to adapt particular expressions by Order and a number of Orders have been made, mostly in relation to Revenue Statutes.[25] Thus the expression 'Subject of Her Majesty' has been adapted for the purposes of section 9 (referred to below) of the Offences against the Person Act, 1861 – but not further – to mean a citizen of Ireland.[26].

Treason

Any Irish citizen or person ordinarily resident in the State may be prosecuted for treason, wherever committed.[27]

Murder and Manslaughter

Where any murder or manslaughter is committed on land outside the area of application of the laws of the State, and whether the person killed was a citizen of Ireland or not, any offence com-

23. Cf. *R. v. Page* [1954] 1 Q.B. 170, per Lord Goddard at 175.
24. For example, the Post Office (Amendment) Act, 1951, s. 14, Decimal Currency Act, 1969, s. 22, 2nd Schedule.
25. A list of such orders made up to 1976 will be found in Part VI of the Index of the Statutes, published by the Stationery Office.
26. Offences against the Person Act, 1861 (Section 9) Adaptation Order, 1973 (S.I. 356 of 1973).
27. Treason Act, 1939, s. 1.

mitted by any citizen of Ireland in respect of any such case, whether the same shall amount to murder or manslaughter, may be dealt with, inquired of, tried, determined and punished in any county or place within the area of application of the laws of the State in which such person shall be apprehended or in custody, in the same manner in all respects as if the offence had been actually committed in that county or place; but this is not to prevent any person from being tried outside England or Ireland for any murder or manslaughter committed out of England or Ireland in the same manner as such person might have been tried before 1861.[28] Thus an Irish citizen (but nobody else) may be dealt with in the State for a murder committed anywhere in the world.[29] The proviso was incorporated in the original Statute and possibly was designed to insure that a British subject might be tried in some colony for an offence committed there, although also triable in England or Ireland; it now appears to be mere surplusage. Whether the indictment must describe the accused as an Irish citizen appears to be doubtful.[30]

Geneva Conventions

The position of Irish citizens has been considered in the foregoing section relating to the universality principle.

Bigamy

Section 57 of the Offences against the Person Act, 1861, provided that any 'subject of Her Majesty' might be dealt with on a charge of bigamy in any county or place in England or Ireland whether the second marriage shall have taken place in England or Ireland or elsewhere. This particular section, however, unlike section 9 of the same Act, has not been adapted and it is submitted that it no longer applies.

Seamen

Section 687 of the Merchant Shipping Act, 1894, provides for the trial of offences against property or persons committed in any

28. Offences against the Person Act, 1861, s. 9 as adapted by S.I. 356 of 1973.
29. As to offences committed in Northern Ireland, see pp. 53 sqq.
30. See Archbold, 25th Edn. p. 828, citing *R. v. Helsham* 4 C. & P. 394, *R. v. de Mattos* 7 C. & P. 458 and *R. v. Jameson* [1896] 2 Q.B. 425.

place either ashire or afloat 'out of Her Majesty's dominions' by any master, seaman or apprentice who at the time the offence was committed was or within three months previously had been employed in any 'British ship', as if such offence had been committed within the jurisdiction of the Admiralty of England. This section does not appear to have been adapted and it is submitted that it is also not now applicable.

Explosives

It is an offence for any Irish citizen to cause an explosion or be in possession of explosives outside the State.[31]

Exchange Control

Any person who is ordinarily resident in the State and commits or aids and abets and so forth the commission of, or conspires with another person to commit an offence, whether he does so within or without the State, is liable to be prosecuted and punished in the State, either summarily or on indictment.[32] It is, for example, an offence to export Irish bank notes without the consent of the Minister for Finance.[33] If therefore a Swiss national who has taken up ordinary residence in Ireland concocts a plan in Switzerland to export Irish bank notes to Switzerland, even if the plan is discovered and never put into operation, he will be liable to prosecution in the Irish courts.

Defence Forces

Any member of the Reserve Defence Force is guilty of a misdemeanour if, while not on active service, and whether within or without the State, he accepts a commission in, or enters into any engagement to serve in, the armed forces of another State.[34]

31. Explosive Substances Act, 1883, ss. 2, 3, as amended by the Criminal Law (Jurisdiction) Act, 1976, s. 4.
32. Exchange Control Act, 1954, s. 20, (continued in force until 31st December, 1986, by the Exchange Control (Continuance) Act, 1982, s. 1).
33. Id. s. 16; permission or exemptions may be granted by the Minister, either for a particular transaction or generally (e.g. for tourists or businessmen up to a certain amount), id. ss. 25, 27; many of the powers of the Minister have been delegated to the Central Bank of Ireland under s. 28 of the Act.
34. Defence Act, 1954, s. 241.

Broadcasting

It is an offence for an Irish citizen to operate or participate in 'pirate' broadcasting on or over the high seas from any ship or aircraft not registered in the State.[35]

II. EXTRADITION

Extradition means, strictly speaking, the surrender by one country to another, in accordance with an extradition treaty or agreement, of persons wanted by the latter country for prosecution or punishment.[1] The term is, however, regularly applied to the surrender by the authorities in the State of persons wanted in Northern Ireland or Great Britain and vice versa. Whilst extraditable offences are not necessarily indictable offences, the process is almost invariably invoked in connection with such offences and may therefore be conveniently dealt with in this work, in so far as it applies to the extradition of offenders from the State.

1. Extradition generally

Extradition in the strict sense is governed by Part II of the Extradition Act, 1965, which repeals the Extradition Acts, 1870 to 1906, and the Fugitive Offenders Acts, 1881 and 1915, and gives effect to the European Convention on Extradition, 1957.[2] The provisions of Part II of the Act of 1965 are similar in many respects to those of Part III which relates to extradition to the United Kingdom, and many judicial decisions under Part III would be applicable to extradition under Part II. It is noticeable that for the most Part II adopts the language of the Convention whilst Part III does not. Some of the distinctions may be justified by distinctions of territorial distance – for example the duration of a provisional warrant for eighteen days under Part II, as against three days under Part III: but others appear anomalous – for an example taken at random, Part III contains no provision for detention of a wanted person in hospital on grounds of health.

35. Broadcasting (Offences) Act, 1968, s. 1.
1. Extradition Act, 1965, s. 3 (1).
2. The text of the Convention is set out in S.I. 286 of 1967.

Part II becomes effective to the extent that it is applied by Ministerial Order in relation to any country with which the State has an extradition agreement or by which the Government is satisfied that reciprocal facilities will be afforded for the surrender of persons wanted for prosecution or punishment.[3] Any such order must be published in Iris Oifigiúil.[4] Since this procedure is very rarely invoked, it will be dealt with comparatively briefly.

Part II of the Act of 1965 is not applicable between the State and Great Britain, which is not a signatory to the European Convention, and it has been observed that even if Great Britain were a party it would be open to Great Britain and the State to exclude its application as between themselves.[5]

Extradition may only be granted in respect of an offence which is punishable, under the laws of the country requesting extradition and of the State,[6] by imprisonment, as defined in the Act,[7] for a maximum period of at least one year or by a more severe penalty and if, in a case where the wanted person has been convicted and sentenced in the requesting country, a sentence of imprisonment for at least four months or a more severe penalty has

3. Extradition Act, 1965, s. 8 (1); a number of Extradition Act, 1965 (Part II) Orders have been made in relation to the following countries: Argentina, Australia, Austria, Bahamas, Bangladesh, Barbados, Belgium, Bolivia, Botswana, Brazil, Bulgaria, Byelo-Russia, Cameroon, Canada, Cape Verde, Chad, Chile, Chinese Republic, Columbia, Costa Rica, Cyprus, Czechoslovakia, Dahomey, Denmark, Dominican Republic, Ecuador, Egypt, Ethiopia, Fiji, Finland, France, Gabon, Gambia, German Democratic Republic, German Federal Republic, Ghana, Greece, Grenada, Guatemala, Guinea-Bissau, Guyana, Hungary, Iceland, Indonesia, Iran, Iraq, Israel, Italy, Ivory Coast, Japan, Jordan, Kenya, Korea, Kuwait, Lebanon, Lesotho, Libya, Liechtenstein, Luxembourg, Malawi, Mali, Mauretania, Mexico, Mongolia, Morocco, Nepal, Netherlands, New Zealand, Nicaragua, Niger, Nigeria, Norway, Oman, Pakistan, Panama, Papua-New Guinea, Paraguay, Peru, Philippines, Poland, Portugal, Qatar, Romania, Salvador, Saudi Arabia, Senegal, Seychelles, Sierra Leone, Singapore, South Africa, Spain, Sri Lanka, Sudan, Surinam, Sweden, Switzerland, Syria, Thailand, Togo, Tonga, Trinidad & Tobago, Tunisia, Turkey, Uganda, Ukraine, Union of Soviet Socialist Republics, United Arab Emirates, United States of America, Uruguay, Yugoslavia and Zaire (S.I. 286 of 1967, 76 of 1969, 151 of 1969, 33 of 1970, 145 of 1971, 229 of 1971, 334 of 1975, 251 of 1976, 322 of 1976, 323 of 1976, 62 of 1977, 102 of 1977, 47 of 1982, 349 of 1982 and 10 of 1983. Reference should be made to the relevant Order for reservations by some countries).
4. Extradition Act, 1965, s. 8 (8).
5. *The State (Holmes) v. Furlong* [1967] I.R. 210 (S.C.) *per* Ó Dálaigh C.J. at 215.
6. Or would have been so punishable if the act had been committed in the State; Extradition Act, 1965, s. 10 (3).
7. Id. s. 3 (1).

been imposed. If the request relates to more than one offence of which one only complies with these conditions as to imprisonment, the order may be made also in respect of the other, if otherwise extraditable.[8]

Extradition may not be granted in respect of an offence which is a political offence or one connected with a political offence, for an offence under military law which is not an offence under ordinary criminal law or for a revenue offence, as defined in the Act;[9] nor may it be granted if there are substantial grounds for believing that the request has been made for the purpose of prosecuting a person on account of his race, religion, nationality or political opinions, or that his position may be prejudiced for any such reason.[10]

Extradition may not normally be granted if the person concerned is a citizen of Ireland,[11] nor where the offence in question is regarded by the law of the State as having been committed in the State, nor where a prosecution is pending in the State against such person for the offence; nor if final judgment has been passed in the State or in some third country, nor in the case of an offence which is an offence under the law of the State, if the Director of Public Prosecutions[12] has decided not to institute or to terminate proceedings, nor where, in effect a prosecution would be statute-barred in the requesting country or in the State.[13]

Extradition may not be granted for an offence which is punishable by death in the requesting country, but for which that penalty is not provided by the law of the State or is not generally carried out in the State, unless a sufficient assurance is given that it will not be carried out.[14]

As a general rule a person who is extradited may not be proceeded against or re-extradited to a third country for an offence

8. Id. s. 10.
9. Id. ss. 11-13; compare s. 44.
10. Id. s. 11 (2).
11. Id. s. 14. If however, the only ground of refusal is citizenship, the person in question is liable to prosecution in the State as if the act had been done within the Dublin Metropolitan District.
12. It is assumed that extradition proceedings are 'criminal proceedings' for the purpose of the Prosecution of Offences Act, 1974.
13. Extradition Act, 1965, ss. 14, 18.
14. Id. s. 19.

other than that for which he is extradited, apart from an offence committed after his surrender – commonly called the rule of speciality – unless the Minister for Justice consents or the person concerned remains in the requesting country of his own volition for forty-five days after disposal of the offence for which he was extradited.[15]

A request for extradition must be communicated in writing by an accredited diplomatic representative, or otherwise as provided by the relevant extradition provisions, supported by evidence of conviction or sentence or of a warrant of arrest, a statement and description of the offence, a statement of the foreign law and a description of the wanted person, with any other relevant information as to his identity and nationality and, in some cases, evidence as to the commission by him of the relevant offence.[16]

If more than one country requests extradition of the same person, it is for the Minister for Justice to decide to which request he should accede.[17]

If the Minister is satisfied that everything is in order he directs a Justice of the District Court to issue a warrant, which may be executed by a member of the Garda Síochána in any part of the State, for the arrest of the wanted person to be brought before a Justice assigned to the Dublin Metropolitan District or such other Justice as the Minister may direct.[18]

In cases of urgency a Justice may issue a provisional warrant, without any Ministerial order, on foot of an information sworn by a member of the Garda Síochána not below the rank of Inspector, stating that a copy of the conviction or sentence or of the foreign warrant exists and the nature and time and place of commission of the alleged offence and giving a description of the wanted person. The Justice must inform the Minister who may direct cancellation of the warrant and release of the person arrested. Otherwise the person arrested must be brought before a Justice assigned to the Dublin Metropolitan District or such

15. Id. ss. 20, 21.
16. Id. ss. 22, 23, 25.
17. Id. s. 24.
18. Id. ss. 26, 28.

other Justice as the Minister may direct, and the Justice may remand him on bail or in custody pending receipt from the Minister of an order that the request for extradition has been duly received. If no such order is received within eighteen days the wanted person must be released, without prejudice to his re-arrest if a request for his extradition is subsequently received.[19]

When the wanted person is brought before the District Court on foot of a warrant or provisional warrant the Justice, if satisfied that the offence is extraditable and that the request for extradition is in order, must commit the person to prison or (if under twenty-one) to a remand institution; otherwise he must discharge him. The Justice may, however, adjourn the hearing and remand the person in custody or on bail. He must inform the wanted person that he will not be surrendered to the requesting country without his consent until after fifteen days and must also inform him of his constitutional right to apply to the High Court for an order of habeas corpus; the Justice must then notify the Minister of the order.[20] It is to be noted that the Justice does not himself make an order for surrender, as in the case of persons wanted by the United Kingdom authorities.

The Minister may order the wanted person to be removed in custody to a hospital on health grounds and may in any case postpone the surrender until that person is proceeded against in the State or serves a sentence for some other offence.[21]

The wanted person may not, without his own consent, given before a District Justice, be surrendered until the expiration of fifteen days after his committal or until the conclusion of any habeas corpus proceedings brought by him, whichever is later.[22]

Unless the Minister is of opinion that the extradition of the person concerned would involve transit through any territory where there is reason to believe that his life or his freedom might be threatened by race, religion, nationality or political opinion, the Minister may order him to be surrendered to somebody authorised by the requesting country, and that person may detain

19. Id. s. 27; cf. s. 49.
20. Id. s. 29.
21. Id. ss. 30, 32.
22. Id. s. 31.

him (in which case he is deemed to be in lawful custody) and convey him out of the State.[23]

If the wanted person is not conveyed from the State within one month of his committal or of the conclusion of habeas corpus proceedings he may apply to the High Court to be released; in addition, if the High Court is satisfied that his state of health or other circumstances beyond the control of the State or of the requesting country have temporarily prevented his being removed from the State, it may set a time limit for his removal.[24] The Minister is also empowered to order the release of the person concerned.[25]

Finally the Garda Síochána is empowered to seize and hand over to the requesting country property which appears to be reasonably required as evidence for proving the alleged offence, or which appears to have been acquired as a result of that offence, and is found in possession of the wanted person when arrested, or is discovered subsequently.[26]

2. Extradition to the United Kingdom

Before the establishment of the State, section 29 of the Petty Sessions (Ireland) Act, 1851, provided a procedure whereby persons found in Ireland could be arrested and sent to some other part of the then United Kingdom for trial or punishment. These provisions were held by the Supreme Court to be no longer applicable in *The State (Quinn) v. Ryan,*[1] and corresponding English legislation suffered the same fate as a result of the decision of the House of Lords in *Metropolitan Police Commissioner v. Hammond.*[2] The result was the enactment of Part III of the Extradition Act, 1965, and in the United Kingdom of the Backing of Warrants (Republic of Ireland) Act, 1965. Part III of the Irish Act of 1965, was challenged unsuccessfully in *The State (Sumers Jennings) v. Furlong,*[3] on the ground that, unlike Part II,

23. Id. s. 33.
24. Id. s. 34.
25. Id. s. 35.
26. Id. s. 36.
1. [1965] I.R. 70.
2. [1965] A.C. 810.
3. [1966] I.R. 183 (S.C.); see also *The State (Whelan) v. Governor of Mountjoy Prison*, unrep. 9th February, 1976, (H.C.).

it did not incorporate what is commonly called the rule of speciality, that a State requesting extradition is under a duty not to prosecute that person for an offence other than that for which he was extradited, but it was held by the Supreme Court that, even if that rule is a generally accepted principle of international law, it is not part of Irish domestic law.

Part III of the Extradition Act, 1965, applies to persons wanted in Northern Ireland, England and Wales, Scotland, the Isle of Man and the Channel Islands.[4] The process must start with the issue by a judicial authority (the term is not defined) in any such part of the United Kingdom of a warrant for the arrest of a person accused or convicted of an offence which is an indictable offence, not being an offence triable on indictment only at the instance or with the consent of the accused,[5] or an offence punishable on summary conviction by imprisonment for a maximum period of at least six months.[6] It seems clear that the warrant must be issued by a judicial authority in the particular part (England and Wales being treated as one) of the United Kingdom in which a charge against the wanted person has been brought or disposed of by conviction.

If the offence specified in the warrant is a summary offence (whether or not also indictable) under the law of the relevant part of the United Kingdom, a warrant is not to be endorsed unless the wanted person

(a) has failed to appear in answer to a summons and, not less than fourteen days before the return date, the summons was served on him personally in that part of the United Kingdom or else a notice of its issue signed by a member of the Garda Síochána not below the rank of Inspector, with a copy of the summons, was served on him by a member of the Garda Síochána or

(b) he has failed to appear in pursuance of a recognisance entered into before the Court in the United Kingdom or

(c) having appeared, he has subsequently failed to appear on an adjournment of the proceedings.[7]

4. Extradition Act, 1965, s. 41.
5. Id. s. 42.
6. Id. s. 43 (1) (a).
7. Id. s. 51; as to service see s. 51 (2).

Delay may occur between the issue of the United Kingdom warrant and its arrival in the State, and in the interval the person named in the warrant might be able to leave the State. Accordingly any member of the Garda Síochána not below the rank of Inspector may lay a sworn information before a District Justice that he has reason to believe that the appropriate warrant has been issued but that it is not yet in his possession, that he has received a request made on grounds of urgency by or on behalf of a police force in the relevant part of the United Kingdom for the arrest of the person for whose arrest the warrant has been issued, and that he has reason to believe that that person may be found in the State. If that person has been convicted, some member of the Gardaí (not necessarily the member who lays the information) must also state on oath that he has reason to believe that the purpose of the arrest is to enable the wanted person to be brought before a court in the relevant part of the United Kingdom for sentence, or to be taken to a place where he is to undergo imprisonment (not merely in default of payment of a fine) under such a sentence. The Justice may then issue a provisional warrant for the arrest of the wanted person.[8] He does not appear to be concerned at this stage with the question whether the offence in question is an extraditable offence.

A provisional warrant may be executed by any member of the Garda Síochána anywhere in the State but is only valid for five days.[9] If the wanted person is arrested within that time he must be brought before a Justice for the District Court Area in which he was arrested, if such a Justice is available, and if not before a Peace Commissioner in that District.[10] If in the meantime the United Kingdom warrant is received and has been duly endorsed the Justice or Peace Commissioner must proceed as if the wanted person had been arrested under that warrant; otherwise the person may be remanded, in custody or on bail, for not more than three days. If he is remanded in custody and if at any time the United Kingdom warrant, duly endorsed, is produced to the person having custody of him, he is thereafter to be treated as if

8. Id. s. 49 (1), (2).
9. Id. s. 49 (8).
10. Cf. *McDonald v. Attorney General* 108 I.L.T.R. 89 (H.C.).

arrested under that warrant, and if it is not so produced during the period of remand he must be released.[11] Presumably if the warrant is received later he may be re-arrested although there is no express provision to that effect, such as to be found in the case of a person arrested on foot of a provisional warrant under Part II of the Act.[12]

Remand

A person remanded in custody may be detained in prison (or, if under twenty-one, in a remand institution) or, for not more than forty-eight hours, in a Garda station.[13]

A person arrested under a provisional warrant or a warrant which has been endorsed may be allowed bail with or without sureties by a District Justice or Peace Commissioner; alternatively the amount of bail may be fixed and he may be detained by the Gardaí until it is forthcoming. He must undertake in his recognisance to surrender at a specified Garda station at a time to be mentioned in a notice from the member in charge of that station served on him, being not more than twenty-four hours before the period of remand is likely to end; if, however, whilst he is in custody after having surrendered it appears that the end of the remand period is likely to be delayed, the member in charge of the station must release him on his entering into a further recognisance in the like terms.[14] Thus if the person in question is arrested on Saturday under a warrant which has been endorsed and in the first instance a District Justice is not immediately available, he may, it appears, be brought before a Peace Commissioner and remanded on bail until the next sitting of the District Court for that area, which may be due to be held on the following Friday, at 11 a.m. The Gardaí must notify him to surrender at any time not earlier than 11 a.m. on the Thursday: but if it then appears that the District Court will be postponed for a week, he must be allowed out on bail again, and notified to surrender not earlier than 11 a.m. on the next following Thursday.

11. Extradition Act, 1965, s. 49 (5)–(7).
12. Id. s. 27 (8).
13. Id. s. 52 (1).
14. Id. s. 52 (2), (4).

If a person fails to surrender in accordance with his recognisance, a District Justice may issue a warrant for his arrest (without prejudice to the enforcement of the recognisance): if re-arrested he is treated as if he had surrendered, save that he has no right to be released on bail unless the member in charge of the station thinks fit to do so.[15]

When the United Kingdom warrant arrives it must be produced to the Commissioner of the Garda Síochána (including a Deputy or Assistant Commissioner)[16] and, if he is satisfied that the person named or described in the warrant may be found in the State, and, in the case of a convicted person, that the purpose of the arrest is to bring that person before a court in the part of the United Kingdom in which he was convicted or sentenced, or to be taken to some place where he is to undergo imprisonment under such a sentence (otherwise than in default of payment of a fine or other sum), the Commissioner must endorse the warrant in the prescribed form for execution, thereby authorising execution of the warrant in the State by any member of the Garda Síochána.[17]

A Garda Commissioner may accept a warrant as duly issued, without further evidence, if it purports to be issued by a judicial authority whose signature is verified by affidavit. He may likewise accept as sufficient a certificate from the clerk or other officer of that authority that the offence is an indictable offence and not also a summary offence, or that it is a summary offence punishable by a specified maximum period of imprisonment. He may also accept a duly certified copy of a summons or of an affidavit or declaration of service or an affidavit of non-appearance sworn by the clerk or other officer of the court.[18]

The endorsement of a warrant is *prima facie* evidence without proof of the signature or office of the Commissioner or that the necessary supporting affidavit was produced to him.[19]

If the warrant is then so executed the person named or described in it must be brought on arrest before a District Justice

15. Id. s. 52 (5).
16. Id. s. 42.
17. Id. s. 43.
18. Id. s. 54.
19. Id. s. 55 (2).

for the District in which he was arrested, or if a Justice for the District in which he was arrested is not available, before a Peace Commissioner in that District.[20] The person concerned should be given a copy of the warrant.[21] If the arrested person is brought before a Peace Commissioner he must be remanded, in custody or on bail, to the earliest practicable sitting of the District Court in that District within eight days after the arrest; and if the arrested person, having been remanded on bail, fails to appear at the Court before which he was bound to appear, the Justice may issue a warrant for his arrest, and his arrest will be the equivalent of an arrest under the previous warrant.[22] The Justice has no power to enquire into the validity of the endorsement,[23] or into the merits of the case, unless, perhaps, it can be shown that there was no evidence justifying the issue of the warrant in the first instance.[24]

When the wanted person is brought before the District Court the Justice has the same powers of adjournment and remand as in the case of a person charged with an indictable offence.[25] The person in question should be given an opportunity to obtain legal advice.[26].

The Justice must be satisfied that the offence specified in the warrant corresponds to an offence under the law of the State which is an indictable offence or one punishable on summary conviction by imprisonment for a maximum period of at least six months; if he is not so satisfied, he must order the person in question to be discharged; otherwise the Justice must make an order for that person to be remanded and delivered at some convenient point of departure from the State into the custody of a member of the police force of the place in which the warrant has issued, for

20. Id. s. 45; an order made by a Justice for a District other than that in which the arrest was made was held to be invalid in *McDonald v. Attorney General* 108 I.L.T.R. 89 (H.C.).
21. *The State (McFadden) v. Governor of Mountjoy Prison,* unrep. 6th August, 1980 (H.C.).
22. Extradition Act, 1965, s. 46.
23. *Molloy v. Sheehan* [1978] I.R. 438 (S.C.).
24. *Archer v. Fleming,* unrep. 21st January, 1980 (H.C.); *Wyatt v. McLoughlin* [1974] I.R. 378, 395 (S.C.).
25. Extradition Act, 1965, s. 47 (4).
26. *The State (McFadden) v. Governor of Mountjoy Prison,* supra.

conveyance to that place.[27]

The point of departure from the State should be specified precisely.[28]

It is desirable that the person to whom the person is to be delivered should be described more specifically than as 'a duly authorised member' of the police force, e.g. as a constable of 'Mid-Anglia constabulary, a police force of England and Wales'.[29]

In addition the order should state the purpose for which it is made, namely the conveyance of the wanted person to some convenient point of departure from the State.[30] If, however, the warrant was valid and it is only the order which is defective, there appears to be nothing to prevent the person in question being re-arrested on the same warrant.[31]

In any proceedings before a court, the court, unless it sees good reason to the contrary, may accept without further evidence that a warrant purporting to be issued by a judicial authority whose signature is verified by affidavit is a valid warrant issued by a judicial authority in the appropriate part of the United Kingdom; it may likewise accept as sufficient a document appearing to be a copy of a summons certified by the clerk or other officer of the appropriate court, or to be an affidavit or other declaration of service, where it is alleged that the person named in it has failed to appear; or a certificate appearing to be given by the clerk or other officer of the appropriate court that the offence in question is an indictable offence and not also a summary offence, or a summary offence punishable by a specified maximum period of imprisonment.[32]

Whilst, however, the Justice may assume that the United Kingdom warrant is in order, if its validity is challenged he must receive otherwise admissible evidence e.g. from an expert in the relevant system of law, English or Scottish and so forth, that the

27. Extradition Act, 1965, s. 47 (1), (3).
28. *The State (Holmes) v. Furlong* [1967] I.R. 210 (S.C.) – not merely 'Dublin' but the place 'where one can say the last goodbye', *per* Ó Dálaigh C.J. at 218.
29. *The State (Furlong) v. Kelly* [1971] I.R.132, 142, 145, 148 (S.C.)
30. *The State (Holmes) v. Furlong* supra.
31. Id. *per* Ó Dálaigh C.J. at 220.
32. Extradition Act, 1965, s. 55.

warrant was properly issued, if that is put in issue;[33] and presumably the same principle is to be applied to other documents which, *prima facie,* 'prove themselves'.

There have been a number of decisions on the question whether the offence specified in the warrant corresponds to an offence under the law of the State. To an extent these have resulted from the fact that although the Larceny Act, 1916, has been repealed in England by the Theft Act, 1968, it is still in force in the State (although in the case of robbery, burglary and aggravated burglary, and to a lesser extent as regards explosives and firearms, the law has been assimilated in the two jurisdictions).[1] Thus it has been held insufficient for the warrant to refer merely to stealing as a trespasser contrary to section 9 of the Theft Act, 1968.[2] On the other hand it has been held by the Supreme Court to be sufficient if the warrant spells out the ingredients of the relevant offence, e.g. larceny, even though it may refer in addition to some provision in the Theft Act;[3] the warrant should show that 'the acts alleged constitute an offence under the law of the requested country'.[4] On the same day the Court held that 'conspiracy to commit theft, i.e. to steal' was not sufficient:[5]

> 'It is not the function of the Irish courts to determine what constitutes stealing or theft in England. A court in this State is not entitled to take judicial notice of the essential ingredients of a particular offence under the law of another State. However, the particular offence may be specified in the warrant by a recital of the particulars.'

Words must, however, be given their ordinary or popular meaning. It was thus held by the Supreme Court to be sufficient if the warrant alleged that the accused 'did rob' M.B. of £281 in cash and, 'immediately before doing so used force to wit personal violence', to the said M.B., having regard to the ordinary meaning of the word 'rob', and to the fact that the form of indictment

33. *Gillespie v. Attorney General* [1976] I.R. 233 (S.C.)
1. Criminal Law (Jurisdiction) Act, 1976, ss. 4-9.
2. *The State (Furlong) v. Kelly* [1971] I.R. 131 (S.C.).
3. *Wyatt v. McLoughlin* [1974] I.R. 378 (S.C.).
4. Id. *per* Walsh J. at 397.
5. *Walsh v. Attorney General,* unrep. 31st July, 1979. *per* Walsh J. at p. 4 of judgment.

in the First Schedule to the Criminal Justice (Administration) Act, 1924, uses merely the word 'rob'.[6] A warrant which referred to evading restrictions on importation of drugs was held to be insufficient, as it did not specify the restrictions.[7] Receiving stolen goods knowing or believing the same to be stolen has, however, been held to be sufficient: even though the Larceny Act, 1916, omits the word 'believing', since, even if knowing does not involve an element of recklessness, all that is required is that the United Kingdom offence should correspond to *some* offence in the State;[8] and it is sufficient for this purpose that *one* offence specified in the warrant is extraditable, even though others are not.[9] It has been stated that:[10]

> '[I]t is a question of looking at the factual components of the offence specified in the warrant, regardless of the name given to it, and seeing if those factual components, in their entirety or in their near-entirety, would constitute an offence which, if committed in the State, could be said to be a corresponding offence of the required gravity.'

It may be permissible to suspect a hardening of the attitude of the courts to what some might suggest were unmeritorious technical objections. It is hard to reconcile some of the decisions, for example to justify distinction between 'stealing' and 'robbery' in their ordinary rather than any special legal sense, or a charge of receiving 'stolen' goods if the meaning of 'steal' is not to be judicially recognised. Furthermore the First Schedule to the Criminal Law (Administration) Act, 1924, uses the word 'steal' in relation to simple larceny, as well as 'rob' in relation to robbery, in the forms of indictment.

It, therefore, appears that the function of the District Justice is to satisfy himself as to the validity of the warrant, if disputed, that the person before him is the person named in the warrant, that the offence specified in the warrant is of sufficient gravity to

6. *Wilson v. Sheehan*, unrep. 23rd June, 1979 (S.C.) apparently disapproving *Whyte v. Sheehan*, unrep. 26th May, 1975 (H.C.), in which the offence specified was an assault with intent to rob.
7. *Rey v. Fleming*, unrep. 29th January, 1980 (H.C.).
8. *Hanlon v. Fleming* [1981] I.R. 489 (S.C.).
9. *Molloy v. Sheehan* [1978] I.R. 438 (S.C.).
10. *Per* Henchy J. in *Hanlon v. Fleming* [1981] I.R. 489, 494; see also *Harris v. Wren*, unrep. 21st March, 1983 (H.C.).

be extraditable, and that it corresponds to some offence in the State; he appears not to be concerned, as are magistrates in England,[11] with the question whether extradition should be refused because of the nature of the offence, for example because it is a political offence; that, as will be seen, is a matter for the High Court or the Minister for Justice.

If the District Justice makes an order for delivery of the wanted person his decision is not subject to appeal to the Circuit Court,[12] but the person in question may not, except with his consent given before a Justice of the District Court or a Peace Commissioner, be delivered up until the expiration of fifteen days from the date of the order, or while an application made by him within that time for an order of habeas corpus or for his release under Section 50 of the Act of 1965 is pending; and the wanted person must be so informed as well as being informed of his right to make such an application; if the application is made to the High Court (as distinct from an application to the Minister for Justice) it is treated as pending until any appeal is disposed of, or not brought within the time for appeal.[13] The time for appealing against an order of the High Court is twenty-one days from the passing and perfection of the order.[14]

Section 50 of the Act of 1965 empowers the High Court to direct the release of the wanted person on any one of a number of grounds which will be considered separately.

The first is that the offence to which the warrant relates is a political offence or an offence connected with a political offence.

A leading case on what is meant by an offence connected with a political offence is *Bourke v. Attorney General.*[1] It has been noted that the phrase appears in the European Convention on Extradition, 1957, to which the United Kingdom is not a signatory, and the United Kingdom has continued in the Backing of Warrants (Republic of Ireland) Act, 1965, to use the phrase 'a political offence or an offence of a political character' which appeared in the earlier Extradition Acts. Whilst the English

11. See Backing of Warrants (Republic of Ireland) Act, 1965, s. 2.
12. Extradition Act, 1965, s. 47 (5).
13. Id. s. 48.
14. Rules of the Superior Courts, O. 58 r. 3 (1) (b).
1. [1972] I.R. 36 (S.C.).

courts have been loath to define such an offence, it has been said that it suggests that the offence connotes the idea of political asylum for political refugees and that a fugitive is at odds with a State which applies for his extradition on some issue connected with the political control of Government of the country,[2] or that an offence is of a political character, either because the wrongdoer had some direct ulterior political motive when he committed the offence, or because the requesting country is anxious to obtain possession of the wrongdoer's person in order to punish him for his politics rather than for the criminal offence referred to in the extradition proceedings.[3] A political conflict between the requesting country and some third country would not be material.[4] It was held insufficient that a person, wanted for murder and armed robbery, was a member of a political organisation which might be, but had not yet been, declared illegal.[5] In Northern Ireland it has been held that an averment by a person named in a warrant issued in the Republic on a charge of murder that the offence was of a political character, and evidence that the victim was a member of an illegal political organisation was insufficient to justify a conclusion that the offence was of a political character.[6]

The facts of *Bourke*'s case (supra) were that a warrant was issued in London and endorsed by the Garda Commissioner for the arrest of the plaintiff, Seán Alphonsus Bourke, on a charge of aiding one George Blake to escape from Wormwood Scrubs Prison in London. Bourke, who was also serving a sentence in the same prison, became friendly with Blake, who was serving a sentence imposed for an offence under the English Official Secrets Acts, which was admitted to be a political offence. The issue was whether Bourke would be guilty of an offence 'connected with a political offence' in assisting Blake to escape. An order for his release on this ground was made by the High Court and affirmed

2. *Schtraks v. Government of Israel* [1964] A.C. 556; applied in *Burns v. Attorney General,* unrep. 4th February, 1974 (H.C.).
3. *R. v. Governor of Winson Green Prison, ex parte Littlejohn* [1975] 3 All E.R. 208, *per* Lord Widgery C.J. at 211.
4. *Tzu-Tsai Cheng v. Governor of Pentonville Prison* [1973] A.C. 931.
5. *Keane v. Governor of Brixton Prison* [1971] 1 All E.R. 1163.
6. *Re Taylor* [1973] N.I. 159.

by the Supreme Court. In the course of his judgment Ó Dálaigh C.J. reviewed the European Convention on Extradition, 1957, and its background as well as a number of English decisions as to what was 'an offence of a political character' and came to the conclusion that:[7]

> '[T]he Convention has added its protection to a wide area of offences which are not necessarily political in character but which are simply connected with a political offence.'

Bourke's assistance of Blake was held to be 'connected with' Blake's political offence.

It also appears from this case that, without questioning the good faith of the English Attorney General, who offered an undertaking that Bourke, if returned to England, would not be prosecuted for any offence other than those specified in the warrant, such undertakings should in principle not be accepted.[8]

In *Burns v. Attorney General*[9] Finlay took the view that possession of explosives entrusted to the plaintiff by an illegal political organisation and intended by it to be used for subversive purposes was a political offence which he equated with an offence of a political character under the earlier Extradition Act, 1870.

In *Hanlon v. Fleming*[10] it had been held by the High Court that there was no evidence that explosives in the possession of the accused were to be used for the purposes of an illegal organisation (the I.R.A.) in such a way as to lend political colour to the offences and the Supreme Court declined to interfere with this finding of fact, but Henchy J.[11] left open the question of whether, if it were shown that the explosives were intended for transmission to the I.R.A., the offence charged would be a political offence or one connected with a political offence.

In *McGlinchey v. Wren,*[12] however, the plaintiff had sought unsuccessfully to object to being extradited to Northern Ireland

7. [1972] I.R. 36, 61.
8. Id. at 64; cf. *R. v. Governor of Brixton Prison, ex parte Armah* [1968] A.C. 192. Such an undertaking from the Irish Attorney General was, however, accepted by the English Court of Appeal in *Keane v. Governor of Brixton Prison* supra.
9. Unrep. 4th February, 1974 (H.C.).
10. [1981] I.R. 489.
11. Id at 495.
12. [1982] I.R. 154.

on a charge of murdering an elderly grandmother as being a political offence or one connected with a political offence, on the ground that an illegal organisation had claimed responsibility. He withdrew his claim in the Supreme Court but O'Higgins C.J. observed that the judicial authorities have in many respects been rendered obsolete by the fact that modern terrorist violence is often the antithesis of what could reasonably be regarded as political either in itself or in its connections, and, whilst stressing that every case must depend on its own circumstances, he suggested that those circumstances would have to show that the person charged was at the relevant time engaged, directly or indirectly, in what reasonable, civilised people would regard as political activity.

The next ground for release is that the offence to which the warrant relates is an offence under military law which is not an offence under ordinary criminal law; an example would be desertion or absence without leave from the British armed forces. It is to be remembered, however, that there are a number of offences under military law which are also offences under the ordinary law, so that the offender may be liable to be dealt with either in the ordinary courts or, as a person subject to military law, by court-martial, and the latter type of offence appears clearly to be extraditable; it is submitted that in so far as the warrant might refer to military law, an order for extradition may be made if it is shown to correspond to *some* offence under the ordinary criminal law of the State.[13]

Another ground for release is that the offence to which the warrant relates is a revenue offence. A revenue offence is an offence in connection with taxes, duties or exchange control, but does not include an offence involving the use or threat of force, or perjury or the forging of a document issued under statutory authority, nor does it include an offence committed by an officer of the revenue in that capacity.[14]

A further ground on which release may be directed by the Court is that in the opinion of the Court there are substantial

13. *Wilson v. Sheehan,* unrep. 23rd June, 1979 (S.C.); cf. *Hanlon v. Fleming* [1981] I.R. 489 (S.C.).
14. Extradition Act, 1965, s. 3 (1).

reasons for believing that the wanted person will, if extradited, be prosecuted or detained for a political offence or an offence connected with a political offence, or an offence under military law which is not an offence under ordinary criminal law; that the offence to which the warrant relates is, in a sense, an excuse for getting a person back to the United Kingdom to be dealt with for a political or politically connected or military offence. It will be noted that reason to believe that the wanted person will be prosecuted for a revenue offence is not a ground for directing his release if the order itself relates to some other extraditable offence. Every such case must, it is submitted, depend on its own particular facts. The grounds for anticipating a prosecution for a political offence and so forth must be substantial: in *The State (Magee) v. O'Rourke*[15] the prosecutor, Magee, was arrested on a Northern Ireland warrant on charges of house-breaking and the unlawful taking of a motor car and assaulting a police officer; he claimed that he would be likely to be prosecuted for a political offence or one connected with a political offence, alleging (and this was not rebutted) that he had already been detained on several occasions in the past.[16] The Supreme Court affirmed an order directing his release on the ground that there were substantial reasons for believing that he was correct; but the onus of establishing it is on the plaintiff or prosecutor. In *Hanlon v. Fleming*[17] the High Court had also[18] declined to direct the release of the applicant, whom it regarded as having pursued a criminal career, on the ground that he had at some time in the past been a member of an illegal political organisation.

The Supreme Court has held that delay by the prosecuting authorities in applying for the order is not a reason for refusing it.[19]

The wanted person may apply to the Court to direct his release on any of the grounds mentioned above. Alternatively he may apply to the Minister who may either direct release or refer the question to the High Court.[20]

15. [1971] I.R. 205 (S.C.).
16. Cf. *McGlinchy v. Wren* [1982] I.R. 154.
17. [1981] I.R. 489.
18. Unrep. s.n. *Hanlon v. Garvey,* 6th October, 1980.
19. *Hanlon v. Fleming,* supra.
20. Extradition Act, 1965, s. 50 (1), (3), (4).

The High Court, but not the Minister,[21] may also direct release of the wanted person on the ground that the offence specified in the warrant does not correspond with any offence under the law of the State which is an indictable offence or is punishable on summary conviction by imprisonment for a maximum period of at least six months.[22] This provision appears, so to speak, to telescope the earlier requirements that the specified offence must be an indictable offence and so forth under the relevant United Kingdom law (if the warrant is to be endorsed), and the requirement that it must correspond to an offence indictable and so forth, under the law of the State (if the District Justice is to make an order).

Any application to the Court under section 50 of the Act of 1965 is to be made by Special Summons which must be served on the person who endorsed the warrant.[23]

If a District Justice makes an order for the delivery of a wanted person and it later appears to him that the United Kingdom police force concerned no longer requires that person to be delivered to it, he must make an order for the discharge of that person;[24] and in any case, if the wanted person is not delivered up within one month after the order was made, he may apply to the High Court which may order his discharge unless reasonable cause is shown for the delay.[25] Presumably the pendency of an application to the High Court or of an appeal would amount to reasonable cause, but it would seem more rational to have provided for the time to run from the affirmation of the order.

III. SPECIAL EXTRA-TERRITORIAL JURISDICTION RELATING TO NORTHERN IRELAND

Difficulties arose in dealing with terrorist crimes, committed in Northern Ireland, because of the facility of movement over the border between the Republic and Northern Ireland, the objection

21. Presumably if the application is made to the Minister he must either refuse it or refer it to the Court.
22. Extradition Act, 1965, s. 50 (2) (c).
23. S.I. 220 of 1973.
24. Extradition Act, 1965, s. 53 (2).
25. Id. s. 53 (1).

in the Republic to extradition for any political offence or any offence connected with a political offence,[1] and the problems of ensuring that evidence should be made available on each side of the border from persons who might be unwilling to leave one jurisdiction for fear of any consequences in the other. These led to discussions between representatives of the Irish and British Governments at Sunningdale in England in December, 1973, and the mutual declarations commonly referred to as the Sunningdale Declarations.[2] One result was the enactment of the Criminal Law (Jurisdiction) Act, 1976; the Bill leading to the Act was referred, under Article 26 of the Constitution, to the Supreme Court, which held it to be constitutional on the ground that it clearly provided for the peace, order and good government of the State.[3] Corresponding legislation for Northern Ireland was enacted in the United Kingdom by the Criminal Jurisdiction Act, 1975.

This work is concerned only with the provisions of the Irish Act which confer jurisdiction on the courts of the Republic over offences committed in Northern Ireland and procedural provisions for the taking of evidence in the Republic for the purpose of a criminal trial proceeding in Northern Ireland and *vice versa;* these latter procedures do not in fact enlarge the jurisdiction of the Irish courts, but may most conveniently be dealt with in this Chapter.

1. Jurisdiction assumed in respect of offences committed in Northern Ireland

The Schedule to the Criminal Law (Jurisdiction) Act, 1976, enumerates a number of common law and statutory offences, which will in general be referred to in this Chapter as scheduled offences. It will be noted that these bear no relation to offences which are made 'scheduled offences' for the purpose of the Offences Against the State Act, 1939.[4] The common law offences are murder, manslaughter, the common law offence of arson,[5]

1. Supra, pp. 48 sqq.
2. As to their effect, see *Boland v. An Taoiseach* [1974] I.R. 338 (S.C.).
3. *Re Criminal Law (Jurisdiction) Bill, 1976,* [1977] I.R. 129.
4. Supra, pp. 18, 19.
5. The malicious and voluntary burning of the house of another; 1 Hale, 566, 1 Hawk: c. 39, ss. 1, 7-15.

kidnapping and false imprisonment. To these are added the statutory extensions of arson in relation to churches and other places of divine worship, or any dwelling while a person is inside, divers buildings with intent to injure or defraud, railway and port installations, public buildings, unspecified buildings, and goods in buildings, and interference with railways;[6] wounding or causing grievous bodily harm or shooting with intent to maim, etc. and malicious wounding or causing grievous bodily harm *simpliciter*;[7] the principal offences relating to explosives;[8] robbery and aggravated burglary;[9] the more serious offences relating to the use and possession of firearms;[10] and the unlawful seizure of aircraft and vehicles.[11]

When a person does an act in Northern Ireland, that, if done in the State, would constitute a scheduled offence, he is guilty of an offence and liable on conviction on indictment to the penalty to which he would have been liable if he had done the act in the State;[12] references to doing an act include references to the making of an omission and references hereunder should be so construed.[13]

It is also an offence for a person to escape from any lawful custody in which he is held in Northern Ireland when charged with or convicted of certain offences; these are:

(i) any offence under the law of Northern Ireland consisting of acts (whether done in the State or in Northern Ireland) that also constitute a scheduled offence or an act which if done in the State could constitute a scheduled offence and

(ii) any offence under the corresponding law of Northern Ireland[14] (which appears to mean escaping from custody in the

6. Malicious Damage Act, 1861, ss. 1 to 7 inclusive and s. 35; it may be noted that a number of other offences under this Act are not scheduled offences.
7. Offences against the Person Act, 1861, ss. 18, 20.
8. Explosive Substances Act, 1883, ss. 2, 3 and 4.
9. Larceny Act, 1916, ss. 23 and 23B, inserted by ss. 5 and 7 of the Criminal Law (Jurisdiction) Act, 1976.
10. Firearms Act, 1925, s. 15, Firearms Act, 1964, ss. 26, 27, 27A and 27B (the last two sections inserted by ss. 8 and 9 of the Criminal Law (Jurisdiction) Act, 1976).
11. Air Navigation and Transport Act, 1973, s. 11; Criminal Law (Jurisdiction) Act, 1976, s. 10.
12. Criminal Law (Jurisdiction) Act, 1976, s. 2 (1).
13. Id. s. 1 (2).
14. Id. s. 3 (1).

State when charged with or convicted of a scheduled offence in the State).

The reference to scheduled offences extends to aiding, abetting, counselling or procuring the commission of such an offence and attempting, conspiring or inciting another person to commit such an offence or, without reasonable excuse, doing any act with intent to impede the apprehension or prosecution of a person who has and whom the accused knows or believes to have committed such an offence.[15]

In addition it is an offence for any person to escape from lawful custody while in Northern Ireland in order to be present at the taking of evidence there for the purposes of a trial by the Special Criminal Court.[16]

Finally it is an offence for a person:

(a) in the State or in Northern Ireland to aid, abet, counsel or procure the commission in Northern Ireland of a scheduled offence or an escape from custody in Northern Ireland or to attempt, conspire or incite another person to commit a scheduled offence in Northern Ireland, or an escape from lawful custody in Northern Ireland, or

(b) in Northern Ireland, to aid, abet, counsel or procure the commission of, or to attempt, conspire or incite another person to commit a scheduled offence

and he may be indicted, tried and punished accordingly.[17]

Where a person is charged with the commission of a scheduled offence in Northern Ireland or escaping from custody there, no further proceedings other than remand may be taken except by or with the consent of the Attorney General[18] (not, it is to be noted, of the Director of Public Prosecutions).

When a person is charged with committing a scheduled offence in Northern Ireland or escaping from custody in Northern Ireland, he may opt to go there in custody for trial instead of being tried in the State and he must be informed of this right by the District Court on his first appearance before it, and also in the court

15. Id. s. 3 (1) (b).
16. Id. s. 3 (2).
17. Id. s. 2 (2), (3).
18. Id. s. 20 (1); on the topic of consents, see pp. 77 sqq. infra.

by which he is to be tried, before entry of his plea on arraignment.[19] If, at any time before entry of the plea of the accused on arraignment, there is in force a warrant duly issued in Northern Ireland on an information laid by a member of the police of Northern Ireland for his arrest for an offence consisting of the acts constituting the offence for which he is to be tried in the State or for escaping from custody in Northern Ireland, and if the accused so requests, the High Court, or the District Court during his preliminary examination or the court of trial (when the accused is before it) may, if satisfied that the warrant has been duly issued, direct that he be delivered into the custody of the police of Northern Ireland.[20]

The accused must then be brought by the Garda Síochána as soon as may be to some convenient point of departure from the State and there be delivered into the custody of the police of Northern Ireland; in the meantime he is to be kept in the custody of the Garda Síochána or in a prison.[21] If after the order has been made the accused either escapes from custody before he is handed over, or escapes from custody in Northern Ireland after being handed over pending disposal of the proceedings there or while serving a sentence imposed on his conviction, and is subsequently found in the State, he must be brought before a judge or justice of any court (and may from time to time be remanded in custody) and an order must be made for his delivery into the custody of the police of Northern Ireland as soon as may be.[22]

If, however, the accused already stands charged with or convicted of some other offence, he is only to be handed over as soon as may be after the conclusion of the proceedings, including any appeal or re-trial, and of any sentence for that offence imposed in those proceedings.[23] A certificate purporting to have been signed by a member of the police of Northern Ireland or the person in charge of a prison or other place of detention in Northern Ireland or by a member or officer of any court in Northern Ireland as to the relevant default by the accused is admissible in evidence in such proceedings.[24]

19. Id. s. 14 (1).
20. Id. s. 14 (2).
21. Id. s. 14 (3).
22. Id. s. 14 (4).
23. Id. s. 14 (5), (7).
24. Id. s. 14 (6).

2. Obtaining evidence from Northern Ireland

Section 11 of the Criminal Law (Jurisdiction) Act, 1976, relates to trials in the State by a special criminal court and appeals from that court and provides in effect that the court of trial or the appellate court may, on the application of either the prosecution or the accused or of its own motion, provide for the issue of a 'letter of request' to the Lord Chief Justice of Northern Ireland, for the taking by a High Court judge in Northern Ireland of evidence from a specified witness in the presence of the members of the court making the order. The accused must be informed of his right to be present in custody (in which case he will be delivered in custody into the custody of the police of Northern Ireland) at the taking of the evidence, and to be represented by counsel or solicitor, or by solicitor alone, whether he is present or not, or else himself to question the witness; and he must also be informed that, while in custody for the taking of the evidence, he will be immune from legal process of any kind in respect of any cause or matter, civil or criminal, arising *before* his arrival in Northern Ireland.[25] If the accused indicates to the Court that he wishes to be present at the taking of the evidence, it must make an order that he be delivered when and so often as may be necessary into the custody of the police of Northern Ireland.[26]

This section also deals with the conditions of admissibility of evidence taken under it.

The accused, if on bail, must be taken into custody not more than 24 hours before he is handed over and kept in custody until handed over; whether he is on bail or not he must be brought to some convenient point of departure from the State and there delivered, as often as may be necessary, into the custody of the police of Northern Ireland.[27] On his return to the State (either upon the conclusion or any adjournment of the taking of evidence) he must be taken into custody by the Garda Síochána, but released on bail if previously on bail; if previously in custody he must be returned as soon as may be to that custody.[28] If, when the

25. Id. s. 11 (2).
26. Id. s. 11 (2).
27. Id. s. 11 (4) (a).
28. Id. s. 11 (4) (b).

order is made, the accused is under sentence in any other proceedings, the order is not to operate so as to interrupt the currency of that sentence.[29]

It will be noted that in such cases the evidence of the witness concerned is not taken by the members of the Special Criminal Court or appellate court but merely in their presence; since they perform the functions of judge and jury in relation to the cases they try, they have the opportunity to assess, as jurors, the weight and credibility of the evidence; but the question of admissibility of the evidence appears still to be open to argument before them, as a matter of law. The Act provides that a statement of the evidence of the witness, certified by the Northern Ireland judge who took it to be a true and accurate statement, and provided that all the members of the special court or appellate court were present throughout the taking of evidence, is to be admissible as evidence of any fact of which evidence would be admissible at the trial or appeal.[30] Supposing, therefore, that the evidence turned out to consist of inadmissible hearsay evidence, the court should presumably exclude it.

So far the Special Criminal Court has never made use of these provisions, although requests from Northern Ireland have been made and disposed of in the converse case considered below.

3. Taking of evidence for trials in Northern Ireland

Section 12 of the Criminal Law (Jurisdiction) Act, 1976, deals with the converse case in which a letter of request has been issued, under the corresponding statutory provisions in Northern Ireland, for the taking of evidence in the State from a specified witness. The letter is to be produced by or on behalf of the Attorney General to the Chief Justice, sitting otherwise than in public, and the Chief Justice must then designate a judge of the High Court to take the evidence in the State. The judge so designated (referred to as the Commissioner) is to take the evidence of the witness on oath.[31] He has power to determine matters of procedure and to secure the attendance of the witness and pro-

29. Id. s. 11 (5).
30. Id. s. 11 (3).
31. Id. s. 12 (1).

duction of documents required; sittings are normally to be held in private.[32] He may direct that the name and address of the witness are not to be disclosed except to interested parties.[33]

The members of the Court in Northern Ireland concerned and any officers of that Court designated by them are entitled to be present,[34] as are the accused and his counsel and solicitor and counsel and solicitor for the prosecution, and they and the accused, if he is not represented, have the right to question the witness and make like representations to the Commissioner as a counsel or solicitor has at a trial on indictment in the State.[35] Barristers and solicitors entitled to practice in Northern Ireland have the right of audience before the Commissioner.[36]

The witness is entitled to claim the same privileges and immunities, to be determined by the Commissioner, as a witness in the Central Criminal Court, and any question as to the exclusion of any oral evidence or the withholding of any document or thing, on the ground of public interest, is to be determined by the Commissioner in accordance with the law of the State.[37]

A witness who fails to attend, having had his expenses tendered to him, or refuses to take an oath or answer any question or produce any document or thing when required to do so by the Commissioner, and any person who disobeys a direction that the name and address of any witness be not disclosed or other direction given by the Commissioner for the purpose of the examination, or does any other thing which, if done in relation to proceedings before the Central Criminal Court by a witness in that Court would be contempt of that court, is guilty of a summary offence,[38] and the giving of false evidence before the Commissioner is the equivalent of perjury.[19]

If the accused elects to be present at the taking of the evidence he must be kept in the custody of the Garda Síochána or in a prison until his removal from the State at the conclusion or any

32. Id. s. 12 (2), (3).
33. Id. s. 12 (2) (d).
34. Id. s. 12 (4).
35. Id. s. 12 (5).
36. Id. s. 16.
37. Id. s. 12 (6).
38. Id. s. 12 (7).
39. Id. s. 12 (8).

adjournment of the taking of evidence;[40] the Commissioner may, upon any adjournment of the proceedings, authorise his temporary return to Northern Ireland.[41]

Whilst, however, the accused is in custody for the purposes of the examination he is immune from detention, and any kind of suit or legal process, in respect of any cause or matter, civil or criminal, arising before his arrival in the State.[42]

IV. LOCAL LIMITATIONS ON JURISDICTION

The jurisdiction of the Circuit Court in respect of indictable offences is to be exercised by the judge of the circuit in which the offence charged has been committed or in which the accused has been arrested or resides.[1]

Similarly the jurisdiction of the District Court in criminal cases may be exercised by any justice for the time being assigned to the District wherein the crime has been committed or the accused has been arrested or resides.[2]

Thus if a person who normally resides in Dublin robs a bank in Cork and is arrested in Limerick he may be tried in any one of these areas.

Certain statutes, however, extend the jurisdiction of both courts as regards certain offences.

Thus, any offence under the Air Navigation and Transport Acts, 1973 and 1975, may be taken and the offence may for all incidental purposes be treated as having been committed in any place in the State,[3] so that regardless of where the accused may reside or have been arrested any District Justice or judge of the Circuit Court would appear to have jurisdiction. There is a similar provision in relation to swearing falsely before the Court of Justice of the European Communities.[4] Certain offences under the

40. Id. s. 13 (1).
41. Id. s. 12 (3) (d).
42. Id. s. 13 (2).
1. Courts (Supplemental Provisions) Act, 1961, s. 25 (3).
2. Courts of Justice Act, 1924, s. 79, as applied by the Courts (Supplemental Provisions) Act, 1961, s. 48 (2).
3. Air Navigation and Transport Act, 1973, s. 2; Air Navigation and Transport Act, 1975, s. 2.
4. Court of Justice of the European Communities (Perjury) Act, 1975, s. 2.

Fisheries Acts, 1959 to 1980, may be dealt with in any District Court or Circuit Court.[5] Proceedings for any offence under the Dumping at Sea Act, 1981, or under section 6 (4) of the Nuclear Energy (An Bord Fuinnimh Nuicleigh) Act, 1971, if committed at sea, may be taken and the offences may for all incidental purposes be treated as having been committed in any place in the State.[6] Summary proceedings against a person for an offence under the Trading Stamps Act, 1980, may be taken by the court having jurisdiction in the place where that person is for the time being or, in the case of a body corporate, in any place where the body corporate for the time being has a place of business.[7] Proceedings for an offence committed in Northern Ireland or escaping from custody there or for causing an explosion or being in possession of explosives may be taken in any place in the State and for all incidental purposes be treated as having been committed in that place;[8] it thus appears that, for example, a person charged with causing an explosion in Waterford (or an Irish citizen in London[9]) and arrested at Shannon Airport could, in theory, be brought before the District Court in Limerick and returned for trial to the Circuit Court there, although, in practice he would in all probability be brought directly to the Special Criminal Court.[10]

V. LIMITATIONS AS TO TIME

At common law proceedings might be brought in respect of an indictable offence at any time, irrespective of when the offence was committed; *nullum tempus occurrit regi*, time does not run against the Crown.[1] Being part of the common law this Crown prerogative appears to have passed to the State by virtue of

5. Fisheries Act, 1980, s. 47.
6. Dumping at Sea Act, 1981, s. 5 (4).
7. Trading Stamps Act, 1980, s. 13. Whether this is applicable to an offence under section 2 (3) of the Act, which is indictable but triable by a District Justice as a minor offence, as distinct from purely summary offences under the Act, seems doubtful.
8. Criminal Law (Jurisdiction) Act, 1976, s. 20 (1).
9. Supra, p. 33.
10. Chapter 14, infra.
1. Archbold, §1-85.

Article 73 of the 1922 Constitution and Articles 49 and 50 of the Constitution of 1937.[2] There appears to have been no positive assertion of this principle since the foundation of the State, but it has never been denied; and whilst there is in general a six month period of limitation from the commission of the offence for the making of complaints in respect of summary offences,[3] it has been held in the High Court[4] that this does not apply to an indictable offence which a District Justice may deal with summarily as a minor offence.[5]

There are, however, a number of statutory exceptions to the general rule in respect of indictable offences, which are mentioned below, although in some cases the charges could be framed by reference to same analogous statute which provides no limitation period.

Riot

Riot itself is an offence at common law so that there is presumably no limit on when proceedings may be brought; but any prosecution for any offence under the Riot Act, 1787, such as failure to disperse after a proclamation under the Act (in so far as it is not obsolete for lack of adaptation) or taking an unlawful oath or publishing a document to incite riot, must be commenced within one year;[6] there is, however, no corresponding limitation on a prosecution for taking an unlawful oath under section 17 of the Offences Against the State Act, 1939, or for publishing such documents contrary to section 3 of the Tumultuous Risings (Ireland) Act, 1831.

2. See generally Kelly, *The Irish Constitution*, 552 sqq. although this prerogative is not mentioned specifically.
3. Petty Sessions (Ireland) Act, 1851, s. 10 (4); some statutes contain specific provisions in relation to particular offences, either extending the time or providing that time should run from some date other than that of commission, such as the date of discovery of the offence.
4. *The State (Kiernan) v. Governor of Mountjoy Prison*, unrep. 19th February, 1973.
5. Supra, pp. 4 sqq.; presumably if a statute declares an offence either to be indictable or a summary offence, the limitation applies to any purely summary proceedings, unless otherwise provided implicitly, as for example, s. 188 (4) and 231 (5) of the Social Welfare (Consolidation) Act, 1981, referred to below.
6. Riot Act, 1787, s. 12.

Unlawful drilling

Any prosecution for unlawful drilling under the Unlawful Drilling Act, 1819, had to be commenced within six months,[7] but such a prosecution could normally be brought, without any time limit, under section 15 of the Offences Against the State Act, 1939.

Customs offences

Any prosecution under the Customs Acts must be brought within three years.[8]

Unlawful carnal knowledge

Any prosecution for having or attempting to have unlawful carnal knowledge of a girl of 15 years or over and under 17 years of age, or of any woman or girl who is an idiot or an imbecile, or is feeble minded, to the knowledge of the accused, must be brought within twelve months after the date on which the offence is alleged to have been committed.[9] It is to be noted that there is no limitation on proceedings for having or attempting to have unlawful carnal knowledge of a girl *under* the age of 15.

Electoral Offences

Any prosecution for personation at an election (which is indictable in the case of a second offence), or injuring ballot boxes and so forth must be brought within one year from the date of the offence or three months after the report of an election court, whichever period last expires, but in any event within two years after the offence was committed.[10]

Merchandise Marks

Any prosecution under the Merchandise Marks Act, 1887, or any statute to which it has been applied, such as the Agricultural Produce (Fresh Meat) Act, 1930, the Agricultural Produce (Potatoes) Act, 1931, and the Seed Production Act, 1955, must

7. Unlawful Drilling Act, 1819, s. 7, repealed Statute Law Revision Act, 1983.
8. Customs (Consolidation) Act, 1876, s. 257.
9. Criminal Law Amendment Act, 1935, ss. 2 (3), 4 (2).
10. Prevention of Electoral Abuses Act, 1923, s. 52.

be brought within three years after the commission of the offence or one year after the discovery of the offence by the prosecutor, whichever expiration first happens.[11]

Social Welfare

Any prosecution for making a false statement and so forth in order to obtain a widow's or orphan's pension (but not an old age pension) or children's allowance must be brought within two years from the date of the offence or three months from the date on which the Minister for Social Welfare certifies in writing under his seal that evidence sufficient to justify the prosecution came into his possession or procurement (whichever is the later).[12]

11. Merchandise Marks Act, 1887, s. 15; Agricultural Produce (Fresh Meat) Act, 1930, s. 27; Agricultural Produce (Potatoes) Act, 1931, s. 19; Seed Production Act, 1955, s. 22; cf. Consumer Information Act, 1978.
12. Social Welfare (Consolidation) Act, 1981, ss. 188, 231.

CHAPTER 4

THE RIGHT TO PROSECUTE

It is an inherent paradox in the criminal process that decisions taken by the judiciary in the course of formal adjudication are usually subject to review by way of appeal, State Side order and habeas corpus applications, while those decisions which are made by the police, who institute virtually all prosecutions, largely escape independent scrutiny. Yet decisions made by the police may have far reaching implications for the operation of the criminal law in society.[1] It is the police who determine the shape and extent of the role which shall subsequently be played by the judiciary and by the Director of Public Prosecutions in the criminal process.

Total enforcement of the criminal law by the courts is an aim which is neither realistic nor desirable. It is unrealistic in that police resources are such that choices must constantly be made as to the best deployment of manpower.[2] The police may, for example, elect to concentrate their scarce resources on apprehending drunken drivers rather than on combing the mountains in search of illicit stills. While full enforcement in relation to all crimes committed is not possible, prosecution by the police, even of those crimes which have been brought to their attention, is by no means a foregone conclusion. The courts have conceded that the police *ought* to enjoy a discretion in the matter of whether or not to prosecute individual offenders. Often the police may consider

1. For discussion of the role of the police in relation to the discretion to prosecute, see generally Wilcox, *The Decision to Prosecute;* also Dickens, *Control of Prosecutions in the United Kingdom* 22 I.C.L.Q. 1; Goldstein, *Police Discretion Not to Invoke the Criminal Process: Low Visibility Decisions in the Administration of Justice* 69 Yale L.J. 543 (1960).
2. See, e.g., *R. v. Commissioner of Police of the Metropolis, ex parte Blackburn* [1968] 2 Q.B. 118.

that society's best interests are best served by not seeking any formal adjudication of guilt or innocence in a particular case. Factors which may prove important in their decision as to whether or not to prosecute include the youth or advanced age of the person involved, the physical or mental health of the suspect and the gravity or otherwise of the offence. These matters are, however, of relevance only in individual cases.

Occasionally the proscription of certain behaviour may, in changed social circumstances, be viewed by senior police officers as anachronistic or even oppressive. This may result in a policy directive that such behaviour is to be ignored. It is this aspect of police discretion which is likely to prove most problematical. Deliberate decisions not to enforce the law arise most frequently in offences involving personal morality. Such decisions might include a direction not to arrest any adult male homosexuals for having sexual relations with each other in private or not to interfere where any woman is known to have had an illegal abortion performed upon her, or not to prosecute anyone for attempted suicide. In Ireland the law in relation to bigamy similarly appears to have given rise to a practice of non-enforcement by the police. The enforcement or otherwise of certain areas of the criminal law will often be dictated by the perception of individual senior police officers of the gravity of the activities in question. This may lead to differential law enforcement. In one area the use of the drug cannabis might be viewed benignly while elsewhere such behaviour might be considered as very serious. It seems clear that the discretion of the police to ignore certain *areas* of criminal behaviour is subject to review by the courts. In *R. v. Commissioner of Police of the Metropolis, ex parte Blackburn,*[3] proceedings were instituted against the Commissioner by a member of the public for failing to enforce the criminal law in relation to certain gaming clubs. The respondent had taken a policy decision based on what he perceived to be the uncertain state of the law then in force. The Court of Appeal differentiated between a discretion not to prosecute in an individual case, which it was prepared to concede, and the taking of a policy decision which involved a total refusal to proceed against any offender in respect

3. Id.

of a particular kind of criminal activity. The extreme example postulated by Salmon L.J. was that of a chief police officer in a particular district issuing an instruction that, as a matter of policy, the police should take no steps to prosecute any house-breaker. He stated, 'I have little doubt but that any householder in that district would be able to obtain an order of mandamus for the instruction to be withdrawn.' In *Ex parte Blackburn* it was accepted by the court that the respondent did owe a duty to the public which he could be compelled by mandamus to perform. It seems likely that the Irish courts would be prepared to follow this decision.

Improper interference with decisions in relation to prosecutions

It is an offence both at common law[4] and by statute[5] to bribe or to attempt to bribe a police officer or any other person involved in the prosecutorial process in order to persuade them to show favour in the discharge of their function. Furthermore, section 6 of the Prosecution of Offences Act, 1974, makes it unlawful to communicate with any police officer, or with the Director of Public Prosecutions or the Attorney General or their respective staffs, with a view to influencing them to withdraw or not to initiate criminal prosecutions. Certain exceptions to this statutory prohibition have been made. These permit *inter alia* communications by defendants or persons who believe that they are likely to be defendants,[6] and also communications by legal or medical advisers.[7]

Those who may conduct a prosecution upon indictment

For many centuries in both England and Ireland the common law not only tolerated the prosecution of serious criminal offences by private citizens but in fact such prosecutions constituted the rule rather than the exception. It was only after very lengthy legislative deliberations that, in 1879, a public prosecuting agency was finally established in England headed by the

4. See Archbold §24-47.
5. Prevention of Corruption Act, 1906, s. 1.
6. Prosecution of Offences Act, 1974, s. 6 (2) (a) (i).
7. Id. s. 6 (2) (a) (ii).

Director of Public Prosecutions.[8] In England today there exists a dual system whereby either the Director of Public Prosecutions or a private individual may prosecute cases upon indictment.[9] One problem with private prosecutions is that they may prove capricious weapons in the hands of certain persons. Recognition of this fact in England has resulted in a situation whereby the Director of Public Prosecutions may, if he considers it appropriate, take over any summary case and seek the leave of the court to offer no evidence against an accused,[10] and, in the case of a trial upon indictment, the Attorney General may enter a *nolle prosequi* which has the effect of terminating the proceedings.[11]

The legislative history in relation to the conduct of prosecutions by public officials in Ireland differs considerably from that of England. In 1801 Ireland saw the appointment of Crown Solicitors for each of the court circuits and in about 1830, at the direction of the Attorney General for Ireland, 'Sessional Crown Solicitors' were appointed to conduct prosecutions at Quarter Sessions and occasionally even in the courts of summary jurisdiction. These two offices were subsequently amalgamated and, in 1922, their functions were taken over by the 'State Solicitor'.[12] Today the Chief State Solicitor has responsibility for all criminal cases in Dublin while local State Solicitors are responsible for work outside Dublin. State Solicitors, acting upon instructions from the Director of Public Prosecutions, undertake the work which would normally be the responsibility of a solicitor in the preparation of a case. They usually prepare the 'Book of Evidence' and conduct preliminary proceedings. In more serious criminal cases the Book of Evidence may be prepared by counsel.

The right to prosecute in relation to a trial upon indictment in Ireland today is largely determined by Article 30.3 of the Constitution and by section 9 of the Criminal Justice (Admini-

8. On this topic generally see Kurland and Waters, *Public Prosecutions in England, 1854-79: An Essay in English Legislative History* (1959) Duke L.J.493-562; Langbein, *The Origins of Public Prosecution at Common Law* 17 Am. J. Legal Hist. 313 (1973).
9. See Dickens, *Control of Prosecutions in the United Kingdom* 22 I.C.L.Q. 1-19 (1973).
10. Prosecution of Offences Act, 1908, s. 2 (3).
11. See infra, pp. 259 sqq.
12. See Delaney, *The Administration of Justice in Ireland,* 44.

stration) Act, 1924. Section 9 of the Act of 1924 provides:

> 1. All criminal charges prosecuted upon indictment in any court shall be prosecuted at the suit of the Attorney General of Saorstát Éireann.
>
> 2. Save where a criminal prosecution in a court of summary jurisdiction is prosecuted by a Minister, Department of State, or person (official or unofficial) authorised in that behalf by the law for the time being in force, all prosecutions in any court of summary jurisdiction shall be prosecuted at the suit of the Attorney General of Saorstát Éireann.

Article 30.3 of the Constitution states:

> All crimes and offences prosecuted in any court constituted under Article 34 of this Constitution other than a court of summary jurisdiction shall be prosecuted in the name of the People and at the suit of the Attorney General or some other person authorised in accordance with law to act for that purpose.

This article clearly provides for the possibility of persons other than the Attorney General to be invested with a prosecutorial function in relation to indictable offences. Today, by virtue of section 3 of the Prosecution of Offences Act, 1974, virtually all the functions capable of being performed by the Attorney General in relation to criminal matters before the passing of that Act have now been transferred to the Director of Public Prosecutions, whose office was first established in Ireland by section 2 of the same Act. Despite the major transfer of functions effected by section 3, the Government, where it is of the opinion that it is expedient in the interests of national security to do so, may declare by order that, in relation to such criminal matters as it shall specify, the functions conferred upon the Director shall revert to be exercised *only* by the Attorney General.[13] No such order has ever been made. The Fisheries (Amendment) Act, 1978, however, gave the prosecutorial functions in relation to maritime fisheries offences upon indictment to the Attorney General instead of the Director. The rationale of this transfer is, presum-

13. Prosecution of Offences Act, 1974, s. 5 (1).

ably, that these offences may involve sensitive political and diplomatic considerations and are therefore more appropriately considered by the Attorney General.[14]

The importance of section 9 of the Criminal Justice (Administ-ration) Act, 1924, lay in the fact that it abolished the right of private prosecution save in courts of summary jurisdiction. Today only the Director of Public Prosecutions or the Attorney General may prosecute a case upon indictment or for sentence after the accused has been sent forward for trial.

Before 1924 private persons were able to prosecute in courts of summary jurisdiction as 'common informers'.[15] A common informer is a member of the public who is capable of giving information in respect of the commission of an offence.

In *Wedick v. Osmond and Son (Dublin) Limited*[16] it was argued in the District Court on behalf of the defendants that the complainant, who was an inspector of the Pharmaceutical Society of Ireland, had no right to prosecute because the right of a common informer to prosecute was taken away by section 9 (2) of the 1924 Act. However, in rejecting this contention, Sullivan P. said:[17]

> '[I]t seems to me that the sub-section in question is not inconsistent with the pre-existing right of a common informer to prosecute in certain cases. If the Legislature had intended to abolish such a right there would be no difficulty in expressing such intention in plain and unambiguous terms. A common informer prosecuting may well be described as a "person (unofficial) authorised in that behalf by the law for the time being in force", and, if that be so, his right to prosecute is expressly preserved by the sub-section.'

Today in the District Court both private individuals and organisations may prosecute as common informers. A common informer does not need to be an eyewitness of the incident which he prosecutes.[18] Where members of the Garda Síochána prose-

14. For detailed discussion of the role of the Attorney General in criminal matters see Casey, *The Office of the Attorney General in Ireland*, 90-144.
15. *Attorney General v. Thompson* 70 I.L.T.R. 161; *Murphy v. Cryan* [1952] I.R. 225 (H.C.); *Kenealy v. O'Keeffe* [1901] 2 I.R. 39 (Q.B.D.); *Lawler v. Egan* [1901] 2 I.R. 589 (K.B.D.).
16. [1935] I.R. 820 (H.C.).
17. Id. at 842-843.
18. *McCormack v. Carroll* 45 I.L.T.R. 7 (K.B.D) ; *R. (Wilbond) v. Armagh JJ.* [1918] 2 I.R. 347 (K.B.D.).

cute in the District Court they frequently do so as common informers.[19]

In *The State (Cronin) v. The Circuit Court Judge of the Western Circuit,*[1] the High Court heard an application for an order of certiorari in a case in which Sergeant Cronin, an officer of the Garda Síochána, had prosecuted one Egan for being drunk in charge of a motor vehicle. The defendant, Egan, appealed against his conviction in the District Court, and in the Circuit Court it was argued that Sergeant Cronin was not a competent prosecutor. The solicitor for the prosecution conceded this point, whereupon the Circuit Court judge struck out the summons and allowed the appeal. The High Court held that Sergeant Cronin was a competent prosecutor and made absolute conditional orders of certiorari and mandamus. Although affirming that Sergeant Cronin was a competent prosecutor, the Supreme Court nevertheless refused the discretionary orders on the ground that the Circuit Court judge's order was good on its face, and the Court also intimated that it should not exercise discretion where a prosecutor had conceded the point in the lower court.

Certain statutes designate specific statutory bodies or Government Ministers to prosecute for offences proscribed by the statute in question. Very many statutory bodies and persons are empowered to prosecute, these include An Chomhairle Oiliúna,[2] Bord na gCon,[3] the Irish Coursing Club,[4] various Health Authorities,[5] the Ministers for Industry and Commerce,[6] Defence[7] and Agriculture.[8]

Where such bodies or Ministers are empowered to prosecute, the offences involved under the various Acts are all of a *summary* nature. Even those Acts which make provision for the disposition of offences either summarily or upon indictment make it clear

19. This situation was criticised by Griffin J. in *The People v. Roddy* [1977] I.R. 177, 190 (S.C.).
1. [1937] I.R. 34 (S.C.).
2. Industrial Training Act, 1967, s. 46.
3. Greyhound Industry Act, 1958, s. 52 (1).
4. Id. s. 52 (2).
5. Health Act, 1953, s. 44.
6. Factories Act, 1955, s. 110.
7. Defence Act, 1954, s. 7.
8. Diseases of Animals Act, 1966, s. 47.

that the power to prosecute is restricted to summary proceedings.[9]

Where a statute empowers a specified body or a Minister to prosecute, such a provision, without more, does not preclude the Director of Public Prosecutions from instituting proceedings himself if no prosecution has been instituted by the body or person empowered by statute to do so. That the Director may be properly described as a prosecutor of last resort seems clear from *Attorney General v. Healy*[10] where the District Justice himself raised a preliminary objection in a case involving the illegal importation of certain items contrary to the Customs Acts. The District Justice was of the opinion that only an officer of Customs or Excise could be the complainant but Sullivan P. said in the High Court:[11]

> 'I do not think we should construe the words "is prosecuted" in that sub-section as equivalent to "may be prosecuted" and I am, therefore, of opinion that the sub-section authorises the Attorney-General to prosecute in any Court of summary jurisdiction in all cases in which a prosecution is not instituted by a Minister, Department of State, or authorised person.'

Title of prosecutions

The question of the correct title to be borne in a prosecution arose in *The People v. Roddy.*[12] In this case summary charges had been brought in the District Court by a member of the Garda Síochána against a number of men. Proceedings against Roddy related to three offences triable summarily, one of which was brought on foot of a charge sheet, the other two being by summons. In the charge sheet the complainant was stated to be 'the People at the prosecution of the Director of Public Prosecutions' while in the summons matters the complainant was described as 'the People at the suit of the Director of Public Prosecutions'. The prosecutions in question were brought by a member of the Garda Síochána who had neither sought nor obtained prior express

9. See, e.g., Restrictive Practices Act, 1972, s. 24 (1).
10. [1928] I.R. 460.
11. Id. at 478; see also *Attorney General v. Dillon* [1959] Ir. Jur. Rep. 53 (Circ.Ct).
12. [1977] I.R. 177.

authorisation from the Director of Public Prosecutions. Before the enactment of the Constitution in 1937 it had been held in *Attorney General v. Thompson*[13] that a common informer was entitled to institute and conduct proceedings in the District Court using the name of the Attorney General, and without his consent, where a District Justice considered it fit and proper to allow this to be done.

In the High Court in *Roddy*'s case McMahon J. stated:[14]

> 'In my opinion. . . the words "The People at the suit of the Director of Public Prosecutions" or "The People at the prosecution of the Director of Public Prosecutions" are not a mere formal title which may be adopted by the real initiator of a prosecution, but bear their ordinary meaning which is that the Director of Public Prosecutions has authorised the proceedings to be brought.'

O'Higgins C.J. agreed in the Supreme Court with this exposition of the law but the majority in that Court took the opposite view.

Griffin J. pointed out that the Constitutional requirement of Article 30.3 did not apply to summary proceedings in the District Court, and he stated that:[15]

> '[S]uch prosecutions are *not* to be brought in the name of "the People at the suit of the Director of Public Prosecutions", which is appropriate only to proceedings brought on indictment. Therefore the complainant in the case of summary offences should be "the Director of Public Prosecutions" simpliciter.'

He further argued that such proceedings did not require the prior consent of the Attorney General or the Director of Public Prosecutions. He was of the opinion that the phrase 'at the suit of' did not infer that the Attorney General or Director had considered the proceedings in question.

Limited rights of private prosecution in respect of offences to be tried on indictment

In *The State (Ennis) v. Farrell*[16] a common informer called Crean charged Ennis with the offence of fraudulent conversion,

13. 70 I.L.T.R. 161.
14. [1977] I.R. 177, 180.
15. [1977] I.R. 177, 189.
16. [1966] I.R. 107.

which was not triable summarily. Despite objections from counsel for the defendant, the District Justice held that he had power to take depositions but that he could not proceed further with the case, nor could he return the defendant for trial unless the Attorney General took over the conduct of the proceedings.

In delivering the judgement of the Supreme Court Ó Dálaigh C.J. said:[17]

> 'The only limitation on the right of the private prosecutor is that a prosecution *on indictment* must be conducted by the Attorney General: s. 9, sub-s. 1, of the Act of 1924. As a consequence, the private prosecutor may conduct the prosecution thus far, i.e., up to the receiving of informations and the order for return for trial. Thereafter the Attorney General becomes *dominus litis*.
>
> The duty of the District Justice in the case of a private prosecution in respect of an indictable offence is therefore clear. He must permit the private prosecutor to direct and conduct the entire of the preliminary investigation – and at the conclusion of the evidence and including any evidence offered by the defendant must consider whether he should refuse informations or return the accused for trial.'

The discretion of the Director of Public Prosecutions

The Director of Public Prosecutions enjoys a wide measure of discretion as to whether proceedings ought to be instituted and, if so, how far a prosecution ought to proceed.

The Director may, upon receipt of a police file, give a direction to the police to discontinue a particular prosecution. Such a direction may result from a variety of factors.

The Director may reassess afresh all those matters which the police will already have considered in the exercise of their discretion in relation to the enforcement of the criminal law in a specific instance.[18] He may also decide that the evidence adduced by the police in a particular case is insufficient to justify the continued involvement of the accused in the criminal process.

Even if a direction issues to proceed with a particular prosecution, a trial upon indictment may still be terminated if counsel on behalf of the Director informs the trial judge that a *nolle prosequi*

17. Id. at 121-122.
18. See p. 66, supra.

is being entered in respect of all the charges in the indictment. Equally counsel may state that a *nolle prosequi* is being entered in respect of one of more charges in the indictment, in which case the trial will proceed only in relation to the remaining charges. The fiat of *nolle prosequi* was originally exercisable only by the Attorney General but since 1974 it is now exercised by the Director in relation to those cases for which he has responsibility. The appropriate time at which to enter a *nolle prosequi* and the effect of the *nolle prosequi* in relation to double jeopardy are discussed elsewhere in this work.[19] Historically this fiat was a prerogative matter,[20] and hence the English courts consistently refused to exercise any judicial control over its operation.[21] Article 49 of the Constitution transferred the prerogative power to the People for exercise by the Government.[22] It would appear that this did not change the view of the Irish courts in relation to the absolute and irresistible nature of the fiat.

In *The State (Killian) v. Attorney General*[23] Killian had been convicted of an offence which he subsequently charged against a man called Synott. Synott pleaded guilty in the District Court to the offence of arson and was returned for trial. Counsel on behalf of the Attorney General entered a *nolle prosequi.* Killian sought an order for mandamus to direct him to proceed with the arraignment of Synott. Maguire C.J., refusing the order, said in the Supreme Court:[24]

> 'The question in this case is whether this Court can interfere with the Attorney General in the exercise of his power of determining whether a prosecution shall go on or not. . .
>
> [I]t would be unjustifiable for this Court to. . . interfere with the Attorney General by ordering him to prosecute, particularly when he has made it quite clear that he does not consider that he ought to do so.'

The Court in this instance appears to have proceeded upon the

19. See pp. 259 sqq.
20. See Wade and Phillips, *Constitutional Law* (7th Ed.) 181; also Dickens, *The Attorney-General's Consent to Prosecutions* 35 M.L.R. 347, 355.
21. *R. v. Allen* 1 B. & S. 850; *R. v. Comptroller of Patents* [1899] 1 Q.B. 909.
22. Kelly, *The Irish Constitution,* 552-570.
23. 92 I.L.T.R. 182.
24. Id. at 183-184.

assumption that so eminent an officer as the Attorney General ought not to be subjected to judicial review in relation to the exercise of his prosecutorial discretion. In *The State (Ennis) v. Farrell,*[25] Ó Dálaigh C.J. reinforced this view by stating that, 'if a District Justice has received informations it may be assumed that the Attorney General would enter a *nolle prosequi* only after the fullest consideration and for good reason. . .' There seems no reason why the Irish courts should not re-examine their approach to this issue and evaluate for themselves whether the Director (or the Attorney General) has taken into account only proper considerations in the exercise of prosecutorial discretion.[26] Other countries have found such judicial review useful.[27]

The consent of the Director of Public Prosecutions or of the Attorney General to the institution of proceedings

An important discretionary power in relation to the institution of criminal proceedings was originally conferred by many statutes upon the Attorney General and is now exercised virtually exclusively by the Director of Public Prosecutions.[1] This relates to the requirement expressed in such statutes that the consent of the Attorney General be obtained before the prosecution of an accused for certain offences contained therein.[2] An important example of one such statute where a 'consent' is required is provided by section 7 (1) of the Explosive Substances Act, 1883, which states:

25. [1966] I.R. 107 (S.C.).
26. See Casey, op. cit. 103-104.
27. In Germany the *Klageerzwingungsverfahren* action enables a victim of serious crime to seek judicial review of a decision by a prosecutor not to prosecute; see German Code of Criminal Procedure, pp. 172-177. Also Langbein, *Controlling Prosecutorial Discretion in Germany* 41 U.Chi.L.Rev. 439, 463-465; Herrman, *The Rule of Compulsory Prosecution and the Scope of Prosecutorial Discretion in Germany* 41 U.Chi.L.Rev. 468.
1. Prosecution of Offences Act, 1974, s. 3.
2. Examples of statutes where 'consents' are required include: Explosive Substances Act, 1883, s. 7 (1); Public Bodies (Corrupt Practices) Act, 1889, s. 4; Prevention of Corruption Act, 1906, s. 2; Law of Property Amendment Act, 1859, s. 24; Punishment of Incest Act, 1908, s. 6. For instances where *only* the consent of the Attorney General will suffice, see Official Secrets Act, 1963, s. 14 (1); Geneva Conventions Act, 1962, s. 3 (3); Genocide Act, 1973, s. 2 (3), Criminal Law (Jurisdiction) Act, 1976, s. 20 (2).

> If any person is charged before a justice with any crime under this Act, no further proceeding shall be taken against such person without the consent of the Attorney-General, except such as the justice may think necessary by remand, or otherwise, to secure the safe custody of such person.

That the consent of the Director is no mere empty form is demonstrated forcibly by *R. v. Downey.*[3] In this case the accused and another were charged with being in possession of a shotgun and ammunition contrary to Section 4 of the Explosive Substances Act, 1883, at 2 Varna Street, Belfast. The written consent of the Attorney General referred to possession at 37 Peel Street, Belfast. This was amended at the trial to read '2 Varna Street' despite the fact that there was nothing to show that the Attorney General had considered any charge relating to that place. Holding that the trial court had no jurisdiction, and quashing the conviction, Lord MacDermott L.C.J. in the Northern Ireland Court of Criminal Appeal said:[4]

> 'The details which a consent should contain depend on its underlying purpose, which is to ensure for the individual in danger of being charged with one or more of the grave offences created by the Act of 1883, the protection that his prosecution may only proceed, if a law officer of the Crown, after such investigation as is requisite, consents thereto. The consent should, therefore, describe the offence or offences with reasonable particularity, and this means that the indictment and the trial thereof cannot rove outside the material particulars stated in the consent.'

Form of consent

Where the consent of either the Director of Public Prosecutions or of the Attorney General is required by statute, counsel for the law officer concerned may inform the court orally that the appropriate consent has been forthcoming.[5] Also where counsel acting on behalf of the Director tenders a document which purports to be issued by the Director and to be signed by him, such a document must be received in evidence, and be deemed to be such a

3. [1971] N.I. 224. On the importance of 'consents', see also *R. v. Taylor* [1960] N.I. 136; *R. v. Breckinridge* (1905) 6 O.W.R. 501; *Berwin v. Donohoe* (1915) 21 C.L.R. 1.
4. [1971] N.I. 224, 228.
5. Prosecution of Offences Act, 1974, s. 4 (3) (b).

document, unless the contrary is shown.[6] Similar provision has been made for documents issued by the Attorney General.[7]

Constitutional challenges to the requirement of a consent

Although it would seem that the case of *The State (Killian) v. Attorney General* currently constitutes a strong authority for the proposition that the courts will not entertain an action to interfere with the discretion of the Director or of the Attorney General, as the case may be, to enter a *nolle prosequi,* it is possible that different considerations may apply in relation to any refusal to grant a 'consent'.[8] The entry of a *nolle prosequi* does not prevent a private prosecutor from bringing the matter before a District Justice and having the accused returned for trial a second time. The effect of such action would be to exert considerable pressure on the Director to prosecute the case at trial.[9] A refusal of a consent, on the other hand, precludes the possibility of a private individual, or in some instances even the Director, from bringing proceedings, and thus serves as an ouster of the jurisdiction of the criminal courts.

The Irish courts have vigorously championed the right of access to the courts by citizens to enable them to vindicate their constitutional rights. An example of one such instance is to be found in *Macauley v. Minister for Post and Telegraphs.*[10] In this case there was a statutory requirement that the plaintiff obtain a fiat from the Attorney General as a pre-requisite to suing the Minister for failing to provide him with a proper telephone service. The Attorney General's consent was not forthcoming and the plaintiff sought to have the section declared repugnant to the Constitution.

Kenny J. held in the High Court:

6. Id. s. 8 (2).
7. Id. s. 8 (1). On the topic of consents, see also Casey, op. cit. 95-96.
8. For a discussion of the English law in this area see Dickens, *The Attorney General's Consent to Prosecutions* 35 M.L.R. 347 (1972).
9. '[A] private prosecutor who has adduced sufficient evidence to effect a return for trial might, as a general rule, rest assured that the Attorney General would thereafter carry the case to trial before judge and jury,' *per* Ó Dálaigh C.J. in *The State (Ennis) v. Farrell* [1966] I.R. 107, 122.
10. [1966] I.R. 345; for the view of the English courts on ouster provisions see *Anisminic Ltd. v. Foreign Compensation Commission* [1969] 2 A.C. 147.

'The refusal of the fiat has the result that a plaintiff who wishes to sue a Minister of State in the High Court cannot validly commence his action: the refusal of it is, therefore, a denial of the right to have recourse to the High Court.'

The section in question was found to infringe the plaintiff's personal rights under Article 40 of the Constitution and was therefore held to be void in so far as it required a fiat.[11]

A major problem for potential plaintiffs seeking similar declarations in respect of the constitutionality of 'consent' provisions in criminal statutes may revolve around the issue of their *locus standi*. It has been stated that:[12]

'The question of *locus standi* of a party wishing to challenge the validity of an Act of the Oireachtas (or the constitutionality of pre-Constitution statutes) has not yet been fully explored.'

Recent Irish decisions suggest that the courts may adopt a less restrictive view of a citizen's *locus standi* to challenge the constitutionality of a statute than was the case in the past.[13] It has even been suggested that:[14]

'It would require only a slight development to bring about the result that, in a matter affecting the public at large, any citizen has a constitutional right of access to the courts to defend or vindicate the rule of law.'

The statutes which still require the specific consent of the Attorney General each enjoy a presumption of constitutionality, as they have all been enacted since 1937.[15]

Mandamus applications in relation to consents

Even if a particular statutory provision requiring a consent were to be found by the courts to be in accordance with the Con-

11. On the topic of fiats generally see: *The Attorney General's Fiat* 68 I.L.T.S.J. 75.
12. See Kelly, *The Irish Constitution*, 223.
13. See, e.g., *McMahon v. Attorney General* [1972] I.R. 69 (S.C.); *Macauley v. Minister for Posts and Telegraphs* [1966] I.R. 345 (H.C.); *O'Brien v. Keogh* [1972] I.R. 144 (S.C.); *Martin v. Dublin Corporation*, unrep. 7th March, 1979 (S.C.).
14. Law Reform Commission Working Paper No. 8 – 1979. *Judicial Review of Administrative Action: The Problem of Remedies*, 56.
15. The statutes in question are the Official Secrets Act, 1963; the Geneva Conventions Act, 1962; the Genocide Act, 1973; and the Criminal Law (Jurisdiction) Act, 1976.

stitution, a question would remain as to whether an order of mandamus would lie to *oblige* the Director or the Attorney General, as the case might be, to give proper consideration to an application for a consent to prosecute.

Although holding the fiat requirement to be unconstitutional in *Macauley*'s case Kenny J., in considering the nature of the fiat itself, said in that case, 'the Attorney General is free to grant or withhold his fiat for proceedings against a Minister of State for any reason and if he decides to withhold it, no proceedings to review his decision can successfully be brought in the Courts.'[16]

The conventional wisdom as represented by this dictum may still hold good. In relation to the matter of the Attorney General's consent to relator proceedings, the English courts have refused to subject the Attorney's consent to any review by the courts.[17] However, Viscount Dilhorne did not accept that there was a true analogy between the giving of a consent to a relator action and the issue of prerogative writs.[18] A strong argument can undoubtedly be made in support of the proposition that the Director or the Attorney General may be obliged to give proper consideration to applications for 'consents' to prosecute.[19]

Although the State Side order of mandamus lies only to compel the performance by a public body of a *duty* imposed upon it by law, the English courts have taken the view that they are free to exercise judicial control to ensure that a discretion conferred by statute is used properly.[20] If the Irish courts were prepared to adopt similar reasoning in relation to 'consents' to prosecute, the other major problem for the applicant seeking an order of mandamus would be one of *locus standi.*

In R. (Irish Union of Distributive Workers and Clerks) v. Rathmines U.D.C. O'Byrne J. said:[21]

> 'It is undoubtedly a rule of law which is well established that a person applying for a writ of mandamus to compel the performance

16. [1966] I.R. 345, 356.
17. *Gouriet v. Union of Post Office Workers* [1977] 3 All E.R. 70.
18. Id. at 94.
19. For a cogent discussion of this proposition in relation to England see Dickens, *The Attorney General's Consent to Prosecute* 35 M.L.R. 347.
20. *Padfield v. Minister of Agriculture, Fisheries and Food* [1968] A.C. 997.
21. [1928] I.R. 260, 291.

of a statutory duty must have a specific interest in the performance of that duty, and that an ordinary member of the public is not entitled to the writ. The nature of the interest, however, in my opinion, must necessarily vary according to circumstances, and to the nature of the particular duty, and, in particular, upon a consideration of the question for whose benefit was the particular duty imposed.'

It has been suggested in a recent Law Reform Working Paper that, subject to one qualification, the above dictum represents an accurate statement of Irish law on the matter. The qualification relates to the right of an ordinary member of the public to seek an order. The Law Reform Commission suggests that:[22]

> 'If the duty is owed to the public at large so that no one person suffers a greater prejudice from its non-performance than another, why should not any individual be entitled to seek mandamus? If, in such a situation, the court insists on a prosecutor with an interest personal to himself, the result may be that the law goes unenforced.'

It is not only private individuals who may seek a consent to prosecute; the Director of Public Prosecutions may also be obliged to obtain a consent from the Attorney General in relation to those matters specifically reserved to the latter.[23] Although in such a case a consent would invariably be forthcoming;[24] if it were not it seems likely that the interest of the Director would be sufficient to support an application for an order of mandamus either to oblige the Attorney General to take a decision on an application for a consent, or to oblige him to exercise his discretion to consent or otherwise in accordance with the objects of the statute in question.

The rights of private citizens in this area are more problema-

22. Law Reform Commission Working Paper No. 8 – 1979 *Judicial Review of Administrative Action: The Problem of Remedies*, 67.
23. I.e. an offence under the Geneva Conventions Act, 1962, s. 3, the Official Secrets Act, 1963, the Genocide Act, 1973, or the Criminal Law (Jurisdiction) Act, 1976, ss. 2 or 3.
24. 'In 1968 the [English] Attorney General granted twenty four consents in twenty six cases referred to him by the Director of Public Prosecutions for his consent to proceed under the Explosive Substances Act, 1883, but authorised no proceedings in any of the thirty cases referred to him under the Race Relations Act, 1965, the latter references consisting mainly of letters from private individuals.' Dickens, *The Attorney General's Consent to Prosecutions* 35 M.L.R. 347, 349.

tical.[25] In the case of *Ex parte Blackburn,*[26] which is analogous to the extent that the applicant was seeking to enforce the criminal law by using the civil process, the English Court of Appeal was assiduously non-committal on the question of whether the applicant had a sufficient interest to be protected to enable him to have *locus standi.*[27] It may well be argued that if an applicant could show some special or particular interest in a prosecution this would provide him with sufficient *locus standi.*[28]

A relative of a child who has allegedly been the victim of incest might well have a sufficiently particular interest in a prosecution to have *locus standi* in an application for mandamus, either to oblige the Director to give a consent to the initiation of criminal proceedings or to ensure that any refusal of a consent is based on proper considerations. Similarly a person who has suffered loss by reason of the corruption of a public official might have a sufficient interest in a prosecution to have *locus standi.*[29] A problem with this latter case, however, is that the courts might take the view that a civil action for damages would suffice and might, therefore, refuse to accept *locus standi.*

25. In discussing the situation in England, Dickens suggests: 'the evolving intention to exclude those with no valid interest from enforcing the criminal law for their own purposes was at the origin of the practice of removing the right of private prosecution and creating governing executive discretions, and the court may be uneasy about seeming to reverse this development through the medium of mandamus'. – op. cit. at 358.
26. [1968] 2 Q.B. 118.
27. See Lord Denning at 137, Salmon L.J. at 145 and Edmund Davies L.J. at 149.
28. 'The court would not listen, of course, to a mere busybody who was interfering in things which did not concern him. But it will listen to anyone whose interests are affected by what has been done. . .' *Per* Lord Denning in *R. v. Paddington Valuation Officer, ex. parte Peachey Corporation Ltd.* [1966] 1 Q.B. 380, 401.
29. See Dickens, op. cit. at 359-360.

CHAPTER 5

INITIATION OF THE CRIMINAL PROCESS

Restraint upon personal liberty

Article 40.4.1 of the Constitution states: No citizen shall be deprived of his personal liberty save in accordance with law.

It is a matter of fundamental importance that a person should not be subjected to any involuntary restraint upon his freedom unless the person who seeks to impose such a restraint is able to point to some lawful justification for his conduct. Widely disparate powers to impose restraints of various kinds upon the liberty of citizens have been granted to police officers (the Garda Síochána or Gardaí) and others both by statute and at common law. Important statutory powers to stop and search vehicles, which invariably involve at least a temporary restraint upon personal liberty, have been made available to Gardaí to assist them in their task of investigating certain serious crimes such as offences against the State and drug offences.[1] By virtue of section 165 of the Mental Treatment Act, 1945, Gardaí may detain persons of unsound mind who may be a danger to themselves or others but if a person is of sound mind a Garda may not detain him even if he believes that person's life to be in danger.[2] There exists no general power of restraint[3] and, other than the kind of statutory powers alluded to above, the only form of deprivation of personal liberty which the law will countenance is that which arises in consequence of a lawful arrest, made for the purpose of making a person amenable to the judicial process. Most persons

1. Infra, pp. 107 sqq.
2. See, e.g., *Connors v. Pearson* [1921] 2 I.R. 51.
3. *Kenlin v. Gardiner* [1967] 2 Q.B. 510; *Ludlow v. Burgess* [1971] Crim. L.R. 238.

who are eventually tried upon indictment will have been arrested at some stage. Those who have not been arrested will have been brought to court by way of summons. The summons procedure tends to be used for most summary offences and sometimes for less serious indictable offences.

Arrest

Although it has been described as 'an ordinary English word'[4] and has been in use for many centuries,[5] both judges and academic writers have experienced considerable problems in determining exactly what it meant by the term 'arrest'.[6] While it clearly involves deprivation of personal liberty, not every such deprivation necessarily constitutes an arrest. The kidnapper is not said to have arrested his victim.[7] Paradoxically the word arrest is often used by judges without any qualifying adjective to connote both lawful and unlawful restraints upon the liberty of the individual. It would avoid much confusion if the term were to be employed *only* in relation to the former restraints. A useful starting point in relation to arrest is provided by the following definition:

> '[A]rrest, in the context of the criminal law, is more than a deprivation of liberty. It is a step in the criminal process; the apprehending or restraining of a person in order that he may be forthcoming to answer an alleged or suspected crime, made in the lawful exercise of an asserted authority with the intention to bring the person within the criminal process, this intention being communicated to the person by words or conduct together with the reasons for the arrest.'[8]

This definition of arrest encompasses only what may be referred to as a formal, lawful arrest. The terms 'unlawful arrest', 'false

4. See *Spicer v. Holt* [1977] A.C. 987, 1000, *per* Viscount Dilhorne.
5. 'An irous man is lik a frentik best in which ther is of wisdom noon arrest': Chaucer (1386).
6. For discussion of the term 'arrest', see generally: Leigh, *Police Powers in England and Wales* 37-38; see also Williams, *Requisites of a Valid Arrest*, [1954] Crim. L.R. 6; Zander, *When is an Arrest not an Arrest*, (1977) 127 New L.J. 352; Kidstone, *A Maze in Law!* [1978] Crim. L. R. 332; Clarke and Feldman, *'Arrest by any Other Name'*, [1979] Crim. L.R. 702; Telling, *Arrest and Detention – The Conceptual Maze* [1978] Crim. L.R. 320.
7. This view is taken by Smith [1977] Crim. L. R. 293 (a case note on *R. v. Brown*).
8. See Kidstone, op. cit. at 336.

arrest', and 'illegal arrest' all denote certain kinds of behaviour whereby persons purporting to effect a lawful arrest have failed to do so, either because they could not lawfully exercise a power of arrest in the particular instance, or because they wrongly failed to notify the arrested person of the reasons for the purported arrest. The consequences of wrongfully depriving a person of his liberty in Ireland may be manifold. Inculpatory statements made by a suspect, or other evidence obtained from him, must normally be excluded from evidence by the Court of trial.[9] A person who is detained unlawfully has the right to seek an order under Article 40 of the Constitution, colloquially referred to as habeas corpus.[10] The law of torts provides such a person with a cause of action for damages for false imprisonment and assault.[11] The reasonable actions of a person in resisting an unlawful arrest will constitute self defence while those of the arrestor in endeavouring to effect such an arrest will constitute a criminal assault.[12] Formal lawful arrest may be said prospectively to legitimise the actions of the arrestor in depriving a person of his liberty for such period as is permitted by law.

The purpose of a lawful arrest

In *The People v. Shaw*,[13] Walsh J. in the Supreme Court described arrest as being, 'simply a process of ensuring the attendance at Court of the person so arrested'.[14] He pertinently commented at a later juncture in the same judgment, 'No person may be arrested with or without a warrant for the purpose of interrogation or the securing of evidence from that person'.[15] Even where a suspect has been lawfully arrested for the purpose of bringing him before a court, the police may nonetheless be tempted to utilise the period which he spends in their custody to question him. It has long been accepted by the courts in Ireland that the police ought not to interrogate any person in relation to

9. *The People v. O'Brien* [1965] I.R. 142 (S.C.).
10. Infra, pp. Chapter 17.
11. Infra, p. 102.
12. Infra, p. 101.
13. [1982] I.R. 1.
14. Id. at 29.
15. Id.; but see Griffin J. at 55.

the offence for which he has been arrested. In *Attorney General v. Cox,*[16] Kennedy C.J. stated:

> 'It has long been settled that once a person has been taken into custody by the police they are not entitled to interrogate him, although, if he then makes a voluntary statement, they may ask him questions within the limits indicated in the *McCabe* case [*Attorney General v. McCabe*][17] for the purpose of clearing up what has already been said.'

It seems clear that the mere fact of questioning a person in relation to the offence for which the arrest has been made, will not *per se* render the ensuing detention unlawful, but in such an instance the trial judge has a discretion to refuse to allow any answers to be given in evidence.[18] The situation is otherwise when the person is arrested for the *purpose* of questioning him. Such a motive would render the detention unlawful.

When a suspect has been lawfully arrested under section 30 of the Offences Against the State Act, 1939, the Gardaí are entitled under s. 52 of the same Act to question him about any offence, including that for which he has been arrested. Unlike other lawful arrests, a lawful arrest under section 30 gives the Gardaí the right to keep the person in question in custody in a Garda station without charge for a period of twenty four hours from the time of his arrest, or if an officer of the Garda Síochána not below the rank of Chief Superintendent so decides, for a further period of twenty four hours.[19] After the expiry of forty eight hours, however, a continued deprivation of liberty is *prima facie* unlawful.[20] It may be argued that the *nature* of an arrest under the Offences Against the State Act, 1939, differs somewhat from other arrests. It cannot simply be described as a process to ensure the attendance of a suspect in court on a specified charge.[21]

16. Unrep. 9th April, 1929. For the discussions of some English courts, see *R. v. Gardner* 11 Cr. App. R. 265; *R. v. Turner* 19 Cr. App. R. 171; *R. v. Dwyer* 23 Cr. App. R. 156. For further discussion of this topic see Brownlie, *Police Questioning, Custody and Caution* [1960] Crim. L. R. 298.
17. [1927] I.R. 124.
18. *R. v. Knight* 20 Cox 711.
19. Offences Against the State Act, 1939, s. 30 (3).
20. See *The People v. Shaw* [1982] I.R. 1. (S.C.).
21. Arrest in the context of emergency legislation in Northern Ireland was briefly discussed by Lowry L.C.J. in *Ex Parte Lynch* [1980] N.I. 126, 131.

Unlawful detention

Acceptance by the Gardaí of the fact that they ought not to question any person (other than one arrested in pursuance of section 30 of the Offences Against the State Act, 1939) in relation to the offence for which he has been arrested has given rise to attempts to circumvent this doctrine by the practice of detaining people or holding them for questioning. The Garda Síochána are not the only police force culpable in this respect.[1] The Irish courts have been consistent in condemning, as unlawful, the detention of persons who have not been lawfully arrested. The important case of *Dunne v. Clinton*,[2] which has been cited before the courts in Ireland[3] and in England,[4] exemplifies police practice in this regard. This was a civil action for damages brought by the Dunne brothers who had been suspected of theft. On the night of Monday, 28th January, 1929, the two plaintiffs had voluntarily gone to the Garda Station in Listowel at about midnight. They remained there along with another man. At about 4.30 a.m. on Tuesday morning a Garda sergeant entered the room and said to the three men, 'You are detained'. The Dunne brothers were not brought before a Peace Commissioner until Wednesday night. They sued Clinton, who was a Chief Superintendent of the Garda Síochána, for false imprisonment and for trespass to the person. The defendant testified, with disarming candour, that the plaintiffs had not been arrested on any charge but were being detained while he pursued his investigations to see whether he could obtain enough evidence to charge them. In giving judgment in the High Court Hanna J. said:[5]

> 'The first question that arises is whether this detention is something different from arrest or imprisonment. In law there can be no half-way house between the liberty of the subject, unfettered by restraint, and an arrest. If a person under suspicion voluntarily

1. For criticism by English judges of the practice of detention, see *R. v. Lemsatef* [1977] 1 W.L.R. 812; *R. v. Houghton* 68 Cr. App. R. 197.
2. [1930] I.R. 366 (H.C.); affirmed by Supreme Court, Frewen, 563.
3. See, e.g., *The People v. Walsh* [1980] I.R. 294 (S.C.); also *The People v. O'Loughlin* [1979] I.R. 85 (C.C.A.).
4. See, e.g., *R. v. Brown* 64 Cr. App. R. 231.
5. [1930] I.R. 366, 372.

> agrees to go to a police station to be questioned, his liberty is not interfered with, as he can change his mind at any time. If, having been examined, he is asked and voluntarily agrees to remain in the barracks until some investigation is made, he is still a free subject, and can leave at any time. But the practice has grown up of 'detention' as distinct from arrest. It is, in effect, keeping a suspect in custody. . . without making a definite charge against him. . . there [can] be no such thing as notional liberty, this so-called detention amounts to arrest, and the suspect has in law been arrested and in custody during the period of his detention.'

This passage was subsequently cited with approval by O'Higgins C.J. in *The People v. Walsh.*[6] However, Hanna J. went on to say: 'They were *lawfully* under arrest because the guards had reasonable grounds for suspecting them to have committed the felony.'[7] As a consequence the two High Court judges hearing the case[8] awarded damages only for that period which had elapsed between the time when the accused persons ought to have been brought before a Peace Commissioner and the time when they were, in fact, so brought. It is submitted that both of the learned judges and, ironically, counsel for the plaintiffs, were incorrect in so calculating the period of detention. Undoubtedly there was an arrest to the extent that the plaintiffs were deprived of their liberty. The Garda who effected the arrest had power to do so, reasonably suspecting as he did that the men were guilty of felony. However, the arrest was not a lawful arrest because it was effected *exclusively* for the purpose of detaining the suspects in order to gather enough evidence to charge them. That was not a lawful purpose and arrest must, as the Supreme Court has stated in the cases of *In Re Ó Laighléis*[9] and *The People v. Walsh,*[10] be for a lawful purpose. While the court in *Dunne v. Clinton* was correct in finding that the plaintiffs were under arrest, 'arrest' in the context of that case was no more than a synonym for deprivation of liberty or detention. The dichotomy between an arrest and a lawful arrest was discerned by Viscount Dilhorne in *Spicer*

6. [1980] I.R. 294, 302.
7. [1930] I.R. 366, 373 emphasis added by authors.
8. Sullivan P. and Hanna J.
9. [1960] I.R. 93.
10. [1980] I.R. 294.

v. Holt,[11] where he stated; 'Whether or not a person has been arrested depends not on the legality of his arrest but on whether he has been deprived of his liberty to go where he pleases.'[12] However, because only a *lawful* arrest can justify a person's involuntary detention it is now vital for the Irish courts to determine not only the *fact* of arrest but also the *legality* thereof. The violation of constitutional rights involved in unlawful detention will normally mean that any evidence obtained during such a period will have to be excluded.[13] The crucial importance of this matter may be seen from *The People v. Walsh.*[14] Here the suspect Walsh was arrested at 9.30 p.m. on 23rd January, 1975. He was suspected of having assaulted a man by hitting him on the head with an object called a 'pillar'. On arrival at the Garda station he was told of the reason for his arrest and was cautioned. Within an hour of his arrival at the station he was fingerprinted. He did not object to this. Although he could, and should, have been brought before a court on 24th January, 1975, he was not charged before a court until 25th January, 1975. The only evidence against him was the fact of his fingerpint on the 'pillar'. In an appeal to the Supreme Court against his conviction, the court was divided 2:1 on the admissibility of the evidence in question. O'Higgins C.J. delivering the majority judgment, relied heavily upon the authority of *Dunne v. Clinton.*[15] He accepted that the imprisonment of the appellant on 24th January, 1975, was invalid because he had not been brought before a court as soon as was reasonable. However, he took the view that the imprisonment of the appellant on 23rd January, 1975, was in pursuance of a lawful arrest and, as such, was a lawful detention. He therefore admitted the fingerprint evidence. In the course of his judgment the Chief Justice said:[16]

> 'It seems to me that *Dunne v. Clinton* is very similar to the present case. As in *Dunne v. Clinton* there was here a *bona fide* arrest at common law but also undue delay in charging the prisoner before a

11. [1977] A.C. 987.
12. Id. at 1000.
13. Infra, pp. 156 sqq.
14. [1980] I.R. 294.
15. [1930] I.R. 366.
16. [1980] I.R. 294, 303.

> court. As in *Dunne v. Clinton* this undue delay ought not of itself to invalidate the entire period of custody but only so much as is covered by the delay.'

He later stated:[17]

> 'I would regard it as illogical and contrary to reason to contend that something done by a person in accordance with the law could be rendered unlawful merely because that person subsequently acted contrary to his obligations under the law.'

Walsh J., the dissenting judge, would have excluded the evidence. He was of the opinion that the object of the arrest on 23rd January, 1975, was to see what evidence could be obtained from the suspect and that it was not the intent of the Gardaí to charge him with any offence at the time when he was taken into custody.[18] Given that this was his conclusion from the evidence, it is submitted that Walsh J. was clearly correct in seeking to exclude the fingerprint evidence on the basis that there had been an unjustifiable violation of the appellant's constitutional right to liberty. It is conceivable that there may be some merit in the majority approach of splitting the period of custody between lawful and unlawful detention although this should not be based, as it purported to be, on the decision in *Dunne v. Clinton*. The arrest in that case *could* not have been lawful even if it was *bona fide;* the arrest in *Walsh*'s case *might* have been lawful if, at the time of that arrest and, it should be said, contrary to Walsh J.'s finding of fact, the Gardaí had intended to charge the suspect and bring him before the courts but that there had been a subsequent failure in this respect. Only in an instance such as this could there ever be a justification for splitting the period spent in police custody into lawful and unlawful components.

In neither *Dunne v. Clinton* nor *The People v. Walsh* was the fact of restraint in question, merely the legality thereof. However, in *The People v. O'Loughlin*[19] it was necessary to determine the fact of restraint. In this case the accused voluntarily accompanied Gardaí to the police station at Carrick-on-Suir when he had been

17. Id. at 303-304.
18. Id at 312.
19. [1979] I.R. 85 (C.C.A.).

found in possession of a muck spreader which he alleged he had bought from a certain dealer. The accused remained at the station while the police sought confirmation of his explanation for being in possession of the machinery. At 2.00 p.m. they informed the accused that the dealer in question had denied selling the machinery to him. At the trial the Detective Garda dealing with the case admitted that after the accused's verbal statement had been disproved he would have been formally arrested and charged had he attempted to leave the station at Carrick-on-Suir. However, the accused remained at the station because Gardaí in Clonmel wished to question him with regard to an offence of cattle stealing. The accused was taken to Clonmel and interrogated at length. At about 9.30 p.m. he indicated that he would tell the truth about the muck spreader. At about 10.00 p.m. and after he had made a statement he was formally taken into custody and charged. Accepting the fact that when the Gardaí had found the accused's story to be unsubstantiated by the dealer then, had the accused tried to leave the Garda station, he could have been arrested, O'Higgins C.J. said:[20]

> 'Had what ought to have been done in this respect been done, the applicant would have been brought before a Peace Commissioner and would have been accorded his rights to bail. Instead, he was not either formally arrested or charged. . . Apart from the special situation in the Offences Against the State Act, 1939, there is no procedure under our law whereby a person may be held in a Garda Station without charge. In particular, our law does not contemplate or permit the holding of a person for questioning. It makes no difference whether the offence for which he is so held is an entirely separate matter to the one with which he is finally charged. "Holding for questioning" and "taking into custody" and "detaining" are merely different ways of describing the act of depriving a man of his liberty. To do such without lawful authority is an open defiance of Article 40, s. 4, sub-s. 1, of the Constitution.'

If a suspect is *de facto* detained, he is under arrest whether or not he knows of this restraint and whether or not he tries to exercise his right to leave. A difficult issue may arise as to whether or not an accused was in fact free to leave at a particular juncture. The police may not always concede the fact of restraint as they did in

20. Id. at 91.

O'Loughlin's case. It would be desirable if there were an obligation on Gardaí to inform any person assisting them in a voluntary capacity that he is free to leave at any time. The English courts, however, have held that where it is not made *clear* to a person in a police station that he is under arrest, he is entitled to leave using reasonable force to do so.[21] It is submitted that although O'Loughlin was under arrest for the purpose of being accorded his legal rights, the absence of any formal arrest would have meant that, if he had tried to leave the Garda station using reasonable force, he would have been justified in so doing.[22]

What constitutes a formal arrest

A formal arrest normally involves the actual seizure or touching of a person's body accompanied by a form of words which indicate to that person that he is under restraint.[1] In *Genner v. Sparks*[2] it was held that bare words would not suffice to constitute an arrest but in *Alderson v. Booth*[3] the court held that there could be an arrest without any physical touching where the person purporting to effect the arrest made it clear to the person being arrested that he was under restraint and the latter submitted and went with the police officer. Words alone are insufficient unless a person submits.[4] No specific verbal formula need be employed by the person effecting the arrest so long as the person being arrested is made aware that he is under compulsion to go. This is most easily done by saying: 'I arrest you'. Excessive

21. *R. v. Inwood* [1973] 2 All E.R. 647.
22. Cf. *Campbell v. Tormey* [1969] 1 All E.R. 961. This case involved an alleged arrest under the English Road Traffic Act. A constable detected the smell of liquor from the respondent's breath. He asked the respondent to go with him to the police station because it was a wet night. The respondent went. At the station he was required to take the breath test. The Road Traffic Act requires an arrest before such a test might be imposed. Ashworth J. stated: '[H]e was never arrested and if there is a distinction between a person under arrest and being arrested, then that would apply to the present case', at 967; see, e.g., *R. v. Jones, ex parte Moore* [1965] Crim. L.R. 222.
1. For a summary of the law on the act of arrest, see *Halsbury's Laws of England* (4th Ed.) Vol. II, Para. 99; also see generally, Williams, *Requisites of a Valid Arrest* [1954] Crim. L. R. 6.
2. 1 Salk. 78.
3. [1969] 2. Q.B. 216; see also *Grainger v. Hill* 4 Bing. N.C. 212.
4. *Alderson v. Booth* [1969] 2 Q.B. 216.

courtesy may prove the undoing of a person making an arrest.[5] If a person is touched through an open window it may suffice to constitute an arrest even though he flees.[6]

Giving reasons for an arrest

If a person is being asked by the law to submit to restraints upon his personal liberty, the law usually insists that he be acquainted in general terms with the reasons for such a restraint because only then is he in a position to decide whether or not it is appropriate to submit. It was held in *Re Ó Laighléis*[7] that a person being arrested without a warrant must be told why he is being arrested unless he otherwise knows. If a suspect runs away or otherwise contrives to produce a situation whereby he cannot be appraised of the reasons for his arrest, then he will be fixed by the law with constructive knowledge of them.[8] Where a person is arrested under section 30 of the Offences Against the State Act, 1939, it is sufficient that he be informed that the arrest is being made under that section.[9] In *The People v. Walsh,*[10] although the Garda effecting the arrest in a public house did not state the reasons for the arrest because of the large number of people present, the arrest was, nonetheless, held to be lawful because the accused had not exercised his right to be informed of the reasons, he had simply submitted. In *R. v. Kulynycz,*[11] the appellant on being arrested was told that a warrant had been issued. Seven minutes later at the police station he was informed of the true situation, namely, that he had been picked up on suspicion of drug offences at the request of another police force. The court accepted that while a person was entitled to know the act giving rise to his arrest he was not entitled to know whether it was by warrant or as a result of reasonable suspicion. This decision has been criticised on the ground that, 'the police are under a duty to refrain from actively misleading persons concerning the source of

5. See, e.g., *Alderson v. Booth* supra; *Campbell v. Tormey* [1969] 1 All E.R. 961.
6. *Sandon v. Jervis* (1859) E.B. & E. 936; see generally, Williams, op. cit. [1954] Crim. L. R. 6.
7. [1960] I.R. 93 (H.C.).
8. *Christie v. Leachinsky* [1947] A.C. 573.
9. *The People v. McDermott*, unrep. 24th May, 1974, Spec. Crim. Ct. *per* Finlay J.
10. [1980] I.R. 294 (S.C.).
11. [1971] 1 Q.B. 367.

powers under which they proceed.'[12] The Court in *Kulynycz* rejected a contention that before the accused could be in lawful custody he would first have to be set free and then re-arrested. A similar submission likewise failed in *The People v. Shaw*.[13] In this case the accused was a passenger in a car which was stopped by Gardaí. The driver of the car was told that he was being arrested on suspicion of being in possession of a stolen car. The accused would have heard the reasons given for the driver's arrest but, when he enquired as to the reasons for his own arrest, he was told merely that he was being taken in for questioning. Costello J. held that this initial arrest was not lawful but that the accused was lawfully arrested when he was told by a Garda Inspector about half an hour later that he was being detained for being in possession of a stolen vehicle and furthermore the judge held that the lawful arrest did not require the release of the accused in order to cure the earlier illegality.

No technical precision need be used when giving reasons for an arrest.[14] It will suffice if the infringement giving rise to the arrest is outlined to the person being arrested.

A bystander who assists a person in seeking an explanation for his arrest is not, *per se,* guilty of obstructing a police office in the execution of his duty.[15]

Persons who may arrest

Arrest without warrant at common law[16]

Every person of full age and, *a fortiori,* a member of the Garda Síochána is obliged by law to endeavour to effect an arrest if treason or a felony is committed in his presence.[17] There are no reported Irish cases where a person has been prosecuted for breach of duty in relation to this matter and the duty is now more in the nature of a *power* of arrest. A private citizen who sees another attempting to commit treason or felony, may arrest him

12. See Leigh, op. cit., 42-43.
13. [1982] I.R. 1.
14. See, e.g., *Christie v. Leachinsky* [1947] A.C. 573; also see generally, Leigh, op. cit., 40-43.
15. See Leigh, op. cit. 42.
16. On this topic, see generaly, Archbold, (35th Ed.) §§2808-13; Leigh, op. cit. *passim.*
17. 2 Hale 75; 2 Hawk. c. 12 ss. 1, 7.

and hand him over to the Gardaí.[18] Private individuals are also empowered to arrest persons who are engaged upon a breach of the peace while that breach is continuing or if there are reasonable grounds for believing that such a breach is imminent.[19] The expression 'breach of the peace' is elusive;[20] it encompasses not only riot, unlawful assembly and fighting but also a unilateral battery where the victim does not retaliate.[21] It is not, however, occasioned merely by verbal quarrels or by swearing unless there is an accompanying threat of personal harm. Although an arrest effected *immediately* after a breach of the peace is permissible, any greater delay will mean that an arrest may only be effected by warrant.[22]

A private person who entertains reasonable grounds for suspecting that a felony has been committed is entitled, but not obliged, to arrest the suspect. Alternatively, he may *direct* a member of the Garda Síochána to effect the arrest. It is essential where any person purports to effect such an arrest or to give such a direction to a Garda, that a felony should actually be proved to have occurred,[23] although the subsequent acquittal of the person arrested is of no consequence. At common law a police officer was said to be bound to arrest a person on a charge of having committed a felony, when directed to do so by a citizen.[24] It has been argued, however, that this rule is now obsolete and that the police must consider the condition and repute of the person making the charge, as well as the gravity of the offence involved.[25] It should also be noted that where a police officer arrests a person on the charge of another, although the person directing the arrest will be liable if no felony has in fact occurred,

18. 2 Hawk. c. 12 s. 19. See also Williams, *Arrest for Felony at Common Law* [1954] Crim. L. R. 408, 422.
19. *Timothy v. Simpson* 1 Cr.M. & R. 757; *Price v. Seeley,* 10 Cl. & F. 18.
20. For discussion of the case law on breach of the peace, see Leigh, op. cit., 83-93; See also Williams, *Arrest for Breach of the Peace* [1954] Crim. L. R. 578.
21. See *Lewis v. Arnold* 4 C. & P· 354; also Williams [1954] Crim. L. R. at 578.
22. Id.
23. *Walters v. W. H. Smith & Son, Ltd.* [1914] 1 K.B. 595.
24. See, e.g., *Ledwith v. Catchpole* Cald. 291.
25. On the topic of a police officer's discretion to arrest when called upon to do so by citizens, see Williams, op. cit. note 18 *passim.*

no similar liability will attach to the officer.[26] A Garda must distinguish carefully between a *direction* given to him by a citizen to arrest and information given to him by a citizen about an offence. The powers of private individuals to arrest are rarely exercised today but they loom largest in cases involving shoplifting. Neither store detectives nor private security officers enjoy any powers of arrest beyond those granted to other citizens. In any instance where a private citizen makes an arrest he ought to hand over his prisoner to the Gardaí as soon as possible.[27] The most important feature differentiating the common law powers of the Gardaí to arrest without warrant from those powers which all other citizens enjoy, is that a Garda may arrest any person whom he reasonably believes to have committed treason or felony, and it is irrelevant in this instance whether or not any offence has taken place. It has been suggested that where a police officer arrests upon reasonable suspicion and the suspect shows no inclination to escape, the officer should make enquiries of the suspect to try to ascertain whether or not his suspicion was justified. There should be an assumption that the *prima facie* suspicion is ill founded.[28] In any instance where arrest is based upon reasonable suspicion, the question of what constitutes 'reasonable suspicion' is a matter of law.[29] There is no power of arrest at common law on suspicion of a misdemeanour, other than in connection with a breach of the peace.

Arrest without warrant authorised by statute

A very large number of statutory provisions confer wide powers to arrest without warrant.[1] Some statutes, mostly those enacted in the nineteenth century, confer a power of arrest upon all citizens which, *a fortiori*, will include members of the Garda Síochána. More frequent in modern statutes, however, has been the tendency to confine the powers of arrest without warrant

26. See *Beckwith v. Philby* (1827) 6 B. & C. 635; *Christie v. Leachinsky* [1947] A.C. 573, 596-7 *per* Lord du Parcq.
27. 1 Hale 589.
28. *Dumbell v. Roberts* [1944] 1 All E.R. 326, 329, *per* Scott, L.J.; see also Leigh, op. cit. 63-64.
29. *Hill v. Yates* 2 Moore C. P. 80; *Mure v. Kaye* 4 Taunt. 34.
1. See Appendix G, infra.

either to specifically authorised persons or officials (who often include Gardaí) or, most commonly of all, to members of the Garda Síochána exclusively. The scope of statutory powers of arrest can only properly be determined by an examination of the language used in each specific provision.[2] In *Barry v. Midland Railway Co.*,[3] George J. was of the opinion that statutes authorising arrest must be strictly construed in favour of liberty.[4] This view has, however, been doubted by Glanville Williams who argues instead that such statutes, 'should be construed in a way that seems best to accord with the intent of the legislature'.[5] This latter view, it is submitted, is correct. A statute which refers, for example, to the arrest of an 'offender' must be interpreted as referring to a person reasonably suspected of the offence in question, because a person cannot become an offender until there has been some formal adjudication of guilt. Modern statutes tend to be more explicit in conferring a power of arrest where there exists a reasonable belief that an offence is being committed[6] or has been committed.[7] More unusual is a power of arrest where it is reasonably believed that an offence is about to be committed, although such powers are conferred by some statutes.[8] It is not uncommon for statutes to make a power of arrest contingent upon the failure of a suspect to do something, e.g. to produce a licence or other authorisation[9] or to give his name and address.[10]

The statutes which authorise arrest without warrant span a period of over 150 years and the different forms of drafting contained in them mean that there now exist what Glanville Williams has referred to as 'extraordinary traps which Parliament has designed for the police and others who try to promote

2. For cases discussing the interpretation of statutes conferring powers of arrest, see *Trebeck v. Croudace* [1918] 1 K.B. 158; *Isaacs v. Keech* [1925] 2 K.B. 354; *Ledwith v. Roberts* [1937] 1 K.B. 232; *Barnard v. Gorman* [1941] A.C. 378.
3. (1867) 1 I.R.C.L. 130.
4. Id. at 141.
5. See Williams, *The Interpretation of Statutory Powers of Arrest Without Warrant*, [1958] Crim. L. R. 73 and 154, at 73.
6. See, e.g., Prohibition of Forcible Entry and Occupation Act, 1971, s. 9.
7. See, e.g., Misuse of Drugs Act, 1977, s. 25.
8. See, e.g., Criminal Law (Jurisdiction) Act, 1976, s. 19; also Official Secrets Act, 1963, s. 15.
9. Betting Act, 1931, s. 25 (3) (a).
10. Id. s. 25 (3) (b).

the ends of criminal justice.'[11]

Arrest on warrant

Because most arrests are not anticipated in advance by the arresting officer and because the powers to arrest without warrant are now very extensive, it will only be in exceptional cases that Gardaí will seek a warrant in order to arrest someone.[12] Warrants may issue in indictable offences even though there exists a common law or statutory power of arrest without a warrant.[13] It has been said that, 'The nature of the warrant procedure is to transfer the discretion from the police officer to the magistrate, and to confer on the police officer, in return for this judicial control, a measure of protection in the execution of the warrant.'[14] Gardaí properly executing warrants are protected by statute when any irregularity or want of jurisdiction may occur in the issue of the warrant,[15] or for any thing done in obedience to the warrant, unless inspection of the warrant has been refused to the person arrested for a period of six days after a demand has been made in writing for a perusal of the warrant.[16] A Garda who makes an arrest on foot of a warrant ought, where possible, to have the warrant in his possession, ready to produce it if it is asked for.[17] This rule, however, does not apply to any case where the Garda has power to arrest without warrant in any event. A warrant to arrest a person on an indictable offence remains in force until it is executed.[18] Gardaí who wish to avail of the protection of a warrant in order to effect an arrest must have a written information sworn before a District Justice or a Peace Commissioner. If the information discloses a criminal offence then the Justice or the Peace Commissioner, in the exercise of his judicial discretion, may cause a warrant to issue. A warrant

11. See Williams, op. cit. n. 5 at 162.
12. For the rules governing the issue and contents of warrants to arrest, see District Court Rules, 1948; also Woods, *District Court Guide,* Vol. 1, 46-49.
13. District Court Rules, 1948, r. 36.
14. Thomas, *The Execution of Warrants of Arrest* [1962] Crim. L. R. 520 and 597, at 520.
15. Constabulary (Ireland) Act, 1836, s. 50.
16. Public Officers Protection (Ireland) Act, 1803, s. 6.
17. See *Codd v. Cabe* 1 Ex. D. 352; also *Galliard v. Laxton* 2 B. & S. 364.
18. Petty Sessions (Ireland) Act, 1851, s. 11 (1); also *District Court Rules,* 1948, r. 35.

should state that a written sworn information has been made.[19] If the judicial officer from whom a warrant is sought believes that the issue of a summons would adequately secure the attendance of the suspect in court, he may cause a summons to issue and the court in *O'Brien v. Brabner*[20] held that a warrant ought to issue only if a summons was likely to prove ineffective to secure the attendance of the subject.

The use of force in effecting arrest

If an arrest is lawful then the law grants to the arrestor the power to use reasonable force to achieve this end. No force is justified if a suspect is prepared to submit to the arrest. Any gratuitous use of violence against a person after he has been subjugated would leave the person making the arrest open to an action in tort for assault and battery[1] as well as to a possible criminal prosecution. The right to arrest does not *per se* confer the right to handcuff an arrested person as a matter of course. He ought to be handcuffed only when it is reasonably anticipated that he may escape or be violent.[2] In *The People v. Walsh*[3] the appellant was handcuffed despite the fact that he appears to have submitted to the arrest and did not even seek the reasons therefor. No issue was taken at the time although the handcuffing could not in any way have affected the legality of the arrest or subsequent detention but, unless the person making the arrest could justify the use of handcuffs, he would be liable for battery.

The concession by the law that a *reasonable* amount of force may be employed to effect an arrest does not mean that the use even of minimal force to achieve this object will always be justifiable. Historically all persons were obliged to arrest felons[4] and the law was that if a felon was killed resisting arrest, such a

19. *Caudle v. Seymour* (1841) 1 Q.B. 889.
20. 49 J.P. 227; see also Woods, op. cit. at 46.
1. Cf. *Reed v. Wastie* [1972] Crim. L. R. 221, where compensation was awarded to an arrested person who was handcuffed when a police officer punched him in the face breaking his nose.
2. *Leigh v. Cole* 6 Cox 329; *R. v. Lockley* 4 F. & F. 155; see generally, Leigh, *Police Powers in England and Wales* at 47.
3. [1980] I.R. 294.
4. On the duty to arrest a felon, see supra, p. 96.

homicide was justifiable.[5] Such a rule was probably uncontroversial at a time when felons were liable to suffer execution in any event. Today, the distinction between felony and misdemeanour has lost most of its original rationale. Felonies may be extremely trivial. Common sense now dictates that some reasonable proportion must obtain between the amount of force employed and the end which it is sought to achieve.[6] To take an extreme example, a Garda protecting an Embassy would not be justified in shooting dead a man whom he saw stealing a milk bottle merely because the culprit ran off when the Garda tried to arrest him and shooting him was the only means left to prevent the felon's escape. The end, of making a man amenable to a court which would probably fine him a small sum, would bear no reasonable proportion to the means invoked to achieve it.

A Garda who is endeavouring to effect an arrest either with or without a warrant, may use reasonable force to break down doors of a house to gain admittance, but only if he has unsuccessfully sought prior admission.[7]

The use of force in resisting arrest

In addition to being a common assault or an assault occasioning actual or grievous bodily harm, it is also a separate statutory offence to resist a lawful arrest.[8] Originally no limit was placed upon the force which a person could use to resist an unlawful arrest.[9] However, by analogy with the position of the person making the arrest, it may today be argued that resistance offered to an unlawful arrest will be permissible only so long as that resistance is reasonable. It is clearly imprudent for any citizen to offer force to a Garda who seeks to effect an arrest because, as has been seen, the powers given to Gardaí both at common law and by statute are extremely varied and any force offered to an

5. See Holdsworth, *A History of English Law*, Vol. III (3rd Ed.) 600.
6. See *R. v. Turner* [1962] V.R. 30; also see generally, Leigh, op. cit. at 43-47; Pearson, *The Right to Kill in Making Arrests* 28 Mich. L. R. 957 (1930).
7. See, e.g., *Seymanne's case* (1604) 5 Co. Rep. 916; *Launock v. Brown* 2 B. & Ald. 593; see generally, Thomas, *The Execution of Warrants of Arrest* [1962] Crim. L. R. 520, 597, 600-604.
8. Offences against the Person Act, 1861, s. 38.
9. *R. v. Woolmer* 1 Mood. C.C. 334.

arrest which proves to be lawful will involve the arrested person in the serious offence of assaulting a Garda in the execution of his duty. In some countries resistance even to an unlawful arrest by a police officer is not permissible.[10] Citizens who believe that they are being unlawfully kept in police custody are better advised to submit to the arrest and then to sue for assault and false imprisonment at a later juncture.[11] The use of lethal force by a citizen in resisting an unlawful arrest by the police will normally constitute manslaughter. This is so even if the suspect is forearmed with a lethal weapon to resist an attempted unlawful arrest by a Garda.[12]

Charging suspects and bringing them before the court

As the purpose of an arrest is solely to make a person amenable to the judicial process, the law is exacting in its requirements that he be brought before the court promptly. Appearance in court is extremely important because it enables accused persons to seek bail, to apply for legal aid and to have some independent scrutiny, albeit often of a perfunctory nature, into the propriety of the actions of the Gardaí.

When the arrest is on foot of a warrant

When a person has been arrested on foot of a warrant, which is a relatively unusual occurrence, the situation is governed by section 15 of the Criminal Justice Act, 1951, which states:

> (1) A person charged with an offence shall on arrest be brought before a Justice of the District Court having jurisdiction to deal with it, if a Justice is immediately available.
>
> (2) If not, he shall be brought as soon as may be before a Peace Commissioner in the district of the Justice.
>
> (3) If he is brought before a Peace Commissioner, the Commissioner, having heard the evidence offered, shall remand him, either in custody or on such bail as the Commissioner

10. For a discussion of the French doctrine of 'rebellion' see Williams, *Requisites of a Lawful Arrest* [1954] Crim. L. R. 6, 8-9.
11. See *Christie v. Leachinsky* [1947] A.C. 573, 599 *per* Lord Du Parcq.
12. See *The People v. White* [1947] I.R. 247 (C.C.A); *R. v. Thompson* 1 Mood. C.C. 80; but see, *R. v. McInnes* [1971] 1 W.L.R. 1600.

thinks fit, and remit the case for hearing before a Justice of the District Court having jurisdiction to deal with it.

(4) If the accused is remanded on bail and there and then finds bail the case shall be remitted to the next sitting of the Court.

(5) In any other event, the case shall be remitted to a sitting of the Court at a named place to be held within eight days after the arrest.

In *Attorney General v. Burke*[1] Davitt P. analysed the wording of section 15 which, as he pointed out, refers to 'a person charged with an offence and arrested' and not to 'a person arrested and charged with an offence'. He took the view that as the great majority of cases in which the charge preceded the arrest were those where a charge was made in writing with a view to securing the issue of a warrant, section 15 could apply *only* to cases in which persons had been arrested on foot of a warrant and that those situations where an arrest was effected without a warrant fell to be governed by the common law rules.[2] It should be noted that if a warrant has been issued which has been endorsed for bail, then section 15 will not apply, because in such an instance the accused must be released as soon as the bail conditions have been fulfilled.[3]

When an arrest is made without a warrant

When an accused has been arrested without a warrant the Gardaí may lawfully adopt any one of a number of courses. First, although arrest is intended to make a person amenable to the judical process, nevertheless, if, after arresting a suspect, Gardaí came across evidence exculpating him, he ought to be released immediately such evidence comes to light. Alluding to this situation in *Wiltshire v. Barrett*,[4] Davies L.J. stated, 'it is in my view plain that, once an officer in charge has satisfied himself that a man is innocent, any further detention in custody would be false imprisonment.'[5]

1. [1955] I.R. 30 (H.C.).
2. Id. at 35.
3. Criminal Procedure Act, 1967, s. 30.
4. [1966] 1 Q.B. 312.
5. Id. at 329.

Secondly, the Gardaí may conclude that, while a reasonable suspicion existed to justify the arrest, there is no admissible evidence upon which a prosecution can properly be initiated. As has already been stated, the question of what constitutes 'reasonable suspicion' justifying an arrest is a matter of law.[6] The actions of the arrestor must be considered at the time he made the arrest and not in the light of any subsequent events. An inference drawn by a Garda from certain facts may be sufficient to constitute a reasonable suspicion justifying an arrest and yet may fall far short of anything which could be considered as *evidence* in a criminal case.[7] Lord Devlin in *Shaaban Bin Hussein v. Chong Fook Kam* neatly isolated the issue when he said:[8]

> 'Suspicion arises at or near the starting point of an investigation of which the obtaining of *prima facie* proof is the end. When such proof has been obtained, the police case is complete: it is ready for trial and passes on to its next stage. . .
>
> There is another distinction between reasonable suspicion and *prima facie* proof. *Prima facie* [proof] consists of admissible evidence. . . Suspicion can take into account matters that could not be put in evidence at all. . . Suspicion can take into account also matters which, though admissible could not form part of a *prima facie* case. Thus, the fact that the accused has given a false alibi does not obviate the need for *prima facie* proof of his presence at the scene of the crime. . .'

Where an arrest has been made on the basis of a reasonable suspicion and yet there exists no evidence against a suspect, he ought to be released. Such a course of action does not preclude the Gardaí from issuing a summons or obtaining a warrant or, in some instances, re-arresting without warrant at a later juncture should admissible evidence come to light.

A third course open to Gardaí in relation to persons against whom there is some admissible evidence is to charge them in the Garda station and then to admit them to bail on condition that they appear before the District Court.[9] The expression 'charging of suspects' is apt to cause confusion as it is often used to connote

6. Supra, p. 97.
7. *Draper v. United States* 358 U.S. 307 (1959).
8. [1969] 3 All E.R. 1626, 1630-31.
9. For rules governing police bail, see pp. 191-192, infra.

two quite distinct situations in the criminal process. The charging of a person in a Garda station refers to a procedure whereby the accused is told that he will be prosecuted for an offence or offences. The particulars of the offence or offences in question are then set out in writing on a charge sheet.[10] When these particulars have been entered on the sheet, a copy must be given to the accused person as soon as may be.[11] The accused is always invited to make a reply to the charge and if any reply is made it is to be recorded in writing and may be given in evidence. A charge sheet must be lodged as soon as possible with the District Court Clerk of the District Court area in which the case is to be heard.[12] When the accused person is thereafter brought before a District Justice or a Peace Commissioner a formal charging takes place. This takes the form of a complaint being made to the Court by a member of the Gardaí who alleges that the offence on the charge sheet has been committed by the accused. He gives evidence of his having arrested and charged the accused with the offence or offences in question and of any reply made thereto by the accused. The accused may then be remanded by the Court either in custody or on bail. It is only when the formal charge is made in court that the judicial process begins.

The final course of action open to Gardaí who wish to proceed against a person arrested without a warrant but who do not wish to admit him to police bail, is to charge him in the Garda station with the offence. They must then, according to common law, bring him before a court 'within a reasonable time'. In considering what constitutes a reasonable time Hanna J. said in *Dunne v. Clinton:*[13]

> 'No hard and fast rule can be laid down to cover every case. It must depend on many circumstances, such as the time and place of the arrest, the number of the accused, whether a Peace Commissioner is easily available, and such other matters as may be relevant.'

In *Doherty v. Liddane,*[14] an action for damages for false im-

10. District Court (Charge Sheet) Rules, 1971, S.I. 225 of 1971, r. 3 (1).
11. Id. r. 3 (2).
12. Id. r. 3 (3).
13. [1930] I.R. 366, 374-375.
14. [1940] Ir. Jur. Rep. 58 (H.C.).

prisonment, Gardaí had detained the plaintiff for twenty-six hours before charging him before a court. Part of this delay had been caused by police efforts to secure bailsmen which had taken place with the acquiescence of the plaintiff. Accordingly, the detention was held not to be unlawful. In *The People v. Shaw*[15] the appellant was invalidly arrested at 11.30 p.m. on 26th September, 1976, at Salthill, Galway. There then took place a valid arrest some forty minutes later at 12.10 a.m. on 27th September, 1976, when he was informed of the reasons for his detention. Although the Galway District Court sat at 10.30 a.m. on the morning of 27th September, the accused was not brought before that Court and was instead detained in Galway Garda Station throughout the day of 27th September and the morning of 28th September. In his consideration of the common law notion of 'reasonable time', Costello J. alluded to and accepted the propositions of law set forth in the case of *John Lewis and Co. Ltd. v. Tims*[16] where the House of Lords considered common law duties attaching to the person effecting the arrest in relation to a person arrested without a warrant. Lord Parker said in that case:[17]

> 'The question throughout should be: Has the arrestor brought the arrested person to a place where his alleged offence can be dealt with as speedily as is reasonably possible? But all the circumstances in the case must be taken into consideration in deciding whether this requirement is complied with. A direct route and rapid progress are no doubt matters for consideration, but they are not the only matters.
>
> Those who arrest must be persuaded of the guilt of the accused; they cannot bolster up their assurance or the strength of the case by seeking further evidence and detaining the man arrested meanwhile or taking him to some spot where they can or may find further evidence. . . Whether there is evidence that the steps taken were unreasonable or the delay too great is a matter for the judge.'

The police do not have greater powers than other persons effecting arrests to delay in bringing a suspect before a court.[18] The Supreme Court in *Shaw*'s case accepted that the detention of Shaw after the District Court had sat on 27th September was

15. [1982] I.R. 1.
16. [1952] A.C. 676.
17. Id. at 691.
18. Leigh, op. cit. at 54.

prima facie unlawful. However, the reason why the accused was not brought before the court was that the Gardaí suspected him of involvement in the abduction of two girls and there remained a possibility, albeit a remote one, that at least one of the girls might still be alive. The Court accepted that the constitutional right of the accused to liberty could be limited or qualified in this particular instance because a choice had to be made by the Garda in charge between the right of the accused to liberty and the possible protection of the right to life of the girls. It therefore held the detention of the accused to be lawful.

Arrest under the Offences Against the State Act, 1939

If the Gardaí arrest a suspect under the Offences Against the State Act, 1939, the common law rule requiring that persons be brought before the court within a reasonable time does not apply. Persons arrested under section 30 of that Act may be detained in a Garda station for twenty-four hours or on the direction of a Garda not below the rank of Chief Superintendent for a further period of twenty-four hours before being brought before a court.

Holding charges

The fact that Gardaí are not permitted to question a person in relation to the offence wherewith he is charged and also the fact that they are obliged at common law to bring suspects before a court within a reasonable time mean that there is a temptation to use a 'holding charge'. A 'holding charge' relates to an offence which it is reasonably believed the accused has committed. However, the main purpose of such a charge is to secure the detention of the suspect while other more serious matters can be investigated. The English courts have accepted the use of holding charges.[19]

Stop and search powers

The involuntary restraint consequent upon a lawful arrest, is, as has been seen, permitted only to enable a suspect to be made

19. See, e.g., *Christie v. Leachinsky* [1947] A.C. 573, 593 *per* Lord Simonds.

amenable to the judicial process. The Gardaí do not have any general power to detain for search or interrogation purposes. A Garda seeking to stop and search or question a citizen against his will and without effecting a lawful arrest must find the authority enabling him to do so in a statute. There exists no power to stop and search at common law. However, wide powers are nowadays given to Gardaí by a number of statutes.

Under section 30 of the Offences Against the State Act, 1939, Gardaí are empowered not only to arrest but also to stop, search and interrogate persons suspected of involvement in offences against the State or scheduled offences. They are empowered under the same section to stop and search vehicles, ships, etc. suspected of containing persons whom Gardaí are empowered by the section to arrest without warrant. Further extensive powers enabling Gardaí to stop and search vehicles and their occupants in a wide number of instances are granted by section 8 of the Criminal Law Act, 1976. This section enables Gardaí, acting on reasonable suspicion, to stop vehicles with a view to ascertaining whether their occupants have committed, are committing or are about to commit any one of the many offences enumerated in the section, e.g. murder, manslaughter, firearms offences, burglary, malicious damage involving the use of fire or explosive substances, etc. It should be noted that, unlike section 30 of the Act of 1939, section 8 of the Act of 1976 does not permit Gardaí to detain for the purpose of *questioning* any person stopped in accordance with its provisions; it merely permits a stop for the searching of the vehicle and its occupants. Nor does this section authorise the kind of blanket road checks which have become familiar in recent years in the aftermath of bank robberies and other serious offences. The 'reasonable suspicion' requirement of section 8 is insufficiently elastic to extend to such police activities. Probably new statutory authority is necessary to justify such checks.

By analogy with statutory powers of arrest, the piecemeal way in which statutory powers of stop and search have evolved throughout the nineteenth and twentieth centuries means that it is virtually impossible to impose any meaningful schematism upon them. Perhaps surprisingly no general power to stop and search is conferred in relation to stolen goods. However, under section 29 of the Dublin Police Act, 1842, a Garda in the Dublin Metropolitan District may stop and detain a vessel, boat, cart or carriage in which he has reason to suspect that anything stolen or unlawfully obtained may be found. The Garda is not required under this section to entertain any suspicion of criminality in respect of the driver of any vehicle involved.[1] Gardaí and other authorised persons have been given stop and search powers in relation to suspected offences involving certain flora and fauna.[2] Customs officials and Gardaí may stop and search vehicles involved in the movement of spirits and stills.[3] Customs and Excise and other authorised officials have wide powers to stop and search persons entering and leaving the country.[4] Under the Road Traffic Act, 1961,[5] Gardaí have wide powers to stop vehicles to check their mechanised condition.

One of the most contentious of all the statutory powers to stop and search is undoubtedly that provided by section 23 of the Misuse of Drugs Act, 1977. This section enables a Garda to search any person whom he has reasonable cause to suspect is in possession of a controlled drug in contravention of the Act. Gardaí are further empowered by the section to stop and search any vehicles, vessels or aircraft where it is suspected that such a drug may be found. In England stop and search powers are very frequently invoked in relation to drug offences.[6] Because drugs may be easily secreted on the person, any search, if it is to be effective, must be extremely thorough and consequently may prove very embarrassing to the person searched.

1. For discussion of the Metropolitan Police Act, 1839, s. 66, which is identical in all material respects to the Dublin Police Act, 1842, s. 29, see Leigh, *Police Powers in England and Wales* at 130-132; also see Williams, *Statutory Powers of Search and Arrest on the Ground of Unlawful Possession* [1960] Crim. L. R. 598.
2. Wildlife Act, 1976, s. 72.
3. Intoxicating Liquor Act, 1960, s. 22 (3).
4. See, e.g., Customs Free Airport Act, 1947, s. 9; Exchange Control Act, 1954, s. 19.
5. S. 20.
6. In 1978 in England and Wales, excluding the Metropolitan Police District, 10,023 drug stops were made and illegal possession of drugs were discovered on 3,116 occasions. This information is contained in The Royal Commission on Criminal Procedure – *The Investigation and Prosecution of Criminal Offences in England and Wales: The Law and Procedure* Cmnd. 8092-1 Appendix 2.

Criticisms of stop and search powers

A factor which is common to almost all of the statutory provisions authorising stops and searches is that the person seeking to avail of such a power must entertain a reasonable suspicion. As has already been seen, most powers of arrest must similarly be on the basis of a reasonable suspicion entertained by the person making the arrest. Opponents of stop and search power plausibly argue that if such a suspicion exists on the part of the person exercising such a power, then such a person would equally be justified in effecting a lawful arrest and that the latter course is much more desirable in that:[7]

> '[A]n arrest initiates a series of steps including normally taking the suspect to a police station, 'booking in' at the station and the like. These steps compel the arresting officer to justify his/her decision to other persons (albeit other police officers). A 'stop and search' power is not subject to the same review or any review at all. Further, an officer possessed of such powers may be tempted to require people or certain categories of people to submit to 'routine' searches or harassment. This raises the problem of differential law enforcement – the fact that certain categories of people are more likely than others to have their behaviour scrutinised by the police.'

This trenchant criticism might equally be applied to the Irish situation. It might even be argued that, as most of the stops and searches in Ireland are aimed at the discovery of either drug offences or offences of violence stemming from political origins, that the potential dangers of the stereotyping of citizens by the Gardaí may be accentuated and allegations of differential law enforcement may, in consequence, be all the more acute than in England. On the other hand, the criticism involves two important presuppositions. The first is that being stopped and searched involves a similar kind of invasion of liberty to being arrested and the second is that reasonable suspicion justifying stopping and searching is of the same degree as that which justifies an arrest. The latter proposition has been doubted by at least one writer.[8] In relation to the former proposition the English Royal Com-

7. Legality in the Criminal Process – Evidence of the Legal Action Group to the Royal Commission on Criminal Procedure, p. 16.
8. See Williams, *Statutory Powers of Search and Arrest on the Ground of Unlawful Possession* [1960] Crim. L. R. 598, 606.

mission on Criminal Procedure takes the view in its report that arrest would normally involve a more significant deprivation of liberty than would be involved in the exercise of a stop and search power.[9] The Commission was also of the opinion that the abolition of stop and search powers might result in more arrests taking place.[10] The solution it proposed, which has much to recommend it, is that powers of stopping and searching be retained but that stops and searches should be recorded in writing and that copies of the record should be made available on request within a reasonable time to any person searched.[11]The Commission also proposes the following rationalisation of stop and search powers to replace all existing powers. It states:[12]

> '[A] police officer should have power to stop and, if need be, search any person in a public place whom he on reasonable grounds suspects of conveying stolen goods or of being in possession of anything whose possession in a public place is itself a criminal offence.'

Remedies for unlawful arrests and stops

If an arrest or a police stop be unlawful, the person deprived of liberty will be able to seek compensation for false imprisonment and possibly also for assault and battery. However, one difficult problem for plaintiffs is that in relation to all stops and most arrests the period of false imprisonment will invariably be very short and damages in consequence will usually be low. In addition to the marginal way in which an accused may be said to be damnified, there may be a distinct reluctance on the part of a judge sitting alone or a jury to penalise a Garda who, through inadvertence or inexperience, has failed to observe the technical requirements for a lawful arrest or stop. Arguably the State ought to encourage such actions. In the United States it has been argued that:[13]

9. Cmnd. 8092 (1981) at 27.
10. Id.
11. Id. at 29.
12. Id. at 27.
13. Foote, *Tort Remedies for Police Violation of Individual Rights* 39 Minn. L. R. 493, 516 (1954-55).

'[T]he tort remedies offer what is perhaps the best hope of achieving increased control over police illegality. By placing the initiative for enforcement in the hands of injured persons who are offered a selfish motive for prosecuting the actions, it is possible to by-pass the insoluble problem of how to make a police force police itself.'

It has been further argued that if private individuals are to bear the brunt of enforcing public policy against police illegality, then adequate inducements to sue ought to be provided.[14] This could be done either by introducing minimum liquidated damages which every successful plaintiff would be certain to secure or alternatively by developing the concept of punitive or exemplary damages. In *Shaaban Bin Hussein v. Chong Fook Kam* [15] the Judicial Committee of the Privy Council acknowledged the fact that scope for compensatory damages was limited in a case such as the one it was hearing, where the arrest had been effected without a reasonable suspicion, and it accepted that:[16]

'[T]he court is not in this category of case confined to awarding compensation for loss of liberty and for such physical and mental distress as it thinks may have been caused. It is also proper for it to mark any departure from constitutional practice, even if only a slight one, by exemplary damages; but these do not have to be large.'

14. Id. 515.
15. [1969] 3 All E.R. 1626.
16. Id. at 1631-32.

CHAPTER 6

THE PREPARATION OF THE PROSECUTION CASE

I. THE QUESTIONING OF SUSPECTS

The questioning of persons suspected of offences may serve either to dispel police suspicion or to confirm it. It is essential to the investigative role of the police that they be permitted to interrogate suspects. Such questioning may elicit a confession from the suspect which, if admitted in evidence, will often suffice to secure a conviction. However, before any confession may be admitted in evidence the prosecution must satisfy the court beyond reasonable doubt in relation to a number of matters. It must show that the taking of the confession involved no deliberate and conscious violation of the accused's constitutional rights because any such violation will invariably lead to the exclusion of evidence obtained in consequence.[1] Also it must establish that the confession was voluntary or again it *must* be excluded from evidence as a matter of law.[2] However even if a confession is accepted by the court to have been obtained voluntarily and without any deliberate and conscious violation of the accused's constitutional rights, the defence may nonetheless urge the trial judge to exercise his discretion to exclude it if it has been obtained in breach of what are known as the Judges' Rules. That judges have such a discretion is quite clear.[3] On occasions some Irish courts appear to have fallen into the error of equating a breach of the Judges' Rules with a circumstance which renders a confession involuntary.[4] These two issues must be kept quite distinct.

1. See pp. 172 sqq., infra.
2. See pp. 125 sqq., infra.
3. *McCarrick v. Leavy* [1964] I.R. 225 (S.C.).
4. This was the error of the District Justice in *McCarrick v. Leavy*. The problem is discussed by Walsh J. in *The People v. Cummins* [1972] I.R. 312, 326-27 (S.C.).

The Judges' Rules

The Judges' Rules originated in response to a request to English High Court Judges from the British Home Secretary. The police were anxious to secure guidance as to the appropriate rubric within which they should conduct interviews of suspects in order to ensure that any evidence thereby gained would be admitted in evidence. The Judges' Rules which are currently accepted by the Irish courts are the old English Judges' Rules of 1918. It is worthy of note that these rules proved so obscure and defective that they were replaced in England in 1964 by a new set of guidelines.[5] However in *The People v. Regan*[6] the Court of Criminal Appeal rejected a submission that these 1964 Judges' Rules had any application in the Irish courts. Before considering the contents of the Rules themselves, it is important that their status be fully appreciated. In *The People v. Farrell,*[7] O'Higgins C.J. said:[8]

> 'The Judges' Rules are not rules of law. They are rules for the guidance of persons taking statements. However, they have stood up to the test of time and will be departed from at peril. In very rare cases, such as *R. v. Mills and Lemon* [1947] K.B. 297 a statement taken in breach may be admitted in evidence but in very exceptional circumstances. Where, however, there is a breach of the Judges' Rules, such as a failure to make a written record of the alleged confession or a failure to invite the accused to accept or reject the statements, each of such breaches calls for an adequate explanation. The breaches and the explanations (if any) together with the entire circumstances of the case are matters to be taken into consideration by the trial judge before exercising his judicial discretion as to whether or not he will admit such statement in evidence. . .'

It should be pointed out that breaches by the police of the Judges' Rules will not involve them in any criminal or tortious liability. However, where police officers fail to observe the guidelines they may be the recipients of barbed judicial comment[9] and, in addition, there exists the possibility that judicial discretion will

5. The Judges' Rules, 1964 are set out in [1964] 1 All E.R. 237.
6. [1975] I.R. 367 (C.C.A.).
7. [1978] I.R. 13 (S.C.).
8. Id. 21; for similar comments by the English Court of Criminal Appeal see *R. v. Voisin* [1918] 1 K.B. 531, 539-540.
9. See, e.g., the comments of Lord Goddard in *R. v. Mills* [1947] K.B. 297, 299.

be used to exclude the evidence so obtained. In *R. v. Allen* [10] the trial judge excluded evidence obtained in breach of the English Judges' Rules 1964 in order to deter the police from similar breaches in future. However, this concept of deterrence has been strongly rejected by subsequent English courts.[11]

The Judges' Rules applicable in Ireland were set out in *The People v. Cummins* by Walsh J.[12] They are as follows:

I. When a police officer is endeavouring to discover the author of a crime there is no objection to his putting questions in respect thereof to any person or persons, whether suspected or not, from whom he thinks that useful information may be obtained.

II. Whenever a police officer has made up his mind to charge a person with a crime, he should first caution such a person before asking him any questions, or any further questions as the case may be.

III. Persons in custody should not be questioned without the usual caution being first administered.

IV. If the prisoner wishes to volunteer any statement, the usual caution should be administered. It is desirable that the last two words of such caution should be omitted, and that the caution should end with the words 'be given in evidence'.

V. The caution to be administered to a prisoner when he is formally charged should therefore be in the following words: 'Do you wish to say anything in answer to the charge? You are not obliged to say anything unless you wish to do so, but whatever you say will be taken down in writing and may be given in evidence.' Care should be taken to avoid the suggestion that his answers can only be used in evidence *against* him, as this may prevent an innocent person making a statement which might assist to clear him of the charge.

VI. A statement made by a prisoner before there is time to caution him is not rendered inadmissible in evidence merely because no caution has been given, but in such a case he should be cautioned as soon as possible.

VII. A prisoner making a voluntary statement must not be cross examined, and no questions should be put to him about it except for the purpose of removing ambiguity in what he has actually said. For instance, if he has mentioned an hour without

10. [1977] Crim. L. R. 163.
11. See, e.g., *R. v. Elliott* [1977] Crim. L. R. 551; cf. *R. v. Sang* [1980] A.C. 402. This was a case of alleged entrapment, where it was stated that it is not part of a judge's function to exercise disciplinary powers over the police.
12. [1972] I.R. 312, 317-318 (S.C.).

saying whether it was morning or evening, or has given a day of the week and day of the month which do not agree, or has not made it clear to what individual or what place he intended to refer in some part of his statement, he may be questioned sufficiently to clear up the point.

VIII. When two or more persons are charged with the same offence and their statements are taken separately, the police should not read these statements to the other persons charged, but each of such persons should be given by the police a copy of such statements and nothing should be said or done by the police to invite a reply. If the person charged desires to make a statement in reply the usual caution should be administered.

IX. Any statement made in accordance with the above rules should, whenever possible, be taken down in writing and signed by the person making it after it has been read to him and he has been invited to make any corrections he may wish.

Many of the Judges' Rules are self explanatory. All, except Rules I and VII, relate specifically to the taking of confessions from suspects. Rule I enables the Gardaí, without administering a caution, to question any person from whom they think useful information may be obtained. It does not matter that the person questioned is suspected by the police of the crime under investigation. Such questioning may take place anywhere. Although there is no time limit imposed on such questioning, a person questioned under Rule I must be assisting the police in a wholly voluntary capacity. If he indicates at any stage that he does not wish to submit to any further questions he must either be told that he is free to go, or alternatively, be formally arrested. In either event the questioning should cease.

Of all the Judges' Rules, Rules II and III pose the greatest difficulties in interpretation.[13] Rule II is intended to cover the situation where a person is not actually in police custody but is about to be arrested. It has been suggested that the reality of this distinction may be questioned.[14] Clearly the time which may have elapsed between a decision by a Garda to charge a suspect and the arrest of the latter may be extremely brief. Indeed it might

13. For discussion of these Rules, see Williams, *Questioning by the Police: Some Practical Considerations* [1960] Crim. L. R. 325; Brownlie, *Police Questioning, Custody and Caution* [1960] Crim. L. R. 298; Smith, *Questioning by the Police, Some Further Points – 1* [1960] Crim. L. R. 347.

14. See Brownlie, op. cit. at 307.

well be that if any person tried to leave after a Garda had made up his mind to charge him he would be formally arrested forthwith. On the authority of *The People v. O'Loughlin,*[15] it would appear that in such an instance a suspect could be said to be in custody from the moment the Garda had made up his mind to charge him. On this interpretation Rule II would be obsolete because persons in custody fall within Rule III. If this interpretation is not correct and there still exists a twilight period between the time when a Garda has made up his mind to charge and the taking into custody of the suspect, then, according to the wording of Rule II, the Garda may question the suspect in this period provided that he first cautions him.[16] The caution is supposed to put the suspect on notice of the gravity of his situation.

Rule III is both the shortest and the most misleading of all the Judges' Rules. An English Home Office Circular issued on 24th June, 1930, with the approval of the English judges stated:[17]

> 'Rule III was never intended to encourage or authorise the questioning or cross examination of a person in custody after he has been cautioned on the subject of the crime for which he is in custody, and long before this rule was formulated and since, it has been the practice of the judges not to allow any answer to a question so improperly put to be given in evidence.'

Rule III does not conflict with Rule VII which prohibits the questioning of a prisoner making a statement except to remove an ambiguity. The very limited kind of situation which Rule III is supposed to cover is that in which a person arrested for an offence such as burglary or larceny has said, before being charged, that he has hidden the goods. He may then, under Rule III be asked, after caution, where the goods are hidden. The expression 'persons in custody' is nowhere defined but it appears to refer to anyone involuntarily detained by the police.[18] Although there are

15. [1979] I.R. 85 (C.C.A.).
16. It should be pointed out that some English courts have been reluctant to admit such questions even when Rule II has apparently been complied with. See, e.g., *R. v. Knight* 20 Cox 711; *Lewis v. Harris* (1913), 110 L.T. 337; *R. v. Booth* 5 Cr. App. R. 177; see also Brownlie, op. cit. n. 13 at 310-311.
17. Home Office Circular S26059/29.
18. In *R. v. Straffen* [1952] 2 Q.B. 911, it was held that a Broadmoor patient was not in custody for the purposes of the Judges' Rules. For discussion of 'custody', see Brownlie, op. cit. at 316-317.

dicta to suggest a willingness by Irish judges to exclude incriminatory answers from persons arrested to questions put to them by the police,[19] judicial practice in this regard may be changing. In commenting on the English position in 1960, Glanville Williams suggested, 'the judges have given up enforcing their own rules, for it is no longer the practice to exclude evidence obtained by questioning in custody'.[20] Questioning in custody in England is now permitted until the police have some information which can be put before a court as the beginning of a case.[21]

Quite how far Irish judges are prepared to countenance breaches of Rule III is unclear. In *The People v. Flynn*,[22] the accused was arrested and brought to a Garda station for the purpose of taking a statement from him. This improper purpose rendered his custody unlawful. He was interrogated while under arrest in palpable breach of Rule III. Although the conviction was quashed, the Court of Criminal Appeal appears to have done so because it was not satisfied as to the voluntariness of the statement. The breach of Rule III was not specifically highlighted. In *The People v. Cummins*[23] the Supreme Court was prepared to admit a voluntary statement despite appearing to accept that breaches of both Rules II and III had occurred.

Questioning of persons arrested under section 30 of the Offences Against the State Act, 1939, is commonplace. In *The People v. Madden*[24] the Court of Criminal Appeal accepted that the obligation of a suspect under section 52 of the 1939 Act to give an account of his movements for any specified period did not prohibit questioning of that person further or by way of repetition by Gardaí. In the subsequent case of *The People v. Kelly*[25] which also involved an arrest under section 30, it was contended

19. 'Our law is definite that a person in custody shall not be interrogated, and that if he wishes to volunteer a statement, he should immediately then be cautioned.' *Per* Judge Fawsitt in *The People v. Lawlor* [1955-56] Ir. Jur. Rep. 38,41; see also *Attorney General v. Cox*, unrep. 9th April, 1929.
20. See Williams, supra note 13, at 331.
21. See The Judges' Rules, 1964 [1964] 1 All E.R. 237; see also *R. v. Osbourne* [1973] 1 Q.B. 678.
22. [1963] I.R. 255 (C.C.A.).
23. [1972] I.R. 312.
24. [1977] I.R. 336.
25. Unrep. 2nd April, 1982 (C.C.A.), 29th October, 1982 (S.C.).

that the accused ought not to have been interrogated after his arrest other than to require an account of his movements in accordance with section 52. Rejecting this contention, Finlay P. said:

> 'So to hold would be to create a uniquely anomalous position whereby a person arrested at common law under suspicion of having committed an ordinary offence could be questioned by the Garda Síochána and provided due procedures and fair treatment were afforded to him, any answers he gave to such questions would be admissible in evidence against him, whereas a person arrested under section 30 of the Offences Against the State Act, 1939, a statute specifically enacted to deal with more serious crimes tending to undermine the stability of the State, could not be so questioned.'

The inescapable conclusion to be drawn from this dictum is that the Irish courts are ignoring the strictures imposed by Rule III and are permitting the questioning of persons arrested in relation to all criminal offences. There are many other reported instances where the courts have exercised their discretion to admit evidence despite breaches of the Judges' Rules. In 1928 in *The State v. Scully*[26] a police officer was questioning the accused in custody which was in itself a breach of Rule III. He read to her a statement made by a co-accused and, in consequence, obtained a confession. The objection to the evidence would seem to have been taken on the basis of a breach of Rule VIII only. The trial judge admitted the statement of the accused. It seems to have been accepted by the court in that case that the English practice was against admitting statements procured in the fashion described but that it was the practice of the Central Criminal Court to admit such statements. The rationale underlying Rule VIII was outlined in *R. v. Mills*[27] by the English Court of Criminal Appeal. In this case the police confronted Lemon with a verbal précis of a written statement made by another accused. This statement implicated Lemon. He was not cautioned. The police behaviour infringed Rule VIII. The Court said:[28]

26. 62 I.L.T.R. 24 (Circ. Crim. Ct.).
27. [1947] K.B. 297.
28. Id. at 299-300.

'What lies at the root of r.8 is the prevention of a police officer giving before a jury by means of his questions a statement of a person also charged of the complicity of the prisoner, when that person may not be called as a witness.
. . . But if after such a question by a police officer, which cannot be given in evidence, the prisoner chooses to dictate or write a confession, there is no authority that if the answer is intelligible without a recital of the question it cannot be given in evidence.'

Several recent reported cases have witnessed attempts by counsel to have evidence excluded which was obtained in breach of Rule IX. In *The People v.Farrell*[29] it was contended that a verbal statement made by an accused ought not to have been admitted in evidence since it had not been reduced to writing at the time it was made, which constituted a breach of Rule IX. However, the Court of Criminal Appeal refused to interfere with the judicial discretion exercised by the trial judge to include the statement. In *The People v. Pringle*[30] the same court stated that:

'[Rule IX] was designed to achieve a situation in which (a) there would be accuracy in the recording of any statement made to be achieved by an early writing down of it so as to obviate errors of recollection and (b) in which an accused person would, at a time when he should have a sufficient memory of what he said, be given an opportunity of challenging the accuracy of the record made.'

The court in this case again refused to exclude evidence obtained in breach of Rule IX. *The People v. Kelly*[31] was a case where the accused had made two oral confessions. The first of these had not been reduced to writing at the time it was made. The second had been reduced to writing and read over to the accused. He had agreed with the contents but was not offered the opportunity to sign it. He subsequently made and signed a written statement. The Court of Criminal Appeal admitted both the oral and the unsigned written confession because the signed written statement was in substance identical to these and therefore confirmed their accuracy.

29. [1978] I.R. 13 (C.C.A.).
30. Unrep. May, 1981.
31. Unrep. 2nd April, 1982 (C.C.A.), 29th October, 1982 (S.C.).

The voluntary confession[1]

The Judges' Rules, despite their obscurity and somewhat erratic enforcement by the courts, constitute an attempt to regulate the way in which statements are taken from suspects. Breaches of the Rules have tended to be overshadowed in recent times by questions pertaining to the voluntariness of confessions and also whether or not there have occurred deliberate and conscious violations of the accused's constitutional rights. Of all the common law exceptions to the rule against hearsay in criminal cases, undoubtedly the most important one is that which permits the prosecution to adduce in evidence admissions and confessions made by an accused person. The value of confession evidence may be gauged from the words of Erle J. in *R. v. Baldry* where he said: 'It appears to me that a clear confession well proved, is the most satisfactory evidence of guilt.'[2] However, over the years judicial scepticism about the manner in which confessions have been obtained has not been lacking.[3] Giving judgment in *R. v. Thompson* in 1893 Cave J. felt constrained to comment:[4]

> 'I always suspect these confessions, which are supposed to be the offspring of penitence and remorse, and which nevertheless are repudiated by the prisoner at the trial. It is remarkable that it is of very rare occurrence for evidence of a confession to be given when the proof of the prisoner's guilt is otherwise clear and satisfactory; but, when it is not clear and satisfactory, the prisoner is not unfrequently alleged to have been seized with the desire born of penitence and remorse to supplement it with a confession; – a desire which vanishes as soon as he appears in a court of justice.'

Of all the stages of immersion in the criminal process the accused is most vulnerable at the time when he is interrogated by the police. There is a clear conflict of interest between the police and the suspect. Interviews are not tape recorded. The suspect need not be appraised of his right to have the services of a solicitor,[5] as is the situation in the United States.[6] Frequently he gains access to

1. On this topic see generally, *Cross on Evidence* (5th Ed.), 541.
2. 5 Cox. 523, 531.
3. See, e.g., *R. v. Thompson* [1893] 2 Q.B. 12; *R. v. Pattinson* 58 Cr. App. R. 417.
4. [1893] 2 Q.B. 12, 18.
5. *The People v. Farrell* [1978] I.R. 13 (C.C.A.).
6. *Miranda v. Arizona* 384 U.S. 436 (1966).

legal advice only after he has made admissions which have irreparably harmed his case. The rules governing the admissibility of confession evidence were largely developed in the nineteenth century. At that time the very severe penalties imposed and the inability of accused persons to testify on their own behalf combined with a residual judicial scepticism about persons involuntarily incriminating themselves to ensure the adoption of a very liberal pro-defendant rule in relation to admissibility. Even in very serious cases apparently slight threats or inducements were deemed sufficient to taint confessions. By the mid-nineteenth century some judges considered the trend had become unacceptably liberal. One such judge was Parke B., who, when giving judgment in *R. v. Baldry,* said:[7]

> 'I look with some shame to the state of the law upon this subject; and when I see the extremely trifling matters,which could not possibly have affected the mind of any man, but which have been allowed to prevail against the reception of confessions in evidence, I cannot but concur in the observation. . . "that justice and common sense seem to have been sacrificed on the shrine of mercy" . .'

The misgivings of Parke B. did not suffice to make inroads into the established authorities and, even today, the rules evolved in the nineteenth century substantially govern the admissibility of statements despite the fact that much of the rationale underpinning their original development no longer exists. Generally speaking, the rules governing signed written statements apply equally to unsigned statements and to oral admissions. However, in *The People v. Keane,*[8] the Court of Criminal Appeal pointed out that where a statement is not signed then the person to whom the statement was made and who reduced it to writing ought to give oral testimony of what the accused said to him. The written record can *only* be put in evidence where oral testimony establishes that the document was acknowledged by the accused to be a correct record of what he said.[9] Where oral testimony is involved it is desirable that the prosecution reproduce the

7. 5 Cox 523, 531.
8. 110 I.L.T.R. 1.
9. A written record acknowledged by the accused but not signed by him was admitted in *The People v. Kelly,* unrep. 2nd April, 1982 (C.C.A.).

ipsissima verba of the defendant, although in *Attorney General v. McCabe* Kennedy C.J. said:[10]

> 'However desirable to have the *ipsissima verba* of a deponent, it is not the law that the statement of an accused person must as a matter of law be rejected if it be not in his *ipsissima verba*. . . It is, however, a matter for careful consideration by the trial Judge, in arriving at his decision as to admission or rejection of the statement. . .'

Confessions and admissions

In 1967 in *Customs and Excise Commissioners v. Harz,*[11] the House of Lords rejected the argument that there was a difference between confessions and admissions which fall short of a full confession and Lord Reid pointed out that, 'there appears to be no English case for more than a century in which an admission induced by a threat or promise has been admitted in evidence where a full confession would have been excluded.'[12]

Inculpatory and exculpatory statements

In *The People v. Cummins,* Walsh J., said, 'a trial judge has no discretion to admit an inculpatory or an exculpatory confession, or statement, made by an accused person which is inadmissible in law because it was not voluntary.'[1] This allusion to exculpatory statements is an interesting one. Should a prosecutor wish to tender in evidence a statement made by the accused which purports to exculpate him of the offence charged, it seems somewhat paradoxical that such a statement must be excluded because the accused has not made it voluntarily. Wigmore was of the view that 'all other admissions than those which directly touch the fact of guilt are without the scope of the peculiar rules affecting the use of confessions. . .'[2]

In *Attorney General v. MacCabe,*[3] the court differentiated between confessions and exculpatory statements and refused to apply the principles applicable to confessions to the statements

10. [1927] I.R. 129, 135 (C.C.A.).
11. [1967] 1 A.C. 760.
12. Id. at 818.
1. [1972] I.R. 312, 322.
2. *Wigmore on Evidence* (3rd Ed.) Vol. 111, 243.
3. [1927] I.R. 129 (C.C.A.).

made by the accused on the ground that the statements in question did not contain anything incriminating the accused, rather they merely contained the outlines of the testimony which he gave in the witness box. Significantly, however, the Chief Justice did concede that:[4]

> '[S]ome statements, without being actually confessions, would be of so incriminating a character as to have the effect of implicating the accused like a confession or admission, and so to come for practical purposes under the latter category, and to require the like strict rules governing their admission in evidence.'

It is submitted that the kind of involuntary exculpatory statement alluded to by Walsh J. in *The People v. Cummins,*[5] is not a genuine exculpatory statement at all but rather is a statement which *appears* to exculpate an accused, but in fact is tendered by the prosecution for precisely the opposite purpose. Such a situation arose in 1970 in *Piche v. The Queen*[6] which was heard by the Supreme Court of Canada. In this case the defendant, Ruth Piche made a statement to the police which the trial judge, after a voir dire, ruled to be inadmissible. The statement was to the effect that the accused had phoned for a taxi, dressed her child and left the house, leaving the man which whom she was cohabiting still asleep. However, in the witness box she testified that the man had died when a rifle she was holding had accidentally discharged. The Supreme Court of Canada refused to differentiate between inculpatory and exculpatory statements. Cartwright C.J.C. commented:[7]

> 'It appears to me to involve a strange method of reasoning to say that an involuntary statement harmful to the accused's defence shall be excluded because of the danger of its being untrue but that a harmful involuntary statement, of which there is not merely a danger of its being false but which the prosecution asserts to be false, should be admitted merely because, considered in isolation, it is on its face exculpatory. . .
>
> I find it difficult to see how the prosecution can consistently urge that a statement forced from an accused is in reality exculpatory

4. Id. 133.
5. [1972] I.R. 312 (S.C.).
6. (1970) 11 D.L.R. (3rd) 700.
7. Id. 701-702.

> while at the same time asserting that its exclusion has resulted in the acquittal of the accused and that its admission might well have resulted in conviction.'

This judgment succinctly encapsulates why inculpatory and apparently exculpatory statements should be subjected to the same test of voluntariness prior to admissibility.

The test of voluntariness

Adopting the often quoted words of Lord Sumner in *Ibrahim v. R.*,[8] Kennedy C.J. stated in *Attorney General v. McCabe:*[9]

> '[I]t is a positive rule of law that such a statement shall not be admitted in evidence against a prisoner unless it is a voluntary statement, in the sense that it has not been obtained from him either by fear of prejudice or hope of advantage exercised or held out by a person in authority, and the onus is on the prosecution tendering the statement to show that it is voluntary in that sense. . .'

The term 'voluntary' when applied to confession statements has acquired a specialised meaning in the course of judicial interpolations. It has been suggested that the word is a misnomer in the sense that even when a judge rules a confession to be involuntary, the accused has nevertheless consciously *chosen* to make the confession, so that voluntariness in this context is wholly different from the notion of voluntary conduct familiar to students of the law on automatism where the automaton has no control over his actions.[10] The concept of voluntariness inherent in the rules governing the admissibility of confessions involves consideration by the trial judge[11] at a 'trial within a trial' of whether an accused's freedom of choice to incriminate himself or otherwise has been overborne by a factor which the law deems to be unfair. Although neither the word 'threat' nor the word 'inducement' appears in Lord Sumner's classic exposition of the law, case law has tended to focus predominantly upon whether or not a threat has been made or an inducement held out to an accused by a person in authority. Nevertheless the law has long accepted that

8. [1914] A.C. 599.
9. [1927] I.R. 129, 134 (C.C.A.).
10. See Heydon, *Evidence Cases and Materials*, 169.
11. But see p. 338 infra.

other matters which could serve to overbear an accused's free will could be taken into account. This was made clear by Hayes J. in *R.v. Johnston* where he pointed out that:[12]

> '[A] confession will be rejected if it appear to have been extracted by the presumed pressure and obligation of an oath, or by pestering interrogatories, or if it have been made by the party to rid himself of importunity, or if, by subtle and ensnaring questions, as those which are framed so as to conceal their drift and object, he has been taken at a disadvantage, and thus entrapped into a statement which, if left to himself, and in the full freedom of volition, he would not have made.'

Threats and inducements

It is difficult to discern from the case law evidence of a consistent approach by the courts to the subject of what will constitute a threat or inducement.[1] In any event Lord Salmon in *Director of Public Prosecutions v. Ping Lin*[2] makes it clear that in any consideration of whether a confession is voluntary, 'it is useless. . . to search for another case in which the facts seem to be similar and treat it as binding'.[3] Threats of a religious nature have been held to be insufficient to taint confessions,[4] yet it has been said that 'even the most gentle. . . threats or slight inducements will taint a confession'.[5]

The Irish courts have considered the problems posed by threats and inducements in a number of reported cases. In *The People v. Moriarty (No. 2.)*[6] the accused was charged with the murder of an illegitimate child of a woman whom he wished to marry. The accused was the only person present with the mother when the

12. (1864) 15 I.C.L.R. 60, 83-84.
1. For examples of cases in which the English courts have excluded confessions because of threats or inducements, see *Sparks v. R.* [1964] A.C. 964; *R. v. Northram* 52 Cr. App. R. 97; *R. v. Zaveckas* [1970] 1 All E.R. 413; *R. v. Smith* [1959] 2 Q.B. 35; *R. v. Cleary* 48 Cr. App. R. 116. Confessions have, on the other hand, been admitted in the following cases: *R. v. Grewal* [1975] Crim. L. R. 159; *R. v. Priestly* 50 Cr. App. R. 183; *Director of Public Prosecutions v. Ping Lin* [1976] A.C. 574. See generally *Cross on Evidence* (5th Ed.) 539-541.
2. [1976] A.C. 574.
3. Id. 606.
4. *R. v. Sleeman* Dears 249; see also *The People v. Galvin* [1964] I.R. 325, 331 *per* Walsh J.
5. *R. v. Smith* [1959] 2 Q.B. 35, 39 *per* Lord Parker C.J.
6. [1947] Ir. Jur. Rep. 30 (Cent. Crim. Ct.).

child was born. He went to the police station and made a statement to the effect that the child had been born dead. A police inspector then told the accused that the State Pathologist would perform a post mortem and that he would be able to say whether the child was born alive or dead and that, if it was born alive, he would be able to tell the cause of death. He also told the accused that the mother of the child had told a maternity nurse that the child was born alive. The inspector then said: 'In view of what I have told you, would you like to reconsider what you have said in that statement?' The accused replied, 'According to that, I might as well tell the truth.' He proceeded to make a fresh statement after caution. The trial judge, in refusing to admit the second statement, said:[7]

> 'I am unable to see why he should have made that statement unless a sense of fear had entered his mind causing him to feel either that the fact of his guilt was known and that he should make the statement he did, or if he was not, in actuality, guilty, that his duty was to stand as a friend to the girl and shelter her, voluntarily taking on himself the sole responsibility for the death of the child. I cannot escape the conclusion that it was one or other of these motives that existed in his mind and induced him to make the statement to the inspector which he did.'

In *Attorney General v. Cleary,*[8] the defendant was charged with the killing of her child shortly after its birth. A police sergeant visited the woman shortly after the incident and cautioned her but also said to her that he intended to take a statement from her. At some stage in the conversation there was mention of a medical examination. The trial judge who admitted the statement said:[9]

> '[I] am satisfied the woman was frightened by reason of the suggestion of medical examination; that is, she was frightened that probably her guilt might be found out. I don't think she was frightened personally by the Sergeant on account of anything in his demeanour or authority, and I don't think her fear was such as would induce her to say anything that was untrue.'

In overruling this decision, Kennedy C.J. delivering the judgment

7. Id. 32 *per* Haugh J.
8. 72 I.L.T.R. 84.
9. Id. 86.

of the Court of Criminal Appeal, held:[10]

> 'We are satisfied that the question of the truth of the statement or whether the person making it has been led one way or the other to make it by the inducement, whether of fear or offer of reward, or whatever it may have been, is not a matter that determines the admissibility of the statement. The question of its admissibility is one entirely of whether it was made voluntarily; whether, even if it is in writing, it is given as an act of the free will of the accused person, or the person making it, so as to be his voluntary statement, and there is no such test to be applied as to whether the suggested inducement was an inducement which could affect a person in the direction of telling the truth or not telling the truth.'

The Chief Justice was here propounding a purely objective test. The vital question is whether the form of words used is *capable* of being construed as a threat or inducement and not whether it *in fact* served as a threat or an inducement to the suspect. Since the decision in *Director of Public Prosecutions v. Ping Lin,*[11] the English courts now concentrate on the subjective question of whether the words used in fact induced the suspect to make a confession. It is submitted that this test is more logical and ought to be adopted by future Irish courts. The present Irish test puts a premium upon the words used rather than upon their effect. In *The People v.Murphy*[12] when a Garda said to the accused, 'Come along with me, Stephen – you are all right,' this was construed by the court as, 'you will be all right,' and thus, it was found to constitute an improper inducement. In *The People v. Flynn*[13] where a sergeant told the suspect that it would be 'just as well for him to tell the truth', the Court of Criminal Appeal accepted that there was strong circumstantial evidence to suggest that the suspect's statement was not voluntary. The suggestion that, in the event of a confession, a friend of the suspect will not be charged will clearly constitute an improper inducement.[14] So also will an offer by the police to facilitate an accused in any application for bail.[15] However, if Gardaí threaten to invoke a statutory provision

10. Id.
11. [1976] A.C. 574.
12. [1947] I.R. 236 (C.C.A.).
13. [1963] I.R. 255 (C.C.A.).
14. *The People v. Pringle*, unrep. May, 1981 (C.C.A.).
15. *R. v. Zaveckas* [1970] 1 All E.R. 413.

which makes it a criminal offence to fail to supply them with certain information and a suspect makes a confession in consequence of such a threat, such a confession will not thereby be inadmissible.[16]

Persons in authority[17]

Where threats or inducements have been made in order to secure a confession, the confession will be inadmissible only if these have emanated from a person in authority. A person in authority is 'anyone who has authority over the accused or over the proceedings or the prosecution against him'.[18] Courts are rarely troubled by the need to resolve whether or not a person can be said to be 'in authority'. Police officers, to whom the vast preponderance of confessions are made, are clearly persons in authority. Other persons who have been held to be in authority by the English courts include an army sergeant in relation to soldiers under his command[19] and a headmistress in relation to girls in her school.[20] The victim of a crime was held in *R. v. Wilson*[21] to be a person in authority on the basis that he was the prosecutor.

In *Sullivan v. Robinson,*[22] Davitt P. was of opinion that a doctor who had been called in by the police to examine a suspect for drunkenness was a person in authority and that it was therefore, incumbent upon the prosecution to prove that any verbal admissions made by the suspect or any test the result of which tended to incriminate him were voluntarily undergone.

It would seem that a person may be 'constructively in authority'.[23] In *The People v. Murphy,*[24] a Garda, who was endeavouring to keep a suspect under observation, without being seen himself, enlisted the help of a citizen. When the accused spoke to the civilian the Garda advanced towards the men and, after a short

16. *The People v. Madden* [1977] I.R. 336 (C.C.A.); *The People v. McGowan* [1979] I.R. 45 (C.C.A.); *The State (McCarthy) v. Lennon* [1936] I.R. 485 (S.C.).
17. See generally, *Cross on Evidence,* (5th Ed.) 541-542.
18. *R. v. Todd* 13 Man. L. R. 364, 376.
19. *R. v. Smith* [1959] 2 Q.B. 35.
20. *R. v. McLintock* [1962] Crim. L. R. 549.
21. [1967] 2 Q.B. 406.
22. [1954] I.R. 161 (H.C.).
23. This phase is used by Heydon, op. cit. 180.
24. [1947] I.R. 236 (C.C.A.).

chase, caught the accused by the sleeve of his coat and said, 'Come along with me, Stephen – You are all right.' When the accused did not want to go, the civilian, Mr Cadden, said, 'Go with the guard – the guard is only for your good.' A few moments later the accused began to say something whereupon the Guard began to caution him but he continued to make a damaging admission before the Guard could complete his caution. O'Byrne J. held:[25]

> 'In view of the fact that Cadden was acting in concert with the guard and on the instructions of the latter and that Cadden's statement to the accused man was uttered in the presence of the guard and without any demur by him, we are of opinion that Cadden's statement to the accused should be treated as a statement by a person in authority.'

It has been suggested that the requirement that a threat or inducement should emanate from a person in authority should no longer be retained. Some of the incongruities of the rule are borne out by the fact that it is irrelevant whether or not the person in authority *intended* to obtain a confession, whether the threat emanates from his authority, or whether or not there has been any impropriety on his part.[26] However, the requirement is one which seems to be well entrenched in law.[27] A threat or inducement by a person not in authority will not suffice to render a confession inadmissible.[28]

Dissipation of threats and inducements

The courts have accepted that in some instances confessions may be admitted in evidence despite the fact that the defendant has been the subject of a threat or inducement from a person in authority. In such a case the prosecution must establish that the effect of the threat or inducement has been obliterated by a super-

25. Id. at 244.
26. *Attorney General v. Cleary* 72 I.L.T.R. 84.
27. See, e.g., *Deokinanan v. R.* [1969] 1 A.C. 20; *Director of Public Prosecutions v. Ping Lin* [1976] A.C. 574.
28. See *R. v. Taylor* 8 C. & P. 733; but for dicta of Winn L.J. suggesting that threats or inducements emanating from persons not in authority may be sufficient to cause a confession to be ruled inadmissible, see *R. v. Richards* [1967] 1 All E.R. 829, 830; *R. v. Northram* 52 Cr. App. R. 97, 103. These dicta do not appear to be good law; on this issue also see generally, Heydon, op. cit. 168.

vening event. In *R. v. Doherty*[1] a constable told a prisoner in the morning that it would be better to tell the truth, and a confession was made that evening to another constable. The court held the confession to be inadmissible. In *The People v. Galvin*,[2] however, the accused had been persistently questioned by Gardaí from 8.50 p.m. until 12.30 a.m. on the following morning. At about 12.10 a.m. a police inspector had said to him: 'You should not be keeping us here all night – tell the truth and be finished with it.' About five minutes later the accused made an incriminatory statement and was then cautioned for the first time but he proceeded to make other statements until 12.30 a.m. At 2.40 a.m. he made a further incriminatory statement to his father. He slept from 4.00 a.m. to 10.00 a.m. At 11.05 a.m. he made a further incriminatory statement and, that night he made yet more incriminatory statements. The trial judge excluded the statements made between 12.15 a.m. and 12.30 a.m. on the ground that the accused was not a free agent by reason of prolonged interrogation. Although it was not argued that the words of the police inspector constituted an inducement, the Court of Criminal Appeal felt that, even on the assumption that the remark *did* constitute an inducement, nevertheless, the effect of such an inducement would have been spent before the accused spoke to his father at 2.40 a.m. In *The People v. Pringle*[3] the Supreme Court accepted that a clear threat uttered by a Garda in relation to the charging of another person had been dissipated as a result of an interview which the accused had subsequently with his solicitor.

Oppression

In *The People v. Galvin* Kenny J., in discussing the law applicable to the admissibility of incriminating statements, said:[4]

> '[T]here are two distinct issues involved: the first is whether a statement is voluntary in the sense that it has not been obtained from an accused person either by fear of prejudice or hope of advantage exercised or held out by a person in authority; the second is that

1. 13 Cox 23,(No. 2) id. 24.
2. [1964] I.R. 325 (C.C.A.).
3. Unrep. May 1981 (C.C.A.).
4. [1964] I.R. 325, 330 (C.C.A.).

> even when a statement is proved by the prosecution to have been voluntary in this sense, the trial Judge may, in his discretion, refuse to allow the statement to be given in evidence when he is of opinion that the statement was obtained under circumstances of such pressure that it ceased to be one freely made.'

It is submitted that the allusion to judicial discretion in this dictum is misleading. If a confession has not been freely given it *must* be excluded. Since the mid 1960's the courts in England and Ireland have tended to employ the term 'oppression' to delineate those situations where confessions are to be ruled inadmissible on grounds other than of threats made or inducements held out by persons in authority. Hayes J. may have had just such a concept in mind when he referred to 'pestering interrogatories' in 1864.[5] In 1964 Lord Parker in *Callis v. Gunn* said:[6]

> 'There is a fundamental principle of law that no answer to a question and no statement is admissible unless it is shown by the prosecution not to have been obtained in an oppressive manner and to have been voluntary in the sense that it has not been obtained by threats or inducements.'

Sachs J. undertook an elaboration of the concept in *R. v. Priestly*[7] where he said:[8]

> '[T]his word [oppression] in the context of the principles under consideration imports something which tends to sap, and has sapped, that free will which must exist before a confession is voluntary. . . Whether or not there is oppression in an individual case depends upon many elements. I am not going into all of them. They include such things as the length of time of any individual period of questioning, the length of time intervening between periods of questioning, whether the accused person has been given proper refreshment or not, and the characteristics of the person who makes the statement. What may be oppressive as regards a child, an invalid or an old man or somebody inexperienced in the ways of this world may turn out not to be oppressive when one finds that the accused person is of a tough character and an experienced man of the world.'

5. *R. v. Johnston* 15 I.C.L.R. 60, 84.
6. [1964] 1 Q.B. 495, 501.
7. For a report of the facts of this case see 50 Cr. App. R. 183.
8. See *Note to Martin Priestly* 51 Cr. App. R. 1.

Allegations of oppression have been made in a number of recent Irish cases.[9] In many of these the accused had been detained for up to forty-eight hours under section 30 of the Offences Against the State Act, 1939. As the existence or otherwise of oppression is a question of fact, there is little to be gained from citing earlier cases as precedents. The Irish courts tend to scrutinise those factors specifically alluded to by Sachs J. in *R. v. Priestly*. The length and frequency of periods of interrogation coupled with the availability of food and rest periods feature largest as indicators of oppression but they are by no means the only determinants. The isolation of a suspect might render an interrogation oppressive in a situation where the presence of the suspect's solicitor could render a similar interrogation not to be oppressive.[10] In *The People v. Lynch,*[11] the court accepted that the lack of veracity of a confession might be an indication that it was obtained by oppressive means, although the obverse does not apply. Much of the case law is an evaluation of oppressive conduct on the part of the police. However, in *R. v. Flynn*[12] Lowry L.C.J. ruled, as inadmissible, confessions of the accused obtained at Holywood Interrogation Centre because the interrogation 'set up' was organised for the purpose of extracting information from persons unwilling to give it. This, the Chief Justice termed 'oppressive circumstances', which he distinguished from oppressive conduct. He said, 'the latter term implies something wrong on the part of those in authority, the former implies the creation of a set up which makes it more likely that those who did not wish to speak would eventually do so.'

The concept of the confession freely given presents both lawyer and layman with an enigma. That a person should wish to inculpate himself is not, of itself, extraordinary. Many persons make confessions and then plead guilty at their trials. But the question

9. See, e.g., *The People v. Madden* [1977] I.R. 336 (C.C.A.); *The People v. McGowan* [1979] I.R. 45 (C.C.A.); *The People v. Breathnach, The People v. McNally* unrep. 12th May, 1980 (C.C.A.); *The People v. Kelly,* unrep. 2nd April, 1982 (C.C.A.), 29th October, 1982 (S.C.); *The People v. Pringle,* unrep. May, 1981 (C.C.A.); *The People v. Lynch* [1982] I.R. 64 (S.C.).
10. Compare *The People v. Lynch* supra with *The People v. Pringle* supra.
11. [1982] I.R. 64 (S.C.).
12. Unrep. 24th May, 1972 (Belfast City Comm.).

remains as to why people who *know* the dire consequences of their act should wish to incriminate themselves during interrogation and yet should challenge the confession at the trial. Has the sense of guilt been artificially heightened during the interrogation process? It is possible that Hayes J. may have exhibited an unwitting prescience when he said in 1864:[13]

> '[I]t is manifest to everyone's experience that, from the moment a person feels himself in custody on a criminal charge, his mental condition undergoes a very remarkable change, and he naturally becomes much more accessible to every influence that addresses itself either to his hopes or fears.'

This change in mental condition has posed a challenge to modern psychologists whose researches may yet reveal our current analyses of oppression to be crude and unreliable.[14] Police interrogators are taught a variety of interrogation techniques which accentuate tension and psychological confusion in the suspect's mind. A familiar tactic is for teams of police interrogators to act in such a way that one officer appears friendly and sympathetic while the other is aggressive and hostile. Another ploy is for a police officer to switch his attitude towards the suspect from one moment to the next. Techniques such as these, which may not appear to be particularly oppressive, often precipitate abnormal brain activity in suspects and induce a state of greatly increased suggestibility and paradoxical behaviour.[15] Courts in future may require to become more circumspect and develop a more sophisticated notion of what constitutes oppression. Matters such as the offer of a meal or a rest (wholly outside the context of an inducement) have hitherto understandably been seized upon by the courts as indicating a solicitude on the part of the police for a suspect's well-being.[16] These may in future have

13. *R. v. Johnston* 15 I.C.L.R. 60.
14. See generally: Driver, *Confessions and the Social Pyschology of Coercion* 82 Harv. L. R. 42, (1968); Sterling, *Police Interrogation and the Psychology of Confession* 14 J. Pub. L. 25, (1965); Horowitz, *Psychology of Confession* 47 J. Crim. L. C. and P.S. 197-204 (1956); Sargant, *The Vital Interrogation Question: Just how voluntary is a voluntary confession? The Times,* 26th May, 1980; Sargant, *Battle for the Mind* 192 (1954); Aubry and Caputo, *Criminal Interrogation* 180 (1965).
15. See Sargant, op. cit. *The Times,* 26th May, 1980.
16. See, e.g., *The People v. Kelly,* unrep. 2nd April, 1982 (C.C.A.), 29th October, 1982 (S.C.).

to be juxtaposed with the preceding attitudes of the police towards the suspect, to see whether they have coalesced so as to induce paradoxical behaviour in the accused which ought to rob any confession of its voluntariness.

Arguably the only way of ensuring that degree of voluntariness to which the law aspires, is to make the admissibility of a confession contingent upon the accused's solicitor being present throughout the interrogation.[17] Even the requirement that interviews be taped would be an improvement on the present position.[18]

II. IDENTIFICATION PROCEDURES

Fingerprinting, measuring and photographing persons in custody

The legal provisions governing the taking of fingerprints are largely to be found in the Regulations as to the Measuring and Photography of Prisoners, 1955.[1] The regulations permit the photographing, measuring and fingerprinting, which in this context includes the taking of palm prints, of a convicted prisoner at any time during his imprisonment.[2] A untried prisoner who has been informed of his right to object, but does not do so, may be photographed, measured and fingerprinted on the application in writing of a Garda officer not below the rank of Inspector. It would seem that the police are not obliged to administer a caution to a suspect as a preliminary to the taking of his fingerprints,[3] nor is there a requirement that the police obtain a consent in writing.[4] If an untried person refuses to give his consent he may nevertheless be photographed, measured and fingerprinted with the authority of the Minister for Justice or upon the application

17. This proposal was made by The Legal Action Group in its evidence to the Royal Commission on Criminal Procedure, *Legality in the Criminal Process*, March, 1979 at 27.
18. On the issue of the tape recording of police interviews, see The Royal Commission on Criminal Procedure Cmnd. 8092 (1981) 75-81.
1. S.I. No. 114 of 1955.
2. Id. r. 3.
3. *The People v. Walsh* [1980] I.R. 294 (S.C.); contra *The People v. Lawlor* [1955-56] Ir. Jur. Rep. 38.
4. This has been recommended in England by the Royal Commission on Criminal Procedure, Cmnd. 8092, at 65.

in writing of a member of the Garda Síochána of not lower rank than Inspector, approved by a Justice of the District Court, or in the Dublin Metropolitan District, by a Commissioner or Deputy Commissioner of the Garda Síochána.[5] In making any such application the applicant must set forth that, either from the character of the offence with which the person has been charged, or for other specified reasons, there are grounds for suggesting that he has been previously convicted or has been engaged in crime or that for other specified reasons the particulars are required for the purposes of justice.[6] The criteria under which a District Justice may refuse a police application to take fingerprints are not clear. Upon the discharge or acquittal of a prisoner who has not previously been convicted of any crime, all photographs, prints or measurements taken under the 1955 Regulations must be destroyed or handed over to the prisoner.[7] There seems little, if any, justification for restricting the return of or destruction of the information gathered to persons who have not previously been convicted of any crime.

In addition to the 1955 Regulations, section 7 (1) of the Criminal Law Act, 1976, provides the Gardaí with considerable powers when a person is detained in custody under section 30 of the Offences Against the State Act, 1939. In this situation any Garda may demand of any such person his name and address, he may search him or cause him to be searched, photograph him or cause him to be photographed and take or cause to be taken his fingerprints and palm prints. In addition to these powers, Gardaí are further empowered to make or cause to be made any test designed to see if the person arrested has been in contact with firearms or explosive substances and for this purpose a Garda may take swabs from that person's skin or samples of his hair. He may also seize and retain for testing anything which an arrested person has in his possession. Section 7 (2) of the same Act makes it a criminal offence to obstruct or impede a Garda in the exercise of any of the powers conferred upon him by subsection (1) or to refuse to give a name and address, or to give a false or misleading

5. S.I. No. 114 of 1955, r. 4 (1).
6. Id. r. 4 (2).
7. Id. r. 5.

name and address. There are no provisions for the destruction of any photographs or prints which have been taken in accordance with section 7 in the event of a person being discharged or acquitted. Another distinction between section 7 and the 1955 Regulations is that under section 7 *any* member of the Garda Síochána can exercise the powers of photography or fingerprinting in respect of a person in custody under section 30 of the Offences Against the State Act, 1939. Section 7 does not contain any provision for the measurement of persons in custody.

The taking of fingerprints or of forensic evidence from suspects without their consent must be justified by reference to a statutory provision. Any attempt to take prints, swabs, hair samples, etc. without statutory justification, therefore, would be an assault, entailing tortious and criminal consequences. It might also constitute a violation of a person's constitutional rights thereby causing evidence so gained to be excluded.[8] The position in relation to the taking of photographs is somewhat different. The law for Gardaí taking photographs is the same as for anyone else taking them. If a photograph of an untried prisoner is taken other than in accordance with one of the statutory provisions already referred to it is not *per se* unlawful unless it has involved an assault upon the prisoner.

Identification from photographs

A device to which the police have frequent recourse is that of asking a witness whether he recognises the perpetrator of a crime from a photograph. There is no objection to such a course being adopted where the police are searching for a clue as to the identity of a culprit. Even where the police have a particular person in mind they ought always to present a witness with a series of at least twelve photographs and then ask whether any of the persons depicted was the perpetrator.[9] These photographs should not bear any names, dates or distinguishing marks. The police should not show a photograph to a witness if a suspect has been *arrested* in connection with the offence.[10] Where one wit-

8. See pp. 170 sqq. infra.
9. *The People v. Mills* [1957] I.R. 106, applying *R. v. Dwyer* [1925] 2 K.B. 799.
10. *R. v. Haslam* 19 Cr. App. R. 59.

ness identifies a person from a photograph, other witnesses should not be shown photographs. Instead a formal identification parade should be held. All witnesses including the witness who has made an identification from a photograph ought to attend at a formal parade. Where witnesses have been shown photographs neither they nor the police ought to reveal this fact in their examination-in-chief, because the jury may then draw an adverse inference from the fact that the police had a photograph of the accused. The defence, however, ought to be informed where photographs have been shown to a witness.

Identification Parades

There is no rule of law which demands that an identification parade must be held in any case.[1] The courts, however, have taken the view that identification evidence has been shown in the past to be fallible.[2] In *The People v. Hughes*[3] the case against the defendant was almost entirely dependant upon the evidence of a Garda who did not know the defendant. The Garda had chased the defendant's car in the middle of the night. The men in the car glanced back occasionally. When the car stopped one of the men was caught while the other man ran off. Later that morning the Garda witness had gone with a detective to the defendant's house and identified him.

Haugh J. said:[4]

> 'Where identification is the only evidence against an accused person an identification parade is essential and when not held the trial Judge must put all the implications of its not having been held to the jury.'

It is, however, submitted that this dictum should be construed in the context of a case involving a Garda witness.

Where an accused asks to be put on a formal identification parade this request should, if possible, be complied with.

1. *The People v. Martin* [1956] I.R. 22 (C.C.A.) (defendant refused to take part in an identification parade and was identified by a Garda).
2. For discussion on the weight to be accorded to identification evidence see pp. 332 sqq. infra.
3. 92 I.L.T.R. 179 (C.C.A.).
4. Id. at 181.

Normally when a formal identification parade is held it should be conducted along the following lines:[5]

1. The parade should be conducted by a Garda Officer who is unconnected with the offence under investigation, but who has familiarised himself with the facts of the case and with the names and addresses of prospective witnesses. He should ensure that the prospective witnesses do not know any person who volunteers to participate in the parade.
2. Where Gardaí are involved in the investigation of the crime they should take no part in the parade and only the member in charge of the investigation should be present thereat.
3. The Garda who intends to conduct a parade should first appraise the suspect of this intention and ask him whether he has any objection to participating in the parade. Where a suspect indicates that he is unwilling to participate in any parade no formal identification parade should then ensue. In *The People v. Martin*[6] the Supreme Court accepted an accused's right not to participate in a formal identification parade. The positive value of a formal identification parade is dependant upon the co-operation of the accused, because an unco-operative accused may simply step forward and identify himself to a prospective witness as the person who is under investigation.
4. The officer conducting the parade should inform a suspect that he is entitled to have a solicitor or friend present when the parade is being carried out. If invited to attend by a suspect, a solicitor should be vigilant to ensure that the parade is carried out fairly and should make a note of the environs in which the parade is being conducted and also of the appearance and dress of both the suspect and the volunteers.
5. A single suspect is normally placed among at least eight volunteers, and often there are more. If there are two suspects of similar appearance, these may be put on a single

5. There appear to be no Regulations in Ireland governing the conduct of formal identification parades. The English rules are contained in Home Office Circular No. 109/78; see also Archbold 14-15.
6. [1956] I.R. 22 (C.C.A.).

parade with at least twelve volunteers. If suspects have quite different appearances, separate parades should be held in respect of each of them because it is important that the volunteers should resemble a suspect in age, dress, height and general appearance.

6. Prospective witnesses should be kept away from the room in which the parade is being carried out. No opportunity should be afforded them to see a suspect in advance of the parade and the interior of the parade room should not be visible from outside. Gardaí should not show any prospective witness a photograph of any suspect or any volunteer nor should they suggest any description of any suspect or volunteer in advance of a parade. When a prospective witness has attended the parade he should not be permitted to have further contact with other witnesses until the parade has been completed.
7. Other than the volunteers, the suspect(s), the conducting officer, the officer in charge of the investigation of the case, and the suspect's solicitor or friend, no other person should be present at the parade. The officer in charge of the investigation of the case should, at all times, be visible to those forming the parade.
8. When the volunteers have lined up, the suspect should be asked whether he has any objections to any of the volunteers, and any reasonable objections should be remedied, e.g. volunteers might be asked to wear spectacles or not to do so.
9. A suspect should be told that he is entitled to take up any position he wishes in a parade and that he may change position after each witness.
10. When the line up is formed, the proceedings should take place in the presence of the suspect. Witnesses should be brought in one by one. The conducting officer should say to each witness:

    'This is an identification parade. I want you to look very carefully at this line of men (women) and see if you can recognise the person (who robbed you or raped you, etc. or the person you saw on the. . . day of . . . etc.). Do not say anything until I ask you a question.'

After each witness has had an opportunity to study the persons in the line up he should then be asked whether or not he can identify anyone.

11. A witness may ask to see a person walk, to hear him talk or to put on or take off an item of clothing. The police will normally comply with a reasonable request from a witness.
12. Where a witness indicates that he has made an identification he should normally be asked to touch the person whom he purports to identify on the shoulder. However, if a witness is a child or an old person or is frightened it will suffice if that witness makes the identification by pointing at and describing the person in question. If any person identified at a parade makes any remark, it should be noted, and any suspect identified should be cautioned, as far as possible, before making any remark.
13. When a parade has been completed a suspect should be asked whether he has any comments to make in relation to the way in which the parade has been conducted. The accused's solicitor and the conducting officer should note any complaints made in this respect.
14. The person conducting the parade must record the proceedings meticulously.

Informal identification

Occasionally, when it is not possible to hold a formal identification parade, the police resort to a more informal procedure. This may occur, for example, where a person approaches a Garda in the street and indicates either that he has witnessed or been the victim of an offence. In such an instance the police may go with the witness in the hope of finding the culprit. Informal identification of persons may properly take place in situations where there are reasonable numbers of persons present e.g. churches, factories, cinemas, etc. The witness ought to touch the person or otherwise give a signal to the Garda conducting such an informal identification procedure. Where this procedure is resorted to the police officer conducting it must record all details relating to the matter, e.g. the number of people in the vicinity, their ages, sexes, etc. In *The People v. Galvin,*[7] the defendant was identified by a witness in a public place and was subsequently picked out at a formal identification parade. The trial judge told the jury that the important identification was the *informal* one. Such informal identifications are also conducted, not infrequently, in the vicinity of the courtroom in which the accused is due to appear, or even in the courtroom itself. It goes without saying that the Garda concerned should do nothing to assist the witness, merely asking him to look around the place where the accused is or is expected; the more conspicuous the accused is, the less will be the value of the identification.

III. POWERS OF SEARCH AND ENTRY

Power to enter premises

Article 40.5 of the Constitution states that the dwelling of every citizen is inviolable and shall not be forcibly entered save in accordance with law.

Entry upon premises contrary to an owner's wishes may be effected either in pursuance of a lawfully issued warrant to arrest a person thereon or to search the premises or alternatively in reliance upon a common law or statutory power to enter certain premises without a warrant.[1]

At common law a private citizen and, *a fortiori,* a member of the Garda Síochána, may enter a dwelling house in order to terminate an affray[2] or to prevent an occupant from causing serious injury to someone else on the premises.[3] A Garda is permitted at common law to effect a non-consensual entry in order to arrest a felon. Where a person has a right to enter premises at common law reasonable force may be employed to effect such an entry although, where possible, a demand for admission ought first to be made and be refused.

7. [1962] I.R. 325.
1. On this topic generally see Leigh, *Police Powers in England and Wales* 167-196.
2. *R. v. Walker* Dears.358.
3. *Handcock v. Baker* 2 Bos. and P. 260.

In 1935 the English Court of King's Bench in *Thomas v. Sawkins*[4] accepted that the police could enter premises without a warrant to prevent a breach of the peace and to prevent the commission of an offence which they believed was likely to occur. It has been suggested that the decision in this case 'certainly enhances the preventive power of the police and, *via* the offences of obstructing and assaulting a constable, imposes a fresh head of criminal responsibility upon persons seeking to exclude constables from private premises.'[5]

In addition to the powers of entry afforded to the police and to private citizens by the common law there exist also many situations in which Gardaí or other specified persons are empowered by statute to enter upon premises without any warrant.[6]

The searching of persons

In addition to the comparatively few statutory provisions which empower members of the Garda Síochána without warrant to stop and search persons, vehicles, vessels, etc. and to seize certain items without effecting an arrest,[1] persons may lawfully be searched in a few other instances. The first is where the person is prepared to give his consent to being searched. This requires no further elucidation. The second situation arises by reason of certain statutory provisions. These permit premises to be searched but, in addition, they allow the searching of any persons found upon the premises. Two important examples of such statutory provisions are provided by the Misuse of Drugs Act, 1977, and the Offences Against the State Act, 1939.

By section 26 (2) of the Misuse of Drugs Act, 1977, Gardaí in possession of a search warrant granted under that section are empowered to search the premises and *any person found thereon.*[2]

4. [1935] 2 K.B. 249, applying *Humphries v. Connor* 17 I.C.L.R. 1, *O'Kelly v. Harvey* 14 L.R. Ir. 105.
5. Leigh, op. cit. 173.
6. A few examples of such statutory provisions are: Air Transport and Navigation Act, 1975, s. 4 (2) (b); Betting Act, 1931, s. 26; Dangerous Substances Act, 1972, s. 40 (1); Gaming and Lotteries Act, 1956, s. 38; Health Act, 1947, ss. 94, 95; Mines and Quarries Act, 1965, s. 131; Misuse of Drugs Act, 1977, s. 24 (1) (a); Pawnbrokers Act, 1964, s. 46 (1); Protection of Animals Act, 1911, s. 5 (2); Public Dance Halls Act, 1935, s. 13 (1); Slaughter of Animals Act, 1935, s. 9.
1. See pp. 107 sqq. supra.
2. Authors' italics.

The Act does not demand that a Garda entertain any suspicion whatsoever in relation to any person whom he proposes to search.[3] As drugs are notoriously easy to secrete, body searches of this kind invariably involve a serious invasion of personal privacy.

An analogous power to search persons present upon premises being searched under a warrant is provided by section 29 of the Offences Against the State Act, 1939.[4] Again this provision does not require Gardaí to entertain any suspicion in relation to a person whom it is proposed to search. A search of a person may be undertaken merely by virtue of the fact that the person is *present* upon the premises in question. However, a warrant to search premises will not bestow any right to search persons thereon *unless* such a right is specifically given by statute.

The final situation in which a person may be searched poses most problems. It is where a person has lawfully been placed under arrest.[5] The power to search as an incident of arrest exists at common law and enables a Garda to search a person whom he has arrested, and to take into custody any dangerous weapon or other item found on that person which may be of evidentiary value.[6]

In *Dillon v. O'Brien*[7] the court considered the position when police officers, armed only with a warrant for the arrest of Dillon, searched the room in which he was arrested and seized certain documents which they believed would be of evidentiary value on a charge of criminal conspiracy against him.

Palles C.B. stated:[8]

> '[T]he interest of the State in the person charged being brought to trial in due course necessarily extends as well to the preservation of material evidence of his guilt or innocence as to his custody for the purpose of trial. His custody is of no value if the law is powerless to prevent the abstraction or destruction of this evidence, without which a trial would be no more than an empty form.'

3. For discussion of an analogous English provision see Leigh, *Police Powers in England and Wales* 182-183; also p. 172 infra.
4. As substituted by the Criminal Law Act, 1976, s. 5.
5. *Bessell v. Wilson* 20 L.T. (O.S.) 233.
6. For a cogent analysis of search on arrest, see Leigh op. cit. 50-53.
7. 20 L.R. (Ir.) 300.
8. Id. at 317.

In consequence, the court in *Dillon v. O'Brien* permitted the detention of material which was found in the same room as Dillon. A United States case suggests that a search of the area under the immediate control of the arrested person is proper.[9] In *Jennings v. Quinn*[10] the Supreme Court considered the situation when, at the time of the arrest of the plaintiff, a search was made of his house and possession was taken of a considerable amount of his property.

O'Keeffe J., in the course of his judgment, outlined the parameters of police powers in relation to the searching of premises and the seizure of material found therein in consequences of a lawful arrest. His Lordship said:[11]

> 'In my opinion the public interest requires that the police, when effecting a lawful arrest, may seize, without a search warrant, property in the possession or custody of the person arrested when they believe it necessary to do so to avoid the abstraction or destruction of that property and when that property is:–
> (a) evidence in support of the criminal charge upon which the arrest is made, or
> (b) evidence in support of any other criminal charge against that person then in contemplation, or
> (c) reasonably believed to be stolen property or to be property unlawfully in the possession of that person.'

This dictum suggests that the police have wide powers of search and seizure for which they do not need to seek the protection of a search warrant. As has been stated, the court in *Jennings v. Quinn*[12] was considering a situation where a search was made of the suspect's house at the time of his arrest and the search was conducted specifically in relation to the offence for which he was arrested. The court appeared to accept that in these circumstances a general search of the house might be made at the time of the arrest. It is possible that the propositions set forth by O'Keeffe J. may require some elucidation and refinement in future cases. It is difficult to know, for example, how an Irish court would react if faced with a factual situation similar to that

9. *Chimel v. California* 23 L.Ed. 2d. 685 (1968); see Leigh op. cit. 51.
10. [1968] I.R. 305.
11. Id. at 309, Ó Dálaigh and Walsh JJ. concurring.
12. Supra.

of the recent English case of *Jeffrey v. Black.*[13] In that case Black was arrested for the theft of a sandwich from a public house. Before he was charged the police told him that they intended to search his house. Black took them to his house, where cannabis and cannabis resin were found by the police. It was accepted by the court of first instance that the search was *not* carried out with the consent of Black and the court refused to permit the material found in the search of the premises to be used in evidence, and it dismissed the charges.

Delivering the judgment of the Court of Appeal on a case stated at the instance of the prosecution, Lord Widgery said:[14]

> 'It may very well be that if the police officers in the instant case had any sort of reason for thinking that the respondent's theft of the sandwich required an inspection of his premises, they might very well have made that inspection without further authority. But it is perfectly clear that when they sought to enter his premises, and did enter his premises, they were not in the least bit concerned about the sandwich. Their concern was something quite different, namely whether they would find drugs on the premises. . .
>
> I do not accept that the common law has yet developed to the point, if it ever does, in which police officers who arrest a suspect for one offence at one point can as a result thereby authorise themselves, as it were, to go and inspect his house at another place when the contents of his house, on the face of them, bear no relation whatever to the offence with which he is charged or the evidence required in support of that offence.'

In *Jeffrey v. Black* the Court of Appeal, while adhering to this view, nevertheless favoured the admission of the evidence obtained because it felt that the failure to obtain a search warrant was, by itself, insufficient to justify the use of judicial discretion to exclude the evidence. For an Irish court the dilemma would probably be more pronounced as the Constitution may fetter the use of judicial discretion. The words of O'Keeffe J. in *Jennings v. Quinn* are wide and could be interpreted in such a way as to render actions similar to those of the police in *Jeffrey v. Black* lawful. Such an interpretation would, it is submitted, constitute a major change in the common law, and would render otiose the need for

13. [1978] 1 All E.R. 555.
14. Id. at 558.

a search warrant in *any* situation where a person had been arrested. It may be argued that *Jennings v. Quinn* ought to be confined to situations where searches of a person's premises have some genuine connection with the offences charged or in contemplation. However, if any material which is reasonably believed to be stolen or to be unlawfully in the possession of a person arrested is thereafter stumbled upon in the course of a search, the Gardaí ought logically to be able to seize it.

The extent to which *Jennings v. Quinn* does authorise a general search of premises incidental to an arrest has become even more crucial since the enactment of section 9 of the Criminal Law Act, 1976,[15] because under this section if a Garda is conducting a search under *any power* (which must include a common law power) he is now entitled to seize *anything* which he believes to be evidence of *any* offence or suspected offence.

Searching premises under warrant

A search warrant is a written legal authority which authorises the person to whom it is addressed to search specified premises and to seize such property as is mentioned in the warrant. Anxiety not to invade peoples' homes and privacy resulted in a situation whereby at common law a search warrant might *only* be granted in the case of stolen goods.[16] The concept of a general warrant to apprehend, which neither named nor described the person to be arrested, was rejected as invalid by the Court in *Leach v. Money*[17] and an argument seeking to justify the issue of a warrant upon the ground of State necessity was similarly rejected in the case of *Entick v. Carrington.*[18]

The common law power to issue warrants today largely finds expression in section 42 (1) of the Larceny Act, 1916, which states:

> If it is made to appear by information on oath before a justice of the peace that there is reasonable cause to believe that any person has in

15. For the full text of this section see pp. 150-151 infra.
16. Lord Coke denied even this exception, 4 Inst. 176, although it was clearly accepted by 1765; see *Entick v. Carrington* 2 Wils. 275, 291 *per* Lord Halifax.
17. 19 St. Tr. 1001.
18. 2 Wils. 275.

> his custody or possession or on his premises any property whatsoever, with respect to which any offence against this Act has been committed, the justice may grant a warrant to search for and seize the same.

Today vast inroads into the strictures of the common law have been made by a large number of statutes.[19] The terms under which search warrants are granted differ widely from statute to statute. Some statutory provisions confer the power to search persons only, others permit searches in relation to premises only while yet others permit searches of both premises and persons found thereon.

Warrants are frequently issued today to permit searches to take place for stolen goods, drugs, firearms, documents in relation to offences against the State, etc. The piecemeal evolution of statute law in relation to search warrants has resulted in some surprising lacunae. Lack of statutory authority precludes the police from seeking warrants *inter alia* to search for the body of a murder victim or for a murder weapon.[20]

The issuing of search warrants

It is almost impossible meaningfully to schematise the conditions under which search warrants may be issued as the empowering statutes differ so widely in their provisions. Warrants are normally issued by either a District Justice or a Peace Commissioner after he has received information upon oath. Some-

19. Statutes which permit search warrants to be issued include: Aliens Act, 1935, s. 7; Betting Act, 1853, s. 11; Bread (Ir.) Act, 1838, s. 10; Broadcasting Authority Act, 1960, s. 12A; Censorship of Publications Act, 1929, ss. 12, 19; Censorship of Publications Act, 1946, s. 17; Children Act, 1908, s. 24; Coinage Offences Act, 1861, s. 27; Customs Consolidation Act, 1876, ss. 204, 205 (ext. Finance Act, 1936, s. 9); Criminal Law Amendment Act, 1885, s. 10; Criminal Law Amendment Act, 1935, s. 19; Dublin Police Act, 1842, s. 54; Defence Act, 1954, s. 260 (5); Excise Management Act, 1841, s. 34; Explosives Act, 1875, s. 73; Firearms Act, 1925, s. 24; Gaming and Lotteries Act, 1956, s. 39; Intoxicating Liquor Act, 1962, s. 26 (9) (a); Licensing (Ir.) Act, 1874, s. 24; Malicious Damage Act, 1861, s. 55; Merchandise Marks Act, 1931, s. 24; Misuse of Drugs Act, 1977, s. 26; Offences against the Person Act, 1861, s. 65; Offences Against the State Act, 1939, s. 29 (1) (as substituted by Criminal Law Act, 1976, s. 5); Official Secrets Act, 1963, s. 16; Spirits (Ir.) Act, 1854, s. 2; Wireless Telegraphy Act, 1926, s. 8.
20. See Street, *Searching without a Warrant* New Society, 16th November 1967; Zander, *Cases and Materials on the English Legal System* 137-39; Leigh, op. cit. 176.

times statutes provide that the information should be laid by a particular person e.g. a member of the Garda Síochána not below the rank of Inspector.

Occasionally senior Garda officers are given the power to issue search warrants without sworn information. Section 29 of the Offences Against the State Act, 1939,[21] for example, permits a member of the Garda Síochána not below the rank of Superintendent to issue a warrant under that section. Section 24 of the Firearms Act, 1925, permits any Superintendent of the Garda Síochána to issue a 'search order' to Gardaí under his command to search any premises or place named if there is reasonable ground for supposing that an offence under that Act has been, is being or is about to be committed.

Invariably it is a condition precedent to the issuing of a warrant that the person issuing it be satisfied that there are reasonable grounds for suspicion. If the person is so satisfied, having considered the evidence presented to him, his decision may not be attacked by way of certiorari.[22]

When issued by a District Justice or by a Peace Commissioner warrants are usually addressed for execution to the Superintendent or to an Inspector of the Garda Síochána who acts for the place where the warrant is issued, but a Justice may address any warrant to any Superintendent or Inspector who acts for any part of the Justice's District.[23] In the case of emergency a Justice may address a warrant to *any* member of the Garda Síochána within his District, although such a member ought to show or deliver the warrant to the Superintendent or to an Inspector if time permits.[24]

Warrants may not be signed in blank by Justices or by Peace Commissioners.[25] A warrant is not vitiated by the death of the person who has signed it.[26] As they are granted for a specific purpose, warrants must normally be executed within the period specified by the statute under which they are granted. Normally

21. As substituted by Criminal Law Act, 1976, s. 5.
22. *The State (Batchelor) v. Ó Floinn* [1958] I.R. 155 (S.C.).
23. District Court Rules, 1948 r. 70 (1).
24. Id. r. 71.
25. Id. r. 45.
26. Id. r. 18.

once a warrant has been used, it is thereafter spent. An important exception to this rule, however, is provided by section 26 (2) of the Misuse of Drugs Act, 1977, which permits execution 'at any time *or times*[27] within one month from the date of issue of the warrant.' This section, therefore, empowers Gardaí to enter and search both premises and persons found therein on as many occasions as they deem appropriate within one month of the date of issue of the warrant, without any necessity to have the warrant renewed.

Material which may be seized where a search warrant has been granted

As search warrants today are exclusively creatures of statute one would expect statutory guidance on the important question of what property may be seized when Gardaí carry out a search of premises in pursuance of a warrant. The many different statutory provisions empowering the issue of warrants invariably specify which items may be seized thereunder. Some permit the seizure of a very limited category of items, e.g. a warrant issued under section 19 of the Censorship of Publications Act, 1929, appears to authorise the seizure and removal of all *indecent pictures* found on the search but it does not seem to permit the seizure of any other material. Other statutes expressly permit a much wider seizure. Pre-eminent among these is the Offences Against the State Act, 1939,[1] section 29 (2) of which permits Gardaí in possession of a search warrant issued under that section to seize *anything* found on the premises or on any person thereon. Such a wide authority is very unusual in statutory provisions authorising the issue of search warrants.

The few authorities which existed in relation to seizure of property under warrants have now been largely superseded by section 9 of the Criminal Law Act, 1976, which states:

> (1) Where in the course of exercising any powers under this Act or in the course of a search carried out under any other power, a member of the Garda Síochána, a prison officer or a member of the Defence Forces finds or comes into possession of anything

27. Authors' italics.
1. As substituted by the Criminal Law Act, 1976, s. 5.

which he believes to be evidence of any offence or suspected offence, it may be seized and retained for use as evidence in any criminal proceedings, or in any proceedings in relation to a breach of prison discipline, for such period from the date of seizure as is reasonable or, if proceedings are commenced in which the thing so seized is required for use in evidence, until the conclusion of the proceedings, and thereafter the Police (Property) Act, 1897, shall apply to the thing so seized in the same manner as that Act applies to property which has come into the possession of the Garda Síochána in the circumstances mentioned in that Act.

(2) If it is represented or appears to a person proposing to seize or retain a document under this section that the document was, or may have been, made for the purpose of obtaining, giving or communicating legal advice from or by a barrister or solicitor, that person shall not seize or retain the document unless he suspects with reasonable cause that the document was not made, or is not intended, solely for any of the purposes aforesaid.

This statutory provision is of major importance because it permits the Gardaí in the course of a search carried out *under any power* which, *a fortiori,* includes a common law power, to seize *anything* which he believes to be of evidence of *any* offence. The section, it may be argued, puts into reverse the whole restrictive approach of the pre-existing law and, *de facto,* erodes the liberties which *Leach v. Money*[2] and *Entick v. Carrington*[3] sought to secure.

Until 1976 the whole philosophy underpinning the notion of issuing warrants for specific purposes was that there should be minimal interference with the inviolability of the person and of private property. So strict were the courts in their construction of police powers in this field that they were only prepared originally to allow police searching for stolen goods to seize those goods mentioned in the warrant or, alternatively, goods which they reasonably, albeit mistakenly, believed to be comprised in a warrant.[4] They subsequently extended this doctrine to permit the seizure of material which was likely to furnish evidence of the

2. 19 St. Tr. 1001, see p. 147 supra.
3. 2 Wils. 275, see p. 147 supra.
4. *Price v. Messenger* 2 Bos. & P. 158.

identity of stolen goods, e.g., in *Crozier v. Cundey*[5] they permitted the seizure of packing cases which had contained stolen cotton.

In December, 1976, the English Court of Appeal delivered judgment in the case of *Chic Fashions (West Wales) Ltd. v. Jones.*[6] In this case the police had obtained a search warrant in respect of clothing made by a particular manufacturer. On searching the premises in question they found items of clothing which they reasonably believed to be stolen but these items were all made by manufacturers other than the manufacturer specifically named in the warrant. Lord Denning, when delivering his judgment, remarked on the paucity of authority on the matter and he put forward the following propositions as representing the law. He stated:[7]

> '[W]hen a constable enters a house by virtue of a search warrant for stolen goods, he may seize not only the goods which he reasonably believes to be covered by the warrant, but also any other goods which he believes on reasonable grounds to have been stolen and to be material evidence on a charge of stealing or receiving against the person in possession of them or anyone associated with him.'

The rationale of his Lordship's view was that if goods reasonably believed to be stolen could not be made the subject of seizure they would disappear by the time the police obtained a warrant and returned.

That the judgments of the court in the *Chic Fashions* case display a change in judicial tack from the strict interpretations of the nineteenth century cases, is undeniable. A purported justification for this change may be gleaned, however, from the judgment of Diplock L.J. who saw the judicial task as being to decide where the balance ought to be struck between the inviolability of private property and the wider public interest. He stated that:[8]

> 'The society in which we live is not static, nor is the common law, since it comprises those rules which govern men's conduct in contemporary society on matters not expressly regulated by legislation.'

5. 6 B. & C. 232.
6. [1968] 2 Q.B. 299.
7. Id. at 313.
8. Id. at 315.

The decision in the *Chic Fashions* case is a judicial attempt to realign the law in England with modern conditions of increased criminality. It has been criticised as being an inaccurate formulation of the law and also on the basis that any erosion of the right of privacy ought more properly to be determined by the legislature.[9] The English approach as evidenced by *Chic Fashions* contrasts interestingly with the attempt by the Irish legislature to counteract violent crime by the enactment of section 9 of the Criminal Law Act, 1976. Although that section has the virtue of clarity, the scope of the powers granted to seize property is so wide that it could face a constitutional challenge. Section 9 would appear, for example, to permit a Garda carrying out a 'stop and search' under the Wildlife Act, 1976, without effecting an arrest and without a warrant, to seize anything he finds in the course of his search even if it has nothing whatever to do with the Act in question. Similarly in a search carried out in consequence of an arrest, as happened in *Jennings v. Quinn*,[10] Gardaí could seize any item whatsoever even if it fell outside the wide parameters set forth by O'Keeffe J. in that case.

The section also seems to render otiose the words in individual statutes which purport to limit the property which may be seized in the course of a search authorised by a warrant issued thereunder.

The only limitation imposed by section 9 is that the search be carried out under a *power*. This could prove important. If a warrant, for example, were to be issued in connection with a stolen clock it seems clear from section 9 that the Gardaí could seize any item which they believe would be of evidentiary value and which they come across *prior* to finding the clock. However, should they find the clock immediately on entering the premises their lawful power to search would thereby be expended and no further search could then be carried out otherwise than as a consequence of the arrest of the occupier.

As the Irish courts operate an exclusionary rule in respect of evidence obtained in deliberate and conscious violation of constitutional rights[11] the interpretation of section 9 may prove vital.

9. Leigh, op. cit. 193.
10. [1968] I.R. 305.
11. See pp. 169 sqq. infra.

Seizure of property without any statutory power and without arrest

While the powers of search and seizure both upon arrest and by virtue of statutory powers either by warrant or by stop and search provisions, are now extensive, there nevertheless remain situations in which certain items may be of vital importance in the investigation of a criminal offence, and yet these may be neither the subject of a statutory power of search and seizure nor may the person in whose custody they are be lawfully placed under arrest. In the important case of *Ghani v. Jones*[12] Lord Denning M.R. instanced a hypothetical situation which involved bank robbers 'borrowing' a private car and subsequently abandoning it. He argued that should the owner of such a car refuse to permit an examination of it to take place that the police could do whatever was necessary and reasonable to preserve the evidence of the crime.[13] It is clear that in such a situation the police could not seize the car under a warrant because there exists no statutory authority for the issue of such a warrant. It is also possible that despite the car owner's attitude the police may have evidence that he was in no way involved in the offence and, if this were so, they would not be justified in arresting him. That the police ought to enjoy a power of seizure to preserve material evidence in these circumstances seems reasonable. However, as has been emphasised, even section 9 does not confer a right to seize unless Gardaí can claim to have been acting under a *power*.

In *Ghani v. Jones* the police, in the course of a suspected murder investigation, entered a house on the invitation of an occupant and searched it. They took from the house two passports which they had been given upon request, and also some letters. On a subsequent occasion they returned and were given a third passport. The plaintiffs sought the return of the passports and letters and the police alleged that some of the items would be of evidential value while others would be of potential evidential value. Lord Denning, giving judgment, said:[14]

12. [1970] 1 Q.B. 693.
13. Id. at 708.
14. Id. at 708-709.

'[I] should have thought that, in order to justify the taking of an article, when no man has been arrested or charged, these requisites must be satisfied:

First: The police officers must have reasonable grounds for believing that a serious offence has been committed – so serious that it is of the first importance that the offenders should be caught and brought to justice.

Second: The police officers must have reasonable grounds for believing that the article in question is either the fruit of the crime (as in the case of stolen goods) or is the instrument by which the crime was committed (as in the case of the axe used by the murderer) or is material evidence to prove the commission of the crime (as in the case of the car used by a bank raider) . . .

Third: The police officers must have reasonable grounds to believe that the person in possession of it has himself committed the crime, or is implicated in it, or is accessory to it, or at any rate his refusal must be quite unreasonable.

Fourth: The police must not keep the article, nor prevent its removal,for any longer than is reasonably necessary to complete their investigations or preserve it for evidence. If a copy will suffice,it should be made and the original returned. As soon as the case is over, or it is decided not to go on with it, the article should be returned.

Finally: The lawfulness of the conduct of the police must be judged at the time, and not by what happens afterwards.'

These dicta have been followed in several subsequent English cases.[15] As was the case in *Chic Fashions,* the court in *Ghani v. Jones* isolated the essential problem as being the need to strike a balance between the interests of society in the prosecution and correct disposition of criminal offences on the one hand, and the right of individual persons to freedom from invasion of privacy and the seizure of property on the other.[16]

However, the decision in *Ghani v. Jones* poses many problems. A major difficulty for any Irish court wishing to adopt the precepts laid down therein would be the State's obligation under the

15. *Garfinkel v. Metropolitan Police Commissioner* [1972] Crim. L.R. 44; *Frank Truman Ltd. v. Police Commissioner* [1977] Q.B. 952.
16. See Lord Denning in *Ghani v. Jones* [1970] 1 Q.B. 693, 708.

Constitution to vindicate the property rights of every citizen from unjust attack.[17] The rule in *Ghani v. Jones* appears to permit the police to seize private property without justifying their action by any affirmative legal rule and to leave an occupier to bear any loss occasioned by the conduct.[18] Such a serious encroachment on the right of the citizen to enjoy his private property, ought only, it is submitted, to be undertaken by the legislature.

Another major difficulty of interpretation in relation to the case arises over what may be said to constitute a 'serious offence'. Such an amorphous concept is likely to vary from one police officer to the next, thus importing imprecision into a very delicate area of law where precision is vital above all else.

The solution to the lacuna in police powers brought to light by *Ghani v. Jones* is the enactment of a measure permitting a senior police officer to obtain a warrant from a District Justice enabling him to search for, to seize and to retain property which he reasonably believes may be of evidential value in relation to a specified indictable offence.

Stop and search powers

These have been discussed in the previous chapter.

IV. IMPROPERLY OBTAINED EVIDENCE

Although the courts of all common law jurisdictions have evolved very similar exclusionary rules to govern the admissibility at the trial of confessions not proved to have been freely given, they have adopted a wide diversity of approaches when faced with the problem of other kinds of evidence obtained from accused persons by wrongful means. Improprieties in the gathering of evidence may assume a variety of forms. They include such matters as the searching of dwellings and the seizure of property without lawful justification, the ill treatment of a person in order to discover the whereabouts of real evidence, the obtaining of evidence from an accused while he is in unlawful detention and resort to tricks and artifices to entrap an accused into incriminat-

17. Article 40.3.2°.
18. See Weir, *Police Power to Seize Suspicious Goods* (1968) C.L.J. 193; also Leigh, op. cit. 193.

ing himself. As the police are charged with the task of gathering evidence it is normally they who will have been responsible where an impropriety has occurred. The dilemma facing all criminal courts when asked by the defence to exclude evidence which has been wrongfully obtained is that such evidence is often of a most cogent kind and may even point inexorably to the guilt of the accused. Its exclusion, therefore, could mean that the perpetrator of a crime will be the recipient of a windfall and may elude justice merely because the police have exhibited incompetence or have been guilty of misbehaviour in their investigative role. Inclusion of evidence improperly obtained, on the other hand, may serve to encourage ignoble police behaviour and to increase the likelihood of further violations of the rights of individuals. The divergent conclusions reached by the courts of different countries reflect their differing views as to the role of the judge in a criminal trial.

The present approach of the Irish courts to this intractable problem is largely set out in *The People v. O'Brien*.[1] The judgments of the Supreme Court in that case suggest that Irish law on this subject represents an amalgam drawn from different legal traditions. Since the *O'Brien* case it would seem that Irish judges must pose for themselves two basic questions in order to determine whether or not to exclude evidence which has been wrongfully obtained. The first is whether the evidence in question was obtained in deliberate and conscious violation of an accused person's constitutional rights. If this is answered in the affirmative, the evidence will almost certainly be excluded. In consideration of this matter the courts appear to have been influenced by case law from the United States. Where a judge decides that the accused's constitutional rights have not been deliberately and consciously violated he must nevertheless pose the question as to whether there are any other reasons why the evidence ought to be excluded. On this question the majority judgment[2] in the *O'Brien* case suggests a predilection for the Scottish viewpoint, while the minority judgment[3] seems to reflect a preference for the views of

1. [1965] I.R. 142.
2. *Per* Kingsmill-Moore J. with Lavery and Budd JJ. concurring.
3. *Per* Walsh J. with Ó Dálaigh J. concurring.

the English courts. A proper understanding of the Irish position is best achieved by considering the case law of England, Scotland and the United States in relation to this matter.

The approach of the English courts

In considering the admissibility of a document in *R. v. Leathem* in 1861 Crompton J. said:[4] '[I]t matters not how you get it if you steal it even, it would be admissible in evidence.' Fidelity to this dictum has exemplified the approach of English courts since that time. Once an English judge is satisfied that evidence is relevant to any count in an indictment then such evidence is admissible. However, despite its admissibility, judges have evolved a discretion to exclude certain evidence. The first example of this arose in England when it was accepted that judges could refuse to permit cross-examination of an accused in relation to certain matters, notwithstanding the fact that such examination was strictly permissible under section 1 of the Criminal Evidence Act, 1898.[5] Thereafter the doctrine of judicial discretion was extended to cover situations where the prosecution sought to adduce similar fact evidence.[6] Finally, Lord Diplock accepted in *R. v. Sang* that:[7]

> '[T]here has now developed a general rule of practice whereby in a trial by jury the judge has a discretion to exclude evidence which, though technically admissible, would probably have a prejudicial influence on the minds of the jury, which would be out of proportion to its true evidential value.'

It is submitted that Irish law and English law are *ad idem* on the question of judicial discretion where the probative weight of the evidence is out-weighed by its potentially prejudicial effect on the defendant. However, the House of Lords in *R. v. Sang* considered the question whether there existed a discretion to exclude evidence because it had been wrongfully gathered by the police. Cases reported from other English courts seemed to point to the existence of such a discretion. In 1955 the Judicial Committee of

4. 8 Cox 498, 503.
5. *R. v. Watson* 8 Cr. App. R. 249; *Selvey v. Director of Public Prosecutions* [1970] A.C. 304.
6. *Noor Mohamed v. R.* [1949] A.C. 182.
7. [1980] A.C. 402, 434.

the Privy Council heard the case of *Kuruma v. R.*[8] The appellant, Kuruma, was a Kenyan who had been travelling home to his reserve during the Mau Mau period. He went down a road on which he knew that there would be a road block. He could easily have opted to have returned home by another route on which there was no such block. He was stopped and illegally searched by an officer below the rank of those who were permitted to undertake searches. Two bullets were found in his possession. His appeal against conviction rested on the basis that the facts of the illegal search ought not to have been admitted in evidence. The Court accepted the admissibility of the evidence because it was manifestly relevant to the charge. But Lord Goddard said:[9]

> 'No doubt in a criminal case the judge always has a discretion to disallow evidence if the strict rules of admissibility would operate unfairly against an accused. . . If, for instance, some admission of some piece of evidence, e.g., a document, had been obtained from a defendant by trick, no doubt the judge might properly rule it out.'

Lord Goddard may have had in mind the situation in *R. v. Barker*[10] in which an accused was unfairly induced to provide evidence against himself and the court held the document in question to be inadmissible. However, the dictum became the foundation for a much wider doctrine. In *Callis v. Gunn* Lord Parker C.J. suggested that evidence might be excluded 'if there was any suggestion of it having been obtained oppressively, by false representations, by a trick, by threats, by bribes or anything of that sort.'[11] In *King v. R.* Lord Hodson suggested that where evidence was obtained 'by conduct of which the Crown ought not to take advantage',[12] it would be excluded. Lord Widgery C.J. in *Jeffrey v. Black,*[13] elaborated further on the theme, and accepted that judicial discretion might be invoked in exceptional cases to exclude evidence obtained by the police in ways which were morally reprehensible. However, although the English

8. [1955] A.C. 197.
9. Id. at 204.
10. [1941] 2 K.B. 381.
11. [1964] 1 Q.B. 495, 502.
12. [1969] 1 A.C. 304, 319.
13. [1977] 3 W.L.R. 895.

courts have not been slow to articulate the existence of discretion when faced by certain improprieties, they have been extremely loth to exercise it.

It was not until *R. v. Sang*[14] that the House of Lords was presented with its first opportunity to consider the line of authority stretching back to *Kuruma*. The House rejected the existence of a discretion to exclude evidence because it had been obtained in a wrongful manner. The Law Lords tended to emphasise the aspect of fairness to the accused. Lord Scarman, for example, accepted that where an accused had been rushed or tricked into providing evidence which incriminated him, the trial judge would have a discretion to exclude it. The test which found most agreement from their Lordships was that suggested during deliberations by Viscount Dilhorne and announced by Lord Diplock. This was that:[15]

> '(1) A trial judge in a criminal trial has always a discretion to refuse to admit evidence if in his opinion its prejudicial effect outweighs its probative value.
>
> (2) Save with regard to admissions and confessions and generally with regard to evidence obtained from the accused after commission of the offence, he has no discretion to refuse to admit relevant admissible evidence on the ground that it was obtained by improper or unfair means.'

R. v. Sang represents a clear direction to English trial judges that it is not their function to attempt to exercise control over the police by excluding admissible evidence. In the minority judgment in *The People v. O'Brien* Walsh J., alluding to the situation where there has been an illegal as distinct from an unconstitutional seizure of evidence, said:[16]

> 'Every Judge in our Courts is bound to uphold the laws and while he cannot condone or even ignore illegalities which come to his notice, his first duty is to determine the issue before him in accordance with law and not to be diverted from it or permit it to be wrongly decided for the sake of frustrating a police illegality, or drawing public attention to it.'

14. [1980] A.C. 402.
15. Id. at 437.
16. [1965] I.R. 142, 167.

The Scottish approach

Until 1950, the Scottish and English courts appear to have treated the discretion to exclude improperly obtained evidence in the same way. However, since the case of *Lawrie v. Muir*[17] the Scottish courts have developed a jurisprudence quite distinct from their English counterparts. In *Lawrie v. Muir* the defendant was convicted of using milk bottles without the consent of the owner. The prosecution had tendered evidence of two inspectors of the Scottish Milk Marketing Board who were entitled to inspect the premises of any producer or distributor in a contractual relationship with the Board, to examine milk bottles in his possession. The defendant, who had no relationship with the Board, nevertheless, on the basis of a misrepresentation made by the inspectors, admitted them to her premises where they found the bottles which formed the subject of the charge. In giving judgment Lord Cooper L.J. Gen. said:[18]

> '[T]he law must strive to reconcile two highly important interests which are liable to come into conflict – (a) the interest of the citizen to be protected from illegal or irregular invasions of his liberties by the authorities, and (b) the interest of the State to secure that evidence bearing upon the commission of crime and necessary to enable justice to be done shall not be withheld from Courts of law on any merely formal or technical ground.'

While accepting that there was no absolute rule of law governing the admissibility of evidence obtained in an irregular fashion nevertheless Lord Cooper said:[19]

> 'Irregularities require to be excused, and infringements of the formalities of the law in relation to these matters are not lightly to be condoned. Whether any given irregularity ought to be excused depends upon the nature of the irregularity and the circumstances under which it was committed. In particular, the case may bring into play the discretionary principle of fairness to the accused which has been developed so fully in our law in relation to the admission in evidence of confessions or admissions by a person suspected or charged with crime.'

17. [1950] J.C. 19.
18. Id. at 27.
19. Id. at 27.

In asserting that irregularities require to be excused, the Scottish courts appear to proceed on the basis that evidence irregularly or illegally obtained is inadmissible and ought to be excluded unless the prosecution can satisfy the court to the contrary. In *Lawrie v. Muir* the evidence was excluded. In *McGovern v. H.M. Advocate*[20] the police scraped the fingernails of a suspect before arresting and charging him. This conduct constituted an assault. Despite the fact that the evidence thereby obtained was confirmed by forensic analysis to contain traces of explosives, Lord Cooper rejected it on the basis that it would have been simple for the police to have adopted the correct procedure. He said, 'unless the principles under which police investigations are carried out are adhered to with reasonable strictness,the anchor of the entire system for the protection of the public will very soon begin to drag.'[21] The court in this instance was specifically grounding its decision on the concept of police deterrence.

Scottish case law suggests that the prosecution may be able to persuade the court to admit evidence wrongfully obtained by showing that the irregularity was of a trivial kind or was one which was dictated by some urgent necessity.[22]

The United States approach

The discretionary approach to the admissibility of evidence obtained illegally, in the sense of having been procured by police officers in violation of constitutional guarantees against search and seizure and self-incrimination, has not found favour with the United States Supreme Court.

The famous *exclusionary rule* for illegally obtained evidence was first accepted in *Boyd v. United States*[23] which involved forfeiture proceedings. In 1914 it was extended to Federal criminal trials[24] and, in 1961, it was further extended to include State criminal trials.[25]

20. [1950] J.C. 33.
21. Id. at 37.
22. See, e.g., *McPherson v. H.M. Advocate* [1972] Scot. L.J. (Notes) 71; *Fairley v. Fishmongers of London* [1951] J.C. 14; *Walsh v. McPhail* [1978] Scot. L.T. 29; *Hay v. H.M. Advocate* [1968] J.C. 40.
23. 116 U.S. 616 (1886).
24. *Weeks v. United States* 232 U.S. 383 (1914).
25. *Mapp v. Ohio* 367 U.S. 643 (1961).

In holding that evidence in a criminal trial which had been obtained by violating constitutional protection against unreasonable search and seizure would be inadmissible, the United States Supreme Court in *Weeks v. United States*[26] appears to have set its face against the earlier English and United States authorities. It has, however, been argued that these authorities, while undoubtedly pre-dating the exclusionary rule by some years, are themselves the creations of the later nineteenth century so that the *volte face* may not in fact be as dramatic as it is frequently projected as being.[27]

The reasons for this change in tack by the Supreme Court in favour of invoking an exclusionary rule in criminal trials centred around the Court's view of the fundamental nature and efficacy of the constitutional guarantee and it came to the conclusion in *Weeks*' case that:[28]

> 'If letters and private documents can thus be seized and held and used as evidence against a citizen accused of an offense the protection of the Fourth Amendment, declaring his right to be secure against such searches and seizures, is of no value, and, so far as those thus placed are concerned, might as well be striken from the Constitution. The efforts of the courts and their officials to bring the guilty to punishment, praiseworthy though they are, are not to be aided by the sacrifice of those greater principles established by years of endeavour and suffering which have resulted in their embodiment in the fundamental law of the land.'

The Supreme Court developed the exclusionary rule bringing within it evidence obtained *indirectly* in consequence of a constitutional violation. This doctrine, known as the 'fruit of the poisoned tree', meant that a lead obtained as a result of an unlawful search would be tainted by the original illegality and would thereby be excluded.[29]

In 1949 in *Wolf v. Colorado*,[30] the Supreme Court, while explicitly adhering to the *Weeks*' doctrine, nevertheless refused to

26. 232 U.S. 383 (1914).
27. See Wilkes, *A Critique of Two Arguments Against the Exclusionary Rule: The Historical Error and the Comparative Myth* 32 Wash. & Lee L. Rev. 881.
28. 232 U.S. 383, 393.
29. See, e.g., *Silverthorne Lumber Co. v. United States* 251 U.S. 385 (1920); also *Wong Sun v. United States* 371 U.S. 475 (1963).
30. 338 U.S. 25 (1949).

impose it on the State Courts. However, in a strident dissenting judgment, Murphy J. rejected the alternatives normally cited by judges to secure the enforcement of the search and seizure clause, namely criminal prosecution and a civil action in tort for trespass, and took the view that:[31]

> 'The conclusion is inescapable that but one remedy exists to deter violations of the search and seizure clause. That is the rule which excludes illegally obtained evidence. Only by exclusion can we impress upon the zealous prosecutor that violation of the Constitution will do him no good. And only when that point is driven home can the prosecutor be expected to emphasise the importance of observing constitutional demands in his instructions to the police.'

The failure to impose the exclusionary rule upon the State courts resulted in a strange anomaly in that State officers could obtain evidence in violation of the Constitution and hand this over to a Federal prosecutor who was then able to adduce it in evidence in the Federal court under what was aptly termed 'the silver platter' doctrine. In 1960 in *Elkins v. United States*[32] the Supreme Court put an end to this pragmatic doctrine and, in the following year, the Court was converted to Murphy J.'s approach when it considered *Mapp v. Ohio.*[33] In this case Miss Mapp was convicted of knowingly having had in her possession and under her control lewd and lascivious books, pictures and photographs. Police officers had gone to her home and had been refused admittance without a search warrant. They then undertook surveillance of the house and three hours later, with the aid of reinforcements, forcibly opened the door. A paper alleged to be a warrant was produced which Miss Mapp grabbed and placed in her bosom. She was then forcibly handcuffed and a search was initiated in the course of which obscene material was discovered. The prosecution at the subsequent trial produced no search warrant. In placing reliance upon *Wolf v. Colorado,* the Ohio Supreme Court held that it was not prevented from using unconstitutionally seized evidence in a criminal trial. However, in reversing this decision, Clark J., delivering the opinion of the

31. Id. at 41.
32. 364 U.S. 206 (1960).
33. 367 U.S. 643 (1961).

United States Supreme Court, said:[34]

> '[N]othing could be more certain than that when a coerced confession is involved, "the relevant rules of evidence" are overriden without regard to "the incidence of such conduct by the police," slight or frequent. Why should not the same rule apply to what is tantamount to coerced testimony by way of unconstitutional seizure of goods, papers, effects, documents, etc?'

The rationale for excluding evidence obtained in violation of constitutional guarantees would appear to be that only by removing any incentive from police officers to break the law can such constitutional guarantees be effectively upheld. It has been suggested that empirical evidence demonstrates that the rule has not been effective in this role of deterrence and one of its most implacable and influential opponents, Burger C.J., while hesitating to abandon the rule until some meaningful substitute could be developed, castigated it in *Bivens v. Six Unknown Federal Narcotics Agents* as being 'conceptually sterile and practically ineffective in accomplishing its stated objective. . .'[35]

At a later juncture in his dissenting judgment in *Bivens* Burger C.J. pointed to an apparent serious weakness in the infrastructure of the rule when he observed that:[36]

> 'Although unfortunately ineffective, the exclusionary rule has increasingly been characterised by a single, monolithic, and drastic judicial response to all official violations of legal norms. Inadvertent errors of judgment that do not work any grave injustice will inevitably occur under the pressure of police work. These honest mistakes have been treated in the same way as deliberate and flagrant violations of the Fourth Amendment. . .
>
> 'Freeing either a tiger or a mouse in a schoolroom is an illegal act, but no rational person would suggest that these two acts should be punished in the same way. From time to time judges have occasion to pass on regulations governing police procedures. I wonder what would be the judicial response to a police order authorising 'shoot to kill' with respect to every fugitive. It is easy to predict our collective wrath and outrage. We, in common with all rational minds, would say that the police response must relate to the gravity and need. . .

34. Id. at 656.
35. 403 U.S. 388, 415 (1971).
36. Id. at 418-419.

> 'I submit that society has at least as much right to expect rationally graded responses from judges in place of the universal "capital punishment" we inflict on all evidence when police error is shown in its acquisition.'

Such a stark view of the exclusionary rule, while possibly in conformity with strict legal theory, is negatived by the ingenuity or, some might claim, casuistry of judges in stretching the doctrine to hold doubtful searches and seizures legal. Writing in 1974 John Kaplan observed, 'The courts have often avoided applying the exclusionary rule in situations in which the consequences of so doing would offend their own sense of proportionality or reach beyond their view of what the public would tolerate.'[37] In support of his argument he instanced two notable cases where United States courts refused to apply the rule. In *Abel v. United States*,[38] the United States Supreme Court affirmed the conviction of Rudolph Abel for conspiracy to commit espionage despite the fact that F.B.I. Agents had conducted a search of Abel's room without a warrant. The Court took the view that the defendant had 'abandoned' the property. Kaplan points out, however, that '[t]he only problem with the use of the abandonment doctrine in this case is that Abel "abandoned" the hotel room only after being arrested by federal authorities armed only with an administrative warrant of deportation.'[39]

In *Wayne v. United States*[40] a dead body was illegally discovered and the District of Columbia Court of Appeals admitted the evidence on the basis that it would eventually have been discovered legally.

Apart from covert adjustments to the exclusionary rule, the courts of the United States have also placed certain specific limitations upon its invocation. The rule does not apply if the evidence was obtained by a violation of the constitutional rights not of the accused but of a third party.[41] Nor does it apply if the evidence in question was obtained by a private citizen as opposed to a State

37. Kaplan, *The Limits of the Exclusionary Rule* 26 Stanford L.R. 1027, 1036 (1974).
38. 362 U.S. 217 (1960).
39. Kaplan, op. cit. at 1037.
40. 318 F.2d.205 (1963).
41. *Alderman v. United States* 394 U.S. 165 (1969).

official.[42] Also where a police officer made a re.
as to fact as opposed to law, the Supreme Court h
to be inapplicable.[43]

The approach of the Irish courts

As has been stated, the Irish Supreme Court was faced ne problem of the admissibility of illegally obtained evidence in *The People v. O'Brien* [1] where a search warrant was issued in respect of premises at '118 Cashel Road' when it should have read '118 Captains Road'. Gardaí searched the appellant's premises at 118 Captains Road and sought to put in evidence at the trial the fruits of this search. The appellants were convicted and had their appeals dismissed by the Court of Criminal Appeal which nevertheless certified that a point of law of general public importance was involved. It, therefore, fell to the Supreme Court to decide whether or not the evidence obtained ought to have been admitted despite the defect in the warrant.

Kingsmill-Moore J. accepted the fact that the Court was obliged to choose between the two desirable but potentially incompatible ends earlier alluded to by Lord Cooper in *Lawrie v. Muir*,[2] and he expressed the view that:[3]

> '[I]n every case a determination has to be made by the trial judge as to whether the public interest is best served by the admission or by the exclusion of evidence of facts ascertained as a result of, and by means of, illegal actions, and that the answer to the question depends on a consideration of all the circumstances. On the one hand, the nature and extent of the illegality have to be taken into account. Was the illegal action intentional or unintentional, and, if intentional, was it the result of an *ad hoc* decision or does it represent a settled or deliberate policy? Was the illegality one of a trivial and technical nature or was it a serious invasion of important rights the recurrence of which would involve a real danger to necessary freedoms? Were there circumstances of urgency or emergency which provide some excuse for the action?'

42. *Burdeau v. McDowell* 256 U.S. 465 (1921).
43. *United States v. Robinson* 94 S.Ct. 467 (1973).
1. [1965] I.R. 142.
2. [1950] J.C. 19.
3. [1965] I.R. 142, 160.

Doubtless this flexible approach would have recommended itself to Burger C.J.,[4] offering as it does the possibility of a 'rationally graded response' from the Irish judiciary to the problem of illegally obtained evidence in contradistinction to the 'capital punishment' visited by the United States exclusionary rule upon all evidence obtained in violation of the accused's constitutional rights. Indeed, in emphatically rejecting such a rule, Kingsmill-Moore J. observed: 'An absolute exclusionary rule prevents the admission of relevant and vital facts where unintentional or trivial illegalities have been committed in the course of ascertaining them. Fairness does not require such a rule and common sense rejects it.'[5]

Walsh J. in his minority judgment seemed less willing to embrace the Scottish view. He adopted the stance that evidence was not rendered inadmissible by reason only of its being obtained illegally as opposed to unconstitutionally. He argued that the primary role of a criminal judge was to conduct a fair trial and that he ought not to be deflected in this task by endeavouring to control the police. Significantly he was not dismissive of the *potential* of an exclusionary rule, should it prove necessary in the future. He specifically adverted to this possibility, pointing out that:[6]

> 'If a stage should be reached where this Court was compelled to come to the conclusion that the ordinary law and police disciplinary measures have failed to secure compliance by the police with the law, then it would be preferable that a rule of absolute exclusion should be formulated rather than that every trial judge, when the occasion arises, should also be asked to adjudicate upon the question of whether the public good requires the accused should go free without full trial rather than that the police should be permitted the fruits of the success of their lawless ventures.'

This view, grounded as it is in the notion that the exclusionary rule is an effective deterrent, is one which, while it can claim many adherents, appears to run contrary to the empirical

4. See pp. 165 sqq. supra.
5. [1965] I.R. 142, 159-160.
6. Id. at 169.

evidence available from the United States.[7]

It may be argued that *if* there is any deterrent value in ruling relevant probative evidence inadmissible, such deterrence could equally well be achieved by increasing judicial discretion to a point where the police would be in no doubt that illegal behaviour on their part would constitute a counter productive exercise. Such a course offers an advantage over the dogmatism of an exclusionary rule in that courts are not forced to retrench behind casuistry or disingenuous reasoning when faced with a case in which the public would be outraged by the exclusion of probative evidence solely on the basis of the illegal way in which it had been obtained.[8] Judges, in such a case, would merely exercise their discretion to admit the evidence.

Deliberate and conscious violations of constitutional rights

Undoubtedly the major evidentiary innovation contained in the *O'Brien* case is to be found in Walsh J.'s meticulous analysis of the legal position where there has been adjudged to have occurred a deliberate and conscious violation of an accused person's constitutional rights. Walsh J.'s formulation of the doctrine was substantially accepted by the other judges.

Constitutional rights comprise, in the first instance, those rights expressly conferred by the text of the Constitution. Such rights include, for example, the right to the inviolability of one's dwelling save where entry is permitted by law,[9] and the right not to be deprived of personal liberty save in accordance with law.[10] This latter right would be infringed if, for instance, a person were arrested other than in accordance with law or if he were detained for longer than the permitted period. However, in the watershed decision of *Ryan v. Attorney General,*[11] the Supreme Court added a new dimension to its approach to constitutional inter-

7. See,e.g., La Fave, *Improving Police Performance Through the Exclusionary Rule – Part 1, Current Police and Local Court Practices* 30 M.L.R. 391 (1965); Spiotto, *Search and Seizure: An Empirical Study of the Exclusionary Rule and its Alternatives,* 2 J. Legal Studies 243 (1973).
8. See p. 166 supra.
9. Article 40. 5.
10. Article 40.4.1°.
11. [1965] I.R. 294.

pretation by accepting the proposition that there existed rights other than those which were specifically adumbrated in the text of the Constitution. Kenny J. said: '[T]here are many personal rights of the citizen which follow from the Christian and democratic nature of the State, which are not mentioned in Article 40 at all. . .'[12] This theme was returned to by Walsh J. in *McGee v. Attorney General* when he held that:[13]

> 'Articles 41, 42 and 43 emphatically reject the theory that there are no rights without laws, no rights contrary to the law and no rights anterior to the law. They indicate that justice is placed above the law and acknowledge that natural rights, or human rights, are not created by law but that the Constitution confirms their existence and gives them protection.'

Today, therefore, it falls to the courts to adjudicate upon the issue of whether or not a right alleged by a defendant to have been infringed is such that it merits the status of a fundamental personal right which is protected by the Constitution. In this delicate and often controversial role of exposition of a nebulous higher law the Supreme Court has sought to reflect, in its evaluation of rights worthy of constitutional protection, changes in social mores. It has adopted a dynamic method of interpretation.[14]

In discussing the preamble to the Constitution in *The State (Healy) v. Donoghue,* O'Higgins C.J. offered the view that:[15]

> '[R]ights given by the Constitution must be considered in accordance with concepts of prudence, justice and charity which may gradually change or develop as society changes and develops, and which fall to be interpreted from time to time in accordance with prevailing ideas. The preamble envisages a Constitution which can absorb or be adapted to such changes. In other words, the Constitution did not seek to impose for all time the ideas prevalent or accepted with regard to these virtues at the time of its enactment.'

Of the many unspecified rights which have been accepted by the Irish courts as being 'fundamental' and entitled to constitutional

12. Id. at 313.
13. [1974] I.R. 284, 310.
14. For fuller treatment of this topic, see Kelly, *The Irish Constitution* 328-343, 360-377.
15. [1976] I.R. 325, 347.

protection, those which are most germane to the gathering of evidence include the right to bodily integrity and the right to have reasonable access to legal assistance while in police custody.[16] The right to bodily integrity was the first of the unspecified rights to be declared. It was this right which the plaintiff alleged had been infringed in *Ryan v. Attorney General.*[17] Kenny J. in the High Court, considering what was meant by a right to bodily integrity, said:[18]

> 'I understand the right to bodily integrity to mean that no mutilation of the body or any of its members may be carried out on any citizen under authority of the law except for the good of the whole body and that no process which is or may, as a matter of probability, be dangerous or harmful to the life or health of the citizens or any of them may be imposed (in the sense of being made compulsory) by an Act of the Oireachtas.'

Counsel for the plaintiff argued in the Supreme Court that this definition was too narrow and that *any* interference with bodily integrity was a violation of the right. The Supreme Court, however, found it unnecessary to define bodily integrity or to consider to what degree or in what circumstances the State could interfere with the right. In the future it may prove vital to determine the extent of this right in relation to the gathering of evidence by the police. Robinson J. in *United States v. Crowder* pointed out that '[a person's] body cannot simply be equated with his car, his clothing or even his home as a repository of evidence.'[19]

Many police actions may serve to raise the issue of whether or not there has been a violation of bodily integrity. Certain relatively trivial intrusions upon a person's body may yield crucial evidence. These include the taking of fingerprints, the scraping of fingernails, the taking of swabs from the skin or the taking of samples of a suspect's hair. These processes, if done without consent or without lawful authority, will constitute assaults with the perpetrator being liable in tort and also in criminal law. Whether

16. *The People v. Madden* [1977] I.R. 336 (S.C.).
17. [1965] I.R. 294.
18. Id. at 313-314.
19. 543 F.2d. 312, 322 (1976).

they would be sufficiently intrusive to constitute a breach of the accused's constitutional right to bodily integrity is less clear. What is clear is that 'a bodily intrusion need not leave the civilised jurist reeling.'[20] While torture, inhuman or degrading treatment would clearly infringe the right, it is submitted that lesser misbehaviour would similarly suffice. Were intimate body fluids such as blood or semen to be unlawfully extracted from a person this would involve a breach of his constitutional rights. Also certain searches of the human body may *per se* violate the right to bodily integrity. As has already been mentioned, the ease with which drugs may be secreted on the person often necessitates searches of a very intimate nature. The right to bodily integrity may require that certain searches should only be carried out by a qualified medical practitioner.[21] In this respect section 26 (2) of the Misuse of Drugs Act, 1977, may be unconstitutional in that it permits Gardaí to search persons found on premises being searched in pursuance of a warrant even though the Gardaí may not entertain any reasonable suspicion in relation to the person searched.[22] The right to bodily integrity encompasses the right not to be detained in conditions which are injurious to health.[23] This right, however, is not an absolute one, and a rigorous regime may be justified to prevent a person from injuring himself.

The consequences of violating an accused's constitutional rights

Discussing the legal consequences where evidence has been obtained in breach of an accused person's constitutional rights Walsh J. said in *The People v. O'Brien:*[1]

> 'When the illegality amounts to infringement of a constitutional right the matter assumes a far greater importance than is the case where the illegality does not amount to such infringement. The

20. Tribe, *American Constitutional Law*, 915 (1978).
21. Cf. *Huguez v. United States* 406 F.2d. 366 (1968) (forced search of the rectum under non medical conditions held unconstitutional); *Blackford v. United States* 247 F.2d. 745 (1957) (search of anal cavity by a doctor held to be constitutional).
22. Cf. *Henderson v. United States* 390 F.2d. 805 (1967) (search of the vagina held to be unconstitutional for lack of clear indication that evidence would be found).
23. See,e.g., *The State (C.) v. Frawley* [1976] I.R. 365; *The State (McDonagh) v. Frawley* [1978] I.R. 131.
1. [1965] I.R. 142, 170 (S.C.).

vindication and the protection of constitutional rights is a fundamental matter for all courts established under the Constitution. That duty cannot yield place to any other competing interest. In Article 40 of the Constitution, the State has undertaken to defend and vindicate the inviolability of the dwelling of every citizen. The defence and vindication of the constitutional rights of the citizen is a duty superior to that of trying such citizen for a criminal offence. The Courts in exercising the judicial powers of government of the State must recognise the paramount position of constitutional rights and must uphold the objection of an accused person to the admissibility at his trial of evidence obtained or procured by the State or its servants or agents as a result of a deliberate and conscious violation of the constitutional rights of the accused person where no extraordinary excusing circumstances exist, such as the imminent destruction of vital evidence or the need to rescue a victim in peril. A suspect has no constitutional right to destroy or dispose of evidence or to imperil the victim. I would also place in the excusable category evidence obtained by a search incidental to and contemporaneous with a lawful arrest although made without a valid search warrant.

In my view evidence obtained in deliberate conscious breach of the constitutional rights of an accused person should, save in the excusable circumstances outlined above, be absolutely inadmissible. It follows therefore that evidence obtained without a deliberate and conscious violation of the accused's constitutional rights is not excludable by reason only of the violation of his constitutional right.'

By adopting a somewhat diluted version of the United States exclusionary rule and subjecting it to certain exceptions Walsh J. acknowledged the paramount nature of constitutional guarantees. However, while he chose to delineate those circumstances which he considered to be 'excusable', the majority of the Court as represented by the judgment of Kingsmill-Moore J., refrained from any such anticipatory schematism. Kingsmill-Moore J. said: 'The facts of individual cases vary so widely that any hard and fast rules of a general nature seem to me dangerous and I would again leave the exclusion or non-exclusion to the discretion of the trial judge.'[2] While it is clear that unless there are excusing circumstances, evidence obtained in deliberate and conscious violation of an accused's constitutional rights should be excluded, the test, as propounded by Walsh J., still leaves dif-

2. Id. at 162.

ficult problems to which trial judges must address their minds before excluding evidence. In addition to assessing the extent of a constitutional right in a given instance, the judge must analyse whether or not a violation of an accused's constitutional right may be said to have been 'deliberate and conscious'. Clearly this requirement leaves open the possibility of a trial judge who is antipathetic towards either the existence of the rule or to its application in an individual case circumventing its effect by finding a violation of constitutional rights not to have been deliberate or conscious. As the question whether or not there has been a deliberate and conscious violation of constitutional rights is essentially one of fact, appellate courts will be loth to interfere with any such finding by a trial judge on the basis that he is in a better position to make such an assessment having, as he does, the opportunity of hearing and seeing the witnesses giving their evidence. However, in *The People v. Madden*[3] the Court of Criminal Appeal was prepared to reverse the decision of a trial judge on this issue. In this case the defendant, Madden, had been arrested and detained under section 30 of the Offences Against the State Act, 1939. As he had been arrested at 7.15 a.m. on 19th June, 1975 he had to be either released or charged by the same time on 21st June, 1975. At 6.40 a.m. on that date he began to make a confession statement which was only completed at 9.00 a.m.

While accepting that the statement was voluntary, the Court of Criminal Appeal nevertheless decided that the violation of the defendant's constitutional rights had been deliberate and conscious. O'Higgins C.J. put the matter thus:[4]

> '[T]he onus on the prosecution of showing that there had been some factor such as inadvertence which might excuse the failure to observe the end of the period of lawful detention, or some other extraordinary circumstance such as envisaged in *O'Brien*'s case, has not been discharged. As matters stand, this statement [i.e. the one begun at 6.40 a.m.] was taken by a senior Garda officer who must have been aware of the lawful period of detention which applied in this defendant's case; it was taken in circumstances which suggest that he deliberately and consciously regarded the taking and completion of the statement as being of more impor-

3. [1977] I.R. 336.
4. Id. at 346-347.

> tance than according to the defendant his right to liberty, should he desire to exercise such right. This Court cannot regard the taking and completion of a statement in these circumstances as any justification or excuse for the continued detention of a person in the position of the defendant.'

The Court of Criminal Appeal in *Madden*'s case felt that the trial judge had erred in requiring an element of *mala fides* on the part of the Gardaí as a pre-condition to finding that a violation of constitutional rights was deliberate and conscious. No such element of *mala fides* was necessary. It is clear that a police officer's knowledge or ignorance of the law may prove a vital determinant in deciding whether or not a constitutional violation has been deliberate and conscious.

The exclusionary rules set out in *O'Brien*'s case applied to *real* evidence in the form of certain articles of clothing found by Gardaí in the accused's house which the prosecution sought to use. However, in *Madden*'s case the Court of Criminal Appeal clearly accepted that the same rule applied to voluntary confessions. The Court continued to accept this view in *The People v. O'Loughlin*.[5] However, when the case of *The People v. Shaw*[6] reached the Supreme Court the whole issue was re-examined minutely by Griffin J. who sought to confine the *ratio decidendi* as set out in *O'Brien*'s case. He stated that:[7]

> '[T]he specific and narrow issue involved in the [*O'Brien*] case prevented its decision from being a vehicle in which to convey an authoritative and binding ruling on the test for the admissibility in evidence of oral, written, or other forms of statements tendered as confessions or admissions.'

His Lordship took the view that in relation to the admissibility of statements only two conditions had to be satisfied by the prosecution. The first was that the statement had to be voluntary. If the statement were voluntary the prosecution had to show that the circumstances in which it was obtained did not fall below the standards of fundamental fairness required by the Constitution. Griffin J. stated:[8]

5. [1979] I.R. 85.
6. [1982] I.R. 1.
7. Id. at 60.
8. Id. at 61.

'The test of basic fairness, based on a due consideration of the rights of the accused coupled with the requirements, in the interests of the common good, of the prosecution, superimposed on the need for voluntariness, has the merit of ensuring, if the judicial discretion is correctly exercised, that an accused person will not be wrongly or unfairly convicted out of his own mouth.'

As three other Supreme Court judges[9] agreed with Griffin J.'s judgment it merits considerable attention. However, in *The People v. Lynch* [10] where an appellant appealed directly from the Central Criminal Court to the Supreme Court, the evidentiary status of confession statements was considered afresh. In this case certain verbal and written statements made by the appellant constituted the only evidence against him. The Supreme Court accepted that the circumstances in which the accused had come to make the statements amounted to harassment and oppression and, in consequence, the confessions were ruled to be inadmissible. In the course of his judgment, however, O'Higgins C.J. trenchantly disagreed with the views expressed by Griffin J. in *The People v. Shaw*. The Chief Justice stated:[11]

'[E]ven if the *O'Brien* case did not effectively decide that statements obtained as a consequence of a deliberate and conscious violation of the constitutional rights of an accused should be excluded except in the circumstances mentioned, it seems to me that such a proposition must be accepted. It does not seem to me possible for any judge, except in such special circumstances as occurred in the *Shaw* case, to countenance or endorse a deliberate violation of the Constitution by the admission of a statement obtained as a consequence of the violation. It is probable that the vast majority of such statements would in any event, be excluded on other grounds, but this is not the point. I do not see that any discretion is possible.

Once the Constitution has been violated for the purpose of securing a confession the fruits of the violation must be excluded from evidence on that ground alone. Nor can it be said that the matter can safely be left to a decision on fairness or the voluntary nature of the statement.'

9. Henchy, Kenny and Parke JJ. For discussion of this case see McAuley and McCutcheon, *Shaw and the Admissibility of Unconstitutionally Obtained Statements* (1982) 4 D.U.L.J. (N.S.) 386.
10. [1982] I.R. 64 (S.C.).
11. Id. at 78.

CHAPTER 7

BAIL

A person is said to have been admitted to bail when he has been released from lawful custody by the courts (including a Peace Commissioner) or by the Gardaí on condition that he will appear before a court at a specified time and place. The concept of admitting persons to bail has an ancient pedigree. The word 'bail' itself derives from the old French verb *bailler* meaning to take charge of, and in earlier times, when the State was less centralised and sophisticated than it is today, it was considered desirable to release accused persons into the custody of others who would have a vested financial interest in ensuring that they would present themselves for trial at a specified future date. Not only did the admission of persons to bail satisfy the inviolable axiom of the criminal law that a man be presumed innocent until proved otherwise but, at a more pragmatic level, it relieved the immediate community of the burden of having to maintain accused persons in custody until their trial.

Today, it is extremely important that judges and others who are entrusted with the power to release accused persons on bail realise the full implications of a remand in custody. Not only does the failure to grant bail mean that the accused is imprisoned without trial, but he may also experience difficulties in the preparation of his defence, he may lose his employment or he may encounter family or other problems.[1] Links have also been discerned between the refusal of bail and the ultimate outcome of criminal trials. Accused persons who have been refused bail have been found, for example, to plead guilty upon arraignment more frequently than persons who have been admitted to bail pending

1. See dicta of Walsh J. in *The People v. O'Callaghan* [1966] I.R. 501, 513.

their trials.[2] It has also been shown in Canada that defendants on bail who plead not guilty are more likely to be acquitted than defendants who have been remanded in custody.[3]

The decision as to whether or not to admit a person to bail is invariably a matter of discretion for the courts. In one instance, however, the High Court is obliged to set a person free on bail. If an accused is charged with a misdemeanour within section 2 of the Habeas Corpus Act, 1781, the Court must admit him to bail so long as it is satisfied as to the sufficiency of the sureties.[4] Bail is not a privilege and must never be withheld by any court in order to punish an accused.[5] Wrongful refusal or delay in admitting an accused to bail constitutes a common law offence. A court, it is submitted, ought to grant bail in all cases where the offence is one which is not normally punished by imprisonment.

Non-Bailable Offences

Irish law does not know the concept of the non-bailable offence. It is clear nevertheless that for certain very grave offences such as murder, treason or capital murder, the courts will be exacting in their requirements before they will consider admitting anyone to bail. In the final analysis, however, bail always remains a possibility, albeit a remote one. In considering bail on a murder charge which carried the death penalty in *The State v. Purcell,* Hanna J. said:[6]

> '[T]hough the Court has power to interfere, it has always been held that it should not do so save under very exceptional circumstances. . . The inducements to avoid the ultimate penalty of death

2. See Davies, *Pre-Trial Imprisonment: A Liverpool Study:* Brit. Jo. Crim. Vol. II 52 (1972); Bottomley, *Prison before Trial,* 33 (London 1970).
3. See Friedland, *Detention before Trial,* 12 (Toronto University Press 1965) (the author's researches revealed that of 6,000 cases in Toronto Magistrates Courts in 1961-1962, 55% of those on bail were acquitted compared with 43% of those in custody. The difference remained even when account was taken of factors differentiating bail from custody cases). This study finding was included in *Legality in the Criminal Process,* Evidence of the Legal Action Group to the Royal Commission on Criminal Procedure, 58.
4. See dicta of Walsh J. in *The People v. O'Callaghan* [1966] I.R. 501, 512; see also *Re Frost* 4 T.L.R. 757.
5. *R. v. Rose* 67 L.J. Q.B. 289.
6. [1926] I.R. 207, 212; see, however, *The People v. Crosbie* [1966] I.R. 426 (S.C.) (bail granted on non-capital murder).

> have been deemed by the Courts to be overwhelming, no matter what the rank, character, or behaviour of the accused; and it has been assumed that, save in very exceptional circumstances, he will endeavour to flee from justice.'

By leaving open the possibility of bail whatever the offence Irish law has assiduously avoided any temptation towards abuse of the judicial process in the matter of bail by the prosecution. Such abuse has been known to occur on occasions in the United States where non-bailable offences exist. In the 1960's, for example, civil rights marchers in Georgia who merely participated in a public march found themselves charged with the non-bailable offence of attempting to incite an insurrection, while in Louisiana pickets outside a cinema which refused admission to black people were charged with criminal anarchy, another non-bailable offence.[7] A major problem with non-bailable offences is that they enable the prosecution to charge a person with such an offence and then subsequently to enter a *nolle prosequi* in respect of that charge and to proceed against the accused on a lesser charge. This, in effect, serves to oust the court's jurisdiction to grant bail.

Excessive Bail

Admission to bail involves the accused and often other persons acknowledging that they will be liable to forfeit a certain sum of money should the accused disobey the conditions of his bail. It has always been part of the common law of Ireland that the amount of bail be not excessive,[8] and this feature is one which all common law jurisdictions share.[9] In addressing himself to this aspect of the law of bail in Ireland, Walsh J. said in *The People v. O'Callaghan*, '[b]ail must not be fixed at a figure so large as would in effect amount to a denial of bail. . .'[10]

7. See National Commission on Causes and Prevention of Violence, *Law and Order Reconsidered*, 432-433 (1969); cited in Goldstein and Orland, *Criminal Procedure Cases and Materials on the Administration of Criminal Law* 422-423 (1974).
8. *The People v. O'Callaghan* [1966] I.R. 501, 518.
9. See, e.g., The Bill of Rights, 1688, which prohibited excessive bail in England; also Eighth Amendment to the U.S. Constitution, which states: 'Excessive bail shall not be required nor excessive fines imposed, nor cruel or unusual punishment inflicted.'
10. *The People v. O'Callaghan* [1966] I.R. 501, 518.

Clearly the whole rationale of the bail system is undermined if the sums fixed are so high that applicants are unable to obtain sureties or 'bailsmen' who are prepared to enter into a bond for the required amount. The courts will consider the gravity of the offence involved as well as the financial circumstances of the accused. As Walsh J. has stated:[11]

> 'If persons come from a humble walk in life or are of little means it is most likely that their friends or those of them who are prepared to go as surety for them are of the same condition and the amount of bail required must be just and reasonable in all the circumstances having regard to the condition and ability of the accused, bearing in mind all the time the overriding test of the probability of the accused failing to appear for trial.'

Judges in Ireland, if they fix bail at a high amount, may take the view that only by setting such a bail can they feel sufficiently confident that the accused will appear to take his trial. Clearly if, for example, on a very serious indictable offence bail were to be fixed at £20 for the accused with one surety in the sum of £20, the accused might well decide to take a chance and remain at large in the knowledge that neither his surety nor himself would suffer unduly in the event of the recognisances being estreated. By fixing bail at a high sum a judge is in a position to exert wholly legitimate pressure on an accused to appear for his trial and also to provide any sureties with an adequate incentive to ensure that he does so.

Walsh J. has pointed out that, 'any bail which a party can in fact procure cannot be considered excessive.'[12] However, the mere fact that an accused is unable to obtain adequate sureties because of the amounts involved does not, of itself, render the bail excessive. It would only be excessive if it could be demonstrated as being unreasonable, in all the circumstances of the case, to secure the attendance of the accused at his trial. One must concede that there are no reported Irish cases of judges indulging in the disarming candour revealed in some cases in the United States. In *The People v. Snow,*[13] for example, the defendant, who

11. Id. at 518-519.
12. Id at 519.
13. 173 N.E. 8 (Ill. 1930); see also Goldstein and Orland, op. cit. 421.

was on a charge of vagrancy, went to the court to give a bond for $10,000 whereupon the prosecutor asked the judge to increase the amount to $50,000 which the latter duly did, adding: 'If I thought he would get out on that I would make it more.' On appeal it was held that the amount fixed had no other purpose than to make it impossible for the accused to get bail and that it was, therefore, unreasonable.

If bail fixed by a District Court is adjudged by the High Court to have been excessive, the latter court will reduce it.[14]

Bailsmen

Where a judge or a Peace Commissioner or a member of the Gardaí feels that it is unsafe to free an accused on his own bail, he may require one or more independent bailsmen to help guarantee the accused's compliance with the conditions of his bail. In Ireland accused persons usually seek their bailsmen from among their friends and relations. The relationship between the accused and his bailsmen is, therefore, in general, one of trust. Except when a Garda is admitting a person to bail, it is a matter for the court which is accepting a bailsman to satisfy itself as to the substance, reliability and independence of that person.[15] Usually this task falls to District Justices, because recognisances are entered into before District Justices not only when the District Court itself admits persons to bail, but also, normally, when the Circuit Court or High Court or Court of Criminal Appeal make bail orders.[16]

However, the Special Criminal Court Rules[17] prescribe that persons must appear *personally* before that Court and acknowledge themselves to be bound in the required sums. The recognisances are signed by the Registrar of that Court. Clearly if it were to come to the attention of any court that a surety was being

14. See, e.g., *Attorney General v. Coleman* 67 I.L.T.R. 183.
15. *The People v. O'Callaghan* [1966] I.R. 501, 518; The Criminal Procedure Act, 1967, s. 27 states: The justice or peace commissioner shall in every case satisfy himself as to the sufficiency of the persons proposed to be accepted as bailsmen.
16. In relation to the Court of Criminal Appeal, the Rules of the Superior Courts O. 86, r. 20 (4) states: 'Unless otherwise ordered by the Court the recognisances of the appellant and his surety (if any) shall be taken before a justice of the District Court.'
17. Reprinted Appendix D, Form x.

pressurised into acting against his wishes he would not be permitted to enter into a recognisance. Such a situation might arise, for example, in the case of highly organised crime or politically motivated violence, where organisations could bring pressure to bear upon a local businessman and thus intimidate him into accepting the role of bailsman against his wishes. However, generally speaking, the *ad hoc* basis on which applicants for bail seek their sureties is indicative of the fact that organised criminal activity on a large scale has not been a feature of Irish society. This stands in stark contrast to the position in the United States where professional bailsmen have long been an integral part of the bail system and have proved to be an object of persistent, and frequently well substantiated, criticism. Insurance companies and individuals in the United States act as bailsmen and in return oblige the applicant to pay insurance premiums of up to 20% of the amount of the bail bond.[18] This big business element of bail has often led to bizarre consequences, accentuated undoubtedly by the fact that there is no longer any personal relationship based on trust between the accused and his surety.[19] Bailsmen must have sufficient resources to answer for the amount of money in which they have bound themselves should the accused fail to obey the conditions of his bail. Nevertheless, as Walsh J. pointed out in *The People v. O'Callaghan:*[20]

> '[T]here is no requirement in law that the bailsmen should be householders or own their own houses. In this country, where more and more persons dwell in houses rented to them by local authorities, particularly in urban areas, such an attitude would rule out as pro-

18. See Goldstein and Orland, op. cit. 413.
19. In *Shine v. State* 204. So. 2d. 817 a defendant obtained an appearance bond from a professional bondsman to appear at his trial. On his appearance the defendant was convicted and his bondsman paid his fine and arranged for his release on an appeal bond. The defendant owed the bondsman $40 and in order to collect this sum the bondsman went to the defendant's house in the middle of the night and broke down his door, thrusting a shotgun into the house. The defendant shot one of the intruders and was convicted of murder on the ground that the surety had a statutory power of arrest. In reversing this decision the Alabama Court of Appeal commented that, 'this "pay or get shot" attitude has too long been allowed to flourish with bonding companies.' On this case, see also Goldstein and Orland, op. cit. 417.
20. [1966] I.R. 501, 518.

> spective bailsmen a large proportion of the population. The question of whether a prospective bailsman does or does not own his own house is of course a relevant factor in considering his financial ability to meet the demands of the bail.'

Certain persons are not acceptable as bailsmen. These include persons under twenty-one years of age, persons in custody, persons who have been convicted of infamous crimes and recently discharged insolvents.[21] The accused's solicitor ought not to be accepted as a surety.[22]

It is unlawful for an accused to indemnify his sureties in the amount of the bail bond and any agreement between persons which involves the indemnification of sureties, albeit without any wrongful intent, constitutes an actionable conspiracy.[23]

Because the reliability of a surety is a matter for the courts, they may not delegate this duty by granting bail subject to the accused finding one or more sureties, 'acceptable to the Gardaí'. The Gardaí are, of course, both entitled and obliged to express to the court their disquiet about any surety offered by an accused and any reasons they may have for such disquiet.

Recognisances

When persons present themselves as prospective sureties for an accused it should be the practice to appraise them of the obligations involved, and to ensure that these are clearly understood. Section 10 of the Fines Act (Ireland), 1851, which was expressly extended to sureties by section 2 of the Fines Act (Ireland), 1851, Amendment Act, 1874, provides that whenever a person enters a recognisance to answer to an indictable offence, and fails to comply with the condition of his recognisance, application may be made, on evidence being given of the breach of condition, to forfeit so much of the recognisance as to the court seems fit, and a warrant may then be issued to levy the amount in question by execution or, in a case where a sum of money has been deposited in court, an order may be made for payment to the Minister for Finance of the amount which is forfeited. The power to estreat a

21. See The Garda Síochána Guide (5th Ed.) 39.
22. *R. v. Scott-Jarvis*, The Times, 20th November, 1876, (Q.B.D.).
23. *R. v. Porter* [1910] 1 K.B. 369; *R. v. Foy* [1972] Crim. L. R. 504.

recognisance of an accused is now given to the court before which the accused was directed to appear.[24]

Seven days notice in writing of the application must be given to the accused or the surety as the case may be, or left at his usual place of abode. The notice must state in substance the cause or matter in which it is intended to sustain the application. Thus the accused and any surety is given an opportunity to be heard. The court has a discretion whether to estreat a recognisance or any part thereof.[25] Where it transpires that a surety has taken all reasonable steps to ensure that a person on bail has obeyed all the conditions of that bail, the court may be prepared to exercise its discretion not to estreat a recognisance.[26] Naturally, however, courts will exercise circumspection before accepting an explanation advanced by a surety in a matter such as this.

Arrest of an accused

Where an accused person has been admitted to bail, a District Justice may, if he thinks fit, on an application by a surety or a member of the Garda Síochána who has sworn an information in writing that the accused is about to abscond for the purpose of evading justice, issue a warrant for the arrest of the accused.[27] When arrested, the accused is to be brought before the District Justice.[28] If the accused is brought before a Justice otherwise than at a sitting of the Court for the District in which the order sending him forward for trial was made, or, if the accused is on remand, of the Court before which he was bound to appear, he must be remanded to appear before such a sitting.[29] That Court may then commit him to prison to await his trial or until he enters a fresh recognisance, or, if he is on remand, further remand him.[30] The Justice has the like powers, as in the case of other remands, to

24. Criminal Procedure Act, 1967, s. 32.
25. *Tynan v. Attorney General* 96 I.L.T.R. 144 (Circ. Ct.).
26. See, e.g., *R. v. Sangiovanni* 68 J.P. 55 (accused absconded while on bail; surety informed the police and telegraphed to the United States to have the accused apprehended on his arrival in that country; through no fault of the surety the accused did not take his trial; estreat previously ordered, withdrawn).
27. Criminal Procedure Act, 1967, s. 33 (1).
28. Id. s. 33 (2).
29. Id. s. 33 (3).
30. Id. s. 33 (4).

remand the accused in custody or on bail or to fix the amount of the bail.[31]

Criteria to be considered when deciding whether or not to admit to bail

It has long been accepted by our courts that on any application for bail by a person who has not stood trial, the fundamental question to which a judge must address himself is whether or not the applicant will seek to evade justice if admitted to bail.[1] The relevance of any evidence adduced by either the prosecution or by the accused on any bail application must be measured against this criterion. In *O'Phelan v. Flood*[2] the defendants, who were members of a trade union, were charged with wrongfully watching and besetting their employer's premises. A District Justice refused bail owing to a refusal by the trade union in question to give an undertaking that there would be no further picketing. It was held by the High Court, however, that the conduct of the trade union could not properly be taken into account, and the defendants were, therefore, admitted into bail.

Traditionally the courts have accorded weight to certain matters which they have viewed as being particularly germane to any consideration of the fundamental question. In the leading case of *The People v. O'Callaghan*[3] the Supreme Court carefully evaluated eleven matters which Murnaghan J., the judge of first instance in that case, had considered ought to be taken into account by any court in deciding whether or not it was likely that an accused would attempt to evade justice. These were as follows:

1. *The seriousness of the charge*

The Supreme Court accepted the proposition that, the more serious the charge was, the greater was the likelihood that the accused would not appear to take his trial. The nature of the

31. Id. s. 33 (3).
1. See *The People v. Crosbie* [1966] I.R. 426 (S.C.); *The People v. O'Callaghan* [1966] I.R. 501 (S.C.).
2. [1938] Ir. Jur. Rep. 70.
3. Supra.

accusation has always been an important factor in bail applications.[4]

2. *The nature of the evidence in support of the charge*

Murnaghan J. held that the more cogent the evidence was, the greater was the likelihood of conviction and consequently the greater was the likelihood that the accused, if admitted to bail, would attempt to evade justice. This had long been the view of Irish courts.[5] The Supreme Court accepted it also. If the evidence against an accused, therefore, is of a tenuous nature, e.g. uncorroborated poor quality identification evidence, the chances of bail will be much better than where, for example, the accused has signed a confession or where there is ample corroborative evidence of guilt.

3. *The likely sentence which will be imposed upon conviction*

Murnaghan J. held that, the greater the sentence was likely to be, the greater was the likelihood of the defendant trying to avoid it. He held, therefore, that because a defendant's previous record could materially affect the question of sentence, it ought to be before any court considering bail. A difference of opinion arose in the Supreme Court over the propriety of the practice of examining the record of past convictions of bail applicants in the course of bail applications. Ó Dálaigh C.J. took the view that previous convictions ought not to be referred to in bail applications.[6] However, Walsh J., with whom Budd J. agreed on this point, stated:[7]

> 'The question of the previous record of the prisoner generally is a delicate one in that it is highly undesirable if it can be avoided that the previous record of any prisoner awaiting trial should be referred to or referred to in a way which may prejudice the pending trial. It is none the less a relevant consideration in my opinion and it may be proper to introduce the evidence in some cases because undoub-

4. See, e.g., *The State v. Purcell* [1926] I.R. 207 (bail refused on a murder charge carrying the death penalty); *Attorney General v. Rooney* [1936] Ir. Jur. Rep. 41 (bail refused on charges of attempted murder, possession of firearms, conspiracy, larceny and intimidation).
5. See, e.g., *R. v. Butler* 8 L.R. Ir. 39; *R. v. McCormick* 17 I.C.L.R. 411; *Attorney General v. Rooney* [1936] Ir. Jur. Rep. 41.
6. [1966] I.R. 501, 510.
7. Id. at 515-516.

> tedly a prisoner with a bad previous record is likely to attract a greater sentence in the event of conviction again and to that extent the existence of a previous record of such a type may act as an inducement to flee justice and avoid the likelihood of a severe sentence. If such existence is to be admitted on bail applications then I think it would be most undesirable that the tribunal which hears such evidence should be the tribunal of trial. If the question of bail arises during the trial itself the interests of justice, on balance, require that such evidence ought not to be adduced. I am furthermore of opinion that such evidence should only be adduced in respect of such previous convictions as would probably cause the trial judge to add substantially to the penalty he might otherwise have imposed in the event of conviction and that such previous record, properly proved, should be open to the same examination and comment on the part of the accused as it would have been if produced after conviction. None of these factors, however serious in the circumstances of any particular case, should be permitted to obscure the fact that bail ought to be allowed unless it appears probable that the accused will not surrender at his trial.'

Apart from the existence of any previous convictions, the character of the accused is irrelevant in any bail application.[8]

4. *The likelihood of the commission of further offences while on bail*

The most dramatic divergence of opinion between the Supreme Court and Murnaghan J. arose over whether it was permissible for a court to refuse bail on the basis that it would afford a person the opportunity to commit further offences while awaiting his trial.

In totally rejecting the view that courts could take into account any such factor, Walsh J. stated:[9]

> 'This is a form of preventative justice which has no place in our legal system and is quite alien to the true purposes of bail. . .
>
> In this country it would be quite contrary to the concept of personal liberty enshrined in the Constitution that any person should be punished in respect of any matter upon which he has not been convicted or that in any circumstances he should be deprived of his liberty upon only the belief that he will commit offences if left at lib-

8. *Re Robinson* 23 L.J. (Q.B.) 286.
9. [1966] I.R. 501, 516-517.

> erty, save in the most extraordinary circumstances carefully spelled out by the Oireachtas and then only to secure the preservation of public peace and order or the public safety and preservation of the State in a time of national emergency or in some situation akin to that.'

5. The possibility of the disposal of illegally acquired property

The Supreme Court accepted the value of this ground for refusing bail but considered it to be more relevant to bail applications entertained prior to committal proceedings. This seems reasonable, because by the time the prosecution has finalised the compilation of the Book of Evidence it will almost invariably be in possession of all the evidence required for the trial of the accused. Walsh J. argued that this ground for refusing bail should exist only where it was *reasonably probable* that disposal of illegally acquired property would occur if bail were granted.[10]

6. The possibility of interference with prospective witnesses or jurors

The Supreme Court also accepted this as a ground for refusing bail, Walsh J. again taking the view that it should only be allowed where it was *reasonably probable* that such interference would occur. The notion of 'interference' with witnesses or jurors must involve some form of intimidation. As Lord Devlin has pointed out:[11]

> '"[I]nterference with witnesses" may mean no more than that the prosecution do not want the accused or his solicitors to ask potential witnesses the same questions as the prosecution have themselves asked, or to get similar statements. The power of refusing bail is not to be used simply to deny to the accused the same freedom of inquiry that the prosecution has.'

This ground for refusing bail may be especially relevant in cases of personal violence where the accused and the victim are known to one another. Much of the potential danger may be eliminated by the inclusion of conditions in the bail order in respect of reporting to the police or in relation to the place of residence of the accused while he is on bail.

10. Id. at 516.
11. Devlin, *The Criminal Prosecution in England,* 80 (O.U.P. 1960).

7. *The prisoner's failure to answer to bail on a previous occasion*
The Supreme Court accepted the relevance of this criterion.

8. *The fact that the prisoner was caught red-handed*
The Supreme Court accepted this criterion. In many ways this ground may be seen as being largely coextensive with ground number two.

9. *The objection of the Attorney General or of the public authorities*
Courts have traditionally accorded weight to objections advanced by the prosecuting authorities. The Supreme Court was prepared to accept Murnaghan J.'s views on this ground, in so far as attention had to be paid to the prosecutor's view when considering the question of bail, but it was nevertheless insistent that any such objection to bail had to be based on some ground on which bail could validly be refused. The court insisted that:[12]

> '[Objections] cannot be simply made *in vacuo* but when made must be supported by sufficient evidence to enable the Court to arrive at a conclusion of probability and objections made must be open to questioning on the part of the accused or his counsel.'

Courts must be circumspect about upholding any objection from prosecuting authorities. If undue credence were seen to be placed on such objections, the threat by the police to oppose bail might be the cause of inducing involuntary confessions.

When an objection is made by the prosecution much will depend on the quality of the evidence upon which that objection is grounded. The hearsay evidence of an accomplice has been held to be of scant evidentiary value.[13] The insistence by the Supreme Court that any objection from the prosecution must be based on some ground on which bail could validly be refused raises a problem when the police objection is motivated by a desire to protect an accused. Murnaghan J. was of the view that the likelihood of personal danger to a defendant might *per se* be a ground for refusing bail. However, in the Supreme Court, Walsh J. rejected this view saying:[14]

12. *Per* Walsh J. at 517.
13. *Attorney General v. Kervick,* unrep.
14. [1966] I.R. 501, 515.

'If an accused wants protective custody he need not ask for bail or accept it. A bail motion cannot be used as a vehicle to import into the law the concept of protective custody for an unwilling recipient. An accused person on bail is entitled to as much protection from the law as may be required.'

Nevertheless in *Re Dolan*[15] Finlay P. allowed an objection by the prosecution and refused bail. The applicant was here charged with conspiracy to murder, and counsel on behalf of the Attorney General opposed bail on the ground that the accused, if admitted to bail, was unlikely to stand trial. This objection was based on the evidence of a Garda Inspector, who testified that, on the basis of information he had received, and which he believed to be true, the accused would be subjected to violence or threats of violence were he to be released, and he believed that this pressure upon him would be such that, whatever his own present intentions were, he would not be likely to stand trial. The Inspector refused to reveal the source of his information saying, that if he did so, it would endanger the safety of the accused. Finlay P. accepted that the fundamental issue was whether the Court believed, as a matter of probability on the evidence before it, that the accused would stand his trial. He continued:

'I am satisfied as a matter of law that if a Court were properly led to the conclusion that an accused would probably not stand trial because he would be prevented by violence or threats of violence from doing so rather than by his own wish such a conclusion would be in accordance with the decisions which would indicate that the Court should exercise its discretion against the granting of bail.'

It would seem, therefore, that if a prosecution objection relates directly to the likelihood of an accused appearing for his trial it must be considered by the court. Finlay P., having considered the decisions in *The People v. O'Callaghan* and the unreported case of *Attorney General v. Kervick,* came to the conclusion that, whereas a bald or mere belief was not something upon which the Court could act, the Court could in specific circumstances and, provided it had itself reached a conclusion of probability, act upon a belief stated by a police officer founded upon information

15. Unrep. 5th November, 1973.

which he believed, even though details of the information were not available to the Court.

10. *The substance and reliability of the bailsmen offered*

The Supreme Court accepted this ground which had been allowed by Murnaghan J. but it re-emphasised that bail must not be excessive. It further pointed out that questions of the independence and reliability of sureties were primarily questions for the Court which was asked to accept the surety.

11. *The possibility of a speedy trial*

The Supreme Court accepted the relevance of this ground to the extent that, if there was no prospect of a speedy trial, a Court might allow bail where it might not otherwise have done so. Presumably the Court in so saying was acting on the assumption that any delay in the trial would be caused by the prosecution, and not by the accused himself. A similar view had earlier been expressed by the Court of Criminal Appeal in *The People v. Kirwan.*[16] However, the Supreme Court in *O'Callaghan*'s case was at pains to point out that the prospect of a speedy trial was not in itself a ground for refusing bail where it ought otherwise to have been granted.

JURISDICTION TO ADMIT TO BAIL

Jurisdiction to admit persons to bail is enjoyed both by the Gardaí and by those Courts exercising criminal jurisdiction.

Gardaí

The sergeant or other person in charge of a Garda station is empowered to admit to bail any person who is brought in custody to the station if he considers it prudent to do so, provided that there is no warrant in force directing the detention of the person in question.[1] Where a Garda releases an accused on bail and takes from him a recognisance, either with or without sureties, for his subsequent appearance at the District Court, then, should the accused fail to appear, the recognisances may be estreated in the same way as recognisances entered into before a

16. 89 I.L.T.R. 120, 123.
1. Criminal Procedure Act, 1967, s. 31 (1).

District Justice.[2] Gardaí are entitled to accept from a person a sum of money in lieu of a surety or sureties. Any money tendered must be deposited by the Garda receiving it with the appropriate District Court Clerk.[3] The Gardaí may not admit to bail anyone arrested under section 251 of the Defence Act, 1954, on suspicion of being a deserter or an absentee without leave from the Defence Forces.[4]

When a District Justice or a Peace Commissioner issues a warrant directing the arrest of any person and the warrant contains an endorsement that the person named therein is to be released on bail upon his entry into a recognisance, either with or without sureties, the Garda in charge of the station to which the person is brought *must* admit him to bail in accordance with the endorsement as soon as any required recognisance, approved by the officer, has been entered into.[5]

Where a young person who appears to be under the age of seventeen has been apprehended, either with or without a warrant, and he cannot be brought before a court forthwith, then a Superintendent, an Inspector or an officer in charge of the Garda station to which he is brought must enquire into the case. The officer making the enquiry is normally obliged to admit any such young person to bail as soon as any recognisances required by the officer have been perfected. The only instances in which the Gardaí appear to have been given a statutory discretion in relation to the granting of bail are:

(a) where the charge is one of homicide or other grave crime;

or (b) where it is necessary in the interest of the young person in question to remove him from association with any reputed criminal or prostitute;

or (c) where the officer has reason to believe that the release of the young person would defeat the ends of justice.[6]

2. Id. s. 31 (2).
3. Id. s. 31 (3).
4. Id. s. 31 (4).
5. Id. s. 30 (2).
6. Children Act, 1908, s. 94, as amended by the Children Act, 1941, s. 24.

District Justices and Peace Commissioners

The powers of District Justices and Peace Commissioners to admit persons to bail are extensive. Bail applications are more numerous in the District Court than in any other court. There are many reasons why this should be so. Usually, where any case is to be tried upon indictment, the accused will in the first instance be remanded by a District Justice from time to time, until the Book of Evidence has been finalised. If an accused has entered into a recognisance to appear at every time and place to which, during the course of proceedings, the hearing may be adjourned,[7] he will be on continuing bail and need not, therefore, enter into fresh recognisances, after each District Court appearance. However, after the committal proceedings, if the accused has been returned for trial, both he and his bailsmen must enter into fresh recognisances conditioned for the appearance of the accused before the Court to which he has been returned.[8]

Even if an accused has been returned for trial in custody, a District Justice may admit him to bail at any time before the first day of the sitting of the Court to which he has been returned.[9] When an accused has been remanded in custody by a District Court or where a District Court hearing has been adjourned and the accused is in custody, an application may be made for bail before the day of the adjourned hearing, and the District Justice before whom the accused is to appear may order that the accused be brought before him for the purpose of being admitted to bail; or alternatively the District Justice may signify to the Prison Governor his consent[10] to the accused being given bail and the amount of bail required.[11]

In those cases in which they are empowered to admit to bail District Justices and Peace Commissioners invariably have a discretion as to whether bail ought to be granted, and, if so, there exists also a discretion to determine the amount of any such bail,

7. Criminal Procedure Act, 1967, s. 23.
8. For the forms of recognisances, see the District Court Rules, 1948, Schedule, Form 2.
9. District Court Rules, 1948, r. 60 (6).
10. This consent may be by an endorsement on the committal warrant or by a separate certificate; District Court Rules, 1948, r. 60 (5).
11. District Court Rules, 1948, r. 60 (5).

the necessity or otherwise of having sureties and the amount in which each surety is to be bound.[12] By section 26 of the Criminal Procedure Act, 1967, a District Justice may direct that a sum of money equivalent to the amount of bail be accepted in lieu of a surety or sureties.

The District Court is empowered by section 22 of the Criminal Procedure Act, 1967, to release a person conditionally upon his entering into a recognisance with or without sureties. Section 28 of the same Act states that a Justice of the District Court or a Peace Commissioner shall admit to bail a person charged before him with an offence, other than an offence to which section 29 of that Act applies, if it appears to him to be a case in which bail ought to be allowed. It should be noted, however, that while Part V of the Offences Against the State Act, 1939, continues in force, further restrictions exist upon the powers of the District Court to admit to bail.

Where an applicant has been refused bail or where he is dissatisfied with any bail order made, section 28 (3) of the Criminal Procedure Act, 1967, states that he has a right to appeal to the High Court. Dissatisfaction with a bail order might result from the amount of bail required,[13] conditions of reporting to the Gardaí or some other restrictions imposed upon the accused.[14] Strictly speaking the use of the word 'appeal' by section 28 (3) is inapposite as any hearing of a bail application by the High Court is *de novo*.[15]

The District Court is precluded from admitting to bail any person charged with any offence enumerated in section 29 of the Criminal Procedure Act, 1967. These offences are treason, an offence against sections 2 or 3 of the Treason Act, 1939, an

12. Id. r. 60 (1); but for the position where a notice of appeal to the Circuit Court has been served: see p. 199, infra.
13. See, e.g., *Attorney General v. Coleman* 67 I.L.T.R. 183 (bail of £15,000 with two sureties of £5,000 each was fixed by a District Justice on a charge of arson with intent to defraud. The High Court reduced the bail to £10,000 with two independent sureties of £2,000 each or four of £1,000 each).
14. For an example of conditions imposed upon bail orders, see *The People v. McCabe* [1944] Ir. Jur. Rep. 41 (bail refused by a District Justice on a charge of conspiracy to commit an abortion. Bail was granted in the High Court but the applicant was obliged to surrender all passports and travel permits); cf. *Attorney General v. Doyle* 75 I.L.T.R. 194.
15. Infra p. 197.

offence under sections 6, 7 or 8 of the Offences Against the State Act, 1939, a grave breach such as is referred to in section 3 (1) (i) of the Geneva Conventions Act, 1962, genocide,[16] an offence against section 9 of the Official Secrets Act, 1963, or an offence under Part II of that Act committed in a manner prejudicial to the safety or preservation of the State, murder, attempted murder and conspiracy to murder, or piracy, including an accessory before or after the fact. An accused who is charged with any of the above offences must apply in the first instance to the High Court in order to be admitted to bail. The activation of Part V of the Offences Against the State Act, 1939, which has resulted in the setting up of the Special Criminal Court means that when a District Justice returns a person to that Court for trial whether charged with an indictable scheduled offence,[17] or with a non scheduled indictable offence,[18] the accused may not be admitted to bail by the District Court without the consent of the Director of Public Prosecutions.

Special Criminal Court

Where a person is charged before the Special Criminal Court or has been sent for trial by a District Court to that Court or has been transferred from any ordinary Court for trial by that Court, the Special Criminal Court has jurisdiction to admit him to bail, both pending his trial and also during and after trial until conviction or acquittal.[19] However, the Special Court does not appear to have jurisdiction to admit an accused to bail after conviction. It is submitted that where any person is dissatisfied with any refusal to grant bail or with any bail order made by the Special Criminal Court, a bail application may be made to the High Court.

The Court of Trial

Although applications are most frequently made before the District Court, the Special Criminal Court and the High Court,

16. Added by the Genocide Act, 1973, s. 7.
17. Offences Against the State Act, 1939, s. 45 (2) as amended by the Prosecution of Offences Act, 1974, s. 3.
18. Offences Against the State Act, 1939, s. 46 (2) as so amended.
19. Offences Against the State Act, 1939, s. 43 (1) (c).

for release on bail pending trial, the trial Court itself has jurisdiction when an accused seeks to be admitted to bail after arraignment or during the course of his trial. The discretion of the trial judge to permit a person to stand out on bail is exercised in accordance with the grounds discussed in *The People v. O'Callaghan.*[20] The Court may, however, be less inclined to permit a defendant who has been arraigned upon a serious offence to stand out on bail during his trial.[21] Certain issues, such as the close proximity of the defendant to the witnesses and jurors, may be more relevant in an application for bail during trial than would be the case in an application for bail pending trial. Also to be taken into account is the fact that the defendant will have already heard part of the prosecution case against him, and may consider that the trial is progressing in a less satisfactory manner than he had hoped.[22] The power of a trial judge to permit a person who has been convicted to stand out on bail if he considers that it is appropriate to do so, is not entirely clear. It has already been stated that the Special Criminal Court does not possess such a power. In the case of the *The People v. Kirwan,*[23] in the Circuit Court, the jury returned verdicts which were inconsistent. The trial judge doubted whether he had the power to admit a defendant to bail in such an instance. After an adjournment to permit legal argument to take place on this point, counsel for the Attorney General conceded that the trial judge did have the power to grant bail if he considered it appropriate. However, despite his preparedness to grant a certificate that the case was fit for appeal, the trial judge refused to admit the defendants to bail. The position of a convicted defendant is quite different from that of a person who has not been convicted. In the Court of Criminal Appeal in *Kirwan*'s case Maguire C.J. said, 'The fact that the applicants have been convicted by a jury weighs down the scales heavily against them.'[24] The power to permit an accused to stand

20. [1966] I.R. 501.
21. *R. v. Chapman* 8 C. & P. 558; cf. *R. v. McCartie* 11 I.R.C.L. 188.
22. The position in England with regard to admission to bail during the trial is governed by the Practice Direction given on 4th June, 1970, by the Lord Chief Justice [1974] 2 All E.R. 794.
23. 89 I.L.T.R. 120.
24. Id. at 123.

out on bail during his trial could prove of importance where the trial judge refers a case to the Court of Justice of the European Communities under Article 177 of the Treaty of Rome.

The High Court

The High Court is vested by the Constitution with full jurisdiction on all matters whether of law or fact, civil or criminal.[25] Applications for High Court bail are made in accordance with the Rules of the Superior Courts,[26] which provide that an application for bail by a person in custody shall be by motion on notice to the Chief State Solicitor, grounded on the affidavit of the applicant, but where an applicant has no solicitor the Court may dispense with a notice of motion and affidavit, and in lieu thereof shall give all appropriate directions, including a direction that the applicant be brought before the Court on a date and time to be specified, and, for the purpose of giving such directions, the Court may hear the applicant. There are no legal aid provisions governing such applications. This is most undesirable because defendants who are unrepresented will be unaware of those matters which they ought to advance in support of their applications.

The High Court has power to grant bail prior to trial for any offence. Where a District Court has refused bail, the applicant, if he does not wish to renew his application before that Court, may apply to the High Court.[27] As Walsh J. pointed out in *The People v. O'Callaghan:*[28]

> 'The jurisdiction of the High Court to grant bail is an original jurisdiction and is in no sense a form of appeal from the District Court or from any other Court which may have dealt with the question of the bail of the applicant.'

This dictum seems to be at variance with that of Murnaghan J., the judge of first instance in the same case, who said:[29]

25. Article 34.
26. O. 84, r. 40.
27. Criminal Procedure Act, 1967, s. 28 (3).
28. [1966] I.R. 501, 511.
29. Id. at 502-503.

'[I]t is in the first place essential that it be shown to this Court that the District Justice has erred in the exercise of his discretion. Some years ago now I decided in the *Attorney General v. Ball*[30] that it was not the function of this Court to substitute its opinion for that of the District Justice, whose function it was to decide whether or not the prisoner should be admitted to bail, and, if he be admitted to bail, the amounts of the recognisances. This decision was upheld by the Supreme Court.'

The apparent dichotomy between the positions of the two judges is possibly reconciled in the Supreme Court judgment of Maguire C.J. in *Attorney General v. Ball*.[31] The main contention by counsel on behalf of the applicant in the Supreme Court in the *Ball* case was that Murnaghan J. had misconceived the position inasmuch as he had considered that he had no jurisdiction to interfere with the discretion of the District Justice. However, in his consideration of this submission, Maguire C.J. commented:[32]

'I do not think that Mr McCarthy is correct in saying that Mr Justice Murnaghan decided he would not be entitled in his discretion to overrule the District Justice, if in fact he had been satisfied that the District Justice had exercised his discretion incorrectly.

The District Justice has, however, had the case before him; he has had to decide on this type of application frequently and has had to consider the circumstances of each case. Mr Clarke refers to the statement of Molony C.J. in *R. v. Israelovitch*[33] that . . . "the Court should be very slow to overrule the magistrate where, in his discretion, he has decided not to accept bail pending the remand". This applies even more strongly in our present judicial system where the District Justice, by his professional training, is very much better qualified to deal with applications of this nature than were the unpaid lay magistrates who had summary jurisdiction in criminal cases at that time when *R. v. Israelovitch* was decided. Save in very exceptional circumstances, this Court should not overrule a District Justice who, in his discretion, has refused bail.'

It is possible to interpret this part of the judgment as suggesting that while High Court judges who entertain bail applications have an unfettered discretion to admit persons to bail for any offence, nevertheless the *de facto* situation is that, if the applicant

30. [1958] I.R. 280.
31. Id.
32. [1958] I.R. 280, 286-7.
33. [1919] 2 I.R. 47.

has been unable to satisfy a legally trained District Justice, then it will be unlikely that in the absence of some arbitrary or capricious behaviour by the latter, he will be able to persuade a High Court judge hearing the same facts, to take the opposite view. One case, however, where this did occur was *The People v. Duffy*[34] where Hanna J. admitted the applicant to bail despite accepting that the discretion of the District Justice in refusing bail had not been wrongly exercised.

As has already been stated, the discretion of a High Court judge to admit a person to bail applies in all cases except those misdemeanour cases falling within section 2 of the Habeas Corpus Act, 1781, when a High Court judge *must* grant bail if he is satisfied about the sufficiency of the bail.[35]

Persons may seek to be admitted to bail by the High Court at a number of different stages of their involvement in the criminal process.

(i) A person awaiting trial upon indictment who has been refused bail by the District Court, or who is dissatisfied with any bail order made by that Court, may apply to the High Court for bail.[36]

(ii) In any instance in which the District Court is precluded by statute from admitting any person to bail such a person may apply to the High Court.[37]

(iii) Any person who has been tried and convicted by a District Court has an automatic statutory right of appeal to the Circuit Court.[38] Such an appeal is by way of full rehearing. It would appear that, as soon as a defendant convicted by the District Court has served a notice of appeal to the Circuit Court, the District Court is then *obliged* to fix recognisances[39] and, when these have been entered into, the appellant must be liberated.[40] Failure

34. [1942] Ir. Jur. Rep. 63.
35. See *The People v. O'Callaghan* [1966] I.R. 501, 512; see also *Re Frost* 4 T.L.R. 757 (this decision relates to the Habeas Corpus Act, 1679, s. 3 which is identical to s. 2 of the 1781 Act).
36. Criminal Procedure Act, 1967, s. 28.
37. Criminal Procedure Act, 1967, s. 29; see also Offences Against the State Act, 1939, ss. 45 (3) and 46 (3).
38. Courts of Justice Act, 1928, s. 18 as amended by Courts of Justice Act, 1936, s. 58.
39. *The People v. McCormack*, unrep. 1972, *per* Griffin J.
40. See the District Court Rules, 1948, r. 194.

by a District Justice to fix recognisances or to admit to bail would appear to give a prospective appellant the right to apply to the High Court for bail. The possibility of bail in this instance is extremely important because the maximum sentences which may be imposed by the District Court are low and, if a defendant were to be refused bail, such a refusal could result in his serving a large part of a prison sentence before an appeal could be heard. The statutory right of appeal would thereby be largely vitiated.

(iv) A person who has been convicted in either the District Court, the Circuit Court or the Special Criminal Court, and who seeks an order of certiorari to remove the proceedings into the High Court for the purpose of having the decision quashed, may be admitted to bail by the High Court pending the making absolute of such an order. Similarly an applicant for an order of prohibition or habeas corpus may be admitted to bail by the High Court pending the making absolute of any such order. In *The State (McKenna) v. Durcan*[41] the prosecutor was convicted on 20th June, 1952 by the District Court and sentenced to three months imprisonment. On appeal to the Circuit Court on 5th November, 1952, this sentence was reduced to two months imprisonment. On 11th November, 1952, the prosecutor, Durcan, began to serve his sentence and on the same day conditional orders of certiorari and habeas corpus were obtained on his behalf. On 5th December, 1952, the prosecutor applied to the High Court for bail pending the making absolute of the conditional orders. Counsel on behalf of the prosecutor urged the Court to accept the authority of the unreported case of *The State (Taylor) v. Kavanagh* in which the prosecutor had been sentenced to one month's imprisonment and counsel on his behalf sought, and was granted, bail pending the making absolute of a conditional order of habeas corpus.

In *The State (McKenna) v. Durcan,* Kingsmill-Moore J. granted the application of the prosecutor on the basis that:[42]

> '[I]f the prosecutor were not admitted to bail he would have served his sentence before the application to have the conditional orders

41. 87 I.L.T.R. 62.
42. Id. at 63.

of certiorari and habeas corpus made absolute was heard, and if he were successful in such an application, an injustice would have been caused.'

(v) The jurisdiction of the High Court to admit to bail any person who has been convicted at a trial upon indictment is unclear as it has not yet been litigated before the Irish courts.[43] In England the High Court has no inherent power to admit a convicted person to bail.[44] However, in *The People v. O'Callaghan* Walsh J. in the Supreme Court stated:[45]

> 'Apart. . . from any question of bail arising on a habeas corpus application the High Court has a jurisdiction to grant bail to a person who has been convicted as the jurisdiction of the High Court in bail matters as in other matters is considerably wider than that of the Court of Criminal Appeal.'

This jurisdiction of the High Court could prove important in a number of instances. If a trial judge has refused, or, as is the case with the Special Criminal Court, has no power to permit an accused person to stand out on bail pending an application for leave to appeal to the Court of Criminal Appeal, the High Court could admit him to bail. Similarly if an accused has been granted a certificate from the Court of Criminal Appeal that his case is fit for appeal to the Supreme Court, he may wish to apply for bail to the High Court.[46]

Any person entitled to apply to the High Court for bail may, if unsuccessful, renew his application on an indefinite number of occasions, although second and subsequent applications are unlikely to succeed unless new grounds can be adduced by the applicant. Alternatively, any applicant dissatisfied with a High Court decision on the granting of bail or as to the amount or conditions thereof, may appeal to the Supreme Court.[47]

Court of Criminal Appeal

The Court of Criminal Appeal, which is a creature of statute, has very limited powers to admit persons to bail. Section 32 of

43. See dicta of Walsh J. in *The People v. O'Callaghan* [1966] I.R. 501, 512.
44. *Ex parte Blyth* [1944] K.B. 532.
45. [1966] I.R. 501, 513.
46. Cf. *The People v. Boggan* [1958] I.R. 67 (S.C.).
47. See Article 34.4.3° of the Constitution.

the Courts of Justice Act, 1924 provides that leave to appeal shall be granted by the Court of Criminal Appeal in cases where the Court is of opinion that a question of law is involved, or where the trial appears to the Court to have been unsatisfactory, or there appears to the Court to be any other sufficient ground of appeal; and that the Court shall have power to make any consequential orders it may think fit, including an order admitting the appellant to bail pending the determination of his appeal. As has been stated, the Court of Criminal Appeal has made it clear that the conviction of a defendant weighs down the scales against him in any bail application.[48] In *Attorney General v. Cashell*[49] the Court refused to admit an applicant to bail pending the granting by it of *leave* to appeal. In *The People v. Boggan*[50] the Court refused bail to an appellant who claimed that the trial judge had no jurisdiction to hear the case, as the District Justice who had conducted the preliminary investigation had refused to return the accused for trial. Although dismissing the appellant's case, the Court of Criminal Appeal granted a certificate that the point of law involved was one of exceptional public importance. Nevertheless it held that it had no jurisdiction to grant bail pending appeal to the Supreme Court, as the particular case was not covered by the Act of 1924. In any event the Court indicated that it would have been very reluctant to grant bail in this case.

The Court of Criminal Appeal may also admit a person to bail pending any re-trial.[51]

The Supreme Court

The Supreme Court has jurisdiction in respect of any refusal of bail by the High Court[52] by virtue of the Constitution.

48. *The People v. Kirwan* 89 I.L.T.R. 120; *The People v. Sigal* [1946] Ir. Jur. Rep. 21.
49. 62 I.L.T.R. 31; applied, *The People v. Hayden*, 10th February, 1930, Frewen 347.
50. [1958] I.R. 67.
51. Courts of Justice Act, 1928, s. 5 (1) (b).
52. Article 34.4.3°.

CHAPTER 8

LEGAL REPRESENTATION

The prevailing ethos of the medieval world that, '[l]egal aid, like other assistance to the *miserabiles personae* of Christendom, was a form of *caritas*',[1] exhibited such remarkable vitality in Ireland that, as late as 1961, the Minister for Justice felt able to say to the Dáil:[2]

> '[I] believe the number of genuine miscarriages of justice in this country is not substantial. I base my belief on the voluntary contribution which the legal profession has made by supplying proper representation in deserving cases and on the high standards which our judges and justices have consistently maintained in ensuring that accused persons who are not legally represented are treated with scrupulous fairness.'

That the movement from charity to right has still not been completed is evidenced by the fact that, in 1976, in *The State (Healy) v. Donoghue*[3] the Supreme Court refrained from making the dogmatic assertion that *all* accused persons have a constitutional right to have professional legal representation in a criminal trial when charged with a serious offence, and that, if they are impecunious, they are entitled to have the costs of their defence met out of State funds, although the Court did propound a constitutional right to professional representation in certain limited instances. To the layman it might appear axiomatic that defendants require to be legally represented in criminal cases and especially in those which are tried upon indictment. The panoply of such a trial with its arcane language and rituals, matters which

1. Cappelletti and Gordley, *Legal Aid: Modern Themes and Variations* 24 Stanford L. Rev. 347, 351 (1972).
2. 193 Dáil Éireann Debates, col. 234.
3. [1976] I.R. 325.

are second nature to trial lawyers, presents a total enigma to defendants, many of whom are inarticulate and uneducated. It, therefore, seems strange that the right to legal representation for persons unable to pay for it has been so slow to establish itself and has not been more vigorously championed by the courts.

A key to the understanding of this apparent lacuna in the criminal process is probably provided by history. The criminal trial of today differs significantly from that of earlier centuries. In the seventeenth and early eighteenth centuries trials proceeded rapidly,[4] with the accused not being permitted the assistance of counsel on treason or felony charges. The Treason Act, 1695, which was repealed in May 1983, enabled an accused to have counsel for the offence of treason although this Act did not extend to persons charged with felony. One paradox to be found in this period lay in the fact that a person charged with a misdemeanour *did* have a right to legal representation as such cases frequently involved property rights and were deemed appropriate matters for lawyers.[5]

The absence of lawyers from felony cases meant that judges played a much greater role in the questioning of witnesses. Although entitled to be represented by counsel in felony cases, the prosecution frequently did not avail of this right, which left the judge much more in the role of inquisitor than that of the dispassionate umpire and arbiter of law that he is in the contemporary adversary system. From the beginning of the eighteenth century the prosecution was increasingly represented by counsel and, as early as the 1730's at the Old Bailey, defence lawyers were present and carried out cross-examinations. Quite why judges should have permitted inroads to be made upon a rule which they had insisted upon for centuries is unclear but it has been suggested that the greater use of prosecuting counsel in the years preceding the advent of defence counsel may have resulted in a disparity, thus influencing the judges to relax their former

4. See Langbein, *The Criminal Trial before the Lawyers* 45 U. Chi. L. Rev. 263 (1978). In this article Langbein instances that in one two-day session in the courtroom at the Old Bailey in December, 1678, thirty two cases were tried. He also points out that the court was under no pressure to induce jury waiver and in consequence plea bargaining was rare.
5. Langbein, op. cit. at 308.

rule.[6]

The final statutory acknowledgement of the role of the defence counsel in the criminal trial was provided by the Trial of Felonies Act, 1836, which stated that all persons tried for felony were entitled, after the close of the prosecution, to make full answer and defence by counsel learned in the law, or by solicitor in courts where solicitors practised as counsel.

It may not be overstating the case to suggest that the contemporary adversary process, forged and fashioned as it has been by the presence of lawyers both for the prosecution and for the defence, has now reached such a degree of complexity and sophistication as to make professional legal representation an indispensible pre-requisite to its effective functioning. One author has even gone so far as to suggest that:[7]

> 'The conduct of a case in court is a peculiar art for which many men, however learned in law are not fitted. . . when clients fully appreciate the dangers they run in entrusting their litigation to so called 'office lawyers' with little or no experience in court, they will insist upon their brief being entrusted to those who make a speciality of court practice. . .'

While nineteenth century legislation entitled accused persons to be legally represented, it failed to provide any mechanism whereby impecunious persons could secure the services of lawyers and undoubtedly there may also have existed a disparity in competence between counsel for the prosecution and counsel for the defence. A judge in the nineteenth century could request a member of the Bar who happened to be present in court to give his services to a defendant charged with murder but no statutory remuneration was provided.[8] This practice continued until 1965. Despite the fact that there existed in England as early as 1903 a statutory scheme whereby legal aid could be made available to defendants tried upon indictment, no similar provision existed in Ireland until the passing of the Criminal Justice (Legal Aid) Act,

6. Id. at 313.
7. Wellman, *The Art of Cross Examination,* (4th Ed.) 23 and 25.
8. In *R. v. Fogarty* 5 Cox 161 the defendant was charged with the murder of his wife. Piggott C.B. accepted that he could not compel counsel to act but he appealed to the sense of feeling at the Bar, saying that he would recommend that counsel's fees be paid by the Crown.

1962.[9] Section 34 of the Courts of Justice Act, 1924, enabled the Court of Criminal Appeal to award costs necessary for the purpose of doing justice in the case before the court. Today that court has no longer jurisdiction to award costs under this section where a legal aid (trial on indictment) certificate or a legal aid (appeal) certificate has been granted in respect of proceedings in relation to which either of those certificates applies.[10]

In the case of any appeal by a person sentenced to death the same court was empowered by the Criminal Appeal Rules of 1924 [11] to assign appropriate legal aid, in the form of either counsel or solicitor and counsel, as appeared to it to be reasonably required. The cost of such legal aid was to be up to an amount allowed by the court and subject to rates and scales of payment made by the Minister for Finance. As late as 1950 no regulations had been made under the 1924 Rules and the State disbursed money to lawyers in accordance with an informal scale in the minutes of the Department of Justice. In commenting upon this state of affairs Gavin Duffy J. remarked, that 'the practice of the State, when bound to pay, of doling out inadequate "token fees" does no credit to the State.'[12]

The Courts of Justice Act, 1928, first gave the Court of Criminal Appeal the power to order a re-trial. Section 5 (1) (b) of that Act also provided that when a re-trial was ordered by either the Court of Criminal Appeal or by the Supreme Court, the costs of the appeal and the re-trial should be borne by the State unless the Court was of the opinion that the necessity for the appeal and the new trial had been caused or contributed to by the defence. The Court of Criminal Appeal no longer has jurisdiction under section 5 where either a legal aid (trial on indictment) certificate or a legal aid (appeal) certificate has been granted in respect of proceedings in relation to which either of those certificates applies.[13]

9. For excellent treatment of the position in Ireland before and immediately after the implementation of the Criminal Justice (Legal Aid) Act, 1962, see Greer, *Legal Services and the Poor in Ireland* [1969] Ir. Jur. 270.
10. Criminal Justice (Legal Aid) Act, 1962, s. 8.
11. Rules of Court made under the Courts of Justice Act, 1924, s. 36; now O. 86, r. 38 R.S.C. 1962.
12. *The People v. Daly* [1951] I.R. 113, 116.
13. Criminal Justice (Legal Aid) Act, 1962, s. 8.

Although Ireland ratified the European Convention on Human Rights which entitles an indigent person charged with a criminal offence to be given free legal assistance when the interests of justice so require,[14] the Government entered a reservation in respect of this provision.

The Criminal Justice (Legal Aid) Act, 1962

The passing of the Criminal Justice (Legal Aid) Act, 1962, the provisions of which were activated on 1st April, 1965, heralded the beginning of a new approach to the problem of indigent defendants. The preamble to the Act describes its purpose as being 'to make provision for the grant by the State of free legal aid to poor persons in certain criminal cases.' Five different kinds of legal aid certificates are contemplated by the Act, all of which provide for *free* legal aid.

These are:

(1) legal aid (District Court) certificate;[15]

(2) legal aid (trial on indictment) certificate;[16]

(3) legal aid (appeal) certificate;[17]

(4) legal aid (case stated) certificate;[18]

(5) legal aid (Supreme Court) certificate.[19]

The different criteria to be applied by a court entertaining an application for one of the above certificates are set forth in the Act.[20]

A legal aid (District Court) certificate will normally be granted at the time of the first remand of an accused who is to be tried upon indictment. This will enable the accused to have the services of a solicitor up to and including the committal proceedings.[21]

14. Art. 6 (3) (c).
15. Criminal Justice (Legal Aid) Act, 1962, s. 2.
16. Id. s. 3.
17. Id. s. 4.
18. Id. s. 5.
19. Id. s. 6.
20. See Appendix A infra. For an excellent commentary on the restrictive wording used in the Act, see Note: Advent of Legal Aid in Ireland 99 I.L.T.S.J. 190, 265 and 297.
21. It should be noted that by the Criminal Procedure Act, 1967, s. 19 (3) no legal aid was available in respect of any preliminary examinations under that Act, unless the accused was charged with murder. This was reversed by the Criminal Procedure (Amendment) Act, 1973, s. 3 (3).

Only in the case of an accused charged with murder may legal aid be granted enabling counsel to be assigned in the District Court.[22]

If the accused is returned for trial, an application is invariably made to the District Justice for a legal aid (trial on indictment) certificate. Application for such a certificate may also be made to the trial judge. This certificate, if granted, entitles an accused to have both a solicitor and counsel assigned to him to enable him to prepare and conduct his defence. By regulation 7 (2) of the Criminal Justice (Legal Aid) Regulations, 1965,[23] a court which is granting a certificate in respect of a trial upon indictment or of any appeal therefrom may direct that two counsel be assigned to act for the accused if the accused is charged with murder, or if the case presents exceptional difficulty and cannot, in the opinion of the court, be conducted adequately without the assistance of two counsel.

If an accused is convicted upon indictment he may seek a legal aid (appeal) certificate. Application is made in the first instance to the trial judge,[24] and, if he refuses, the applicant may apply to the court to which an appeal from the conviction lies. This will normally be the Court of Criminal Appeal.[25]

If a defendant is tried upon indictment in the Circuit Court and the trial judge refers a question of law arising in the proceedings to the Supreme Court by way of case stated, an applicant may be granted a legal aid (case stated) certificate by the Circuit Court judge[26] and, in the event of a refusal of the application, he may apply to the Supreme Court.[27]

A legal aid (Supreme Court) certificate is available *inter alia* in those instances when an appeal is brought from the Court of Criminal Appeal. The application is made in the first instance to the Court of Criminal Appeal,[28] and, in the event of a refusal by that Court, the applicant may apply to the Supreme Court.[29]

22. Criminal Justice (Legal Aid) Act, 1962, s. 2 (1).
23. S.I. 12 of 1965; excerpts are reprinted in Appendix A infra.
24. Criminal Justice (Legal Aid) Act, 1962, s. 4 (2).
25. Id. s. 4 (3).
26. Id. s. 5 (2).
27. Id. s. 5 (3).
28. Id. s. 6 (2).
29. Id. s. 6 (3).

In addition to the courts empowered to grant free legal aid by the 1962 Act, the Special Criminal Court is now similarly empowered to grant certificates in relation to cases heard by it and appeals therefrom.[30]

Assessment of means of applicant

In dealing with each of the five certificates for free legal aid the court must assess whether the applicant's means are 'insufficient to enable him to obtain legal aid.' By section 9 of the Act a court or judge may require an applicant to furnish a written statement of his means before a legal aid certificate is granted. The use of the word 'may' in the section indicates that the need for a written statement as to means is not mandatory and that the court is entitled to be, and very often is, satisfied after hearing oral evidence as to an applicant's means. The Second Schedule to the Criminal Justice (Legal Aid) Regulations, 1965[1] provides the form of the statement of means of an applicant for free legal aid where a written statement is required. This form requires information about the financial commitments of prospective applicants, e.g., rent, mortgages, dependant relatives, and so forth. It also enquires whether the applicant has money or assets which could be deployed to enable him to obtain legal aid at his own expense and, if the applicant is under 21, whether his parents or guardian are willing to provide or assist in the provision of legal aid.

Assignment of solicitor and counsel

The Act contemplates the provision of a solicitor in respect of all five certificates for free legal aid and the provision of counsel in respect of all except the legal aid (District Court) certificate. In proceedings before the District Court that Court may only assign counsel on a charge of murder. Counsel may be of considerable use in the committal proceedings in such a case. The Act provides for the assignment of legal representatives in such a manner as may be provided by regulations made under section 10 of the

30. Special Criminal Court Rules, S.I. No. 147 of 1972, reprinted, Appendix D, infra.
1. S.I. 12 of 1965; see Appendix A infra.

Act.[2] This section empowers the Minister to make such regulations as are necessary for carrying the Act into effect. He has in consequence issued a large number of such regulations.[3] The statutory regulations have provided for a system whereby solicitors, who have notified the County Registrar of their willingness to act for persons who are granted free legal aid certificates, are placed on a list which in turn is sent to officials of the various courts.[4] Similarly the Bar Council sends the Minister the names of counsel who have indicated a willingness to act under the scheme[5] and copies of this list are sent to the various courts.[6] The Regulations also provide for the inclusion and deletion of counsel from the list.

Regulation 7 (1) of the 1965 Regulations states that:

> Upon the grant of a certificate for free legal aid, the court granting the certificate shall, having taken into consideration the representations (if any) of the person to whom the certificate was granted, assign to him a solicitor from the appropriate list kept pursuant to Regulation 4 of these Regulations to act for him in the preparation and conduct of his case.

The question of the right of an applicant to the legal representation of his choice arose in *The State (Royle) v. Kelly.*[7] In this case the prosecutor was granted free legal aid by the Special Criminal Court,[8] and on the day fixed for the trial the solicitor intimated to the Court that, as he had only just received the Book of Evidence, he was not in a position to proceed with the defence; and he further intimated that he would have to withdraw if compelled to go on with the case. This application was refused although the case in fact did not proceed on that day as the Court acceded to an application for adjournment by a co-accused. Subsequently correspondence ensued between the Registrar of the Special

2. Ss. 2 (1), 3 (1), 4 (1), 5 (1), and 6 (1).
3. The principal regulations are contained in the Criminal Justice (Legal Aid) Regulations, 1965, (S.I. 12 of 1965). Most of the subsequent regulations merely deal with updating the financial remuneration of lawyers.
4. S.I. 304 of 1978, r. 3.
5. S.I. 12 of 1965, r. 5 (1).
6. Id. r. 5 (2).
7. [1974] I.R. 259.
8. Pursuant to r. 28 of the Special Criminal Court Rules, 1972, reprinted in Appendix D infra.

Criminal Court and the prosecutor, in which the prosecutor, Royle, was appraised of the fact that his solicitor had withdrawn from the case and he was invited to nominate another. On receiving no reply to his initial letter, the Registrar wrote again to the prosecutor inviting him to nominate a solicitor, and this time the letter indicated that the person chosen should be someone other than the solicitor who had withdrawn. The prosecutor refused to be represented by anyone other than his original solicitor, and he was subsequently tried and convicted without legal representation. In agreeing with the view expressed by Butler J. in the High Court, Walsh J. in the Supreme Court held:[9]

> '[T]he Special Criminal Court was acting within the powers granted to it under the statutory free legal aid provisions in refusing to assign Mr. Concannon, and that the court had a discretion as to whom it would assign. What the limits of that discretion are it is not here necessary to decide; but in view of the fact that Mr. Concannon had expressly withdrawn from the case the court was entitled to hold him to that withdrawal.'

It would seem, therefore, that, so long as the court takes into consideration the representations (if any) of the person to whom a free legal aid certificate has been granted, it may assign any solicitor from the legal aid panel to appear and conduct the defence.

Constitutional aspects of legal representation

Before 1975 no defendant in Ireland had ever sought to impeach a conviction or sentence on the basis that a court had failed to vindicate his constitutional rights, in that he had been convicted or sentenced without having the assistance of professional legal representation.

Unlike the Sixth Amendment to the United States Constitution, which specifically provides that accused persons shall enjoy the right to have the assistance of counsel in criminal prosecutions, the Irish Constitution does not set out with particularity any such right to counsel.

The most important express constitutional provisions with

9. [1974] I.R. 259, 265.

regard to the right to professional legal assistance are those contained in Articles 38.1, 40.3 and 40.4.[10] The issue whether or not the right to professional legal assistance could constitute a fundamental personal right arose in *The State (Healy) v. Donoghue.*[11] In this case the prosecutor, who was aged eighteen years but whose formal education had ceased when he was thirteen years old, was brought before the Children's Court on a charge of breaking and entering a building. He pleaded guilty and, after a number of adjournments, was convicted on 15th January, 1975, and sentenced to three months detention. He did not apply for free legal aid, nor was he informed of any right so to apply. On 13th December, 1974, the prosecutor had appeared in the District Court on charges of larceny which were unconnected with the other court appearance. He consented to being dealt with summarily and was remanded in custody pending the imposition of sentence. On 30th December, 1974, he applied for and was assigned a solicitor in respect of these charges and on 29th January, 1975, he was sentenced to six months detention, although the solicitor assigned to him was not present as he had withdrawn from the statutory scheme for legal aid in the intervening period. In view of the absence of any legal representation, the prosecutor had sought to have the case adjourned on 29th January, 1975, but was unsuccessful.

On 21st February, 1975, he applied to the High Court and obtained a conditional order of certiorari in respect of the three orders made on 29th January, 1975, and also a conditional order of habeas corpus. On 4th March, 1975, he applied for and obtained a conditional order of certiorari in respect of the order made on 15th January, 1975. The grounds on which this order was granted were that he had been denied his rights under Article

10. Article 38.1. No person shall be tried on any criminal charge save in due course of law.
Article 40.3.1° The State guarantees in its laws to respect, and, as far as practicable, by its laws defend and vindicate the personal rights of the citizen.
2° The State shall, in particular, by its laws protect as best it may from unjust attack, and in the case of injustice done, vindicate the life, person, good name, and property rights of every citizen.
Article 40.4.1° No citizen shall be deprived of his personal liberty save in accordance with law.

11. [1976] I.R. 325 (S.C.).

38.1 of the Constitution.

The prosecutor then sought to have the order made absolute. In his interpretation of the phrase 'in due course of law' in Article 38.1 of the Constitution, Gannon J. said:[12]

> 'It is a phrase of very wide import which includes in its scope not merely matters of constitutional and statutory jurisdiction, the range of legislation with respect to criminal offences, and matters of practice and procedure, but also the application of basic principles of justice which are inherent in the proper course of the exercise of the judicial function.'

Gannon J. accepted that an individual whose freedom was in jeopardy had a number of natural rights including the right to be tried in his presence by an impartial court, to hear and test by examination the prosecution evidence, to give or call evidence in his defence, etc. but the learned judge specifically rejected the contention that an accused person had a natural or constitutional right to professional legal representation, although he *did* accept that the basic rights previously referred to by him, 'might effectively and manifestly be denied to an accused person, whether impecunious or not, in some instances if he were not to be afforded the professional assistance of a practising lawyer.'[13]

In so far as the proceedings on 29th January, 1975, were concerned, Gannon J. made absolute the orders of certiorari, on the ground that, once the District Justice made the decision that it was *essential* in the interests of justice that the indigent prosecutor be accorded free legal aid, to proceed thereafter with the disposition of the case deprived the prosecutor of his constitutional rights and resulted in his being tried otherwise than 'in due course of law'. However, in relation to the order of 15th January, 1975, Gannon J. refused to make absolute the order of certiorari because the accused had not applied for free legal aid and the learned judge took the view that neither the 1962 Act nor the Constitution created a right in an accused person to be informed by the court of the purport of the Act of 1962, nor did they impose upon the court a duty to subject an accused to interrogation concerning his means, his intelligence or his knowledge of the

12. Id. 335.
13. Id. 339.

provisions of the statutory scheme.

The Supreme Court, however, took a different view of the need to be informed of the right to free legal aid. O'Higgins C.J. said:[14]

> '[I]f a person who is ignorant of his right fails to apply and on that account is not given legal aid then, in my view, his constitutional right is violated. For this reason it seems to me that when a person faces a possible prison sentence and has no lawyer, and cannot provide for one, he ought to be informed of his right to legal aid. If the person charged does not know of his right, he cannot exercise it; if he cannot exercise it, his right is violated.'

Henchy J. held:[15]

> 'It is true that the Criminal Justice (Legal Aid) Act, 1962, requires the District Court to allow free legal aid only when an application is made for it, and that the Act does not spell out any duty on the court to inform an accused in any particular case of his right to apply for it. Nevertheless, where the known circumstances, or the circumstances that ought to have been known to the court, are such as to show that the accused would have been entitled to free legal aid, and where he was not so informed but was convicted and deprived of his liberty in default of legal aid, he has good reason to complain that the conviction and detention stem from a disregard of his constitutionally-guaranteed rights as an accused person.'

It would appear that the propositions of law which may properly be extrapolated from this case are that, if an accused faces a serious charge, namely one in which his liberty is in jeopardy or in which a severe penalty which may affect his livelihood may be imposed, a court must analyse first whether or not he is indigent and secondly whether or not his circumstances are such that, by reason of his ignorance, lack of education, youth or other incapacity, justice demands that he be legally represented. This second consideration, involving the intellectual capacity of accused persons, should invariably be resolved in the accused's favour because Griffin J. is unquestionably correct when he points out that:[16]

> 'Very few laymen, when charged in court where their liberty is in jeopardy, can present adequately their own cases, much less identify and argue legal questions.'

14. Id. 352.
15. Id. 356.
16. Id. 357.

These sentiments merely echo the powerful words of Sutherland J. in *Powell v. Alabama* in which he said:[17]

> 'The right to be heard would be, in many cases, of little avail if it did not comprehend the right to be heard by counsel. Even the intelligent and educated layman has small and sometimes no skill in the science of law. If charged with crime, he is incapable, generally, of determining for himself whether the indictment is good or bad. He is unfamiliar with the rules of evidence. Left without the aid of counsel he may be put on trial without a proper charge, and convicted upon incompetent evidence irrelevant to the issue or otherwise inadmissible. He lacks both the skill and knowledge adequately to prepare his defense, even though he have a perfect one. He requires the guiding hand of counsel at every step of the proceedings against him. Without it, though he be not guilty, he faces the danger of conviction because he does not know how to establish his innocence.'

The United States Supreme Court expressly approved this statement in the case of *Gideon v. Wainwright.*[18]

If in a serious case an Irish court answers both the question of indigence and that lack of intellectual capacity in the affirmative, then it is incumbent upon it to vindicate the accused's constitutional rights by appraising him of his right to free legal aid under the statutory scheme. It would also seem that if the first question is answered in the negative but the second in the affirmative the accused ought to be appraised of his right to have legal assistance at his own expense, and the court ought not to proceed with the disposition of the case in the absence of legal representation unless the defendant makes an intelligent waiver of his right.

Waiver of legal representation

In *The State (Healy) v. Donoghue* Griffin J. held, 'If [the] defendant indicates that he does not wish to have legal aid, the District Justice should satisfy himself that the defendant intelligently and understandingly waives his right to legal aid.'[19]

O'Higgins C.J. held in the same case that, 'no one can be compelled to accept legal aid, and a person charged is entitled to

17. 287 U.S. 45, 68-69 (1932).
18. 372 U.S. 335 (1963).
19. [1976] I.R. 325, 361 (S.C.).

waive his right in this respect and to defend himself.'[20]

The issue of waiver of legal representation raises some deceptively complex problems. Once a court makes the evaluation that it is essential in the interests of justice that an accused be afforded professional legal representation it is, in effect, averring that the accused is, in its opinion, incapable of effectively vindicating his legal rights if he conducts his own defence. A question to be posed therefore is whether a court *can* permit an inept accused to waive his right to legal representation. It is interesting to note that courts in the United States have differentiated between the right to waive counsel on the one hand and the right to conduct a defence *pro se* on the other.[21] A waiver may properly be described as 'an intentional relinquishment or abandonment of a known right or privilege',[22] while the question of self representation usually involves the *assertion* of a right.

In the *United States v. Plattner*[23] it was stated that the right to counsel supplemented the other rights of the defendant and did not impair 'the absolute and primary right to conduct one's own defence *in propria persona*,'[24] and in 1975 the United States Supreme Court affirmed a constitutional right to self representation to a defendant who knowingly and intelligently chose to adopt this course, basing its decision on the Sixth Amendment guarantee of the right to counsel.[25]

Undoubtedly the Irish courts will continue to accept the right of any defendant to defend himself and it may be argued that the right of *pro se* representation is, in effect, guaranteed either by the 'due course of law' provision of Article 38. 1 of the Constitution or alternatively that it is one of the unspecified personal fundamental rights guaranteed by the Constitution. If, however, an accused applies for a legal aid certificate and is assigned a solicitor and counsel thereunder, it is submitted that the court has a right to consider this as a waiver of the right to defend the case *pro se* and to hold the accused to his election.

20. Id. 352.
21. See Weiner, *A criminal defendant who makes an intelligent and knowing choice has a constitutional right to self-representation* 53 J. of Urban Law 333 (1976).
22. *Johnson v. Zerbst* 304 U.S. 458, 464 (1938).
23. 330 F. 2d. 271 (2nd Cir. 1964).
24. Id. 274.
25. *Faretta v. California*, 95 S.Ct. 2525 (1975).

Should an accused purport to waive his right to legal assistance any such waiver must, according to Griffin J. in *The State (Healy) v. Donoghue,* be 'intelligently and understandingly' made. The United States courts operate a strong presumption against waiver of fundamental constitutional rights[26] and in *Von Moltke v. Gillies,*[27] it was said that trial judges must ensure that any waiver by an accused of the right to counsel is made:[28]

> '[W]ith an apprehension of the nature of the charges, the statutory offenses included within them, the range of allowable punishments thereunder, possible defenses to the charges and circumstances in mitigation thereof, and all other facts essential to a broad understanding of the whole matter.'

A trial judge in Ireland, in a case being heard upon indictment, ought, it is submitted, to adopt these or similar guidelines before accepting any decision by an accused person to waive his right to counsel, because only by ensuring that the accused is appraised of these matters can a judge be satisfied that a purported waiver has been made 'intelligently and understandingly'. However, once the gravity of his position has been clearly put to the accused the judge ought to accept a subsequent waiver irrespective of whether or not he considers the defendant's election in the matter to be appropriate.[29] Almost inevitably a waiver of counsel by a defendant will result in a situation whereby the protagonists in the adversary system will be of unequal ability and to this degree any ensuing trial could be viewed as 'unfair'. However, with lay persons usually being the arbiters of fact, forensic skill may play a smaller part in the trial process than lawyers may care to imagine. A defendant may have his own reasons for waiver. He may, for example, seek to project himself to the jury as a person engaged in an unequal battle against the resources of the State. He may feel that the interposing of counsel between himself and the jury detracts from his sincerity.[30] He may be trying to force an unsym-

26. *Johnson v. Zerbst* 304 U.S. 458.
27. 332 U.S. 708 (1948).
28. Id. 724.
29. On the general question of waiver of Irish constitutional rights, see Kelly, *The Irish Constitution,* 336-339.
30. Philo, *Self Representation in Criminal Trials – The Pro Se Defendant* 9 Wake Forest L.Rev. 265 (1973).

pathetic trial judge to intervene on his behalf to ensure that justice is *seen* to be done, and judges certainly tend to be meticulously watchful in the case of a defendant who is unrepresented.

Ineffectual legal representation

As the Supreme Court has now accepted that in certain instances an accused person's constitutional rights may only be effectively vindicated if he receives professional legal representation, there falls to be determined the problem of what in fact constitutes 'legal representation'. It can scarcely be argued that, merely because an indigent person has been assigned a solicitor and counsel, albeit the solicitor and counsel of his choice, the court's duty of ensuring the vindication of his constitutional rights in this respect has thereby been discharged. Given that there is a limited constitutional right to legal representation, the nature and quality of such representation must, perforce, become an area susceptible of constitutional challenge. Lawyers, whether they be assigned in accordance with the provisions of the statutory legal aid scheme or retained by accused persons at their own expense, may prove wholly inadequate to their task. This inadequacy may take a large variety of forms including inexperience at criminal defence work, inability to devote time to considering the evidentiary issues arising out of the depositions, a failure to consult adequately with a client before the trial, omission to consider all possible legal defences to counts in the indictment or to ask appropriate questions at the trial.[1]

Because the judicial exposition of the right to be legally represented in certain instances is of recent origin there exists, as yet, no Irish case law on the matter of the adequacy of legal representation in criminal cases. Courts in the United States, on the other hand, have been obliged to evaluate whether or not legal representation has in fact been effective and the large amount of case law thereby generated has in turn stimulated

1. For a detailed treatment of the ways in which counsel can prove ineffective: see Finer, *Ineffective Assistance of Counsel* 58 Cornell L. Rev. 1077 (1973).

much academic discussion of this extremely difficult issue.[2]

While the enunciation of a right to counsel without the concomitant right to question the effectiveness of such a counsel would be meaningless,[3] it is scarcely possible to envisage a more tempting ground for a disappointed defendant to attempt to impeach a conviction than that the responsibility for the verdict rests with his counsel.

Few could disagree with Arnold J. in the United States case of *Diggs v. Welch*[4] where he argued that:

> 'To allow a prisoner to try the issue of the effectiveness of his counsel under a liberal definition of that phrase is to give every convict the privilege of opening a Pandora's box of accusations which trial courts near large penal institutions would be compelled to hear. . .'

In deference to this obvious danger, the courts in the United States, whether entertaining appeals on the ground of inadequate representation or some form of collateral attack on convictions, for example, by way of habeas corpus, have sought to construe the phrase very strictly. The courts in that country have grounded the right to effectual counsel upon the 'due process' provision of the United States Constitution as well as upon the Sixth Amendment guarantee of the right to the assistance of counsel. The Irish courts, when they face this issue, will doubtless measure the effectiveness of assistance against the Irish Constitution's guarantees of trial 'in due course of law'[5] and of no deprivation of liberty save in accordance with law,[6] in conjunction with those unspecified fundamental rights which are also guaranteed by the Constitution.

2. Waltz, *Inadequacy of Trial Defence Representation as a Ground for Post Conviction Relief in Criminal Cases* 59 Nw.U.L.Rev. 289 (1964); Little, *Criminal Defendants Entitled to Reasonably Competent Assistance of Counsel – United States v. De Coster* 12 Am. Crim. Law Rev. 193 (1974); Bazelon, *The Defective Assistance of Counsel* 42 U. Cin. L. Rev. 1 (1973); Flynn, *Adequacy of Counsel: the emerging fair trial issue for the seventies?* New York State Bar Journal, 19 January 1975. Note: *Effective Assistance of Counsel for the Indigent Defendant* 78 Harv. L. Rev. 1434 (1965).
3. Chief Justice Bazelon describes the right to counsel without the assurance that counsel will perform competently as 'the crack in the house that Gideon built.' 42 U. Cin. L. Rev. 1, 2. (1972).
4. 148 F. 2d. 667 (D.C. Cir. 1945).
5. Article 38. 3.
6. Article 40. 4.

The standard most widely adopted by the United States courts has demanded that the defendant demonstrate that he has been denied the fundamental fairness required by due process, in that his trial was a 'farce and a mockery of justice'.[7] Other courts have enquired whether 'gross incompetence ... blotted out the essence of a substantial defence',[8] or whether the representation 'withdrew a crucial defence from the accused's case'.[9] In a liberal judgment in 1970 the Court of Appeals decided in *Moore v. United States* that the appellant's counsel had not satisfied 'the standard of adequacy of legal services [which] as in other professions is the exercise of the customary skill and knowledge which normally prevails at the time and place.'[10]

In recent years a test which has found favour with courts in many subsequent cases was propounded in *MacKenna v. Ellis* where the court said:[11]

> 'We interpret the right to counsel as the right to effective counsel. We interpret counsel to mean not errorless counsel, and not counsel judged ineffective by hindsight, but counsel reasonably likely to render *and rendering* reasonably effective assistance.'

In *United States v. De Coster* the court held that, 'a defendant is entitled to the reasonably competent assistance of an attorney acting as his diligent conscientious advocate'[12] and it based its decision on both the 'due process' provisions and the Sixth Amendment right to counsel. It seems likely that Irish courts, when faced with an allegation that legal representation has been inadequate, will be as stringent in their requirements as courts in the United States have been, and irrespective of how the test of

7. *Diggs v. Welch* 148 F. 2d. 667 (D.C.Cir.), cert. denied, 325 U.S. 889 (1945); *Bottiglio v. United States* 431 F. 2d. 930 (1st Cir. 1970); *Mitchell v. United States* 259 F. 2d. 787 (D.C.Cir. 1958), cert. denied, 358 U.S. 850 (1958).
8. *Bruce v. United States* 379 F. 2d. 113, 117 (D.C.Cir. 1967); *Scott v. United States* 427 F. 2d 609 (D.C.Cir. 1970).
9. *Smith v. United States* 428 F. 2d. 1183 (4th Cir. 1971).
10. 432 F. 2d. 730, 736 (3d Cir. 1970).
11. 280 F. 2d. 592, 599 (5th Cir. 1960); followed *West v. Louisiana* 478 F. 2d. 1026 (5th Cir. 1973), *Beasley v. United States* 491 F. 2d. 687 (6th Cir. 1974), where the test in *MacKenna v. Ellis* was followed in preference to the 'farce and mockery' test which Celebrezze J. said had no instrinsic meaning. It is submitted that Finer is correct when he argues that the test in *MacKenna v. Ellis* begs the question. See p. 218 supra, n. 1.
12. 487 F. 2d. 1197, 1202.

inadequacy is formulated, it will be difficult to set aside convictions on the basis that the legal assistance rendered has failed to ensure the vindication of constitutional rights.

The right to legal representation in the police station

If one accepts the proposition evinced by Gannon J. in *The State (Healy) v. Donoghue* that certain constitutional rights, 'might effectively and manifestly be denied to an accused person, whether impecunious or not, in some instances if he were not to be afforded the professional assistance of a practising lawyer,'[13] a question remains to be posed as to the extent of such a right. The Supreme Court in *The State (Healy) v. Donoghue* confined itself to affirming a right to legal representation at the *trial* of certain serious cases.

In *The People v. Madden*[14] it was contended by counsel for one of the appellants that it should be held by the court that the failure of the police to provide a lawyer for the accused at the time of, or prior to the making of a statement was a deprivation of his constitutional right. Counsel contended that this was the position irrespective of whether or not the accused asked for a lawyer. However, in rejecting this contention O'Higgins C.J. held:[15]

> 'This Court is satisfied that a person held in detention by the Garda Síochána, whether under the provisions of the [Offences Against the State] Act of 1939 or otherwise, has got a right of reasonable access to his legal advisers and that a refusal of a request to give such reasonable access would render his detention illegal. Of course, in this context the word 'reasonable' must be construed having regard to all the circumstances of each individual case and, in particular, as to the time at which access is requested and the availability of the legal adviser or advisers sought. However, the court is not satisfied that there is any obligation on the Garda Síochána when detaining a person either under s. 30 of the Act of 1939 or under any other authority, to proffer to such person the assistance of a legal adviser without request. The finding of fact in this case made by the Special Criminal Court that the accused did not at any time during his detention request the assistance or the presence

13. [1976] I.R. 325, 339.
14. [1977] I.R. 336.
15. Id. 355-356.

of a legal adviser was based upon evidence which that court was entitled to accept. Therefore, this Court is satisfied that the accused was not deprived in that context of any constitutional or other lawful right.'

If one contrasts this view with that expressed by the Chief Justice in *The State (Healy) v. Donoghue* where, in referring to a failure to apply for free legal aid, he commented, '[i]f the person charged does not know of his right he cannot exercise it, if he cannot exercise it, his right is violated',[16] one is left with a perplexing dichotomy. The Irish courts appear to view the pre-court rights of accused persons differently from the rights which they may enjoy *during* the adjudicatory process. Whether or not such a diversity in treatment is justified seems doubtful.

In *Gideon v. Wainwright,*[17] the United States Supreme Court held that there existed a right to counsel at trial and it further stated that this right was one which extended to States themselves. In *Escobedo v. Illinois,*[18] the same court was invited to explore the issue whether there existed a right to counsel in the pre-trial process and, in delivering the judgment of the court Goldberg J. held:[19]

> 'We have learned the lesson of history, ancient and modern, that a system of criminal law enforcement which comes to depend on the "confession" will, in the long run, be less reliable and more subject to abuses than a system which depends on extrinsic evidence independently secured through skilful investigation. . .
>
> We have also learned the companion lesson of history that no system of criminal justice can, or should, survive if it comes to depend for its continued effectiveness on the citizens' abdication through unawareness of their constitutional rights. No system worth preserving should have to *fear* that if an accused is permitted to consult with a lawyer he will become aware of, and exercise, these rights. If the exercise of constitutional rights will thwart the effectiveness of a system of law enforcement, then there is something very wrong with that system.'

In *Massiah v. U.S.* the court held that:[20]

16. [1976] I.R. 325, 352.
17. 372 U.S. 335 (1963).
18. 378 U.S. 478.
19. Id. 488-490.
20. 377 U.S. 201, 204 (1964) quoting Douglas J. in *Spano v. New York,* 360 U.S. 315, 326 (1959).

> '[A] Constitution which guarantees a defendant the aid of counsel at . . . trial could surely vouchsafe no less to an indicted defendant under interrogation by the police in a completely extra-judicial proceeding. Anything less . . . might deny a defendant "effective representation by counsel at the only stage when legal aid and advice would help him" . . .'

Many criminal trials are undoubtedly rendered foregone conclusions by reason of evidence gained at preceding police interrogations. As Black J. held in his dissenting judgment in *Re Groban*, 'The right to use counsel at the formal trial [would be] a very hollow thing [if], for all practical purposes, the conviction is already assured by pre-trial examination.'[21] If this dictum is correct it could be argued that to refuse a defendant a right to legal assistance at the only time when it would be of value to him is not only to visit a cruel wrong upon him but also to infringe his constitutional rights.

In *The People v. Farrell*,[22] the defendant was convicted of causing an explosion on the basis of oral and written statements made by him to the police while he was being detained for an extended period under section 30 of the Offences Against the State Act, 1939. He applied to the Court of Criminal Appeal for leave to appeal against his conviction and counsel urged on his behalf, *inter alia*, that the appellant, being a person in custody on suspicion of, or intended to be charged with, the commission of a criminal offence, was entitled to the right of the benefit of legal advice and assistance and that he had a concomitant right to be *informed* of this right to have legal assistance. The appellant relied *inter alia* upon *The State (Healy) v. Donoghue* but, in distinguishing the latter case, the Chief Justice said:[23]

> 'It should be noted that *The State (Healy) v. Donoghue* was a case in which the exercise of the judicial functions of the State by the Courts as guardians under the Constitution of the personal rights of the citizen was examined in relation to the performance of such functions by the Courts. In the present instance it is being submitted that the Courts, as such guardians under the Constitution, should direct or control or supervise that area of the executive function of

21. 352 U.S. 330, 344.
22. [1978] I.R. 13.
23. Id. 18.

the State which is involved in the prevention, detection and investigation of criminal offences'.

The contrary argument can be made, namely that the right to have a lawyer present, whether requested by the person in custody or not, may be necessary to ensure the adequate vindication of an accused person's constitutional rights *during* the judicial process by ensuring that evidence presented by the prosecution at the trial, whether in the form of oral or verbal admissions or confessions, has been acquired in a correct fashion. This prevents the possibility of evidence being admitted wrongly by the courts owing to their lack of awareness of the facts whereby such evidence was obtained.[24] The importance of confession statements is discussed elsewhere.[25]

In *The State (Harrington) v. Commissioner of the Garda Síochána*[26] Finlay P. held that the accused person's right of access to his legal adviser was not effectively given unless he had the opportunity to consult with his legal advisers out of the hearing of the members of the Gardaí. He further held that the right to a legal adviser existed not only in relation to an accused who had personally sought to exercise it but also when a *bona fide* request for legal assistance was made on behalf of an accused, and he held that where a solicitor appeared, alleging to be instructed on behalf of an accused, an enquiry should thereafter be made of the detained person as to whether he wished the advice of such solicitor.

24. It should be noted that Direction 7 of the English Home Office Administrative Directions provides that every person in custody must be told of his/her right to communicate with and consult a solicitor.
25. Supra pp. 121 sqq.
26. Unrep. 14th December, 1976 (H.C.).

CHAPTER 9

PROCEDURE IN THE DISTRICT COURT

When an accused person comes before the District Court charged with an indictable offence the District Justice may, in certain cases, deal with the case summarily; if he does not do so, then in most cases he may accept a plea of guilty, if forthcoming from the accused, and send him forward to the Circuit Court for sentence; otherwise the Justice must conduct a preliminary examination of the charge, unless such examination is waived by the defence. In any serious case, however, it is unlikely that the case will be disposed of when it first comes before the Court, so that the accused must be remanded, or put back to a later date.

I. REMAND

If the accused is on bail, when he appears he surrenders to his bail, and if he is to be released again fresh bail will be required. Remand is governed by Part III of the Criminal Procedure Act, 1967. Section 21 of that Act provides that where an accused person is before the District Court in connection with an offence the Court may, subject to the provisions of Part III, remand him from time to time as occasion requires.

Where the District Justice remands a person or sends him forward for trial or sentence, the Court may either commit him to prison[1] or other lawful custody,[2] or, save in the case where only

1. The only remand prisons are at present Mountjoy Prison in Dublin and Cork Prison for males, and Mountjoy and Limerick Prisons for females.
2. If the remand period does not exceed four days, the accused may be committed to the custody of the Gardaí, provided that (outside the Dublin Metropolitan District) suitable facilities are shown to be available for his custody; Criminal Procedure Act,1967, s. 25.

the High Court may grant bail,[3] release him conditionally on his entering into a recognisance, with or without sureties.[4]

Any recognisance is to be conditioned for the appearance of the accused before the Court at the end of the period of remand, and at every place and time to which, during the course of the proceedings, the hearing may be adjourned.[5] The Court is expressly empowered to grant further remands,[6] and the fixing of a time for the next appearance is deemed to be a remand.[7]

The accused may not be remanded in custody for more than eight days on his first appearance; on a subsequent appearance he may be remanded for up to thirty days if he and the prosecutor consent.[8] The accused may be remanded on bail, with his consent and that of the prosecution, for any period.[9] If there is no sitting of the Court on the day to which a person is remanded, he stands remanded to the sitting of the Court next held in the same District Court district.[10] If the accused is unable, by reason of illness or accident, to appear or be brought before the Court at the expiration of the period of remand, he may be remanded in his absence for such further period, which may exceed eight days, as the Court considers reasonable.[11]

A District Justice is bound to admit the accused to bail, where he has power to do so, if the case appears to him to be one in which bail should be allowed,[12] but refusal of bail on one occasion is not a bar to a subsequent application.[13] The principles on which bail should be allowed, and consequences of its being refused in the District Court, and the remedies of the prosecution or a bailsman if it appears that the accused may abscond, have already been considered.[14]

3. Supra pp. 194-195.
4. Criminal Procedure Act, 1967, s. 22 (1).
5. Id. s. 23 (1).
6. Id. s. 22 (4), 23 (3).
7. Id. s. 23 (2).
8. Id. s. 24 (1), (3).
9. Id. s. 24 (2).
10. Id. s. 24 (5).
11. Id. s. 24 (4).
12. Id. s. 28 (1).
13. Id. s. 28 (2).
14. Supra, Chapter 7.

II. SUMMARY DISPOSAL OF INDICTABLE OFFENCES

The Criminal Justice Act, 1951,[1] provides that the District Court may on certain conditions try summarily a person charged with:

(a) any offence specified in the First Schedule to the Act, or

(b) any indictable offence declared to be a scheduled offence by order of the Minister for Justice, approved by resolution of each House of the Oireachtas.[2]

The offences specified in the First Schedule to the Act of 1951, (as amended) include public mischief, perjury, indecent assault and assaults occasioning bodily harm or on police officers, gross indecency, offences under the Larceny Acts, 1861 and 1916, and the Forgery Act, 1913, obtaining by false pretences, some minor offences under the Malicious Damage Act, 1861, any attempt to commit an indictable offence triable summarily, and attempted carnal knowledge of young girls.

Similar provisions are contained in a number of other, mostly more recent, statutes dealing with other specific offences.

The conditions for summary trial are:

(1) that the Court is of opinion that the facts proved or alleged constitute a minor offence fit to be tried summarily;[3]

(2) that the accused, on being informed by the Court of his right to be tried by a jury, does not object to being tried summarily; and

(3) that in the case of certain offences, sometimes only where the value of the property involved exceeds a certain amount, the Director of Public Prosecutions has consented to such trial.[4] Any such consent may be conveyed in

1. Criminal Justice Act, 1951, s. 2, and First Schedule, as amended by the Criminal Procedure Act, 1967, s. 19, and the Criminal Law (Jurisdiction) Act, 1976, s. 21 (6).
2. No such order has been made.
3. Before the Court can form such an opinion it must know the facts, *The State (Nevin) v. Tormey* [1976] I.R. 1 (H.C.); but the Justice may change his mind during the case, *The State (O'Hagan) v. Delap*, unrep. 18th October, 1982 (H.C.).
4. In certain cases relating to sea-fishing boats, the Attorney General retains jurisdiction, transferred in other cases to the Director by the Prosecution of Offences Act, 1974; Fisheries Act, 1978, s. 18 (2).

writing by the Director or orally by any person prosecuting at the suit of the Director or appearing on his behalf.[5]

If the Justice deals with the case summarily his powers of sentencing are restricted; he cannot impose a fine exceeding a certain amount or a sentence of imprisonment for a term exceeding 12 months,[6] sometimes less, but may impose both any such fine and imprisonment.[7]

In the Table of Offences, Appendix H, infra, indictable offences triable summarily, and the appropriate penalties, are marked*, or, where the consent of the Director of Public Prosecutions is required**, or, if such consent depends on the value of the property**†.

It is to be noted that the normal time limit of 12 months for dealing with summary offences does not apply to the summary trial of an indictable offence,[8] although any general limit on the prosecution of the offence would continue to be applicable.

III. PLEA OF GUILTY IN THE DISTRICT COURT

Under the Criminal Procedure Act, 1967, where an accused is before the District Court charged with an indictable offence other than an offence under the Treason Act, 1939,[9] murder, attempt to murder, conspiracy to murder, piracy, genocide or a grave breach of the Geneva Conventions Act, 1962, including an offence by an accessory before or after the fact of any such offence, the District Justice may ascertain, at any stage, that the accused wishes to plead guilty.[10] The Justice must be satisfied that the accused understands the nature of the offence and the facts alleged; if so satisfied, and if the accused signs a plea of guilty, the

5. Criminal Procedure Act, 1967, s. 20. The order should show that such consent has been given: all three conditions must have been satisfied, *The State (Browne) v. Feran* [1967] I.R. 147 (S.C.), *The State (Kiernan) v. Governor of Mountjoy Prison,* unrep. 19th February, 1973 (H.C.).
6. The maximum fine for cases falling under the Criminal Justice Act, 1951, was £100, but later statutes have taken inflation into account.
7. Criminal Justice Act, 1951, s. 4 and later particular statutes.
8. Criminal Justice Act, 1951, s. 7, *The State (Kiernan) v. Governor of Mountjoy Prison,* supra.
9. Presumably this includes treason, although the offence is created by the Constitution and the Treason Act, 1939, s. 1, merely prescribes the penalty.
10. Criminal Procedure Act, 1967, s. 13, as amended by the Genocide Act, 1973, s. 6.

Justice may send him forward to the Circuit Court with that plea. Alternatively, if the Director of Public Prosecutions does not object, the Justice may deal with the offence summarily, but in such cases the maximum penalties correspond to those which the Justice may impose on summary conviction of an indictable offence.[11]

If the accused is sent forward to the Circuit Court, further charges may not be added,[12] but any defect in the charge may be corrected by the court to which he is sent forward, provided that, in the opinion of the court, the correction will not result in injustice; the plea will then be treated as a plea of guilty to the corrected charge.[13]

The accused is, however, entitled to withdraw his written plea and plead not guilty.[14] In that case a plea of not guilty must be entered, and this has the same operation as if he had been sent forward for trial, and the prosecution must serve on the accused any documents required to be supplied to him and not already served.[15]

IV. THE PRELIMINARY EXAMINATION

Unless the case is either tried summarily or the accused signs a plea of guilty,[1] or waives his right to a preliminary examination,[2] the District Justice is obliged to conduct a preliminary examination of the charge.

Historically the preliminary examination of serious offences originated in an English statute enacted in 1554.[3] This statute obliged a magistrate to examine an accused and to discharge him if, but only if, the case against him was so weak that there was no probable cause to believe that he might be guilty. Otherwise the duty of the magistrate was to commit the accused for trial. This

11. Supra, p. 228.
12. *The State (Brien) v. Kelly* [1970] I.R. 69 (S.C.).
13. Criminal Procedure (Amendment) Act, 1973, s. 2.
14. Criminal Procedure Act, 1967, s. 13 (4) (a).
15. Id. s. 13 (4) (b).
1. Criminal Procedure Act, 1967, s. 13 (2).
2. Id. s. 12.
3. 1 & 2 Ph. & M. c. 13, s. 43; see generally: Puttkammer, *Administration of Criminal Law*, 87-92 (1953).

was followed in Ireland in 1634.[4] In an age when there was no public prosecuting agency and no professional police force, the preliminary examination of offences by magistrates served to ensure that some independent scrutiny was carried out in order to justify the continued involvement of an accused person in the criminal process.

Although it may have been deprived of much of its rationale and prestige, the procedure initiated by the English and Irish Acts mentioned above, and elaborated in Ireland by the Petty Sessions (Ireland) Act, 1851, still survives and is now carried out in accordance with the provisions of the Criminal Procedure Act, 1967.[5]

Before the enactment of this latter statute, committal proceedings involved the taking and recording of 'depositions'. The witness gave his testimony on oath, it was taken down in writing and read over to him and then signed by him and also by the Justice.[6] Although depositions are not obsolete today they have become the exception rather than the rule.

Before the Justice embarks upon the preliminary examination of a case, the prosecutor must serve on the accused what is commonly called a Book of Evidence. This consists of a statement of the charges, a copy of any sworn information in writing upon which the proceedings were initiated, a list of the witnesses whom it is proposed to call at the trial, a statement of the evidence that is to be given by each of them and a list of exhibits, if any.[7] Exhibits are documents or things which it is proposed to produce at the trial, e.g. a statement signed by the accused, plans or photographs, stolen property which has been recovered, a weapon alleged to have been used, clothing worn by the accused or his victim and submitted to scientific tests. The usual practice is to number the exhibits for convenience of reference at the trial.

4. 10 Car. 1, Sess. 2, c. 18.
5. See generally, Petty Sessions (Ireland) Act, 1851, ss. 14-16; the procedure was one described as basic and as essential for the general purposes of the adminstration of justice as it was for the protection of the accused; *per* Pigot, C.B., *Lawrenson v. Hill* 10 Ir. C.L.R. 177, 185.
6. 'It is a curious reflection that today, as in the reign of Charles I, the justice is to examine the witnesses – but his order is of less importance.' *Per* Lavery J. *The People v. Boggan* [1958] I.R. 67, 84 (S.C.).
7. Criminal Procedure Act, 1967, s. 6 (1).

A copy of the Book of Evidence must be furnished to the Court[8] and the accused has the right to inspect all exhibits.[9]

The Statements of Evidence will usually be based, in the case of a prosecution by the Director of Public Prosecutions, upon statements made or reports furnished to the police. It may often happen that further evidence becomes available after the Book of Evidence has been prepared, and in such a case the prosecutor may cause to be served on the accused and furnish to the Court a further statement of the evidence of any witness who appears in the Book.[10]

The prosecutor and the accused are each entitled to give evidence on sworn deposition, and also to require the attendance of any person (whether or not included in the list of witnesses) and to examine him by way of sworn deposition.[11] Any person so examined may be cross-examined and re-examined on his evidence and his deposition must be taken down in writing, read over to him and signed by him and the Justice.[12]

The Justice must ask the accused if he has anything to say in answer to the charge. The Justice must caution the accused that he is not obliged to say anything unless he wishes to do so and that whatever he does say will be taken down in writing and, if he is sent forward for trial, may be given in evidence at the trial.[13] Whatever the accused says in answer must be read over to him and must be signed by him and by the Justice.[14] The statement, if appearing to be so signed, may be given in evidence at the trial unless it is proved that it was not signed by the Justice.[15] Subject to that there seems to be a presumption that the accused signed the statement if his signature appears on it.

When the preliminary examination is complete, various options are open to the Justice. He may or may not be satisfied that the accused has a case to answer either on the charge pre-

8. Id. s. 6 (2).
9. Id. s. 6 (3).
10. Id. s. 6 (4).
11. Id. s. 7 (2); even before the Book of Evidence is served, *The State (Williams) v. Director of Public Prosecutions,* unrep. 20th July, 1982 (H.C.).
12. Id. s. 7 (3).
13. Id. s. 7 (4) (a).
14. Id. s. 7 (4) (b).
15. Id. s. 7 (4) (c).

ferred or on some alternate charge. The function of the Justice is to examine the evidence and decide whether it discloses a *sufficient* case. A *sufficient* case will be made out if the evidence adduced is of such cogency that a reasonable jury, properly charged, could convict upon it. In considering whether or not such a case has been made out the Justice will almost invariably only be assessing the prosecution evidence because, although the accused is entitled to give evidence himself, he normally does not do so, since by so doing he may disclose his defence, thereby putting the prosecution on warning and affording it an early opportunity to rebut it. Supposing, for example, the defence is an alibi of which the accused has not informed the police (and he is under no obligation to make any statement to the police although failure to do so, or produce some explanation or defence, may be a matter of comment at a later stage) then, if he gives evidence in the District Court that he was somewhere else when the crime was committed, the prosecution will thereby gain a chance to investigate and to cast doubt upon the alibi before the trial. It is not the function of the Justice to decide the facts, or the weight of the evidence, since those are matters for the jury.

If the Justice is of the opinion that a sufficient case has been made out to justify putting the accused on trial for the offence with which he is charged, he must send him forward for trial.[16] The Act of 1967 does not specify the court to which the accused is to be returned. In practice, only cases, such as murder, which are within the exclusive jurisdiction of the Central Criminal Court are returned for trial to that Court, whilst cases within its jurisdiction are returned to the Circuit Court, and it is submitted that in cases within the jurisdiction of the Circuit Court, in the absence of special circumstances, this practice should be followed. In so far, however, as the Central Criminal Court has general jurisdiction, there appears to be no legal reason why *any* case should not be returned to it for trial, and occasionally this might be desirable, as, for example, a case in which a number of persons are concerned in different capacities in the same incident, starting with accessories before the fact to robbery and culminat-

16. Id. s. 8 (1).

ing in attempted murder by the principals in the first degree. Return to the Special Criminal Court is dealt with in Chapter 14 infra.

If the Justice is of opinion that there is a sufficient case to put the accused on trial for some other indictable offence, he must cause him to be charged with that offence and ask him, after cautioning him, if he has anything to say, record his answer and then send him forward for trial on that charge. An order returning an accused for trial on the new charge[17] must be written and signed by the Justice.[18] These provisions are, however, without prejudice to the powers of the Justice to deal with the offence summarily as a minor offence.[19].

If the Justice is of opinion that only a summary offence is disclosed, he may then have the accused charged with that summary offence and deal with it himself, but only if the Director of Public Prosecutions consents.[20] Such consent may be conveyed in writing by the Director or may be given orally by anyone prosecuting on his behalf.[21] In any other case the Justice must order the accused to be discharged in relation to the offence which is the subject of the preliminary examination.[22]

If a Justice causes an accused to be discharged, formerly called 'refusing informations', the Director of Public Prosecutions may nevertheless make an order directing that the accused be sent forward for trial to any specified court to which the Justice might have returned him for trial.[23]

In *The People v. Boggan,*[24] the defendant was in fact returned for trial after a preliminary investigation had been held. At the trial, however, it was contended by the defence that the depositions taken were defective, in that some of them had not been taken in accordance with the Rules of the District Court, 1948. The defence application was refused and the defendant was con-

17. Id. s. 8 (2).
18. Id. s. 8 (6).
19. Id. s. 8 (3); see pp. 227-228 supra.
20. Id. s. 8 (4).
21. Id. s. 20.
22. Id. s. 8 (5).
23. Courts of Justice Act, 1936, s. 62 (1), as amended by the Schedule to the Criminal Procedure Act, 1967.
24. [1958] I.R. 67 (S.C.).

victed. He appealed to the Court of Criminal Appeal. Although dismissing his appeal, that Court gave leave to the appellant to appeal to the Supreme Court to determine whether a valid preliminary investigation by a District Justice was necessary before the Attorney General could prefer an indictment. The law on this subject was carefully surveyed in the Supreme Court by Lavery J. who concluded that the Court system as laid down by the Courts of Justice Act, 1924, was inconsistent with the creation of a power of arbitrary indictment by the Attorney General and he was fortified in his opinion by the subsequent decisions of the courts. He adverted to the case of *Attorney General v. Colleary*[25] where the trial judge held that he had no jurisdiction to try the case when the Attorney General presented an indictment after the District Justice had conducted a preliminary investigation and had held that there was no *prima facie* case to justify the accused being sent forward for trial. The Legislature, in deference to this case, stepped in and, by section 62 of the Courts of Justice Act, 1936,[26] enabled the Attorney General to direct that an accused be sent for trial where a District Justice had refused to return him.

Lavery J. interpreted this section as *enabling* the Attorney General to reverse the order of the District Justice refusing informations and he continued:[27]

> 'It would be strange indeed if a "direction" by the Attorney General should in the particular case be given the efficacy of an order returning for trial if such an order was unnecessary.
>
> In my opinion the clear implication of this enactment is that though the Attorney General is given the power to give a direction and in pursuance of that to prefer an indictment, in this particular case he did not enjoy the general power to prefer an indictment now claimed.
>
> The provision seems to emphasise that a preliminary investigation and the taking of depositions in accordance with the Rules of

25. 69 I.L.T.R. 233 (Circ. Ct.).
26. Where a person is brought before a justice of the District Court charged with an indictable crime, and such charge either cannot lawfully be or is not disposed of summarily by such justice, and such justice [refuses to receive informations in relation to such charge or] to send such person forward for trial on such charge, then and in every such case it shall be lawful for the Attorney General to direct that such person be sent forward for trial to a specified Court to which such justice could lawfully have so sent such person, s. 62 as amended.
27. [1958] I.R. 67, 82-83.

the District Court is a condition precedent to the placing of a person on trial on indictment.'

In placing this interpretation on section 62 (1) of the 1936 Act Lavery J. was refusing to follow the case of *The State (Attorney General) v. Fawsitt.*[28]. At the conclusion of his judgment in *Boggan*'s case Lavery J. succinctly stated his view of the law which was that: [29]

> '[The] basis of the jurisdiction to try a criminal charge on indictment is a preliminary investigation conducted by a Justice of the District Court on a valid order receiving informations and sending the accused forward for trial, or an order refusing informations when the powers of s. 62 of the Act of 1936 are invoked.'

The constitutionality of the relevant section was questioned in *The State (Shanahan) v. Attorney General*[30] where it was alleged that the exercise of the power by the Attorney constituted, *inter alia*, an unwarranted interference with the operation of the courts in a purely judicial domain. The Supreme Court, however, took the view that the power to give a direction, which was accorded to the Attorney General, was not one to change or modify the District Court order. Walsh J., with whom the other members of the Court agreed, said:[31]

> '[T]he direction of the Attorney General is not an intervention in the particular controversy before the District Court which has, in the event, already been brought to an end by the refusal of informations. Rather is the direction of the Attorney General the initiation of a different justiciable controversy, namely, the trial upon indictment. Unlike the preliminary investigation this new justiciable controversy is one whose object is to determine the guilt or innocence of the accused person. In my opinion, s. 62 of the Courts of Justice Act, 1936, is not inconsistent with the Constitution and it was continued in force by Article 50 of the Constitution.'

Since 1974 the power to give a direction has rested with the Director of Public Prosecutions.[32]

28. [1955] I.R. 39 (H.C.).
29. [1958] I.R. 67, 85.
30. [1964] I.R. 239.
31. [1964] I.R. 239, 258.
32. Prosecution of Offences Act, 1974, s. 3.

The constitutionality of the Director's powers was again questioned in *The State (Connolly) v. Director of Public Prosecutions*[33] when the District Justice had declined to return the accused for trial on charges of perjury at a public inquiry into a disaster resulting from the explosion of an oil tanker in Bantry Bay. The Director gave a direction that the accused be returned for trial and a conditional order of certiorari was refused by the High Court. The case was, at the time of going to press, under appeal to the Supreme Court. In *The State (Costello) v. Director of Public Prosecutions*[34] Gannon J. again upheld the constitutionality of section 62 of the Act of 1936.

Publicity at the preliminary examination

The preliminary examination must normally be held in open court; if, however, the Court is satisfied, because of the nature or circumstances of the case or otherwise in the interests of justice, that it is desirable, it may exclude the public or any particular portion of the public, or any particular person or persons (except *bona fide* representatives of the Press);[35] but this provision is without prejudice to the right of a parent or other relative or friend of an accused who is under 21, or of the victim of an offence of an indecent or obscene nature who is under that age or is a female, to be present.[36]

The publication of any information as to any particular preliminary examination, other than a statement of the fact that it was held in relation to a named person on a specified charge and of the decision thereon, is prohibited,[37] except for such information as the Justice, at the request of the accused, may permit to be published.[38] If anyone appears to have contravened this provision, the Director of Public Prosecutions may apply to a Justice for a certificate to that effect to the High Court; and that Court may then inquire into the offence, hear any witnesses who may be produced against or on behalf of the alleged offender, hear any

33. Unrep.
34. Unrep. 11th February, 1983 (H.C.).
35. Criminal Procedure Act, 1967, s. 16.
36. Criminal Justice Act, 1951, s. 20 (4).
37. Criminal Procedure Act, 1967, s. 17 (1).
38. Id. s. 17 (3).

statement that may be offered in defence, and either punish or take steps for the punishment of the offender in like manner as if he had been guilty of contempt of the Court;[39] the Act of 1967 does not specifically state that the application for a certificate must be made to the Justice who conducted the examination.

Waiver of a preliminary examination

Any accused (but in the case of a person under the age 17 only with the consent of the parent or guardian who has actual possession and control of him) may waive the preliminary examination and elect to be sent forward for trial with a plea of not guilty, unless the prosecutor requires the attendance of a witness to give evidence on deposition. The Justice may then send the accused forward for trial and he must be served with any documents, such as a Book of Evidence or statements of additional evidence, which have not already been served, and copies must also be furnished to the trial court.[40]

Any defect in the charge may, if in the opinion of the Court it will not cause injustice, be amended in stating the charge in the indictment.[41]

The taking of evidence upon deposition

As has already been stated, either the prosecution or the defence at the preliminary examination may require a witness to attend and be examined, cross-examined and re-examined by way of sworn deposition;[1] the permission of the District Justice is not required where this section is invoked by either the prosecution or the defence.

Apart from their right to have evidence taken on deposition at the preliminary hearing, either the prosecution or the defence may apply to a District Justice (not necessarily it would seem the Justice having seisin of the case) to have the evidence of a prospective trial witness taken on deposition; a District Justice may make such an order only if he is satisfied that the witness in

39. Id. s. 17 (2).
40. Id. s. 12; Children Act, 1908, s. 131, Children Act, 1941, s. 29.
41. Criminal Procedure (Amendment) Act, 1973, s. 2.
1. Criminal Procedure Act, 1967, s. 7 (2), (3).

question may be unable to attend or may be prevented from attending to give evidence at the trial of the accused, and that it is necessary in the interests of justice to have his evidence taken on deposition.[2] The deposition must be taken in the presence of the Justice and of the accused; it must be taken down in writing, read over to the deponent and signed by him and by the Justice.[3] A person making such a deposition may be cross-examined and re-examined upon it.[4] Before the deposition is taken the Justice must inform the accused of the circumstances in which the deposition may be read as evidence at his trial.[5] There is no similar requirement imposed in relation to depositions required to be taken as of right at the preliminary hearing. When an accused has been returned for trial the right given to the prosecutor to apply to a District Justice to have such depositions taken from prospective trial witness is exercisable only by the Director of Public Prosecutions.[6] The reason for this is that a private prosecutor becomes *functus officio* as soon as an accused's return for trial has been effected.

Because of the time and labour involved in taking down the evidence in writing, it frequently happens that if a statement of evidence from a prosecution witness already appears in the Book of Evidence, he is merely asked whether that statement is correct; but if that is done, and if the deposition is to be given in evidence at the trial, it is important that a copy of the statement, as it appears in the Book, or of the Book containing it, should be identified by the witness and the Justice, and it is also submitted that this procedure should only be adopted with the consent of the defence.

The use of depositions as evidence in a criminal trial

Although depositions constitute sworn documents by prospective witnesses in criminal cases, the trial of the accused is based almost exclusively upon the oral evidence given by the wit-

2. Id. s. 14 (1).
3. Id. s. 14 (2).
4. Id. s. 14 (4).
5. Id. s. 14 (3).
6. Id. s. 14 (6), as adapted by the Prosecution of Offences Act, 1974.

nesses called. In certain limited instances, however, it is permissible for a deposition properly taken under the Criminal Procedure Act, 1967, to be read to the court as *evidence* in the trial. It is necessary in the first place to prove at the trial that:

(a) the deponent is dead or is unable to attend or is prevented from attending to give evidence at the trial, and

(b) the deposition was taken in the presence of the accused, and

(c) an opportunity was given for the cross-examination and re-examination of the deponent.[7]

Subject to the foregoing conditions it appears that, if the deponent has died, either party is entitled to read his deposition at the trial. In any other case, however, an ordinary deposition taken at the preliminary hearing on the application of the prosecutor may not be read unless the accused consents; and a deposition from a prospective witness who might be unable to attend or prevented from attending the trial may not be read if the trial judge considers that to do so would not be in the interests of justice.[8]

One effect of these provisions is that an accused will not be able to elude justice in the event of the death of the prosecution deponent before the trial, although if his own witness has died he too has a right to have the deposition read. It is submitted that it is right that there should be restrictions upon the production of depositions as evidence. Where, for example, a deposition has been taken at the instance of the prosecution at the preliminary examination, the defence may well decline to cross-examine, preferring to reserve cross-examination until the trial, thus ensuring that the prosecution witness is not given a rehearsal of what he may expect at the trial. There appears, however, to be a justification for the differentiation in treatment between depositions taken at the instance of the prosecution at the preliminary examination, which, except in the event of the deponent's death, require the accused's consent before they can be read as evidence at the trial, and those taken where the District Justice is of

7. Id. s. 15 (1).
8. Id. s. 15 (2).

opinion that a prospective witness may be unable to attend or be prevented from attending the trial, in that in the latter situation, unlike the former, the defence is on notice of the *possibility* of non-attendance, and will be aware of the consequences should it choose not to exercise the right of cross-examination.

In other jurisdictions the depositions of witnesses made at the committal proceedings may often by used *in lieu* of oral testimony at the trial.[9]

Procedure when a District Justice has decided to return for trial

If the District Justice decides to send the accused forward for trial, he must make a 'witness order' in respect of each person a statement of whose evidence has been supplied or who has made a deposition, to attend and give evidence before the court by which the accused is to be tried and to produce any document or thing specified in the order.[10] A person disobeying an order to attend before any court without just cause is guilty of contempt of that court.[11] If, on the application of the Director of Public Prosecutions or an accused, the Justice is satisfied by evidence on oath that a particular person is unlikely to comply with a witness order, the Justice may bind him by recognisance, that is, he may require him to enter into a bond, to appear at the trial, and if he refuses to be so bound the Justice may by warrant commit him to custody until the trial or until he enters into the recognisance required.[12]

The Justice has the same powers for enforcing the attendance of and giving of evidence on deposition by a prospective witness, or by a witness who is unlikely to comply with a witness order, as the District Court has in relation to witnesses in criminal proceedings.[13]

Apart from witness orders, a 'witness summons' may, on the application of the Director of Public Prosecutions, or the accused,

9. See Graham and Letwin, *The Preliminary Hearing in Los Angeles* (1971) 18 U.C.L.A. Law Rev. 636 and 916 at 931 (75% of trials in Los Angeles County are tried on the basis of depositions).
10. Criminal Procedure Act, 1967, s. 9 (1).
11. Id. s. 9 (2).
12. Id. s. 9 (3).
13. Id. ss. 9 (3), 14 (5).

be issued out of the Court to which the latter has been sent forward for trial, requiring the person to whom it is addressed to attend before the trial court and give evidence at the trial and produce any document or thing specified in the summons. Since, however, this provision could be employed to abuse the judicial process, e.g. if an accused sought to have summoned a person such as his Bishop or a Minister of State who has nothing to do with the case, the Court may decline to issue the summons if it is of the opinion that the person to whom it is to be addressed cannot give any material evidence, or, as the case may be, produce any document or thing likely to be material evidence.[14] A person who, without just cause, disobeys a witness summons is guilty of contempt of the Court out of which the summons was issued.[15]

A witness order directs the witness to attend before the court to which the accused is sent forward at the next sittings of that court and would then appear to be spent. Similarly a witness summons appears to be effective only as regards the court which issues it, so that if it is issued out of the Circuit Court outside Dublin it will cease to be effective if the trial is transferred to the Dublin Circuit Court. In practice, however, so far as the prosecution witnesses are concerned, witness summonses will be issued even though a witness order has been made, and if a trial is transferred to the Dublin Circuit Court, fresh summonses will be issued out of that Court.

It may well happen that after the accused is returned for trial the prosecution wishes to produce further evidence at the trial. The Book of Evidence, and any further documents already furnished should disclose a sufficient case, but it may be desired to supplement it, for example by the production of a map, or of a medical report, or an additional witness who might not be essential but corroborative, or additional evidence from a witness whose name had been supplied. In any such case the Director must cause to be served on the accused a list of any further witnesses whom he proposes to call at the trial together with a state-

14. Id. s. 10 (1).
15. Id. s. 10 (2).

ment of the evidence that is to be given by each, a list of any further exhibits, and a statement of any further evidence to be given by any witness whose name appears on the list already supplied. The accused must also be served with a copy of any statement made by him in answer to the Justice at the preliminary hearing, and a copy of any deposition which may have been taken. Copies of all documents must also be furnished to the trial court.[16]

The contemporary significance of the preliminary examination

It is undoubtedly the case that the preliminary examination of an offence is today of little significance in comparison with the trial itself. It is merely perceived as a low standard which the prosecution must attain in order to justify the continued immersion of the accused in the criminal process. Very few cases in Ireland result in the discharge of an accused as a consequence of a finding by a District Justice that there is no case to answer.The picture is the same in other countries which have an analogous procedure.[17]

Probably a major reason why defence counsel do not make an all out effort to have some cases against the accused dismissed at the end of the preliminary examination is because of the Director of Public Prosecution's power, considered above, to direct that a person be sent forward for trial despite the finding of the District Justice that a *sufficient* case has not been made out.

16. Id. s. 11.
17. In England in 1964 and 1965 almost 96% of defendants brought before examining justices were committed for trial; see Krulwich, *The Committal Proceeding in England* (Institute of Criminal Law and Procedure, Georgetown University Law Center, 1969) cited in Goldstein and Orland, *Criminal Procedure* (1967), 285.

CHAPTER 10

THE INDICTMENT

When an accused person is sent forward for trial the prosecution must prepare an indictment, that is to say the formal charge to be preferred by the People of Ireland (acting by or 'at the suit of' the Director of Public Prosecutions or, in the few cases reserved to him, of the Attorney General) against the accused. The prosecution should give serious consideration to the form of the indictment and the proofs required to sustain it.[1]

Perusal of old law reports will reveal the complexity and the length of indictments in the past and the technicality which was often necessary to ensure that an indictment was sufficient. The form of the indictment has, however, been greatly simplified by the Criminal Justice (Administration) Act, 1924, and the Rules and Appendix thereto contained in the First Schedule.[2] Furthermore, even a faulty indictment may be made good, since the Act provides that where before trial or at any stage of a trial it appears to the Court that the indictment is defective, the Court shall make such order for the amendment of the indictment as the Court thinks fit to meet the circumstances of the case, unless the required amendment cannot, in the opinion of the Court, be made without injustice. It should postpone the trial if necessary, and may make such order as it thinks fit as to the payment of any costs incurred owing to the necessity of the amendment.[3] It has been said that the Court has a duty to make the proposed amendment unless it will result in injustice.[4] It appears that the amend-

1. *Attorney General v. Armitage* 67 I.L.T.R. 179 (C.C.A.).
2. Corresponding to the English Indictments Act, 1915; the Schedule to that Act has been replaced by the Indictment Rules, 1971, (S.I. 1971 No. 1253).
3. Criminal Justice (Administration) Act, 1924, s. 6.
4. *R. v. Fraser* 17 Cr. App. R. 182.

ment may be made before or after arraignment, and may be by way of adding or substituting a new count, although the longer the interval between arraignment and the application to amend the less likely it is that the amendment can be made without injustice;[5] and, if a substantial amendment is made after arraignment, it is desirable that the accused should be re-arraigned on the amended indictment.[6] It appears that an insubstantial amendment, e.g. as to a date, may be made to give effect to the jury's verdict after it has been delivered and before the jury has been discharged but not after the verdict has been accepted by the Court and the jury discharged, when the trial judge is considering the matter of sentence. For example in *R. v. Dossi,*[7] the verdict was 'with regard to the date March 19th not guilty, if the indictment covers other dates guilty' (of a charge of indecent assault on a child). The trial judge amended the indictment by substituting 'on someday in March' for 'on March 19th' and the jury found the accused guilty on the amended indictment: but in *The State (McGinley) v. Durkin*[8] where the accused had been charged with dealing with uncustomed goods to the value of £500 and found guilty in respect of some but not all of the goods, it was held that the trial judge could not, before passing sentence (to which the value of the goods was material), amend the indictment by substituting £482 for £500 (even though the result was to the benefit of the accused), although he might hear evidence as to the value of the goods to which the verdict related.

An indictment may charge one or more offences; if there is more than one, each offence is the subject of a separate '*count*'. The counts should be numbered consecutively.[9] They may relate to completely different incidents, such as a series of thefts; or to offences varying in degree such as wounding with intent and assault occasioning bodily harm; or to alternatives such as larceny or receiving stolen goods. The joinder of counts will be considered further below. There is no need for separate counts where

5. *R. v. Johal* [1972] 3 W.L.R. 210.
6. *R. v. Radley* 58 Cr. App. R. 394.
7. 13 Cr. App. R. 158.
8. Unrep. 5th May, 1975.
9. Indictment Rules, r. 4 (6).

it is open to the jury to convict of a lesser offence having no distinct characteristic, for example, to convict an accused of manslaughter when charged with murder, or where conviction of an alternative offence or an attempt to commit any offence is permitted by statute.[10]

The Appendix of Forms to the Rules in the Schedule to the Criminal Justice (Administration) Act, 1924, contains forms of indictment covering many of the more serious or common crimes.[11] An indictment is to contain, and is sufficient if it contains, a statement of the specific offence or offences with which the accused is charged, together with such particulars as may be necessary for giving reasonable information as to the nature of the charge, and no indictment is to be open to objection in respect of its form or contents if it is framed in accordance with the Rules. In cases to which the forms apply, the forms in the Appendix, or forms conforming thereto as nearly as may be, are to be used; in other cases forms to the like effect are to be used, the statement and particulars of the offence being varied according to the circumstances of each case.[12]

The commencement of the indictment is to be entitled. 'The Attorney General of Éire v. A.B.' and is then to state the Court of Trial, e.g. Central Criminal Court (or) the Circuit Court of Justice – but the form of indictment in common use is entitled 'The People of Ireland, (at the suit of the Director of Public Prosecutions)' against A.B., and the specific court in which the indictment is to be preferred is stated, e.g. Dublin, or Cork, Circuit Court. It then sets out the charge or charges to be preferred to the jury.

> 'A.B. is charged with the following offence (offences).'[13]

Each count is to commence with a *statement of the offence*, describing it shortly in ordinary language, avoiding as far as possible the use of technical terms, and without necessarily

10. See pp. 366 sqq. infra.
11. See Appendix B post; forms designed to cover virtually every kind of common indictable offence are to be found in successive editions of Archbold.
12. Indictment Rules, r. 4 (5); some forms are no longer appropriate because of changes in the law, e.g. as to burglary.
13. Criminal Justice (Administration) Act, 1924, s. 4, Indictment Rules, r. 2.

stating all the essential elements of the offence but the gist of the offence must be clear[14] – e.g. 'murder'. If the offence charged is created by statute the count must contain a reference to the section of the statute creating the offence,[15] but there is no need to state that it is contrary to common law, and an unnecessary reference to a statute may be regarded as mere surplusage.[16] If the statute has been amended a reference to the amending statute should be inserted e.g. 'Burglary, contrary to section 23A of the Larceny Act, 1916, as inserted by section 6 of the Criminal Law (Jurisdiction) Act, 1976.'[17] It should, however, be noted that a statute frequently provides the penalty for a common law offence; if the statute does no more than that, reference to it is unnecessary but if the penalty depends on some particular feature, the result has been described as creating a 'hybrid offence', and in such cases reference to the statute appears to be desirable,[18] although not essential. Furthermore an attempt to commit a statutory offence is an offence at common law and reference to the statute creating the complete offence has been held to be unnecessary.[19]

On the other hand, whilst murder is an offence at common law, capital murder has been held to be a new offence created by the Criminal Justice Act, 1964,[20] so that reference to the section is presumably necessary.

After the statement of the offence, *particulars* must be set out in ordinary language, in which the use of technical terms is not

14. Indictment Rules r. 4 (3); cf. *Attorney General v. Cunningham* [1932] I.R. 28 (C.C.A.) (breach of the peace); *The People v. Gilmore* 85 I.L.T.R. 99 (S.C.) (false pretences).
15. Indictment Rules, r. 4 (3).
16. *The State (O.) v. O'Brien* [1971] I.R. 42 (S.C.) (assault occasioning bodily harm).
17. *The State (Duggan) v. Evans* 112 I.L.T.R. 61 (H.C.) (burglary).
18. For example section 47 of the Offences against the Person Act, 1861, prescribes the penalty for an assault, if it occasions actual bodily harm, *The State (O.) v. O'Brien* supra; the Court was, however, only directly concerned with whether an indictable offence had been charged. Various sections of the Larceny Act, 1916, prescribe different penalties according to what is stolen; it is convenient and common practice to refer to the relevant section, but omission to do so is not fatal: *The State (Foley) v. Director of Public Prosecutions,* unrep. 23rd July, 1979 (H.C.); *The State (Scott) v. Clifford,* unrep. 14th July, 1980 (H.C.) (indecent assault).
19. *Attorney General v. Sullivan* [1964] I.R. 169 (S.C.).
20. *The People v. Murray* [1977] I.R. 360 (S.C.).

necessary; but if under any rule of law or any statute the particulars required are limited, more particulars need not be given.[21]

The rules themselves are to some extent restrictive of particulars, e.g. in the description of persons or property. The forms give a good indication of how much – or how little – may be required. A reference to the County or town is often enough. 'On a date unknown' between two dates is not uncommon and the time is usually omitted – although if the time at which an offence was committed is material, it should be stated; such as, for example, on a charge of possession of house-breaking implements, the fact that the offence was committed 'in the night'. It is enough to allege that the accused murdered someone, or stole something, without specifying all the ingredients of murder or larceny. The precise date is usually unnecessary[22] except in the few cases, for example, unlawful carnal knowledge of young girls, where there is a time limit for bringing the prosecution.[23] On a charge of receiving stolen property it is not necessary to state where the property was stolen.

The *description of property* is to be in ordinary language and such as to indicate with reasonable clearness the property referred to, and it is not necessary to name the person to whom the property belongs or its value, unless the offence depends on the special ownership of property or special value of the property.[24] The 'special ownership' would be material on a charge of embezzlement, in that the accused must be a clerk or servant of the owner. Value would be material on a charge of malicious damage if the amount of the damage were to exceed £50. Where the property is vested in more than one person and the owners are referred to, it is sufficient to describe the property as owned by one of them by name 'and others', and if the owners are a body of persons with a collective name such as 'Trustees', 'Commissioners' or 'Club' or some other such name, then the collective name is sufficient without the name of any individual.[25]

21. Indictment Rules, r. 4 (4).
22. *R. v. Dossi* 13 Cr. App. R. 158; *The People v. Melody* unrep. 11th May 1967, Frewen 319.
23. See Chapter 3, supra.
24. Indictment Rules, r. 6 (1).
25. Id. r. 6 (2).

As regards *persons* the description or designation of the accused or of any other person mentioned in the indictment is to be such as is reasonably sufficient to identify him, without necessarily stating his correct name, or his abode, style, degree or occupation; and if his name is not known or it is impracticable to give such a description or designation, such description or designation is to be given as is reasonably practicable in the circumstances, or he may be described as 'a person unknown'.[26]

The *age* of a person is normally irrelevant, but it may be material in certain cases, such as offences of a sexual nature involving young girls, and in any such case the age of the accused (if material) and of the injured party (if material to the offence or to negative some element of defence, such as consent) should be stated.[27]

As regards *documents,* where it is necessary to refer to any document or instrument, it is sufficient to describe it by any name or designation by which it is normally known or by its purport, and a copy need not be set out in the indictment.[28]

As regards *description* generally, the Act of 1924 provides that it is in general sufficient to describe any place, time, thing, matter, act, or omission whatsoever, to which it is necessary to refer in the indictment, in ordinary language in such a manner as to indicate with reasonable clearness the particular place, time and so forth.[29]

When the offence involves an *intent to* defraud, deceive, or injure some person, the identity of that person need not be stated unless it is an essential ingredient of the offence.[30]

It is not necessary in the case of a statutory offence to *negative* any exception from or qualification to the operation of the statute.[31]

26. Id. r. 7.
27. *R. v. Martin* 9 C. & P. 213, *R. v. Stephenson* [1912] 3 K.B. 341.
28. Indictment Rules, r. 8.
29. Id. r. 9.
30. Id. r. 10.
31. Id. r. 5 (2), cf. *R. v. James* [1902] 1 K.B. 540.

Duplicity

Whilst an indictment may contain any number of counts it is a cardinal rule that no count (and the same principle applies to summary charges, to which some of the authorities refer) should relate to more than one offence.

Thus the accused should not be charged *in the same count* with a number of separate burglaries or assaults, although when the offence contains different elements each of which would be an offence in itself, there is no objection to charging the aggregate offence; thus robbery involves both an assault and theft, but robbery is, so to speak, an aggregate offence in itself; similarly burglary may involve an entry with intent to commit a further offence, the entry being an offence under paragraph (a) of sub-section (1) of section 23A of the Larceny Act, 1916.[1] The intended offence may be stealing, causing grievous bodily harm, rape, or malicious damage. If a person, having entered a building as a trespasser, steals or inflicts grievous bodily harm he is guilty of a distinct offence under paragraph (b) of the same sub-section and will normally be charged accordingly. If, however, he enters with intent to rape and subsequently rapes a woman, he should presumably be charged in separate counts with the entry and the rape, since the two are not a 'combined offence', under paragraph (b).

The rule against duplicity applies to offences such as embezzlement and fraudulent conversion, but it is not always practicable where there has been a series of takings or appropriations to distinguish each one. In *R. v. Tomlin*[2] the appellant was the manager of a shoe shop; a stock-taking revealed a deficiency of over £400 of the proceeds of stock sold since the previous stock-taking; he was charged that on a date unknown between the dates of the two stock-takings he embezzled the total amount of the deficiency, and it was held by the Court of Criminal Appeal in England that, as it was impossible to split up the aggregate sum and to trace individual items, it was proper to include the total

1. Inserted by the Criminal Law (Jurisdiction) Act, 1976, s. 6.
2. [1954] 2 Q.B. 274, approving *R. v. Lawson* 36 Cr. App. R. 30, and not following *R. v. Jones* 8 C. & P. 288, *R. v. Chapman* 1 C. & K. 119, *R. v. Morris* 24 Cr. App. R. 105; see also *Attorney General v. Gleeson* 64 I.L.T.R. 225 (C.C.A.).

sum in a count alleging a general deficiency. Giving the judgment of the Court, Pearson J. said:[3]

> 'Where separate offences can be charged in separate counts the court regards as improper an "omnibus" count in an indictment charging an aggregate of offences over a long period (see for instance *R. v. Robertson*[4]) but here no splitting up of the aggregate sum was possible. . . We feel that, if the technical rule alleged on behalf of the appellant [that the count was bad for duplicity] prevails, justice will in truth, in many cases, be defeated.'

He cited Erle J. in *R. v. Lambert:*[5]

> 'There would be constant failure of justice if I were to decide otherwise, since it is impossible, in cases like the present, where a number of different amounts of money have been received, to specify which sum or sums, or the parts of which sum or sums, have been embezzled.'

He concluded, however, by saying:[6]

> '[I]n the ordinary case, where it is possible to trace the individual items and to prove a conversion of individual property or money, it is undesirable to include them all in a count alleging a general deficiency. What we are not willing to do is to elevate a rule of practice, applicable to circumstances where it may be required to avoid injustice, into a rule of law applicable to circumstances where it will defeat justice.'

Whilst, however, the question most commonly arises in cases of embezzlement or fraudulent conversion, it may also be relevant in cases of larceny. If a person takes a number of things from the same place at or about the same time, there may in a sense be a series of takings, but in such cases the proximity of time or place may be such that there is really only one offence involving a single activity, though a number of acts; it is a question of fact and degree.[7] One test appears to be whether the larceny is to be regarded as having been committed 'at one time, or in such a way

3. [1954] 2 Q.B. 274, 279-280.
4. 25 Cr. App. R. 208.
5. 2 Cox 309, 310; see also *R. v. Balls* L.R.1 C.C.R. 328.
6. [1954] 2 Q.B. 274, 282.
7. See *Jemmison v. Priddle* 56 Cr. App. R. 229 in which two deer were shot within seconds at the same place; *R. v. Wilson* 69 Cr. App. R. 83, where the accused was charged with the theft of separate items from different departments in the same store.

as to form one "continuous taking".'[8] In *R. v. Bleasdale*[9] the accused was held to have been properly convicted on a count of taking coal belonging to a large number of different proprietors from the same mine shaft. A count of stealing gas on a certain date, although it had been taken over a number of years, was held good in *R. v. Firth*,[10] as was one count of stealing eight trees over a single season in *R. v. Shepherd*.[11] A number of persons might have goods stored in the same store, or sheep grazing on the same commonage, and daily checks might not be practicable; after a periodic check it might be found that a quantity of goods or a number of sheep were missing, in circumstances that would render it improbable or impossible that all were taken at the same time, whilst it would be equally impossible to prove whose particular chattels were taken at any one time. It is submitted that a single omnibus count would be preferable to a number of separate counts, each alleging that some particular article or animal belonging to each particular owner had been stolen on a date unknown within the period over which the deficiency was discovered.

The rule against duplicity is to some extent modified by the Criminal Justice (Administration) Act, 1924, which provides that, where an enactment constituting an offence states the offence to be the doing or the omission to do any one of any different acts in the alternative, or the doing or the omission to do any act in any one of any different capacities, or with any different intentions, or states any part of the offence in the alternative, the acts, omissions, capacities, or intentions or other matters stated in the alternative in the enactment may be stated in the alternative in the indictment.[12]

It is submitted that an example of an enactment stating the offence to be the doing of any one of any different acts in the alternative would be wounding or causing grievous bodily harm. Larceny by a clerk or servant would be an example of an offence

8. *R. v. Henwood* 11 Cox 526, 528.
9. 2 Car. & Kir. 765.
10. L.R. I.C.C.R. 172.
11. 11 Cox 119.
12. Indictment Rules, r. 5 (1).

involving the doing of an act in any one of different capacities. Wounding with intent to maim, disfigure or disable or cause other grievous bodily harm would be an example of an offence involving alternative intentions.

It is, however, not always easy to determine whether a parti cular enactment involves the creation of a single offence which may be committed in different ways or with varying intentions, or two or more separate and distinct offences. Thus before the amendment by section 4 of the Road Traffic Act, 1968, of section 53 of the Road Traffic Act 1960, (which now relates to driving in a manner (*including* speed) which is dangerous to the public), it was held that statutes which made it an offence to drive in a manner *or* at a speed which was dangerous to the public in fact created two offences, and a charge which alleged a single offence in the terms of the statute was bad for duplicity.[13] A charge alleging the use of violence and intimidation with a view to compelling a person to abstain from doing something he was entitled to do has been held to be good.[14] Similarly a charge of driving under the influence of intoxicating liquor or drugs has been held to be good;[15] as has been a charge of a breach of police regulations by 'falsehood or prevarication',[16] and a person may be charged in a single count with obtaining credit 'under false pretences or by means of any other fraud',[17] or with using threatening words with intent to commit a breach of the peace, or whereby a breach of the peace might be occasioned.[18]

Joinder of charges

At one time charges of felony and misdemeanour could not be joined in the same indictment because the right of an accused person to challenge jurors varied according to the nature of the

13. *The State (McLoughlin) v. Shannon* [1948] I.R. 439 (H.C.); *The People v. Blogh* [1958] I.R. 91 (C.C.A.).
14. *The State (Hardy) v. O'Flynn* 83 I.L.T.R. 58 (H.C.)
15. *The State (McGroddy) v. Carr* [1975] I.R. 275 (S.C.).
16. *The State (Sheehan) v. Commissioner of Garda Síochána*, unrep. 1st March, 1976 (H.C.) reversed on other grounds, 25th October, 1977 (S.C.); s.n. *The State (Sheehan) v. McMahon*, unrep. 25th October, 1977.
17. *R. v. Perry* 31 Cr. App. R. 16.
18. *The State (Lynch) v. Delap*, unrep. 23rd June, 1980 (H.C.); cf. *Minister for Social Welfare v. Johnston* [1960] I.R. 185 (H.C.).

offence; this was altered by the Criminal Justice (Administration) Act, 1924,[1] and there is now no distinction under the Juries Act, 1976.[2] The Act of 1924 provides that charges for both felonies and misdemeanors may be joined in the same indictment if they are founded on the same facts or are part of a series of offences of the same or a similar character.[3] Thus a person might be charged in different counts with burglary of a building, robbing one of the occupants, and causing damage to the building and on a further count of entering another building with intent to steal, or he might be charged in different counts with a series of larcenies committed over a period, or on a number of counts alleging that he obtained or attempted to obtain money by false pretences. It was once regarded as improper to join any other count with a count of murder, but it has now been held both in Ireland and in England that this is permissible.[4] The Court of Criminal Appeal has, however, disapproved the undue proliferation of counts.[5]

The joinder of counts in an indictment does not, however, mean that all counts will necessarily be tried together. The question of separate trials on different counts will be considered later.[6]

Joinder of offenders

Two or more persons may be charged in the same indictment.[7] They may have been concerned jointly in the commission of a crime, as where a brother and sister were charged with the murder of another brother,[8] as where two persons burgle a house or are concerned, albeit in different capacities, in robbing a bank, or they may have been concerned in the same incident, although each acted separately,[9] as where a number of acts of a similar

1. S. 5.
2. S. 20.
3. Indictment Rules, r. 3; see also *The People v. Wallace,* unrep. 22nd November, 1982 (C.C.A.).
4. *The People v. Murray* [1977] I.R. 360 (S.C.); *Connelly v. Director of Public Prosecutions* [1964] A.C. 1254.
5. *The People v. Coughlan,* 2nd February, 1967, Frewen 325.
6. Infra, pp. 291 sqq.
7. 2 Hale, 173.
8. *Attorney General v. O'Leary* [1926] I.R. 445 (C.C.A.).
9. 2 Hale 173, *Director of Public Prosecutions v. Merriman* [1973] A.C. 584.

nature are connected in the time and place of their commission.[10] It is specifically provided that in the case of receiving, any number of persons who have at different times received the same property may be charged and tried together;[11] and it has been held that two defendants may be joined in receiving, at different times, parts of the same stolen property.[12] One or more counts may charge several persons with the same crime and another or others may charge some only of the accused. A. and B. might be charged with entering a house with intent to steal, and in the same indictment A. might be charged with assaulting X. and B. with assaulting Y.

It does not, however, necessarily follow that because several persons have been joined in the same indictment they will be tried together, and this question will be considered later.[13]

The indictment may include either in substitution for or in addition to a count charging the offence for which the accused was sent forward for trial, any count founded on any of the documents (including depositions and any statement by the accused to the Justice in answer to the charge) and exhibits considered by the Justice at the preliminary examination, provided that it is a count which may be lawfully joined[14] i.e. is founded on the same facts or forms part of a series of offences of the same character. Thus if the accused was sent forward on a charge of larceny from A., and the Book of Evidence contained evidence of a larceny from B. also, a count might be included in respect of the second larceny; or if the accused was sent forward on a charge of assaulting a police officer in the execution of his duty and the Book contained evidence that the officer had suffered actual bodily harm, the indictment might include a count in respect of the actual bodily harm, as well as or in substitution for the count of assaulting the officer in the execution of his duty.[15]

10. Id.
11. Larceny Act, 1916, s. 40 (3).
12. *R. v. Tizard* [1962] 2 Q.B. 608.
13. Infra, pp. 293 sqq.
14. Criminal Procedure Act, 1967, s. 18.
15. The joinder of such counts is common, although it is arguable that the offence in each case is the same, viz. assault, and that the relevant sections (38 and 47) of the Offences against the Person Act, 1861, merely prescribe the penalty.

The indictment may also contain a count in respect of a summary offence provided that the accused has been charged with it and that it arises out of the same set of facts,[16] and the summary offence then becomes an indictable offence.[17] Thus the accused might have been sent forward for trial on a charge of burglary; he might also have been charged in the District Court with malicious damage to the building he entered, to an extent not exceeding £50; the latter is a summary offence on which he could not have been returned for trial, but a count in respect of it may be included in the indictment, thus enabling all charges to be disposed of together. At the same time, it is submitted that discretion should be used in the inclusion of summary counts not directly related to the principal charge to which a jury will have to direct its attention; the accused may have been charged with dangerous driving causing death, and also with having no driving licence or insurance, charges requiring evidence, immaterial and only incidental to the principal charge, with which a jury should not be troubled.

Where an accused person is charged before a District Justice with both indictable and summary offences, it is common for the Justice, if he sends the accused forward for trial on the indictable offences to adjourn consideration of the summary offences until after the trial of the major offences; but there is no objection in that event and in an appropriate case to including some or all of the summary offences in the indictment, when they should be struck out in the District Court.[18]

Conspiracy

If the evidence discloses the commission of a substantive offence a count of conspiracy should not normally be added.[19]

16. Criminal Justice Act, 1951, s. 6.
17. *The State (Harkin) v. O'Malley* [1978] I.R. 269 (S.C.); overruling *The People v. Doyle* 101 I.L.T.R. 136. In *Harkin*'s case a jury had found the accused not guilty of an indictable offence but disagreed on the summary charge which had been included, and it was held that the accused might be re-tried on indictment for the latter offence.
18. See *The State (Cahill) v. President of the Circuit Court* [1954] I.R. 128 (S.C.).
19. *The People v. Keane* 110 I.L.T.R. (C.C.A.); but see Archbold §§28-27, 28-28.

CHAPTER 11

ARRAIGNMENT

After an accused person has been sent forward for trial to the Central Criminal Court or Circuit Court the next formal procedure will normally be his arraignment, that is to say, calling him before the Court of trial, reading the indictment to him and asking him whether he pleads guilty or not guilty.

Section 6 of the Habeas Corpus Act, 1781, provides that if a person who is in custody for treason or felony shall, in the first week of term or first day of sessions, pray for trial, and shall not be indicted during the next term or sessions after commitment, he shall on motion on the last day of term or sessions be discharged on bail unless there is evidence on oath that a witness for the Crown cannot be produced; and, if not indicted and tried in the second term or sessions, he is to be discharged. This particular enactment has not been repealed but it has not been adapted, and whilst the authors are not aware of any case in which it has been judicially considered since the establishment of Saorstát Éireann, it is submitted that it is obsolete.

Quite apart from this, however, every person charged with a criminal offence is presumed to be innocent until his guilt is proved and is entitled to have the question determined as soon as possible, but so also is the prosecution on behalf of the People. Addressing the House of Lords in *R. v. Lawrence* Lord Hailsham L.C. said:[1]

> '[I]t is a truism to say that justice delayed is justice denied. But it is not merely the anxiety and uncertainty in the life of the accused, whether on bail or remand, which are affected. Where there is delay

1. [1982] A.C. 510, 517.

the whole quality of justice deteriorates. Our system depends on the recollection of witnesses, conveyed to a jury by oral testimony. As the months pass, this recollection necessarily dims, and juries who are correctly directed not to convict unless they are assured of the reliability of the evidence for the prosecution, necessarily tend to acquit as this becomes less precise, and sometimes less reliable. This may also affect defence witnesses on the opposite side.'

It is furthermore accepted that if the accused is in custody awaiting trial, still with the presumption of innocence, he should be given priority — although it may be questioned whether the like priority which is given to a person who has been refused bail or cannot satisfy the conditions on which bail has been allowed should be given to a person who has merely declined to accept bail allowed with no onerous conditions, or one who has deprived himself of the opportunity of a trial by failing to answer to his bail, at the expense of others anxiously awaiting trial.

Order 85 of the Rules of the Superior Courts provides that the Registrar of the Central Criminal Court is to give notice of the date fixed for trial to the Chief State Solicitor, the accused, and to a solicitor who represents the accused and has given notice to that effect to the Registrar.[2] The indictment is to be lodged with the Registrar[3] and the accused or his solicitor is entitled, on application, to obtain a copy of the indictment.[4] The accused is also entitled on application to copies of any depositions made in the District Court, on payment of the prescribed fees, or, if he has been granted a legal aid certificate, free of charge.[5] The Registrar is to have custody of all original depositions and of all exhibits put in evidence, and must retain them until directed by the Central Criminal Court to return home.[6] He must keep a register of all cases awaiting trial in that Court.[7] Apart from these Rules, however, there are no rules of Court relating to arraignment or trial of an accused person either in the Central Criminal Court or in the Circuit Court.

2. Rules of the Superior Courts, O.85, r. 2.
3. Id. r. 3.
4. Id. r. 4.
5. Id. r. 5 as amended.
6. Id. r. 6.
7. Id. r. 7.

I. PRESENCE OF THE ACCUSED

'It is an essential principle of our criminal law that the trial for an indictable offence has to be conducted in the presence of the accused, and for this purpose trial means the whole of the proceedings; including sentence.'[8] Until comparatively recently the accused was arraigned and remained throughout the trial in the dock of the Court. Since every accused person is presumed innocent until the contrary is proved, this ancient practice is nowadays generally considered to be undesirable unless special circumstances, in particular security, make it necessary, and the accused is usually seated in the well of the Court. There are, however, exceptions to the rule that the accused must be present throughout. Thus the trial may proceed in the absence of an accused if he proves disorderly,[9] unless his conduct may be attributable to mental illness,[10] or if he absents himself in the course of the trial.[11] If the accused is taken ill he may be allowed to leave court and the trial may proceed in his absence.[12] If there is reason to fear that the accused may intimidate a witness, he may be removed from the sight of the witness so long as he can hear the evidence.[13]

In the case of a company,[14] charged with an indictable offence, other than one punishable *only* by death or imprisonment, which a corporation of its nature cannot suffer, it may appear at all stages by a representative duly appointed by the company to represent it; the representative need not be appointed under the seal of the company, and a statement in writing, signed by the managing director or some other person having himself or with others the management of the affairs of the company, is sufficient proof of the representative's appointment.[15]

8. *Per* Lord Atkin in *Lawrence v. R.* [1933] A.C. 699, 708, cited in *The People v. Messitt,* infra.
9. *The People v. Jasinski,* 11th March, 1963, Frewen 283.
10. *The People v. Messitt* [1972] I.R. 204 (C.C.A.).
11. Archbold, §3-49, 3-50.
12. *R. v. Orton alias Castro* , noted Archbold §3-47.
13. *R. v. Smellie* 14 Cr. App. R. 128.
14. I.e. a company registered under the Joint Stock Companies Acts or the Companies Acts of 1862, 1908 or 1963, or one registered outside the State which has an established place of business in the State; Companies Act, 1963, ss. 2 (1), 382 (7).
15. See generally Companies Act, 1963, s. 382.

II. NOLLE PROSEQUI

The Attorney General had power at common law to discontinue the prosecution of an accused by entering a *nolle prosequi* and might exercise this power to prevent the further prosecution of a trial by a private prosecutor: many of the older cases were concerned with this.[1] As has been already stated, once an accused has been returned for trial, a private prosecutor has to yield place to the Attorney General[2] so that those cases are no longer relevant. The powers of the Attorney General are now exercisable by the Director of Public Prosecutions.[3]

The power of the Director to discontinue a prosecution does not appear to be subject to control by the Court.[4]

Section 12 of the Criminal Justice (Administration) Act, 1924, as adapted by the Prosecution of Offences Act, 1974, provides that at the trial of a prisoner on indictment, a *nolle prosequi* may be entered at any time after the indictment is preferred to the jury and before a verdict is found, and every such *nolle prosequi* is to be in the following form.

> On the day of 19 at the trial of AB on the prosecution of the Director of Public Prosecutions on an indictment for the said Director in his proper person (or by his Counsel) stated to the court that he would not further prosecute the said AB on the said indictment, whereupon it was ordered by the Court that the said AB be discharged of and from the indictment aforesaid.

In giving judgment in *The State (O'Callaghan) v. Ó hUadhaigh*[5] Finlay P. adverted to the fact that the entering of a *nolle prosequi* under this section had for over 50 years been the exception rather than the rule and that the practice, except in very exceptional circumstances, is for it to be entered before the indictment is preferred. He adverted to the following passage from the judgment of Maguire C.J. in *The State (Killian) v. Attorney General:*[6]

1. *The State (O'Callaghan) v. Ó hUadhaigh* [1977] I.R. 42, 48, *per* Finlay P.; and see *The State (Killian) v. Attorney General* 92 I.L.T.R. 182 (S.C.); also pp. 76 sqq.
2. *The State (Ennis) v. Farrell* [1966] I.R. 107 (S.C.).
3. *The State (O'Callaghan) v. Ó hUadhaigh*, supra.
4. *The State (Killian) v. Attorney General*, 92 I.L.T.R. 182; see also supra p. 75.
5. [1977] I.R. 42, 49 (H.C.).
6. 92 I.L.T.R. 182, 183-184.

> 'It is contended that section 12 of [the Criminal Justice (Administration) Act, 1924] prevents the Attorney General exercising any power to enter a *nolle prosequi* until the accused has been given in charge to the jury. Such an interpretation has not been acted upon at any time. The section appears to make it clear that the Attorney General can stay the proceedings at any time up to the conclusion of the trial. Even if it were arguable that the procedure adopted was not strictly regular, it would be unjustifiable for this Court to do what is asked, namely, to interfere with the Attorney General by ordering him to prosecute, particularly when he has made it quite clear that he does not consider that he ought to do so.'

As has been seen in Chapter 4, supra, *Killian*'s case involved an application by a person who had instituted proceedings as a common informer for an order of mandamus directing the Attorney General to prosecute upon an indictment notwithstanding the entry by him of a *nolle prosequi,* and the order was refused.

In *O'Callaghan*'s case the facts were more complicated. On the 17th January, 1976, the prosecutor was arrested and charged with four offences arising out of an alleged armed robbery from a Post Office in Walkinstown. On 16th February 1976, he was charged with four further offences of larceny and receiving a motor bicycle and motor car from different places in Dublin. He was returned for trial on each of these eight charges to the Dublin Circuit Court and the trial was there adjourned to the next sittings, when the prosecution applied for a further adjournment. An indictment containing a single count of receiving in connection with the Post Office robbery was lodged and the trial was transferred to the Central Criminal Court; before it came on, an indictment was lodged containing eight counts relating to the Post Office robbery, the motor car and the motor cycle, and two others against another accused; subsequently a third indictment was lodged, containing a repetition of the original eight and two further alternative counts. When the case came on for trial a jury was sworn, but the accused was at no time put in charge to it. That jury was discharged and a fresh jury sworn some days later, after legal argument, but the accused was again not put in charge. The trial judge indicated his view that the only count he had jurisdiction to try was the single count in the indictment originally lodged in the Circuit Court, whereupon counsel for the prosecution entered a *nolle prosequi*, informing the Court that it was intended to have the accused re-arrested and re-charged on all counts. This was in fact done, and the application to Finlay P. was to make absolute a conditional order of prohibition against the further hearing of the charges by the District Justice.

In the course of his judgment in *O'Callaghan*'s case Finlay P. referred to the judgment of Kenny J. in *Macauley v. The Minister for Posts and Telegraphs*,[7] to the effect that the office of Attorney General created in 1924 was a new office, and he concluded that the sole right to enter a *nolle prosequi* was to be found in section 12 of the Criminal Justice (Administration) Act, 1924, that the consequences of so doing are therefore to be found in the same statute and that decisions which concerned the powers of the Attorney General in England or Ireland before 1924, as Law Officers of the Crown, to enter a *nolle prosequi*, and, in particular, statements or decisions which would appear to confirm an unqualified right on his part subsequently to institute a fresh proceeding arising out of the same matter, did not appear to be directly applicable although they might be of some assistance.

Having regard, however, to the facts of the case the learned Judge indicated that he could only deal with it on the basis that a valid *nolle prosequi* had been entered and reserved his decision on the general question whether it is open to the Director of Public Prosecutions, having entered a valid *nolle prosequi*, to institute fresh proceedings arising out of the same alleged offence. He said:[8]

> 'If the contention of the respondent in this case is correct, then it means that in any criminal trial the Director, on meeting a situation in which a ruling or proposed ruling by the trial judge on a matter within his discretion at the trial is unsatisfactory, from the point of view of the prosecution, can deal with that problem by entering a *nolle prosequi* and so avoid the consequences of technical matters that may have arisen in the course of the proceedings up to that time by instituting an entirely fresh prosecution freed from, or cured of, the difficulties which have arisen and which are likely to favour the accused.'

7. [1966] I.R. 345 (H.C.).
8. [1977] I.R. 42, 52.

Having quoted from the judgment of O'Higgins C.J. in *The State (Healy) v. Donoghue,*[9] and stated the facts of the case, he concluded:

> 'If the contention of the respondent is correct the prosecutor, having undergone that form of trial (and remand awaiting trial) and having succeeded in confining the issues to be tried, would be deprived of all that advantage by the simple operation of a statutory power on the part of the Director of Public Prosecutions. In this way the prosecutor would have the entire of his remand awaiting trial set at naught and he would have to start afresh to face a criminal prosecution in which the prosecution, by adopting different procedures, could avoid the consequences of the learned trial judge's view of the law. No such right exists in the accused: if the trial judge makes decisions adverse to the interests of the accused, the latter cannot obtain relief from them otherwise than by appeal from the Central Criminal Court, or by appeal or review in the case of an inferior court.
>
> It seems to me that so to interpret the provisions of s. 12 of the Act of 1924 as to create such an extraordinary imbalance between the rights and powers of the prosecution and those of the accused respectively, and to give the Director such a relative independence from the decision of the court in any trial, would be to concur in a proposition of law which signally failed to import fairness and fair procedure. . .
>
> Therefore, I am satisfied that on the facts of this particular case the Director of Public Prosecutions has not got a right to institute a fresh prosecution against the accused in respect of the matters which were the subject matter of the three charge sheets, and in respect of which the accused was returned by the learned District Justice for trial to the Circuit Court.'

The fact that entry of a *nolle prosequi* was no bar to further proceedings for the same offence was in fact accepted by the Supreme Court in *The State (Walsh) v. Lennon.*[10] Whilst in *O'Callaghan*'s case the learned judge expressed the view that the only right the Director had to enter a *nolle prosequi* was that conferred by Section 12 of the Act of 1924, it is submitted that this view was *obiter,* and he in fact stated[11] that it was not necessary

9. [1976] I.R. 325 (S.C.).
10. [1942] I.R. 112 (H.C.); see also *The State (Quirke) v. Carr,* unrep. November, 1974 (H.C)., neither case appears from the report to have been cited in *O'Callaghan*'s case.
11. [1977] I.R. 42, 51-2.

in that case for him to decide, as a general matter, whether, having entered a *nolle prosequi,* it was not possible under any circumstances for the Director to institute a fresh prosecution arising out of that offence, and he reserved his decision on that matter. Furthermore, the same Judge considered the question again in *The State (Coveney) v. The Special Criminal Court;*[12] in that case the accused had been sent forward to the Circuit Court on a plea of guilty and later changed his plea, whereupon the prosecution entered a *nolle prosequi* and then had the accused charged before the Special Criminal Court. The learned judge refused to make absolute an order of prohibition to restrain the Special Court from proceeding with the trial, but based his decision on the laches of the prosecutor, i.e. the unwarranted delay on the part of the accused in applying for the order; he did, however, refer to *The State (Walsh) v. Lennon*[13] and accepted that the entry of a *nolle prosequi* was not a bar in an appropriate case to the institution of fresh proceedings, indicating that while the only power now enjoyed by the Director of Public Prosecutions was that derived from Section 12 of the Act of 1924, the nature and effect of the *nolle prosequi* was the same as at common law. Dealing with the question whether it is still open to the Director to enter a *nolle prosequi* before the preferment of the charge to the jury he said:[14]

> 'It is difficult to see what end of justice and in particular what right or interest of the accused could be secured by inhibiting the Director of Public Prosecutions as it now is from entering a *nolle prosequi* before the accused had been given in charge to a jury. In many cases as in this case the entry of a *nolle prosequi* before that time expedites the discharge of the accused and, of course, in the very great majority of cases in which a *nolle prosequi* is entered no further proceedings are instituted. In a case such as the present where the entry of a *nolle prosequi* is a precedent to the institution of fresh proceedings in respect of the same charge its early rather than its late entry merely achieves one of the known objectives of justice, namely the speedy dispatch of criminal proceedings. Furthermore, expense incurred by an accused in his own defence and the

12. [1982] I.L.R.M. 284.
13. [1942] I.R. 112.
14. [1982] I.L.R.M. 284, 288.

> anxiety associated with a pending criminal charge would be intensified if strict adherence were in all cases paid by the Director of Public Prosecutions to the provisions of the section appearing to provide that it was only when the accused had been put in charge of the jury that he could and should enter a *nolle prosequi*.
>
> Having regard to all of these considerations I conclude that the commencement time limit contained in s. 12 appearing as it clearly does appear to limit the right of the Director of Public Prosecutions to the entry of a *nolle prosequi* until after the accused has been put in charge of the jury must be considered as directive in its nature only and not as mandatory and that therefore the fact that a *nolle prosequi* has been entered prior to that stage, cannot of itself invalidate the entry of the *nolle prosequi*.'

An alternative answer may be that, as suggested in *O'Callaghan*'s case, the Director may have the same right as any other litigant before the courts not to proceed with a case; but in any event the conclusion appears to be that the Director may enter a *nolle prosequi* before the trial or before a verdict is given, and he may still be entitled to institute fresh proceedings but has no absolute right to do so.

III. APPLICATIONS FOR TRANSFER

(1) **Transfer to the Dublin Circuit Court**

Before the enactment of the Courts Act, 1981, when the accused had been sent forward for trial to the Circuit Court (including the Dublin Circuit Court) either the prosecution or the defence might apply to have the trial transferred to the Central Criminal Court under section 6 of the Courts Act, 1964. Either the prosecution or the defence might feel that a local jury might be unlikely to convict (or acquit), for fear or prejudice. So far as the prosecution was concerned such applications were rare (save where one only of several accused applied for a transfer and it was desired to have all tried together), since in most cases the Special Criminal Court provided an alternative. An accused on the other hand might fear the reputed severity of a particular Circuit Judge (or the judge's previous knowledge of the accused) or that the notoriety of the case locally might prejudice his chances before a local jury. One result was gross overloading of the lists of cases for trial in the Central Court.

Section 31 of the Courts Act, 1981, (which repeals the last-mentioned provision) now provides that when an accused person has been sent forward for trial to the Circuit Court sitting other than within the Dublin Circuit, either the prosecution or the accused may apply to the Circuit Judge before whom the accused is triable to have the trial transferred to the Circuit Court sitting within the Dublin Circuit. If there is more than one accused any one or more may so apply.

It is to be noted that if a person is returned for trial to the Dublin Circuit Court, there is no provision for transfer to any other Circuit or to the Central Criminal Court. It is submitted that if the accused is returned to the Circuit Court elsewhere on a plea of guilty, the Circuit Court has no jurisdiction to transfer the case to Dublin, even if the accused alters his plea; but it might be argued that in so far as it was always open to the accused to change his plea, he might be said to have been returned for trial in the event of his so doing, and apply to have his trial, but not the matter of the sentence, transferred to Dublin.

If the party making the application gives seven days notice of it to the other party, the Circuit Judge is bound to grant it.[1] The Circuit Judge is also bound to grant the application if there are less than seven days between the date on which the accused was sent forward and the date of commencement of the trial.[2] In addition, if two or more accused are sent forward for trial and it is proposed to try them together, and an application for transfer is made by one or more, but not all, and granted, then the prosecution, without notice to the accused, may apply to the Judge who granted the application, to transfer the trial of the remaining accused and the judge is bound to grant that further application.[3] The prosecution is thus given the alternative, where there is more than one accused, of proceeding in the Circuit Court against any who has not applied for a transfer, or having all the accused tried together in the Dublin Circuit Court.

In any other case the Circuit Judge has a discretion to grant or refuse the application, and his decision is final and unappealable.[4]

1. Courts Act, 1981, s. 31 (1) (a).
2. Id. s. 31 (3).
3. Id. s. 31 (2).
4. Id. s. 31 (1) (b).

(2) Transfer within the Circuit

Either the prosecution or the accused may apply to the judge of the Circuit Court before which any criminal issue is pending to transfer the trial from the place on his circuit where it is required by law to be held to any other place on that circuit. The trial is to be held with a jury drawn from the jury district or other area prescribed for trials by the Circuit Court sitting in the place to which the trial is transferred.[5] The Circuit Judge has a discretion whether or not to transfer the trial, and the order for transfer may provide for matters ancillary or incidental to it, but any order for transfer is final and unappealable, and an accused person has no right to be tried by a jury from any particular area or district.[6] These provisions appear to apply only to those Circuits in which there are several towns and separate jury districts for the hearing of criminal cases.

(3) Transfer to the Special Criminal Court.

This subject is dealt with elsewhere in this work.[7]

IV. POSTPONEMENT OR ADJOURNMENT

Postponement is strictly speaking putting back the commencement of a trial to a later date, whilst adjournment is more appropriate to deferring the further hearing of a trial in progress to the following or some later day, but the term 'adjournment' is commonly used in reference to postponement.

The Criminal Justice (Administration) Act, 1924,[1] specifically provides that where, before trial or at any stage of a trial, the court is of the opinion that, in consequence of an amendment of the indictment or an order for the separate trial of any count, the postponement of the trial is expedient, it is to make such order as to postponement as appears necessary. If such an order is made during a trial the court may order that the jury be discharged from giving a verdict on the count or counts the trial of which is postponed, or on the whole indictment, as the case may be; on

5. Courts (Supplemental Provisions) Act, 1961, s. 26.
6. *The State (Hughes) v. Neylon* [1982] I.L.R.M. 108 (H.C.).
7. See Chapter 14, infra.
1. S. 6 (4).

the separate trial of a count, the procedure is to be the same as if it had been found in a separate indictment; if the jury is discharged during the trial the procedure on the postponed trial is as if the trial had not commenced; the court may make such order as to costs and as to bail and the enlargement of recognisances and otherwise as the court thinks fit.[2]

These statutory powers are, however, in addition to and not in derogation of any other powers the court may have.[3] Thus, the trial may be postponed to the next session of the court on the application of the prosecution or the accused on account of the illness of the accused or the unavoidable absence or illness of a material witness, the existence of prejudice in the jury and so forth.[4]

If the accused is returned in custody for trial to the next sitting of the Circuit Court for the discharge of criminal business, and he is not indicted at the then current or next such sitting of the Circuit Court the warrant of committal lapses;[5] but the original return for trial is still good, and the accused may be re-arrested and arraigned before a subsequent sitting,[6] and, if the accused is arraigned before the next sitting and then remanded in custody by the Court until the following sitting, the remand is good.[7]

V. STANDING MUTE

It may happen that, apart from any question of mental capacity, the accused may say nothing when called upon to plead to the indictment. This may be because he is deaf or dumb,[1] or is a foreigner who does not understand the language (although in such a case the prosecution would invariably provide an interpreter), in which case he is said to stand mute by visitation of God; or he may deliberately refuse to plead, when he is said to be

2. Criminal Justice (Administration) Act, 1924, s. 6 (5).
3. Id. s. 6 (6).
4. See Sandes, 114; cf. *The People v. Chaney*, 6th December, 1963, Frewen 290 (accused under misapprehension as to reason for attendance).
5. *Re Singer* 97 I.L.T.R. 130 (S.C.).
6. *Re Singer* (No. 2) 98 I.L.T.R. 112 (S.C.).
7. *Re Francis* 97 I.L.T.R. 151 (S.C.).
1. *R. v. Pritchard* 7 C. & P. 303; Archbold §4-113.

mute of malice. Formerly the issue was triable by a jury,[2] but now no jury is to be sworn and the judge must himself hear such evidence (if any) relevant to the issue whether the accused stands mute of malice or by visitation of God as may be adduced before him; if evidence is adduced and the judge is satisfied that the accused is mute by visitation of God the like consequences ensue as would have ensued if a jury had been sworn for the purpose and had so found; but if the judge is not so satisfied or if no such evidence is adduced he must direct a plea of 'not guilty' to be entered.[3] If the prosecution claims that the accused is mute by visitation of God, it must establish it beyond reasonable doubt.[4] A finding that the accused is mute by visitation of God is not a bar to the trial proceeding, if he can read or write, or if intelligence can be conveyed to him by signs or symbols.[5]

Somewhat similarly, if the accused is a foreigner who does not understand English, the evidence must be interpreted; the judge may dispense with translation if the accused, knowing English, indicates that he understands the evidence or any part of it, or if he is represented by counsel and he and his counsel are willing to dispense with translation; the judge should in any event be satisfied that the accused substantially understands the proceedings, and, if there are substantial divergences between the statements in the Book of Evidence or depositions and the evidence as given in Court, the evidence should be translated regardless of the attitude of the accused.[6]

The accused is entitled by virtue of Article 5 of the Constitution to give his evidence, but not to insist on the proceedings being conducted entirely, in Irish;[7] but it is submitted that, if he does, the judge should insist on everything being translated into English, for the benefit of the jury if of nobody else.

An interpreter must be sworn: no form of oath is prescribed by statute, but the recognised formula is:[8]

2. This is still the position in England; Archbold §4-112.
3. Juries Act 1976, s. 28, re-enacting Courts of Justice Act, 1936, s. 80.
4. *R. v. Sharp* 41 Cr. App. R. 197.
5. *R. v. Steel* 1 Leach 451, *R. v. Jones* 1 Leach 102, Archbold §4-113.
6. *R. v. Lee Kun* [1916] 1 K.B. 337.
7. *Ó Monacháin v. An Taoiseach*, unrep. 27th February, 1980 (H.C.).
8. Archbold §4-15.

I swear by Almighty God that I will well and faithfully interpret and true explanation make of all such matters and things as shall be required of me according to the best of my skill and understanding.

VI. UNFITNESS TO PLEAD

Where a person detained in a mental hospital is charged with an indictable offence before a Justice of the District Court and evidence is given which, in the opinion of the Justice, constitutes *prima facie* evidence that such person has committed the offence and that he would, if placed on trial, be unfit to plead, the Justice must certify that he is suitable for transfer to the Central Mental Hospital.[1] In making such an order the Justice is exercising his criminal jurisdiction,[2] but it is not necessary that the accused should be present.[3]

If any question arises as to the competence of an accused person to plead, the issue must be determined by a jury specially empanelled for the purpose;[4] the form of oath to be administered to the jurors is 'I will well and diligently inquire whether [name] the prisoner at the bar be insane or not and a true verdict give according to the best of my understanding.'[5]

The invariable practice is for medical evidence to be called, although it would appear that the jury may also pay attention to the demeanour of the accused in court.[6]

The test of whether the accused is mentally fit to plead does not appear to be the same as that to be applied on the question of insanity at the date of the alleged offence, but rather, whether he is of sufficient intellect to comprehend the course of the proceedings, so as to make a proper defence, to challenge a juror to whom he might wish to object, and to understand the details of the evidence.[7]

1. Mental Treatment Act, 1945, s. 207 as adapted by the Mental Treatment Act, 1961, and the Mental Treatment Acts (Adaptation) Order, 1971, (S.I. 108 of 1971), *The State (M.) v. O'Brien* [1971] I.R. 169 (S.C.).
2. *The State (O.) v. O'Brien* [1971] I.R. 42 (S.C.).
3. *The State (O'Reilly) v. Director of the Central Mental Hospital*, unrep. 7th July, 1977 (S.C.).
4. Criminal Lunatics Act, 1800, s. 2; in England the procedure is now governed by the Criminal Procedure (Insanity) Act, 1964.
5. Juries Act, 1976, s. 19 (2).
6. *R. v. Goode* 7 A. & E. 536.
7. *R. v. Pritchard* 7 C. & P. 303, *R. v. Robertson* [1968] 1 W.L.R. 1767 and other cases cited in Archbold §4-117.

If the issue is raised by the prosecution, the onus is on the prosecution to establish it beyond reasonable doubt;[8] but if raised by the defence it appears sufficient to establish unfitness as a matter of probability.[9] If the jury find the accused fit to plead, he has no right of appeal to the Court of Criminal Appeal on this issue.[10]

If the jury find the accused unfit to plead he must be detained in the Central Mental Hospital at the pleasure of the Government.[11]

There appears to be no definite authority as to what is to be done if, during the trial, the accused is alleged to be or becomes unfit to comprehend the course of the proceedings;[12] it is submitted that the proper course is for the judge to discharge the jury[13] and for the accused to be re-arraigned, when the issue of fitness can be dealt with by a fresh jury in the usual way.

VII. DEMURRER

A demurrer was an objection in writing by the accused to the indictment on the ground that, admitting the facts alleged to be true, they did not, in point of law, constitute him guilty of an offence sufficiently charged against him. The plea appears to be obsolete.[1]

VIII. MOTION TO QUASH THE INDICTMENT

At common law either the prosecutor or the defence may move to quash the indictment on the ground that it is bad on its face or so insufficient as to make any judgment given on it erroneous.[2] Since the Director of Public Prosecutions has control of the conduct of the proceedings in every case once the accused has been returned for trial, and appears to have power to enter a *nolle prosequi* or discontinue the proceedings at any time,[3] a motion by

8. *R. v. Robertson,* supra.
9. Archbold, §4-118.
10. *The People v. Fennell (No. 2)* [1940] I.R. 453 (S.C.).
11. Criminal Lunatics Act, 1800, s. 2; Lunacy (Ireland) Act, 1821, s. 17; Central Criminal Lunatic Asylum (Ireland) Act, 1845, s. 8; Mental Treatment Act, 1961, s. 39.
12. In England the issue is to be determined by a separate jury or by the trial jury as the court may direct; Criminal Procedure (Insanity) Act, 1964, s. 4 (4) (b).
13. Cf. *R. v. Streek* 2 C. & P. 413, *The People v. Messitt* [1972] I.R. 204 (C.C.A.).
1. Sandes, 116, Archbold §4-65.
2. 2 Hawk. c. 25, s. 146.
3. Supra, p. 259.

the prosecution to quash the indictment would appear to be unnecessary; and having regard to the simplified form of indictments under the Criminal Justice (Administration) Act, 1924, and to the extensive powers of amendment given to the Court by section 6 of that Act, an application by the defence would be unlikely to succeed.[4] Nevertheless cases may occur where an amendment may be refused on the grounds that it could not be made without injustice, and it is conceivable that an indictment might be bad as disclosing on its face no offence known to the law,[5] or only an offence triable summarily,[6] or an offence not within the jurisdiction of the Court,[7] or on the ground that the accused had not been properly committed for trial.[8]

The motion may be made to the Court of trial, but if the case is to be tried by the Circuit Court application may alternatively be made to the High Court for an order of prohibition.[9] A motion by the accused should ordinarily be made before he pleads to the indictment but may be made at any time during the trial. If the indictment is clearly bad the Court will quash it but in a case of doubt the accused may be left to his remedy by way of motion in arrest of judgment.[10]

IX. PLEAS IN BAR OF THE INDICTMENT

The only pleas in bar of the indictment which need be considered[1] are the pleas of *autrefois acquit* and of *autrefois convict,* that the accused has already been acquitted or convicted, as the case may be, of the offence with which he is charged. It was an

4. Supra, p. 243.
5. See Archbold, §§1-110 sqq., (bearing in mind that there is no provision in the State corresponding to the English Administration of Justice (Miscellaneous Provisions) Act, 1933, s. 2) and 25th Edn. 98-100.
6. If, however, a summary offence is properly included in an indictment but left undetermined after disposal of any indictable offences, the summary offence is still triable on indictment; *The State (Harkin) v. O'Malley* [1978] I.R. 269 (S.C.); overruling *The People v. Doyle* 101 I.L.T.R. 136 (S.C.); *aliter* if the summary offence was not properly included in the indictment, e.g. because not charged in the District Court; *R. v. Hall* [1891] 1 Q.B. 747, *The People v. O'Brien* [1963] I.R. 92 (S.C.).
7. Sandes, 116.
8. *R. v. Jones* 59 Cr. App. R. 120.
9. Chapter 17, infra.
10. *R. v. Lynch* [1903] 1 K.B. 444, infra, p. 375.
1. As to the special plea of pardon, see Archbold, §4-110, 4-111.

established rule of the common law that a man might not be put twice in danger of his life for the same offence,[2] sometimes called the rule against double jeopardy.

> 'When a man is once fairly found not guilty upon any indictment, or other prosecution, before any court having competent jurisdiction of the offence he may plead such acquittal in bar of any subsequent accusation for the same crime.'[3]

As regards statutory offences it is provided that, where an act or omission constitutes an offence under two or more Acts or under an Act and at common law (whenever such Act was passed), the offender shall, unless the contrary intention appears, be liable to be prosecuted and punished under either or any of those Acts, but shall not be liable to be punished twice for the same offence;[4] but this does no more than extend the common law rule to statutory offences.[5] A simple example would be that, if a person has been charged with larceny and acquitted, he cannot be subjected again to a charge for the same larceny based on fresh evidence; but the precise meaning of and limitations on the operation of the rule require careful consideration.

Firstly, the accused must have been in jeopardy or peril of conviction on the previous occasion. Thus, if a previous indictment or charge was defective and quashed and struck out on that account, that is no bar to the preferment of a fresh charge.[6]

The rule, and this aspect of it in particular, was considered at length by the Supreme Court in *The People v. O'Shea*[7] in which the majority of the Court held that the Director of Public Prosecutions was entitled to appeal to the Supreme Court from an

2. 2 Hawk. c. 35, s. 1.
3. 4 Bl. Comm. 335.
4. Interpretation Act, 1937, s. 14; see *The People v. Dermody* [1956] I.R. 307 (C.C.A.) (rape and unlawful carnal knowledge).
5. *R. v. Miles* 24 Q.B.D. 423, *R. v. Thomas* [1950] 1 K.B. 26.
6. *R. (McDonnell) v. Tyrone JJ.* [1912] 2 I.R. 44 (K.B.D.) (summons withdrawn); *Minister for Supplies v. Connor* [1945] I.R. 231 (H.C.) (summons struck out); *The State (McLoughlin) v. Shannon* [1948] I.R. 439 (H.C.) (defendant charged in wrong name); *The State (Tynan) v. Keane* [1968] I.R. 348 (S.C.) (previous conviction quashed as made without jurisdiction); *Attorney General (O'Gara) v. Callaghan* 92 I.L.T.R. 74 (H.C.), (summons defective); *The State (Hogan) v. Carroll*, unrep. 12th May, 1981, (S.C.) (summons struck out in District Court for want of Book of Evidence).
7. Unrep. 2nd November, 1982.

acquittal by a jury by direction of the Judge in the Central Criminal Court.[8] In the course of his judgment O'Higgins C.J. said:[9] 'The plea is founded on natural justice and is based on the common law maxim *"nemo debet bis vexari pro una et eadem causa"*,' adding the quotation from Blackstone's Commentaries cited above.

After referring to *The People v. O'Brien*[10] and the judgment of Ó Dálaigh, J. (later Chief Justice) in *The State (Attorney General) v. Binchy*[11] he continued:[12]

> 'While that case turned on what was wrongly directed as a jurisdictional acquittal, it seems to me that the reasoning behind this Court's judgment as pronounced by the late Chief Justice applies equally to any verdict of acquittal directed by a trial judge. The significant feature of such a verdict is that the acquittal results in no trial because it is not in fact the verdict of the jury. It follows therefore that the person accused has not been in jeopardy.'

It is, however, to be noted that the issue in *O'Shea*'s case was whether the prosecution had a right to appeal to the Supreme Court on a matter of law from an acquittal by a jury by direction of the trial judge in the Central Criminal Court. It is implicit in the judgments of the minority (Finlay P. and Henchy J.), rejecting such a right, that the accused could not be re-tried after such an acquittal. Hederman J. who agreed with the majority as to the right of appeal expressed no view on whether a re-trial might be ordered.[13]

Secondly the previous verdict must have been final. The decision of a justice not to return an accused for trial is no bar to his being returned for trial by the Director of Public Prosecutions.[14] If a conviction is quashed by the Court of Criminal Appeal and a new trial ordered the plea of *autrefois convict* is not available.[15] If the jury disagrees there is no verdict and the

8. Infra, pp. 435 sqq.
9. At p. 28 of judgment.
10. [1963] I.R. 92 (S.C.).
11. [1964] I.R. 395 (S.C.).
12. At p. 30 of judgment; but see p. 439, infra.
13. The appeal was eventually dismissed in January, 1983.
14. *The State (Shanahan) v. Attorney General* [1964] I.R. 239 (S.C.); see pp. 233, sqq. supra.
15. Courts of Justice Act, 1928, s. 5 (2).

accused may be re-tried.[16] Acquittal on a charge of dangerous driving which was not properly before the court was no bar to an indictment for manslaughter, arising out of the same accident.[17] But if the accused is found not guilty by direction of the judge, it is specifically provided that the statement of a case by the prosecution to the Supreme Court on a question of law is to be without prejudice to the verdict of the jury.[18]

The third requirement is that the second indictment is for the same offence or for an offence of which the accused might have been found guilty on a previous trial, or is based on identical facts. This aspect of the principle was considered at length by the Court of Criminal Appeal and the House of Lords in England in *Connelly v. Director of Public Prosecutions*,[19] and there appears to be no substantial difference between Irish and English Law.

In *Connelly*'s case the accused had been charged with others with murder in the course of theft and with robbery, both charges arising out of the same incident; the trial proceeded on the count of murder alone and the accused was convicted but his conviction was quashed on appeal. He was then arraigned on the count of robbery and pleaded *autrefois acquit*. The House of Lords, affirming the Court of Criminal Appeal, held that the plea must fail.

In the course of his opinion Lord Morris of Borth y Gest expressed the view that both principle and authority established the following propositions:[20]

> '(1) that a man cannot be tried for a crime in respect of which he has previously been acquitted or convicted; (2) that a man cannot be tried for a crime in respect of which he could on some previous indictment have been convicted; (3) that the same rule applies if the crime in respect of which he is being charged is in effect the same, or is substantially the same, as either the principal or a different crime in respect of which he has been acquitted or could have been convicted or has been convicted; (4) that one test as to whether the rule

16. *Director of Public Prosecutions v. Nasralla* [1967] 2 A. C. 238 (accused found not guilty of murder, jury disagreeing on manslaughter); *R. v. Robinson* [1975] Q.B. 508 (no verdict recorded).
17. *The People v. O'Brien* [1963] I.R. 92 (S.C.).
18. Criminal Procedure Act, 1967, s. 34 (1).
19. [1964] A.C. 1254.
20. [1964] A.C. 1254, 1305.

applies is whether the evidence which is necessary to support the second indictment, or whether the facts which constitute the second offence, would have been sufficient to procure a legal conviction upon the first indictment either as to the offence charged or as to an offence of which, on the indictment, the accused could have been found guilty; (5) that this test must be subject to the proviso that the offence charged in the second indictment had in fact been committed at the time of the first charge; thus if there is an assault and a prosecution and conviction in respect of it there is no bar to a charge of murder if the assaulted person later dies; (6) that on a plea of *autrefois acquit* or *autrefois convict* a man is not restricted to a comparison between the later indictment and some previous indictment or to the records of the court, but that he may prove by evidence all such questions as to the identity of persons, dates and facts as are necessary to enable him to show that he is being charged with an offence which is either the same, or is substantially the same, as one in respect of which he has been acquitted or convicted or as one in respect of which he could have been convicted; (7) that what has to be considered is whether the crime or offence charged in the later indictment is the same or is in effect or is substantially the same as the crime charged (or in respect of which there could have been a conviction) in a former indictment and that it is immaterial that the facts under examination or the witnesses being called in the later proceedings are the same as those in some earlier proceedings; (8) that, apart from circumstances under which there may be a plea of *autrefois acquit*, a man may be able to show that a matter has been decided by a court competent to decide it, so that the principle of *res judicata* applies; (9) that, apart from cases where indictments are preferred and where pleas in bar may therefore be entered, the fundamental principle applies that a man is not to be prosecuted twice for the same crime.'

Lord Devlin said:[21]

'For the doctrine to apply it must be the same offence both in fact and in law. Robbery is not in law the same offence as murder (or as manslaughter, of which the accused could also have been convicted on the first indictment) and so the doctrine does not apply in the present case.'

Strictly speaking a plea of *autrefois convict* or *acquit* is appropriate only to a trial on indictment,[22] but, in so far as it is to some

21. Id. at 1339-1340.
22. *Attorney General v. Mallen* [1957] I.R. 344 (S.C.) citing Blackburn J. in *Wemyss v. Hopkins* L.R. 10 Q.B. 378.

extent an application of the principle of *res judicata,* this appears to be academic, and many of the cases relate to summary offences; that principle is, however, to be distinguished from 'issue estoppel', the rule that a party to a cause may not raise an issue which has been decided against him already. Where a jury has brought in a verdict of guilty or not guilty it is often not possible to know whether the verdict involves a particular conclusion or determination; 'issue estoppel' has been held to be applicable to criminal cases in Australia and Canada,[23] and there appears to have been some difference of opinion in *Connelly*'s case,[24] but it has since been held by the House of Lords that 'issue estoppel' has no place in the criminal law.[25] It has been held by the Supreme Court in Ireland that issue estoppel is, at any rate, not available to the prosecution in a criminal case.[26]

The following examples of the application of the principle of the plea of *autrefois acquit* or *convict* to the question whether the later charge is in respect of the same offence or based on the same facts as the offence to which a previous charge related, or is one of which the accused previously might have been convicted, are intended to be illustrative and not exhaustive.

A general verdict of not guilty on an indictment of murder is a bar to a later indictment for manslaughter in respect of the same killing; but where a jury having considered the question of murder and manslaughter found the accused not guilty of murder, but disagreed on the question of manslaughter, it was held that the accused might be re-tried on the latter charge.[27]

An acquittal of larceny would be a bar to a charge of obtaining the same goods by false pretences, since the accused might by statute have been found guilty in effect of the latter offence at the first trial.[28]

An acquittal on a charge of dangerous driving causing serious bodily harm, on the ground that the evidence did not disclose serious bodily harm, is a bar to a subsequent charge of dangerous

23. *Mraz v. R.* (No. 2) 96 C.L.R. 62, *Sealfon v. United States* 332 U.S. 575.
24. [1964] A.C. 1254.
25. *Director of Public Prosecutions v. Humphrys* [1977] A. C. 1.
26. *Dublin Corporation v. Flynn,* unrep. 20th December, 1979 (S.C.).
27. *Director of Public Prosecutions v. Nasralla* [1967] 2 A. C. 238.
28. *The People v. Heald* [1954] I.R. 58 (C.C.A.).

driving *simpliciter*.[29] Acquittal on a charge of dangerous driving causing serious bodily harm is a bar to a subsequent charge of careless driving.[30] An acquittal or conviction of a summary charge of dangerous driving is a bar to an indictment for dangerous driving causing death on the same occasion, since the relevant section of the Road Traffic Act, 1961, creates a single offence, with the choice of procedure by indictment where the driving causes death or serious bodily harm.[31]

An acquittal on a charge of murder is a bar to a subsequent indictment for manslaughter in connection with the same death,[32] but a conviction or acquittal on a charge of assault is no bar to a subsequent indictment for murder or manslaughter when the victim of the assault subsequently dies.[33]

An acquittal on a charge of burglary *and* larceny is a bar to a subsequent indictment for larceny,[34] but an acquittal of burglary with intent is not a bar to an indictment for larceny on the same occasion and conversely, if acquitted of larceny, the accused might still be indicted for burglary with intent on the same night. In *Connelly*'s case Lord Morris held:[35]

> 'It matters not that incidents and occasions being examined on the trial of the second indictment are precisely the same as those which were examined on the trial of the first. The court is concerned with the charges of offences or crimes. The test is, therefore, whether such proof as is necessary to convict of the second offence would establish guilt of the first offence or of an offence for which on the first charge there could be a conviction.'

An acquittal by a foreign court, if properly verified by the record of the foreign court, is a bar to an indictment for the same offence in Ireland;[36] and it is specifically provided by the Criminal Law (Jurisdiction) Act, 1976,[37] that a person who has been acquitted or convicted of an offence under the law of Northern Ireland is

29. *Attorney General (Ó Maonaigh) v. Fitzgerald* [1964] I.R. 458 (S.C.).
30. *Attorney General (McElwain) v. Power* id.
31. *Attorney General (Ward) v. Thornton*, id.
32. 2 Hale 246.
33. *R. v. Friel* 17 Cox 325, *R. v. Thomas* [1950] 1 K.B. 26.
34. 2 Hale 245-6, *R. v. Vandercomb* 2 Leach 708.
35. [1964] A.C. 1254, 1309.
36. *R. v. Roche* 1 Leach 134, *R. v. Aughet* 13 Cr. App. R. 101.
37. S. 15.

entitled to plead his acquittal or conviction as a bar in any proceedings in the State for an offence consisting of the acts (or omissions) that constitute the offence of which he has been so acquitted or convicted.[38]

The plea in bar of the indictment will normally be made on arraignment but may be made at any stage of the proceedings.[39] It should be reduced to writing and signed by counsel and if the prosecution disputes the plea it should do so by replication.[40] It is submitted that the following forms of plea and replication are appropriate:

Plea

The People (Director of Public Prosecutions) v. A.B.
A.B. says that the People ought not further to prosecute the indictment against him because he has been lawfully acquitted (convicted) of the offence charged therein.

Replication

The Director of Public Prosecutions joins issue on behalf of the People.

If the plea is disputed a jury must be sworn to try the issue.[41] The onus of proof, as a matter of probability, is on the accused.[42] The previous conviction or acquittal should be established by a copy of the record certified by the appropriate officer of the Court,[43] but the accused is not confined to a comparison between the earlier and later indictments, and may prove by evidence all such questions as to the identity of persons, dates and facts as may be necessary.[44]

On an indictment for felony, if the plea fails the accused might 'plead over', i.e. plead not guilty. Apparently the issue is to be tried by the same jury.[45] In the case of a misdemeanour it appears that he had no such right, but might be allowed by the Court to plead over.[46] If the plea succeeds, the accused must be dis-

38. See Chapter 3, supra.
39. *Connelly v. Director of Public Prosecutions* [1964] A.C. 1254, 1331.
40. See Archbold, §§4-101 sqq.
41. *R. v. Scott* 1 Leach 401, *The People v. O'Shea,* unrep. 2nd November 1982, *per* Henchy J. at p. 33 of judgment.
42. *R. v. Coughlan* 63 Cr. App. R. 33.
43. Evidence Act, 1851, s. 13.
44. *Connelly v. Director of Public Prosecutions,* supra.
45. See Archbold, 25th Edn. p. 156; there is no statutory provision in Ireland corresponding to the English Juries Act, 1974, s. 11, which specifically empowers the same jury to try the main issue as tried the preliminary issue.
46. Sandes, 118.

charged[47] in respect of the indictment or count in the indictment to which the plea relates.

X. THE PLEA OF GUILTY

The accused may plead guilty to the indictment as laid, or he may plead guilty to one or more counts, or to some alternative or lesser offence. The indictment may well contain alternative counts, e.g. for larceny and receiving, or counts charging offences differing in degree but arising out of the same incident, such as occasioning grievous bodily harm with intent and malicious wounding.

If the counts are alternative the usual practice is for the prosecution to enter a *nolle prosequi* on the count to which the accused has not pleaded guilty. If they are, so to speak, cumulative, and the accused pleads guilty to the major count, a similar course will be adopted in respect of the lesser ones. If the accused pleads guilty to a subsidiary count only, or pleads guilty to an offence less than that charged – e.g. to manslaughter on an indictment for murder, or to an attempt on an indictment for the substantive offence, it is a matter for the prosecution whether it will accept the lesser plea. If the accused is prepared to enter, and the prosecution to accept, a plea of guilty to an offence different from that charged, and of which he could be found guilty on the indictment as laid,[1] he may plead not guilty to the offence charged and guilty to such other offence,[2] but, if he could not be found guilty of such other offence in the indictment as laid, then the proper course appears to be to have the indictment amended, by substitution of the other offence for the offence charged, and for the accused to plead to the amended indictment.

The adversary process by which the criminal trial upon indictment is conducted demands that on a plea of not guilty the prosecution must prove every item of evidence necessary to establish an accused person's guilt 'beyond a reasonable doubt'. In *R. v. Sims* Lord Goddard said:[3]

47. 2 Hale 391.
1. See Chapter 13, infra.
2. Criminal Justice Administration Act, 1914, s. 39 (1).
3. [1946] K.B. 531, 539.

> '[W]henever there is a plea of not guilty, everything is in issue and the prosecution have to prove the whole of their case, including the identity of the accused, the nature of the act and the existence of any necessary knowledge or intent.'

The high onus and standard of proof invariably means that the criminal trial upon indictment is an expensive, cumbersome and often protracted affair. Not only does it engage the energies of a judge, counsel, solicitors, court officials and jurors but it may also take doctors and other professional persons away from other work and it similarly diverts the police away from other duties.

Not every defendant in Ireland seeks to avail himself of his constitutional right to a trial; indeed it is probably correct to state that only by virtue of the fact that a significant number of accused persons relieve the prosecution of the necessity of proving its case does the administration of criminal justice continue to function with reasonable efficiency.

It may seem paradoxical that accused persons should waive the important constitutional right to be tried by a jury of their peers, a form of trial traditionally considered to favour defendants, in favour of a course of action which inevitably results in their conviction. A number of reasons may be advanced for this phenomenon. Some accused persons may merely wish to acknowledge their guilt, have the matter dealt with speedily and accept the consequences. For the great majority of accused, however, the decision to plead guilty at a trial upon indictment is only taken at a late stage, sometimes even during the trial itself, and is taken in the belief that they will thereby be dealt with more leniently by the court.

Although historically the courts discouraged pleas of guilty believing that it was safer to have a formal adjudication of guilt,[4] today they implicitly encourage them by affording leniency in sentencing where such pleas are entered. Discount in sentencing on a guilty plea may assume a variety of forms. It may, for example, take the form of a non-custodial sentence where a custodial one might otherwise have been anticipated. On the other hand, it

4. See Alschuler, *The Prosecutor's Role in Plea Bargaining*, 36 U. Chi. L. Rev. 50 (1968).

may be that the defendant may receive a lesser custodial sentence than the normal 'tariff', or normal penalty, for the offence would indicate as being appropriate.

The justification traditionally advanced by the judiciary for according leniency on pleas of guilty is that persons so pleading are thereby exhibiting remorse. One English writer has suggested that sentence reductions in England for persons who plead guilty are probably not automatic and will only be given where there is actual evidence of remorse and repentence.[5] In practice, defence counsel rarely experience too much difficulty in persuading judges to accept the proposition that a plea of guilty *per se* is at least some evidence of remorse.

It may be that the courts are hiding behind a fiction in appearing to extrapolate from a plea of guilty a presumption of contrition. Judicial sentencing policy means that most guilty pleas are self-serving. There are many reasons other than remorse which could be advanced for the current policy of the courts. The accused's waiver of his right to trial upon indictment will invariably result in a saving to society, in terms both of money and of manpower. In some instances children, old people, the victims of rapes or of other traumatic assaults may be spared the ordeal of having to testify. Also, if there is a large backlog of cases (as can occur in Ireland where there has been an almost unprecedented expansion in criminal activity in recent years without any corresponding increase in courts or personnel), the accused, in addition to securing the speedy disposition of his case may, by pleading guilty, also ensure that other persons on remand, either on bail or in custody, will be dealt with more expeditiously. Reasons such as these may well lie at the heart of judicial sentencing policy, although judges prefer to seek refuge in the notion of remorse, it being perhaps a penologically more respectable consideration

5. See Davis, *Sentences for Sale: A New Look at Plea Bargaining in England and America* [1971] Crim. L.R. 150, 152-153; *contra*, Thomas, *Plea Bargaining and the Turner Case* [1970] Crim. L.R. 559. In *R. v. DeHaan* [1968] 2 Q.B. 108 the only mitigating factor found by the trial judge was that the defendant had changed his plea during the trial and had not tried to lie his way out of the offences; the sentence was effectively reduced from 4½ years to 3 years because the Court of Appeal felt that insufficient consideration had been given to this mitigating element.

than that of mere administrative expediency.

The knowledge that there exists a judicial policy to grant leniency in exchange for a plea of guilty may serve to put pressure on an accused not to contest his case, which may be undesirable. However, despite their avowed preparedness to exercise clemency on a guilty plea, the courts have equally been at pains to emphasise that the exercise by a defendant of his right to a trial must never be fettered by judges deliberately increasing sentences merely because the right has been exercised.[6]

As D. A. Thomas puts it:[7]

> 'If the norm for a given set of circumstances is in the region of three years imprisonment, the principle allows some deduction from that figure in favour of the offender who pleads guilty, but prohibits an increase beyond that point for the man who pleads not guilty and is convicted by a jury.'

In *R. v. Harper* which was an appeal from a plea of not guilty Lord Parker C.J. said:[8]

> 'This court feels it is quite improper to use language which may convey that a man is being sentenced because he has pleaded not guilty, or because he has run his defence in a particular way. It is, however, of course proper to give a man a lesser sentence if he has shown genuine remorse, amongst other things by pleading guilty.'

The notion of remorse being in some way evidenced by a plea of guilty becomes even more detached from reality when the plea of guilty has been secured from the defendant in consideration for some specific concession extracted from the prosecution in the process of what is referred to as 'plea bargaining'.

6. See, e.g. *R. v. Regan* [1959] Crim. L.R. 529 (sentence of three years imprisonment for receiving stolen goods reduced to eighteen months because the trial judge took into account the fact that the accused had refused to plead guilty); *R. v. Harper* [1968] 2 Q.B. 108 (sentence of five years reduced to three years where the judge used words which might have conveyed that he had taken into account the plea and the nature of the defence).
7. *Appellate Review of Sentences*, 20 Ala. L. Rev. 193, 201 (1968).
8. [1968] 2 Q.B. 108, 110.

Plea bargaining

Plea bargaining has been the subject of heated academic discussion in the United States[9] and to a lesser extent in England.[10] On this topic, perhaps more than any other, it is extremely dangerous to draw analogies with other jurisdictions. Especially is this so in the case of the United States, where the role and powers of the prosecutor are very different from those in Ireland. Furthermore it is believed that until now, at least, the objectionable features of plea bargaining referred to below have not been apparent in Irish courts. Lest they should tend to be, however, further consideration of the problem seems desirable.

Plea bargaining occurs when a defendant is unprepared to plead guilty to the indictment as it stands, but may be willing to change this stance if he receives some benefit from the prosecution.

The Director of Public Prosecutions may be prepared to countenance a plea bargain in the interests of the kind of administrative expediency already referred to, or to save his witnesses from the ordeal of having to testify. His counsel may be concerned about the quality of some of the prosecution evidence and may prefer to accept a plea to a lesser charge rather than risk a complete acquittal. There also exists the human possibility, albeit remote, that counsel for the prosecution, behaving unethically, could seek an accommodation with the defence on the ground of his own personal convenience.

It is submitted that the prosecution, having once decided to indict the accused for specific offences, should never, save in the most exceptional circumstances, *offer* to accept a plea of guilty to some lesser or alternative offence, or even *invite* the defence *to treat,* but should, in an appropriate case, be prepared to consider acceptance of an offer to plead guilty made spontaneously by the defence.

9. See, e.g., Alschuler, *The Prosecutor's Role in Plea Bargaining* 36 U. Chi. L. Rev. 50 (1968); Note: *The Unconstitutionality of Plea Bargaining* 83 Harv. L. Rev. 1387; Note: *Plea Bargaining and the Transformation of the Criminal Process* 90 Harv. L. Rev. 564; Whitman, *Judicial Plea Bargaining* 19 Stan. L. Rev. 1082 (1967).
10. See, e.g., Baldwin and McConville, *Negotiated Justice* (1977).

Inducements which may be offered to defendants by the prosecution

The prosecution may be prepared to accept a plea of guilty from an accused person for a number of reasons. Firstly, charges are often preferred in such a way as to encompass every possible offence that the evidence appears to disclose. This may result in a person being returned for trial on a large number of counts arising out of the same incident.[11] As a result of such a multiplicity of counts counsel for the prosecution may agree to enter a *nolle prosequi* in respect of a more serious charge in return for a plea to an offence of lesser gravity. The entry of a *nolle prosequi* cannot be questioned by the judge.[12] Such a reduction in the offence charged may, *de facto*, result in a fettering of the judicial power of sentencing within certain margins. If, for example, an accused is charged under section 27B of the Firearms Act, 1964, with the possession of a firearm with intent to endanger life, he may be sentenced to imprisonemnt for a period of up to ten years. If counsel for the prosecution is willing to enter a *nolle prosequi* in respect of the count under section 27B in return for a plea of guilty to possession in suspicious circumstances under section 27A of the same Act, the maximum sentence which the trial judge may impose is one of five years.

Alternatively the prosecution may indicate that, although it is not prepared to enter a *nolle prosequi* in respect of any count in the indictment, it is nonetheless prepared to accept a plea by an accused to a lesser charge. Thus, for example, in an indictment containing a single count of rape an accused, on arraignment, might plead not guilty to the charge of rape but guilty of indecent or common assault. In such a situation, irrespective of any indication by the prosecution to the defence in advance of the arraignment of its willingness to accept such a plea, it is a matter for the trial judge as to whether or not he is prepared to accept the plea entered by the defendant.

Another situation sometimes encountered is for the prosecutor, in exchange for a plea of guilty, to agree to outline the

11. See, however, pp. 252 sqq. supra, as to joinder of counts.
12. Supra, p. 76.

salient facts of the case to the trial judge in a way which presents the defendant in the most favourable light. The defendant may be prepared to accept this, even though the prosecutor is unwilling to countenance any change in the indictment as drafted or any plea to a lesser charge.

It has been stated that:[13]

> 'While it is impossible to lay down a hard and fast rule in any class of case upon when a plea for a lesser offence should be accepted by counsel for [the prosecution], (a) it must always be in the discretion of the judge whether he will allow it to be accepted, and (b) where nothing appears on the depositions which can be said to reduce the crime from the more serious offence charged to some lesser offence for which a verdict may be returned, the duty of counsel for [the prosecution] would be to present the offence charged in the indictment'.

This latter rule is one which is possibly more honoured in the breach than in the observance.

The role of the defendant in plea bargaining

It is axiomatic that any plea entered into by a defendant must be entirely voluntary. Any improper pressure exerted upon a defendant will render the subsequent disposition of the case a nullity. The parameters within which plea bargaining may legitimately take place must be clear.

Although the assent of the defendant must clearly be obtained to any arrangement finally arrived at by counsel, his active participation in the process of negotiation is extremely limited. A criticism of plea bargaining which is often advanced is that the defendant is often asked to assent to an agreement immediately before, or even during his trial, at a time when he is undergoing considerable stress.

Allegations are sometimes made by defendants that they have been improperly pressurised by their own counsel into adopting a course of action upon arraignment which they had never intended. Unfortunately the confidentiality which attaches to discussions between counsel for the two sides and between the defendant and his own counsel means that public scrutiny in the

13. Archbold, §4-60.

form of the Press or of an official transcript will not be available to test the validity or otherwise of any assertions that a defendant may make in this respect. Therein lies the real danger of the plea bargaining process because, whilst a disappointed defendant has a strong motive improperly to impugn the conduct of his counsel, it would nonetheless be unrealistic to exclude the possiblility that, in some instances, counsel may exert improper pressures on accused persons. Further as Baldwin and McConville point out:[14]

> 'If a barrister transgresses rules laid down by the courts or fails to conform to accepted ethical standards of behaviour, the accused is left very largely without redress'.

The role of defence counsel in advising his client as to his plea

The role of the defence counsel in advising his client as to the appropriate plea to enter, whether in exchange for some concession offered by the prosecution or otherwise, is a crucial one. In *R. v. Turner* Lord Parker said:[15]

> 'Counsel must be completely free to do what is his duty, namely to give the accused the best advice he can and if need be advice in strong terms. This will often include advice that a plea of guilty, showing an element of remorse, is a mitigating factor which may well enable the court to give a lesser sentence than would otherwise be the case. Counsel of course will emphasise that the accused must not plead guilty unless he has committed the acts constituting the offence charged.'

For the diligent and ethical counsel there may be a dilemma between trying to prevent an accused person from harming himself by contesting an extremely strong prosecution case while, at the same time, trying to ensure that the defendant makes a choice in the matter which is both informed and voluntary. Even the *Turner* guidelines do not obviate all the dangers inherent in such a situation. For example, where the defence counsel strongly advises a plea, acting, as he believes, within the limits of *Turner*, the defendant's perception of the same advice may be that he is being pressurised into a course of action which he does not wish to take. Paradoxically it must also be recognised that breaches of

14. Op. cit. at 54.
15. [1970] 2 Q.B. 321, 326.

ethical standards by counsel may be in the best interests of their clients, given current judicial sentencing policy.[16] By their failure to give any incentive whatever to a defendant to plead guilty, the courts in earlier centuries may have exhibited a greater wisdom than their modern counterparts.

The role of the trial judge before arraignment

Counsel for both the prosecution and the defence may wish to approach a trial judge, before the accused is arraigned, in connection with a number of matters. They may wish to ascertain, for example, whether the judge is prepared to accept a plea of guilty to a lesser charge or to try and ascertain whether or not a non-custodial sentence might be appropriate. However, any approach by counsel to the trial judge, whether before or indeed during the course of a trial, is fraught with danger. The Court of Appeal (Criminal Division) in England considered the proprieties of this practice in *R. v. Turner*.[17] In this case the defendant, who had a number of previous convictions, pleaded not guilty on arraignment to a charge of theft. During an adjournment his counsel who, to the knowledge of the defendant, had spoken to the trial judge, advised his client that in his opinion he would get a non-custodial sentence if he were re-arraigned and pleaded guilty, whereas if he continued to contest the charge there was a real possibility that he would go to gaol. Counsel emphasised that the ultimate choice of plea rested with the defendant. The defendant mistakenly thought his counsel was only amplifying the trial judge's view, and he agreed to be re-arraigned and to plead guilty.

The Court rejected any suggestion of undue influence by counsel but Lord Parker, in referring to the 'vexed question of so called "plea bargaining",' said:[18]

> 'There must be freedom of access between counsel and judge. Any discussion, however, which takes place must be between the judge and both counsel for the defence and counsel for the prosecution.

16. See Baldwin and McConville, op. cit. at 45.
17. [1970] 2 Q.B. 321.
18. Id. at 326-327.

If a solicitor representing the accused is in the court he should be allowed to attend the discussion if he so desires. This freedom of access is important because there may be matters calling for communication or discussion, which are of such a nature that counsel cannot in the interests of his client mention them in open court.

Purely by way of example, counsel for the defence may by way of mitigation wish to tell the judge that the accused has not long to live, is suffering maybe from cancer, of which he is and should remain ignorant. Again, counsel on both sides may wish to discuss with the judge whether it would be proper, in a particular case, for the prosecutor to accept a plea to a lesser offence. It is, of course, imperative that so far as possible justice must be administered in open court. Counsel should, therefore, only ask to see the judge when it is felt to be really necessary, and the judge must be careful only to treat such communications as private where, in fairness to the accused person, this is necessary.

The judge should, subject to the one exception referred to hereafter, never indicate the sentence which he is minded to impose. A statement that on a plea of guilty he would impose one sentence but that on a conviction following a plea of not guilty he would impose a severer sentence is one which should never be made. This could be taken to be undue pressure on the accused, thus depriving him of that complete freedom of choice which is essential. Such cases however are in the experience of the court happily rare. What on occasions does appear to happen however is that a judge will tell counsel that, having read the depositions and the antecedents, he can safely say that on a plea of guilty he will for instance, make a probation order, something which may be helpful to counsel in advising the accused. The judge in such a case is no doubt careful not to mention what he would do if the accused were convicted following a plea of not guilty. Even so, the accused may well get the impression that the judge is intimating that in that event a severer sentence, maybe a custodial sentence would result, so that again he may feel under pressure. This accordingly must also not be done.

The only exception to this rule is that it should be permissible for a judge to say, if it be the case, that whatever happens, whether the accused pleads guilty or not guilty, the sentence will or will not take a particular form, e.g. a probation order or a fine, or a custodial sentence.

Finally, where any such discussion on sentence has taken place between judge and counsel, counsel for the defence should disclose this to the accused and inform him of what took place.'

In *R. v. Quartey*[19] an appeal was taken against a sentence of two years imprisonment for conspiracy to evade the prohibition on the importation of cannabis. It was disclosed that counsel, during the trial, had gone to see the judge, who intimated that he would impose a sentence of eighteen months irrespective of whether the defendant was convicted or changed his plea. This was in itself clearly a breach of the guidelines laid down in *Turner*'s case. However, on hearing further evidence, the judge decided to increase the period of imprisonment in the event of conviction and informed counsel accordingly. In a second interview with the judge defence counsel was told that the judge was considering a period of three years imprisonment, but that there would be a reduction if the defendant were to plead guilty. The defence appealed on the basis that the judge was wrong to take the view that further evidence made the case against the appellant more serious, and also that the appellant had a grievance in view of the fact that he had lost the chance of an eighteen month sentence and was under pressure to change his plea. The Court of Appeal (Criminal Division) held that:[20]

> 'It was regrettable and wrong that information as to the sentence was sought and received on both occasions. It was regrettable that information was given that the sentence would be reduced if there were a change of plea because such information must be passed to the defendant and might result in a wrong plea being made under pressure.'

They nevertheless refused to interfere with the sentence which they thought was a light one. In *R. v. Inns*[21] the defendant was minded to plead not guilty to the theft of some wire which he told his counsel he believed had been abandoned. The judge in his chambers intimated to defence counsel that, if Inns were convicted, there would be a sentence of detention but, if he pleaded guilty, a more lenient course might be possible. Inns still refused to plead and the judge, on being informed of this, indicated that he was still of the same mind and refused an application by counsel for the defence to discharge himself from hearing the case.

19. [1975] Crim. L.R. 592.
20. Id.
21. 60 Cr. App. R. 231.

Inns then decided to plead guilty. The Court of Appeal, in ordering a new trial, said that the whole basis of a plea on arraignment was that the accused had a free choice. The law attached so much importance to a plea of guilty in open court that no further proof was required. A plea made under pressure of threats was not a proper plea and the proceedings thereafter were a nullity.

One of the great shortcomings of plea bargaining surfaced in Inns because the trial judge reported that the defence counsel had misunderstood him and that he had not intended any threat but only to indicate how his mind was working. In the absence of any record of such a meeting, misunderstanding cannot be tested by appellate courts. In any event, clearly what had been done infringed the *Turner* guidelines, and when counsel for the defence informed his client of the judge's comment, inevitably the client would feel pressurised.

In July,1975, the English Court of Appeal (Criminal Division) in *R. v. Plimmer*[22] stated that while it did not wish to depart from *Turner,* the practice of counsel going to see judges was, in general, undesirable.

Change of plea

A plea of guilty may be withdrawn by leave of the judge at any time before but not after sentence;[23] and, if the accused has pleaded not guilty and been put in charge of a jury, a plea of guilty may be substituted by leave of the judge.[24]

Consequences of plea

The procedure after reception of a plea of guilty is similar to that following conviction after a trial,[25] save that it will be necessary to outline the facts of the case to the judge, normally by calling a police officer in charge of or concerned with the case to do so, in addition to giving the antecedents of the accused. It is submitted that this is desirable in all cases since, even though the Judge may have read the Book of Evidence, if there is an appeal

22. 61 Cr. App. R. 264.
23. *R. v. Plummer* [1902] 2 K.B. 339.
24. Archbold §4-121; the practice in Ireland is then to discharge the jury.
25. Chapter 13, infra.

against sentence alone the Book will not form part of the transcript before the Court of Criminal Appeal.

XI. PLEA OF NOT GUILTY

If the accused pleads not guilty to the indictment, or to any count in the indictment which the prosecution does not withdraw, a jury must be empanelled to try him.

XII. APPLICATION FOR SEPARATE TRIALS

It has already been seen that a single indictment may contain a number of distinct counts or may be preferred against several accused.

Separate trials of different counts

The joinder of counts may be unsatisfactory from the point of view of the prosecution or from that of the defence. Too many counts, e.g. relating to a series of elaborate frauds, may tend to confuse the jury, and the prosecution may elect to proceed for the time being on some one or more of the counts, probably those which are the most serious, or in respect of which the evidence is strongest. Conversely, the presentation of a number of counts before the same jury may prejudice the accused. He is presumed to be innocent until his guilt is established, and evidence of his previous bad character is usually inadmissible. A jury having to try an accused person for a number of quite distinct offences may well be tempted to think that there cannot be smoke without fire, that the accused would hardly be facing such a variety of charges unless he was guilty of some at least. The Criminal Justice (Administration) Act, 1924,[1] provides that where, before trial or at any stage of a trial, the court is of opinion that the accused may be prejudiced or embarrassed in his defence by reason of being charged with more than one offence in the same indictment, or that for any other reason it is desirable to direct that he should be tried separately for any one or more offences charged in an indictment, the court may order a separate trial of any count or counts. In such a case the prosecution will be put to its election as

1. S. 6 (3).

to the charge or charges which are to proceed. The court has a discretion in the matter but must exercise it judicially so that the accused will not be embarrassed. A person might be identified by two different people in relation to two separate incidents – neither may be corroborated, but the jury, even after being warned as to the danger of acting on such visual identification, may well be tempted to think that each witness corroborates the other. A similar situation may exist as regards corroboration in the case of sexual offences.[2] The prosecution should not, however, be put to its election if there is no risk of embarrassment to the accused.[3]

It is submitted that the following statement by Lord Pearson in the House of Lords in *Ludlow v. Metropolitan Police Commissioner*, represents the law in Ireland:[4]

> 'The judge has no duty to direct separate trials [under the corresponding section of the English Indictments Act, 1915] unless in his opinion there is some special feature of the case which would make a joint trial of the several counts prejudicial or embarrassing to the accused and separate trials are required in the interests of justice. In some cases the offences charged may be too numerous and complicated; *R. v. King;*[5] *R. v. Bailey;*[6] or too difficult to disentangle; *R. v. Norman;*[7] so that a joint trial of all the counts is likely to cause confusion and the defence may be embarrassed or prejudiced. In other cases objection may be taken to the inclusion of a count on the ground that it is of a scandalous nature and likely to arouse in the minds of the jury hostile feelings against the accused: *R. v. Southern,*[8] *R. v. Muir,*[9] and *R. v. Fitzpatrick.*[10]'

Thus in *The People v. O'Connor*[11] it was held that the trial had not been prejudiced by the inclusion (before the Special Criminal Court) of forty-four charges relating to offences infringing an

2. See generally Archbold, §§1-75 sqq.
3. *R. v. Lockett* [1914] 2 K.B. 720.
4. [1971] A.C. 29, 41; see also *The People v. Wallace,* unrep. 22nd November, 1982 (C.C.A.) following *Harris v. Director of Public Prosecutions* [1952] A.C. 694.
5. [1897] 1 Q.B. 214.
6. [1924] 2 K.B. 300.
7. [1915] 1 K.B. 341.
8. 22 Cr. App. R. 6.
9. [1938] 2 All E.R. 516.
10. [1963] 1 W.L.R. 7.
11. 26th July, 1943, Frewen 42.

Order as to the sale of tea, flour and other commodities, when a full opportunity had been given to the defence to consider the evidence and an adjournment had been offered if necessary. Similarly, it was held in *Attorney General v. Reilly*[12] that the trial had not been prejudiced by the joinder of a large number of counts alleging the obtaining by false pretences or fraudulent conversion of different sums of money. On the other hand in *Attorney General v. Duffy*[13] it was held that the accused had been prejudiced by the trial together of a number of charges of gross indecency, with the danger of the jury's acceptance of corroboration in relation to one charge as corroboration in relation to others.

Separate trials of different accused.

It is in general desirable that where two or more persons are charged with the same offence, they should be tried together, not merely to save time and expense but also to secure that the same jury should deal with the entire case, but there are undoubtedly exceptions to this rule.[14]

Just as an accused may be prejudiced by the trial together of a number of counts, so several accused may be prejudiced by being tried together because the jury may be tempted to act on evidence admissible only against one when considering the case against another. A common example is where one accused has made a statement which implicates another. The statement, if admissible, is evidence against the person who made it, but it is not evidence against anybody else; although the jury must be so warned, the temptation will be there to overlook the warning.

Another example would be where the prosecution or defence wishes to call a witness who could not be called if two accused were tried together. The prosecution might want to call the wife of one accused (who would not usually be a competent witness for the prosecution against him) as a witness against the other accused; or might want to obtain a conviction against a thief, and then call him against a person charged on the same indictment

12. [1937] I.R. 118 (C.C.A.).
13. [1931] I.R. 144 (C.C.A.).
14. See Archbold, §§1-73, 1-74.

with receiving the stolen property. In such cases the prosecution may elect to proceed separately against separate accused. Alternatively one of the accused may wish to call his co-accused or the latter's wife, neither of whom would be compellable, and might ask for separate trials on that ground.

The trial judge has, accordingly, power to order separate trials whenever justice so requires. As Sullivan P. said in the Court of Criminal Appeal:[15]

> 'Where. . . persons jointly indicted plead not guilty, the trial Judge may direct that they be separately tried if, in his opinion, separate trials are desirable in the interests of justice. The trial Judge has a discretion in the matter which must be exercised judicially. The exercise of such discretion may be reviewed by this Court, and a re-trial directed, if we are satisfied that a refusal to direct separate trials has resulted in a miscarriage of justice.'

A mere statement by counsel that he would be seriously embarrassed, without indicating the nature or cause of that embarrasment, is not sufficient to require the judge to exercise his discretion to order separate trials.[16]

Kenny J. held in *The People v. Murtagh:*[17]

> '[T]he fact that one of the accused has made a statement which incriminates another of the accused is not by itself a matter which compels the trial Judge to grant separate trials: this is always a matter for the discretion of the trial Judge. When two or more accused are charged in connection with one transaction, the interests of justice may require that they should be tried together even if a statement made by one of them incriminates another of them. When two or more persons are charged in connection with a single transaction, it is possible for each of the accused to cast the entire blame for the transaction on the other if they are tried separately and this may result in the acquittal of both.'

Quoting Hewart L.C.J. in *R. v. Bywaters*[18], Kenny J. continued:

15. *Attorney General v. Joyce* [1929] I.R. 526, 537; approved in *The People v. Carney* [1955] I.R. 324; *The People v. Mulcahy* 87 I.L.T.R. 137 (C.C.A.).
16. *The People v. Carney*, supra.
17. [1966] I.R. 361, 363 (C.C.A.); and see *Attorney General v. Corcoran* 63 I.L.T.R. 145 (C.C.A.).
18. 17 Cr. App. R. 66, 68.

> '[W]hat is meant by miscarriage of justice? It means that a person has been improperly found guilty. It is idle to suppose that a miscarriage of justice has taken place if a prisoner against whom there is overwhelming evidence suffers some further evidence, because another prisoner goes into the witness-box.'

The fact that the statements of two accused although not inculpating each other are incompatible is not a ground for ordering separate trials.[19]

19. *The People v. Sykes* [1958] I.R. 355 (C.C.A.).

CHAPTER 12

THE JURY

Juries were formerly selected from a panel summoned from time to time and restricted to persons having a certain property qualification, and in practice to men, in accordance with the provisions of the Juries Act, 1927. The property qualification and exclusion in practice of women was held by the Supreme Court to be unconstitutional in *de Búrca v. The Attorney General.*[1] Eligibility for jury service is now governed by the Juries Act, 1976.[2] The Act lays down who are qualified to act as jurors and distinguishes between persons who are ineligible and persons who, although otherwise eligible, may be disqualified, and provides also for persons who, although eligible and qualified, may be excused if called upon to serve.

Eligibility

For the purposes of the Act each county (including any county borough[3] within its geographical boundries) is a jury district, but the Minister for Justice may by order divide a county into two or more districts or limit a jury district to a part or parts of a county.[4] Every issue triable with a jury is triable with a jury called from a panel drawn from the jury district in which the court is sitting.[5]

Subject to the provisions of the Act, every citizen aged 18 years

1. [1976] I.R. 38 (S.C.).
2. The corresponding enactment in England is the Juries Act, 1974, as amended by the Criminal Law Act, 1977, s. 43.
3. Juries Act, 1976, s. 5 (1).
4. Id. s. 5 (2); see Jury Districts Order, 1976 (S.I. 57 of 1976), Jury Districts Order, 1977 (S.I. 59 of 1977).
5. Juries Act, 1976, s. 5 (4).

and upwards and under the age of 70 years who is entered in a register of Dáil Éireann electors in a particular jury district is qualified and liable to serve as a juror for the trial of all issues which are for the time being triable with a jury drawn from that district unless for the time being ineligible or disqualified.[6]

Apart from the age limits, however, certain persons are declared to be ineligible,[7] and accordingly may not serve even if they wish to do so. They are listed in Part 1 of the First Schedule to the Act and include the President of Ireland, persons concerned with the administration of justice (e.g. practising barristers and solicitors, solicitors' apprentices and clerks, court officials, court stenographers, members of the Garda Síochána and prison and welfare officers), members of the Defence Forces, and persons who are illiterate or deaf, or mental patients.

Disqualification

A person is disqualified for jury service, and may likewise not serve even if he wishes, if he has been convicted of an offence in any part of Ireland and has at any time been *sentenced* to imprisonment or penal servitude for life or for a term of five years or more or to detention under section 103 of the Children Act, 1908 (which relates to the detention of children and young persons convicted of a capital offence) or under the corresponding law of Northern Ireland,[8] and in such a case it is irrelevant whether he served the sentence or any part of it. He is also disqualified if, within ten years, he has been convicted of an offence in any part of Ireland and has *served* any part of a sentence of penal servitude, or of a sentence for a term of imprisonment of at least three months, or a sentence of detention in Saint Patrick's Institution or in a corresponding institution in Northern Ireland.[9] A conviction outside Ireland involves no disqualification, although, if known to the prosecution, it might well result in the juror being challenged.[10]

6. Id. s. 6.
7. Id. s. 7; the complete list will be found in Appendix C, Part I, infra.
8. Id. s. 8 (a).
9. Id. s. 8 (b).
10. Infra, pp. 302 sqq.

Excusal

Certain persons, who are entitled to serve if they wish, may be excused as of right if they inform the County Registrar that they wish to be,[11] whilst others may be excused at the discretion of the County Registrar or the Court.[12]

Those excusable as of right include any person who has served on a jury or attended for jury service in the three years before service of the jury summons on him, or still enjoys the benefit of an excusal from service given at the conclusion of a trial. In addition a number of others who have a right to be excused are listed in Part II of the First Schedule to the Act. These include members of the Oireachtas, persons in Holy Orders and members of religious communities, registered medical practitioners, nurses and chemists, wholetime students at educational establishments and persons aged from 65 to 70 years. Others are excusable as of right on production of a certificate from the head of their department or the like that they cannot be spared, and these include Civil Servants, employees of local authorities, professors, lecturers and teachers.[13]

If the person concerned is ill or unable for any other reason to do so himself, some other person may apply on his behalf[14] to the County Registrar to be excused from attending during the whole or any part of the sittings in question and the County Registrar may excuse him accordingly, if satisfied there is good reason so to do.[15] If the County Registrar refuses the application, the person concerned may appeal to the court at which he has been summoned to attend;[16] the procedure for the appeal (including the designation of the judge to hear it and the time within which and the manner in which it is to be brought) is to be directed by the President of the High Court or the Circuit Court as appropriate; and the decision of the court is final.[17] The judge presiding over the court during a sitting has a like discretion to excuse a juror

11. Juries Act, 1976, 9 (1).
12. Id. s. 9 (2).
13. The complete list will be found in Appendix C, Part II, infra.
14. Juries Act, 1976, s. 9 (3).
15. Id. s. 9 (2).
16. Id. s. 9 (4).
17. Id. s. 9 (5), (6).

from attendance or further attendance.[18]

Jurors are selected from the current register of Dáil Éireann electors and a panel (omitting any person whom the County Registrar knows or believes not to be qualified) is to be drawn up whenever necessary by some random or other non-discriminatory selection.[19]

A written summons, in the form prescribed by regulations,[20] must then be delivered to each juror by hand, or sent by post addressed to him at his address in the current register,[21] requiring him to attend the court on a specified day and at a specified time and thereafter as the court may direct.[22] The summons must be accompanied by a notice informing him of the effect of the sections of the Act relating to qualification, ineligibility, disqualification and excusal as of right, and of the penalties for making false representations, and for serving when ineligible or disqualified,[23] and the notice should indicate that the person concerned may apply to the County Registrar to have the summons withdrawn, if for any reason he is not qualified or wishes or is entitled to be excused.[24]

The number summoned will depend on the number of cases to be tried, it being remembered that some people may not turn up and that some may be challenged in any particular case. In practice the whole panel may be required to attend on the first day of the relevant sittings but in the Central Criminal Court and Dublin Circuit Court part only of the panel is required to attend on the first day, and the remainder on some later day or days. If, however, it appears to the judge that there will or may not be enough to try any issue he may require the County Registrar to make up the deficiency by summoning more persons who are qualified and liable to serve.[25] The judge may specify the area from which such persons are to be summoned (which may be the

18. Id. s. 9 (7).
19. Id. ss. 10, 11.
20. Jury Summons Regulations, 1976 (S.I. 56 of 1976).
21. Juries Act, 1976, s. 13 (1).
22. Id. s. 12 (1).
23. Infra, pp. 300-301. The notice need not, apparently, state the penalties for non-attendance.
24. Juries Act, 1976, s. 12 (2).
25. Id. s. 14 (1).

area in the vicinity of the Court).[26] If any such person applies to the County Registrar to be excused and is refused, he has no right of appeal;[27] but, presumably, he may still be excused by the judge.

A person employed under a contract of service or apprenticeship is deemed to be so employed during any period when he is absent in order to comply with a jury summons, and is entitled to be paid accordingly; and any contractual provision to the contrary is void.[28]

The names and addresses of those required to attend on the day in question are called out; if any fail to answer, their names and addresses will usually be called out a second time, and if they still fail to answer the procedure for prosecution may be put in hand.

Offences

Formerly, if a person failed to attend court when required to do so, he might be fined by the judge on the spot, but this has been altered and he is now liable to prosecution in the District Court.

If a person who has been duly summoned fails without reasonable cause to attend in compliance with the summons on any day when required by the court, he is liable on summary conviction to a fine not exceeding £50.[29] He is also liable to a similar penalty if, having attended, he is not available when called upon, or is unfit to serve by reason of drink or drugs.[30] He is, however, not liable for non-attendance (except when an order has been made by the judge to make up a deficiency) unless the summons was served at least fourteen days before the date specified for his attendance.[31]

A similar penalty may also be imposed on a person who has been duly summoned and makes a false representation,[32] or causes or permits such a representation on behalf of another in

26. Id. s. 14 (2).
27. Id. s. 14 (3).
28. Id. s. 29.
29. Id. s. 34 (1).
30. Id. s. 34 (2).
31. Id. s. 34 (3).
32. Id. s. 35 (1).

order to enable the latter to be excused from jury service;[33] or on a person who fails without reasonable excuse to answer a question, or recklessly gives a false answer, when questioned by a judge to determine whether he is qualified;[34] or if he serves on a jury knowing that he is ineligible,[35] or if he refuses to be sworn;[36] the penalty for serving when a person knows he is disqualified is a fine not exceeding £200.[37]

Empanelling the jury

The selection of persons to serve on a particular jury is to be made by ballot in open court,[1] but a ballot is not required in the case of persons who have been summoned to make up a deficiency after the balloting has begun.[2] The practice is for the Registrar of the court to call a certain number of jurors towards the jury box, usually more than the minimum required (in anticipation of possible challenges) and then for him to call on each individually to be sworn. The Act provides[3] that, before the selection is begun, the judge must warn the jurors present that they must not serve if they are ineligible or disqualified and as to the penalty for so doing; and he must invite anyone who knows that he is not qualified or is in doubt, or who may have an interest in or in connection with the case or the parties to communicate the fact to the judge, orally or otherwise, if he is selected. It is to be noted that having an interest is not itself a disqualification but it may be a ground for a challenge, and the judge may at any stage direct that a person summoned shall not serve if he for any stated reason considers it is desirable in the interests of justice to give such a direction.[4] The mere fact, however, that a juror may have some indirect interest is not a ground for treating the trial as unsatisfactory.[5]

33. Id. s. 35 (2).
34. Id. s. 35 (3).
35. Id. s. 36 (1).
36. Id. s. 37.
37. Id. s. 36 (2).
1. Id. s. 15 (1).
2. Id. s. 15 (2).
3. Id. s. 15 (3).
4. Id. s. 24.
5. *The People v. Singer* [1975] I.R. 408 (C.C.A.).

Challenges

A challenge is an objection to a particular juror. It may be 'peremptory' or 'for cause'. Anyone is entitled to reasonable facilities to inspect a particular panel free of charge, and either the prosecution or the accused is entitled to a copy of the panel, free of charge, on application to the County Registrar.[6] These rights are exercisable at any time between the issue of the summons and the close of the trial or the time when it is no longer possible to have a trial with a jury.[7] The right includes a right to be shown, on request, all alterations to the panel and the names of any persons summoned to make up a deficiency, and to be told of any excusals.[8]

A peremptory challenge is one for which no reason is given. The prosecution may have reason to believe that, because of the previous history or associations of a juror, he would be prejudiced against it.[9] The defence may well think that, for one reason or another, a juror may be prejudiced against the accused. It might, for example, consider a shop-keeper to be undesirable on a jury to try the accused for burglary of a shop. Whilst only the names and addresses of voters appear on the Dáil register, the notice accompanying the summons may request the addressee to inform the Registrar of his occupation, so that it may be included on the panel; but there appears to be no obligation on the addressee to supply the information.

The Crown formerly enjoyed the right to require any number of jurors to 'stand by' i.e. to postpone consideration of challenge of the juror for cause until the panel had been 'gone through' and a full jury for the case in question had not been sworn. A similar right was given to the Attorney General by section 59 of the Juries Act, 1927, now repealed, but having regard to the observations of Finlay P. in *The State (O'Callaghan) v. Ó hUadhaigh,*[10] it appears no longer to be exercisable in Ireland, although it may still be exercised in England, where the prosecution has a

6. Juries Act, 1976, s. 16 (1).
7. Id. s. 16 (2).
8. Id. s. 16 (4).
9. Cf. *R. v. Mason* [1981] Q.B. 881.
10. [1977] I.R. 42 (H.C.).

further safeguard against jurors likely to be prejudiced, in that majority verdicts are permissible.[11]

The Juries Act, 1976,[12] provides that the prosecution and each accused person may, on the trial of a criminal issue triable with a jury, challenge seven jurors and no more without showing cause and any person so challenged is not to be included in the jury.[13] It is to be noted that if there are several accused each has an individual right to challenge seven, but the prosecution may only challenge seven, regardless of the number of accused.

The Act further provides[14] that in any such trial the prosecution and each accused person may challenge any number of jurors for cause shown. The cause of the challenge must be shown immediately upon its being made and it is then a matter for the judge to allow or disallow it as he thinks proper.[15] Thus it appears not to be permissible for the party challenging the juror to question him before doing so, but presumably that party or the judge may question the juror in order to establish or test the validity of the cause;[16] it might relate to the qualification of the juror, but much more probably to the danger of prejudice.[17]

Every challenge must be made immediately after the name of the juror is called out, i.e. before he is asked to go into the jury box, and before the administration of the oath to him has begun, i.e. before the Registrar of the court begins to say the words of the oath to the juror.[18] The Act does not specifically provide that an accused person who is not represented by solicitor or counsel must be informed of his right to challenge, but this is invariably done. If he is represented, the practice is for any challenge to be made by his solicitor, and for any challenge on behalf of the prosecution to be made by the solicitor for the prosecution, and it is generally regarded in Ireland as undesirable for a challenge to be made by counsel, although there appears to be no rule against it.

11. See Archbold, §4-139.
12. S. 20 (2).
13. Juries Act, 1976, s. 20 (3).
14. Id. s. 21 (2).
15. Id. s. 21 (3).
16. See Archbold, §4-162.
17. See Archbold, §4-160, 4-161.
18. Juries Act, 1976, s. 17 (4).

Even if a juror is not challenged the court ought to excuse him if he is obviously unfit to perform his duty.[19]

Formerly jurors were sworn in groups but now they must be sworn separately.[20] The Registrar must call out the juror's name and direct him to take the Testament[21] in his hand and must then administer an oath to him; if the juror objects to being sworn in the ordinary manner, he must do so immediately after he is called to go into the jury box and before the administration of the oath has begun.[22] If he refuses to be sworn, or insists on being sworn in a manner not authorised by the Juries Act or otherwise, he must not be included in that jury.[23] Subject to the foregoing remarks the juror must hold the Testament in his uplifted hand and repeat after the Registrar:[24]

> I swear by Almighty God that I will well and truly try the issue whether the accused is (or are) guilty or not guilty of the offence (*or* the several offences) charged in the indictment preferred against him (*or* her, *or* them) and a true verdict give according to the evidence.

If, however, the juror states that he professes no faith or that the taking of an oath is contrary to his religious belief, he may make an affirmation instead of taking an oath or may take an oath in any other manner provided by statute,[25] and if he states that he has a religious belief but is neither of the Christian nor the Jewish faith he may, by permission of the judge, be sworn in any manner which the juror states to be binding on him;[26] but the oath must be administered to every juror in the ordinary manner without question, unless the juror appears to be physically incapable of taking the oath in that manner, or objects to taking the oath in that manner and satisfies the judge that he is entitled to take the oath in some other manner.[27] The form of affirmation is

19. *Mansell v. R.* 8 St. Tr. (N.S.) 831, Archbold, §4-164.
20. Juries Act, 1976, s. 17 (2).
21. The New Testament for Christians and the Old for Jews; Juries Act, 1976, s. 17 (7).
22. Id. s. 17 (1), (3).
23. Id. s. 17 (5); but he will be guilty of an offence under section 37 of the Act.
24. Juries Act, 1976, ss. 18 (1), 19 (1).
25. Id. s. 18 (2), Oaths Act, 1888, s. 1.
26. Juries Act, 1976, s. 18 (3).
27. Id. s. 18 (4).

'I, (AB), do solemnly, sincerely, and truly declare and affirm' followed by the words of the oath.[28]

In addition it seems that if the juror desires to swear with uplifted hand, in the form and manner in which an oath is usually administered in Scotland he must be permitted to do so without further question.[29]

Once the oath has been administered, and taken, the fact that the person taking it had no religious belief does not invalidate the oath.[30]

The number of jurors to be sworn is, by long tradition, twelve.[31] If less than twelve are sworn the verdict will be ineffectual; but if more are sworn it appears that the subsequent proceedings will be valid, the jury consisting of the first twelve sworn.[32]

Further consideration of the functions and duties of the jury, and so forth, when empanelled, is postponed to Chapter 13.

28. Oaths Act, 1888, s. 2.
29. Id. s. 5.
30. Id. s. 3.
31. Bacon, Abr. Juries, A.
32. 2 Hale, 296.

CHAPTER 13

THE TRIAL

I. PRELIMINARY

Functions of the judge, the jury and counsel[1]

The functions of judge and jury in a criminal trial are distinct. The judge presides over the court and directs its procedures, and on all matters of law he is the only judge and the jury is bound to accept his directions; on all matters of fact, on the other hand, the judge may comment, but the sole arbiters are the jury and he should so inform them. It has been said that:[2]

> '[The constitutional right to a trial with a jury envisages] a trial before a judge and jury, at which the judge would preside, ensure that all conditions necessary for a fair and proper trial of that nature are complied with, decide all matters deemed to be matters of law, and direct the jury as to the legal principles and rules they are to observe and apply; and in which the jury, constituted in a manner calculated to ensure the achievement of the proper exercise of their functions, would under the governance of the judge, be the arbiters of all disputed issues of fact and, in particular, the issue of guilt or innocence.'

The function of counsel is to present and conduct the case on behalf of the prosecution or the accused, whichever he represents.

In the Central Criminal Court and Circuit Court counsel for the prosecution are invariably nominated by the Director of Public Prosecutions or, in certain fishery cases, by the Attorney General.[3]

1. The term counsel is normally used throughout this Chapter as including a solicitor, who is entitled to appear in all courts by virtue of the Courts Act, 1971, s. 17.
2. *The People v. O'Shea*, unrep. 2nd November, 1982 (S.C.) *per* Henchy, J. at p. 30 of judgment.
3. Fisheries Act, 1978, s. 18.

The accused is fully entitled, if he wishes, to conduct his own case, although if he has briefed counsel who has begun to conduct the defence the judge appears to have a discretion whether to allow him to dispense with the services of his counsel.[4] He is, however, entitled to be represented by counsel, and, as has been seen, may often be entitled to free legal aid.[5] The English custom whereby an accused person might retain any counsel whom he saw robed in court to accept a 'dock brief' for a nominal fee was never applied in Ireland.

If either counsel refers to matters of law he should make it clear that he is expressing his own views, which are subject to any directions to be given by the judge.[6]

Throughout the case counsel for the prosecution should regard himself as assisting in the administration of justice rather than as advocating a cause.[7] It is not his duty to obtain a conviction by all means, but fairly and impartially to exhibit all the facts to the jury, giving them such guidance as to the law, subject to the directions of the judge, as may be necessary for them to apply the facts to the case.[8]

Counsel for the defence is, however, in a different position, in so far as his primary duty, within certain limits, is to his client. The importance of that duty has been stressed by several rulings of the General Council of the Bar of Ireland. He should never accept a brief for the defence 'subject to commitments'; once he has accepted the brief, whether under legal aid or otherwise it takes priority over other matters; he should follow the case through to the end, even though it takes a course not anticipated when the brief was originally accepted, and should not accept any other commitment which conflicts with this obligation.[9] He should remain with his client, even though the latter refuses to accept his advice and counsel is convinced that, if the accused

4. Archbold §4-19; *R. v. Lyons* 68 Cr. App. R. 104; see p. 214, supra.
5. Chapter 8, supra; see *The State (Healy) v. Donoghue* [1976] I.R. 325 (S.C.) discussed in that Chapter.
6. Archbold §4-177; *R. v. Courvoisier* 9 C.& P.362.
7. Boulton, *Conduct and Etiquette at the Bar*, 6th Edn. (1975); cf. *The People v. Kerins* [1945] I.R. 339 (C.C.A.); see also Code of Conduct of the Bar of England and Wales (1980) 46, sqq.
8. *R. v. Puddick* 4 F. & F. 497; *R. v. Banks* [1916] 2 K.B. 621.
9. Bar Council Rulings, 21st June, 1974, 5th March, 1979.

appeared in person, he might be treated more leniently.[10] He should not withdraw from the case because of remarks made by the judge, and indeed such remarks may make it more incumbent upon him to remain with his client and protect the latter's interests.[11] He has in an appropriate case an absolute discretion as to what consultations and what interviews he holds, and no obstacle should be placed in his way which might hamper his conduct of the defence.[12]

At the same time counsel's duty to his client means that, if he is to perform that duty properly, and to do his best for his client he must be properly instructed; and he also owes a duty to the court. The Bar Council has ruled (although no doubt emergencies may arise) that a barrister should not conduct a criminal case on indictment unless given instructions a week ahead of the hearing, including the Book of Evidence, a statement from the accused taken by his solicitor, the indictment, the statements of any witnesses to be called on behalf of the accused, and confirmation that any proofs advised by him have been carried out.[13] Bearing in mind his duty to the court, counsel 'may not assert that which he knows to be a lie. He may not connive at, much less attempt to substantiate, a fraud',[14] although defence counsel is not obliged to disclose any previous convictions which his client may have, even if the prosecution has mistakenly led the court to believe that no such convictions exist.[15] It is conceived that in general there are no differences between the practice and traditions of the Irish Bar and the English Bar.

Counsel for the accused may well believe his client to be guilty, but it is for the prosecution to prove it beyond a reasonable doubt. Problems may arise, however, if the accused confesses his guilt; if he does so before proceedings begin, counsel probably will not accept the brief, but if the brief has been accepted, counsel's withdrawal may prejudice his client. In such cases he clearly cannot put his client into the witness box to give evidence which

10. Id. 5th December, 1972.
11. Id. 20th October, 1961.
12. Id. 15th December, 1972.
13. Id. 21st May, 1979.
14. Boulton, op. cit. 71; Code of Conduct, supra, para. 149.
15. Boulton, op. cit. 76.

will, to his knowledge, be perjured; nor may he adduce evidence which he also knows to be false as a result of the confession, nor may he suggest that somebody else committed the crime. He may, however, raise any technical objections or objections to the admissibility of evidence and, within the limits to which the confession may have restricted him, cross-examine the witnesses for the prosecution.[16]

Subject to the foregoing remarks it is submitted that the following statement of principle by the Chairman of the English Bar, made in 1976,[17] is equally applicable in Ireland:

> 'It is the duty of counsel when defending an accused on a criminal charge to present to the court, fearlessly and without regard to his personal interests, the defence of that accused. It is not his function to determine the truth or falsity of that defence, nor should he permit his personal opinion of that defence to influence his conduct of it. No counsel may refuse to defend because of his opinion of the character of the accused nor of the crime charged. That is a cardinal rule of the Bar, and it would be a grave matter in any free society were it not. Counsel also has a duty to the court and to the public. This duty includes the clear presentation of the issues and the avoidance of waste of time, repetition and prolixity. In the conduct of every case counsel must be mindful of this public responsibility'.

In conclusion, it may be appropriate to cite an extract from the speech of Lord Diplock in a recent case in the House of Lords:[18]

> 'It cannot be too often stressed that verbose justice is not necessarily good justice. There is virtue, both from the point of view of the prosecution and from the point of view of the defence, in incisiveness, decisiveness and conciseness, not only in addressing juries but in the general conduct of a case, the examination and cross-examination of witnesses, the submission of legal argument, and in summing up. A long trial is not necessarily a better one if a shorter one would have sufficed.'

The jury

When a jury has been empanelled and the trial is ready to start the accused is given into their charge – the count or counts to which he has pleaded not guilty are read over to them and they

16. Id. pp. 78-79; see also Archbold §4-317.
17. Reproduced, 62 Cr. App. R. 193-194.
18. *R. v. Lawrence* [1982] A.C. 510, 517.

are told that the issue they have to try is whether the accused is guilty or not guilty of the offence or offences with which he is charged.

By custom communications from the jury to the judge are made and their verdict is verified by their foreman. Until 1976, the first juror sworn acted as foreman; but now the choice is to be made by the jurors themselves, at such time as the judge may direct (usually before the trial begins) or, in the absence of a direction, before the jury bring in their verdict or any other communication to the judge.[1]

The jurors may separate at any time before considering their verdict, except where the judge otherwise directs.[2] They should, however, be warned not to discuss the case with anybody other than among themselves,[3] and in particular they should not speak to a witness, although, if it is shown that the result of such conversation could not have prejudiced the accused, the trial may not be regarded as unsatisfactory:[4] but even mixing with strangers over a prolonged period by members of the jury, as such, may render a trial gravely unsatisfactory, notwithstanding that the accused is not shown to have been prejudiced.[5]

The judge may at any stage direct that a person summoned to serve as a juror shall not serve, or continue to serve, as a juror, if he considers that for any stated reason it is desirable in the interests of justice that he should give such a direction.[6] It may happen that after the trial has progressed some juror may realise that he knows the injured party when he sees him, or has some prior knowledge of the case. In addition, the judge may, for good reason, excuse a juror during the course of a trial from further service in the trial.[7]

1. Juries Act, 1976, s. 15 (4).
2. Id. s. 25.
3. *R. v. Prime* 57 Cr. App. R. 632.
4. *R. v. Twiss* [1918] 2 K.B. 853.
5. Cf. *The People v. Heffernan (No. 2)* [1950] I.R. 206 (C.C.A.) following *R. v. Taylor* [1950] N.I. 57; both cases related to trials for murder during which separation of the jury was not at the time permitted; see, however, *The People v. Quinn* [1965] I.R. 366 (S.C.) in which brief conversation between a juror and the accused was held not to have been such as to prejudice a fair hearing.
6. Juries Act, 1976, s. 24.
7. Id. s. 9 (7). This sub-section relates also to excusal from service, supra, p. 298; excusal during a trial is presumably to be considered in the same context. The trial

Whenever in the course of a trial a juror is discharged owing to his being incapable through illness or any other cause,[8] or because the judge excuses him or directs that he should not continue to serve, as indicated in the foregoing paragraph, the jury remains properly constituted and the trial will proceed and a verdict may be given by the reduced number of jurors, unless the judge otherwise directs or the number of jurors is reduced below ten.[9] If, as a result of jurors being discharged or excused, only nine or fewer jurors are left, those who are left are no longer competent to act and must be discharged; otherwise the judge appears to have complete discretion, although he may, particularly in a serious case, invite the views of the prosecution and defence.

If the judge directs that the jury should not separate, or if they have retired to consider their verdict, they are put in charge of an officer of the court or police officer, who takes an oath that he will not permit separation or allow conversation and so forth with others.[10]

View by jury

The judge may at any time before the jury have given their verdict direct that the jurors shall have a view of any specific place, which in his opinion it is expedient that they should see, and may adjourn the trial at such stage and for such time as appears to be convenient.[11] He may, however, only make such an order on the application of the prosecution or of the accused.[12] He must give such directions as appear to him to be expedient for the purpose of preventing any communication with the jurors during the execution of his order.[13] If it is alleged that on the view the jury has received evidence in the absence of the judge and of the

does not begin until the accused has at least been put in charge of the jury: *The People v. Moriarty* [1945] Ir. Jur. Rep. 63 (Cent. Crim. Ct.).

8. Perhaps because prevented by weather or accident from attending the Court; the question appears to be one for the exercise of judicial discretion.
9. Juries Act, 1976, s. 23.
10. Archbold §4-441; 2 Hale 296.
11. Juries Act, 1976, s. 22 (1).
12. Id. s. 22 (3); the expenses of conveyance of the jurors are payable out of public funds; id.
13. Id. s. 22 (4).

accused, it is apparently for the judge to investigate the facts and ascertain whether such an irregularity has occurred.[14]

Publicity of proceedings

At common law every trial on indictment had to be held in a public court with open doors.[1] The Constitution[2] now provides that, save in such special and limited cases as may be prescribed by law, justice shall be administered in public. Reference has already been made to the exclusion of members of the public in the course of a preliminary examination in the District Court;[3] other exceptions are as follows:

(a) All proceedings under the Punishment of Incest Act, 1908, must be held *in camera*.[4]

(b) The Court may in any criminal proceedings of an indecent or obscene nature exclude all persons other than officers of the Court, persons directly concerned in the proceedings, *bona fide* representatives of the Press and such other persons as the Court may, in its discretion, permit to remain.[5]

(c) Where a person who is, in the opinion of the Court, under the age of 17 years is called as a witness in any proceedings in relation to an offence against, or any conduct contrary to, decency or morality, the Court may direct the exclusion of all persons other than the members or officers of the Court, the parties to the case, their counsel or solicitors, persons otherwise directly concerned in the case, and *bona fide* representatives of a newspaper or press agency.[6] If, however, the accused is under 21, or where the offence is of an indecent or obscene nature and the person with or against whom the offence is alleged to have been committed is under that age or is a female, a parent or other relative or friend is entitled to remain in Court during the whole of the hearing.[7]

14. *R. v. Martin* L.R. 1 C.C.R. 378; see also Archbold §4-41, bearing in mind that in England there is no statutory provision corresponding to those in the Juries Act, 1976, governing views by the jury.
1. Archbold §4-1.
2. Article 34.1.
3. Chapter 9, supra.
4. Punishment of Incest Act, 1908, s. 5.
5. Criminal Justice Act, 1951, s. 20 (3).
6. Children Act, 1908, ss. 114, 131, as amended by the Children Act, 1941, s. 29.
7. Criminal Justice Act, 1951, s. 20 (4).

(d) Children under 15 (other than infants in arms) may not be present in Court during the trial of other persons except for so long as their presence is required as witnesses or otherwise for the purposes of justice.[8]

(e) In the course of proceedings for the major offences under the Official Secrets Act, 1963, the Court must order that part of the hearing should be *in camera* if the prosecution makes an application to that effect on the ground that the publication of any evidence given or statement made during that part of the hearing would be prejudicial to the safety or preservation of the State; but the verdict and sentence (if any) must be given in public.[9]

(f) Members of the general public may in certain circumstances be excluded from a hearing by a Special Criminal Court.[10]

(g) Whilst there is no statutory provision to that effect, it is submitted that every Court retains for the conduct of its own proceedings an inherent power to exclude or eject persons who disturb the proceedings.[11]

Adjournment of the Trial

If a trial is not concluded on the day on which it began the judge may adjourn it from day to day, and so on from time to time.[12] An adjournment from Wednesday to the following Monday has been held to render the trial unsatisfactory,[13] but not an adjournment over the week-end after the conclusion of the final address by counsel for the accused.[14]

II. THE CASE FOR THE PROSECUTION

When the trial is ready to start counsel for the prosecution 'opens' the case, i.e. he summarises, in greater or less detail according to the nature of the case, the facts that it is intended to prove before the jury. His opening should be such as to give the jury the opportunity of considering any discrepancy between

8. Children Act, 1908, ss. 115, 131, as amended.
9. Official Secrets Act, 1963, s. 12.
10. Chapter 14, infra.
11. Archbold §§4-1, 4-2.
12. *R. v. Castro* L.R. 9 Q.B. 350, 5 Q.B.D. 490.
13. *The People v. Jackson* [1972] I.R. 345 (C.C.A.).
14. *Re Lucey* [1972] I.R. 347 (S.C.).

what a witness is expected to prove and his actual evidence. He should not, however, open evidence to which objection may be taken on the ground that it is inadmissible, such as a statement made by the accused.[1] If he does, and the evidence is eventually ruled to be inadmissible, the jury may have to be discharged and a new trial ordered.[2] If in doubt he should ascertain from the defence, if it is willing at this stage to disclose its attitude, whether objection may be taken.

Having opened the case, counsel for the prosecution calls the witnesses for the prosecution. He should call or make available all witnesses whom he considers to be material and whose attendance can be secured,[3] even though some of them may be prejudicial to the case for the prosecution.[4] He may hand in documents which 'prove themselves', but apart from that virtually all the evidence must be given orally and there is no provision for 'admissions' in a criminal trial, such as exists in England.[5]

The defence is, however, entitled to know the case to be answered, and accordingly evidence of which the substance is not contained in the Book of Evidence, and of which no notice has been given, should not be adduced, although it may still be admissible.[6] A witness may unexpectedly add something prejudicial to the defence which would not have been in his statement to the police; it is submitted that in an appropriate case the prosecution or the defence may ask for a reasonable adjournment of the trial in order that notice of additional evidence may be served or that the evidence which has been given may be considered by the defence; in some cases, however, the damage may have been such as to require discharge of the jury and a new trial.

If the return for trial is questioned, it should be proved; but

1. *Attorney General v. Stevens* [1934] L.J. Ir. 118; *The People v. O'Shea*, 27th July, 1943, Frewen 50.
2. Archbold §4-177.
3. *The People v. Byrne* [1974] I.R. 1 (C.C.A.).
4. *The People v. Kerins* [1945] I.R. 339. (C.C.A.); the duty of counsel who has evidence which he considers false was left open in that case, but it is submitted that he is not bound to call it.
5. Criminal Justice Act, 1967, s. 10. A similar provision was introduced in Ireland by the Criminal Justice Bill, 1967, s. 25, but was never enacted.
6. *R. v. Wright* 25 Cr. App. R. 35.

there is a *prima facie* presumption of its validity.[7]

The former practice whereby counsel for the prosecution read the answer, if any, made by the accused to the District Justice at the conclusion of the preliminary examination, is no longer the rule in practice, although any such statement *may* be read as part of the evidence.[8]

Record of proceedings

The Criminal Appeal Act, 1907, which established the Court of Criminal Appeal in England provided that a shorthand note was to be taken of the proceedings at the trial of any person on indictment, if the accused, if convicted, might be entitled to appeal. In Ireland there appears to be no such requirement save by implication, in that any appeal to the Court of Criminal Appeal is to be heard on the basis of a transcript of the evidence.[9]

This note or transcript, taken by an official stenographer, contains the evidence, any objection to the evidence, legal arguments, any statement by the accused,[10] the summing-up and the sentence imposed; but unless the trial judge so orders it does not include counsel's addresses to the jury. In *Attorney General v.Joyce*,[11] in which the evidence had been given in Irish and translated into English, it was held on appeal to the Court of Criminal Appeal that a transcript of the translation was sufficient where there was no question as to its accuracy, but Kennedy C.J. observed:[12]

> '[I]t is the duty of the official stenographers to report every case fully and in every detail, and certainly, in a case where evidence is given in the Irish language, it is the duty of the stenographer employed for that purpose to record every word of the evidence so given in that language, and, if he fails to do so, it may have very grave consequences. . . I therefore take this opportunity of impressing upon the stenographers the importance of an absolutely complete report of the trial, and of every word spoken in the course of it.'

7. *The People v. Hannigan* [1958] I.R. 378 (C.C.A.); *The State (Attorney General) v. Binchy* [1964] I.R. 395 (S.C.); *The State (Smith) v. Governor of Mountjoy Prison* 102 I.L.T.R. 93 (S.C.).
8. Criminal Procedure Act, 1967, s. 7 (4).
9. Courts of Justice Act, 1924, s. 33.
10. *The People v. Riordan* [1948] I.R. 416. (C.C.A.).
11. [1929] I.R. 526 (C.C.A.).
12. Id. 533-534.

In *Joyce*'s case the note was taken of the evidence in Irish and in English but the Irish version was mislaid. It would be absurd to suggest that if the evidence was given in Chinese or even in French there should be a shorthand note of the original version.

In practice, it is usual for the stenographer to be present throughout the proceedings, but it is submitted that, having regard to the absence of any statutory requirement, this is unnecessary save to the extent that there may be an appeal, for example, on applications for adjournment, special pleas, applications for separate trials, empanelling the jury and so forth, considered in the last two Chapters; and indeed it has been held that even the express statutory English provision is merely directory, and that the absence of a shorthand writer did not invalidate the trial itself.[13]

Evidence for the prosecution

It is not the purpose of this work to deal at any length with the law of evidence, either in relation to the examination of witnesses, or as to the admissibility of evidence, still less to deal with the evidence required to substantiate particular charges, but it has nevertheless been thought appropriate to deal with certain matters of procedure which may commonly arise in the course of a trial, and the law relating to competence and compellability of witnesses, and also with some matters relevant to criminal cases in general; the question of admissibility of statements made by an accused person has already been covered.[1]

It is not the usual practice, as in England, to require the witnesses to remain outside the court until called to give evidence. There appears, however, to be no objection to either party asking for that to be done in the case of witnesses as a whole, or

13. *R. v. Elliott* 2 Cr. App. R. 171; *R. v. Le Caer* 56 Cr. App. R. 727 decided under Criminal Appeal Act, 1907, s. 16; in England the Criminal Appeal Act, 1968, permits Rules of Court to provide for the making of a record by means of shorthand notes, by mechanical means or otherwise; and the Criminal Appeal Rules, 1968, provide that the record may be made by mechanical means by permission of the Lord Chancellor and prescribes what is to be included in a shorthand note. Archbold §7-109.

1. Supra, pp. 121 sqq.; a statement taken down in writing and acknowledged to be correct may be put in evidence even though unsigned; *The People v. Wickham* [1949] I.R. 180 (C.C.A.).

as regards particular witnesses, in order to prevent a later witness from fortifying or even varying his evidence as a result of what he has heard in the course of the examination or cross-examination of an earlier one; the question appears to be one for the exercise of the judge's discretion.

The giving of evidence

The rule at common law was that all evidence in a criminal case must be given on oath.[2] In some cases, however, a witness may be entitled to affirm instead of taking an oath, and, as will be seen, young children may be permitted to give unsworn evidence and an accused person is entitled to make an unsworn statement 'from the dock'.

In the normal way a person takes the oath by holding the New Testament, or, in the case of a Jew, the Old Testament, in his uplifted hand and by saying, or repeating after the Registrar of the Court who administers the oath, the words: 'I (A.B.) swear by Almighty God that' followed by the words of the oath.[3] The Registrar must administer the oath in that manner or form unless the person about to take the oath voluntarily objects thereto or is physically incapable of taking the oath, but in the case of a person who is neither a Christian nor a Jew the oath is to be administered in any other lawful manner.[4]

The accepted words of the oath are that 'the evidence I shall give to the Court on this trial shall be the truth, the whole truth and nothing but the truth'.

If a person objects to being sworn and states, as the ground of his objection, either that he has no religious belief or that the taking of an oath is contrary to his religious belief, he is entitled to make a solemn affirmation, which has the same effect as an oath: 'I (A.B.) do solemnly, sincerely and truly declare and affirm' followed by the words of the oath;[5] but, where an oath has been duly administered, the fact that the person taking it had no religious belief does not affect the validity of that oath.[6]

2. Archbold §4-254; Phipson, *Law on Evidence* (12th Edn. 1976) §1516; Cross, *Evidence* (5th Edn. 1979), 164.
3. Oaths Act, 1909, s. 2 (1).
4. Id. s. 2 (2).
5. Oaths Act, 1888, ss. 1, 2.
6. Id. s. 3.

In addition a person who desires to swear 'with uplifted hand', in the form and manner usual in Scotland, must be permitted to do so.[7]

Special provision is also made for persons who are or were Quakers or Moravians and the form prescribed is: 'I (A.B.) being one of the people called Quakers (or of the persuasion of the people called Quakers or of the United Brethren called Moravians, as the case shall be) do solemnly, sincerely and truly declare and affirm', or in the case of former members of those denominations 'I (A.B.) having been one of the people, called Quakers', etc. and 'entertaining conscientious objection to the taking of an oath, do solemnly', etc, followed by the words of the oath.[8]

There is furthermore a general provision that a person is bound by an oath administered in any form which he declares to be binding.[9]

Competence of witnesses

A witness is said to be 'competent' if he is capable in law of offering admissible testimony pertaining to an issue in the trial.[10] Whether he is 'compellable' is another matter, considered below. Generally speaking in any instance where a witness is competent for either the prosecution or the defence he is also compellable. There are, however, important exceptions to this rule which are considered below.

A witness is competent to give, and entitled to give his evidence in any language, provided that, if necessary, it can be interpreted so that all concerned in the case can understand it. In *Attorney General v. Joyce,* Kennedy C.J. stated:[11]

7. Id. s. 5.
8. Quakers and Moravians Acts, 1833 and 1839.
9. Oaths Act, 1838, s. 1; in the Canadian case of *R. v. Ah Wooey* (1902) 8 C.C.C. 25, which involved a murder prosecution in British Columbia, the trial judge permitted a witness to take a 'chicken oath'. This form of swearing involved the witness signing a document in which he humbled himself before Heaven and invited severe punishment if he testified falsely. He then chopped the head of a rooster as part of the ceremony in which the written document was burned.
10. On this topic, see generally Cross, op. cit., 163 sqq.
11. [1929] I.R. 526, 531 (C.C.A.).

'It would seem to me to be a requisite of natural justice, particularly in a criminal trial, that a witness should be allowed to give evidence in the language which is his or her vernacular language, whether that language be Irish or English, or any foreign language and it would follow, if the language used should not be a language;known to the members of the Court, that means of interpreting the language to the Court (Judge and jury), and also, in the case of evidence against a prisoner, that means of interpreting it to the prisoner, should be provided.'

In *Ó Monacháin v. An Taoiseach,*[12] a case which originated in the District Court, Henchy J. expressed the view that it could not be lawful to hear any case in any language (even in Irish, the national language) without giving those who do not speak that language, the Justice, parties, or witnesses (to whom, if he had been dealing with a jury trial, he would doubtless have added the jury) a full opportunity to understand the case.

The absence, however, of an interpreter during part of the trial of a person who was legally represented and had a good knowledge of English has been held not to render the trial unsatisfactory.[13]

Likewise persons who suffer from a physical disability such as deafness or dumbness are not thereby rendered incompetent, provided that they understand the nature of the oath and that they are capable of conveying their evidence by some means, e.g. writing or signs, through an interpreter.[14]

Where an interpreter is required he must be unbiased, and sworn.[15]

A trial judge may permit a person of defective intellect to be sworn if he is satisfied that the person understands the nature of the oath,[16] although the degree of credibility attaching to any such evidence is a matter within the domain of the jury.[17]

Children

Undoubtedly the issue of competence to testify arises in its

12. Unrep. July, 1982 (S.C.).
13. *The People v. Saunders,* 11th March, 1963, Frewen 283.
14. See Phipson, op. cit. §1543.
15. Phipson, op. cit. §1543.
16. *The People v. Rossiter,* 3rd May, 1951, Frewen 118.
17. *R. v. Hill* 2 Den. 254; *R. v. Dunning* [1965] Crim. L.R. 372.

most acute form in relation to the evidence of children.[1] In the early case of *R. v. Brasier* a court of twelve judges decided:[2]

> '[A]n infant, though under seven years of age, may be sworn in a criminal prosecution, provided such infant appears, on strict examination by the Court, to possess a sufficient knowledge of the nature and consequences of an oath. . . for there is no precise or fixed rule as to the time within which infants are excluded from giving evidence; but their admissibility depends upon the sense and reason they entertain of the danger and impiety of falsehood, which is to be collected from their answers to questions propounded to them by the Court. . .'

At the time of this decision only sworn testimony could be entertained in a criminal court. Today, however, if a judge decides that a child is incapable of giving sworn testimony it may be permitted to give unsworn testimony. Section 30 of the Children Act, 1908, as amended by section 28 (2) of the Criminal Justice Administration Act, 1914, provides that, when there is tendered as a witness in any criminal proceedings a child of tender years who, in the opinion of the court, does not understand the nature of an oath, the unsworn evidence of such a child may nevertheless be received if in the opinion of the court, the child has sufficient intelligence to justify the reception of the evidence and understands the duty of speaking the truth.

The major significance of whether or not a child is permitted to testify upon oath lies in the fact that if such evidence is sworn then, as a matter of law, it need not be corroborated, whereas if it is unsworn it must be.[3] This, therefore, renders it essential to know whether or not a child may be sworn.

The test propounded in *R.v.Brasier* demands that the trial judge examine a child to ensure that it understands the 'nature and consequences' of an oath. In *Attorney General v. O'Sullivan*[4] the Supreme Court considered a case in which an accused had been convicted, on the sworn evidence of a boy of about ten years of age, of an attempt to commit sodomy. The first ground of appeal lay in the fact that the trial judge had not held an investi-

1. See *Children's Evidence* 90 I.L.T.R. 231 and 237.
2. (1772) 1 Leach 199.
3. Infra, p. 328.
4. [1930] I.R. 552.

gation in respect of the capacity of the boy to understand the nature of an oath. Counsel for the defendant had not taken objection to the swearing of the boy at the trial, because he was aware of a ruling in another case by the same trial judge which was such that he felt able to anticipate that any objection on his part would be futile. The court rejected the contention of the appellant that some form of inquiry was a condition precedent to the swearing of a child. In relation to the law permitting sworn testimony Kennedy C.J. said:[5]

> '[I]t was and is a question, not of age, for there is no precise limit of age fixed by any rule within which the evidence of children on oath is to be excluded, but it is a question of the intelligence and actual mental capacity of the child witness, "its sense and reason of the danger and impiety of falsehood" *R. v. Brasier.*'

The implications of the old authority of *R. v. Brasier* were subjected to careful scrutiny in the Canadian case of *R. v . Bannerman,*[6] in which the defendant was convicted of having unlawful sexual intercourse with a girl under 14 years of age and of gross indecency with her brother. The prospective witness, Frankie Spence, was 13 years of age according to his own evidence, but 12 according to the testimony of his mother. In an examination conducted before he was sworn, the boy indicated that he went to catechism and that he knew that it was bad not to tell the truth, but he did not know what would happen to him if he did not tell the truth, and counsel for the defendant therefore argued on appeal that, while the witness understood the *nature* of the oath, he did not understand the *consequences*. In rejecting this contention Dickson J. said:

> '[C]ounsel for the accused contended that Frankie Spence should have replied, "I will go to Hell", or given some other answer acknowledging the sureness of Divine punishment. It seems to me that such thinking is wrong theologically and in all other respects.'

Later in his judgment he continued:

> 'In my opinion all that is required when one speaks of an understanding of the "consequences" of an oath is that the child appreciates it is assuming a moral obligation.'

5. Id. 556.
6. 55 W.W.R. 257 (1966), Court of Appeal for Manitoba.

Dickson J. further indicated in the course of his judgment that he felt that it was 'entirely proper' for leading questions to be put to the child by the trial judge when assessing the fitness of a potential witness to give sworn testimony.

In England in *R. v. Hayes*,[7] which was an application for leave to appeal against a conviction on three counts of incitement to gross indecency with a child and one count of an act of gross indecency with a child, the Court of Appeal (Criminal Division) considered the issue of judicial discretion to permit a child to give sworn testimony where a boy of 12 years of age said that he had not heard of God but, when later asked did he think there was a God, replied, 'Yes'. In delivering the judgment of the court Bridge L.J. said:[8]

> 'It is unrealistic not to recognise that, in the present state of society, amongst the adult population the divine sanction of an oath is probably not generally recognised. The important consideration, we think, when a judge has to decide whether a child should properly be sworn, is whether the child has a sufficient appreciation of the solemnity of the occasion, and the added responsibility to tell the truth, which is involved in taking an oath, over and above the duty to tell the truth which is an ordinary duty of normal social conduct.'

Irish judges may take the view that the test propounded in *R. v. Hayes* is more easily operated than one which has its origins in the more simplistic theology of earlier centuries.

Compellability of witnesses

The defendant's spouse as a prosecution witness

The general rule at common law was that the spouse of a defendant was not competent as a witness for the prosecution in a criminal case. This rule applies equally to a joint trial, even where the spouse's testimony would inculpate only a co-accused. The rationale of the rule would seem to lie in the fact that it was felt that any law which permitted a wife to testify against her husband:

> '[W]ould occasion implacable divisions and quarrels, and destroy the very legal policy of marriage that has so contrived it, that their

7. [1977] 1 W.L.R. 234.
8. Id. 237.

> interest should be but one; which it could never be if wives were admitted to destroy the interest of their husbands and the peace of families could not easily be maintained if the law admitted any attestation against the husband.'[1]

Various inroads have, however, been made into this rule both at common law and by statute.

At common law there is somewhat dubious support for the proposition that in cases of high treason a wife was competent.[2] In cases of forcible abduction and marriage the 'wife' is competent. This exception to the general rule can be based either on the proposition that such a marriage is null and void or that force was perpetrated upon the wife.[3] Undoubtedly the major deviation from the common law norm of incompetence arose in the case of personal injury perpetrated by one spouse upon the other.[4] The ambit of 'personal injury' was extended by the judiciary to include not only assaults of all kinds but also the commission of unnatural offences by husbands against wives.[5]

The decision of the English Court of Criminal Appeal in *R. v. Lapworth* [6] was that, for the purposes of the common law, the notion of competence included compellability, and, therefore, spouses were obliged to testify in any case which involved a common law exception to the general rule of incompetence. This decision contrasted starkly with the decision of the House of Lords in *Leach v. R.*[7] which was that the statutory exceptions to the rule of incompetence were such as to render a spouse competent but not compellable as a witness for the prosecution. In *Hoskyn v. Commissioner of Police for the Metropolis*[8] the House of Lords rejected the rationale of *R. v. Lapworth* and held[9] that a

1. Gilbert, *Law of Evidence* (3rd Ed. 1769) 136, quoted by Lord Wilberforce in *Hoskyn v. Commissioner of Police for the Metropolis* 67 Cr. App. R. 88, 95.
2. *R. v. Griggs* 2 Hawk. c. 46, 582; see generally Cross, op. cit. 167.
3. *R. v. Wakefield* 2 Lew. C.C. 279; *Reeve v. Wood* 5 B. & S. 364.
4. *R. v. Lapworth* [1931] 1 K.B. 117.
5. *R. v. Blanchard* [1952] 1 All E.R. 114.
6. Supra.
7. [1912] A.C. 305.
8. [1978] 2 W.L.R. 695 *per* Lords Wilberforce, Salmon and Keith and Viscount Dilhorne, Lord Edmund-Davies (dissenting).
9. Adopting the conclusion reached by the House of Lords in *Leach v. R.* [1912] A.C. 305, considering the provisions of the English Criminal Evidence Act, 1898, which bears great similarity to the Irish Act of 1924.

wife was competent as a witness, but that she could not be compelled to testify against her husband on a charge of personal violence at the instance of a prosecutor.

Statutory enactments affecting spouses' testimony for the prosecution

By the Evidence Act, 1877, an accused's spouse is both competent and compellable as a prosecution witness in a case of public nuisance.

Section 4 of the Criminal Justice (Evidence) Act, 1924, provides that:

> (1) The wife or husband of a person charged with an offence under any enactment mentioned in the Schedule to this Act may be called as a witness either for the prosecution or defence and without the consent of the person charged.
> (2) Nothing in this Act shall affect a case where the wife or husband of a person charged with an offence may at common law be called as a witness without the consent of that person.

This section renders the accused's spouse competent but not compellable in so far as an offence mentioned in the Schedule to the Act is concerned.[10]

In *McGonagle v. McGonagle*[11] the Supreme Court considered whether the wife of an accused ought to have been permitted to testify in a prosecution alleging the wilful neglect of a six year old child contrary to section 12 of the Children Act, 1908, an offence for which she would not have been competent at common law and which was not included in the Schedule to the 1924 Act. The appellant argued that as the offence was not contained in the Schedule his wife's evidence was consequently inadmissible and the court was obliged to resolve the issue whether or not the Schedule was conclusive as regards the offences for which a spouse could be a competent witness. Section 133 (28) of the Children Act, 1908, provided that in any proceeding for an offence under Part II of that Act,[12] or for any of the offences

10. The enactments set out in the Schedule are the Vagrancy (Ireland) Act, 1847, s. 2; and Offences against the Person Act, 1861, ss. 48, 52, 53, 54 (so far as unrepealed) and 55; and Prevention of Cruelty to Children Act, 1904; to which was later added the Public Assistance Act, 1939, s. 83.
11. [1951] I.R. 123.
12. Part II of the Act comprises ss. 12-38 inclusive and the offences are contained in ss. 12-17 inclusive.

mentioned in the First Schedule to the Act,[13] the wife or husband of an accused would be competent although not compellable to give evidence. The court accepted that there existed a general rule of statutory interpretation whereby a prior statute was impliedly repealed by a subsequent statute which was inconsistent with and repugnant to the prior one, but according to O'Byrne J. this rule did not apply where the prior statute was 'special' and the subsequent one 'general' in which instance the court applied the maxim *generalia specialibus non derogant.* The court accepted that the 1908 Act was special, thus enabling this latter doctrine to be invoked.

The court also seized upon the fact that included in the Schedule to the 1924 Act was the whole of the Prevention of Cruelty to Children Act, 1904, which, according to O'Byrne J.:[14]

> '[W]ould seem to indicate that, *per incuriam,* the Legislature overlooked the fact that a great deal of the Act of 1904 had been repealed and re-enacted in the Act of 1908.'

Bearing the above matters in mind the court accepted that the legislature at the time of passing the 1924 Act had not manifested an intention to repeal section 133 (28) of the Children Act, 1908, and held that section 133 (28) remained operative even though not included in the Schedule to the 1924 Act.

By section 18 of the Unemployment Assistance (Amendment) Act, 1935, a spouse is competent but probably not compellable for the prosecution in any case under that Act or under the Unemployment Assistance Act, 1933.

The Married Women's Status Act, 1957, renders a spouse competent against the other spouse for the protection and security of his or her own property.

The accused as a prosecution witness

Where an accused is being tried alone he is incompetent as a

13. The First Schedule comprises any offence under the Offences against the Person Act, 1861, ss. 27, 55 and 56 and any offence against a child or young person under ss. 41, 42, 43, 51 or 62 of that Act or under the Criminal Law Amendment Act, 1885; any offence under the Dangerous Performances Acts, 1879 and 1897; any other offence involving bodily injury to a child or young person.
14. [1951] I.R. 123, 128.

witness for the prosecution, except in the rare case of a prosecution for public nuisance under the Evidence Act, 1877, when he is both a competent and a compellable prosecution witness.

In the case of a joint trial an accused is incompetent to testify against a co-accused, although the prosecution may be in a position to remedy this situation by adopting one of a number of courses the consequence of which would be to render an accused both competent and compellable for the prosecution. Firstly, it may refuse to offer any evidence against an accused who has pleaded not guilty thus enabling an acquittal to be recorded against the accused. In such circumstances the plea of *autrefois acquit* would be open to the accused if any attempt were made to re-indict him. Secondly, it may enter a *nolle prosequi* indicating that it does not propose to proceed against the accused in relation to the charges in the indictment. While such a course would not necessarily operate *de jure* in the same way as an acquittal[15] it would nevertheless leave the accused *de facto* immune from further prosecution in relation to the charges in question. Thirdly, if the prosecution can secure separate trials for the accused and a co-accused then, if proceedings against the accused have been completed, it may call him against the former co-accused. Finally, it can call the accused against his co-accused in a case where the accused has been arraigned and has pleaded guilty and preferably been sentenced in connection with the charges.[16]

Diplomats

The provisions of the Vienna Convention on Diplomatic Relations, signed on 18th April, 1961, were accorded the force of law by section 5 (1) of the Diplomatic Relations and Immunities Act, 1967.

Article 31 (2) of the Convention states that a diplomatic agent is not obliged to give evidence as a witness, and this privilege is extended to members of the family of such an agent forming part of his household provided that they are not nationals of the receiving state.[17] A similar privilege attaches to members of the

15. Supra, pp. 259 sqq.
16. *R. v. Payne* [1950] 1 All E.R. 102; cf. *The People v. Shribman* [1946] I.R. 431 (C.C.A.).
17. Art. 37 (1).

administrative and technical staff of the mission together with members of their family forming part of their respective households, if they also are not nationals of or permanently resident in the receiving state.[18] Such persons are thus competent but not compellable.

Corroboration

As a general rule a person may be convicted on the evidence of a single witness. To this rule there are a few exceptions in respect of specific offences at common law, in the case of perjury,[1] or by statute,[2] when, if there is no corroboration, the jury *must* be directed to find the accused not guilty, and there are qualifications to the rule, generally developed out of rules of practice, as regards the evidence of young children, evidence of a complainant in the case of a sexual offence, evidence of accomplices and evidence of visual identification when, according to the circumstances, the jury must be warned of the dangers of acting on the evidence of one or more witnesses without corroboration or supporting evidence.

The law was concisely summarised by Kingsmill Moore J. in giving the judgment of the Supreme Court in *The People v. Casey (No. 2)*:[3]

> '[A]ccumulated judicial experience eventually tends to crystallise into established rules of judicial practice, accepted rules of law and statutory provisions. Thus the general directions which must be given in every case as to the onus of proof and necessity of establishing guilt beyond reasonable doubt have arisen from experience of the fallibility of human testimony in general, whether due to mendacity, imperfect observation, auto-suggestion or other causes. The suggestibility and lack of responsibility of children of tender age find recognition in the statutory provision that their unsworn evidence shall not be sufficient to convict of an offence, unless

18. Art. 37 (2).
1. 2 Hale, 2 Hawkins, c. 46; Archbold, 25th Ed. 1134-35; in England, the matter is governed by the Perjury Act, 1911, ss. 13, 25.
2. Treason Act, 1939, ss. 1 (4), 2 (2);Road Traffic Act, 1961, s. 105; Children Act, 1908, infra, Criminal Law Amendment Act, 1885, infra; the provisions of the Ballot Act, 1872, referred to in Sandes, 138 were repealed by the Electoral Act, 1963.
3. [1963] I.R. 33, 37

corroborated by other material evidence implicating the accused, and even when such evidence is received under oath it is customary for judges to tell juries that they should not convict unless they have weighed the evidence with the most extreme care. Similarly, the opportunities for giving false evidence afforded to an accomplice and to a person who alleges that a sexual offence has been committed against him or her, coupled with the extreme temptation to give false evidence frequently present in such cases, have given rise to the rule that a judge must warn the jury that it is always dangerous to convict on the evidence of such persons unless it is corroborated in some material particular implicating the accused.

The category of circumstances and special types of case which call for special directions and warnings from the trial judge cannot be considered as closed.'

Children

Where a child of tender years is permitted by the trial judge[4] to give unsworn evidence on behalf of the prosecution, the accused may not be convicted *unless* the child's testimony is corroborated by some other material evidence implicating the accused.[5] Where a child is sworn it is customary for the judge to tell the jury that they should not convict unless they have weighed the evidence with most extreme care.[6] It has been held by the House of Lords in England that the sworn evidence of one child may be corroborated by the unsworn evidence of another and *vice versa,* but that the unsworn evidence of one child cannot be corroborated by the unsworn evidence of another.[7] In some cases, however, the child may also fall into the category of victims of sexual assaults or accomplices, considered below.

Sexual Offences

No person is to be convicted of an offence under sections 2 or 3 of the Criminal Law Amendment Act, 1885 (which relate to procuration of women to have unlawful carnal knowledge or to become prostitutes and so forth, and procuration of unlawful carnal knowledge by intimidation, false pretences or the admini-

4. Supra, pp. 319 sqq.
5. Children Act, 1908, s. 30.
6. *The People v. Casey (No. 2)* [1963] I.R. 33.
7. *Director of Public Prosecutions v. Hester* [1973] A.C. 296.

stration of drugs and so forth) upon the evidence of one witness unless corroborated in some material particular by evidence implicating the accused.[8] Apart from this it is an established rule of practice, to the extent that it is virtually now a rule of law, that in cases of rape,[9] unlawful carnal knowledge,[10], indecent assault,[11] sodomy,[12] and gross indecency between males,[13] a jury should be warned that it is dangerous to convict on the evidence of the complainant alone, unless corroborated (which is a matter for the jury), but that they are entitled to convict without such corroboration if they are satisfied of the truth of the evidence beyond a reasonable doubt.

Thus in *The People v. Williams* O'Sullivan C.J. said:[14]

> '[I]n all cases in which there is no corroboration of the girl's evidence the attention of the jury should be directed to that fact, and they should be told that they should weigh her evidence with great care before they decide to convict. In many cases no further warning may be necessary; that is a matter to be determined in the first instance by the trial Judge. When an adequate warning has been given the jury should be told that they are entitled to act on the girl's evidence if they are satisfied beyond all reasonable doubt that it is truthful.'

The rule was re-iterated by Maguire C.J. in *The People v. Cradden:*[15]

> 'As the question whether evidence offered as corroborative of the story of the prosecutrix does in fact corroborate her is a matter for

8. Criminal Law Amendment Act, 1885, ss. 2 (4), 3 (3). The suggestion in Sandes, 131, 135 that there is a like statutory requirement of corroboration for other offences under this Act and under the Criminal Law Amendment Act, 1935, is not borne out by these Acts.
9. *James v. R.* 55 Cr. App. R. 299.
10. *The People v. Williams* [1940] I.R. 195 (S.C.); *The People v. Powell* [1945] I.R. 305 (C.C.A.); *The People v. Moore* [1950] Ir. Jur. Rep. 45 (C.C.A.); *The People v. Quinn* [1955] I.R. 57 (C.C.A.);*The People v. Trayers* [1956] I.R. 110 (C.C.A.).
11. *Attorney General v. Corcoran* 63 I.L.T.R. 145 (C.C.A.); *The People v. Cradden* [1955] I.R. 130 (C.C.A.); *The People v. Casey* [1961] I.R. 264 (C.C.A.).
12. *Attorney General v. O'Sullivan* [1930] I.R. 552 (C.C.A.); *The People v. Troy* 84 I.L.T.R. 193 (C.C.A.)
13. *Attorney General v. Duffy* [1931] I.R. 144 (C.C.A.); *The People v. Ward* 78 I.L.T.R. 64 (C.C.A.).
14. [1940] I.R. 195, 204 (S.C.).
15. [1955] I.R. 130, 140-141 (C.C.A.).

the jury, it would seem proper to give the warning together with the admonition that if they find corroboration in the other testimony they should ignore the warning. It may be in certain cases, that the evidence which is offered in corroboration of the prosecutrix is so clear and cogent that a reasonable jury would hold it to be so. In such a case this Court could, of course, apply the provisions of s. 5, sub-s. (1) (a) of the Courts of Justice Act, 1928. . . [that there has been no miscarriage of justice]. . .

In our opinion, therefore, however it be phrased, the warning to be given should convey to a jury in unmistakable terms the danger of acting upon the unconfirmed testimony of a prosecutrix if that testimony stands alone.

We wish, however, to emphasise that the degree and gravity of the warning called for may vary with the degree and gravity of the risk involved in accepting the evidence which requires corroboration. It will be for the trial Judge in each case to measure the strength of the warning having regard in cases such as this to what Hale in the passage (1 P.C. 633) cited by the Chief Justice in *Williams'* case, calls "concurring circumstances which give greater probability" to the evidence of the prosecutrix.'

It should be noted that whilst evidence is admissible of a complaint, including particulars of the complaint, made by the injured party on the first opportunity which reasonably offers itself after the offence, such evidence is admitted only as evidence of the consistency of the story told by the injured party, and of lack of consent (where material), but it does not amount to corroboration.[16]

Accomplices

A similar principle has been established as to the desirability of corroboration of the evidence of a person who was himself or herself concerned in some way with the commission of the offence. The jury must be warned that it is dangerous to convict on the uncorroborated evidence of an accomplice, but that if, having heard the warning, they are satisfied of its truth beyond a reasonable doubt they may accept it. Such a warning should always be given:[1]

16. *R. v. Lillyman* [1896] 2 Q.B. 167; *R. v. Lovell* 17 Cr. App. R. 163; Archbold §§4-308 sqq.
1. *Davies v. Director of Public Prosecutions* [1954] A.C. 378, 399, *per* Lord Simonds L.C. (adopting the words of counsel for the appellant); see generally O'Connor, *Corroboration and the Testimony of Accomplices in the Irish Law of Evidence* (1982) 4 D.U.L.J. (n.s.) 12.

> 'Where the judge fails to warn the jury in accordance with this rule, the conviction will be quashed, even if in fact there be ample corroboration of the evidence of the accomplice, unless the appellate court can apply the proviso [corresponding to section 5 (1) (a) of the Courts of Justice Act, 1928, that there has been no miscarriage of justice].'

Sometimes this rule coincides with those considered above in relation to children and sexual offences, as where a female is a consenting party to an alleged act of incest,[2] or a boy to one of gross indecency.[3]

In *Attorney General v. Linehan* Kennedy C.J. said:[4]

> '[A] person implicated either as principal or as accessory in the crime under investigation is an "accomplice" within the rule, though the degree and gravity of such complicity may vary, and inasmuch as the extent of the effect of such complicity upon the credit of the witness or the weight of his uncorroborated testimony will vary accordingly, so should the degree and gravity of the warning be measured'

O'Byrne J. stated in *The People v. Carney*:[5]

> 'It is clear. . . that a very slight degree of complicity, either as principal or accessory, in the crime charged is sufficient to render a person an accomplice for the purpose of the rule requiring that the jury should be warned of the danger of acting on his uncorroborated testimony.'

It appears that the spouse of a witness or of an accomplice may have to be treated as an accomplice.[6]

The evidence of one accomplice cannot normally be taken as corroborative of that of another.[7]

The term 'accomplice' extends to those who actually take part in the commission of the crime, and, on a charge of receiving

2. *R. v. Dimes* 7 Cr. App. R. 43.
3. Cf. *The People v. Ward* 78 I.L.T.R. 64 (C.C.A.).
4. [1929] I.R. 19, 23 (C.C.A.); see also *The People v. Shaw* [1960] I.R. 168 (C.C.A.); *The People v. Ryan*, 5th August, 1966, Frewen 304; *The People v. Lawless*, 6th November, 1968, Frewen 338.
5. [1955] I.R. 324, 345 (S.C.).
6. *Attorney General v. Durnan* [1934] I.R. 308 (C.C.A.); *The People v. Coleman*, [1945] I.R. 237; *Id. (No. 2)* 14th June, 1945, Frewen 64.
7. *Director of Public Prosecutions v. Hester* [1973] A.C. 296; but see *Director of Public Prosecutions v. Kilbourne* [1973] A.C. 729.

stolen goods or larceny it includes both thief and receiver.[8] The term does not, however, extend to an *agent provocateur*.[9] Where evidence of similar facts is admissible[10] it appears that the evidence of an accomplice in relation to such facts also requires corroboration.[11]

The meaning of corroboration

In *R. v. Baskerville,*[12] approved in *The People v. Phelan,*[13] Lord Reading giving the judgment of the English Court of Criminal Appeal said that:

> '[E]vidence in corroboration must be independent testimony which affects the accused by connecting him or tending to connect him with the crime. In other words, it must be evidence which implicates him, that is, which confirms in some material particular not only the evidence that the crime has been committed, but also that the prisoner committed it. The test applicable to determine the nature and extent of the corroboration is thus the same whether the case falls within the rule of practice at common law or within that class of offences for which corroboration is required by statute.'

Whether evidence is *capable* of being corroboration is a question of law to be detemined by the trial judge, but whether it *does* corroborate other evidence is a matter of fact for the jury.[14]

Identification

In every criminal case the prosecution must establish not only the commission of the offence but also that it was committed by the accused. In many cases the implication of the accused in the incident giving rise to the charge may not be disputed. He may merely dispute the criminality of his involvement, for example, that he acted in self defence or that a blow was accidental when charged with an assault, or that on a charge of larceny he had no intent to defraud or to deprive the complainant permanently of

8. *R. v. Jennings* 7 Cr. App. R. 242; *R. v. Dixon* 19 Cr. App. R. 36.
9. *R. v. Bickley* 2 Cr. App. R. 53.
10. Infra, p. 335.
11. *Davies v. Director of Public Prosecutions* [1954] A.C. 378.
12. [1916] 2 K.B. 658, 667.
13. 15th January, 1951, Frewen 98.
14. *R. v. Farid* 30 Cr. App. R. 168; *The People v. Lynch* [1982] I.R. 64.

the property in question. In other cases, however, whilst the genuineness of the complaint is not really disputed, the accused may simply claim that he was not the person responsible. His involvement or presence on the scene may have been alleged by the victim or by somebody else. He may or may not have been previously known to the witness. Even if the accused was a close friend of the witness the latter might have been mistaken as to his presence in a particular place at a particular time, especially if identification was the result of a fleeting look, or at a distance, or in bad light. The witness may never have met the accused before and identified him later in the street, or on an identification parade, or even for the first time in court,[1] where the accused may be prominent from his position. There have been notorious cases, when a person has been found guilty of an offence which it was afterwards proved beyond doubt he could not have committed.

The leading Irish case on this subject, to which reference has already been made, is *The People v. Casey (No. 2)* in which Kingsmill Moore J. said:[2]

> 'We are of opinion that juries as a whole may not be fully aware of the dangers involved in visual identification nor of the considerable number of cases in which such identification has been proved to be erroneous; and also that they may be inclined to attribute too much probative effect to the test of an identification parade. In our opinion it is desirable that in all cases, where the verdict depends substantially on the correctness of an identification, their attention should be called in general terms to the fact that in a number of instances such identification has proved erroneous, to the possibilities of mistake in the case before them and to the necessity of caution. Nor do we think that such warning should be confined to cases where the identification is that of only one witness. Experience has shown that mistakes can occur where two or more witnesses have made positive identifications. We consider juries in cases where the correctness of an identification is challenged should be directed on the following lines, namely, that if their verdict as to the guilt of the prisoner is to depend wholly or substantially on the correctness of such identification, they should bear in mind that there have been a number of instances where responsible witnesses, whose honesty was not in question and whose opportunities for

1. Generally undesirable; see Archbold §14-6.
2. [1963] I.R. 33, 39-40.

> observation had been adequate, made positive identifications on a parade or otherwise, which identifications were subsequently proved to be erroneous; and accordingly that they should be specially cautious before accepting such evidence of identification as correct; but that if after careful examination of such evidence in the light of all the circumstances, and with due regard to all the other evidence in the case, they feel satisfied beyond reasonable doubt of the correctness of the identification they are at liberty to act upon it.'

The principles laid down by the Supreme Court in *Casey*'s case were applied by the Court of Criminal Appeal in *The People v. Goulding,*[3] *The People v. Bond,*[4] *The People v. O'Brien,*[5], *The People v. O'Driscoll,*[6] *The People v. Fagan,*[7] *The People v. Stafford,*[8] *The People v. Wallace,*[9] whilst more elaborate guide lines were indicated by the English Court of Appeal (Criminal Division) in *R. v. Turnbull.*[10] After reiterating the need for a warning as in *Casey*'s case, Lord Widgery C.J. observed that the trial judge should direct the jury in an appropriate case as to the *quality* of the identification, how long the witness saw the accused, how well he knew the accused (if at all), the light, distance, impediments to observation, and so forth, as to any discrepancies between a description given to the police and the appearance of the accused when seen by the jury in court, and as to apparent discrepancies in the evidence of identification; he suggested that if the prosecution was aware of material discrepancies they should supply the defence with particulars of the description given by the witness to the police.[11] He also suggested that in some cases the opportunity for observation might be so poor that if there was no other evidence to support the identification the judge should withdraw the case from the jury, but he added that such other evidence need not be corroboration in the ordinary

3. 31st March, 1964, Frewen 292.
4. [1966] I.R. 214.
5. 103 I.L.T.R. 109.
6. 3rd March, 1972, Frewen, 351.
7. 13th May, 1974, Frewen 375.
8. Unrep. 7th December, 1981.
9. Unrep. 22nd November, 1982.
10. [1977] Q.B. 224; see Archbold §14-2.
11. In practice this would normally be apparent from the Book of Evidence.

legal sense. It was such as to make the jury sure there was no mistake. And while Kingsmill Moore J. made the statement as to corroboration in general at the start of his judgment in *Casey*'s case,[12] he, also, did not use the word 'corroboration' with reference to evidence in support of identification.

It must, moreover, be stressed that both *Casey*'s case and *Turnbull*'s case laid down general principles, the application of which must depend on the circumstances of the particular case.[13] Whilst *Turnbull*'s case has frequently been cited in the Irish courts, it has not, so far as is known, been considered in detail in any reserved judgment of the Court of Criminal Appeal or the Supreme Court.[14]

Examination of witnesses

When the witness has been sworn he is examined by counsel for the prosecution. This 'examination-in-chief' is designed to elicit the evidence from the witness in his own words, keeping him as far as possible to the statement of his evidence which appears in the Book of Evidence, lest the defence complain of being taken by surprise by some material or damaging statement which does not appear in the Book. 'Leading questions' which suggest the answer to the witness are not normally permissible, except on formal matters or matters as to which there is no dispute.[1]

Similar fact evidence

As a general rule the evidence tendered by the prosecution must relate to the issue whether the accused committed the particular crime with which he is charged, so that evidence to show that he has committed some other crime is not admissible.

As Lord Herschell L.C. said in *Makin v. Attorney General for New South Wales:*[2]

12. [1963] I.R. 33, 36, cited supra, p. 327.
13. See *R. v. Keane* 64 Cr. App. R. 248; *R. v. Oakwell* [1978] 1 W.L.R. 32; *R. v. Weeder* 71 Cr. App. R. 228.
14. It was referred to in *The People v. Wallace,* unrep. 22nd November, 1982.
1. Archbold §4-292; Cross, op. cit. 226.
2. [1894] A.C. 57, 65 (P.C.) approved in *The People v. Kirwan* [1943] I.R. 279 (S.C.) and applied in *The People v. Mohangi,* 14th May, 1964, Frewen 297, and *The People v. Wallace,* unrep. 22nd November, 1982 (C.C.A.); see generally Archbold §§13-1 sqq.; Cross, op. cit. 355 sqq.

'It is undoubtedly not competent for the prosecution to adduce evidence tending to shew that the accused has been guilty of criminal acts other than those covered by the indictment, for the purpose of leading to the conclusion that the accused is a person likely from his conduct or character to have committed the offence for which he is being tried. On the other hand, the mere fact that the evidence adduced tends to shew the commission of other crimes does not render it inadmissible if it be relevant to an issue before the jury, and it may be so relevant if it bears upon the question whether the acts alleged to constitute the crime charged in the indictment were designed or accidental, or to rebut a defence which would otherwise be open to the accused.'

Bankers' Books

The admissibility under the Bankers' Books Evidence Act, 1879, of secondary evidence of bank records is dealt with in Archbold,[3] but this must be read in conjunction with the Bankers' Books Evidence (Amendment) Act, 1959. The extent to which the latter Act, and the decision in *Barker v. Wilson*[4] extend to the final computerised records produced by Banks has been left open by the Court of Criminal Appeal.[5]

Hostile witnesses

It sometimes happens that a witness who has been called by the prosecution in the expectation that he will give evidence on the lines of a statement made to the police and included in the statement of his evidence in the Book of Evidence fails to do so – fails, in the colloquial phrase to 'swear up'. It may be that he is forgetful, or has thought things over and come to the honest conclusion that his original statement was wrong, or he may be afraid to give evidence for fear of retaliation by the accused or his friends, or he may even be positively hostile to the prosecution.

Section 3 of the Criminal Procedure Act, 1865, (Denman's Act)[6] provides that:

3. §§10-79 to 10-81.
4. [1980] 1 W.L.R. 884.
5. *The People v. Murray*, unrep. 25th July, 1983.
6. See generally, Archbold §§4-305 sqq., Phipson, op. cit. §§1576-8; Cross, op. cit. 252.

> A party producing a witness shall not be allowed to impeach his credit by general evidence of bad character, but he may, in case the witness shall, in the opinion of the judge, prove adverse, contradict him by other evidence, or, by leave of the judge, prove that he has made at other times a statement inconsistent with his present testimony; but before such last-mentioned proof can be given, the circumstances of the supposed statement, sufficient to designate the particular occasion, must be mentioned to the witness, and he must be asked whether or not he has made such statement.

If the witness proves adverse, i.e. hostile and not merely unfavourable, then counsel for the prosecution may, by leave of the judge, put leading questions to him by way of cross-examination,[7] but so far as the jury is concerned it is his evidence given in court, and not the previous statement which matters, although the statement is something which goes to his credibility.

The procedure to be followed and consequences were dealt with in *The People v. Taylor* in which Walsh J. said:[8]

> 'The proper procedure, if it is desired to have a witness treated as hostile, is make the application to the judge and put before him the material upon which it is sought to have the witness declared to be a hostile witness. This, of course, should be done in the absence of the jury and, if the judge rules that the witness may be treated as hostile, *then the witness may be cross-examined.* That is something quite different and distinct from the rules and procedure which govern the admissibility of written statements in cross-examination. This particular witness had been allowed to be treated as hostile and, when the jury were recalled to court, the proper procedure for the prosecution was to have put to the witness that she had on another occasion made a statement which differed materially from or contradicted the one she was making in the witness-box. If she were to deny that, then the proper procedure would have been to have her stand down from the box, and to prove in fact that she did in fact make a statement by putting into the box the person who took the statement, proving it in the ordinary way without revealing the contents of the statement at that stage. The earlier witness should then have been put back in the box and the statement put to her for identification, and then her attention should have been directed to the passage in which the alleged contradiction or material variation appears. If she had agreed that there was such a contradiction or

7. *Price v. Manning* 42 Ch. D. 372.
8. [1974] I.R. 97, 99 (C.C.A.) (emphasis added by authors).

> material variation, that should have been the end of the matter *in so far as the question of impugning her credibility was concerned* because there would then have been before the jury an admission from the witness to the effect that she had made contrary statements on the same matter. The statement might then put in evidence, though that would not be strictly necessary at that stage when the admission had been made. If she had persisted in denying the contradiction, then the statement, having already been proved, would have gone in as evidence of the fact that the witness had made a contrary statement.
>
> It must at all times be made clear to the jury that what the witness said in the written statement is not evidence of the fact referred to but is only evidence on the question of whether or not she has said something else – it is evidence going only to her credibility.'

It is submitted that the stresses indicated by the authors show the dual purpose of having a witness treated as hostile – on the one hand to impugn the credibility of the witness in the box, and on the other, whether the previous statement is admitted or denied, to permit the cross-examination of the witness under oath in the hope that he or she might ultimately admit that the original statement was the true one, in which case, of course, the facts admitted on oath would be part of the evidence at the trial, although the jury should be warned of its unreliability.[9]

Objections to admissibility of evidence

The normal rule is that all evidence is to be given in the presence of the jury.[1] If, however, the defence claims that certain evidence, e.g. as to similar facts[2] or as to an alleged confession or other statement by the accused,[3] ought not to be admitted, the whole purpose of the objection would be defeated if the jury were to hear the evidence in question and it were then disallowed. The question of admissibility is one which is to be decided by the judge alone, and the question will, therefore, be argued in the absence of the jury.

9. See also *The People v. Kerins* [1945] I.R. 339, 352 and generally, Archbold §§4-305,4-306; Phipson, op. cit. §1592; Cross, op. cit. 251-54.
1. Cf. *R. v. Reynolds* 34 Cr. App. R. 60 (evidence as to the mental capacity of a young girl).
2. Supra, p. 335.
3. Supra, pp. 123 sqq.

This question arises most commonly in the case of confessions. As has been seen a statement made by an accused person is only admissible if voluntary, and in general it is for the judge to determine that issue.[4] That means that he must hear the circumstances in which the statement was made, resulting in a 'trial-within-a-trial' in the absence of the jury. It may, however, happen that this involves determination of disputed issues of fact, such as whether force was used by a police officer or whether the accused was at the time under arrest or unlawfully detained, and whether, if he was unlawfully detained, he was so detained as a result of a deliberate denial of his constitutional rights, where the judge has no discretion in the matter save in the most exceptional circumstances.[5] The authors are not aware of any positive decision by the Court of Criminal Appeal or the Supreme Court and the practice adopted by judges appears to vary. A number of judges, however, take the view, apparently based on the judgments in the Supreme Court in *The People v. Lynch*,[6] that such issues of fact ought to be decided by the jury itself in the course of a trial-within-a-trial.

If the evidence is admitted by the judge in the absence of the jury it must be adduced again before the jury, but an admission by the accused in the absence of the jury has been held in Northern Ireland and the House of Lords not to be admissible as evidence for the prosecution before the jury.[7]

Argument in the absence of the jury

Whilst the evidence is to be given in the presence of the jury, they are not concerned with purely legal arguments, and normally retire in the course of such arguments.[8]

Cross-examination

When counsel for the prosecution has concluded his examination-in-chief the defence may, if it wishes, cross-examine the

4. Supra, pp. 113 sqq.
5. Supra, pp. 172 sqq.
6. [1982] I.R. 64.
7. *R. v. Brophy* [1982] A.C. 476.
8. Supra, p. 338.

witness. The object of cross-examination is either to elicit information favourable to the defence or to cast doubt on the accuracy of the evidence given by the witness. If it is proposed to challenge any part of that evidence the matter in question should be put to the witness so that he may deal with it specifically. Leading questions are permissible.[1]

If the defence suggests that the witness has made a previous statement inconsistent with his testimony, and if the statement is not admitted, the circumstances of the supposed statement, sufficient to designate the particular occasion, must be mentioned to the witness and he must be asked whether or not he made such a statement; if he persists in his denial the defence may adduce evidence in due course to prove that he made it,[2] but only for the purpose of challenging the credibility of the witness, not in order to make the previous statement evidence in the case.[3] If the statement is alleged to have been made in writing, the same procedure should apparently be adopted as in the case of a hostile witness.[4]

As a general rule questions may be put to the witness designed to discredit him on the ground of his bad character. If, however, the accused is charged with a rape offence[5] to which he has pleaded not guilty, then, except with the leave of the judge, no evidence may be adduced and no question may be asked in cross-examination at the trial,[6] by or on behalf of the accused,[7] about any sexual experience of a complainant with a person other than the accused. An application to adduce any such evidence or ask any such question must be made to the judge in the absence of the jury.[8] The judge may only give leave if he is satisfied that it would be unfair to the accused to refuse the application, i.e. that, on the

1. Archbold §§4-314 sqq.; Phipson, op. cit. §1578; Cross, op. cit. 256 sqq.
2. Criminal Procedure Act, 1865, s. 4.
3. Archbold §§4-326 sqq.; Phipson, op. cit. §1578; Cross, op. cit. 258.
4. Supra, pp. 336 sqq.
5. I.e. rape, attempted rape, aiding, abetting, counselling and procuring rape or attempted rape, and incitement to rape; Criminal Law (Rape) Act, 1981, s. 1 (1); the Act appears to relate only to rape at common law, and not to unlawful carnal knowledge of young girls, sometimes called 'statutory rape', or other sexual offences.
6. Such questions appear to be permissible on the taking of a deposition in the District Court.
7. Criminal Law (Rape) Act, 1981, s. 3 (1).
8. Id. s. 3 (2) (a).

assumption that if the evidence or question were not allowed the jury might be satisfied that the accused was guilty, the effect of allowing the evidence or question might reasonably be that they would not be so satisfied.[9] If the evidence or question is allowed, it must be kept within the limits of the leave given.[10]

Re-examination

After the close of the cross-examination the prosecution is entitled to re-examine the witness on matters arising out of the cross-examination and the same general rules apply as in the case of the examination-in-chief. If the prosecution wishes to introduce any fresh matter which it may have overlooked, it may only do so by leave of the judge, and the defence will be entitled to cross-examine on it.[11]

Direction to the jury to acquit

At the conclusion of the case for the prosecution the defence may ask the judge, or the judge may determine of his own volition, to direct the jury as a matter of law to find the accused not guilty on some one or more or all of the counts in the indictment, on the ground that on the evidence the accused has no case to answer. This may be because the evidence does not disclose any offence,[12] or because it does not establish the offence with which the accused is charged or some other offence of which he might be found guilty on the indictment, or because the evidence as it stands is such that no reasonable jury properly charged could convict.[13]

If such a direction is refused and the accused had some case, however tenuous, to answer it appears that the conviction may stand if the defence goes into evidence and supplies what might have been lacking in the evidence adduced by the prosecution;[14] but it seems that if at the close of the case for the prosecution the

9. Id. s. 3 (2) (b).
10. Id. s. 3 (3).
11. Archbold §4-381; Phipson, op. cit. §1611; Cross, *Evidence* (5th Edn) 268.
12. *Attorney General v. Cunningham* [1932] I.R. 28 (C.C.A.); *The People v. Edge* [1943] I.R. 115 (S.C.).
13. Archbold §§4-385 sqq.
14. *R. v. Fraser* 7 Cr. App. R. 99; *R. v. Hogan* 16 Cr. App. R. 182; *R. v. Power* [1919] 1 K.B. 572; *R. v. Garside* 52 Cr. App. R. 85.

accused had *no* case to answer and a direction was nevertheless refused, and if evidence is then adduced as a result of which the accused is convicted, the conviction should be quashed on appeal.[15]

Apart from any such direction it is open to the jury, at any time after the close of the case for the prosecution, to inform the judge that the evidence they have heard is insufficient to justify a conviction, although the extent to which the judge should invite them to do so or draw attention to their right to do so appears doubtful.[16]

III. THE CASE FOR THE DEFENCE

A number of courses are open to the accused and the subsequent order of proceedings depends on which course is adopted.

The defence may elect to call no evidence, in effect inviting the jury not to accept the evidence tendered by the prosecution as establishing the guilt of the accused beyond a reasonable doubt. It is for the jury to assess the credibility of the witnesses, and to draw their own inferences from the facts. Alternatively the accused may elect to call witnesses as to his own good character, to induce the jury to consider whether they think it likely that a person with such a character would have committed the offence.[1] The accused may call other persons to testify as to the facts of the case, in support, for example, of a defence of *alibi,* that he was somewhere else at the time the offence was committed, or to put a different complexion on what the facts proved by the prosecution might appear to mean. He may himself give evidence on oath, a right not enjoyed in Ireland until 1924,[2] or he may make an unsworn statement 'from the dock'. If he gives evidence on oath he will be liable to cross-examination, within certain limits considered below, but he cannot be cross-examined on an unsworn statement, although such a statement is an integral part of the

15. *R. v. Abbott* [1955] 2 Q.B. 497.
16. Archbold §4-385.
1. *R. v. Bryant* [1979] Q.B. 108.
2. Criminal Evidence Act, 1924; in England the right was given by the Criminal Evidence Act, 1898.

trial and should be included in the transcript of evidence.[3]

Order of proceedings on the defence case

Assuming that the judge does not withdraw the case from the jury the order of procedure to be followed varies according to whether the accused is legally represented and the course which he elects to follow.

If any defendant is defended by counsel, but not otherwise, it is the duty of the presiding judge, at the close of the case for the prosecution, to ask such counsel if he intends to adduce evidence, and if no counsel announces his intention to do so counsel for the prosecution is allowed to address the jury a second time in support of his own case, for the purpose of summing up the evidence.[4] If the accused alone is to be called as a witness this right is postponed until he has done so,[5] when the prosecution may comment on the evidence given by the accused.[6] This right to sum up should, however, be exercised only in exceptional cases.[7]

If the accused is not defended by counsel the judge should inform him of the options open to him, and of his right to address the jury. It has been held in the past that failure by the judge to inform the accused of his rights may not invalidate a conviction, but it is submitted that the case is now of doubtful authority.[8]

If the accused is not represented by counsel and only wishes to give evidence himself or call witnesses as to character, he may give or call the evidence he wishes and then address the jury on his own behalf. If he wishes to call witnesses as to the facts, he may open his case, give evidence himself, if he wishes, and call his witnesses. The prosecution may sum up its case and the accused may then address the jury.[9]

If the accused is represented by counsel who proposes to call no witnesses as to the facts other than the accused, counsel is not

3. *The People v. Riordan* [1948] I.R. 416 (C.C.A.).
4. Criminal Procedure Act, 1865, (Denman's Act) s. 1.
5. Cf. Criminal Justice Evidence Act, 1924, s. 3.
6. *R. v. Gardner* [1899] 1 Q.B. 150, decided under the earlier English statute.
7. Cf. *R. v. Bryant* [1979] Q.B. 108; *The People v. Kerins* [1945] I.R. 339 (C.C.A.).
8. Cf. *R. v. Carter* 44 Cr. App. R. 225.
9. Sandes 121; Archbold §4-390.

entitled to open the case, but he may call the accused to give evidence or to make an unsworn statement, if he wishes, and any witnesses to character. The prosecution may sum up its case and counsel for the defence then addresses the jury. If, however, counsel for the defence proposes to call witnesses as to the facts other than the accused, he may open the case for the defence to the jury, then call his witnesses, and sum up his case. In that event counsel for the prosecution may reply.[10]

If no witnesses as to the facts are called, or if only the accused gives evidence, and if the accused is not represented, counsel for the prosecution appears to have no *right* to address the jury for a second time.[11] But even if, in such a case, the accused calls witnesses to the facts the prosecution seldom exercises its right to sum up its case.

If the accused is represented by counsel and no witnesses to the facts, or only the accused are called, counsel for the prosecution has the right to reply, before counsel for the defence addresses the jury, but this right should only be exercised in exceptional circumstances, and even if witnesses to the facts are called prosecuting counsel does not normally exercise his right of reply in straightforward cases.

Documents put in evidence have the same effect as witnesses to the facts.[12]

If witnesses are called, the same procedure as to examination-in-chief, cross-examination (subject to the restrictions on cross-examination of the defendant himself, considered below) and re-examination, and as to the admissibility of evidence and the giving and recording of evidence, is followed as in the case of witnesses for the prosecution. If there are several accused it seems the proper course is for counsel for the defence to cross-examine witnesses and address the jury in the order in which they appear on the indictment.[13]

10. Sandes 122; Archbold §4-390.
11. See, however, *Attorney General v. Lawless* [1930] I.R. 247 (C.C.A.); whether he may reply is apparently a matter for the discretion of the trial judge; cf. *The People v. Thompson*, 13th October, 1960, Frewen 201.
12. The rule in England is different: see Archbold §4-420.
13. See Archbold §4-316; *R. v. Richards* 1 Cox 62.

The role of the defendant in the trial

Silence

A defendant is entitled to remain silent throughout his trial. Although granting him *competence* to testify in his own defence, section 1 (b) of the Criminal Justice (Evidence) Act, 1924, clearly provides that the failure of any person charged with an offence, or the wife or husband, as the case may be, of the person so charged, to give evidence shall not be made the subject of any comment by the prosecution.

The Act only forbids comment by the prosecution, hence the trial judge is entitled to comment to the jury in relation to the defendant's silence when he is summing up the case.[1] Counsel for any co-accused involved are similarly entitled to make such comment.[2] The judge's comments must not be excessive,[3] and the English courts have sanctioned as being appropriate the form of words advanced by Lord Parker in *R. v. Bathurst*,[4] namely:

> '[That the accused] is not bound to give evidence, that he can sit back and see if the prosecution have proved their case, and that while the jury have been deprived of the opportunity of hearing his story tested in cross examination the one thing they must not do is to assume that he is guilty because he has not gone into the witness box.'

Some cases may justify more forceful judicial comment than others.[5]

Unsworn statement from the dock

The right to make an unsworn statement had existed for a long time before the 1924 Act and was expressly preserved by it.[6] In the past the statement was always made from the dock but today Irish defendants who wish to make such a statement do so from their normal place in the courtroom, or wherever they may best be heard. The right to make an unsworn statement to the jury is

1. *R. v. Rhodes* [1899] 1 Q. B. 77.
2. *R. v. Wickham* 55 Cr. App. R. 199.
3. See *Waugh v. R.* [1950] A.C. 203; cf. *The People v. Riordan* [1948] I.R. 416 (C.C.A.).
4. [1968] 2 Q.B. 99, 107-108; see *R. v. Mutch* [1973] 1 All E.R. 178.
5. See, e.g., *R. v. Sparrow* 57 Cr. App. R. 352.
6. Criminal Justice (Evidence) Act, 1924, s. 1 (h).

rarely availed of by defendants today. If such a statement is made, the prosecution has no right to cross-examine the defendant upon it.

The statement is meant to be that of the defendant and hence, although counsel may advise his client in relation to the matters which it might be appropriate to include, it appears that the language of the statement is a matter for the defendant himself.[7] The fact that many defendants in criminal trials prove inarticulate and incapable of delivering a monologue unaided usually renders unsworn statements of little consequence. The evidentiary value of such a statement is not clear.[8] In *The People v. Riordan*[9] the trial judge, although commenting severely upon the failure of the defendant to testify, failed to put the defence to the jury in his charge. The defendant had made an unsworn statement which had been omitted from the transcript of the trial. The Court of Criminal Appeal, quashing the conviction and ordering a re-trial, stated that the transcript should include all of the defendant's unsworn statement.

As a co-accused is not permitted to cross-examine upon it, an unsworn statement cannot constitute *any* evidence against him.

Cross-examination of the defendant who testifies upon oath

Although conferring upon defendants the right to testify for the defence at their own trials, the 1924 Act nevertheless did not place such defendants in the same exposed position as other witnesses in relation to the scope of the matters upon which they could be cross-examined. A defendant has a 'shield' which he may lose or abandon. The extent to which cross-examination of a defendant is permitted, is governed by paragraphs (e) and (f) of section 1 of the Act.

Section 1 (e) states:

> [A] person charged and being a witness in pursuance of this Act may be asked any question in cross-examination notwithstanding that it would tend to criminate him as to the offence charged.

7. See English Bar Council Annual Statement, 1977-1978, 29; also Barnard, *The Criminal Court in Action,* (2nd Ed.) 112.
8. Cross, op. cit. 186.
9. [1948] I.R. 416 (C.C.A.).

This paragraph removes the privilege against self-incrimination from a defendant who exercises his right to testify in his own defence. The exact scope of the questions which may be put to a defendant under this section has been the subject of some judicial disagreement,[10] although the majority view of the House of Lords is that only questions which *directly* criminate a defendant in relation to the offence wherewith he is charged may be asked under this section.[11]

Section 1 (f) states:

> [A] person charged and called as a witness in pursuance of this Act shall not be asked, and if asked shall not be required to answer, any question tending to show[12] that he has committed or been convicted of or been charged with any offence other than that wherewith he is then charged, or is of bad character, unless:
> (i) the proof that he has committed or been convicted of such other offence is admissible evidence to show that he is guilty of the offence wherewith he is then charged; or
> (ii) he has personally or by his advocate asked questions of the witnesses for the prosecution with a view to establish his own good character, or has given evidence of his good character, or the nature or conduct of the defence is such as to involve imputations on the character of the prosecutor or the witnesses for the prosecution; or
> (iii) he has given evidence against any other person charged with the same offence.

Section 1 (f) is cast in the form of a clear prohibition which is made subject to certain exceptions. The first exception alluded to does not depend, in order to be activated, upon any action whatsoever on the part of the defence. It permits the introduction of similar fact evidence by the prosecution to assist it in showing that the defendant in fact *committed* the offence wherewith he is charged. The section allows only a proof of the *commission* or *conviction* of the accused in relation to similar offences. Similar fact evidence may, therefore, be admitted in those circumstances where it would be admitted at common law.[13]

10. See *Jones v. Director of Public Prosecutions* [1962] A.C. 635.
11. This was the view of Lords Simonds, Reid and Morris in *Jones'* case; the minority view permitted questions which *indirectly* criminate the accused as to the offence charged, and was propounded by Lords Denning and Devlin.
12. 'Tending to show' means 'tending to reveal to the jury for the first time' – *Jones v. Director of Public Prosecutions*, supra.
13. Supra, p. 335; see also *The People v. Lehman* [1947] I.R. 133 (C.C.A.).

In stark contrast to paragraph (i), paragraph (ii) of section 1 (f) can be activated solely in consequence of the manner in which the defendant has conducted his defence. The defendant may activate this paragraph and thereby leave himself open to be asked any of the otherwise prohibited questions, in any one of a variety of ways.

The defendant or his counsel may ask a question of a prosecution witness *with a view* to establishing the good character of the defendant. Here it is the *intent* of the person cross-examining which is crucial and not the *effect* of any such question.

The word 'character' in this sub-section, whether or not it is qualified by any adjective, relates to both 'disposition' and 'reputation'.[14] If the defence asks a question of any witness for the prosecution with a view to establishing the good character of the defendant, or if the defendant gives evidence of his own good character, a trial judge may exercise his discretion to permit the otherwise prohibited questions. English authorities illustrate that a defendant may set up his own good character in any one of a wide variety of ways.[15]

Character is said to be indivisible and hence even if, for example, a defendant is charged with an offence involving dishonesty he may be cross-examined as to previous sexual misconduct. The 'dropping of his shield' by a defendant may thus entail serious consequences for his case. The prosecution must not, therefore, frame the cross-examination in such a way as to set a trap for a defendant and thus cajole him into dropping the shield.[16]

14. *The People v. Coleman* [1945] I.R. 237 (C.C.A.) approving *Stirland v. Director of Public Prosecutions* [1944] A.C. 315; see also *Malindi v. R.* [1967] A.C. 439; *Selvey v. Director of Public Prosecutions* [1970] A.C. 304.
15. For cases where trial courts accepted that character had been put in issue see: *R. v. Ferguson* 2 Cr. App. R. 250 (an assertion by a defendant that he attended Mass regularly); *R. v. Coulman* 20 Cr. App. R. 106 (questions which were aimed to show that the accused was a married man with a family and in regular work); *R. v. Samuel* 40 Cr. App. R. 8 (in a case of larceny by finding, an assertion by the defendant that he had previously found money and had returned it to its owners); cf. *R. v. Hamilton* [1969] Crim. L. R. 486 (defendant told improperly by the trial judge to remove a regimental blazer or he would be putting his character in issue); see generally, Cross, op. cit. 425 sqq.
16. In *Selvey v. Director of Public Prosecutions* [1970] A.C. 304, it was suggested that a warning ought to be given by a trial judge where the defence appears to be reaching a stage where the shield will be dropped.

Another way in which the prohibited questions may be put to the accused, with the judge's permission, is if the nature or conduct of the defence involves imputations being made upon the character of the prosecutor or upon any of the witnesses for the prosecution. Several Irish cases exemplify what constitute such imputations.

In *Attorney General v. Campbell,*[17] it was held that evidence given by the defendant to the effect that two witnesses for the prosecution had taken part in a conspiracy constituted an imputation. In *The People v. Coleman,*[18] the defendant was charged with carrying out an abortion and he alleged in his evidence that one prosecution witness had in fact committed the crime with which he was charged and that the same witness had conspired with another prosecution witness to have the defendant charged. The Court of Criminal Appeal accepted the view of the trial judge that such allegations constituted imputations and deprived the accused of the protection of section 1 (f).

To allege in the trial itself (as opposed to a trial-within-a-trial in the absence of the jury) that police officers had extracted a confession by force, threats or inducements, or implying that they had fabricated it, would constitute imputations if the officers concerned were prosecution witnesses. Similarly, allegations of vices or faults in relation to prosecution witnesses, whether they be true or false, will constitute imputations upon their character.[19]

The courts are prepared to accept the right of defendants to contradict prosecution witnesses and to probe, albeit by a very severe cross-examination, the veracity of any prosecution witness.[20] Even calling a prosecution witness a 'liar' has been held insufficient to permit the prohibited questions to be asked.[21] In rape cases allegations that the prosecutrix consented will not be deemed to be imputations.[22]

17. 62 I.L.T.R. 30 (C.C.A.)
18. [1945] I.R. 237 (C.C.A.); (No. 2) 14th June, 1945, Frewen 64.
19. Cf. *R. v. Britzman* [1983] 1 All E.R. 369 (implication that the police had fabricated statement); *R. v. Bishop* [1974] 3 W.L.R. 308 (allegations of vice).
20. *Attorney General v. O'Shea* [1931] I.R. 713 (C.C.A.).
21. *R. v. Rouse* [1904] 1 K.B. 184.
22. *R. v. Turner* [1944] K.B. 463; as to restrictions on cross-examination, see p. 340 supra.

Even if the nature of the defence *necessarily* involves an imputation being made upon the character of a prosecution witness the prohibited questions may still be asked.[23]

If the defendant gives testimony on oath,[24] and has been adjudged by the trial judge to have dropped the shield in any of the ways referred to in section 1 (f) (ii) then, with the judge's permission, the prosecution may cross-examine the defendant about his bad character and/or about any previous offences which he may have *committed*, or been *convicted* of, or been *charged* with. Even an offence which has occurred after the offences in the indictment may be raised.[25] However, scarcely, if ever, will the previous acquittal of a defendant be admissible, as it will invariably fail to satisfy the judge that it possesses sufficient relevance to justify admission.[26] In *The People v. Havelin*[27] the defendant attacked the character of a prosecution witness and the trial judge permitted the prosecution to disclose that the accused was 'wanted' for another offence. The Court of Criminal Appeal quashed the resulting conviction.

Purpose of evidence of bad character or previous conviction

The purpose of similar fact evidence adduced under section 1 (f) (i) can only be to help prove the guilt of the defendant. The purpose, however, of the prohibited questions under section 1 (f) (ii) is not quite so clear. It seems manifestly reasonable that, if a defendant seeks to set up his good character, the prosecution should be entitled to rebut such an assertion; equally where the character of a prosecution witness is attacked, retaliation against the defendant seems fair. To what purpose, however, should evidence of a defendant's bad character or previous convictions be

23. *Selvey v. Director of Public Prosecutions* [1970] A.C. 304; but see *The People v. Coleman* [1945] I.R. 237 (C.C.A.).
24. *R. v. Butterwasser* [1948] 1 K.B. 4; it should be noted that the prosecution cannot introduce any evidence of previous convictions or bad character under section 1 (f) (ii) unless the defendant testifies; cf. *R. v. de Vere* [1981] 3 All E.R. 473. (An unsworn statement from the dock making imputations on prosecution witnesses does not put an accused's character in issue; nor can section 1 (f) (ii) apply.)
25. *R. v. Wood* [1920] 2 K.B. 179.
26. *Maxwell v. Director of Public Prosecutions* [1935] A.C. 309.
27. 86 I.L.T.R. 168.

put? This question arose in *The People v. Bond,*[28] where the defendant's defence was one of alibi, but it also involved the casting of imputations on the character of the prosecution witnesses. It was urged upon the Court of Criminal Appeal that injustice might have been occasioned to Bond by reason of the fact that the trial judge had failed to instruct the jury that the evidence of Bond's previous convictions was generally inadmissible, but that its admission in the instant case had been due to the fact that Bond had attacked the character of prosecution witnesses, and being so admitted it could only be used by the jury to consider the credibility of Bond and *not* in relation to the probability of his having committed the offence charged. The Court of Criminal Appeal stated:[29]

> 'The way in which this evidence was to be used by the jury was vital to the interests of the applicant. It certainly necessitated a careful direction from the Judge as to why it was admitted, and as to how it was to be used; that it went to his credit only, and should on no account be used to show the probability of his guilt.'

This conclusion, so emphatically reached by the court, was diametrically opposed to an earlier one posited by eminent writers[30] one of whom suggested,

> 'If . . . it is decided that such cross-examination goes to credibility alone and not to guilt, and that juries should be so instructed, we shall be faced with a most extreme example of the operation of what Wigmore so aptly terms "the principle of multiple admissibility". Evidence will be allowed to go to the jury for one proper purpose, to be used by them, despite the most categorical of instructions, for another quite improper purpose. For it is usually relevant not merely to the credibility of the defendant *qua* witness but to the guilt of the witness *qua* defendant.'[31]

While *Bond*'s case remains law in Ireland, it places a heavy onus upon the trial judge to explain specifically to the jury the

28. [1966] I.R. 214.
29. Id. at 223.
30. See generally, Stone, *Cross Examination by the Prosecution at Common Law and under the Criminal Evidence Act, 1898: A Commentary on Maxwell v. Director of Public Prosecutions* 51 L.Q.R. 443; also Stone, '*Further Problems in the Interpretation of the Criminal Evidence Act, 1898, s. 1, Proviso (f.)* 58 L.Q.R. 369.
31. Stone, op. cit., 51 L.Q.R. 443, 463.

limited purpose for which they have received the evidence admitted under section 1 (f) (ii). It seems difficult to expect a jury to be able to differentiate between evidence which goes merely to credibility and evidence which goes to proof of guilt. It would also seem to be the case that, when a defendant asserts his good character, he is inviting the jury to accept that he is not the kind of person who would commit the offence charged, and therefore logically the evidence of a defendant's bad character ought to be capable of evaluation by the jury as showing the opposite to be the case.[32]

Cross-examination as to previous convictions and/or bad character may be admissible under section 1 (f) (iii) if the defendant has given evidence against any other person charged with the *same* offence. When considering this provision it is the *effect* of a defendant's testimony rather than his intent which is relevant to the decision whether or not the shield has been dropped. Counsel for each co-accused charged with the same offence against whom evidence has been given is entitled *as of right* to put the otherwise prohibited questions, and the trial judge enjoys no discretion in the matter. It is, however, desirable that any defence counsel wishing to undertake such a cross-examination as to bad character or previous offences should first inform the court and the counsel whose client is involved. Prosecuting counsel wishing to ask similar questions under section 1 (f) (iii) requires the court's permission to do so.

It should be noted that section 1 (f) (iii) is only applicable where co-accused are indicted upon the same charges.[33] Where this is not the case, for example where one defendant is charged with theft and another with receiving, then, if imputations are made by one defendant against another, the position is not clear.[34] It is possible that in such a situation counsel for a co-defendant might be able to cross-examine with the judge's permission under section 1 (f) (ii), although a strict reading of this

32. English courts appear to share the view of the Irish Court of Criminal Appeal that cross-examination in relation to section 1 (f) (ii) matters goes to credibility only; see *R. v. Vickers* [1972] Crim. L.R. 101.
33. *R. v. Russell* [1971] 1 Q.B. 151.
34. See *R. v. Lovett* [1973] 1 W.L.R. 241.

section would appear not to justify such a result, as it refers only to 'imputations on the character of the *prosecutor* or witnesses for the *prosecution*.'

Competence and compellability of defence witnesses other than the defendant

Although it is subject to a number of important exceptions, the general rule is that any person who can offer testimony relevant to the defence case is competent and also compellable as a defence witness.[35] It is rare for the defence to seek to compel an unwilling witness to testify. Those persons excepted from the general rule of compellability are:

(i) *Co-defendants:* By virtue of section 1 of the Criminal Justice (Evidence) Act, 1924, a defendant is competent but may not be compelled to testify in the defence case where another person is being jointly tried with him. Any person who has been or is to be tried separately from the defendant is a compellable witness. A person who has pleaded guilty in a joint trial is compellable as a witness for a co-defendant.[36] The only other instance in which a co-defendant in a joint trial is compellable as a defence witness is on a charge of public nuisance under the Evidence Act, 1877.

(ii) *The spouse of a defendant:* The position of a defendant's spouse as a prosecution witness has already been discussed. In every criminal case the spouse of the defendant is competent as a defence witness but only in a prosecution under the Evidence Act, 1877, is the spouse of a defendant compellable.

(iii) *A defendant's spouse as a witness for a co-defendant:* By virtue of section 1 (c) of the Criminal Justice (Evidence) Act, 1924, the spouse of one defendant is competent but not compellable in any criminal case as a witness for a co-defendant, if the defendant gives his consent. The consent of the defendant, however, is unnecessary in any case which falls within the Schedule to the Act of 1924, as amended,[37] or in any case to which section 9 of the Married Women's Status Act, 1957, applies or in any pro-

35. On the topic of competence and compellability of witnesses generally, see Cross, op. cit. 163-188.
36. *R. v. Boal* [1965] 1 Q.B. 402.
37. Supra, pp. 324-325.

secution for an offence under the Unemployment Assistance Act, 1933, or the Unemployment Assistance (Amendment) Act, 1935.[38] In each of these instances a spouse would appear to be competent but not compellable.[39] Under the Evidence Act, 1877, a spouse of a co-defendant is compellable.

Further evidence

The normal rule of practice, though not of law, is that evidence upon which the prosecution intends to rely should be adduced before the close of the case for the prosecution. It may happen that evidence becomes available to the prosecution after that, or that the prosecution inadvertently omits to adduce some evidence, or wishes to rebut evidence adduced by the defence.

Whether further evidence should be allowed after the close of the case for the prosecution and the case for the defence appears to be entirely within the discretion of the judge, bearing in mind that:

> '[I]n a criminal trial the administration of justice means justice for the People and for the accused and the admission of matters which either side wishes to produce must be decided by the same principle.'[1]

If the evidence for the defence introduces new matters which the prosecution could not foresee, the court has a discretion to permit rebutting evidence to be adduced by the prosecution.[2] There is no rule corresponding to that introduced in England,[3] that advance notice should be given of witnesses to a defence of alibi.

The trial judge may himself call a witness who has not been called by either party, but should only do so in exceptional circumstances, particularly after the case for the defence has

38. Unemployment Assistance (Amendment) Act, 1935, s. 18.
39. *Leach v. R.* [1912] A.C. 305.
1. *Per* Kenny J., in *The People v. O'Brien*, 22nd October, 1969, Frewen 343, 345. See generally, Archbold §§4-408, 4-414; *R. v. Rice* [1963] 1 Q.B. 857; *R. v. Doran* 56 Cr. App. R. 429; *R. v. Kane* 65 Cr. App. R. 270 (in which the evidence was improperly introduced by way of cross-examination of the accused); *R. v. Halford* 67 Cr. App. R. 318.
2. *R. v. Whelan* 8 L.R. Ir. 314 (Q.B.D.); *Attorney General v. Gleeson* 64 I.L.T.R. 225 (C.C.A.); Archbold §§4-409, 4-410.
3. Criminal Justice Act, 1967, s. 11.

closed.[4] Although neither party is entitled to cross-examine such a witness as of right, each should be given leave to do so if the witness proves adverse to that party.[5] Moreover, the judge is entitled to question or cross-examine any witness, whether for the prosecution or for the defence, including the defendant if he gives evidence on oath, providing that his questioning is fair; but constant interruptions of the defence case may render the trial unsatisfactory.[6]

The trial judge may, at any stage of the case and without the consent of the defence, require the jury to retire and may hear argument and evidence in their absence.

> 'We think it is a prudent course that the judge should read the depositions before the trial and if he has any doubt about the admission of evidence, even though it is not objected to by any counsel, he should ask the jury to retire.'[7]

Closing addresses

As has been seen, prosecuting counsel in addressing the jury is not entitled to comment on the failure of the accused or the spouse of the accused to give evidence.[8] Nor should he comment on the absence of other witnesses, unless it might be fairly expected that witnesses would be called to support a story presented by the accused, nor should he urge a conviction on the ground that acquittal would damage the character or reputation of the complainant.[9]

Counsel for the defence, on the other hand, should not state to the jury, as existing facts, matters which the accused has told him but which have not been put in evidence,[10] nor suggest, without evidence, that the crime was committed by some specific person not on trial,[11] although he is entitled to draw the attention of the

4. Archbold §4.413; *R. v. Harris* [1927] 2 K.B. 587.
5. *Coulson v. Disborough* [1894] 2 Q.B. 316.
6. *The People v. McGuinness* [1978] I.R. 189 (C.C.A.); Archbold §4-382.
7. *Per* Kenny J. delivering the judgment of the Court of Criminal Appeal in *The People v. O'Brien*, 22nd October, 1969, Frewen 343, 347; some judges, however, prefer not to read the Book in order to hear the case with an open mind.
8. Criminal Justice (Evidence) Act, 1924, s. 1 (b).
9. *R. v. Rudland* 4 F. & F. 495; *R. v. Puddick* 4 F. & F. 497.
10. *R. v. Shimmin* 15 Cox 122.
11. *Attorney General v. O'Leary* [1926] I.R. 445 (C.C.A.).

jury to any evidence which might reasonably show that *some* other person was responsible.[12] He should exercise restraint in referring to the consequences of conviction of a capital crime,[13] and he should not invite the jury to add a rider to their verdict.[14]

In a recent case in the English Court of Appeal (Criminal Division), involving charges of conspiracy to defraud. Lawton L.J. in giving the judgment of the Court said:[15]

> 'The first 73 days of the trial were taken up with Crown counsel's opening speech, submissions and evidence. The last days of winter passed into high summer. By the beginning of July the jury must have had the evidence well in mind. What they wanted at that stage of the case was a clear and concise summary of what each party was putting forward. What they got was 11 days of counsel's speeches followed by 6 days of summing up. Crown counsel's speech went on for 4 days, the speeches of the defending counsel taking up 7 days. We have no reason for thinking that counsel were unduly prolix by the standards of present day forensic fashion. The fault lies partly in the fashion but also in the present tendency to overload cases. The great advocates of the past did not find it necessary to address juries at such great length. We can see no good reason for such prolixity nowadays. If the object of a closing speech is to ensure that the jury keep in mind when considering their verdict the points which counsel wish to bring out, they are unlikely to do so if, as in the case of the counsel's speech for the Crown, they heard it three weeks before.'

IV. SUMMING UP

At the close of the evidence and after any addresses by counsel or the accused it is normally the duty of the judge to sum-up the case, or 'charge' the jury,[1] although it appears that in a simple case where the facts and the law are clear, this is not essential.[2]

In *R. v. Landy* Lawton L.J. said:[3]

> 'A summing up should be clear, concise and intelligible. If it is overloaded with detail, whether of fact or law and follows no obvious

12. *R. v. Wainright* 13 Cox 171.
13. *Attorney General v. O'Leary* [1926] I.R. 445.
14. *R. v. Black* [1963] 1 W.L.R. 1311.
15. *R. v. Landy* [1981] 1 W.L.R. 355, 363.
1. *R. v. Finch* 12 Cr. App. R. 77.
2. *R. v. Newman* 9 Cr. App. R. 134; *R. v. Attfield* [1961] 1 W.L.R. 1135.
3. [1981] 1 W.L.R. 355, 367.

plan, it will not have any of the attributes it should have. This summing up suffered from the fact that the judge was over-conscientious. He seems to have decided that the jury should be reminded of nearly all the details of the evidence and directed as to every facet of the law which applied. He must have spent hours preparing his summing up but in the end he got lost in the trees and missed the wood.'

Some three months later in *R. v. Lawrence* Lord Hailsham L.C. said in the House of Lords:[4]

'It has been said before, but obviously requires to be said again. The purpose of a direction to a jury is not best achieved by a disquisition on jurisprudence or philosophy or a universally applicable circular tour round the area of law affected by the case. The search for universally applicable definitions is often productive of more obscurity than light. A direction is seldom improved and may be considerably damaged by copious recitations from the total content of a judge's notebook. A direction to a jury should be custom built to make the jury understand their task in relation to a particular case.'

Where, as almost invariably, the judge does sum up the case he must present the case for the defence as well as the case for the prosecution, and a verdict of guilty delivered by the jury before they have heard the summing up of the defence case may be quashed.[5]

Matters of law may be of general application to any criminal trial or matters particular to a given trial or a given charge. It has also been said that the judge's directions on law should be such as to aid the common sense of the jury in arriving at a verdict,[6] and avoid matters which are in fact irrelevant, such as a disparaging reference to a previous trial and acquittal of the accused.[7]

Of general application are the respective functions of the judge and jury; the fact that the jurors, whilst entitled to avail of their general knowledge and their common sense,[8] are otherwise restricted to the evidence which has been adduced in court to the exclusion of what they may have read or heard elsewhere; the

4. [1982] A.C. 510, 519.
5. *R. v. Young* [1964] 1 W.L.R. 717.
6. *R. v. Bonnyman* 28 Cr. App. R. 131.
7. *Attorney General v. Hurley* 71 I.L.T.R. 29 (C.C.A.).
8. *R. v. Rosser* 7 C. & P. 648; *R. v. Jones* 54 Cr. App. R. 63.

fact that their verdict, if they agree, must be unanimous for conviction or acquittal (but that they are entitled to disagree); that in a case in which an aggrieved party may have suffered loss or injury, their verdict will have no effect on civil proceedings which that party might take. The judge should not invite a rider to the verdict.[9]

The most important direction to be given in all cases is that, if the jury are to convict the accused, they must be satisfied of his guilt beyond a reasonable doubt. Precisely how this should be done has given rise to much divergence of judicial opinion, both in Ireland and in England. It has been suggested in some English cases that use of the words 'reasonable doubt' should be avoided,[10] but there is considerable authority to the contrary.[11] Certainty is not required but the use of such expressions as 'sure', 'satisfied', 'pretty certain', 'reasonably sure', 'pretty sure' may be unsuitable; a distinction has been drawn between 'the sort of doubt which might affect you in the conduct of your everyday affairs' and 'the sort of doubt which may affect the mind of a person in the conduct of important affairs'.[12] It had been said that by the time he begins to sum up, the judge has had an opportunity of observing the jurors and should use the most appropriate words in which to make that particular jury understand that they must not return a verdict against the accused unless they are sure of his guilt.[13]

Irish cases in which the question has been considered include *Attorney General v. Murray,*[14] and *The People v. Casey.*[15] The most recent reported pronouncement in the Court of Criminal Appeal was in *The People v. Byrne,* in which Kenny J., giving the judgment of the Court, reviewed a number of English and Australian cases and said:[16]

9. *R. v. Larkin* [1943] 1 K.B. 174; *R. v. Black* [1963] 1 W.L.R. 1311.
10. See, e.g., *R. v. Summers* [1952] 1 All E.R. 1059; *R. v. Hepworth* [1955] 2 Q.B. 600.
11. See, e.g., *Woolmington v. Director of Public Prosecutions* [1935] A.C. 462); *McGreevy v. Director of Public Prosecutions* [1973] 1 W.L.R. 276; *Ferguson v. R.* [1979] 1 All E.R. 877.
12. See *Walters v. R.* [1969] 2 A.C. 26; *R. v. Gray* 58 Cr. App. R. 177, and generally, Archbold §4-426.
13. *Walters v. R.* [1969] A.C. 26.
14. [1926] I.R. 266 (C.C.A.).
15. [1938] Ir. Jur. Rep. 56 (C.C.A.).
16. [1974] I.R. 1, 9 (C.C.A.).

'The correct charge to a jury is that they must be satisfied beyond reasonable doubt of the guilt of the accused, and it is helpful if that degree of proof is contrasted with that in a civil case. It is also essential, however, that the jury should be told that the accused is entitled to the benefit of the doubt and that when two views on any part of the case are possible on the evidence, they should adopt that which is favourable to the accused unless the State has established the other beyond reasonable doubt.

In this case the trial judge used the words "satisfied" and "to your satisfaction" on many occasions when explaining the onus of proof. He then said that "being satisfied" means the same thing as "beyond a reasonable doubt". This is not correct because one may be satisfied of something and still have a reasonable doubt. The judge made no attempt to explain to the jury what degree of satisfaction is required and it is in this respect that the time-honoured words "beyond reasonable doubt" are of such assistance; nor did the judge tell the jury that the accused were entitled to the benefit of the doubt. The Court thinks that jurymen understand the meaning of the expression "beyond reasonable doubt" particularly when it is associated with a comparison of the standard of proof in a civil case.'

Whilst, however, the judge should make it clear that the onus of proof of the guilt of the accused lies at all stages on the prosecution and that if they have any doubt on any particular matter they should give the benefit of that doubt to the accused,[17] this does not mean that doubt on any one matter entitles the accused to be acquitted; the jury may have doubts about the credibility or accuracy of one witness, in which case they should ignore his evidence, but still be satisfied beyond reasonable doubt from the evidence of other witnesses of the guilt of the accused.

It is sometimes stated that the jury should first consider the evidence for the prosecution and that only if they are not then satisfied should they consider the evidence for the defence. It is submitted that such a direction is not in accordance with the authorities; if the defence goes into evidence, that evidence becomes part of the case as a whole,[18] and that, provided that the

17. *Attorney General v. O'Connor* [1935] Ir. Jur. Rep. 1 (C.C.A.); *The People v. Berber* [1944] I.R. 405 (C.C.A.); *The People v. Quinn* [1965] I.R. 366 (S.C.); *The People v. Oglesby* [1966] I.R. 162 (C.C.A.); *The People v. Power,* unrep. 31st July, 1975.
18. *R. v. Rudd* 32 Cr. App. R. 138.

accused has *some* case to answer and a direction to acquit has been refused, the prosecution may rely on evidence given by or on behalf of the accused to make good any defects in the evidence for the prosecution.[19] It would seem absurd that a defendant who has a case to answer and who goes into the witness box and admits his guilt should be entitled to an acquittal. It is, therefore, submitted that a more proper direction would be that the jury should first consider the case for the prosecution and then, if satisfied that the accused *may* be guilty, they should consider any evidence for the defence, bearing in mind that *throughout* the case the onus of establishing the guilt of the accused from the evidence as a whole remains with the prosecution.

More particularly, if there are several accused the judge should warn the jury that they must deal with each separately and by reference to so much only of the evidence as is material to the guilt or innocence of the particular accused with whom they are dealing. If there are several counts he should warn them that each count constitutes a distinct charge on which they may convict only on such of the evidence as is material to it and that they should not, so to speak, supplement the evidence material to one count with evidence material *only* to another.[20] To take a simple example, the accused might be charged in different counts of the indictment with several distinct larcenies: in considering each count the jury must confine themselves to the evidence (including any admission made by the accused) relevant to that larceny and must not, if satisfied as to the guilt or innocence of the accused on that count, permit themselves to take it into consideration when passing on to the next. The same evidence or much of it may, however, be material to more than one count, as where the counts are alternative, such as larceny or receiving stolen goods, or when the counts vary in degree, as where the accused is charged with wounding with intent to cause grievous bodily harm and with an assault occasioning actual bodily harm.

If, by mistake, inadmissible evidence has been given before the jury they should be warned to ignore it.[21]

19. *R. v. Abbott* [1955] 2. Q.B. 497.
20. *The People v. Wallace,* unrep. 22nd November, 1982 (C.C.A.); Archbold §4-424.
21. *R. v. Gibson* 18 Q.B.D. 533.

The judge should warn the jury of the danger in certain cases of convicting on uncorroborated evidence and as to what may constitute corroboration,[22] and as to the risk of error on matters of visual identification.[23]

He is entitled to give the jury the benefit of his experience, for example, that medical evidence has not been adduced by the defence, as is usual, in support of a plea of insanity.[24]

If the case depends on circumstantial evidence, the judge should warn the jury that they should not convict unless satisfied that it is consistent only with the guilt of the accused.[25]

When dealing with the particular charge the judge should instruct the jury as to the necessary ingredients of the offence.[26]

In some cases the legal burden of proof is to a certain extent shifted by statute to the defence. For example, if a person is charged with possession of housebreaking implements at night without lawful excuse the proof of the excuse lies on the accused,[27] but the burden of proof when cast upon the accused is that of the balance of probability,[28] as in the case of a defence of insanity;[29] the wording of the statute in question must, however, be considered in every such case.

As regards the facts, the length and detail of the charge to the jury must depend on the relative simplicity or complexity of the case and it may not be fatal to a conviction that there was no discussion of the facts.[30] The judge is entitled to express his opinion, even strongly, as to the facts, provided that he makes it clear to the jury that they alone are the judges of the facts and should ignore his views if they disagree with him.[31] He may comment on the evidence given and on the absence of evidence which might have been given, and, unlike the prosecution, he may comment

22. Supra, pp. 207 sqq.
23. Supra, pp. 210 sqq.
24. *The People v. Manning* 89 I.L.T.R. 155 (C.C.A.).
25. *Attorney General v. Finkel,* 31st January, 1951, Frewen 123.
26. *R. v. Lincoln* [1944] 1 All E.R. 604; *The People v. Bristow,* 7th November, 1961, Frewen 249.
27. Larceny Act, 1916, s. 28.
28. *R. v. Carr Briant* [1943] K.B. 607.
29. Infra, p. 372.
30. *R. v. Attfield* 45 Cr. App. R. 309.
31. *R. v. O'Donnell* 12 Cr. App. R. 219; *R. v. Canny* 30 Cr. App. R. 143.

on the failure of the accused or his wife to give evidence, or to call evidence in support of some aspect of the defence, but should only do so if, in the circumstances, such comment is fair and just.[32] He may comment on the failure of the accused to disclose his defence before the trial, as in the case where the accused pleads an alibi, but bearing in mind that an accused is not bound to disclose his defence and is indeed, so cautioned at the conclusion of the preliminary hearing.[33] He should not refer to the possibility of a verdict of guilty being reversed on appeal, although, if he does, it may not amount to a misdirection.[34] If there is evidence which might entitle the jury to acquit or to bring in a verdict of guilty of an offence lesser than that charged, as when for example, on a charge of murder there is evidence to suggest the possibility of accident or provocation, the judge should direct the jury accordingly even though the particular defence is not raised;[35] but he need not do so if there is no such evidence,[36] and may exceptionally direct the jury that on the evidence they cannot, as a matter of law, bring in the lesser verdict.[37]

Retirement of jury

At the conclusion of the judge's charge the jury normally retire to consider their verdict, an officer of the court being sworn to keep them and suffer none to speak to them or to speak to them himself, without leave of the court, except only to ask them whether they are agreed upon their verdict.[1]

If either the prosecution or the defence wishes to object to any portion of, or suggest any omission from, any part of the judge's charge they should do so when the jury retire, by submitting 'requisitions' asking the judge to correct anything and so forth,

32. *The People v. Trayers* [1956] I.R. 110 (C.C.A.); *The People v. Reynolds*, 6th June, 1958, Frewen 184; Archbold §4-431.
33. *Attorney General v. Fleming*]1934] I.R. 166 (C.C.A.); Archbold §4-431.
34. *Attorney General v. Murray* [1926] I.R. 266 (C.C.A.).
35. *Bullard v. R.* [1957] A.C. 635; Archbold §4-425.
36. *The State v. McMullen* [1925] 2 I.R. 9 (C.C.A.); *The People v. Kelly*, 31st August, 1953, Frewen 147.
37. *The State v. McMullen* supra; cf. *The People v. Cadden*, 24th December, 1956, Frewen 157; *The People v. McGrath*, 4th May, 1960, Frewen 192; *R. v. Vickers* 61 Cr. App. R. 48; Archbold §4-437.
1. 2 Hale 296.

and the judge may, if he thinks fit, recall the jury and direct them further, but he should not invite argument after the jury has retired.[2] Failure by the defence to raise any such objection may put it at a disadvantage in making the objection on appeal.[3]

It appears that once they have retired to consider their verdict the jury may not separate without the special permission of the court, and they were at one time 'to be kept together without meat, drink, fire or candle' until they were agreed.[4]

The jury, having retired, may ask for any witness to be recalled, and the judge has a discretion whether to acceded to such a request.[5]

The jury may ask for further assistance from the judge, and such assistance must be given in open court in the presence of counsel,[6] and even without such a request the judge may himself wish to correct some direction he has given.

When the jury retire they are given an 'issue paper', a formulation of the charges and indication of the issues to be determined and to be delivered by the foreman; although a list of questions may sometimes be sufficient.[7] They should also be given, or have made available to them if they want to examine them, such exhibits as have been put in evidence, particularly any written statement by the accused. Care should be taken that only documents which have been admitted in evidence are given to the jury since if, when they retire, they are given anything which was not in evidence, the trial may be held to have been unsatisfactory and a conviction quashed.[8] In addition a statement by the accused may need to be 'edited' before being given to the jury, where, for example, it includes admissions of other crimes not relevant to the issue, or where it implicates a co-accused; in the latter case a

2. *R. v. Cocks* 63 Cr. App. R. 79.
3. Chapter 16, infra.
4. 2 Hale 297. They may now in practice be allowed refreshment both during the trial and after they have retired, at the expense of the State (in England at their own expense, Juries Act, 1974, s. 15).
5. *The State v. Kelly* [1925] 2 I.R. 73 (C.C.A.); *Attorney General v. McDermott* [1933] I.R. 512 (C.C.A.); *The People v. O'Brien* [1963] I.R. 65 (S.C.); the rule in England appears to be different; see Archbold §4-383.
6. *R. v. Willmott* 10 Cr. App. R. 173.
7. *The People v. McCormack,* 5th July, 1944, Frewen 55.
8. *The People v. Moran,* 27th June, 1979, Frewen 380.

practice has developed of substituting in the edited version, words like 'another man', instead of the co-accused by name.

V. THE VERDICT

Generally

The verdict of the jury, whether it be for conviction or acquittal, must be unanimous.

> '[It is a fundamental principle] that every accusation, whether preferred in the shape of an indictment or information, shall afterwards be confirmed by the unanimous suffrage of twelve of the party's equals and neighbours, indifferently chosen, and superior to all suspicion.'[1]

There is no provision in Ireland, as there is in civil cases,[2] and as there is in England in criminal cases when the jury have failed after a reasonable time to agree on a verdict,[3] for accepting the verdict of a certain majority. All twelve jurors (or if their number has been reduced, all of those who remain) must agree that the accused is either guilty or not guilty on each count. If they fail to agree on any count, they must be discharged and a new trial ordered;[4] if they agree on some counts and disagree on other counts a new trial will be ordered on the counts on which they have failed to agree, unless the verdict which they have given amounts in substance to a conviction or acquittal on the outstanding counts or the prosecution is satisfied to accept the verdict on the counts on which the jury have agreed and to enter a *nolle prosequi* on the remainder.[5] It is generally considered undesirable that the new trial should be by a jury selected from the same panel as the last, since some of the jurors may have been present during the earlier trial, and the new jury may only try the case on the evidence presented during the trial before it.

The jury may bring in either a general verdict or a special verdict. A general verdict is that the accused is guilty or not guilty. If

1. Gabbett, *Criminal Law*, (1843) Vol. 2, p. 362.
2. Courts of Justice Act, 1924, s. 94, as amended by the Courts of Justice Act, 1928, s. 20 and the Courts Act, 1971, s. 6.
3. Juries Act, 1974, s. 17.
4. *The State v. McMullen* [1925] 2 I.R. 9 (C.C.A.).
5. Archbold §4-447.

there are several counts, he may be convicted on all, or acquitted on all, or may be found guilty on some counts and not guilty on others; if different counts relate to the same type of offence but vary in degree, such as wounding with intent, and assault occasioning actual bodily harm, then if the jury acquit on the more serious they may convict on the lesser charge; but if they convict on the more serious they should be directed to return no verdict on the lesser charge. If there are several defendants some may be found guilty and others not guilty, but when the particular crime involves the implication of more than one person, such as riot or conspiracy[6] then the acquittal of some may necessarily involve the acquittal of the rest. Thus conspiracy necessarily involves at least two persons. If two accused are charged with conspiring together, and with nobody else (such as a third person or a person unknown), the acquittal of one necessitates the acquittal of the other.[7]

Alternative verdicts

In certain cases the jury may, either at common law or by statute, find the accused guilty of an offence other than that charged in the indictment.

At common law

At common law a person charged with the commission of a felony could not be found guilty of a misdemeanour.[1]

The common law rule has been modified by statute to a small extent, in that, if, on the trial of a person for any misdemeanour, it appears that the facts given in evidence amount to a felony, he is not by reason thereof to be acquitted of the misdemeanour, but he is not afterwards to be prosecuted for felony on the same facts unless at the first trial the court shall have discharged the jury and directed that the accused be indicted for felony.[2] If, however, the accused is charged with a felony or a misdemeanour with some form of aggravation he may be convicted of an unaggravated or

6. 2 Hawk. c. 47, s. 8.
7. But see Archbold §28-33.
1. *R. v. Thomas* L.R. 2 C.C.R. 141.
2. Criminal Procedure Act, 1851, s. 12; cf. *R. v. Garland* [1910] 1 K.B. 154.

less aggravated felony or misdemeanour as the case may be.[3] Most commonly, perhaps, if the accused is charged with murder he may be found guilty of manslaughter, if malice aforethought is not established.[4] On a charge of riot, the accused may be convicted of rout (if the crowd had not started to put their purpose into effect) or unlawful assembly (if it had not set out to achieve that purpose) or, if an assault has been charged, of assault.[5] Similarly when a statute prescribes a higher penalty for a common law offence in certain circumstances, such as an assault occasioning actual bodily harm or an indecent assault, and the special circumstances are not proved, the accused may be convicted of the simple common law offence, such as common assault.[6]

By statute

By statute the accused may be found guilty of an offence other than that charged in a number of cases, and when the statute enables such a verdict to be given by a jury it may be pronounced by a court sitting without a jury, such as the Special Criminal Court.[7]

A person charged with a substantive offence may be convicted of an attempt to commit the offence.[8] Whether the attempt must be to commit precisely the same offence appears to be doubtful, as is also the question whether the accused may be convicted of an attempt declared by statute to be a felony as distinct from one which is a mere misdemeanour.[9]

A person charged with capital murder may be convicted of ordinary murder or manslaughter,[10] if, for example, the charge relates to the murder of a police officer and it is not established that he was known to be acting in the course of his duty.

3. Archbold, 25th Edn. p. 204.
4. *The People v. White* [1947] I.R. 247 (C.C.A.).
5. Archbold, 25th Edn. p. 1165.
6. Id. p. 204.
7. Criminal Justice (Verdicts) Act, 1976, s. 1, negativing the effect of *The People v. Yates,* unrep. 12th November, 1975 (C.C.A.).
8. Criminal Procedure Act, 1851, s. 9.
9. See Archbold, 25th Edn. p. 208. The position has to some extent been modified in England by the Criminal Law Act, 1967, s. 6.
10. Criminal Justice Act, 1964, s. 3 (2); cf. *The People v. Murray* [1977] I.R. 360 (S.C.).

If the accused is charged with murder of a child he may be convicted of concealment of birth.[11]

If the accused is a woman charged with murder she may be found guilty of infanticide.[12]

On an indictment for robbery the accused may be found guilty of an assault with intent to rob,[13] but not, it appears, of a common assault.[14]

If a person aged over 17 is charged with manslaughter of a person under 16, he may be convicted of cruelty to the child.[15]

If the accused is charged with administering poison with intent to endanger life or inflict grievous bodily harm he may be convicted of the misdemeanour of administering poison with intent to injure, aggrieve or annoy.[16]

If the accused is charged with rape at common law, he may be found guilty of unlawful carnal knowledge or attempted carnal knowledge of a girl under 15, or of a girl of 15 to 17 years of age, procuring carnal knowledge or indecent assault. On a charge of unlawful carnal knowledge of a girl under 15, the accused may be found guilty of the statutory offence of the attempt (supposing the complete offence is not established) or of carnal knowledge or attempted carnal knowledge of a girl between 15 and 17 years (supposing that it is established that she was between those ages but not that she was under 15), procuring carnal knowledge or indecent assault.[17]

On an indictment for incest the accused may be found guilty (supposing, for example, that the necessary degree of relationship between him and his victim is not established) of carnal knowledge or attempted carnal knowledge of a girl under 15 or between the ages of 15 and 17 years.[18]

A person charged with a corrupt practice at an election may be

11. Offences against the Person Act, 1861, s. 60.
12. Infanticide Act, 1949, s. 1 (2).
13. Larceny Act, 1916, s. 44 (1).
14. *R. v. Woodhall* 12 Cox 240.
15. Children Act, 1908, s. 12 (4) as amended by the Children (Amendment) Act, 1957, s. 4.
16. Offences against the Person Act, 1861, s. 25.
17. Criminal Law Amendment Act, 1935, s. 3.
18. Punishment of Incest Act, 1908, s. 4 (3) as amended by the Criminal Law Amendment Act, 1935, s. 12.

convicted of an illegal practice.[19]

On a charge of riotously demolishing a building the accused may be convicted of riotous damage.[20]

On a charge of larceny the accused may be convicted of embezzlement or fraudulent application, and if charged with embezzlement he may be convicted of stealing,[21] but not, it would seem, of fraudulent conversion.[22] If charged with larceny he may likewise be convicted of obtaining by false pretences,[23] whilst if he is charged with the latter offence, he is not entitled to be acquitted if the evidence establishes that he stole the property.[24] It should, however, be noted that these statutory provisions do not equate the offences for all purposes. It would seem doubtful whether if the accused is charged with larceny he may be convicted of *attempting* to obtain by false pretences; and the distinction may also be relevant on a charge of receiving, where the quality of the offence and, more important, the penalty, depends on whether the primary offence was a felony, such as larceny, or a misdemeanour, such as obtaining by false pretences.[25]

A person charged with an offence under section 2 (which relates to offences committed in Northern Ireland) or section 3 (which relates to escape from custody in Northern Ireland) of the Criminal Law (Jurisdiction) Act, 1976, may be convicted of impeding the apprehension or prosecution of the primary offender.[26]

On a charge of dangerous driving (which is indictable if it causes death or serious bodily harm to another) the accused may be found guilty of driving without due care and attention, or without reasonable consideration for other persons.[27]

If the indictment charges the accused with any felony (other than murder or manslaughter) and alleges that the accused cut, stabbed or wounded any person the jury may acquit the accused

19. Prevention of Electoral Abuses Act, 1923, s. 53.
20. Malicious Damage Act, 1861, s. 12.
21. Larceny Act, 1916, s. 44 (2).
22. *R. v. Stevens* 24 Cr. App. R. 85.
23. Larceny Act, 1916, s. 44 (3).
24. Id. s. 44 (4).
25. Id. s. 33 (1).
26. Criminal Law (Jurisdiction) Act, 1976, s. 2 (5).
27. Road Traffic Act, 1961, s. 53 (4).

of the felony charged (e.g. wounding with intent) but find him guilty of unlawful wounding.[28] It is, nevertheless, usual to charge an accused with wounding with intent to maim, disfigure or disable, or cause grievous bodily harm to some person, contrary to section 18 of the Offences against the Person Act, 1861, and with a separate count of malicious wounding under section 20 of the same statute.[29]

In the case of purely statutory offences, as distinct from offences at common law for which a statute has prescribed the penalty, the extent to which the jury, in the absence of any specific provision such as those mentioned above, may find the accused guilty of an offence other than that charged in the indictment is less clear. The common law may be compared to a conglomerate and statute law to a number of distinct globules. Every statutory offence is a distinct offence. Every wounding involves an assault, but wounding, as such, appears to be a purely statutory offence; there is, however, authority for the proposition that a person charged with malicious wounding may be found guilty of a common assault if the wounding is not established.[30]

Larceny and burglary, the breaking and entering of the dwellinghouse of another in the night with intent to commit a felony therein,[31] were offences at common law; housebreaking by day, or shop-breaking were not. It was common to frame a single count charging both burglary or housebreaking and larceny, thereby in effect alleging two distinct offences,[32] and it appears that if the evidence established the stealing but not the breaking and entering the accused might be found guilty of larceny or, if the value of the goods exceeded £5, of larceny in a dwellinghouse.[33] Robbery was also a common law offence, the felonious and forcible taking from the person of another and against his will of any money or goods by violence or putting him in fear.[34] As has been observed, if the accused is charged with robbery, he

28. Prevention of Offences Act, 1851, s. 5.
29. See Archbold, 25th Edn. p. 899.
30. *R. v. Taylor* L.R. 1 C.C.R. 194.
31. Archbold, 25th Edn. p. 634.
32. *R. v. Hungerford* 2 East P.C. 518; supra, p. 249.
33. Archbold, 25th Edn. pp. 634, 650.
34. Id. citing 4 Bl. Comm. 243, 1 Hawk c. 34.

may be found guilty of an assault with intent to rob,[35] supposing that the stealing is not established. There is no statutory provision, and appears to be no authority for the converse situation where the stealing but not the use of force or putting in fear is established. It appears, however, that if the accused was charged with aggravated robbery, but the particular form of aggravation was not established, he might be convicted of simple robbery.[36]

Sections 5, 6 and 7 of the Criminal Law (Jurisdiction) Act, 1976, however, introduced into the Larceny Act, 1916, definitions of robbery and burglary and a new offence of aggravated burglary, and correspond to sections 8, 9 and 10 of the English Theft Act, 1968. Robbery is now committed by a person who steals and, immediately before or at the time of doing so, and in order to do so, uses force on any person or seeks to put any person in fear of being then and there subjected to force.[37] There has been no repeal of the provision, referred to above, that a person charged with robbery may be convicted of an assault with intent to rob. There is, however, no express provision that a person charged with robbery may be found guilty of larceny, or of larceny from the person, if the use of force and so forth is not established. A person is guilty of burglary if he either:

(a) enters any building or part of a building as a trespasser with intent to steal in the building or inflict any grievous bodily harm on any person or rape any woman therein, or to do unlawful damage to the building or anything therein or,

(b) having entered any building or part of a building as a trespasser, he steals or attempts to steal anything therein or inflicts on any person therein any grievous bodily harm.[38] A person is guilty of aggravated burglary if he commits any burglary and at the time has with him any weapon or imitation firearm, any weapon of offence or any explosive.[39] A weapon of offence includes any article intended by the person having it to cause injury to or incapacitate a person.[40]

35. Supra, p. 367; Larceny Act, 1916, s. 44 (1).
36. Archbold, 25th Edn. p. 622.
37. Larceny Act, 1916, s. 23.
38. Id. s. 23A; if the accused enters a building as a trespasser with intent to rape and in fact rapes a woman therein, he should presumably be charged with one count alleging the entry of the building and another, the rape.
39. Larceny Act, 1916, s. 23B (1).
40. Id. s. 23B (1) (c).

If a person charged with robbery cannot be convicted of larceny, it would seem necessary to add a second count of larceny or larceny from the person in any case where there might be a doubt as to the sufficiency of the evidence as to the use of force or putting a person in fear of being subjected to force. If a person charged with aggravated burglary cannot be convicted of simple burglary because of a doubt as to whether something which the accused had, such as a spanner, was intended by him to cause injury, it would seem necessary to include two counts in the indictment, one charging aggravated burglary and the other simple burglary. If a person charged with burglary, in the form of entering and stealing cannot be convicted of larceny alone because of a doubt whether the accused actually entered the building, or whether his entry amounted to trespass,[41] it would seem necessary to include one count of entering with intent, or of entering as a trespasser and stealing, and another of larceny alone, or larceny in a dwellinghouse.

Such proliferation of counts cannot be desirable. It is submitted that in any case in which a statute creates in a single section a combination of offences, it should be open to the jury to convict on any one of them, the indictment being amended, if necessary, to specify the section creating or prescribing the penalty for the offence on which the accused is found guilty.[42]

In England the position has been simplified in that where on a person's trial on indictment for any offence except treason or murder the jury find him not guilty of the offence specifically charged in the indictment, but the allegations in the indictment amount to or include (expressly or by implication) an allegation of another offence falling within the jurisdiction of the court of trial, the jury may find him guilty of that other offence.[43]

Special verdict

Apart from the special verdict of insanity, a special verdict is one by which the facts alone of the case are found by the jury and the legal inferences therefrom are to be drawn by the court. Thus

41. Cf. *R. v. Collins* [1973] Q.B. 100; *R. v. Smith* [1976] 1 W.L.R. 672.
42. Cf. *R. v. Dossi* 13 Cr. App. R. 158, supra, p. 246.
43. Criminal Law Act, 1967, s. 6 (3); but see *R. v. Woods* [1969] 1 Q.B. 447.

in *R. v. Dudley and Stevens*,[1] in which the accused were charged with the murder of a boy when shipwrecked at sea, the jury found as facts that the accused had killed the boy and eaten his flesh to save themselves from starvation, leaving it to the court to decide that this nevertheless amounted to murder. The jury have a right to bring in such a verdict,[2] and this right is recognised by section 5 of the Defamation Act, 1961, re-enacting in effect section 3 of the Libel Act, 1793, but such verdicts are exceedingly rare and it has been laid down in England that they should only be obtained in the most exceptional cases.[3]

Special verdict of insanity

The only special verdict now returned in practice is a verdict of guilty but insane. If at the time of commission of the alleged crime the accused was insane in the legal sense,[4] he lacks the *mens rea* normally required for the commission of a crime and is, therefore, innocent of the crime. Where, however, in any indictment any act or omission is charged against any person as an offence, and it is given in evidence on the trial of such person that he was insane, so as not to be responsible, according to law, for his actions at the time of the act or omission, then, if it appears to the jury that he did the act or made the omission charged but was insane at the time, the jury must bring in a verdict that the accused was guilty of the act or omission charged against him but was insane at the time.[5] The onus of proving beyond a reasonable doubt that the accused did the act or was guilty of the omission rests on the prosecution, and if it is not discharged, the accused is entitled to be acquitted, regardless of his state of mind at the time.[6] Subject to that, the onus is on the accused to establish insanity as a matter of probability,[7] but if the jury are satisfied

1. 14 Q.B.D. 273.
2. Archbold §4-468.
3. *R. v. Bourne* 36 Cr. App. R. 125.
4. See generally, *Doyle v. Wicklow County Council* [1974] I.R. 55 (S.C.). The onus of proof as a matter of probability lies on the accused: *Sodeman v. R.* [1936] W.N. 190, cited *Attorney General v. Boylan* [1937] I.R. 449, 458 (C.C.A.).
5. Trial of Lunatics Act, 1883, s. 2 (1); in England the special verdict is now one of not guilty by reason of insanity, Criminal Procedure (Insanity) Act, 1964, s. 1.
6. Archbold §17-35.
7. *R. v. Smith* 6 Cr. App. R. 19.

that the accused was probably insane, any further doubt is irrelevant.[8] The prosecution is under no obligation to furnish the defence with all medical reports it has received.[9] Pleas of insanity were common when every form of murder was a capital offence (although the plea is not reserved for indictments for murder) but now, having regard to the consequences of such a verdict, and to the fact that since the verdict is in effect one of acquittal the accused has no right of appeal,[10] such pleas are comparatively rare. If the accused is found to have been insane, the court must order that he be kept in custody in the Central Mental Hospital at the will and pleasure of the Government.[11]

Receiving the verdict

Whilst the jury are entitled to insist on the judge accepting the first verdict they return, the judge is not otherwise bound to receive it, and may ask the jury to reconsider it, giving them any necessary directions;[1] but if the verdict is clear and unambiguous, it appears that the judge has no discretion to refuse to accept it and that it is most undesirable for him to ask the jury to reconsider it.[2] The verdict is, however, not complete until the jury have dealt with all possible alternative verdicts open to them on the indictment.[3]

The jury may add a rider to their verdict. If it does not vary the effect of the verdict, such as a recommendation to mercy after a verdict of guilty, it does not vitiate the verdict,[4] and words added to a verdict which do not vary its effect, such as 'guilty but under the influence of drink' may be disregarded,[5] but not if the effect is to negative *mens rea*.[6]

8. *Attorney General v. Boylan* [1937] I.R. 449.
9. *The People v. Kelly*, 31st July, 1962, Frewen 267.
10. *Felstead v. R.* [1914] A.C. 534.
11. Criminal Lunatics Act, 1800, s. 1; Lunacy (Ireland) Act, 1821, ss. 1, 8; Central Criminal Lunatic Asylum (Ireland) Act, 1845, s. 8; Mental Treatment Act, 1961, s. 39.

1. *Attorney General v. Lane* 63 I.L.T.R. 6 (C.C.A.), in which the verdict was ambiguous; *The People v. Byrne*, 10th March 1966, Frewen 303, in which it was held that the jury might amend an inconsistent verdict; Archbold §§4-445 sqq.
2. *R. v. Robinson* [1975] Q.B. 508; *R. v. Lester* 27 Cr. App. R. 8.
3. Cf. *R. v. Carter* [1964] 2 Q.B. 1; Archbold §4-454.
4. 2 Hawk c. 47, s. 10; cf. *Attorney General v. O'Shea* [1931] I.R. 713 (C.C.A.).
5. *R. v. Moore* 23 Cr. App. R. 138.
6. *The People v. Keogh* [1944] I.R. 309 (C.C.A.); *The People v. E.* [1945] Ir. Jur. Rep. 67 (C.C.A.).

Ambiguous or inconsistent verdicts

If the verdict appears to be ambiguous the judge should endeavour to clear up the ambiguity,[7] and may question the jury as to what they mean,[8] but he should not to do so if the effect of the verdict is clear and unambiguous.[9]

If the verdict appears to be inconsistent, the onus of establishing that lies on the defence;[10] but an apparently inconsistent verdict does not necessarily mean that it cannot stand; every case must depend on its own facts.[11] If the intention of the jury to convict is clear, although the words of the verdict are confused or ambiguous, the Court of Criminal Appeal may decide that no miscarriage of justice has occurred and decline to quash the conviction.[12] If, however, the verdict is such that no judgment can properly be entered, a re-trial may be ordered.[13]

Delivery of verdict

The verdict, when delivered, is entered on the record of the court, but the judge may amend it before it is entered on the record, or even afterwards if it is done before the jury have left the jury-box.[14]

Finality of verdict

Once the verdict has been recorded and the jury has left the box, the verdict is final save that the judge may apparently correct the record if there is clear evidence that it does not represent the actual verdict.[15] Thus in *The People v. Longe*[16] the Court of Criminal Appeal held that, apart from the well established principle that the deliberations of a jury in a criminal case

7. Id.; *R. v. Hawkes* 22 Cr. App. R. 172; cf. *Attorney General v. Lane* 63 I.L.T.R. 6 (C.C.A.).
8. *R. v. White* 45 Cr. App. R. 34.
9. *R. v. Larkin* [1943] K.B. 174.
10. *R. v. Hunt* [1968] 2 Q.B. 433; *R. v. Durante* [1972] 1 W.L.R. 1612.
11. *R. v. Drury* 56 Cr. App. R. 104; Archbold §4-457.
12. Infra, p. 430.
13. *Attorney General v. O'Connell* [1937] Ir. Jur. Rep. 57 (C.C.A.).
14. Archbold §4-453; *R. v. Vodder* Dears. 229, when the accused had been discharged after a verdict of acquittal; *R. v. Wooller* 2 Stark. 111.
15. Archbold, 25th Edn. p. 212, citing *R. v. Virrier* 12 Ad. & E. 317.
16. [1967] I.R. 369 (C.C.A.).

should not be revealed or investigated, it would be irregular and against all precedent and practice, to act on the unsworn statement of one member of the jury, then *functus officio*, in order to alter the verdict, as given in court and entered on the issue paper which had been signed by the foreman.

In *The People v. Kennedy*,[17] where it was discovered, after the accused had been convicted and sentenced, that the jury was improperly constituted, the trial judge decided that he had no power to take any action; but it appears that the accused was released by order of the Minister for Justice.

Verdict of acquittal

If the accused is found not guilty on all counts of the indictment, and is not in custody on any other matter, he is entitled to be discharged immediately.[18]

Arrest of judgment

If the accused is found guilty the next step is for the court to pass sentence;[1] the accused may, however, at any time after conviction and *before* sentence move the court to arrest judgment, and even if no such application is made the court may, in an appropriate case, itself arrest the judgment; arrest of judgment has the effect of an acquittal, save that it is no bar to a fresh indictment.[2] Judgment will only be arrested because of some defect arising on the face of the record, such as want of sufficient certainty in the indictment which has not been amended, or because the conviction does not relate to an offence known to the law, but not because of any defect in the evidence or alleged irregularity at the trial.[3]

Costs

The court has jurisdiction to award costs to an accused person who is acquitted, although in the great majority of cases, free

17. 90 I.L.T.R. 48 (Circ. Ct.).
18. Archbold §4-453; *Mee v. Cruikshank* 20 Cox 210.
1. Chapter 15, infra.
2. *Vaux's Case* 4 Co. Rep. 44a.
3. Archbold §4-471.

legal aid will have been granted, and the question will be academic.[4] An award of costs involves no reflection on the Director of Public Prosecutions,[5] but will not normally result from the mere acquittal of the accused.[6]

4. *The People v. Bell* [1969] I.R. 24 (S.C.).
5. Id. at 38.
6. Id.; the decision of the Supreme Court related only to the question of jurisdiction; in the Central Criminal Court Kenny J. allowed costs to one accused who had been found not guilty by direction of the trial judge, but not to five others who were found guilty without such direction.

CHAPTER 14

SPECIAL CRIMINAL COURT PROCEDURE

An accused person may be returned for trial from the District Court to the Special Criminal Court, and the High Court may direct the transfer to the Special Criminal Court of a case awaiting trial in the Central Criminal Court or in the Circuit Court. In addition, however, a person may be charged before the Special Criminal Court in the first instance and the great majority of cases today being tried in that Court begin in this way.

I. CASES ORIGINATING IN THE DISTRICT COURT

Scheduled Offences

If a person is brought before the District Court charged with a scheduled offence[1] which the Justice has jurisdiction to dispose of summarily, the Justice must, if the Director of Public Prosecutions so requests, send him (in custody or on bail) for trial by a Special Criminal Court.[2] This appears to relate both to purely summary offences and also to those indictable offences which a Justice may deal with summarily under the Criminal Justice Act, 1951,[3] and it seems to be irrelevant whether an accused wishes to plead guilty or not. So far as can be ascertained, such a request has never been made since the establishment of the present

1. For the meaning of this term see pp. 18-20, supra.
2. Offences Against the State Act, 1939, s. 45 (1). The reference in this section to *a* Special Criminal Court was discussed in *The State (Littlejohn) v. The Governor of Mountjoy Prison*, 18th March, 1976. The Supreme Court unanimously rejected a contention that a District Court order could be defective merely because it referred to *the* Special Criminal Court rather than *a* Special Criminal Court. Since 1972 there has been only one Special Criminal Court.
3. See pp. 227, 228, supra.

Special Criminal Court. This is possibly because a Justice may be expected to be less subject to influence or intimidation than members of a jury,[4] and also because the offences concerned will rarely be of a very serious nature.

If a person is brought before the District Court charged with a scheduled offence which is an indictable offence and the Justice 'receives informations' and sends him forward for trial, the Justice *must,* unless the Director of Public Prosecutions otherwise directs, send him forward in custody, or with the consent of the Director on bail, for trial by a Special Criminal Court.[5] If an accused is sent forward in custody for trial he may be allowed bail by the High Court.[6]

It is submitted that if an accused has been sent forward for trial by the District Court either to the Circuit Court or to the Central Criminal Court, in respect of an unscheduled indictable offence, e.g. burglary, and if the Book of Evidence discloses a scheduled indictable offence, e.g. malicious damage, the indictment may include a count in respect of the latter offence.[7]

Neither the Offences Against the State Act, 1939, nor the Special Criminal Court Rules, 1972,[8] stipulate how a direction by the Director of Public Prosecutions in relation to a scheduled offence is to be given, and, in particular, whether it ought to be given in writing. In practice such a direction is often communicated to the Justice verbally by whoever conducts the case on behalf of the prosecution in the District Court. It is submitted that it is desirable that any order returning an accused for trial on a scheduled offence to the Central Criminal Court or to the Circuit Court should show on its face that a positive direction from the Director of Public Prosecutions, enabling this course to be adopted, has been given, since the return would otherwise be bad. If the order returning for trial contains no such reference it may prove necessary at a later stage to provide oral evidence that a direction was communicated to the Justice, in order to establish the validity of the return.

4. Cf. *The State (Coveney) v. Special Criminal Court* [1982] I.L.R.M. 284 (H.C.).
5. Offences Against the State Act, 1939, s. 45 (2).
6. Id. s. 45 (3).
7. See p. 254, supra.
8. S.I. No. 147 of 1972.

Non-scheduled offences

Whenever a person is brought before the District Court charged with an offence which is not a scheduled offence, and is one which the Justice has jurisdiction to deal with summarily, he *must* send the accused forward for trial by the Special Criminal Court, if the Director of Public Prosecutions so requests and certifies *in writing* that the ordinary courts are, in his opinion, inadequate to secure the effective administration of justice and the preservation of public peace and order in relation to the trial of the accused on the charge.[9] The District Justice would appear to have a discretion to admit the accused to bail in this instance.[10]

When a person is brought before the District Court charged with an indictable offence which is not a scheduled offence, and the Justice receives informations and sends him forward for trial, then if an application is made by or on behalf of the Director of Public Prosecutions, grounded upon the Director's certificate that the ordinary courts are, in his opinion, inadequate to secure the effective administration of justice and the preservation of public peace and order in relation to the trial of the accused on the charge, the Justice *must* send the accused forward to the Special Criminal Court either in custody or, with the consent of the Director, on bail.[11] Any accused who is sent forward in custody may be admitted to bail by the High Court.[12]

Sending accused persons forward from the District Court for sentence only

Sections 45 and 46 of the Offences Against the State Act, 1939, require the District Justice to return accused persons for *trial* to the Special Criminal Court where an appropriate intervention by the Director of Public Prosecutions either 'negatively' in the case of indictable scheduled offences, or 'positively' in the case of all other offences, has taken place. The sections in question, however, do not address the problem of the accused person who pleads guilty to an indictable offence, whether scheduled or

9. Offences Against the State Act, 1939, s. 46 (1).
10. Id.
11. Id. s. 46 (2).
12. Id. s. 46 (3).

otherwise, and is sent forward for *sentence* only.

This apparent lacuna formed the basis of the important unreported case of *The State (Littlejohn) v. Governor of Mountjoy Prison.*[13] This was an application for habeas corpus questioning the lawfulness of the prosecutor's detention under the order of the Special Criminal Court. The prosecutor, Littlejohn, had appeared before the District Court charged with armed robbery, a non-scheduled offence. The Attorney General, whose functions had not at the relevant time been transferred to the Director, gave a certificate in writing that the ordinary courts were inadequate to secure the effective administration of justice and the preservation of peace and order in relation to the trial of the accused. Littlejohn, however, pleaded guilty and the District Justice sent him forward for sentence to the Special Criminal Court. In his application for habeas corpus Littlejohn contended that the District Court order was bad, as the certificate of the Attorney General was ineffective to secure a return to the Special Criminal Court. The certificate had referred to *the trial* of the defendant, but in fact at that juncture it appeared that there would be no full trial. As it transpired, the defendant changed his plea to not guilty when he reached the Special Criminal Court.

The Supreme Court decided unanimously that the word *trial* also comprehended a sentence, unless the context of a particular statute required otherwise.[14] Henchy J., with whom the other members of the Court agreed, said:

> 'The context of the use of "trial" in s. 46 of the 1939 Act contains nothing that would require the word to be cut down in its connotation to a judicial hearing of the issue of guilt or innocence and not to cover merely the question of sentence.'

Counsel for Littlejohn further sought to persuade the Supreme Court that, if jury intimidation lay at the heart of the policy to set up special non-jury courts, this danger was obviated where an accused was sent forward for sentence only. The Court, however, did not accept that potential jury intimidation was the only basis

13. Unrep. 18th March, 1976 (S.C.).
14. The Court accepted, e.g. that the Criminal Procedure Act, 1967, s. 13 (2) (b) did require an opposite interpretation; on this section, see *The State (Williams) v. Kelly (No. 2)* [1970] I.R. 271 (S.C.).

upon which the Attorney General might certify that the ordinary courts were, in his opinion, inadequate. It also rejected a contention that it was incongruous for the Attorney General to certify in effect that either a District Justice, a Circuit Court judge or a High Court judge was inadequate to secure the effective administration of justice, when the *effect* of a certificate was to put an accused before a Special Criminal Court consisting of a High Court judge, a Circuit Court judge and a District Justice. The Court took the view that although a judge is clearly identifiable when he passes sentence in an ordinary court, the absolute bar on disclosure which obtains in the Special Criminal Court in regard to sentence or to any other question means that it is impossible to identify any particular member of the Special Criminal Court as having assented to or dissented from a sentence imposed, or the determination of any other question.

II. TRANSFER TO THE SPECIAL CRIMINAL COURT

When the Special Criminal Court was re-established in 1972, there were several cases, already pending in the ordinary courts, which would have been within the province of the Special Court. Provision was made by the Act of 1939 for the transfer of trials from the ordinary courts to the Special Criminal Court, and applications by the prosecution were not uncommon when the Court was re-established. Today, since most cases now start in the Special Court, such applications would be rare but it may sometimes appear to the prosecution in the progress of a case that the ordinary courts are not suitable and there seems no reason why an application for transfer cannot be made. The procedure for transfer is governed by section 48 of the Act of 1939, and applies whenever a person is sent forward by a District Court for trial, which, as has been seen, includes sentence, by the Central Criminal Court or the Circuit Court. The Director of Public Prosecutions must certify that in his opinion the ordinary courts are inadequate to secure the effective administration of justice and the preservation of public peace and order in relation to the trial of the charge. If he so certifies, he must then cause application to be made to the High Court (not, it is to be noted, to the court to which the accused has been sent forward) for the transfer of the trial to the Special Criminal Court. The High Court appears to be bound to grant any such application and the accused is then deemed to have been sent forward to the Special Criminal Court for trial on the charge in question.[15]

When an order for transfer has been made a copy of it must be served on the accused by a member of the Garda Síochána and a copy must be sent to the appropriate County Registrar; the Special Court fixes the place and time of trial. If the accused is in custody he remains in custody, subject to his right to apply to the High Court for bail. If he is on bail, his bail is deemed to be conditioned for his attendance before the Special Court at the appropriate time and place.[16]

III. CASES ORIGINATING IN THE SPECIAL CRIMINAL COURT

Whenever it is intended to charge a person with a *scheduled* offence, the Director of Public Prosecutions may direct that the person be brought before the Special Criminal Court instead of the District Court. Where such a direction has been given the person will be brought before the Special Criminal Court and will be charged and eventually tried there.

Whenever it is intended to charge a person with some *non-scheduled* offence, e.g. murder, and the Director certifies that the ordinary courts are, in his opinion, inadequate to secure the effective administration of justice and the preservation of public peace and order in relation to the trial of the accused on the charge, the Director may, if he so thinks proper, direct that such person be brought before the Special Criminal Court instead of the District Court. Where such a direction has been given the accused will be brought before the Special Criminal Court and will be charged and tried there.[17]

Whenever any person is required to be brought before the Special Criminal Court, that Court may issue a warrant for him to be arrested and brought before the Court.[18]

15. Offences Against the State Act, 1939, s. 48 (a).
16. Id. s. 48 (b).
17. Id. s. 47 (2) as adapted by the Prosecution of Offences Act, 1974, s. 3.
18. Id. s. 47 (3).

Challenging the powers of the Director of Public Prosecutions in relation to the placing of cases before the Special Criminal Court

It is clear that the various powers originally accorded to the Attorney General, and now exercisable by the Director,[19] to require that cases be put before the Special Criminal Court, are very extensive.

Today theoretically *any* criminal offence could be put before the Special Criminal Court despite the fact that this Court was set up to deal specifically with crimes of a politically motivated nature. The exercise of the powers in question has been challenged in two unreported cases.

In 1972 in *The State (Bollard) v. The Special Criminal Court*[20] Kenny J. heard an emergency application in which the prosecutor, Bollard, sought an order of prohibition to prevent the Special Criminal Court from hearing his case. The judgment in some respects is slightly unclear, reflecting, perhaps, the nature of the application. Bollard had been returned for trial by a District Justice charged with a scheduled offence and two non-scheduled offences. The specific offences are not set out in the judgment.

In relation to the non-scheduled offences, the Attorney General had certified in writing that the ordinary courts were, in his opinion, inadequate to secure the effective administration of justice and the preservation of peace and order in relation to the trial of Bollard on the charges in question. Kenny J. rejected the contention of the prosecutor that, in so doing, the Attorney General was exercising the judicial power of the State.

In relation to the single scheduled offence involved, counsel for the prosecutor appears to have advanced two arguments in the alternative. The first was that, if the offence was one which could be disposed of summarily, then the request of the Attorney General to the District Justice to send Bollard for trial to the Special Criminal Court constituted an exercise of the judicial power of the State and was, therefore, invalid. The trial judge did not accede to this argument. The second proposition advanced was that, if the offence were an indictable scheduled offence, then

19. Prosecution of Offences Act, 1974, s. 3.
20. Unrep. 20th September, 1972 (H.C.).

the *failure* of the Attorney General to intervene and direct that the accused should *not* be sent to the Special Criminal Court for trial was an exercise of judicial power. This contention prompted Kenny J. to say, 'I do not understand how not giving a direction can be an exercise of judicial power.'

In 1980 Finlay P. heard the cases of *Savage and McOwen v. Director of Public Prosecutions.*[21] The plaintiffs here sought declarations that certificates in writing which had been issued by the Director requesting the return for trial of the plaintiffs on indictable non-scheduled offences were void, and that the District Court order made in pursuance thereof was also void.

The plaintiffs did not allege that the Director had not *formed* an opinion; the essential question involved in the case was whether the opinion formed by him pursuant to section 46 (2) of the Act 1939, was reviewable by the Court and, if so, to what extent this was the case.[22]

Finlay P. embarked upon a careful analysis of a number of issues pertaining to the establishment of the Special Criminal Court and the placing of cases before it. Accepting the right of the Government to proclaim the establishment of Special Criminal Courts in the first instance, he stated that the courts ordinarily sitting had no power to question in any particular circumstances whether Special Courts were necessary or, alternatively, had ceased to be necessary. Only the Dáil could annul such a Government proclamation.

In relation to scheduled offences, Finlay P. viewed the powers presently vested in the Director of Public Prosecutions as constituting a graft upon the unrestricted right of the Government to declare an offence to be scheduled. The courts, he believed, could not review any decision by the Director either to require the trial of a person on a scheduled summary charge or, alternatively, to abstain from directing otherwise in the case of a person on a indictable scheduled charge, in order to avoid, in either case, trial by a Special Criminal Court.

21. Unrep. 31st July, 1980 (H.C.).
22. In *The State (Littlejohn) v. The Governor of Mountjoy Prison,* unrep. 18th March, 1976, the Supreme Court unanimously decided that it was not entitled to speculate as to the grounds on which the Attorney General formed his opinion that the ordinary courts were inadequate in relation to sentencing a prisoner.

On the question of non-scheduled offences being put before the Special Criminal Court in pursuance of section 46 of the Offences Against the State Act, 1939, Finlay P. accepted the view of Gavan Duffy J. in *Re MacCurtain* where he held [23] that the question as to whether or not a particular trial for a non-scheduled offence should be carried out by the Special Criminal Court was essentially within the domain of the Attorney General as the State authority in charge of prosecutions under the Constitution.

Finlay P. felt that the opinion of the Attorney General was clearly not reviewable by the courts, and he was not prepared to accept that the substitution of the Director for the Attorney General could affect this situation. As well as basing his decision on the precedent of *Re MacCurtain*, the judge took the view that, if the opinion of the Director were to be subjected to review by the courts, serious consequences could ensue. If a plaintiff were able to establish a *prima facie* case that some of the matters upon which the Director had formed his opinion were untrue, or based on false information, it would be necessary for the Director, in order to vindicate the issuing of a certificate, and for the Special Criminal Court to have jurisdiction, to reveal in open court and in the presence of the accused all the information, knowledge or facts upon which he based his opinion. This, according to Finlay P., would make impossible the operation of Part V of the Offences Against the State Act, 1939, in relation to the trial of non-scheduled offences and would vitiate the whole purpose of Special Courts.

IV. PROCEDURE IN THE SPECIAL CRIMINAL COURT

Procedure in the Special Criminal Court is governed partly by the Offences Against the State Act, 1939, and partly by the Special Criminal Court Rules, made under section 41 (1) of that Act, which provides that it shall have power in its absolute discretion to appoint the time and place of its sittings.

When sitting for the purpose of the trial of a person or the making of any order as to the exercise of any other jurisdiction or

23. [1941] I.R. 83, 87 (H.C., S.C.).

function the Court must consist of an uneven number (not less than three) of its members present at and taking part in such sittings,[1] but subject to that it may exercise any power, jurisdiction or function notwithstanding one or more vacancies in its membership.[2] The Court normally sits with three members.

Subject to the provisions of the Act, the practice and procedure applicable to the trial of a person on indictment in the Central Criminal Court apply to the trial of a person by the Special Court and the like rules of evidence apply.[3] In *The People v. Yates*[4] it was held that to find an accused guilty of an offence lesser than that charged – manslaughter when the accused was charged with murder – was not a mere matter of 'practice and procedure'. This situation was remedied by the Criminal Justice (Verdicts) Act, 1976, which provides that where a person is lawfully before a court for trial of an offence, and the trial is being or is to be held without a jury, the court shall have the same jurisdiction and powers to give any verdict or make any findings as the court or jury would have (a) if the court were sitting with a jury, and (b) (in case the offence is triable only summarily) if the offence were triable on indictment, and enactments and rules of law relating to a verdict or finding of a jury, shall, with any necessary modification, apply accordingly. The Act goes on to provide that where a person is lawfully before a court charged with an offence, the court shall have jurisdiction to convict that person, on a plea of guilty, of another offence with which he is not specifically charged and of which he could be convicted by that court after trial for the offence specifically charged. This replaces the more limited provisions of section 39 (1) of the Criminal Justice Administration Act, 1914.

A Special Criminal Court is given specific jurisdiction to try and to convict or acquit any person lawfully brought before it for trial and is also given the following ancillary jurisdictions:[5]

1. Offences Against the State Act, 1939, s. 41 (2).
2. Id. s. 41 (3); the number of members of the present Court is 11: 4 from the High Court, 3 from the Circuit Court, and 4 from the District Court.
3. Offences Against the State Act, 1939, s. 41 (4).
4. Unrep. 12th November, 1975 (S.C.).
5. Offences Against the State Act, 1939, s. 43 (1).

(a) to sentence every person convicted of an offence to the punishment provided by law in respect of such offence;
(b) in lieu of or in addition to any other order to require a person to enter into a recognisance before the Court or before a Justice of the District Court, in such amount, and with or without sureties, as the Court shall direct, to keep the peace and be of good behaviour for such period as the Court shall specify;
(c) to order the detention of and to detain in civil or military custody, or to admit to bail, in such amount, and with or without sureties, as the Court shall direct, pending trial and until conviction or acquittal, any person sent forward, transferred to or otherwise brought for trial by the Court;
(d) power to administer oaths;
(e) power to punish in the same manner and in the like cases as the High Court, persons whom it finds in contempt of the Court or any member thereof, whether such contempt is or is not committed in the presence of the Court;
(f) power to estreat recognisances and bail bonds entered into before it, in like manner and in like cases as the District Court.

Where a person is sent forward for trial to a Special Criminal Court, or the High Court transfers a trial to that Court, the relevant order is not to specify the particular Special Court: if, as at the present time, there is only one Special Court in existence the relevant order is deemed to refer to that Court. If more than one are in existence, the Director may apply to such one as he thinks proper for an order that the accused be tried before that Court.[6]

The determination of every question before a Special Court is to be according to the opinion of the majority of its members present at and taking part in such determination. No member or officer of the Court is to disclose whether any such determination was or was not unanimous or, when it was not, the opinion of any individual member of the Court. Every decision is to be pronounced by such member as the Court shall determine and no other member is to pronounce or indicate his concurrence or dissent.[7]

6. Id. s. 49 (e).
7. Id. s. 40.

Every order, conviction and sentence by a Special Court is to have the like consequences in law as an order, conviction or sentence made or pronounced by the Central Criminal Court, and every order or sentence is to be carried out likewise.[8]

Every order or other act of a Special Court must be authenticated by the signature of the Registrar and is receivable in evidence accordingly.[9]

Whenever a person stands mute when called upon to plead, the Court shall hear such evidence (if any), relevant to the issue whether the accused stands mute of malice or by visitation of God, as may be then and there adduced. If the Court is satisfied that the accused is mute by visitation of God, the like consequences ensue as if he had been so found in the Central Criminal Court. If the Court is not so satisfied, or if no such evidence is adduced, it must direct a plea of 'not guilty' to be entered on behalf of the accused.[10]

Whenever an accused fails or refuses in any way, otherwise than by standing mute, to plead to the charge, the Court must likewise direct a plea of not guilty to be entered on his behalf.[11] In addition, however, whenever a person, at any stage of his trial, by any act or omission refuses to recognise the authority or jurisdiction of a Special Court, or does any act (other than lawfully objecting in due form of law to the jurisdiction of the Court to try him) which in the opinion of the Court is equivalent to a refusal to recognise it or its authority or jurisdiction, he is guilty of contempt of the Court and liable to be punished accordingly.[12]

Section 41 (1) of the Offences Against the State Act, 1939, provides that every Special Criminal Court shall have power, in its absolute discretion to appoint the times and places of its sittings, and shall have control of its own procedure in all respects and shall for that purpose make, with the concurrence of the Minister for Justice, rules regulating its practice and procedure, and may in particular provide by such rules for the issuing of summonses, the procedure for bringing, in custody or on bail, persons before

8. Id. s. 50.
9. Id. s. 42.
10. Id. s. 51 (1).
11. Id. s. 51 (2).
12. Id. s. 51 (3).

it for trial, the admission or the exclusion of the public to or from its sittings, the enforcing of the attendance of witnesses, and the production of documents. Such Rules, to be cited as the Special Criminal Court Rules, 1972, were made on the 9th June, 1972,[13] and are reprinted in Appendix D.

The Court decides where and when it is to sit.[14] The Registrar must give notice of the place and time of each sitting to the Chief State Solicitor and to any person to be tried, and may also give notice to the solicitor representing any such person.[15]

The members of the Court take their seats in order of seniority, the senior member present acting as President.[16]

The Court is an open Court to which the public generally have access so far as the same can conveniently contain them, and subject to such conditions as the Court may from time to time impose. Where, however, the Court is satisfied, because of the nature or the circumstances of the case, or otherwise in the interests of justice, that it is desirable, the Court may exclude the public or any particular person or persons except *bona fide* representatives of the Press from the Court during the hearing. The Court may permit a witness to give his name in writing to the members of the Court. The Court may further direct that such name, or the evidence or part of the evidence of any witness, shall not be published.[17]

The Court may direct that no witness shall remain in Court while the evidence of another witness is being given and may make provision for the separation of witnesses from each other.[18]

When an accused person is not defended he must, at the close of the case for the prosecution, be informed by the President of the Court that:

(a) he may give evidence in his defence on oath and will then be liable to be cross-examined and to be questioned by the Court, or
(b) he may make a statement not on oath and will then not be

13. S.I. 147 of 1972.
14. Special Criminal Court Rules, 1972, r. 4.
15. Id. r. 5.
16. Id. r. 6.
17. Id. r. 7.
18. Id. r. 8.

liable to be cross-examined or to be questioned by the Court, or (c) he may make no statement.

An accused person must also be informed that he may address the court in his defence and may call witnesses in his defence.[19]

In other respects the Rules are designed to bring procedures in the Special Court into line with proceedings in the ordinary courts. They deal with the transmission of documents,[20] filing and form of indictment,[21] furnishing of copies of documents to the accused in the case of indictable offences where the accused has been sent forward from the District Court or his trial transferred by the High Court, and in summary cases sent forward from the District Court to the Special Court. They deal separately with cases in which the accused is charged in the first instance before the Special Court under section 47 of the Act, with provisions similar to those of the Criminal Procedure Act, 1967, and provisions for the issue of warrants and summonses, and committal to prison or into military custody pending trial.[22] The Rules also deal with the procuring of the attendance of persons in custody,[23] and requiring persons on bail to surrender to their bail,[24] detention during adjournments,[25] and securing the attendance of witnesses for the prosecution or defence.[26] They provide for the mode and proof of service of documents,[27] for the attendance of an official stenographer,[28] for the form of recognisances,[29] the location and functions of the Registrar,[30] abridgment and extension of time [31] and granting of legal aid.[32]

Finally, there is a Schedule of Forms of Committal Warrant, Notice of Trial, Warrants for Arrest, Witness Summons, Declarations of Service, Recognisance and Summons.

19. Id. r. 23.
20. Id. rr. 9-14.
21. Id. r. 10.
22. Id. r. 15-16.
23. Id. r. 17.
24. Id. r. 18.
25. Id. r. 19.
26. Id. r. 20.
27. Id. r. 21-23.
28. Id. r. 24.
29. Id. r. 25.
30. Id. r. 26.
31. Id. r. 27.
32. Id. r. 28.

CHAPTER 15

SENTENCE

The imposition of sentence is essentially a matter for the trial judge and not for the jury. It is improper, indeed, for the latter to be informed by counsel for the defence what the consequences of a conviction may be.[1] Whilst, as has been seen, it is permissible for the jury to add a rider, such as, a recommendation for mercy, to their verdict,[2] and whilst the judge is likely to be influenced by it, he is no way bound by it, and it will be seen that before passing sentence the judge will probably know a great deal more about the previous character of the accused than the jury were permitted to know; the jury had before them a man or woman presumed to be, and quite possibly presenting the guileless appearance, of an innocent person, whom the judge (and the jury if they choose to remain in court after delivering their verdict) may learn later to have been an habitual criminal, a fraud, or a blackguard.

It is not the purpose of this work to present the arguments for or against capital punishment, corporal punishment, or the adequacy or inadequacy of the prison and reformatory systems.

The objects of punishment have been described as punitive, deterrent, reformatory and preventative: that a person should be punished for his crime; that he or others may be deterred from committing the same type of crime in the future; that a person should be given an opportunity to mend his ways; and that a person should, if necessary, be prevented from repeating his crime. It has been stated that:[3]

1. *Attorney General for South Australia v. Brown* [1960] A.C. 432.
2. Supra, p. 373.
3. *The State (Stanbridge) v. Mahon* [1979] I.R. 214, 218 (H.C.) *per* Gannon J., citing *R. v. Ball* 35 Cr. App. R. 164.

'The first consideration in determining the sentence is the public interest, which is served not merely by punishing the offender and showing a deterrent to others but also by affording a compelling inducement and an opportunity to the offender to reform. The punishment should be appropriate not only to the offence committed but also to the particular offender.'

The concept of punishment is the most primitive: the offender should be made to pay; if he has taken the life of another he should forfeit his own life, an eye for an eye and a tooth for a tooth; 'let the punishment fit the crime'. The concept of deterrence derives from the need of society to protect itself. This, no doubt, was the reason for imposing a penalty as severe as death for crimes such as larceny and assaults which endangered the common weal. The idea that the criminal should be reformed seems to have developed much later, but to have become the most positive object. Walsh J. has observed:[4]

'The objects of passing sentence are not merely to deter the particular criminal from committing a crime again but to induce him as far as possible to turn from a criminal to an honest life and indeed the public interest would be best served if the criminal could be induced to take the latter course.'

The preventative concept may have first found its expression in the Criminal Law (Ireland) Act, 1828, which recited that it was expedient to provide for the more exemplary punishment of offenders who commit felony after a previous conviction of felony,[5] but it may be preferable to regard that as an application of the punitive principle. The Prevention of Crime Act, 1908,[6] dealt with the problem of the habitual criminal; it provides that, where a person is convicted on indictment of a crime and sentenced to penal servitude, if he admits that he is or is found by a jury to be an habitual criminal, and if the Court is of opinion that by reason of his criminal habits and mode of life it is expedient for the protection of the public that the offender should be kept in detention for a lengthened period of years, then the Court may

4. *The People v. O'Driscoll*, 3rd March, 1972, Frewen 351, 359.
5. As to this and other 19th century enactments, see Archbold, 25th Edn. pp. 1390-1400.
6. S. 10.

order that he undergo a period of not less than five nor more than ten years preventative detention on the determination of the sentence of penal servitude already imposed. There are, however, no facilities in the State for providing such detention, so that in practice the Act cannot be applied.

Antecedents of the accused.

It follows from the considerations mentioned above that, except in cases of treason and murder where the sentence is mandatory, the sentence is in the discretion of the judge, within such limits as may be prescribed by law for the particular offence, and having regard to the circumstances of the case and of the accused. Statutes commonly prescribe that an offence is punishable by a sentence of up to a certain term of detention or up to a certain fine,[7] and it is to be presumed that the legislation regarded the maximum penalty as appropriate only to an extreme instance of the offence in question. But in every case there may be mitigating circumstances, and the particular offender may be deserving of greater or less consideration in the light of his personal circumstances and previous character.[8]

Accordingly, if the accused has pleaded guilty, the facts should be furnished to the judge (and in case of an appeal against sentence the facts so furnished, but not the Book of Evidence, will be included in the transcript to be considered by the appellate court).[9] Whether the accused has pleaded guilty or been convicted by a jury, his circumstances and any previous convictions (but not other complaints against the accused)[10] will be presented to the Court, normally by a police officer familiar with the case. The accused must, however, be given an opportunity of disputing the testimony, usually by hearsay, of the police officer,[11] and if he disputes a particular conviction and if the prosecution is not con-

7. If a statute prescribes a sentence on conviction on indictment it may be imposed on a person sent forward on a plea of guilty to the Circuit Court for sentence; *The People v. Gurr*, unrep. 3rd December, 1979 (C.C.A.).
8. *The People v. Poyning* [1972] I.R. 402 (C.C.A.).
9. Infra, p. 427.
10. *The People v. Riordan* [1948] I.R. 416 (C.C.A.).
11. *The State (Stanbridge) v. Mahon* [1979] I.R. 214 (H.C.); the evidence may be given on the voir dire, i.e. the witness swears that he will give true answers to such questions as may be put to him by the court.

tent to leave the judge to impose sentence without regard to it, an opportunity should be given to the prosecution to prove it by formal evidence.[12]

Death

Writing in 1863, Stephen stated[1] that: 'the history of English punishments is a history of a transition from almost barbarous severity to excessive lenity'.

He listed the following scale of punishments as having gradually become established before 1848:

> 'In cases of high treason, hanging, drawing, and quartering for a man, and burning for a woman.
> In cases of petit treason (a form of murder), hanging and drawing for a man, and burning for a woman.
> In cases of felony, except petit larceny, death by hanging.
> In cases of petit larceny, whipping.
> In cases of misdemeanour, fine and imprisonment, both or either, at the discretion of the court; to which were sometimes added whipping, cutting the ears, and the pillory.'

So much for the past; the death penalty was abolished except in cases of treason, murder and piracy with violence in the course of the nineteenth century and abolished by the Criminal Justice Act, 1964, except in the case of treason, capital murder,[2] and certain offences,[3] by persons subject to military law.

In the cases in which it may be imposed, the death penalty is mandatory: no lesser sentence may be imposed by the Court,[4] and any commutation or mitigation of the penalty is a matter for the Executive. If, however, the accused stands convicted on other charges, it appears to be proper for the court to impose prison sentences on those charges as well as sentencing him to death, in case the conviction for murder is quashed.[5]

12. *R. v. Turner* 18 Cr. App. R. 161, cited in *The State (Stanbridge) v. Mahon* supra.
1. *Criminal Law of England,* 74.
2. As defined in section 1 (1) (b) of the Act; in England capital murder was introduced, but differently defined by the Homicide Act, 1957, but the death penalty was abolished, except in the case of treason and piracy with violence, by the Murder (Abolition of Death Penalty) Act, 1965.
3. Such as treacherous desertion to the enemy or mutiny with violence.
4. Offences against the Person Act, 1861, s. 2.
5. *The People v. Murray* [1977] I.R. 360, 390 (S.C.) *per* Walsh J.

In the ordinary way, the sentence is to be carried out by hanging,[6] and:

> 'If at the first attempt the criminal is not thoroughly hanged, and is afterwards revived, he shall be hanged again, for the former hanging was not an execution of the sentence which implies a completion of the punishment.'[7]

but in the case of persons subject to military law it may be carried out in such manner as the officer confirming the sentence, which must also be approved by the Government, may direct.[8]

Sentence of death is not to be carried out on a person for the time being of unsound mind,[9] and in the case of a woman who is pregnant, so found by a jury of matrons, it must be stayed until the child is born.[10] According to Hale:[11]

> 'This privilege is however to be allowed but once; for if she be a second time with child she shall not thereby delay execution, but the gaoler shall be punished for not looking to her.'

One would clearly not find such rigidity in modern times and even some 150 years ago Gabbett observed that:[12]

> '[T]he execution of the law in the first instance is respited not from a regard for the mother, but from tenderness toward the innocent infant, if then it should happen that she becomes quick of a second child, this, surely, is as much an object of compassion and humanity as the first.'

Deprivation of liberty

A convicted person may be deprived of his liberty by being sentenced to undergo penal servitude, imprisonment, or, in the case of certain young persons, detention.

6. See the form of sentence, Archbold §5-18; *The People v. Pringle*, unrep. 22nd May, 1981 (C.C.A.); the sentence must, however, be carried out within the walls of the prison in which the prisoner was confined up to the time of execution; Capital Punishment Amendment Act, 1868, s. 2.
7. 2 Hale 412.
8. Defence Act, 1954, s. 227.
9. 4 Bl. Comm. 395.
10. Archbold, 25th Edn. p. 221.
11. 2 Hale 413.
12. *Criminal Law*, vol.II, 582, and see Article 40.3.3° and Eighth Amendment of the Constitution, September, 1983.

Penal servitude

In the course of the 18th and early 19th centuries it became usual to commute the death penalty in cases other than treason or murder to a sentence of deportation to a convict settlement in one of the British colonies, where the status of the convict corresponded in theory to that of a slave: with the abolition of slavery a sentence of penal servitude was substituted for deportation.[1]

Section 2 of the Prisons (Ireland) Act, 1856, as adapted,[2] provides that the Minister for Justice may, by order to be published in Iris Oifigiúil, set apart places of confinement for prisoners under sentence of penal servitude, to be described as 'convict prisons', and section 11 of the same Act provides for the transfer of such persons from one such prison to another. It appears, however, that no such order has ever been made, and that persons sentenced to penal servitude are for this purpose in no different position from that of persons sentenced to imprisonment, and are subject to the provisions of section 17 of the Criminal Justice Administration Act, 1914, considered below.[3]

A sentence of penal servitude may only be imposed by statutory authority.[4] In the case of non-capital murder the only penalty which may be imposed is penal servitude for life,[5] but in most cases the particular statute authorising the sentence specifies the minimum or maximum term which may be imposed. Subject to that, however, a sentence of penal servitude may only be imposed for a term of not less than three years nor more than seven years.[6] The effect of the material enactments appears[7] to be that when, in any statute in force on the 5th August, 1891, an offence was declared to be a felony and no punishment was specifically provided for it, the offence remains punishable with penal servitude for any period not exceeding seven years; but where an offence was declared to be punishable with penal servitude, the maximum term is five years, unless a particular statute authorises a longer term.

1. *Russell on Crime* (7th Edn.) 209.
2. Adaptation of Enactments Act, 1922, s. 11.
3. See *Re McLoughlin* [1970] I.R. 197 (S.C.).
4. *The State (Jones) v. O'Donovan* [1973] I.R. 329 (H.C.).
5. Criminal Justice Act, 1964, s. 2; *The People v. Murtagh* [1966] I.R. 361 (S.C.).
6. Criminal Law (Ireland) Act, 1828, s. 15; Penal Servitude Act, 1857, s. 2; Penal Servitude Act, 1891, s. 1.
7. Archbold, 25th Edn. p. 230.

Imprisonment

Penal servitude was abolished in England by the Criminal Justice Act, 1948, and, whilst it has not been abolished in the State, and a sentence of penal servitude may have consequences stemming from the convict status of the prisoner, it appears that for practical purposes there is no distinction in the treatment of prisoners sentenced to penal servitude or imprisonment, or between imprisonment with or without hard labour.[8] It is, moreover, to be observed that many recent statutes prescribe only a sentence of imprisonment, even for life.[9] The result is anomalous; a person may plead guilty to burglary which now entails a sentence of imprisonment, and to a series of larcenies which carry a possible sentence of penal servitude: it is submitted that, technically, if the judge decided to impose a sentence of five years imprisonment on the burglary count, any concurrent sentence[10] on the larceny counts should also be of imprisonment, not exceeding two years. Bearing in mind that there is now no practical difference between penal servitude and imprisonment, one may note that it has been held in the past that a sentence of penal servitude to follow on a term of imprisonment should not normally be imposed,[11] nor a sentence of imprisonment to follow on a term of penal servitude.[12]

Many of the older statutes prescribe that an offence shall be punishable by penal servitude for a term of not less than three years or imprisonment, with or without hard labour, for a term not exceeding two years. Apart from that, whenever a court is empowered or required to impose a sentence of penal servitude the court may, unless any Act otherwise provides,[13] award imprisonment with or without hard labour for a term not exceeding

8. Reply by the Minister for Justice to a question in Dáil Éireann, 22nd July, 1962; for the distinction between imprisonment with or without hard labour, see Archbold, 25th Edn. pp. 231-5.
9. E.g. Criminal Law (Jurisdiction) Act, 1976, s. 5 (robbery); id. s. 7 (aggravated burglary). The last statute to prescribe a sentence of penal servitude was the Criminal Justice Act, 1964, s. 2.
10. Cf. *R. v. Jones* 1 Cr. App. R. 196; *R. v. Bruce* 5 Cr. App. R. 213 and 233.
11. *R. v. Jones*, supra; *R. v. Baumgarten* 9 Cr. App. R. 212.
12. *R. v. Johnson* 7 Cr. App. R. 97.
13. E.g. in the case of non-capital murder, when the sentence of penal servitude for life is mandatory: *The People v. Murtagh* [1966] I.R. 361 (S.C.).

two years.[14] Whilst the court may impose consecutive sentences of imprisonment it has been held (in so far as in practice it may still be material) that no one should be required to suffer imprisonment with hard labour, which can only be imposed by statutory authority, and should be specified in the sentence,[15] for a continuous period exceeding two years.[16]

There was, however, no limit at common law to the term of simple imprisonment which might be imposed[17] and this is still the rule as regards any common law offence,[18] although in the case of an offence such as an attempt to commit, and normally in the case of conspiracy to commit, a statutory offence, the term should not exceed the maximum term of imprisonment or penal servitude which might be imposed for the substantive offence.[19]

Section 17 of the Criminal Justice Administration Act, 1914, as applied by section 43 of that Act and adapted by section 11 of the Adaptation of Enactments Act, 1922, replacing the corresponding section in the General Prisons (Ireland) Act, 1877, provides that the Minister for Justice may from time to time by any special rules under the Prisons (Ireland) Acts, 1826 to 1907,[20] appropriate, either wholly or partially, particular prisons to particular classes of prisoners sentenced to imprisonment or committed to prison on remand or pending trial or otherwise, and to direct the transfer of prisoners from one prison to another. 'Imprisonment' in this context includes penal servitude.[21]

Portlaoise and Limerick Prisons have been appropriated to male prisoners convicted of offences treated as subversive, although they also accommodate a number of male prisoners engaged in maintenance and cleaning work. Arbour Hill Prison is

14. Penal Servitude Act, 1891, s. 1 (2); s. v. *The People v. Power*, unrep. 31st July, 1975 (C.C.A.).
15. *R. (Taverner) v. Tyrone JJ.* [1909] 2 I.R. 763 (K.B.D.).
16. *Attorney General v. Duffy* [1931] I.R. 144 (C.C.A.).
17. *R. v. Castro* 5 Q.B.D. 490, 509.
18. *The People v. Giles* [1974] I.R. 422 (S.C.), citing *Re O'Keeffe*, unrep. 4th October, 1965 (S.C.); *R. v. Morris* [1951] 1 K.B. 394.
19. *R. v. Pearce* [1952] 2 All E.R. 718; *Verrier v. Director of Public Prosecutions* [1967] 2 A.C. 195.
20. Now the Prisons Acts, 1826 to 1980; Prisons Act, 1980, s. 2 (2).
21. See generally, *The State (Gorman) v. Governor of Portlaoise Prison* [1964] Ir. Jur. Rep. 50 (S.C.); cf. *Re McLoughlin* [1970] I.R. 197 (S.C.).

appropriated to prisoners serving sentences of three years or more. Mountjoy and Cork Prisons cater for other male prisoners serving sentences or on remand. Apart from a few convicted of subversive offences, who are in Limerick, female prisoners, whether serving sentences or on remand, can only be taken to Mountjoy or Limerick, but a new women's prison is planned. Shelton Abbey, Co. Wicklow, and Loughan House, Co. Cavan (for males over 18 years of age) are 'open prisons'.

Section 2 of the Prisons Act, 1972, authorised the Minister for Justice, in certain circumstances, to direct the transfer of prisoners to military custody, but the Act ceased to have effect on 31st May, 1983.[22]

Commencement and duration of sentence

Rule 9 of Order 85 of the Rules of the Superior Courts provides that every order of the Central Criminal Court, when drawn up, shall be dated the day of the week, month and year in which it was made, unless that Court shall otherwise direct, and shall take effect accordingly. There is no corresponding Circuit Court rule.

In the days of Assizes and Gaol Delivery the sessions were for most purposes considered in law as one day[1] and accordingly the sentence ran from the first day of the sittings unless otherwise stated;[2] but in the case of Quarter Sessions it ran, in England, from the date it was pronounced, unless otherwise stated.[3] Whilst no authority can be found, it is submitted that the first of these rules should apply to sittings of the Circuit Court, which are fixed according to the law terms, and *may* likewise be applied, if the Court thinks fit, to sittings of the Central Criminal Court. The question may to some extent be academic, since in the case of a sentence of imprisonment it is not infrequently made retrospective, normally if the accused has been in custody awaiting trial, but a sentence of penal servitude cannot be so imposed, pre-

22. As to the constitutionality and effect of these provisions see: *The State (Boylan) v. Governor of Mountjoy Detention Barracks,* unrep. 3rd March, 1981 (S.C.); *The State (Smith) v. Governor of Curragh Military Detention Barracks,* unrep. (H.C.); *The State (Fox) v. Same,* unrep. 14th October, 1980 (H.C.).
1. *Whitaker v. Wisbey* 6 Cox 109.
2. *R. v. Wilkes* 4 Bro. P.C. 360, 367.
3. Stipendiary Magistrates Act, 1858, s. 12; this Act did not apply to Ireland.

sumably because a person could not be transported from a past date, and the sentence runs continuously from the time it was imposed, even though the prisoner may not have actually served part of the term, as occurred in *The State (Woods) v. Governor of Portlaoise Prison,*[4] where the convicted defendant was released in pursuance of a High Court order of habeas corpus; the order was later reversed in the Supreme Court and a warrant was issued for his re-arrest. Where a prisoner is already serving a sentence, he may be sentenced, on conviction of a subsequent offence,[5] to a further term of penal servitude or imprisonment to commence on the expiry of the existing sentence.[6] Where, however, the prisoner is already serving a sentence, or is sentenced on a number of counts in the same indictment or on more than one indictment at the same sittings, it is usual for the court to direct that the sentences be served concurrently.[7]

In England the day on which a sentence of imprisonment begins is included in the term, and months mean calendar months, so that if the accused is sentenced on the 15th day of any month the sentence will expire on the 15th day of the last calendar month of the term;[8] but if the last day of the term, whether penal servitude or imprisonment, would be a Sunday, Christmas Day or Good Friday, the prisoner is to be released on the day before.[9] There appears, however, to be no corresponding statutory provision in Ireland.

Suspension of Sentence

There is no statutory authority in Ireland as there is in England,[10] enabling the court to suspend the operation of a prison

4. 108 I.L.T.R. 54 (H.C.); see generally *The People v. Poyning* [1972] I.R. 402 (C.C.A.); *The State (Jones) v. O'Donovan* [1973] I.R. 329 (H.C.); *The State (McNally) v. O'Donovan* [1974] I.R. 272 (S.C.); *The State (Langan) v. Donoghue* [1974] I.R. 251 (S.C.).
5. Whether this means one committed after, rather than dealt with after, the offence for which the accused has already been sentenced appears not to be decided; *R. v. Hemming* 7 Cr. App.R. 236.
6. *The State (Jones) v. O'Donovan* supra; *The State (McNally) v. O'Donovan* supra. The apparently superfluous provision of the Prisons Act, 1828, was repealed by S.L.R.A., 1983.
7. See, e.g., *The State (Brien) v. Kelly* [1970] I.R. 69 (S.C.).
8. Prisons Act, 1898, s. 12 (1); *Migotti v. Colvill* 4 C.P.D. 233.
9. Prisons Act, 1898, s. 12 (2).
10. Powers of Criminal Courts Act, 1973, ss. 22-26, replacing the Criminal Justice Act, 1967.

sentence, but the judges have long assumed such power.[11] Another practice which has sometimes been adopted is for the court to impose a sentence for a given term, and then to direct that after serving a certain part of that term the offender should be brought before the court to have the operation of the remainder of the term suspended, and this practice appears to have had the implicit approval of the Supreme Court.[12] An order of this kind was imposed by the trial Judge in *Woods'* case referred to above. The more usual order is to impose the sentence, often somewhat more severe than what would have been imposed as a 'custodial sentence', i.e. one to take effect immediately, and then to suspend its operation upon the offender entering into a recognisance, with or without sureties, to keep the peace and to be of good behaviour for a specified period, and further conditions may be imposed: if the offender is in breach of his recognisance, then the sentence comes into full operation without any further order.[13]

The court is not entitled to suspend a sentence imposed on a person convicted of certain offences under the Air Navigation and Transport Acts, 1973 and 1975 (hijacking and endangering aircraft).

Another course sometimes adopted is for the court simply to adjourn the matter of sentence for a certain time in order to see how the offender behaves, or to enable him to pay compensation to an injured party.

Whipping

Whilst corporal punishment appears in practice to have become obsolete,[1] a small number of statutes[2] still authorise the

11. *The State (McIlhagga) v. Governor of Portlaoise Prison* unrep. (S.C.).
12. Id.
13. No reported authority for the proposition can be found, but it appears to be generally accepted; cf. *R. v. Spratling* [1911] 1 K.B. 77.

1. It was abolished in England by the Criminal Justice Act, 1948, s. 2, and the Criminal Justice Act, 1967, s. 65.
2. Offences against the Person Act, 1861, s. 21, and Garrotters Act, 1863, s. 1 (attempting to choke, etc., with intent); Criminal Law Amendment Act, 1885, s. 2 (procuration of women) as amended by the Criminal Law Amendment Act, 1912, s. 3 and the Criminal Law Amendment Act, 1935, s. 7; Inebriates Act, 1898, s. 1 (pimps) as extended by the Criminal Law Amendment Act, 1912, s. 7 (5).

whipping of adult males, and provision is to be found in modern prison regulations as to how the punishment is to be inflicted.[3]

The European Court of Human Rights has, however, ruled that whipping constitutes degradation under the European Convention on Human Rights and Fundamental Freedoms, to which Ireland is a signatory.

Fine

In the case of felony the court appears to have no power to impose a fine except in the case of manslaughter,[4] although it may direct payment of compensation when applying the provisions of the Probation of Offenders Act, 1907.[5] The court has, however, at common law, power to impose a fine on conviction for any misdemeanour, and there appears to have been no limit in Ireland on the amount of the fine which might be imposed. Numerous statutes expressly provide for the imposition of fines, usually up to a maximum amount, for misdemeanours and unclassified offences. There appears no longer to be any reason, as there was at common law, why a fine should not be imposed on a married woman.[6]

Recognisances

A person convicted of any felony, except murder, may be required, in addition to any other sentence imposed by the court, to enter into a recognisance, with or without sureties, to keep the peace, and if he fails, when required, to find sureties, he may be sentenced to imprisonment for a term not exceeding one year.[7] Any person convicted of a misdemeanour, which presumably includes any indictable offence other than felony even though not specifically declared to be a misdemeanour,[8] may, either in addition to or in substitution for any other sentence, be required to

3. Rules for the Government of Prisons, 1947, S.R.O. 320 of 1947, rr. 72, 73.
4. Offences against the Person Act, 1861, s. 5.
5. Infra, pp. 403 sqq.
6. Archbold, 25th Edn. p. 237.
7. See Archbold, 25th Edn. p. 238. It is submitted that the form of recognisance often adopted, when a sentence is imposed but *suspended,* requiring the offender to come up for judgment when called upon to do so is incorrect.
8. See Stephen, *Criminal Law of England,* (1863) 57.

enter into a recognisance, with or without sureties, to be of good behaviour for a reasonable time,[9] and he may be imprisoned for not more than one year if he fails, when required, to find sureties in the case of any offence under certain statutes[10] authorising this procedure in the case of felony.

Probation

Where any person has been convicted on indictment of any offence punishable with imprisonment, and the court is of opinion that, having regard to the character, antecedents, age, health or mental condition of the person charged, or to the trivial nature of the offence, or to the extenuating circumstances under which the offence was committed, it is inexpedient to inflict any punishment or any other than a nominal punishment, or that it is expedient to release the offender on probation, the court may, in lieu of imposing a sentence of imprisonment, make an order discharging the offender conditionally on his entering into a recognisance, with or without sureties, to be of good behaviour and to appear for sentence when called on at any time during such period, not exceeding three years, as may be specified in the order.[1] The court has inherent power to pass sentence subsequently.[2]

The court may, in addition to any such order, order the offender to pay such damages for injury or compensation for loss, and to pay such costs of proceedings, as the court thinks reasonable.[3]

The court may make it a condition of the recognisance that the offender be under the supervision of such person as may be named in the order during the period specified in the order, and may impose such other conditions for securing such supervision as may be specified in the probation order.[4] The court may also impose conditions with respect to residence, abstention from

9. *R. v. Dunn* 12 Q.B. 1026; *R. v. Edgar* 23 Cox 558.
10. Malicious Damage Act, 1861, s. 73; Coinage Offences Act, 1861, s. 38; Offences against the Person Act, 1861, s. 71; Forgery Act, 1913, s. 12; Larceny Act, 1916, s. 37 (5).
1. Probation of Offenders Act, 1907, s. 1 (2); the Act is far more frequently applied in the District Court, when the Court need not proceed to conviction.
2. *R. v. Spratling* [1911] 1 K.B. 77.
3. Probation of Offenders Act, 1907, s. 1 (3).
4. Id. s. 2 (1).

intoxicating liquor and any other matters as the court may, having regard to the particular circumstances of the case, consider necessary for prevention of a repetition of the same offence or the commission of other offences; it must furnish the offender with a notice stating in simple terms any conditions he is required to observe.[5]

The provisions of the Act may not be applied to certain offences under the Air Navigation and Transport Acts, 1973 and 1975 (hijacking and endangering aviation), nor to certain summary offences.

The Court of Criminal Appeal has disapproved further application of the Act to the same offender for serious offences.[6]

The Act of 1907 contains detailed provisions for the appointment of Probation Officers.[7] If it appears to the court before which the offender was bound over, on application of the Probation Officer, that the terms of the recognisance should be varied, it may summons the offender before it and, if he fails to show cause why the variation should not be made, it may vary the terms of the recognisance by extending (up to a maximum of three years from the original order) or diminishing the duration of the order, or by altering the conditions, or by inserting additional conditions, or it may, if satisfied that the conduct of the offender has been such as to make it unnecessary that he be any longer under supervision, discharge the recognisance.[8] It is to be noted that any such application may only be made by the Probation Officer, not by the offender himself.

If an information is sworn that an offender has failed to observe any of the conditions of his recognisance, the court before which the offender was bound over, or any District Justice, may issue a warrant for his arrest, or require him and his sureties, if any, to attend before the court on summons. If the offender is arrested, and is not brought forthwith before the court before which he was bound over, he is to be brought before

5. Id. s. 2 (2).
6. *The People v. Buckley,* 14th December, 1959, Frewen 190.
7. Ss. 3, 4; a professional probation and welfare service under the control of the Department of Justice is now available throughout the State.
8. Probation of Offenders Act, 1907, s. 5, as subtituted by Criminal Justice Administration Act, 1914, s. 9.

the District Court; and any offender brought before the District Court on arrest or summons may be remanded, in custody or on bail, to appear before the court in which he was bound over.[9] If that court is satisfied that he has failed to observe any condition of his recognisance, it may forthwith, without further proof of his guilt, convict[10] and sentence him for the original offence.[11]

Community Service

In June 1981, the Minister for Justice laid a White Paper before the Oireachtas in which he proposed the introduction of legislation whereby offenders instead of going to prison might be permitted to undertake certain projects in the community. He outlined the working of the proposed scheme, the advantages to the offenders, to the community, to the courts and to prison administration, apart from the saving of expense. The White Paper indicated tasks which might be suitable, such as personal service in various forms in children's and old people's homes and in youth clubs, assistance for handicapped persons, as well as practical help in renovation, construction and decoration for community groups and the like.

The Criminal Justice (Community Service) Act, 1983 enables any court other than the Special Criminal Court to make a Community Service Order in respect of any offender over 16 who has been convicted of an offence for which the appropriate sentence would otherwise be one of penal servitude or detention in St Patrick's Institution. Under such an order the offender is obliged to complete between 40 and 240 hours of unpaid work under the supervision of a Probation Officer. The court may only make such an order if the offender consents and if it is satisfied, having considered the offender's circumstances and a report about him, the offender is suitable to perform work under such an order. The court must explain to the offender that if he fails to perform the required work he will be guilty of an offence under section 7 of the Act.

The Act is to be brought into force by ministerial order.

9. Id. s. 6.
10. Presumably this only applies where the accused was bound over before the District Court and no conviction was recorded.
11. Probation of Offenders Act, 1907, s. 6 (5); cf. *R. v. Spratling* [1911] 1 K.B. 77.

Youthful Offenders[1]

In determining the penalty which may be imposed on a young person, having regard to his or her age, the relevant date appears to be that on which the sentence is passed and not the date of the crime.[2]

A person attains a particular age on the day before the relevant anniversary of his birth.[3] The court should hear evidence on oath as to the age of the offender, but it appears that the order of the court is not invalidated if the age is incorrectly stated, even though the court has been misled, and its determination of age appears to be final.[4]

The relevant statutes distinguish between 'young persons' and 'children': a child means a person under the age of 15 years, a young person is a person aged 15 years or upwards and under the age of 17.[5] Statutory provision is also made for the punishment of juvenile offenders between the ages of 17 and 19 years although the statutes do not use this specific term. It is however, to be remembered that, whilst in the case of a person between the ages of 7 and 14, there is a *rebuttable* presumption that he has not the *mens rea* necessary to establish criminal responsibility, a child under the age of 7 is still regarded as *doli incapax,* or wholly incapable of committing a crime. The vast majority of cases involving children are dealt with in the Children's Court or District Court.

No person under the age of 17 may be sentenced to *death,* but in lieu thereof the court must sentence the accused to be detained, and he is then liable to be detained in such place and under such conditions as the Minister for Justice may direct.[6]

1. See generally the Report furnished by Denis C. Mitchell to the Director of Public Prosecutions in October, 1977, and the Kennedy Report on the Reformatory and Industrial School Systems, 1970, both published by the Government Publications Office.
2. *R. v. Fitt* [1919] 2 I.R. 35. In England the relevant date in the case of treason and piracy is the date of commission of the crime; Children and Young Persons Act, 1933, s. 53; Murder (Abolition of Death Penalty) Act, 1965, s. 1.
3. *Re Shurey, Savory v. Shurey* [1918] 1 Ch. 263.
4. Children Act, 1908, s. 123 (1), as amended by the Children Act, 1941, s. 27; *The State (Kenny) v. Ó hUadhaigh* [1979] I.R. 1 (H.C.).
5. Children Act, 1908, s. 131, as amended by the Children Act, 1941, s. 29.
6. Children Act, 1908, s. 103; *The State (O.) v. O'Brien* [1973] I.R. 50, 71 (S.C.) *per* Walsh J.

A male juvenile offender may, under the provisions of the Criminal Justice Act, 1960, in lieu of being sentenced to penal servitude or imprisonment, be sentenced to detention in St Patrick's Institution in Dublin for a period not exceeding the term for which he might be sentenced to penal servitude or imprisonment.[7] There is no corresponding institution for female juveniles, who must accordingly be sent to prison or released. St Patrick's Institution corresponds to what in earlier statutes was referred to as a Borstal Institution.[8] St Patrick's has been described as:[9]

> '[A] special custodial unit for young male offenders of the specified ages which aims at their reformation, and the prevention of crime, by providing a regime calculated to lead to that result.'

Detention in St Patrick's Institution is not the equivalent of imprisonment;[10] a person should not be sent there,

> '[If] he is unfitted, able to benefit from the curriculum of that institution, or if he is likely to prevent other inmates from benefiting from it. Each case, therefore, requires that the particular offender be dealt with in the framework of his known particular circumstances. A sentence of detention in St Patrick's Institution, being a specially allowed alternative to prison, must always be chosen as such alternative by the exercise of a sound judicial discretion.'[11]

It cannot, therefore be imposed to run from a future date.[12]

In addition to its power to sentence to detention under the Act of 1960 the court may, when a person is convicted on indictment and is not less than 16 nor more than 19 years of age, in lieu of passing a sentence of penal servitude or imprisonment, sentence him to detention in St Patrick's Institution for a term of not less than one year, nor more than three years, if it appears to the court that, by reason of his criminal habits or tendencies or association with persons of bad character, it is expedient that he be subject to such detention and under such instruction and direction as

7. Criminal Justice Act, 1960, ss. 1, 13 (1), as amended by the Prisons Act, 1970, s. 6.
8. Criminal Justice Act, 1960, s. 12.
9. *The State (White) v. Martin* 111 I.L.T.R. 21, 24, *per* Henchy J.
10. Id. at 23.
11. Id. at 24.
12. Id.

appears most conducive to his reformation and the repression of crime.[13]

If a young person is over the age of 16, and would be liable to be sentenced to penal servitude or imprisonment if over the age of 17, he may be sentenced to be detained in St Patrick's Institution for a period not exceeding the term of penal servitude or imprisonment to which he would be liable if over 17, if the court considers that none of the other methods by which the case may be legally dealt with is suitable.[14]

The Minister for Justice may, for the purpose of promoting the rehabilitation of offenders, provide places other than prisons for the detention of persons sentenced to penal servitude or imprisonment or to detention in St Patrick's Institution.[15] The offender's suitability for such treatment must first be assessed by the institution, but no such institution has yet been provided.

Whenever the Minister is of opinion that it is necessary to do so for the purpose of relieving congestion in St Patrick's Institution he may direct the transfer to prison of any offender, not under 17 years of age, serving a sentence in St Patrick's, whose transfer is in his opinion necessary. If he does so he must commute the unexpired residue of the term of detention of any such person to such term of imprisonment (not exceeding such residue) as he may determine.[16]

In addition to his general power to transfer prisoners from one prison to another, the Minister may also direct the transfer of persons to a prison from a place of detention other than a prison, and *vice versa*.[17]

No *child* or *young person* may be sentenced to penal servitude, a child may not be sentenced to imprisonment in any circumstances and a *young person* may not be sentenced to imprison-

13. Prevention of Crime Act, 1908, s. 1, as modified by the Prisons Act, 1970, s. 6; similar provisions in respect of persons convicted in the District Court are to be found in the Criminal Justice Administration Act, 1914, s. 10.
14. Criminal Justice Act, 1960, s. 13 (2); and see *The People v. Boylan* [1963] I.R. 238 (C.C.A.).
15. Prisons Act, 1970, s. 2.
16. Id. s. 7. This power is only to be operative for such period as the Minister, after consultation with the Visiting Committee of St Patrick's Institution, may specify; so far as can be ascertained no such order has been made.
17. Prisons Act, 1970, s. 5.

ment or committed to prison in default of payment of a fine, damages or costs, unless the court certifies that he is of so unruly a character that he cannot be detained in a place for the detention of young persons, or that he or she is so depraved in character as not to be a fit person to be so detained.[18] The court should not so certify without sworn evidence, and if it does so without evidence it acts without jurisdiction, and the sentence, in the case of an inferior court, may be quashed by certiorari:[19] presumably if the sentence were imposed in such circumstances by the Central Criminal Court, the remedy would be by way of appeal or habeas corpus. The maximum term of imprisonment prescribed by section 106 of the Children Act, 1908, does not apply to such a case. In addition, where a person detained in St Patrick's Institution is reported by the Visiting Committee to be incorrigible or to be exercising a bad influence on other inmates of the Institution, the Minister may commute the term of detention to a term of imprisonment, not exceeding the residue of the term of detention.[20]

Apart from the power to sentence a young person to prison, the only way in which a person under the age of 16 may be detained is in a Reformatory School or Industrial School. Such schools are now, in practice, described as 'Special Schools',[21] and are approved by the Department of Education. Reformatory Schools are established at Trinity House, and at Scoil Ard Mhuire (for boys aged between 12 and 16), both in Dublin. Industrial Schools are established at St Lawrence's, Finglas, County Dublin (for boys of 11 and 12 years of age), and St Joseph's, Clonmel, County Tipperary for boys (mainly between the ages of 10 and 12), and at St Ann's Kilmacud, County Dublin, St Joseph's Convent, Limerick, The Good Shepherd Convent in Waterford and The Good Shepherd Convent, Maymount, Cork for girls. Before a boy under 16 is sent to a Special School he must

18. Children Act, 1908, s. 102 (3).
19. *The State (Holland) v. Kennedy* [1977] I.R. 193 (S.C.). See also *The State (Donoghue) v. Kennedy*, unrep. 23rd July, 1979 (H.C); confidential reports from social workers may, however, be considered, with the consent of the defence, subject to their being made available to the defence for comment and submissions.
20. Prevention of Crime Act, 1908, s. 7, as adapted; see *The State (Holden) v. Governor of Portlaoise Prison* [1964] I.R. 80 (H.C.); *The State (Dickenson) v. Kelly* [1964] I.R. 73 (H.C.).
21. *The State (Laffey) v. Esmonde*, unrep. 22nd July, 1982 (S.C.).

normally be remanded for three weeks for assessment at St Michael's, Finglas, County Dublin, provided that accommodation is available, but in exceptional circumstances assessment may be dispensed with before a boy under 16 is sent to Trinity House. There is no assessment centre for girls. A girl may be placed on probation on condition that she resides in a hostel willing to accept her.

Children present a particular problem. As has been seen, nobody under the age of 16 can be sent to prison unless certified to be unruly, or to St Patrick's or to any alternative institution, if established. In the first place, a child under the age of 12 cannot be detained at all, save that he may be sent to a certified Industrial School if the court thinks it expedient so to deal with him without his being convicted. If he is convicted and is between the ages of 12 and 15 he may be sent to a certified Reformatory School[22] or, if he has not previously been convicted, and if the court is satisfied that his character and antecedents are such that he will not exercise an evil influence over other children, *and* if the manager is willing to receive him, to an Industrial School: but in that case the manager may ask the Minister for Justice for an order transferring him to a Reformatory School.

A child may be sent to an Industrial School for such period as the court deems proper, but may not be detained there beyond the age of 16 unless the Minister for Education, with the consent of the child's parents or guardians, directs that he should stay on for a further year for the purpose of completing his education.[23] A child may be sent to a Reformatory School for any period not less than two nor more than four years, and in any case not beyond the age of 19, save that, if the Minister for Justice feels that it is necessary for his protection and welfare, the offender may be detained for a further period up to a maximum of 21 years of age.[24] It would seem that, if a School declines to accept, or has no vacancy for, a child under 15, he can only be detained in some other place of detention, other than a prison, for a term of one month.[25]

22. Children Act, 1908, ss. 57, 58, as amended, Children Act, 1941, s. 10.
23. Children Act, 1908, s. 65 as extended; Children Act, 1941, s. 12, and Children (Amendment) Act, 1949, s. 6.
24. Children Act, 1908, ss. 65, 68 as amended; Children Act, 1941, ss. 11, 14.
25. See the Mitchell Report, op. cit., 44.

Whipping[26]

If a male child is found guilty of an indictable offence in the District Court, the court may, instead of any other punishment, adjudge him to suffer not more than six strokes of the birch, to be inflicted privately by a police officer in the presence of a senior police officer, the Governor and Medical Officer of the Prison and, if he desires to be present, of the parent or guardian of the child.[27] Paradoxically, there does not appear to be any general power to inflict such a punishment on a young person, nor to inflict it on a child or young person convicted on indictment, but many statutes authorise the whipping of males under the age of 16, if convicted of specific offences.[28]

Monetary payments

A child or a young person, who is dealt with on a charge of an indictable offence in the District Court, may be fined or ordered to pay damages or costs. The maximum fine or damages which a child may be directed to pay is £2, and he may only be required to pay if the parent or guardian of the child cannot be found, or has not contributed to the commission of the offence by neglecting to exercise due care of the child. The amount of the costs must not exceed the amount of the fine and fees paid by the prosecutor. If the parent or guardian can be found, and unless the court is satisfied that he has not so contributed, the fine, etc. is paid by the parent or guardian; the court need not proceed to a conviction, and the parent or guardian may be required to give security for the good behaviour of the child. The parent or guardian must be given an opportunity to attend the court and to be heard. The like procedure may be adopted in the case of young persons, save that the making of an order that the fine, damages or costs should be paid by the parent or guardian is discretionary, and the maximum amount of fine or damages is raised to £10.[29]

26. Whipping was abolished in England by the Criminal Justice Act, 1948, s. 2.
27. Summary Jurisdiction over Children (Ireland) Act, 1884, s. 4 (1) as adapted, Children Act, 1908, s. 128 (1) and Children Act, 1941, s. 28; Rules for the Government of Prisons, 1947 (S.I. 320 of 1947).
28. See, however, p. 401, supra, as to whipping generally.
29. See Summary Jurisdiction over Children (Ireland) Act, 1884, s. 7; Children Act, 1908, s. 99.

The position where a child or young person is convicted on indictment appears to be similar as regards whipping to that obtaining on conviction in the District Court.

Probation

The provisions of the Probation of Offenders Act, 1907,[30] apply equally to children and young persons as they do to persons over the age of 17. In addition a child or young person may be placed in the care of the Court Probation Officer, who, in the case of a child, must be named in the order, unless there is good reason to the contrary.[31]

In addition there have been established a number of Probation Hostels, sometimes called halfway houses between closed institutions, such as a Reformatory School, and the community. They usually take a small number of boys between the ages of 14 and 16 years who have been in trouble with the law. The boys live in the hostel under trained supervision, but continue their schooling, if still at school, or, if they have left school, are given a programme of work or apprenticeship.

Two such hostels have been established in Dublin and one in Waterford, and at the time of going to press one is to be established in Cork.

The boys are not committed to any particular hostel, but are given the benefit of the Probation of Offenders Act, 1907, on condition that they reside there, which they must agree to do. They are subject to the supervision of the court, through the Probation Liaison Officer, which means in practice that supervision can only be applied to cases dealt with in the District Court, which sits much more frequently than the Circuit Court when dealing with criminal cases.

A similar hostel for girls has been opened in Clontarf, Dublin. Although not a Probation Hostel, Sarsfield House in Dublin will accept boys placed on probation.

30. Supra, pp. 403 sqq.
31. Probation of Offenders Act, 1907, s. 2.

Disqualifications

If a person is convicted of an offence under certain provisions of the Road Traffic Acts, 1961 to 1977, the court may make an order disqualifying him from holding a driving licence for such period as the court thinks fit. In other cases disqualification is mandatory.[1] In these and some other cases the court must make an order endorsing the conviction on the offender's driving licence.[2]

Apart from conviction of an offence under those Acts, a court may also make an order disqualifying a person from holding a driving licence for such period as the court thinks fit if the offender is convicted of an offence and a motor vehicle was used in the course of commission of the offence.[3] In such cases, however, the court must consider, upon hearing the appropriate evidence, and as a separate matter, the issue of whether the person is unfit to hold a driving licence.[4]

A person who has been convicted of any offence and been sentenced to or has served a sentence, a term of imprisonment or penal servitude may in certain cases be disqualified from jury service.[5]

At one time conviction of treason or felony entailed forfeiture of the convict's property but forfeiture was finally abolished by the Forfeiture Act, 1870. Any such 'convict' is, however, still disqualified from bringing an action, entering into a contract or alienating his property whilst serving a sentence of penal servitude.[6] If necessary a curator or administrator may be appointed to deal with the property of the convict.[7] The appointment of a curator is not an additional punishment.[8]

A number of statutes provide for forfeiture of property connected with the commission of an offence.[9] Conviction of treason

1. Road Traffic Act, 1961, ss. 26, 27.
2. *Attorney General v. Keane* 106 I.L.T.R. 5 (H.C.).
3. Road Traffic Act, 1961, s. 27.
4. *The People v. Poyning* [1972] I.R. 402 (S.C.); cf. *The People v. Hogan,* 30th June, 1972, Frewen 360 (C.C.A.).
5. Juries Act, 1976, s. 8, supra, pp. 297.
6. Forfeiture Act, 1870, s. 8.
7. Id. ss. 9, 12.
8. *Woods v. Attorney General,* unrep. 20th December, 1974 (H.C.).
9. See, e.g., Firearms Acts, 1925 to 1971; Fisheries Acts, 1959 to 1980; Misuse of Drugs Act, 1977, s. 30.

or felony may also result in the forfeiture of certain public offices.[10]

A person undergoing a sentence of penal servitude or imprisonment with hard labour for a period exceeding six months, which has been imposed by a court in the State, is disqualified from being elected to the Oireachtas.[11]

Where a person is convicted on indictment of any offence in connection with the promotion, formation or management of a company, or of any offence including fraud or dishonesty, whether in connection with a company or not, the court may, on the application of the Director of Public Prosecutions, order that such person shall not, without the leave of the High Court, be a director of or be concerned with the management of any company for such period as may be specified in the order.[12]

Some other statutes disqualify persons from pursuing a particular profession or vocation in consequence of a criminal record, depending on the terms of the statute.[13]

Some twenty or so statutes which establish Public Boards, committees and so forth provide that a person may be disqualified from membership of the body in question.[14]

Pardon, commutation and remission of sentence

The Crown enjoyed the prerogative of granting a free pardon to any person convicted of a criminal offence[1] and the effect is to

10. Forfeiture Act, 1870, s. 2, so far as not repealed.
11. Electoral Act, 1923, ss. 51 (2) (a), 57 (2) (a).
12. Companies Act, 1963, s. 184; see also Building Societies Act, 1976, ss. 42, 68; Unit Trusts Act, 1972, s. 16.
13. See, e.g., Auctioneers and House Agents Act, 1947, s. 18; Veterinary Surgeons Act, 1931, s. 34, as amended by Veterinary Surgeons Act, 1960, s. 1; Solicitors Act, 1954, s. 34.
14. A few examples are: Harbour Authorities (Harbours Act, 1946, s. 19); Bord na Móna (Turf Development Act, 1946, s. 11); Fógra Fáilte (Tourist Traffic Act, 1952, Sched. 4 (5); Bord na gCon (Greyhound Industry Act, 1958, s. 9); Bord na gCapall (Horse Industry Act, 1970, s. 8); Voluntary Health Insurance Board (Voluntary Health Insurance Act, 1957, s. 8 (2)); Restrictive Practices Commission (Restrictive Practices Act, 1972, Second Sched. 4 (6)); The Arts Council (Arts Act, 1973, s. 7); Bord na Gaeilge (Bord na Gaeilge Act, 1978, s. 6 (2), Sched. 7 (2)); Fisheries Boards (Fisheries (Consolidation) Act, 1959, ss. 26, 30, 35); Central Bank Board of Directors (Central Bank Act, 1942, s. 25 (c)); Prices Advisory Committee (Prices Act, 1972, s. 7).
1. *Hay v. Tower Division Justices* 24 Q.B.D. 561.

place the person in the same position as he was in before conviction. The right of pardon is now conferred by the Constitution[2] on the President, acting on the advice of the Government. The President is given like power to commute or remit punishment imposed by any court exercising criminal jurisdiction, but such power may, except in capital cases, also be conferred on other authorities. In accordance with the latter power, the Government is empowered to commute or remit in whole or in part any punishment imposed by a court exercising criminal jurisdiction, subject to such conditions as they may think proper, and may remit in whole or in part any forfeiture or disqualification imposed by such a court and restore or revive, in whole or in part, the subject of the forfeiture; the Government may delegate these powers to the Minister for Justice.[3]

Section 1 of the Prisons (Ireland) Act, 1907, enables provision to be made by Prison Rules for enabling a prisoner sentenced to imprisonment for a period specified by the Rules, to earn by special industry and good conduct a remission of a portion of his imprisonment, and on his discharge his sentence is deemed to have expired.[4]

The Minister for Justice is also empowered to make rules providing for the temporary release, subject to such conditions (if any) as may be imposed in each particular case, of persons serving a sentence of penal servitude or imprisonment or detention in St Patrick's Institution;[5] any such condition must be notified in writing to the person concerned at the time of his release.[6] The Minister may also suspend, wholly or in part, the currency of the sentence of a person so released.[7]

2. Article 13.6.9°; see *The State (O.) v. O'Brien* [1973] I.R. 50; Kelly, *The Irish Constitution,* 55-56.
3. Criminal Justice Act, 1951, s. 23.
4. Provided that the prisoner has been sentenced, or served, at least one month, the normal remission is for one fourth of the sentence, but see Byrne, Hogan, McDermott, *Prisoners' Rights, A Study in Irish Prison Law,* 103 sqq.
5. Criminal Justice Act, 1960, ss. 2, 4; similar provisions apply to criminal lunatics: id. s. 3. The rules are the Prisoners (Temporary Release) Rules, 1960 (S.I. 167 of 1960).
6. Id. s. 4.
7. Id. s. 5.

CHAPTER 16

APPEALS

A right of appeal can only be conferred by the Constitution or by statute.[1]

I. TO THE HIGH COURT

Whilst a person convicted or bound to the peace in the District Court may appeal to the Circuit Court against a conviction or sentence or both,[2](or against an order dismissing the case under the Probation of Offenders Act, 1907),[3] and the Circuit Court will then re-hear the case, both on the facts and on the law, no such right of appeal against conviction, still less on the ground that the sentence was too lenient, is available, save in exceptional cases, to the prosecution.[4]

Either party to *summary* criminal proceedings in the District Court may, however, request the Justice to state a case for the opinion of the High Court on any question of law, after he has given his decision. Once he has done so he is *functus officio* and the case should not be referred back to him for any further finding of fact.[5] Any such case may be stated by virtue of section 2 of the Summary Jurisdiction Act, 1857,[6] as extended by section 51 of the Courts (Supplemental Provisions) Act, 1961. This power is distinct from that given by section 52 of the Act of 1961,[7] which

1. *The People v. Kennedy* [1946] I.R. 517, 532 (S.C.) *per* O'Byrne J.; *The People v. O'Shea,*unrep. 2nd November, 1982 (S.C.) *per* Henchy J. at p. 3 of judgment.
2. Courts of Justice Act, 1928, s. 18, Criminal Justice Act, 1951, s. 24.
3. Courts of Justice Act, 1953, s. 33.
4. *Foley v. Clifford* [1946] Ir. Jur. Rep. 53 (Circ. Ct.).
5. *M.T.T. v. N.T.,*unrep. 1st April, 1982 (S.C.).
6. The corresponding English statutes were the Summary Jurisdiction Act, 1857, which applied to both England and Ireland and the Summary Jurisdiction Act, 1879, which applied only to England.
7. Reproducing the Courts of Justice Act, 1924, s. 83.

provides that a District Justice shall, if requested by any person who has been heard in any proceedings whatsoever before him (other than proceedings relating to an indictable offence which is not being dealt with summarily by the court), unless he considers the request frivolous, and may (without request) refer any question of law arising in such proceedings to the High Court for determination. Under the Act of 1961[8] the case may be stated *before* the Justice has given his decision whilst the Act of 1857 provides, in effect, an *appeal* from his decision on a question of law. The great majority of reported decisions relate to cases stated under the Act of 1857 – probably because neither party is anxious to incur the expense of further proceedings before there is a decision against him, and also because the right of appeal to the Supreme Court from a decision under section 52 of the Act of 1961 is restricted.

Section 2 of the Act of 1857, as so extended, provides that after the hearing and determination by a Justice of any proceedings (other than proceedings relating to an indictable offence which was not dealt with summarily) any party to the proceedings, if dissatisfied with the determination as being erroneous on a point of law, is entitled to apply in writing within fourteen days after such determination to the Justice to state and sign a case setting forth the facts and grounds of his decision for the opinion thereon of the High Court. For this purpose a 'party' means any party who was entitled to be heard and was heard in the proceedings,[9] and the party requesting the case stated is described as the appellant.[10] The determination of the proceedings is suspended, if the application is granted, until the case stated has been heard and determined or, if the application is refused, until it is refused.[11] If the application is made by or under the direction of the Director of Public Prosecutions, it must be granted. Otherwise the Justice may refuse the application if he considers it merely frivolous.[12] His refusal is, however, open to review on an

8. S. 52.
9. Courts (Supplemental Provisions) Act, 1961, s. 51 (4).
10. Summary Jurisdiction Act, 1857, s. 2.
11. Courts (Supplemental Provisions) Act, 1961, s. 51 (2).
12. Summary Jurisdiction Act, 1857, s. 4.

application to the High Court for an order of mandamus requiring him to state a case.[13] If the Justice, having considered judicially whether a request for a case stated was frivolous, refuses to state it, the High Court will not interfere with his order.[14] If the Justice decides to state a case, notice must be given to the respondent before the case is transmitted to the High Court.[15]

A case may only be stated under the Act of 1857 if the Justice, acting within his jurisdiction, has determined the complaint. If he makes an order without jurisdiction, the remedy of the aggrieved party is to apply for an order of certiorari to quash the decision.[16] If he declines to accept jurisdiction, or to state the case within the time prescribed by the rules, the remedy is to apply for an order of mandamus requiring him to hear the complaint, or state the case.[17]

A case may only be stated on a question of law, and the Justice's findings of fact are conclusive, provided there was evidence to support those findings, which is a matter of law,[18] as is any question of the admissibility of the evidence.[19] The High Court is not, however, confined to consideration of the particular matter of law referred by the Justice, but may consider other arguments, provided they are compatible with the evidence adduced in the District Court.[20]

In so far as this work is concerned primarily with indictable offences, it is not proposed to deal with the details of procedure for statement of a case, either under the Act of 1857 or under the Act of 1961.[21]

If a case is stated under the Act of 1857 an appeal lies from the

13. *The State (Turley) v. Ó Floinn* [1968] I.R. 245 (S.C.).
14. *The State (Reilly) v. Clones District Justice* [1935] I.R. 908; *R. (Murphy) v. Cork JJ.* [1914] 2 I.R. 249 (K.B.D.).
15. *Thompson v. Curry* [1970] I.R. 61 (S.C.).
16. *Attorney General (McNamara) v. Beirne* [1943] I.R. 480 (H.C.).
17. *Wakefield Local Board v. West Riding Railway Co.* 30 J.P. 628; *Prendergast v. Porter* [1961] I.R. 440 (H.C.).
18. *Donaghy v. Walsh* [1914] 2 I.R. 261 (K.B.D.).
19. *Dwyer v. Larkin* 5 N.I.J.R. 25; *R. (Murphy) v. Cork JJ.* [1914] 2 I.R. 249.
20. *Revenue Commissioners v. Bradley* 76 I.L.T.R. 87 (S.C.).
21. See Crotty, *Practice and Procedure in the District Court* (1961), Ch. 14; Woods, *District Court Guide,* Vol. 1, 295 sqq.; District Court Rules, 1948, rr. 199-206; District Court Rules, 1955, rr. 16-18; Rules of the Superior Courts, O. 62.

High Court to the Supreme Court,[22] but if it is stated under the Act of 1961 only by leave of the High Court.[23]

II. TO THE COURT OF CRIMINAL APPEAL

Until the beginning of this century it might be said that the verdict of a jury in a criminal case was, in general, conclusive; if the accused was convicted and any question of law had arisen at the trial, the judge might defer that question and refer it to the Court for Crown Cases Reserved under the Crown Cases Act, 1848, and that Court might either quash or affirm the conviction, or if there was any irregularity at the trial, the accused might, with the consent of the Attorney General, obtain a writ of error and an order for a re-trial.[1]

In England a Court of Criminal Appeal [2] was established by the Criminal Appeal Act, 1907, and a similar Court was established in Ireland by the Courts of Justice Act, 1924,[3] and re-established by the Courts (Establishment and Constitution) Act, 1961,[4] and the jurisdiction of the former Court was transferred to the present Court by the Courts (Supplemental Provisions) Act, 1961.[5]

The prosecution has no right of appeal to the Court of Criminal Appeal from an acquittal although, as will be seen later, it may be able to refer a matter of law,[6] and sometimes to appeal, to the Supreme Court.

Even an accused person who has been convicted has no absolute right of appeal against either conviction or sentence, save, perhaps, in so far as he may appeal direct to the Supreme Court from the Central Criminal Court.[7] He must first obtain leave to appeal.

22. *Attorney General (Fahy) v. Bruen* [1936] I.R. 750 (S.C.).
23. Courts (Supplemental Provisions) Act, 1961, s. 52 (2); cf. *Minister for Industry and Commerce v. Healy* [1941] I.R. 545 (S.C.), decided under s. 83 of the Courts of Justice Act, 1924.
1. Stephens, *Criminal Law of England,* 224; see generally *The People v. Kennedy* [1946] I.R. 517 (S.C.).
2. Now the Criminal Division of the Court of Appeal; Criminal Appeal Act, 1966.
3. S. 8.
4. S. 3.
5. Ss. 12, 48.
6. Criminal Procedure Act, 1967, s. 34 (1).
7. Infra, pp. 435 sqq.

In the case of an offence tried on indictment in the Circuit Court an appeal lies to the Court of Criminal Appeal under like conditions as apply in respect of an appeal from the Central Criminal Court;[8] and this has been extended to appeals against sentence in cases where the accused has pleaded guilty in the District Court and been returned to the Circuit Court for sentence.[9]

A person convicted on indictment before the Central Criminal Court may appeal to the Court of Criminal Appeal if he obtains a certificate from the trial judge that the case is a fit case for appeal, or in case of refusal of such certificate, if the Court of Criminal Appeal on appeal from such refusal, grants leave to appeal.[10] Even if the accused pleaded guilty when arraigned, he may still seek leave to appeal against his conviction, but this will only be granted in exceptional circumstances, as where it is clear that the plea was entered under a misapprehension.[11] It appears that a verdict that, in effect, the accused was guilty but insane is a verdict of acquittal, from which the accused may not appeal to the Court of Criminal Appeal, since it is not a conviction.[12]

The rules relating to such appeals and forms to be used are contained in Order 86, and Appendix U, as amended, to the Rules of the Superior Courts, 1963, set out in Appendix E, infra.

Time for appeal

An application for a certificate from the trial judge that a case is a fit case for appeal must be made at the close of the trial or within three days thereafter.[13] The Court of Criminal Appeal has no jurisdiction to extend the time for making such an application,[14] and may itself only grant leave to appeal if such an application has been refused, so that counsel will usually be prudent to make the application, even if it is a formality in that the judge will in most cases refuse it; but it has been held in England that a

8. Courts of Justice Act, 1924, s. 63.
9. Criminal Procedure (Amendment) Act, 1973, s. 1, nullifying the effect of *The People v. Tyrrell* [1970] I.R. 294 (S.C).
10. Courts of Justice Act, 1924, s. 31.
11. *The People v. Marshall* [1956] I.R. 79 (C.C.A.).
12. *Felstead v. R.* [1914] A.C. 534; as to appeals from the Central Criminal Court to the Supreme Court, see pp. 435 sqq., infra.
13. Rules of the Superior Courts, O. 86, r. 3.
14. *The People v. Cronin* [1972] I.R. 159 (S.C.).

solicitor is not entitled to *appeal* without the authority of his client.[15] If the appellant is granted or refused a certificate, he must serve a notice of appeal, or a notice of application for leave to appeal, as this case may be setting out the grounds of appeal, within seven days[16] but the Court of Criminal Appeal has power to extend the time for notice of appeal to it, on such terms as justice may require, on an application by the appellant specifying both the grounds on which he seeks an extension and the grounds of appeal.[17] If, however, an application for leave to appeal is granted, the original notice is deemed to be the notice of appeal.[18]

Where the applicant had appealed unsuccessfully against conviction only, an application for extension of the time to appeal against sentence was refused in *The People v. Tynan,*[19] on the grounds that no satisfactory explanation of the delay had been given and that there was no substance in the grounds of appeal. The jurisdiction of the Court of Criminal Appeal to extend the time was, however, considered at length by the Supreme Court in *The People v. Kelly.*[20] The accused had been convicted with two others, Bernard McNally and Osgur Breatnach in December, 1978, before the Special Criminal Court on charges of larceny of mail bags and of stopping a mail train with intent, and sentenced to twelve years penal servitude. He had in fact absconded to the United States of America before the conclusion of his trial. In May, 1980, the other two accused appealed to the Court of Criminal Appeal and their convictions were quashed on the ground that the only evidence against them consisted of statements which the Court held not to be admissible because of the circumstances in which they had been taken. Kelly returned to

15. *R. v. McCready* [1978] 1 W.L.R. 1376; *R. v. Jones* [1971] 2 Q.B. 456.
16. Rules of the Superior Courts, O. 86 rr. 4, 5 as amended by the Rules of the Superior Courts, 1967 (S.I. 219 of 1967): the grounds of appeal may be amended or added to by leave of the Court; *The People v. Kerins* [1945] I.R. 339 (C.C.A.); *The People v. Hughes* 92 I.L.T.R. 179 (C.C.A.); but as to the duty of counsel in drafting such grounds and the risk that a ground of appeal will not be entertained, see Archbold §1-47.
17. Rules of the Superior Courts, O. 86, r. 8.
18. Id. O. 86, r. 6.
19. [1964] Ir. Jur. Rep. 28: the dictum of Lavery J. that 'an appeal against conviction puts everything in issue including sentence', was in effect overruled by the Supreme Court in *The People v. Earls* [1969] I.R. 414.
20. [1982] I.R. 90 (S.C.).

the State in 1980, when he was arrested and ordered by the Special Court to serve the sentence imposed on him. He applied to the Court of Criminal Appeal to enlarge the time for appeal against his conviction, and that application was refused on the grounds that:[21]

> 'Whether justice requires that the time be enlarged to enable an application to be made for leave to appeal would appear to depend upon: (a) whether the application is bona fide in that an intention was genuinely in mind while the trial and verdict were still fresh, and the proposed grounds for appeal existed and were in contemplation while the trial and verdict were still fresh;
> (b) whether there are facts properly brought to the attention of the Court concerning the trial of the applicant which prima facie could import unfairness in the trial or an unsatisfactory trial; or (c) whether on the facts proved at the trial there are arguable grounds for finding error of law in relation to the trial of the applicant on such facts.'

The Court, however, granted a certificate for leave to appeal to the Supreme Court as to the criteria to be applied.

In the Supreme Court O'Higgins C.J. and Walsh J. (with whom Hederman J. agreed) expressed the view that an application for leave to enlarge the time was not essential, relying on the general provisions of rule 40 of Order 86 of the Rules of the Superior Courts, that non-compliance by an appellant with any other rule (such as that stipulating the time for appeal) shall not prevent the further prosecution of his appeal unless the Court shall so direct; but Henchy J. (with whom Kenny J. agreed) did not accept that proposition; in the event, however, the distinction appears in the particular case to have been unimportant, since all members of the Court were agreed that the appellant should be permitted to appeal. The criteria to be applied, whether in considering an appeal which is out of time or an application to enlarge the time, appear to be what is just and equitable in all the circumstances of the particular case. All members of the Supreme Court expressed the view that the criteria applied in the Court below were too close to those prescribed for civil cases in *Eire Continental Trading Co. Ltd. v. Clonmel Foods Ltd.*[22]

21. [1982] I.R. 90, 99 *per* Gannon J.
22. [1955] I.R. 170 (S.C.).

In the course of his judgment O'Higgins C.J., after commenting on the reprehensible behaviour of the appellant and the unsatisfactory nature of his affidavit in support of the application, observed:[23]

> 'This Court has before it the judgment of the Court of Criminal Appeal giving its reasons for allowing the appeals of the appellant's co-accused (McNally and Breatnach). I cannot overlook or ignore the fact that each of those appeals related to the admission in evidence of statements obtained as a result of an interrogation of those two accused throughout the same three days as the appellant was questioned or the fact that such interrogation occurred in the same place of detention (the Bridewell) and in respect of the same offences. McNally's appeal was allowed because of a failure to observe the Judges' Rules. However, in Breatnach's case, the Court of Criminal Appeal was of the view that the statements had been obtained in circumstances of oppression, and that basic fairness had not been observed in the process of interrogation. It seems to me that where the appellant (having been involved in the same detention and the same interrogation) makes the same complaints of oppression, this does raise a question which at least requires examination. It may well be that his complaint is ill-founded and that the circumstances of his interrogation differed materially from that of his co-accused. Nevertheless, in my view, justice requires, at least, that the matter be considered and investigated.'

Henchy J. differed from the English Court of Appeal (Criminal Division) in *R. v. Jones*[24] as to the consequences of an appellant 'jumping bail'. He too commented on the conduct of the appellant which he said might be fatal to an application for extension of time, and he continued:[25]

> 'In a case such as the present, the onus is on the convicted applicant to bring to the attention of the Court of Criminal Appeal circumstances which would enable the court to hold that justice requires that his claim (that he should not be shut out by lapse of time from seeking leave to appeal against what he alleges to be a bad or unsafe conviction) should prevail over the claim of the prosecution that justice requires that in all the circumstances time should not be extended to allow the conviction to be assailed.'

23. [1982] I.R. 90, 108-109.
24. [1972] 1 W.L.R. 887.
25. [1982] I.R. 90, 115.

> But for one factor, I would be inclined to hold that the appellant should be refused the extension of time he seeks. That factor is that the evidence on which his conviction rests was a self-incriminating admission made in circumstances akin to those in which his two co-accused made admissions which led to their convictions, but which admissions were later held by the Court of Criminal Appeal to have been unfairly obtained so that their convictions and sentences were quashed. The self-incriminating admissions of all three accused appear to have been made in the same place of detention, during the same period of detention and as a result of methods of interrogation which had certain common features.'

He concluded by saying that:

> '[D]espite the appellant's contumelious treatment of the court of trial, despite his premeditated and well-planned efforts to frustrate and set at naught the process of that court, and despite his evasiveness and lack of candour in making this application to the Court of Criminal Appeal, I would consider that the risk of a miscarriage of justice is so real that the prescribed time should be enlarged to enable the appellant to apply for leave to appeal.'

The appellant's application for leave to appeal was later heard and refused by the Court of Criminal Appeal and this decision, distinguishing the circumstances in which the admissions of the applicant's co-accused were made, was affirmed by the Supreme Court.[26]

A notice of appeal must normally be signed by the appellant but provision is made for cases where the appellant is unable to write, or is alleged to be insane, or is a corporation.[27] Notices must be addressed to and served in the manner provided by the Rules on the Registrar of the Court of Criminal Appeal, who must give notice to the persons affected.[28]

If only a fine was imposed on an accused and has been paid it must be retained by the person who receives it pending determination of any appeal and, if the appeal is successful, the fine must be repaid. If the trial judge who imposes the fine gives a certificate of leave to appeal he may require the appellant to enter

26. Unrep. 2nd April, 1982.
27. Rules of the Superior Courts, O. 86, r. 32. Other notices may be signed by the accused or his solicitor.
28. Rules of the Superior Courts, O. 86, rr. 4-7.

into a recognisance, with or without sureties, to prosecute his appeal.[29] Where the trial judge makes any order consequential on conviction, such as an order for restitution of property or for payment of costs, a reward or compensation, the rules provide for the suspension or annulment of any such order pending appeal.[30]

Bail

An *appellant* who is, as a result of his conviction, in custody may apply for bail pending an appeal. He must do so on notice to the Registrar of the Court of Criminal Appeal. If it grants bail the Court must specify the amount in which the appellant and any surety is to be bound by recognisance; any recognisance is taken before a District Justice. The appellant, if admitted to bail, must attend every hearing of his appeal, when he must surrender himself (and may be searched) into custody until re-admitted, and, if he fails to do so, a warrant may be issued for his arrest. A surety who suspects that the appellant is about to abscond or to fail to observe the conditions of his bail may (apart from his right himself to apprehend the appellant) apply to a District Justice for a warrant for the arrest of the appellant.[31]

The principles to be applied on an application for bail pending appeal have already been considered.[32]

Presence of the accused

In the case of preliminary and interlocutory applications any party may be represented by his solicitor.[1] If, however, the appellant is in custody and so desires,[2] he is entitled to be present at the hearing of all interlocutory applications and at the hearing of his appeal or of an application for leave to appeal or for extension of time for appeal;[3] but if the appellant has been admitted to bail and fails to appear the Court may proceed in his absence.[4]

29. Id. r. 9, which also deals with estreatment of recognisances.
30. Id. rr. 10-13.
31. Id. rr. 20, 37.
32. Supra, pp. 201-202.
1. Rules of the Superior Courts, O. 86, r. 31.
2. See Form of Notice of Appeal, Appendix E, infra.
3. Rules of the Superior Courts, O. 86, r. 26.
4. Id. r. 20 (8).

Abandonment of appeal

At any time after an appellant has served notice of appeal or of application for leave to appeal or for enlargement of time, he may serve notice on the Registrar in the appropriate form abandoning his appeal and the Registrar must notify the persons affected.[5] Even assuming that the Court has jurisdiction to grant leave to withdraw a notice of abandonment, such jurisdiction will only be exercised in special circumstances.[6] If such notice of abandonment is given the Court of Criminal Appeal no longer has any jurisdiction in the matter.[7] Whether informal abandonment before the start of the appeal is permissible without leave of the Court appears to be doubtful, and it has been held in England that an appeal may not be withdrawn without such leave after it has opened.[8]

Non-compliance with rules

Non-compliance by an appellant with the Rules of Court or with any rule of practice will not prevent the further prosecution of his appeal unless the Court so directs.[9]

Hearing of appeals

The Registrar must keep a register, which is open to public inspection, of all cases in which he receives notice of appeal, or of any application for leave to appeal, and must publish from time to time a list of cases to be dealt with.[10] If the appellant is in custody he must notify the appellant, the Prison Governor and the Department of Justice of the probable day on which the case will be heard, and the Department must, if necessary, take steps to transfer the appellant to a prison convenient for his appearance before the Court at such a reasonable time before the hearing as will enable him to consult his legal adviser.[11]

5. Id. r. 24.
6. *The People v. Rushe* [1944] I.R. 66 (C.C.A.); *R. v. Medway* [1976] Q.B. 779.
7. *The State (Woods) v. Attorney General* [1969] I.R. 385 (S.C.).
8. *R. v. de Courcy* [1964] 1 W.L.R. 1245.
9. Rules of the Superior Courts, O. 86, r. 40; cf. *The People v. Kelly* [1982] I.R. 90 (S.C.).
10. Rules of the Superior Courts, O. 86, r. 21.
11. Id. r. 23.

The Court of Criminal Appeal normally deals with an appeal only on the basis of the transcript of the evidence taken at the trial of the accused,[12] and the stenographer must, on request, furnish the Registrar of the Court of Criminal Appeal with the original note and a typewritten transcript certified as correct, or of so much of it as may be required, after having had the transcript certified by the trial judge.[13] The Court may also require the trial judge to furnish a report in writing, giving his opinion upon the case generally or upon any particular point; no part of such a report is to be furnished to anyone other than the Court, except by leave of the Court.[14] Any interested party may obtain a copy of any document upon payment of the proper charges,[15] and any person is to be given a free copy of the transcript if he has been granted a legal aid (appeal) certificate or (if not) by order of the Court of Criminal Appeal.[16] The means and circumstances of the appellant must be furnished to the Registrar, if the latter so requires, by the Garda Síochána.[17]

If, however, it appears to the Registrar that an application for leave to appeal does not show any substantial ground for appeal he may in the first instance list the case for hearing without obtaining the transcript.[18]

Documents, etc.

The Registrar must apply to the court of trial for any original depositions taken before a District Justice, the indictment or indictments against the appellant, a copy of the record of the trial from the Trials Book, any exhibits retained in the court of trial, and a list of the exhibits. On determination of the appeal, these must be returned to the court of trial.[19]

The Registrar may on application by the appellant or the prosecution, or if he considers it necessary or is so directed by the

12. Supra, pp. 315-316.
13. Rules of the Superior Courts, O. 86, r. 14.
14. Id. r. 19.
15. Id. r. 18 (1).
16. Id. r. 18 (3) as amended by the Rules of the Superior Courts, 1971 (S.I. 226 of 1971).
17. Id. r. 34.
18. Id. r. 27.
19. Id. r. 16.

Court, obtain any documents, exhibits or other things (which are to be open to inspection) relating to the proceedings before the Court, and the Court may order production of such things by the person having the custody or control thereof; service of such an order must normally be personal and may be effected by the Gardaí.[20] Copies of any documents in the possession of the Registrar may be obtained from him on payment of the proper charges, or free of charge if counsel is assigned to the appellant or by order of the court, or, if the accused is unrepresented, at the discretion of the Registrar.[21]

Interlocutory applications

Any interlocutory application in relation to an appeal or an application for leave to appeal may be dealt with by the Chief Justice or by a Judge of the Supreme Court designated by him.[22]

Fresh evidence

If the appellant wishes to call new or additional evidence he must apply to the Court for leave to do so, and it appears that the application should be made at the hearing of the appeal or of the application for leave to appeal and not as a preliminary application.[1] If, however, an application for leave to appeal has been refused, the application will not be reinstated for the purpose of seeking to adduce fresh evidence.[2]

Notice of the application must be given in the prescribed form and must state the name and address of the witness, whether he was examined at the trial and, if not, the reason, and the matters on which it is proposed to examine him. It must be accompanied by a statement, signed by the witness, of the evidence which he proposes to give and of the reason why he did not give it at the trial, but the Court may dispense with such statement.[3] If the appellant is legally represented it appears that the statement of

20. Id. r. 17.
21. Id. r. 18.
22. Courts of Justice Act, 1928, s. 7; *Attorney General v. Scuffil* [1936] I.R. 469 (C.C.A.).
1. Sandes, 33.
2. *The State v. Killian,* 17th January, 1951, Frewen 115.
3. Rules of the Superior Courts, O. 86, r. 25 (1), App. U. Form 21.

the witness should be taken by the appellant's solicitor.[4]

If leave is given the evidence will normally be heard by the Court itself, but the Court may order that it be taken by way of deposition before an examiner, normally in private.[5] The Court may make an order for the attendance of any witness, whose expenses may be ordered to be defrayed by the State.[6] The appellant and the prosecution are entitled to be present and to take part in the examination of any witness.[7]

Fresh evidence which was available and was not used will only be admitted in the most exceptional cases, and fresh evidence will not be admitted to make a new case inconsistent with that made at the trial, or merely to supplement evidence given at the trial[8] and the Court may have regard also to the credibility of the evidence.[9]

At the same time one of the principal objects of a criminal trial is to ensure that an innocent man is not convicted.[10]

If the Court admits fresh evidence then, having assessed its credibility,[11] it may either affirm the conviction, (or presumably vary it), or quash the conviction entirely or allow the appeal and order a re-trial on the grounds that the weight of the evidence ought to be determined by a jury rather than by the Court itself.[12]

The order of the court

The grounds on which an accused person seeks *leave* to appeal are usually substantially the same as those of his appeal, so that in practice, if the Court of Criminal Appeal decides to grant leave, it will usually treat the preliminary application as the hearing of the appeal, and so dispense with repetition of the arguments.

The judgment of the Court is to be pronounced by the President of the Court, i.e. such member as is entitled to precedence

4. *Attorney General v. McGann* [1927] I.R. 503 (C.C.A.).
5. Rules of the Superior Courts, O. 86, r. 25 (3)-(7).
6. Id. r. 25 (2), (8).
7. Id. r. 25 (10).
8. *Attorney General v. McGann* supra; *The People v. Keane* 110 I.L.T.R. 1 (C.C.A.).
9. *R. v. Hamilton* 13 Cr. App. R. 32; *Braddock v. Tillotson's Newspapers Ltd.* 65 T.L.R. 553; Archbold §7-44.
10. *Attorney General v. Kelly* [1937] I.R. 315 (C.C.A.).
11. *R. v. Parks* [1961] 1 W.L.R. 1484; *R. v. Flower* [1966] 1 Q.B. 146.
12. *Attorney General v. Kelly* [1937] I.R. 315.

over the other members, or by such other member as the President directs; it is according to the opinion of the majority of the members present and, unless the Court otherwise directs, no judgment with respect to the determination of any question may be pronounced separately by any other member.[13]

The Court may either affirm or reverse the conviction in whole or in part, and may remit, reduce, increase, or otherwise vary the sentence.[14] If, however, the appellant has appealed against conviction *only,* he is *dominus litis* and the Court is not entitled to increase the sentence.[15] The Court has jurisdiction to quash a conviction even where proper directions have been given by the trial Judge, if it considers that the verdict is unreasonable or cannot be supported, having regard to the evidence.[16] The Court may substitute a verdict of guilty of a charge less than that of which the appellant was convicted, e.g. a verdict of manslaughter in place of a conviction for murder.[17] It may make such further order as may be necessary for the purpose of doing justice in the case before the Court, including an order as to costs, except where the accused has a legal aid certificate,[18] and this appears to extend to an order in relation to the costs of the trial, as distinct from the costs of the appeal, although such order will only be made in exceptional cases.[19]

It may happen that the appellant succeeds on some comparatively minor or technical ground of appeal. In such a case it is provided that the Court may, notwithstanding the fact that the point might be decided in favour of the appellant, dismiss the appeal if it considers that no miscarriage of justice has actually occurred.[20] The corresponding English proviso is in section 2 (1)

13. Courts of Justice Act, 1924, s. 28.
14. Id. s. 34.
15. *The People v. Earls* [1969] I.R. 414 (S.C.).
16. *Attorney General v. Lloyd alias Sugden,* 19th May, 1936, Frewen 32 (conviction dependent on evidence of a single questionable witness which no reasonable jury could accept); *Attorney General v. Doyle,* 1st March, 1943, Frewen 39 (appellant prejudiced by improper questions put to co-accused).
17. *The People v. White* [1947] I.R. 247 (C.C.A.); *The People v. Messitt* [1974] I.R. 406 (S.C.); cf. *The People v. Murray* [1977] I.R. 360 (C.C.A.) (capital murder reduced to murder).
18. Courts of Justice Act, 1924, s. 34; cf. *The People v. Bell* [1969] I.R. 24 (S.C.); see also Criminal Justice (Legal Aid) Act, 1962, s. 8.
19. *The People v. Harte* [1946] I.R. 110 (S.C.).
20. Courts of Justice Act, 1928, s. 5.

of the Criminal Appeal Act, 1968, replacing section 4 (1) of the Criminal Appeal Act, 1907.[21]

Every case must necessarily depend on its own facts and the weight of the evidence. The test would appear to be whether, 'in the face of the volume of evidence which was given at the trial, an overwhelming case was proved which the jury could not, without perversity, have ignored so as to find an acquittal.'[22]

Thus the Court declined to quash a conviction in *Attorney General v. Hurley*[23] notwithstanding disparaging references by the trial judge, which it held should not have been made, to a previous acquittal of the accused; in *Attorney General v. Richmond,*[24] where the trial judge had failed sufficiently to distinguish between preparation for and an attempt to commit a crime; and in *Attorney General v. Doyle,*[25] in spite of an incorrect direction that certain evidence amounted to corroboration. On the other hand in *Attorney General v. McLoughlin,*[26] where a complaint by the victim of a sexual assault was held to have been wrongly admitted, on the ground that it was not made spontaneously as soon as practicable after the incident, the Court declined to apply the proviso, as it also did in *The People v. Bruton*[27] in which the prosecution had failed to adduce an essential proof.

The Court may in effect substitute a verdict of 'guilty but insane' for a verdict of guilty, i.e. it may find that, although the appellant was guilty of the act or omission charged, he was insane at the time, and in that case it may quash the sentence and order the appellant to be kept in custody in the same manner as if the verdict had been found by the jury to that effect.[28]

21. See Archbold §7-46; for a full treatment of the subject, see Knight, *Criminal Appeals,* 9-53 (1970 and supp.).
22. *Attorney General v. Hurley* 71 I.L.T.R. 29, 34 (C.C.A.) *per* Kennedy, C.J.
23. Id.
24. 4th December, 1935, Frewen 28.
25. 75 I.L.T.R. 41, Frewen 33.
26. 71 I.L.T.R. 247.
27. 76 I.L.T.R. 56.
28. Courts of Justice Act, 1924, s. 35; in *The People v. Fennell* [1940] I.R. 445 (C.C.A.), the court was invited to substitute such a verdict, but, after commenting on the difficulty of its being required to perform the function of a jury, declined to do so having regard to the evidence. In England a new trial may only be ordered by the Court of Appeal as a result of its hearing new evidence under the Criminal Appeal Act, 1968, s. 23.

If the Court wholly reverses a conviction it may order the appellant to be re-tried for the same offence, and may, except where the appellant has a legal aid certificate, order the costs of the appeal and of the re-trial to be paid by the State, unless the Court is of opinion that the necessity for the new trial has been caused or contributed to by the defence;[29] it may remand the appellant in custody or on bail on such terms as it thinks fit.[30]

Whether an order for a new trial is to be made must depend on the facts of the particular case. If, for example, the only evidence against the appellant is a confession which the Court decides to have been wrongly admitted in evidence, a new trial would be purposeless.[31] If on the other hand the Court finds that the trial judge failed properly to direct the jury, it may conclude that, if the jury had been properly directed, they might nevertheless have convicted and it might normally be expected to order a new trial.[32] A re-trial may be ordered where there was an irregularity at the trial,[33] and may be ordered on certain counts of the indictment only;[34] but not on different charges.[35] A re-trial should not be ordered if the conviction is quashed because of the failure of the prosecution to adduce an essential proof.[36]

As a matter of law, the accused may be re-tried any number of times until a jury agrees on a verdict;[37] but in practice the prosecution will normally enter a *nolle prosequi* after three disagreements.

29. Courts of Justice Act, 1928, s. 5 (1) (b) as modified by Criminal Justice (Legal Aid) Act, 1962, s. 8; costs were refused in *The People v. Hopkins,* 20th April, 1953, Frewen 142; *The People v. Moran,* 27th June, 1974, Frewen 380.
30. Courts of Justice, 1928, s. 5 (1) (b).
31. *Attorney General v. Armitage* 62 I.L.T.R. 174; but a re-trial was ordered in *Attorney General v. Cleary* 72 I.L.T.R. 84, in which only the inadmissible evidence had been adduced but other evidence was available.
32. *Au Pui-Kuen v. Attorney General of Hong Kong* [1979] 1 All E.R. 769.
33. Cf. *The People v. Heffernan (No 2.)* [1951] I.R. 206 (C.C.A.) (contact between jury and public); *The People v. Moran,* 27th June, 1979, Frewen 380 (inadmissible statements inadvertently given to jury on retirement).
34. *The People v. Singer,* 23rd June, 1961, Frewen 214.
35. *The People v. Gilmore* 85 I.L.T.R. 99 (S.C.).
36. *The People v. Griffin* [1974] I.R. 416 (S.C.).
37. *The People v. Kelly (No. 2)* [1938] I.R. 109 (C.C.A.).

Appeal against sentence

There are few reported decisions of the Irish courts dealing with the principles on which they will act in relation to appeals against sentence, since such appeals are seldom the subject of considered judgments. The Court of Criminal Appeal has, however, repeated, in line with its English counterpart, that it will not interfere with a sentence, even though the members of the Court might themselves have been more or less severe if dealing with the case themselves, unless the trial judge has erred in principle[38] – although in practice the Court may seem occasionally to make an exception to prove its rule. The fact that a co-accused may have received too lenient a sentence is not a ground for interfering with a sentence properly imposed on an appellant.[39] The Court will, however, vary the sentence if the trial judge was not informed or misinformed as to some material factor,[40] and if there is merely a technical flaw in the sentence, the proper course is for the Court of Criminal Appeal to vary it, for example by substituting a sentence of imprisonment for one of penal servitude.[41]

It should be noted that, unlike the Irish Court, the English Court of Appeal has no power to *increase* a sentence.

III. TO THE SUPREME COURT

References by the Director of Public Prosecutions

Where on a question of law a verdict in favour of an accused person is found not guilty by direction of the trial judge, the Director of Public Prosecutions may, without prejudice to the verdict in favour of the accused, refer the question to the Supreme Court for decision.[1] The statement of the question to be referred must be settled by the Director after consultation with the trial judge, and must include any observations which the judge may wish to add, and the Supreme Court must assign counsel to argue in support of the decision.[2]

38. See Archbold §7-633 sqq.; *R. v. Ball* 35 Cr. App. R. 164.
39. *The People v. Poyning* [1972] I.R. 402 (C.C.A.).
40. *The People v. Earls* [1969] I.R. 414 (S.C.).
41. *The People v. Power*, unrep. 31st July, 1975 (C.C.A.); *The State (McDonagh) v. Frawley* [1978] I.R. 131.

1. Criminal Procedure Act, 1967, s. 34 (1), as adapted by the Prosecution of Offences Act, 1974.
2. Criminal Procedure Act, 1967, s. 34 (2), (3).

The Director is not entitled to refer a question by virtue of the foregoing provisions after a verdict of not guilty in the Special Criminal Court.[3] Whether the Director is entitled to refer the question whether evidence rejected by the trial judge was properly rejected is apparently undecided; in *The People v. Cummins*[4] the Supreme Court considered the admissibility of such evidence, but whether that question was properly referred was not argued; in *The People v. Crinnion*[5] Henchy J. expressed the view *obiter* that the admissibility of such evidence was not properly referable, the other two judges of the Court expressing no view.

By case stated from the Circuit Court

Section 16 of the Courts of Justice Act, 1947, provides that a Circuit Judge may, on application by any party to any matter pending before him, refer any question of law arising in such matter to the Supreme Court by way of case stated, but the Supreme Court has held that this section does not apply in the case of a criminal trial before a jury after the accused has been given in charge and before the jury has delivered its verdict.[6]

From the Court of Criminal Appeal

The decision of the Court of Criminal Appeal affirming or varying conviction or sentence is final, unless that Court or the Director of Public Prosecutions certifies that the decision involves a point of law of exceptional public importance and that it is desirable in the public interest that an appeal should be taken to the Supreme Court, whose decision will then be final.[7] Such a certificate may not be granted by the Court of Criminal Appeal to the Director if the conviction is quashed, and in such a case the Supreme Court will not hear an appeal if the Director himself

3. *The People v. Crinnion* [1976] I.R. 29.
4. [1972] I.R. 312.
5. Supra.
6. *The People v. McGlynn* [1967] I.R. 232; Walsh J. expressed the view that such a case stated would lie before the accused was put in charge, or after the jury had returned its verdict, but that particular question was not before the Court and the other two judges expressed no opinion.
7. Courts of Justice Act, 1924, s. 29; the Supreme Court cannot itself grant the certificate; *Attorney General v. Murray* [1926] I.R. 300.

issues a certificate.[8] It is submitted that the dual requirement for the certificate is unnecessary in so far as it would seem to be necessarily in the public interest that an appeal should be taken whenever the case involves a point of law of exceptional public interest; a somewhat similar formula is, however, to be found in the corresponding English legislation.[9]

If the appropriate certificate is granted the Supreme Court is not limited to the point of law certified as being of public importance, but may also, in an appropriate case, consider other grounds of appeal.[10]

From the Central Criminal Court

Article 34.4.3° of the Constitution provides that the Supreme Court shall, with such exceptions and subject to such regulations as may be prescribed by law, have appellate jurisdiction from all decisions of the High Court and shall also have appellate jurisdiction from such decisions of other Courts as may be prescribed by law. The Supreme Court is given no such appellate jurisdiction from decisions of the Circuit Court or Special Criminal Court in respect of conviction or sentence, or in respect of an acquittal (save by way of case stated from the Circuit Court after an acquittal by direction of the trial judge referred to above) or from decisions of the Court of Criminal Appeal (save on foot of a special certificate also referred to above). The Central Criminal Court is, however, the High Court exercising its criminal jurisdiction.[11]

The question whether a person convicted in the Central Criminal Court may appeal *direct* to the Supreme Court was considered by the Supreme Court in *The People v. Conmey*.[12] In that case the accused had been convicted in the Central Criminal Court and appealed against conviction and sentence to the Court

8. *The People v. Kennedy* [1946] I.R. 517 (S.C.). In England the Attorney General may, in the event of an acquittal, refer a point of law to the Court of Appeal or House of Lords; Criminal Justice Act, 1972, s. 36; Archbold §7-136.
9. Cf. Criminal Appeal Act, 1968, s. 33 (2).
10. *The People v. Giles* [1974] I.R. 422 (S.C.); *The People v. Shaw* [1982] I.R. 1 (S.C.); *The People v. Kelly (No. 2)* [1982] I.R. 90 (S.C.).
11. Courts (Supplemental Provisions) Act, 1961, s. 11 (1).
12. [1975] I.R. 341.

of Criminal Appeal which dismissed the appeal and refused to grant a certificate enabling him to appeal to the Supreme Court. He then applied to the Supreme Court for an order extending the time for appeal to the Supreme Court against conviction.[13] His application was dismissed on the ground that, having appealed in the first instance to the Court of Criminal Appeal, his appellate rights were exhausted. O'Higgins C.J. and Walsh J. (with whom Doyle J. agreed) did, however, express the view that the Constitution conferred a right on an accused person convicted in the Central Criminal Court, or on the prosecution in the case of an acquittal, to appeal direct to the Supreme Court, a question on which Griffin J. (with whom Budd J. agreed) expressed no opinion. In the later case of *The People v. O'Shea* referred to below, O'Higgins C.J. (with whose judgment Walsh J. and Hederman J. concurred) took the view that this was a clear and authoritative decision that, pending appropriate changes prescribed by law, the Constitution conferred on the Supreme Court jurisdiction to entertain appeals against conviction in the Central Criminal Court, observing that since *Conmey*'s case such appeals against conviction had in fact been dealt with.[14]

The converse case of the right of the Director of Public Prosecutions to appeal against an acquittal by a jury in the Central Criminal Court was considered by the Supreme Court in *The People v. O'Shea,*[15] which resulted in a sharp division of eminent judicial opinion on the preliminary issue whether such a right existed. The accused had been charged in the Circuit Court on an indictment on several counts relating to possession of firearms, ammunition and drugs and the trial was transferred on the application of the Director of Public Prosecutions to the Central Criminal Court.[16] The trial judge directed the jury to find the accused not guilty and the verdict, already entered on the issue paper, was 'Not guilty by direction'. The majority of the Court (O'Higgins C.J., Walsh and Hederman JJ.) interpreted Article 34.4.3° of the

13. Under the Rules of the Superior Courts, O. 58, r. 3, the time would have been 21 days from the date of conviction, unless extended by O. 108, r. 71.
14. See, e.g., *The People v. Lynch* [1982] I.R. 64 (S.C.).
15. Unrep. 2nd November, 1982.
16. Such an application would not now be possible; supra, p. 264.

Constitution strictly as conferring such a right of appeal on the prosecution. O'Higgins C.J. said:[17]

> 'The Constitution as the fundamental law of the State must be accepted, interpreted and construed according to the words which are used and these words, where the meaning is plain and unambiguous, must be given their literal meaning. Of course the Constitution must be looked at as a whole and not merely in parts, and where doubt or ambiguity exists, regard may be had to other provisions of the Constitution and to the situation which obtained and the laws which were in force when it was enacted. Plain words must, however, be given their plain meaning unless qualified or restricted by the Constitution itself. The Constitution brought into existence a new State, subject to its own particular and unique basic law, but absorbing into its jurisprudence such laws as were then in force to the extent to which these conformed with that basic law. It follows that existing laws or formerly accepted legal principles or practices cannot be invoked to alter, restrict or qualify the plain words used in the Constitution unless the authority for so doing derives from the Constitution itself. Indeed the very existence of an inconsistency between what was formerly the law and what the words of the Constitution, according to their literal meaning declare, repeals and abrogates what has been the law.'

He continued:[18]

> 'In the first place I think it proper to raise the question whether, in this case, we are, in fact, dealing with the verdict of a jury or merely with the decision of the trial Judge, . . . [From the transcript] it appears that the trial Judge, having informed the jury of the decision he had come to on the legal submissions made to him, then said:
>
>> "Now I have an issue paper here. What we have done, ladies and gentlemen . . . we have taken it upon ourselves to write in the verdict of 'Not Guilty by direction', by my direction, so that now, will be the verdict of the jury and Mr Muldoon, the foreman, you will sign the bottom to say that this jury, on my direction, recorded this verdict."
>
> 'Can it seriously be suggested that, in such circumstances, the findings of "Not Guilty" represented the verdict of the jury? The word "verdict" derives from the Latin words"verus" and "dictum" and has always been taken to indicate an important decision truly

17. At pp. 9-10 of judgment.
18. At pp. 16-18.

spoken after careful deliberation by the deciding body. Here the jury's only association with what is described as their verdict was to watch while the foreman, in obedience to the order of the trial Judge, signed his name on an issue paper which already had written on it the words "Not Guilty by direction" in respect of the seven counts standing on the indictment. Whatever appearance old established custom and procedure may require in criminal jury trials, the reality is that such a verdict of "Not Guilty" was never pronounced by the jury and resulted from the Judge's decision and his alone.'

He went on, however, to say:[19]

> 'While, in my view, Article 34.4.3° of the Constitution gives to this Court an appellate jurisdiction in respect of all verdicts resulting from criminal trials in the Central Criminal Court, this means no more than that the Court is given a competence to entertain such appeals. How, and to what extent, that competence will be exercised is a matter for decision by the Court. A clear practice has developed in relation to appeals brought in respect of civil jury trials. I see no reason why this practice, with appropriate changes, should not apply to appeals resulting from jury trials on criminal charges. Verdicts, properly arrived at and supported by evidence, while in theory appealable, would not be disturbed. This Court would be bound by findings of fact made at the trial. A conviction would be open to challenge on the sufficiency of the evidence relied on to support it or on the trial Judge's directions or rulings on law. An acquittal duly recorded by a jury on a consideration of the evidence would be immune . . .
>
> It should be remembered that the Constitution is concerned with justice, and in the context of this case, with criminal trials being fairly conducted in due course of law. While these considerations provide safeguards for the person accused they also guarantee to the State, which accuses him and which has a duty to detect and suppress crime, that he will in fact be tried fairly and properly on the evidence adduced against him and in accordance with law. If, as a result of an error made by the trial Judge, the jury is not permitted to consider the evidence of the charge brought against him or to pronounce on his guilt or innocence, can it be said that justice has been accorded to the State and to society? In my view, it cannot and, if this be so, a situation would exist which the Constitution prohibits.'

The Chief Justice disposed of the contention that an order for re-trial would be contrary to the doctrine of *autrefois acquit* on

19. At pp. 24-26.

the basis that it does not apply where the accused was acquitted by direction of the judge, since the accused was never in jeopardy.[20] It is submitted, however, that these observations were *obiter dicta* in that the Court was not at this stage required to determine whether a new trial should be ordered, and, with respect to the Chief Justice, it is difficult to see how the accused was not *in jeopardy* from the time that he was put in charge of the jury on a valid indictment.

Walsh J. agreed with the judgment of the Chief Justice and that of Hederman J. referred to below, and in the course of his judgment said:[21]

> 'Jury trial in criminal cases, which is made mandatory by the Constitution save in the exceptions provided for, is a most valuable safeguard for the liberties of the citizen. It must therefore be permitted to operate properly. It would be totally abhorrent if a conviction which had been obtained by improper means, such as the corruption or coercion of a jury, should be allowed to stand. It should be equally abhorrent if an acquittal obtained by the same methods should be allowed to stand. If attempts to sway the verdicts of jurors by intimidation or other corrupt means were allowed to go unchecked they could eventually bring about the destruction of the jury system of trial.'

Hederman J. agreed with the judgment of the Chief Justice on the preliminary issue, whether there was any right of appeal, excluding the question whether a re-trial might be ordered.

Finlay P. differed with the majority on the effect of an acquittal by direction. He said:[22]

> 'The fundamental question which arises necessarily for determination in this case is as to whether one of the essential ingredients of the trial with a jury as contained in the Constitution is the immunity of the verdict of "not guilty" by a jury arrived at within its jurisdiction and without corruption from appeal to any appellate tribunal. In my view, it is.
>
> A consideration of the decisions of the Irish Courts over the past 100 years or so would seem to indicate that there is not a single instance of a decision by any court at any level that an appeal lay with the prosecution against the acquittal of a person tried on a

20. Supra, pp. 271 sqq.
21. At p. 7 of judgment.
22. At pp. 12, 13 of judgment.

criminal charge with a jury. It would further appear that until the present case (notwithstanding the fact that historically, over that period, very many of jury acquittals must have seemed extremely unsatisfactory to the prosecuting authorities) no attempt has been made to assert such a right.'

He concluded:[23]

> 'For these reasons, I have come to the conclusion that the right of trial with a jury provided for in the Constitution includes the right to a trial with a jury, one of the ingredients or essential characteristics of which is the fact that a jury's verdict reached of "not guilty", is not subject to appeal to any other court. I am satisfied that this right expressly dealing with the question of criminal trials must take precedence over the general right of appeal provided for from decisions of the High Court to the Supreme Court. . .'

The President expressed no opinion as to whether an accused person was entitled to appeal direct to the Supreme Court from conviction in the Central Criminal Court.

Henchy J. took the view that the sole question which arose was whether the prosecution could appeal to the Supreme Court from a verdict of acquittal in the Central Criminal Court, whether or not that verdict was reached by direction of the trial judge. He commented on the fact that the case had originated in the Circuit Court, from which there was manifestly no right of appeal, and transferred to the Central Criminal Court, from which it was contended that such a right subsisted, by the Director of Public Prosecutions who now claimed that right. He differed from the Chief Justice on the interpretation of Article 34.4.3° of the Constitution. He emphasised that this right of appeal is but a component in an ensemble of interconnected and interacting provisions, adding:[24]

> 'It may be said of a constitution, more than of any other legal instrument, that "the letter killeth, but the spirit giveth life". No single constitutional provision (particularly one designed to safeguard personal liberty or the social order) may be isolated and construed with undeviating literalness.'

23. At p. 20.
24. At pp. 17-18 of judgment.

He took the view[25] that : 'appellate jurisdiction from all decisions of the High Court' meant 'appellate jurisdiction from all *appealable* decisions' and that:[26]

> '[A] quintessential feature of the jury trial required [by Article 38.5 of the Constitution] is the consequence that when that trial properly takes place within jurisdiction and results in the jury's verdict of not guilty, whether directed by the judge or not, that verdict can never again be questioned in any court by way of appeal or otherwise.'

O'Shea's case is thus a clear authority for the proposition that the prosecution has a right of appeal, on a question of law, from any acquittal by a jury in the Central Criminal Court, but whilst there are strong judicial dicta to the effect that the accused has a like right to appeal on a question of law from conviction or sentence in that Court, apart from his right to appeal by leave to the Court of Criminal Appeal, that particular question does not appear yet to have been positively decided. The Director's appeal in *O'Shea*'s case was, in the end, dismissed.[27] The question whether, if he had succeeded, he could have obtained a new trial appears still to be open.

IV. REFERENCES TO THE COURT OF JUSTICE OF THE EUROPEAN COMMUNITIES

The Treaty of Rome provides[1] that where a question is raised before any court or tribunal of a Member State, and the question is within the jurisdiction of the Court of Justice of the European Communities,[2] that court or tribunal may, if it considers that a decision on the question is necessary to enable it to give judgment, request the European Court to give a ruling thereon. The Treaty further provides[3] that where any such question is raised in a case pending before a court or tribunal of a Member State, against whose decisions there is no judicial remedy under national law, that court or tribunal *shall* bring the matter before

25. At p. 25.
26. At. p. 32.
27. Unrep. 6th May, 1983.
1. Article 177 (2).
2. Hereinafter referred to as the European Court: for the constitution and jurisdiction of that Court, see pp. 22 sqq., supra.
3. Article 177 (3).

the European Court. Domestic courts are obliged by the doctrine of the supremacy of Community law to accept any ruling given by the European Court on a reference under Article 177 of the Treaty.

Interpretation of Article 177

Article 177 of the Treaty essentially involves a separation of jurisdiction, between the domestic courts on the one hand and the European Court on the other, where the interpretation of a point of Community law arises in the course of domestic proceedings. Such a bifurcation of jurisdiction has no historical precedent within the common law systems.[4] However, the frequent invocation of this Article by domestic courts in all Member States of the Communities has resulted in the accumulation of a large body of case law which has served to throw light upon the respective jurisdictional competences of the domestic courts and the European Court.

Article 177 itself draws a distinction between those domestic courts from whose decision there is a remedy under national law and courts of final resort within the national hierarchy. In so far as the courts exercising criminal jurisdiction in Ireland are concerned the position is not entirely clear. In some instances the criminal court of final resort is easily identifiable. Examples of such courts include the Circuit Court when exercising criminal appellate jurisdiction from the District Court, and the Supreme Court in the exercise of appellate jurisdiction in a criminal case. These courts are *obliged* by Article 177 (3) to refer any question in relation to any of the matters referred to in Article 177 (1) to the European Court if they consider that a decision on such a question is *necessary* to enable them to give judgment.

Where a case is tried upon indictment the position of the trial court is not quite so clear. In the case of the Central Criminal Court there may be a *right* of appeal to the Supreme Court,[5] in

4. French courts have long operated a system of referring preliminary questions to a Tribunal des Conflits. On this see Lagrange, *The European Court of Justice and National Courts. The Theory of Acte Clair: A Bone of Contention or a Source of Unity?* (1971) 8 C.M.L. Rev. 313, 313-315.
5. Supra, pp. 435 sqq.

which case this Court would seem to be *empowered* by Article 177 (2) to refer a question for a preliminary ruling rather than *obliged* to do so by Article 177 (3).

Where a trial upon indictment takes places in the Circuit Court or in the Special Criminal Court, there is, as has been seen, no right of appeal, save by leave of the court of trial or the Court of Criminal Appeal,[6] and there is likewise no *right* of appeal from the Court of Criminal Appeal except on foot of a certificate from that Court or the Director of Public Prosecutions.[7] Where an automatic right of appeal is available, the trial court will fall within Article 177 (2) but it is submitted that where leave is *essential* to enable a defendant to appeal and no such leave is given by the trial court, such a court ought to consider itself bound by the obligation to refer which is imposed by Article 177 (3). Similarly where the Court of Criminal Appeal hears any appeal, unless it intends to give a certificate that the case involves a point of law of general public importance, thereby enabling an appellant to appeal to the Supreme Court, it ought to consider itself *bound* to refer under Article 177 (3).[8]

Criteria to be applied by a domestic court

It has been suggested that 'in fact very few differences separate the application of Article 177 (2) from that of Article 177 (3). . .'[9] Whether domestic courts consider that they fall within the category of courts which are empowered by Article 177 (2) or alternatively are required by Article 177 (3) to make a preliminary reference, nevertheless *all* domestic courts still enjoy a wide measure of discretion in relation to the initial decision whether or not to refer any matter for a preliminary ruling.

Where a domestic court is not a court of final resort and a question of the correct interpretation of some aspect of Com-

6. Supra, pp. 420.
7. Supra, pp. 434.
8. This seems to follow from the decision of the Court of Justice in *Hoffman-La Roche v. Centrafarm* [1977] 1 E.C.R. 957; *contra, Bulmer v. Bollinger* [1974] Ch. 401. On this see generally Jacobs, *Reference to the European Court in interlocutory proceedings* (1977) 2 E.L. Rev. 354; Wyatt and Dashwood, *The Substantive Law of the E.E.C.* 69-71.
9. See Lagrange, op. cit at 320.

munity law arises, the trial judge ought to *consider* the matter but he is entitled to exercise his discretion not to refer, in the safe knowledge that the question may always be reopened before a domestic appellate tribunal. The European Court has tended to encourage lower courts to refer preliminary matters to it and has criticised any attempts by higher domestic courts to fetter the power of referral given by the Treaty.[10] Indeed, it is worthy of note that many of the most important decisions of the European Court have been as the result of referrals by lower courts.[11]

English courts and judges have, as a rule, tended to deprecate the practice of referrals from lower courts.[12] In *Bulmer v. Bollinger*[13] the English Court of Appeal suggested certain guidelines to be considered by judges before making a reference. These included consideration of the time factor involved in making such a reference, the importance of not overloading the European Court, the difficulty and importance of the point of law, the expense involved and the wishes of the parties themselves.[14] However, the somewhat restrictive views of some English judges have not inhibited the constant stream of cases to the European Court under Article 177[15] and the Article has proved most useful in integrating even the lowest national courts into the Community framework.

Even in the case of courts of final resort, the fact that they are enjoined by Article 177 (3) to refer matters for preliminary rulings is still contingent upon certain factors. First, the court of last resort may consider that, while a genuine point on the inter-

10. See, e.g., *Rheinmühlen-Düsseldorf v. EV St. (No. 1)* [1974] E.C.R. 33.
11. See, e.g., *Costa v. E.N.E.L.* [1964] 3 C.M.L.R. 425 (referral from the Giudice Conciliatore in Milan).
12. See Bridge, *Community Law and English Courts and Tribunals: General Principles and Preliminary Rulings* (1975) 1 E.L. Rev. 13, 18.
13. [1974] Ch. 401.
14. Id. at 421-423 *per* Lord Denning. See also Collins, *European Community Law in the United Kingdom* (2nd Ed.) 115-116.
15. Recent referrals in criminal cases from English courts include *R. v. Saunders* [1979] 2 C.M.L.R. 216 (referral on a plea of guilty from Bristol Crown Court); *R. v. Thompson* [1978] 1 C.M.L.R. 390 (referral from Court of Appeal (Criminal Division) (s.n. *R. v. Johnson*). Recent referrals from Irish courts include: *North Kerry Milk Producers v. The Minister for Agriculture* [1976] 2 C.M.L.R 680 (from the High Court); *The Minister for Fisheries v. Schonenberg* [1978] 1 E.C.R. 473 (criminal case referred by Cork District Court); *An Bord Bainne v. The Minister for Agriculture* [1978] 1 E.C.R. 497.

pretation of Community law has arisen in a case before it, nevertheless a decision in the case may be given without the point being resolved. If a court refuses to refer on this basis it is acting entirely within the sphere of competence left to it by the Treaty. Secondly, a court of final resort is not obliged to refer where there is already in existence a ruling from the European Court on the same question on an earlier occasion.[16] Even, however, where the European Court has given a ruling, a domestic court may, if it considers it appropriate, refer an identical point to the Court in order to attempt to secure a reconsideration of the matter.[17] The third and most problematical issue in this area of law has arisen over the so-called doctrine of *acte clair*.[18] The axiom *clara non sunt interpretanda* has long been articulated in the French courts through the application of the doctrine of *acte clair*.

French courts of final resort have often refused to refer under Article 177 (3) on the basis that Community law was so clear on a particular point that no question of interpretation could be said to have been raised.[19] Opponents of *acte clair* suggest that this is a usurpation of the sphere of competence of the European Court and is a case of begging the question.[20] However, in his defence of the doctrine former Advocate-General Lagrange has suggested that:[21]

> '[I]t is the *abusive use* of the *acte clair* that is to blame, and not the principle, which is sound. In this respect it should be observed that everything depends on the good faith and goodwill of the national courts. In fact, if they use the theory of the *acte clair* as a pretext for retaining certain cases for themselves more or less systematically, the situation would practically amount to a deadlock.'

16. In *Da Costa en Schaake v. Nederlandse Belastingadministratie* [1963] E.C.R. 31, the Court of Justice accepted seisin despite having answered the same question in *van Gend en Loos v. Nederlandse Administratie der Belastingen* [1963] E.C.R. 1.
17. See, e.g., *Renato Manzoni v. Fonds National* [1977] 2 E.C.R. 1647 (reference from a Belgian Court).
18. On the topic of *acte clair* see generally: Collins, op. cit. 101-105; Lipstein, *Law of the European Economic Community* 329-330; Lagrange, *The Theory of Acte Clair* 8 C.M.L. Rev. 313; Pescatore (1970) Rev. trim dr. europ. 300.
19. See, e.g., *Re Shell-Berre* [1964] C.M.L.R. 462 (Conseil d'État); also *State v. Cornet* [1967] C.M.L.R. 351 (Cour de Cassation Ch. Crim.); *Lapeyre v. Administration des Douanes* [1967] C.M.L.R. 362 (Cour de Cassation Ch. Crim.).
20. See Pescatore, op. cit. *passim*.
21. Lagrange, op. cit. at 322.

National courts, if they use *acte clair* prudently, will merely be protecting the European Court from having to adjudicate upon 'issues' which are manifestly devoid of any foundation. The English Court of Appeal appears to have sanctioned such a use of the doctrine in *Bulmer v. Bollinger.*[22] However, as domestic tribunals are unfamiliar with the complexities of Community law they may frequently err if they attempt to be dogmatic as to the meaning of any Treaty provision. A clear illustration of this appears to be provided by the interpretations of the meaning of the phrase 'quantitative restrictions' in Article 30 of the Treaty in the English case of *R. v. Henn, R. v. Darby,*[23] by the House of Lords and lower courts. The European Court itself appears to accept the desirability of the screening which is provided by *acte clair.*[24]

The stage in criminal proceedings at which a preliminary reference should be sought from a national court

Article 177 (2) uses the expression 'Where . . . a question is raised before any court'. Either the defence or the prosecution may *request* a court to make a reference under Article 177. Alternatively, the court itself may raise the matter. However, the decision as to whether or not to make a reference belongs *exclusively* to the court, and no party to proceedings may make a reference directly.

Article 177 is silent as to the appropriate stage of proceedings at which to seek a reference. In a criminal case this may prove particularly problematical. A defendant may not dispute the facts alleged against him, but may argue that these facts do not amount to a criminal offence if an issue of Community law is interpreted in accordance with his contention. Alternatively, the defendant may dispute the facts alleged by the prosecution, but may further contend that even if the prosecution's version of the facts is accepted, these facts do not constitute a criminal offence

22. [1974] Ch. 401, 423 *per* Lord Denning.
23. [1981] A.C. 850 (E.C.J. and H.L.); [1978] 3 All E.R. 1190 (C.A.).
24. *Da Costa en Schaake v. Nederlandse Belastingadministratie* [1963] E.C.R. 31.

due to the superimposition of Community law on the national legal order.

As defendants in criminal trials may spend some time in custody before and more particularly *during* their trials the time factor in Article 177 referrals assumes a greater importance in criminal cases than in civil actions.

There would appear to be several alternatives open to the defendant who wishes to obtain a preliminary ruling on the basis that the criminality of the act charged is contingent upon a particular interpretation of Community law. In a case to be heard upon indictment before an inferior court, an order of prohibition might be sought from the High Court on the ground that the indictment discloses no criminal offence. If an indictment is preferred in the Central Criminal Court it may alternatively be possible to seek a declaration in similar circumstances, although in *Imperial Tobacco v. Attorney General,*[25] the House of Lords held that it was not a proper exercise of discretion of a judge in a civil case to grant to a defendant in criminal proceedings a declaration on the basis that the counts did not disclose any offence. The court in that case felt that such a use of discretion usurped the function of the criminal court.

When a criminal trial begins the defence may attempt to raise an issue of Community law by way of a motion to quash the indictment. Such an application was rejected by the trial court in *R.v. Henn, R. v. Darby*[26] where the appellants faced a number of charges arising out of the importation of pornography into the United Kingdom. The defence alleged that in respect of one count in the indictment the statutory provision under which the accused had been charged had ceased to have any effect as it conflicted with a Treaty provision. After the motion to quash was refused, counsel for the defendants again sought a referral at the end of the prosecution case but this application was also refused.[27] After conviction by the jury the appellants appealed to

25. [1981] A.C. 718.
26. [1981] A.C. 850; but see *R. v. Goldstein* [1983] 1 All E.R. 434.
27. For another case in which a defence application for a referral was refused at the conclusion of the prosecution case: see *R. v. Johnson* [1978] 1 C.M.L.R. 390 (whether the term 'capital' in Articles 67 to 73 of the Treaty of Rome included certain gold and silver coins).

the Court of Appeal (Criminal Division) as of right on a point of law. Although refusing the appellants' appeal, the Court of Appeal both refused to refer the case and refused leave to appeal to the House of Lords. However, the House of Lords itself gave leave to the appellants to appeal to it and then referred the matter to the European Court. After receiving the preliminary ruling on the matter, the House of Lords dismissed the appeal. In the course of his judgment Lord Diplock stated:[28]

> '[I]n a criminal trial upon indictment it can seldom be a proper exercise of the presiding judge's discretion to seek a preliminary ruling before the facts of the alleged offence have been ascertained, with the result that the proceedings will be held up for nine months or more in order that at the end of the trial he may give to the jury an accurate instruction as to the relevant law, if the evidence turns out in the event to be as was anticipated at the time the reference was made – which may not always be the case. It is generally better, as the judge himself put it, that the question be decided by him in the first instance and reviewed hereafter if necessary through the hierarchy of the national courts.'

Dogmatism is probably ill advised as to the appropriate juncture for a lower court to refer any case. It is a matter which ought to remain within the *exclusive* discretion of the trial judge. If the factual situation is not in dispute a referral at a very early stage may be desirable.

One problem with the vast majority of jury verdicts is that they do not articulate any specific findings of fact. It is possible that in some cases, where an issue as to the applicability of some point of Community law is involved, the trial judge ought to consider eliciting from the jury a special verdict in which the facts as found by them are clearly set forth. Such a verdict could enable a court to decide whether it was necessary to refer a case at all, and in the event of any referral it would enable the trial court to enter the appropriate judgment when an authoritative statement of the applicable law had been gained.

The effect of any reference to the European Court is to suspend the case at hearing until a ruling has been obtained.

28. [1981] A.C. 850, 904.

Issues arising out of the formulation of the questions to be put to the European Court by the referring court have frequently featured in the case law of the European Court. That Court has demonstrated a willingness to reframe any questions from a national court in order to make it conform with the dictates of the Treaty. It will even extrapolate an appropriate question where no effort has been made by the national court to do so. The European Court never refuses seisin of a case on the basis that a question has been badly framed or even on the basis that a referral is, in its opinion, wholly unnecessary given the facts of the case. In *Salgoil v. Italy* the Court held:[29]

> 'The Court of Justice has no jurisdiction to decide whether one or other of the provisions referred for an interpretation is applicable to the case at issue; this is a matter for the court making the reference.'

English courts have held in criminal trials that a legal aid certificate granted for the case continues to be valid for a reference to the European Court.[30] Although no Irish court appears as yet to have considered this specific point it seems that they should grant legal aid.

29. [1968] E.C.R. 453, 459-460.
30. *R. v. Marlborough Street Stipendiary Magistrate, ex parte Bouchereau* [1977] 1 W.L.R. 414.

CHAPTER 17

STATE SIDE ORDERS

Order 84 of the Rules of the Superior Courts governs the procedures to be followed when an applicant is seeking a 'State Side order'. These orders issue from the High Court and were formerly known as 'prerogative writs'. Those orders which have most relevance to the criminal process are habeas corpus, mandamus, certiorari and prohibition. The liberty of the individual was, for centuries, effectively secured by the writ of *habeas corpus ad subjiciendum* and it is now similarly protected by Article 40.4 of the Constitution. Relief under Article 40.4 is colloquially still referred to as habeas corpus and this nomenclature has been retained in the Rules of the Superior Courts.[1] The order of mandamus lies to command an inferior court or a person or body to perform a public duty. The orders of certiorari and prohibition frequently prove useful to challenge the jurisdiction of inferior criminal courts. In Ireland the inferior courts comprise the District Court, the Circuit Court, and the Special Criminal Court. No application for mandamus, prohibition or certiorari may be maintained against any order of the Central Criminal Court as this is itself the High Court exercising criminal jurisdiction.

I. HABEAS CORPUS

Article 40.4 of the Constitution states:[2]

> 2° Upon complaint being made by or on behalf of any person to the High Court or any judge thereof alleging that such person is being

1. O. 84, rr. 2-8.
2. Article 40.4.2-5 were enacted as part of the Second Amendment of the Constitution in May, 1941. For an exhaustive treatment of the constitutional aspects of habeas corpus, see Kelly, *The Irish Constitution*, 421-435.

unlawfully detained, the High Court and any and every judge thereof to whom such complaint is made shall forthwith enquire into the said complaint and may order the person in whose custody such person is detained to produce the body of such person before the High Court on a named day and to certify in writing the grounds of his detention, and the High Court shall, upon the body of such person being produced before that Court and after giving the person in whose custody he is detained an opportunity of justifying the detention, order the release of such person from such detention unless satisfied that he is being detained in accordance with the law.

3° Where the body of a person alleged to be unlawfully detained is produced before the High Court in pursuance of an order in that behalf made under this section and that Court is satisfied that such person is being detained in accordance with a law but that such law is invalid having regard to the provisions of this Constitution, the High Court shall refer the question of the validity of such law to the Supreme Court by way of case stated and may, at the time of such reference or at any time thereafter, allow the said person to be at liberty on such bail and subject to such conditions as the High Court shall fix until the Supreme Court has determined the question so referred to it.

4° The High Court before which the body of a person alleged to be unlawfully detained is to be produced in pursuance of an order in that behalf made under this section shall, if the President of the High Court or, if he is not available, the senior judge of that Court who is available so directs in respect of any particular case, consist of three judges and shall, in every other case, consist of one judge only.

5° Where an order is made under this section by the High Court or a judge thereof for the production of the body of a person who is under sentence of death, the High Court or such judge thereof shall further order that the execution of the said sentence of death shall be deferred until after the body of such person has been produced before the High Court and the lawfulness of his detention has been determined and if, after such deferment, the detention of such person is determined to be lawful, the High Court shall appoint a day for the execution of the said sentence of death and that sentence shall have effect with the substitution of the day so appointed for the day originally fixed for the execution thereof.

Relief under Article 40.4 of the Constitution lies in such a wide number of instances that attempts to impose any meaningful schematism thereon seem futile. However, it is clear that habeas corpus does not lie as an adjunct to the normal system of criminal appeals, and the High Court will not re-open any factual issues in pursuance of such an application.

Habeas corpus is intended by the Constitution to provide a means whereby the legality of any detention of one individual by another may be scrutinised by the court. Relief under Article 40.4 is thus not confined to matters touching the criminal process.

Where an applicant seeks relief of this kind, the illegality which he alleges must be of such a nature that the court will conclude that he has been deprived of his liberty otherwise than in accordance with law. This is clear from the judgment of O'Higgins C.J. in the Supreme Court in *The State (McDonagh) v. Frawley:*[3]

> '[T]he phrase [in accordance with law] means that there must be such a default of fundamental requirements that the detention may be said to be wanting in due process of law. For habeas corpus purposes, therefore, it is insufficient for the prisoner to show that there has been a legal error or impropriety, or even that jurisdiction has been inadvertently exceeded.'

An irregularity or a procedural deficiency which is of such a nature as to invalidate any essential step in the proceedings leading ultimately to detention will entitle an applicant to relief because in such an instance his detention may be said to be other than in accordance with law.[4] There are dicta from other jurisdictions to the effect that the judicial power of review by way of habeas corpus exists only where the decision is a nullity,[5] but the modern dynamic interpretation of constitutional rights by Irish judges makes such dogmatism ill advised.

Habeas corpus lies to correct widely diverging kinds of unlawful detention. A person unlawfully detained without being arrested will be entitled to relief, as will a person who is under arrest but who has been held beyond the time permitted by law. In *The State (Hoey) v. Garvey*[6] Finlay P. directed the release of

3. [1978] I.R. 131, 136.
4. See *The State (McKeever) v. Governor of Mountjoy Prison,* unrep. 19th December, 1966 (S.C.); also Kelly, op. cit. 433.
5. See, e.g., *R. v. Governor of Brixton Prison, ex parte Schtraks* [1962] 3 W.L.R. 1013; *Estep v. United States* 327 U.S. 114 (1946).
6. [1978] I.R. 1 (H.C.).

the prosecutor, who had been arrested upon reasonable suspicion, released without charge, and then arrested on a second occasion in relation to the same matter and upon the same suspicion. The President of the High Court accepted that the second arrest had been made on the basis of additional information given to the police but he stated:[7]

> '[T]here does not appear to me to be any justification for making a distinction between a suspicion in the mind of a Garda Officer which has grown by reason of obtaining additional information and one which has merely grown in his mind.'

Another instance in which Irish courts will grant habeas corpus is when a court has purported to make an order depriving a person of liberty but has failed to observe the statutory preconditions leading to the imposition of such a sentence.[8]

As has already been mentioned,[9] there may exist the possibility of applying for relief where legal representation has been so perfunctory as to render a criminal trial a farce or a sham.

Sometimes it is not the *fact* of detention that is objected to by a prosecutor but the *place* of detention or the *conditions* under which such detention is carried out. In *The State (Dillon) v. Kelly*[10] the High Court ordered the release of the prosecutor because the place of his detention was not in accordance with law. In *The State (McDonagh) v. Frawley*[11] the prosecutor alleged that he was not receiving proper medical attention for a pain in his back while in prison and that his constitutional right to bodily integrity had thereby been infringed. The Supreme Court, however, disallowing his appeal, held that the prosecutor had failed to prove a breach of a fundamental requirement of the law.

It is clear that where a person is imprisoned in consequence of

7. Id. at 5.
8. *The State (Holland) v. Kennedy* [1977] I.R. 193 (S.C.).
9. See Chapter 8, supra.
10. [1970] I.R.174; cf. *The State (Hanley) v. Governor of Mountjoy Prison* 108 I.L.T.R. 102.
11. [1978] I.R. 131; see also *The State (C.) v. Frawley* [1976] I.R. 365 (prosecutor with personality disturbance, kept in solitary confinement much of the time; no suitable facilities for the long term psychiatric treatment needed by the prosecutor; order of habeas corpus refused).

an order of a competent court he is '*prima facie* detained according to law, and it would require most exceptional circumstances for [the] Court to grant even a conditional order of habeas corpus to a prisoner so convicted.'[12]

Persons who may apply for relief under Article 40.4

Article 40.4.2 of the Constitution makes references to a 'complaint being made by or on behalf of any person to the High Court'.

In many instances it may be possible for the imprisoned person himself to swear an affidavit seeking a conditional order, i.e. an order directing his release unless cause to the contrary is shown. A prosecutor may even appear and present his case in person. If he is incapable of so doing, however, there is no objection to another person applying on his behalf and indicating to the Court that the prisoner is incommunicado and is incapable of making the application himself. Such a situation could arise if a person were under police interrogation and his legal adviser were to be refused access. The right of a stranger to maintain an application for an order under Article 40.4 where the prisoner himself was not incommunicado was left open by Gavan Duffy J. in *The State (Burke) v. Lennon*[13] although in the more recent case of the *Re Woods*[14] an application was made on behalf of Woods who was not incommunicado, by a fellow prisoner, alleging that the transfer of Woods from one prison to another in pursuance of a warrant and transfer order rendered his detention unlawful. Accepting that a person has a right to apply to the court on behalf of another Ó Dálaigh C.J. said, '[t]his right includes a right to state the grounds which are put forward for alleging that such other person is being unlawfully detained.'[15] The court, however, rejected the proposition that a stranger had the further right to argue the case on behalf of the person detained. Even where it is clear that no *de facto* authority has been given to a stranger to

12. *Per* Maguire P. in *The State (Cannon) v. Kavanagh* [1937] I.R. 428, 435 approved, *The State (McDonagh) v. Frawley* [1978] I.R. 131.
13. [1940] I.R. 136 (S.C.).
14. [1970] I.R. 154 (S.C.).
15. Id. at 157.

seek habeas corpus on behalf of another, the courts will strive to ensure the vindication of the constitutional rights of the imprisoned person, by permitting the application to be brought.[16]

The appropriate respondent

The appropriate respondent in an application for habeas corpus is always *primarily* the person in whose custody the prisoner is at the time of the application.[17] It has been stated[18] that 'habeas corpus is not formulated or intended to serve as a challenge to the decision ordering the imprisonment. It is directed against the gaoler who should not be charged with the additional duty of having to defend the tribunal's errors, if any.' Frequently orders of certiorari and habeas corpus are sought at the same time. This enables the impugned conviction to be quashed, where appropriate. In such consolidated applications the appropriate respondents will include the Prison Governor, the Attorney General, the Director of Public Prosecutions and the Judge(s) or District Justice who has made the order which is under scrutiny.[19]

As the court will not make an ineffectual order, it is incumbent upon the prosecutor to demonstrate that the respondent has the prisoner in his control. In *The State (Quinn) v. Ryan*[20] the Supreme Court refused to make absolute, conditional orders of habeas corpus against members of the Gardaí who had improperly handed the prosecutor over to British police officers. The court based its decision upon the fact that it would have been absolutely impossible for the respondents to resume custody over

16. *The State (Quinn) v. Ryan* [1965] I.R. 70 (S.C.) (prisoner removed from jurisdiction without having the opportunity to consult his legal advisors); Kelly, op. cit. at 426 suggests that the absolute nature of the right of strangers such as an officious volunteer acting without the prisoner's wishes is unclear. On this, see also de Smith, *Judicial Review of Administrative Action* (4th Edn) at 598, where the author states that it is implicit in the English rules that the application be made with the concurrence of the detainee (unless he is incommunicado) or is incapable in law or in fact of consenting to the application.
17. The technical custody of bailsmen is insufficient. Cf. *Attorney General v. Blennerhassett* 67 I.L.T.R. 136.
18. See Rubinstein, *Habeas Corpus as a Means of Review* 27 M.L.R. 322, 324 (1964).
19. See, e.g., *The State (Browne) v. Feran* [1967] I.R. 147 (habeas corpus and certiorari).
20. [1965] I.R. 70

the prosecutor. In *The Secretary of State for Home Affairs v. O'Brien*[21] when the British Secretary for Home Affairs had deported the applicant to the Irish Free State, the English Court of Appeal was disposed to make the Secretary of State a respondent on the basis that he might *de facto* still be able to influence the release of the defendant.

Where a Ministerial Order relating to a detention is being questioned, the Minister involved is joined as a respondent.[22]

Procedure

The procedure for applying for relief under Article 40 is set forth in the Rules of the Superior Courts.[1] The application is initiated by an *ex parte* motion for a conditional order. Although this procedure antedates the Constitution and finds no endorsement therein, the courts appear to accept it, although in *Re Singer* Lavery J. did advert to the possibility that:[2]

> 'It may be necessary to consider in some appropriate case whether the procedure prescribed by the Constitution should not be used in place of the old procedure by conditional order, cause shewn, and motion to make absolute, or to discharge the conditional order.'

A conditional order means that unless the respondents, to whom it is directed, show cause to the contrary, the court will make the habeas corpus order absolute and direct the release of the person imprisoned. It is the almost invariable practice of the Irish courts to grant conditional orders of habeas corpus, although, as has been seen, if the applicant is a convicted prisoner he may experience difficulty even in getting a conditional order.[3] The court has power to make an absolute order in the first instance, although it would only make such an order if satisfied that it was impossible for the respondent to show lawful cause. There is no time limit for making an application for relief under Article 40.4.[4]

21. [1923] A.C. 603.
22. See, e.g., *The State (Dillon) v. Kelly* [1970] I.R. 174 (S.C.).
1. O. 84, rr. 44-50; see Appendix F.
2. 97 I.L.T.R. 130, 139 (S.C.); see also Kelly, op. cit. at 423.
3. See, e.g., *The State (Cannon) v. Kavanagh* [1937] I.R. 428 (H.C.).
4. In this, habeas corpus differs from certiorari, at least in so far as challenges to District Court and Circuit Court orders are concerned, as these must be challenged within six months.

The application for the conditional order is grounded upon an affidavit sworn either by the person who is himself under restraint or by some other person who swears as to the fact of restraint.

The grounding affidavit, in addition to stating the fact of restraint, also sets out those grounds upon which it is alleged that the detention is contrary to law. In those instances in which an order of a court is sought to be impugned, the details of such order are stated.

If a conditional order is granted the judge directs those persons upon whom the order is to be served, and also any persons to whom notice is to be given.[5] When the conditional order is directed to a gaoler such as a prison governor or other public official, it is served by leaving a copy of the order with the gaoler or his servant at the place of confinement, while at the same time exhibiting an attested copy of it, or in such manner as the court may direct. In all other cases, the conditional order is served personally, unless the court otherwise directs.[6]

Every conditional order granted must be filed in the Central Office within ten days from the day on which it was pronounced unless the court grants further time for filing. Failure to comply will mean that the order will stand discharged.[7] After the order has been filed and served, the respondent must show cause as to why the conditional order should not be made absolute. This must be done within the time specified in the conditional order or, if no time is specified, within ten days after service.[8] Cause may be shown on affidavit, although, if a respondent wishes to show cause but does not wish to adduce any evidence, he may show cause by a notice served upon the prosecutor or his solicitor, stating concisely the ground upon which the respondent relies.[9]

As soon as cause has been shown the prosecutor is *obliged* to apply to the court to make absolute the conditional order not-

5. O. 84, r. 44 (1).
6. O. 84, r. 44 (2).
7. O. 84, r. 45.
8. O. 84, r. 46.
9. O. 84, r. 47; see Form No. 12 (Appendix T) Rules of the Superior Courts.

withstanding the cause shown.[10] Notice of motion is served upon the party showing cause, or his solicitor, within six days of the filing of the cause shown or, where there exists a multiplicity of persons showing cause, within six days of the service of the last of the notices.[11]

If the prosecutor fails to serve the required notice of motion, the respondent will be entitled to an order allowing the cause shown as well as an order for costs.[12]

On the other hand should the respondent fail to show cause as required, the prosecutor must file an affidavit of service of the conditional order and a certificate that no cause has been shown. The prosecutor will then be entitled (unless the conditional order has otherwise directed) to a side bar order from the Master of the High Court making absolute the conditional order.[13]

Where the prosecutor has served notice of motion to make absolute a conditional order, notwithstanding cause shown by the respondent, he must deliver, two days before the hearing, to the Central Office, books of the proceedings for use by the court, unless otherwise directed.[14] If the relevant books are not delivered the other side may deliver them and the defaulting party is not heard until he has defrayed the cost of the books. In default, the case may be struck out.[15]

At the hearing of the notice the court will consider the affidavits, and if the respondent is unable to justify the detention the order is made absolute, and the prisoner is released. If the respondent is able to establish the legality of the detention (and the onus normally rests upon him to do so), then the conditional order will stand discharged.

Successive applications for an order of habeas corpus

The somewhat confused history of successive applications for the old writ of habeas corpus may be largely responsible for the phrase in Article 40.4.2 of the Constitution which contemplates

10. O. 84, r. 49 (1).
11. O. 84, r. 49 (2).
12. Id.
13. O. 84, r. 50.
14. O. 84, r. 54.
15. O. 84, r. 56.

complaints being made 'to the High Court or any judge thereof'. This phrase is identical to that used in Article 6 of the Constitution of 1922.

Prior to the Judicature (Ireland) Act, 1877, it was clearly the case that successive applications could be made to different divisions of the High Court in respect of the same detention. Thus, for example, a refusal by the Court of Queen's Bench would not preclude the Court of Exchequer from deliberating upon an identical application. While it is not entirely clear, it seems very unlikely that prior to the 1877 Act an applicant could apply to any individual *judge* as opposed to any *court* for a writ of habeas corpus.[1]

The reason for permitting successive applications to different *Divisions* of the High Court prior to 1877 may, it has been suggested, be traceable to an erroneous dictum by Lord Coke in *Bonham's Case* in 1609.[2] In that case[3] Lord Coke held *inter alia* that if a writ of error could not be brought in respect of proceedings it remained open to the parties to traverse the facts found. As habeas corpus proceedings resulted in an 'award' or 'order' rather than a 'judgment' no writ of error lay in respect of them and, therefore, there would be no *res judicata*.

However, Lord Coke's view in *Bonham's Case* as to the inconclusive nature of proceedings not reviewable by writ of error has been widely repudiated.[4] No writs of error lay against the refusal of mandamus (without pleadings) or certiorari[5] and yet the courts never allowed successive applications in these instances after they were dismissed on the merits.[6] It has been suggested[7] that, 'there was not, and never has been, any good reason for not applying the principle of *res judicata* to habeas corpus just as to all other branches of the law. . . '

1. See Heuston, *Habeas Corpus Procedure* 66 L.Q.R. 79 (1950).
2. (1609) 8 Rep. 1216. For criticism of the rule, see Gordon, *The Unholy Writ of Habeas Corpus* 26 M.L.R. 520 (1963).
3. The case involved a physician who had been convicted by the College of Physicians of practising without a licence. It was not a habeas corpus matter.
4. See, e.g., *Groenvelt v. Burwell* (1699) 1 Ld. Raym. 454 (where the dicta were specifically rejected); also Gordon, op. cit. at 527.
5. See, e.g., *R. v. The Dean and Chapter of Dublin* 1 Str. 536; see also Lord Goddard, *A Note on Habeas Corpus* 65 L.Q.R. 34-35 (1949).
6. Gordon, op. cit. at 528-529.
7. Id. at 529.

However, even after the passing of the Judicature (Ireland) Act, 1877, successive applications could still be made to the different Divisions of the High Court.[8] In *Egan v. Macready*[9] it was suggested that an applicant could apply not only to every *court* but to every *judge*. The origin of this doctrine may be traced to a dictum of Lord Halsbury in *Cox v. Hakes.*[10] Other judges in *Cox v. Hakes* referred only to the right of an unsuccessful applicant to go from *court* to *court* and indeed Lord Esher M.R., in the same case in the Court of Appeal, was quite specific, saying, 'It is not correct to say that under the old system there could be an application to all the judges in succession.'[11]

In 1928 in *Eshugbayi Eleko v. Nigeria*[12] the Judicial Committee of the Privy Council sanctioned the proposition that a detained person could seek to have the propriety of his detention adjudicated upon by every judge of any court which had jurisdiction to grant a writ of habeas corpus. One reason suggested for the decision in *Eleko* is that:[13]

> '[T]he Judicial Committee may have realised that before 1875 the right was to go from court to court, and yet, in its reluctance to reach a conclusion apparently adverse to the rights of the subject, have decided that there was now a right to apply successively to every High Court judge.'

However, the implications of permitting a multiplicity of applications to different High Court judges forced the Supreme Court to reach a conclusion different from that of the Judicial Committee. In *The State (Dowling) v. Kingston (No. 2)*[14] the prosecutor, Dowling applied for and was granted a conditional order of habeas corpus. The application to make absolute the order was refused by a majority of two-to-one in the High Court.[15] The prosecutor then sought an order from the dissenting judge. This order was refused and the prosecutor then appealed to the Supreme Court, asking that Court to draw up an order in

8. *Re Sullivan* (1888) 22 L.R. Ir. 98 (Ex. Div.).
9. [1921] 1 I.R. 265 (Ch.D.).
10. (1890) 15 App. Cas. 506.
11. 20 Q.B.D. 1, 13.
12. [1928] A.C. 459.
13. Heuston, *Habeas Corpus Procedure* 66 L.Q.R. 79, 85-86 (1950).
14. [1937] I.R. 699.
15. *Per* Maguire P. and Hanna J., Gavan Duffy J. dissenting.

accordance with the opinion given by Gavan Duffy J. in the High Court. After a careful analysis of the history of the right of a prosecutor to apply *seriatim* to different judges of the High Court for independent adjudications, Fitzgibbon J. concluded:[16]

> 'I can find no possible ground for the suggestion that an application may be made to a Judge, after the Court of which he is a member has refused a writ, for the issue of a new writ. Each Judge is bound to administer the law, and when once the law has been declared by a competent Court, whether by a majority or unanimously, the law so declared is in my opinion binding upon the individual members of the Court.'

Today in Ireland the prosecutor, assuming that he is relying upon the same facts, is entitled to only one *determination* from the High Court on the issue of whether or not to make absolute a conditional order. The situation is otherwise when the prosecutor is merely seeking a conditional order. In this case there is no objection to a prosecutor 'forum shopping' and making repeated applications *ex parte,* because there has been no judicial determination that the detention is in accordance with law.[17] If, however, he is represented by counsel, his counsel should, as a matter of professional etiquette, inform the judge to whom he makes the fresh application that an earlier application has been refused.

If there has been a refusal to make absolute a conditional order the prosecutor is entitled to a further *determination* by the High Court on the propriety of his detention but only if he can advance new grounds in support of such an application.[18] In *Re Woods* the President of the High Court declined jurisdiction on the basis that the Supreme Court had already determined that the applicant was in lawful custody. The President believed that he was bound by the provision of the Constitution which states:[19] '[T]he decision of the Supreme Court shall in all cases be final and conclusive.'

16. [1937] I.R. 711, 746.
17. See Murnaghan J. in *The State (Dowling) v. Kingston (No. 2)* [1937] I.R. 699, 751-752.
18. *Re Woods* [1970] I.R. 154.
19. Article 34.4.6°.

However, on appeal to the Supreme Court, Walsh J. said:[20]

> 'In my view it was never contemplated by the Constitution that the dismissal of such an application for habeas corpus precluded for all time any further application being made in respect of the same detention of the same person. Information might subsequently come to light which would be sufficient to satisfy any court of the illegality of the detention. Even if it were the fact that such information could have been obtained at the time of the original application, in my opinion it would not alter the situation. . .
>
> When in a new application the High Court is asked to consider the complaint upon grounds formerly ruled by the Supreme Court in earlier proceedings, the High Court is not entertaining an appeal against a decision of the Supreme Court because the earlier proceedings concluded in the Supreme Court. However, the High Court should rule the new application in the light of the decision given by the Supreme Court in the earlier proceedings. Where grounds are advanced which had not been formerly considered then, *a fortiori*, the High Court must consider and rule upon these grounds according to its own judgment.'

It is now accepted that the appellate jurisdiction conferred upon the Supreme Court from all decisions of the High Court by virtue of Article 34.4.3° of the Constitution is such that either a prosecutor who has failed in his attempt to have a conditional order made absolute in the High Court[21] or a respondent who has failed in the opinion of that Court to show cause[22] may appeal to the Supreme Court. In the latter instance, if the Supreme Court allows the respondent's appeal, a warrant will issue for the arrest of the prosecutor.[23]

II. MANDAMUS

This order lies to compel an inferior court or a person or body to perform a public duty. Within the criminal process the area of greatest potential for the order of mandamus is in relation to the discretion to prosecute, the decision to enter a *nolle prosequi*, and the requirements contained in various statutes that the con-

20. [1970] I.R. 154, 167-168.
21. *R. (Johnstone) v. O'Sullivan* [1923] 2 I.R. 13 (C.A.)
22. *The State (Browne) v. Feran* [1967] I.R. 147 (S.C.).
23. Cf. *The State (Woods) v. Governor of Portlaoise Prison* 108 I.L.T.R. 54 (H.C.).

sent of the Director of Public Prosecutions, the Attorney General or some other specified person be obtained before a prosecution may be instituted. These matters have already been discussed in Chapter 4. Mandamus may also issue to compel an inferior court to hear an appeal or to state a case.[1] It may also lie to oblige a judge of an inferior court to consider such matters as applications for legal aid.

III. PROHIBITION

The order of prohibition issues to ensure that no person acts outside his competence or that no inferior court exceeds its jurisdiction. In *The State (O'Callaghan) v. Ó hUadhaigh*[2] an order was made to prevent the Director of Public Prosecutions from renewing a prosecution after a *nolle prosequi* had been entered. The orders of prohibition and certiorari bear a close affinity to one another. The essential difference between these two orders is that prohibition is anticipatory, in that it is frequently sought before an inferior court embarks upon the hearing of a case.[3] Alternatively, it may be applied for to prevent such a court from continuing with a hearing in excess of its jurisdiction. Prohibition is sometimes sought in conjunction with certiorari because if an order of certiorari issues to quash a conviction or sentence, prohibition may prove useful to prevent a further irregularity occurring in the future. In *The State (de Búrca) v. Ó hUadhaigh*[4] the sentences imposed by the District Justice were quashed by certiorari, and the prosecutrix succeeded in obtaining an order of prohibition to prevent the Justice from entering the correct sentences on the charge sheets. The Supreme Court held in that case

1. *The State (Turley) v. Ó Floinn* [1968] I.R. 245; *Prendergast v. Porter* [1961] I.R. 440 (H.C.).
2. [1977] I.R. 42.
3. See, e.g., *The State (Bollard) v. The Special Criminal Court*, unrep. 20th September, 1973, where an order of prohibition was unsuccessfully sought to prevent the Special Criminal Court from trying Bollard; see, p. 383, supra; also *The State (Harkin) v. O'Malley* [1978] I.R. 269 (S.C.) where an order of prohibition was refused to prevent the Circuit Court from proceeding with a further trial of the prosecutor on a summary offence only, after the jury had found him not guilty of an indictable offence but had disagreed on the summary offence which had been included in the indictment.
4. [1976] I.R. 85.

that where a sentence was quashed on certiorari the order had the effect of quashing the conviction also. The grounds justifying an order of prohibition are similar to some of those justifying an order of certiorari which are discussed below.

IV. CERTIORARI

The old writ of certiorari originally took the form of a royal demand for information. The orderly administration of justice and the policy of ensuring that inferior courts acted only within those powers accorded to them by statute was deemed to be the concern of the Crown and hence, until 1922, applications for prerogative writs were taken in the name of the Crown at the prosecution of individuals, e.g. *R. (McSwiggan) v. Londonderry JJ.*[5] Today the State continues to be a nominal prosecutor and, as such, is seen to collaborate with the citizen to ensure that justice is carried out according to law. Consequently State Side orders bear such titles as *The State (Cunningham) v. District Justice Ó Floinn.*[6] It has been suggested that this practice is no longer appropriate[7] and that, in future, actions ought to bear only the names of the parties involved.[8]

For largely historical reasons the order of certiorari will issue only in limited instances. The applicant must show either that there is an error of law on the face of the record of the inferior court, or that there was no jurisdiction in that court to take a decision, or that the procedure leading to the decision has been vitiated by a failure to observe natural justice or constitutional requirements, or that the order was obtained by fraud. The High Court will not review any decision on matters of fact by way of certiorari.

Error of law on the face of the record

The relevance of this ground in criminal proceedings is extremely limited. In the early nineteenth century justices made

5. [1905] 2 I.R. 318; on writs of certiorari generally, see de Smith, *Judicial Review of Administrative Action* 381-428.
6. [1960] I.R. 198.
7. See *Byrne v. Ireland* [1972] I.R. 241, 274-5.
8. See Law Reform Commission Working Paper No. 8 – 1979: *Judicial Review of Administrative Action: The Problem of Remedies* 74-76.

'speaking orders' which set out, as part of the record, the judgment of the court and the evidence leading to it. The replacement of speaking orders by a more cryptic form of conviction meant that, in the words of Lord Sumner, '[t]he face of the record "spoke" no longer: it was the inscrutable face of a sphinx.'[9]

Although the truncation of the record might appear to render the possibility of injustice more likely, judges took the view that the possibility of stating a case would obviate any suggestion of grievance that might arise from evidence not being embodied in a conviction.[10]

The 'uncontrollable verity of the record' was held by the courts to be conclusive in the absence of a manifest error upon its face. In *R. (Martin) v. Mahony* the record was held to consist of the statement of the charge, of the adjudication of guilt and of the imposition of a penalty warranted by law.[11] Recent English decisions appear to take a wider view of the concept of the record and it has been held to include both documents forming the basis of a judicial decision[12] and also an oral announcement from the bench of the reasons for a particular decision.[13] In Ireland the allegation that there exists an error on the face of the record is not usual in an application for certiorari.[14]

Want or excess of jurisdiction to take a decision

The demise of error of law on the face of the record as a ground for certiorari has been rendered less contentious by the growth in the concept of lack of jurisdiction. In *R. (Martin) v. Mahony* Lord O'Brien C.J. sought to make a clear distinction between *lack* of jurisdiction and an error in the *exercise* of jurisdiction. He rejected the contention that a mere want of evidence to justify a conviction would create a cesser of jurisdiction.[15] Clearly a lack of jurisdiction is involved if a court is improperly constituted,[16] or

9. *R. v. National Bell Liquors Ltd.* [1922] 2 A.C. 128, 159.
10. See, e.g., *R. (Martin) v. Mahony* [1910] 2 I.R. 695, 717 (K.B.D.) *per* O'Brien L.C.J.
11. Id. at 718.
12. *R. v. Patents Appeal Tribunal* [1962] 2 Q.B. 647.
13. *R. v. Chertsey JJ.* [1961] 2 Q.B. 152.
14. Law Reform Commission Working Paper No. 8, op. cit. 11.
15. [1910] 2 I.R. 695, 707.
16. *The State (Walsh) v. Murphy,* unrep. December, 1981.

has no statutory authority to hear a particular kind of case,[17] or to make a particular kind of order.[18]

In *R. (Harrington) v. Clare JJ.*[19] the Court granted an order of certiorari where the Justices refused to adjourn a criminal case at the instance of the defendant who claimed that he had been given insufficient time in which to prepare a defence.

The basic problem facing the applicant who is alleging that an inferior court has erred in law is to show that the error of law can be said to amount to a lack or cesser of jurisdiction. Recent English decisions in this area exemplify a new approach to this intractable problem. In one of the widest judicial interpretations of lack of jurisdiction, Lord Denning M.R. said in *Pearlman v. Harrow School:*[20]

> 'The way to get things right is to hold thus: no court or tribunal has any jurisdiction to make an error of law on which the decision of the case depends. If it makes such an error, it goes outside its jurisdiction and certiorari will lie to correct it.'

No Irish court has yet gone so far in its interpretation of lack of jurisdiction, and in *Walsh v. Minister for Local Government*[21] the Supreme Court accepted that an erroneous determination of a matter of law could be attacked only if it was apparent on the face of the record. In that case it appears to have been assumed that the error of law alleged did not affect jurisdiction.

While it seems probable that the concept of jurisdictional error will become increasingly wide in future, nevertheless in *The State (Stanbridge) v. Mahon*[22] Gannon J. showed a continued awareness of the distinction between those errors giving rise to excess of jurisdiction and other, non-jurisdictional errors.

17. *The State (Nevin) v. Tormey* [1976] I.R. 1 (H.C.).
18. *The State (Holland) v. Kennedy* [1977] I.R. 193 (S.C.); *R. (McCann) v. Belfast JJ.* [1978] N.I. 153 (Q.B.D.).
19. [1918] 2 I.R. 116 (K.B.D.); see also *R. (Roche) v. Clare JJ.* 46 I.L.T.R. 80 (K.B.D.).
20. [1979] 1 Q.B. 56, 70; see also *Anisminic Ltd. v. Foreign Compensation Commission* [1969] 2 A.C. 147.
21. [1929] I.R. 377.
22. [1979] I.R. 214 (H.C.).

Failure to observe natural justice or constitutional requirements

Any failure on the part of an inferior court to observe the basic precepts of natural justice, namely that no man should be a judge in his own cause and that each party has a right to be heard,[23] will provide an aggrieved party with an opportunity to seek an order of certiorari and/or prohibition.

The maxim *nemo judex in sua causa* means that, if any judge participates in a cause or matter in which he has an interest either of a pecuniary or a non-pecuniary nature, then any decision at which he purports to arrive may be the subject of review by way of certiorari.[24] In addition, an order of prohibition will lie to prevent any hearing in which a judge has an interest or bias from proceeding.[25] As well as those rules of natural justice derived from the common law, the decision in *Garvey v. Ireland* has made it clear that:[26]

> '[T]he Constitution incorporates into our laws and their administration the requirements of natural justice, and by Article 40.3 there is guaranteed to every citizen whose rights may be affected by decisions taken by others the right to fair and just procedures. This means that under the Constitution powers cannot be exercised unjustly or unfairly.'

Certiorari will issue if a procedural defect results in the trial having been conducted other than in due course of law.[27] It seems likely that, in future, constitutional provisions will be increasingly invoked by applicants for certiorari and prohibition.

Fraud

If an inferior court purports to make any order which has been obtained by fraud or collusion, such an order may be quashed by certiorari. The fraud must be clear and manifest.[28] If the court has been materially misled by fraudulent evidence an order of certiorari may lie to quash the order. In *R. (Burns) v. Tyrone County*

23. See *The State (Gleeson) v. The Minister for Defence* [1976] I.R. 280 (S.C.); *The State (Shannon Atlantic Fisheries) v. McPolin* [1976] I.R. 93 (H.C.).
24. *R. (Giant's Causeway Tramway Co.) v. Antrim JJ.* [1895] 2 I.R. 603 (Q.B.D.).
25. *R. (Courtney) v. Emerson* [1913] 2 I.R. 377 (K.B.D.).
26. [1981] I.R. 75, 97 (S.C.) *per* O'Higgins C.J.; see also *The State (Healy) v. Donoghue* [1976] I.R. 325 (S.C.).
27. *The State (Kenny) v. Ó hUadhaigh* [1979] I.R. 1 (H.C.).
28. See de Smith, op. cit. at 408-409; *R. v. Gillyard* (1848) 12 Q.B. 527.

Court Judge[29] an affiliation order had been procured by perjured testimony. Before the application for certiorari one witness had pleaded guilty to perjury and the woman seeking the affiliation order was herself charged with subornation of perjury but was acquitted. The Court rejected the argument that it was necessary for an applicant for certiorari to show that the perjury was instigated or connived at by the party who obtained the challenged decision and, in so doing, distinguished the case of *R. v. Ashford Justices.*[30]

In *Burns'* case the Court did not consider, as definitive, dicta in *R. v. Ashford Justices* to the effect that:[31]

> '[A]n order of certiorari to quash proceedings on the ground that they were procured by fraud or perjury should seldom if ever be made unless the facts regarding the alleged fraud or perjury have either been the subject of a conviction in regular criminal proceedings against the person to whom the fraud or perjury is imputed, or else have been admitted by something amounting to a confession by such person.'

Although in criminal matters the order of certiorari is invariably sought with a view to quashing a conviction or sentence, it may also prove useful in respect of preliminary matters such as the quashing of arrest warrants,[32] search warrants[33] or witness summonses.[34] Certiorari has been held not to lie against a decision of a Justice returning a defendant for trial,[35] although more recent English authorities suggest otherwise.[36]

V. PROCEDURE WHEN SEEKING MANDAMUS, PROHIBITION OR CERTIORARI

The procedure to be followed when seeking a State Side order is set forth in Order 84 of the Rules of the Superior Courts[1]. This

29. [1961] N.I. 167.
30. [1956] 1 Q.B. 167.
31. Id. at 177 *per* Jenkins L.J.
32. *R. v. Thompson* [1909] 2 K.B. 614.
33. *The State (Batchelor) v. Ó Floinn* [1958] I.R. 155.
34. *R. v. Cheltenham JJ.* [1977] 1 W.L.R. 95.
35. *R. (Blakeney) v. Roscommon JJ.* [1894] 2 I.R. 158; *R. (Hastings) v. Galway JJ.* 43 I.L.T.R. 185.
36. *R. v. Coleshill JJ. ex parte Davies* [1971] 1 W.L.R. 1684; *R. v. Rugby JJ. ex parte Prince* [1974] 1 W.L.R. 736.
1. See Appendix F, infra.

procedure has already been outlined in relation to habeas corpus and it is basically similiar for certiorari, prohibition and mandamus. Nevertheless it must be stated that each State Side order retains its own distinctive procedural requirements and these must be meticulously complied with. In the case of mandamus, for instance, unlike habeas corpus, certiorari and prohibition, the motion for the conditional order is not made *ex parte*, i.e. without notice to the other side. Furthermore, in an application for prohibition the procedure is the same as for certiorari, except that a plenary hearing may be directed at any stage of the proceedings for prohibition, while no such power exists in the case of an application for certiorari.[2] However, despite the fact that there are no provisions for a plenary hearing with pleadings, discovery, etc., in certiorari applications, the court nevertheless has the power to compel the attendance of deponents for the purpose of cross-examination. It has been suggested that the approach of the Irish courts in this regard may be less restrictive than that of their English counterparts.[3] In *R. v. Stokesley, Yorkshire JJ., ex parte Bartram* Lord Goddard C.J., while reluctantly permitting cross-examination in an application for certiorari, added:[4]

> 'I desire to say that it is the first time in my experience, and I think the first time in anyone else's experience, in Crown proceedings for prerogative writs, that cross-examination has ever taken place. I do not want this to be thought to as an easy precedent. We allowed cross-examination in this case because it is a case of a very remarkable character.'

However, in *The State (Stanbridge) v. Mahon*[5] Gannon J. merely mentioned *en passant* the fact that he had heard oral evidence from two prosecutors who had been required to attend court by the respondent for the purpose of being cross-examined. The High Court is empowered to order the attendance for the purpose of cross-examination of any person who makes an affidavit.[6] Orders for discovery are also available in Ireland on

2. See O. 84, r. 51; also Law Reform Commission Working Paper No. 8, op. cit. 43-44.
3. Law Reform Commission, op. cit. 18-19.
4. [1956] 1 W.L.R. 254, 258.
5. [1979] I.R. 214.
6. Rules of the Superior Courts, O. 40, r. 1.

certiorari applications, and in this respect, Irish law differs from English law.[7]

VI. THE DISCRETIONARY NATURE OF ORDERS OF CERTIORARI, PROHIBITION AND MANDAMUS

Unlike an order of habeas corpus, which issues as of right, the orders of certiorari, prohibition and mandamus are discretionary remedies, although the exercise of the court's discretion is not a matter of caprice but follows well settled precedents. While certain dicta suggest that a stranger may have sufficient *locus standi* to apply for an order of certiorari or prohibition,[1] it seems unlikely that in the absence of exceptional circumstances a court would exercise its discretion in favour of anyone other than a person prejudicially affected by the order made,[2] to whom an order will issue *ex debito justitiae*.

The English court in *R. v. Greater London Council, ex. parte Blackburn*[3] appears to have accepted that Mr Blackburn had sufficient *locus standi* to support a writ of prohibition to restrain the defendant's exercise of its censorship functions, by virtue of his being a ratepayer and a parent whose children might be harmed by pornographic films. The trend in England appears to be moving away from a strict judicial stance on *locus standi*.[4]

Undoubtedly the conduct of the applicant is germane to the exercise of judicial discretion. An applicant who delays in seeking an order may fail to secure the exercise of the court's discretion. In any event, an applicant for an order of certiorari against an order of either the District Court or the Circuit Court must apply within six months;[5] an application from a decision of the Special Criminal Court is at the discretion of the High Court. No time limits are prescribed to govern applications for prohibition although these, of necessity, are dictated by the timing of the hearing against which the prohibition is to be directed. The ques-

7. Id. O. 31.
1. See, e.g., *The State (Doyle) v. Carr* [1970] I.R. 87, 93 *per* Henchy J.; also Law Reform Commission Working Paper, op. cit. 22.
2. See de Smith, op. cit. at 418.
3. [1976] 3 All E.R. 184.
4. See, e.g., *R. v. Lewes JJ. ex parte Home Secretary* [1973] A.C. 388.
5. Rules of the Superior Courts, O. 84, r. 10.

tion of whether the State is bound by the time limits set out in the Rules of the Superior Courts is unclear.[6]

In addition to the matter of delay, the prosecutor may disentitle himself to relief by reason of his own acquiescence. Acquiescence may exist where a defendant fails to take objection to the qualifications of a judge or justice to hear a case, if he is aware of such a defect[7] or he fails similarly to take objection to the jury.[8]

Although a defendant cannot confer jurisdiction by means of a waiver in a situation where there exists a total lack of such jurisdiction[9] nevertheless such a waiver could conceivably result in a refusal by the court to exercise its discretion in favour of a prosecutor.[10] However, the Supreme Court has made it clear in *The State (Vozza) v. Ó Floinn*[11] that it would require exceptional circumstances for it to exercise its discretion against a prosecutor where a conviction was made without jurisdiction.

If a party to proceedings either expressly or by implication waives his objection to a justice or judge hearing the case, such a waiver will almost certainly operate to disentitle the prosecutor to an order based on an allegation of bias.[12]

Utmost candour at all stages of State Side proceedings is vital for any applicant. Suppression of material facts in any application for a conditional order may suffice to discharge the order.[13]

Even in those instances where a court is satisfied that there may have been a failure in procedure affecting the basic principles of the administration of justice, it may nevertheless refuse to issue an order of certiorari, in the exercise of its discretion, if the matter can be put right on appeal.[14]

6. *Re an Application for Certiorari* [1965] N.I. 67 (Crown not bound by usual time limits).
7. *R. v. Comptroller General of Patents and Designs, ex parte Parke Davis & Co.* [1953] 2 W.L.R. 760.
8. *The State (Byrne) v. Frawley* [1978] I.R. 326.
9. See de Smith, op. cit. 422.
10. 'Whether the tribunal lacked jurisdiction is one question; whether the court, having regard to the applicant's conduct, ought in its discretion to set aside the proceedings is another': de Smith, op. cit. 422.
11. [1957] I.R. 227.
12. See, e.g., *R. (Giant's Causeway Tramway Co.) v. Antrim JJ.* [1895] 2 I.R. 603.
13. *The State (Vozza) v. Ó Floinn* [1957] I.R. 227; *R. (Marshall) v. Tyrone JJ.* 32 L.R. Ir. 201; *R. (Shannon) v. Carlow JJ.* [1902] 2 I.R. 142.
14. *The State (Stanbridge) v. Mahon* [1979] I.R. 214.

APPENDIX A

CRIMINAL JUSTICE (LEGAL AID) ACT, 1962

(No. 12 of 1962)

1.—In this Act, except where the context otherwise requires—
"justice" means justice of the District Court and includes the President of the District Court;
"the Minister" means the Minister for Justice.

2.—(1) If it appears to the District Court—

(a) that the means of a person charged before it with an offence are insufficient to enable him to obtain legal aid, and

(b) that by reason of the gravity of the charge or of exceptional circumstances it is essential in the interests of justice that he should have legal aid in the preparation and conduct of his defence before it,

the Court shall, on application being made to it in that behalf, grant in respect of him a certificate for free legal aid (in this Act referred to as a legal aid (District Court) certificate) and thereupon he shall be entitled to such aid and to have a solicitor and (where he is charged with murder and the Court thinks fit) counsel assigned to him for that purpose in such manner as may be prescribed by regulations under section 10 of this Act.

(2) A decision of the District Court in relation to an application under this section shall be final and shall not be appealable.

3.—(1) Where—

(a) a person is returned for trial for an indictable offence, and

(b) a certificate for free legal aid (in this Act referred to as a legal aid (trial on indictment) certificate) is granted in respect of him by the District Court, upon his being returned for trial, or by the judge of the court before which he is to be or is being tried,

the person shall be entitled to free legal aid in the preparation and conduct of his defence at the trial and to have a solicitor and counsel assigned to him for that purpose in such manner as may be prescribed by regulations under section 10 of this Act.

(2) A legal aid (trial on indictment) certificate shall be granted in respect of a person returned for trial for an indictable offence if (but only if)—

(a) application is made therefor,

(b) it appears to the District Court or the judge of the court before which the person is to be or is being tried that the means of the person are insufficient to enable him to obtain legal aid, and

(c) either

(i) the return for trial is upon a charge of murder, or

(ii) it appears to the District Court or the judge of the court before which the person is to be or is being tried (as the case may be) that, having regard to all the circumstances of the case (including the nature of such defence (if any) as may have been set up), it is essential in the interests of justice that the person should have legal aid in the preparation and conduct of his defence at the trial.

4.—(1) Where—

(a) a person is convicted on an offence, and

(b) a certificate for free legal aid (in this Act referred to as a legal aid (appeal) certificate) is granted in respect of him by the District Court or by the judge of the court before which he was tried or under subsection (3) of this section,

the person shall be entitled to free legal aid in the preparation and conduct of an appeal from the conviction or the penalty (if any) imposed on conviction and to have a solicitor and (where the appeal lies to the Court of Criminal Appeal) counsel assigned to him for that purpose in such manner as may be prescribed by regulations under section 10 of this Act.

(2) A legal aid (appeal) certificate shall be granted in respect of a person convicted of an offence if (but only if)—

(a) application is made therefor,

(b) it appears to the District Court or the judge of the court before which the person was tried that his means are insufficient to enable him to obtain legal aid, and

(c) either

(i) the conviction is for murder, or

(ii) it appears to the District Court or the judge of the court before which the person was tried that, by reason of the serious nature of the offence or of exceptional circumstances, it is essential in the interests of justice that the person should have legal aid in the preparation and conduct of an appeal.

(3) Where a person is, on being convicted of an offence, refused a legal aid (appeal) certificate, he may apply for the certificate to the court to which an appeal from the conviction lies either—

(a) by letter addressed to the registrar of that court setting out the facts of the case and the grounds of the application, or

(b) to the court itself,

and the court shall grant the certificate if (but only if)—

(i) it appears to the court that the means of the person are insufficient to enable him to obtain legal aid, and

(ii) either—

(I) the conviction is of murder, or

(II) it appears to the court that, by reason of the serious nature of the offence or of exceptional circumstances, it is essential in the interests of justice that the convicted person should have legal aid in the preparation and conduct of an appeal.

5.—(1) Where—

(a) a person is charged with an offence before the District Court or the Circuit Court or appeals to the Circuit Court against a conviction of an offence by the District Court and the justice or judge (as the case may be) of the court before which the charge or appeal (as the case may be) is heard refers a question of law arising in the proceedings to the High Court or Supreme Court (as the case may be) by way of case stated or the justice states a case in relation to the proceedings for the opinion of the High Court, and

(b) a certificate for free legal aid (in this Act referred to as a legal aid (case stated) certificate) is granted in respect of the person by the court before which the charge or appeal (as the case may be) is heard or under subsection (3) of this section,

the person shall be entitled to free legal aid in the preparation and conduct of his case in relation to the case stated and to have a solicitor and counsel assigned to him for that purpose in such manner as may be prescribed by regulations under section 10 of this Act.

(2) Where a person is charged with an offence before the District Court or the Circuit Court or appeals to the Circuit Court against a conviction of an offence by the District Court and the justice or judge (as the case may be) of the court before which the charge or appeal (as the case may be) is heard refers a question of law arising in the proceedings to the High Court or Supreme Court (as the case may be) by way of case stated or the justice states a case in relation to the proceedings for the opinion of the High Court, a legal aid (case stated) certificate shall be granted in respect of the person if (but only if)—

(a) application is made therefor,

(b) it appears to the court before which the charge or appeal (as the case may be) is heard that the means of the person are insufficient to enable him to obtain legal aid, and

(c) it appears to the court before which the charge or appeal (as the case may be) is heard that, by reason of the serious nature of the offence with which the person is charged or of exceptional circumstances, it is essential in the interests of justice that a legal aid (case stated) certificate should be granted in respect of the person.

(3) Where, in relation to a case stated, a person is refused a legal aid (case stated) certificate by the District Court or Circuit Court, he may apply for the certificate to the court in which the case stated is to be heard either—

(a) by letter addressed to the registrar of that court setting out the facts of the case and the grounds of the application, or

(b) to the court itself,

and the court shall grant the certificate if (but only if)—

(i) it appears to the court that the means of the person are insufficient to enable him to obtain legal aid, and

(ii) it appears to the court that, by reason of the serious nature of the offence with which the person is charged or of exceptional circumstances, it is essential in the interests of justice that a legal aid (case stated) certificate should be granted in respect of the person.

6.—(1) Where—

(a) a person is charged with an offence,

(b) an appeal is brought to the Supreme Court from a determination of the Court of Criminal Appeal in relation to the offence or the penalty (if any) imposed in respect thereof or from a determination of the High Court on a case stated by a justice in relation to the proceedings in the District Court in regard to the offence or in relation to a question of law arising in those proceedings, and

(c) a certificate for free legal aid (in this Act referred to as a legal aid (Supreme Court) certificate) is granted in respect of the person charged with the offence to which the appeal relates by the Court of Criminal Appeal or the High Court (as the case may be) or under subsection (3) of this section,

the person shall be entitled to free legal aid in the preparation and conduct of his case in relation to the appeal and to have a solicitor and counsel assigned to him for that purpose in such manner as may be prescribed by regulations under section 10 of this Act.

(2) A legal aid (Supreme Court) certificate shall be granted if (but only if)—

(a) application is made therefor,

(b) it appears to the Court of Criminal Appeal or the High Court (as the case may be) that the means of the person charged with the offence are insufficient to enable him to obtain legal aid, and

(c) in the case of an appeal from a determination of the High Court on a case stated by a justice, it appears to the High Court that, by reason of the serious nature of the offence with which the person is charged or of exceptional circumstances, it is essential in the interests of justice that a legal aid (Supreme Court) certificate should be granted in respect of the person.

(3) Where a person is refused a legal aid (Supreme Court) certificate, he may apply for the certificate to the Supreme Court either—

(a) by letter addressed to the registrar of the Supreme Court setting out the facts of the case and the grounds of the application, or

(b) to the Supreme Court itself,

and the Court shall grant the certificate if (but only if)—

(i) it appears to the Court that the means of the person are insufficient to enable him to obtain legal aid, and

(ii) in the case of an appeal from a determination of the High Court on a case stated by a justice, it appears to the Supreme Court that, by reason of the serious nature of the offence with which the person is charged or of exceptional circumstances, it is essential in the interests of justice that a legal aid (Supreme Court) certificate should be granted in respect of the person.

7.—(1) Where a legal aid (District Court) certificate or a legal aid (trial on indictment) certificate has been granted in respect of a person, any fees, costs or other expenses properly incurred in preparing and conducting the defence to which the certificate relates shall, subject to the regulations under section 10 of this Act, be paid out of moneys provided by the Oireachtas.

(2) Where a legal aid (appeal) certificate, a legal aid (case stated) certificate or a legal aid (Supreme Court) certificate has been granted in respect of a person, any fees, costs or other expenses properly incurred in preparing and conducting the person's case in relation to the appeal or case stated (as the case may be) to which the certificate relates shall, subject to the regulations under section 10 of this Act, be paid out of moneys provided by the Oireachtas.

8.—(1) Where a legal aid (trial on indictment) certificate is granted in respect of a person, the Court of Criminal Appeal shall not have jurisdiction under section 34 of the Courts of Justice Act, 1924, or section 5 of the Courts of Justice Act, 1928, to award costs to the person in respect of court proceedings in relation to which the certificate applies.

(2) Where a legal aid (appeal) certificate is granted in respect of a person, the Court of Criminal Appeal shall not have jurisdiction under the said section 34 or the said section 5 to award costs to the person in respect of court proceedings in relation to which the certificate applies.

9.—(1) Before a person is granted a legal aid certificate he may be required by the court or judge, as the case may be, granting the certificate to furnish a written statement in such form as may be prescribed by the Minister by regulations under section 10 of this Act about matters relevant for determining whether his means are insufficient to enable him to obtain legal aid.

(2) In this and in the next following section "legal aid certificate" means a legal aid (District Court) certificate, a legal aid (trial on indictment) certificate, a legal aid (appeal) certificate or a legal aid (Supreme Court) certificate.

10. [Regulation].

11. [Offences].

12. [Operative date].

13. [Expenses incurred by Minister].

14. [Citation].

CRIMINAL JUSTICE (LEGAL AID) REGULATIONS, 1965

(S.I. No. 12 of 1965)

I, BRIAN LENIHAN, Minister for Justice, in exercise of the powers conferred on me by section 10 of the Criminal Justice (Legal Aid) Act, 1962 (No. 12 of 1962), and in so far as these regulations are in relation to rates or scales of payment of fees, costs or expenses payable out of moneys provided by the Oireachtas pursuant to certificates for free legal aid with the consent of the Minister for Finance, hereby make the following regulations:

1. [Citation].

2. [Pending proceedings].

3. In these Regulations—

"the Act" means the Criminal Justice (Legal Aid) Act, 1962 (No. 12 of 1962);

"the Minister" means the Minister for Justice.

4. [Compilation of lists of solicitors willing to act].

5. [Compilation of lists of counsel willing to act].

6.—(1) The registrar of the Supreme Court, the registrar of the Court of Criminal Appeal, the registrar of the High Court managing the Central Office of the High Court, the registrar of the Central Criminal Court, each county registrar and each District Court clerk shall keep a register of all cases in which application is made to the court of which he is an officer for a certificate for free legal aid and shall record therein in respect of each case—

(a) the date of the application;

(b) the name of the applicant;

(c) in general terms, the charge or charges involved and the nature of the proceedings;

(d) the result of the application, and

(e) if the application is granted, the names of the solicitor and of the counsel (if any) assigned.

(2) Each officer specified in paragraph (1) of this Regulation shall send to the Department of Justice, at such times as the Minister may from time to time direct, a copy of the entries in the register kept by him pursuant to the provisions of that paragraph.

7.—(1) Upon the grant of a certificate for free legal aid, the court granting the certificate shall, having taken into consideration the representations (if any) of the person to whom the certificate was granted, assign to him a solicitor from the appropriate list kept pursuant to Regulation 4 of these Regulations to act for him in the preparation and conduct of his case.

(2) The court granting a certificate (other than a legal aid (District Court) certificate) for free legal aid may, if the person to whom it is granted is charged with murder or the case concerning him appears to present exceptional difficulty and is not an appeal to the Circuit Court and the court is of opinion that the defence or appeal, as the case may be, cannot be conducted adequately without the assistance of two counsel, direct that two counsel be assigned to the person to act for him in the preparation and conduct of his case.

(3) Where a certificate for free legal aid is granted to a person and the certificate entitles the person to have counsel assigned to him—

(a) in case the certificate includes a direction under paragraph (2) of this Regulation, any two counsel whose names are included in the list kept by the Minister pursuant to Regulation 5 of these Regulations, and

(b) in any other case, any one counsel whose name is included in such list,

may be retained on behalf of the person by the solicitor who has been assigned pursuant to the certificate to act for the person in the preparation and conduct of his case and, upon such retention, the counsel shall be deemed to have been assigned to the person pursuant to the certificate to act for the person in the preparation and conduct of his case.

(4) Where two or more certificates for free legal aid are granted to a person and the cases in relation to which they are granted are heard together or in immediate succession, one certificate only shall (unless the Court, being satisfied that there is good reason for so doing, otherwise directs) be deemed, for the purposes of these Regulations, to have been granted to the person.

8.—(1) Where a certificate for free legal aid is granted by any court in respect of free legal aid in another court, a copy of the certificate shall be sent by the court officer concerned to the registrar of the other court.

(2) Where an application by a person under subsection (2) of section 4, 5 or 6 of the Act for a certificate for free legal aid is refused, the registrar of the court to which the person may then apply for a certificate shall be notified of such refusal by the court officer concerned.

9. [Forms].

10. [Fees to the solicitor and counsel].

11. (1) (a) Allowances to witnesses summoned and attending on behalf of the defence at the hearing of a case in relation to which a certificate for free legal aid has been granted shall be payable under the Act on a scale corresponding to the scale for the time being at which allowances to similar witnesses summoned and attending on behalf of the prosecution at the hearing or at similar hearings are paid.

(b) The fees and expenses of witnesses who are qualified medical practitioners summoned and attending on behalf of the defence to give professional evidence at the hearing of a case in relation to which a certificate for free legal aid has been granted shall be payable under the Act on a scale corresponding to the scale for the time being at which fees and expenses of such witnesses summoned and attending on behalf of the prosecution to give professional evidence at the hearing or at similar hearings are paid.

(c) The fees and expenses of witnesses (other than those referred to in paragraph (b) of this Regulation) holding a professional qualification summoned and attending on behalf of the defence to give professional evidence at the hearing of a case in relation to which a certificate for free legal aid has been granted shall be payable under the Act at a rate corresponding to the rate for the time being at which fees and expenses to such witnesses summoned and attending on behalf of the prosecution to give professional evidence at the hearing or at similar hearings are paid.

(d) The expenses of obtaining medical and technical reports necessarily required for use by the defence in a case in relation to which a certificate for free legal aid has been granted shall be payable under the Act at a rate corresponding to the rate for the time being at which the expenses of obtaining such reports for use by the prosecution in the case or in similar cases are paid.

(2) Subject to paragraphs (4) and (5) of this Regulation, the travelling expenses actually and necessarily incurred by a solicitor in attending sittings of the Circuit or District Court on any day in any place (other than the county or county borough of Dublin) in connection with a case in relation to which he has been assigned pursuant to a certificate for free legal aid shall be payable under the Act as follows:

(a) in case the solicitor makes the whole journey in his own motor-car, a sum calculated at the rate of 10d. per mile of the journey shall be paid, and

(b) in any other case, a sum equal to the lesser of the following shall be paid, namely:

(i) the actual cost of the journey,

(ii) the cost of the journey by public transport and (to the extent (if any) that public transport is not available) hired car, or if no public transport is available for the journey, hired car.

(3) Subject to paragraphs (4) and (5) of this Regulation, the travelling and subsistence expenses actually and necessarily incurred by a solicitor practising elsewhere than in the county or county borough of Dublin in attending sittings of a court (other than the Circuit or District Court) in connection with a case in relation to which he has been assigned pursuant to a certificate for free legal aid and travelling and subsistence expenses actually and necessarily incurred by a solicitor in travelling to and from any place visited for the purposes of the case shall be payable under the Act as follows:

(a) in the case of travelling expenses—

(i) in case the solicitor makes the whole journey in his own motor-car, a sum calculated at the rate of 10d. per mile of the journey shall be paid, and

(ii) in any other case, a sum equal to the lesser of the following shall be paid—

(I) the actual cost of the journey,

(II) the cost of the journey by public transport and (to the extent (if any) that public transport is not available) hired car, or if no public transport is available for the journey, hired car.

and

(b) in the case of subsistence allowances, on a scale corresponding to the scale for the time being at which the subsistence expenses of civil servants of the highest grade are paid.

(4) No travelling or subsistence expenses shall be paid under the Act to a solicitor assigned in relation to any particular case in pursuance of a certificate for free legal aid in respect of any day on which the hearing of the case consists only of one or more of the following, that is to say, the delivery of a reserved judgment, consideration of the penalty (if any) to be imposed on conviction of an offence and the imposition or non-imposition of a penalty, an application for an adjournment or remand or in relation to bail.

(5) Where a solicitor is engaged on court business other than business in connection with a case in relation to which he has been assigned pursuant to a certificate for free legal aid in any place on any day, no travelling or subsistence expenses shall be payable under the Act to the solicitor in connection with the hearing on that day in that place of a case in relation to which he has been assigned in pursuance of a certificate for free legal aid.

12.—(1) Notwithstanding anything contained in these Regulations, where a certificate for free legal aid has been granted to a person and a payment has been made or agreed to be made by or on behalf of the person towards the costs or expenses of the case in relation to which the certificate was granted, a payment shall not be made under the Act in respect of those costs or expenses.

(2) If the Minister so thinks fit, he may refuse to make a payment under the Act in relation to a case in respect of which a certificate for free legal aid has been granted unless the person in respect of whom the payment falls to be made, furnishes to the Minister a document stating that he has not made or agreed to make and will not make or agree to make a payment towards the costs or expenses of the case in relation to which the certificate was granted and is not aware of a payment or intention to make a payment by any other person (other than under the Act) towards such costs or expenses.

FIRST SCHEDULE

[Forms of certificate]

SECOND SCHEDULE

STATEMENT OF MEANS OF AN APPLICANT FOR FREE LEGAL AID IN A CRIMINAL CASE

As an applicant for free legal aid, you are hereby required in pursuance of section 9 of the Criminal Justice (Legal Aid) Act, 1962, to furnish on this form particulars relevant for determining whether your means are insufficient to enable you to obtain legal aid.

You must enter true and correct particulars against each numbered heading. If the answer is "None" or "No," this must be written in.

The declaration at the end must be signed and the form returned to:
....

1. Name of applicant (in block letters) ....
2. Full postal address ....
....
3. State whether single man/woman, married man/woman, widow or widower
....
4. Occupation ....
5. Average weekly income from all sources, including overtime £ : :
6. If you pay rent, please state the weekly amount £ : :
7. If you own your own house, please state amount of
    (a) ground rent (annual)
    (b) rates, and
    (c) monthly mortgage repayments (if any)
8. What persons do you support? If any are children at school state their ages ....
....
9. What money have you, or is likely to be available to you that could be used for obtaining legal aid at your own expense? ....
....
10. What other assets have you that could be used for obtaining legal aid at your own expense? ....
....
11. If you are under twenty-one, are your parents or guardian able and willing to provide legal aid for you or to assist you in providing yourself with legal aid? ....

DECLARATION*

I declare that to the best of my knowledge and belief the above particulars are true.

Date .... Signature ....

*WARNING.—If any person in furnishing this statement of means knowingly makes any false statement or false representation he is liable, on summary conviction, to a fine not exceeding one hundred pounds or to imprisonment for a term not exceeding six months or to both the fine and the imprisonment.

APPENDIX B

FORMS OF INDICTMENT

(Criminal Justice (Administration) Act, 1924)
(Appendix to Rules)

No. 1.

Statement of Offence

Murder

Particulars of Offence

A.B., on the day of in the County of , murdered J.S.

No. 2.

Statement of Offence

Accessory after the fact to murder

Particulars of Offence

A.B., well knowing that one H.C. did on the day of in the County of murder, C.C., did on the day of in the County of and on other days thereafter receive, comfort, harbour, assist and maintain the said H.C..

No. 3.

Statement of Offence

Manslaughter

Particulars of Offence

A.B., on the day of in the County of , unlawfully killed J.S.

No. 4.

Statement of Offence

Rape

Particulars of Offence

A.B., on the day of in the County of , had carnal knowledge of E.F. without her consent.

No. 5.

First Count

Statement of Offence

Wounding with intent, contrary to section 18 of the Offences against the Person Act, 1861.

Particulars of Offence

A.B., on the day of in the County of , wounded C.D., with intent to do him grievous bodily harm, or to maim, disfigure, or disable him, or to resist the lawful apprehension of him the said A.B.

Second Count

Statement of Offence

Wounding, contrary to section 20 of the Offences against the Person Act, 1861.

Particulars of Offence

A.B., on the day of in the County of , maliciously wounded C.D.

No. 6. *Statement of Offence*

Cruelty to a child, contrary to section 12 of the Children Act, 1908

Particulars of Offence

A.B., between the day of and the day of in the County of , being a person over the age of sixteen years having the custody, charge, or care of C.D., a child, ill-treated or neglected the said child, or caused or procured the said child to be ill-treated or neglected in a manner likely to cause the said child unnecessary suffering or injury to its health.

No. 7. *Statement of Offence*

Larceny, contrary to section 17 (1) (a) of the Larceny Act, 1916.

Particulars of Offence

A.B., on the day of in the County of , being clerk or servant to M.N., stole from the said M.N. ten yards of cloth.

No. 8. [Obsolete].

No. 9. First Count

Statement of Offence

Larceny after a previous conviction.

Particulars of Offence

A.B., on the day of in the County of , stole a bag, the property of C.D. A.B. has been previously convicted of burglary on the day of at the Court sitting at Galway.

Second Count

Statement of Offence

Receiving stolen goods, contrary to section 33 (1) of the Larceny Act, 1916.

Particulars of Offence

A.B., on the day of in the County of , did receive a bag, the property of C.D., knowing the same to have been stolen.

No. 10. [Obsolete].

No. 11. *Statement of Offence*

Threatening to publish a libel, contrary to section 31 of the Larceny Act, 1916.

Particulars of Offence

A.B., on the day of in the County of , sent, delivered or uttered to or caused to be received by C.D., a letter accusing or threatening to accuse the said C.D. of an infamous crime with intent to extort money from the said C.D.

No. 12. *Statement of Offence*

Obtaining goods by false pretences, contrary to section 32 (1) of the Larceny Act, 1916.

Particulars of Offence

A.B., on the day of in the County of , with intent to defraud, obtained from S.P. five yards of cloth by falsely pretending that he, the said A.B., was a servant to J.S., and that he, the said A.B., had been sent by the said J.S. to S.P. for the said cloth, and that he, the said A.B., was then authorised by the said J.S. to receive the said cloth on behalf of the said J.S.

No. 13. *Statement of Offence*

Conspiracy to defraud.

Particulars of Offence

A.B. and C.D., on the day of and on divers days between that day and the day of in the County of , conspired together with intent to defraud by means of an advertisement inserted by them, the said A.B. and C.D., in the H.S. newspaper, falsely representing that A.B. and C.D. were then carrying on a genuine business as jewellers at , in the County of , and that they were then able to supply certain articles of jewellery to whomsoever would remit to them the sum of two pounds.

No. 14. First Count

Statement of Offence

Arson, contrary to section 2 of the Malicious Damage Act, 1861.

Particulars of Offence

A.B., on the day of in the County of , maliciously set fire to a dwelling house, one F.G. being therein.

Second Count

Statement of Offence

Arson, contrary to section 3 of the Malicious Damage Act, 1861.

Particulars of Offence

A.B., on the day of in the County of , maliciously set fire to a house with intent to injure or defraud.

No. 15. *Statement of Offences*

A.B., arson, contrary to section 3 of the Malicious Damage Act, 1861; C.D., accessory before the fact to the same offence.

Particulars of Offences

A.B., on the day of in the County of , set fire to a house with intent to injure or defraud.

C.D., on the same day, in the County of , did counsel procure, and command the said A.B. to commit the said offence.

No. 16. First Count

Statement of Offence

Offence under section 35 of the Malicious Damage Act, 1861.

Particulars of Offence

A.B., on the day of in the County of , displaced a sleeper belonging to the Great Southern and Western Railway with intent to obstruct, upset, overthrow, injure, or destroy any engine, tender, carriage or truck using the said railway.

Second Count

Statement of Offence

Obstructing railway, contrary to section 36 of the Malicious Damage Act, 1861.

Particulars of Offence

A.B., on the day of in the County of , by unlawfully displacing a sleeper belonging to the Great Southern and Western Railway did obstruct or cause to be obstructed an engine or carriage using the said railway.

No. 17. *Statement of Offence*

Damaging trees, contrary to section 22 of the Malicious Damage Act, 1861.

Particulars of Offence

A.B., on the day of in the County of , maliciously damaged an oak tree there growing.

A.B. has been twice previously convicted of an offence under section 22 of the Malicious Damage Act, 1861, namely at , on the day of , and at , on the day of .

No. 18. First Count

Statement of Offence

Forgery, contrary to section 2 (1) (a) of the Forgery Act, 1913.

Particulars of Offence

A.B., on the day of in the County of , with intent to defraud, forged a certain will purporting to be the will of C.D.

Second Count

Statement of Offence

Uttering forged document, contrary to section 6 of the Forgery Act, 1913.

Particulars of Offence

A.B., on the day of in the County of , uttered a certain forged will purporting to be the will of C.D., knowing the same to be forged and with intent to defraud.

No. 19. *Statement of Offence*

Uttering counterfeit coin, contrary to section 9 of the Coinage Offences Act, 1861.

Particulars of Offence

A.B., on the day of at the shop kept by C.D. in the County of , uttered a counterfeit half-crown, knowing the same to be counterfeit.

No. 20. *Statement of Offence*

Uttering counterfeit coin, contrary to section 12 of the Coinage Offences Act, 1861.

Particulars of Offence

A.B., on the day of at the shop kept by C.D. in the County of
, uttered a counterfeit sovereign, knowing the same to be counterfeit.

A.B. has been previously convicted of a misdemeanour under section 9 of the Coinage Offences Act, 1861, on the day of at

No. 21. *Statement of Offence*

Libel

Particulars of Offence

A.B., on the day of in the County of , published a defamatory libel concerning E.F., in the form of a letter (book, pamphlet, picture, or as the case may be.)

(Innuendo should be stated where necessary.)

No. 22. First Count

Statement of Offence

Publishing obscene libel.

Particulars of Offence

E.M., on the day of in the County of , sold, uttered and published and caused or procured to be sold, uttered, and published an obscene libel the particulars of which are deposited with this indictment.

(Particulars to specify pages and lines complained of where necessary, as in a book.)

Second Count

Statement of Offence

Procuring obscene libel (or thing) with intent to sell or publish.

Particulars of Offence

E.M., on the day of in the County of , procured an obscene libel (or thing), the particulars of which are deposited with this indictment, with intent to sell, utter or publish such obscene libel (or thing).

No. 23. First Count

Statement of Offence

Falsification of accounts, contrary to section 1 of the Falsification of Accounts Act, 1875.

Particulars of Offence

A.B., on the day of in the County of , being clerk or servant to C.D., with intent to defraud, made or concurred in making a false entry in a cash-book belonging to the said C.D., his employer, purporting to show that on the said day £100 had been paid to L.M.

Second Count

Statement of Offence

Same as first count.

Particulars of Offence

A.B., on the day of in the County of , being clerk or servant to C.D., with intent to defraud, omitted or concurred in omitting from or in a cash-book belonging to the said C.D., his employer, a material particular, that is to say, the receipt on the said day of £50 from H.S.

No. 24.

First Count

Statement of Offence

Fraudulent conversion of property, contrary to section 20 (1) (iv) (a) of Larceny Act, 1916.

Particulars of Offence

A.B., on the day of in the County of , fraudulently converted to his own use and benefit certain property, that is to say £100, entrusted to him by H.S., in order that he, the said A.B., might retain the same in safe custody.

Second Count

Statement of Offence

Fraudulent conversion of property, contrary to section 20 (1) (iv) (b) of Larceny Act, 1916.

Particulars of Offence

A.B., on the day of in the County of , fraudulently converted to his own use and benefit certain property, that is to say, the sum of £200, received by him for and on account of L.M.

APPENDIX C

JURIES ACT, 1976

FIRST SCHEDULE

PART I

Persons Ineligible

Uachtarán na hÉireann.

Persons concerned with administration of justice

Persons holding or who have at any time held any judicial office within the meaning of the Courts (Establishment and Constitution) Act, 1961 (No. 38).

Coroners, deputy coroners and persons appointed under section 5 (2) of the Local Authorities (Officers and Employees) Act, 1926 (No. 39) to fill the office of coroner temporarily.

The Attorney General and members of his staff.

The Director of Public Prosecutions and members of his staff.

Barristers and solicitors actually practising as such.

Solicitors' apprentices, solicitors' clerks and other persons employed on work of a legal character in solicitors' offices.

Officers attached to a court or to the President of the High Court and officers and other persons employed in any office attached to a court or attached to the President of the High Court.

Persons employed from time to time in any court for the purpose of taking a record of the proceedings of the court.

Members of the Garda Síochána.

Prison officers and other persons employed in any prison, Saint Patrick's Institution or any place provided under section 2 of the Prisons Act, 1970 (No. 11) or in any place in which persons are kept in military custody pursuant to section 2 of the Prisons Act, 1972 (No. 7) or in any place specified to be used as a prison under section 3 of the latter Act; chaplains and medical officers of, and members of visiting committees for, any such establishment or place.

Persons employed in the welfare service of the Department of Justice.

A person in charge of, or employed in, a forensic science laboratory.

Members of the Defence Forces

Every member of the Permanent Defence Force, including the Army Nursing Service.

Every member of the Reserve Defence Force during any period during which he is in receipt of pay for any service or duty as a member of the Reserve Defence Force.

Incapable persons

A person who because of insufficient capacity to read, deafness or other permanent infirmity is unfit to serve on a jury.

A person who suffers or has suffered from mental illness or mental disability and on account of that condition either —

(a) is resident in a hospital or other similar institution, or

(b) regularly attends for treatment by a medical practitioner.

PART II

Persons Excusable as of Right

Members of either House of the Oireachtas.

Members of the Council of State.

The Comptroller and Auditor General.

The Clerk of Dáil Éireann.

The Clerk of Seanad Éireann.

A person in Holy Orders.

A regular minister of any religious denomination or community.

Vowed members of any religious order living in a monastery, convent or other religious community.

The following persons if actually practising their profession and registered (including provisionally or temporarily registered), enrolled or certified under the statutory provisions relating to that profession:

Medical practitioners;

Dentists;

Nurses;

Midwives;

Veterinary surgeons;

Pharmaceutical chemists.

A member of the staff of either House of the Oireachtas on a certificate from the Clerk of that House that it would be contrary to the public interest for the member to have to serve as a juror because he performs essential and urgent services of public importance that cannot reasonably be performed by another or postponed.

Heads of Government Departments and Offices and any civil servant on a certificate from the head of his Department or Office that it would be contrary to the public interest for the civil servant to have to serve as a juror because he performs essential and urgent services of public importance that cannot reasonably be performed by another or postponed.

Any civilian employed by the Minister for Defence under section 30 (1) (g) of the Defence Act, 1954 (No. 18) on a certificate from the Secretary of the Department of Defence that it would be contrary to the public interest for the civilian to have to serve as a juror because he performs essential and urgent services of public importance that cannot reasonably be performed by another or postponed.

Chief officers of local authorities for the purposes of the Local Government Act, 1941 (No. 23), health boards established under the Health Act, 1970 (No. 1) and harbour authorities within the meaning of the Harbours Act, 1946 (No. 9) and any employee of a local authority, health board or harbour authority on a certificate from its chief officer that it would be contrary to the public interest for the employee to have to serve as a juror because he performs essential and urgent services of public importance that cannot reasonably be performed by another or postponed.

The head or principal teacher of the college of a university, of a school or other educational institution, and any professor, lecturer or member of the teaching staff of any such institution on a certificate from such head or principal teacher that the person concerned performs services in the institution that cannot reasonably be performed by another or postponed.

Whole-time students at any such educational institution as is mentioned in the preceding paragraph.

The secretary to the Commissioners of Irish Lights and any person in the employment of the Commissioners on a certificate from the secretary that the person concerned performs services for the Commissioners that cannot reasonably be performed by another or postponed.

Masters of vessels, duly licenced pilots and duly licenced aircraft commanders.

Persons aged sixty-five years or upwards and under the age of seventy years.

APPENDIX D

SPECIAL CRIMINAL COURT RULES, 1972

(S. I. No. 147 of 1972)

1. These Rules shall come into operation on the 12th day of June, 1972, and may be cited as the Special Criminal Court Rules, 1972.
2. The Interpretation Act, 1937, shall apply to these Rules.

INTERPRETATION

3. In these Rules

"the Act" means the Offences against the State Act, 1939, (No. 13 of 1939);

"the Court" means the Special Criminal Court established by Instrument made by the Government on the 30th day of May, 1972;

the word "exhibits" includes all books, papers and documents, and all other property, matters and things whatsoever connected with the proceedings against any person if the same have been transmitted to the Court or have been produced and used in evidence during such proceedings or on any application made to the Court in reference to any such proceedings or intended proceedings and any written statement handed into Court by such person but does not include the statement of the evidence that is to be given by each of the witnesses, or the original deposition of any witness examined before the Justice of the District Court or any indictment against any such person;

the word "person" includes a corporation;

the expression "the Registrar" means the Registrar of the Court;

the expression "Offical Stenographer" means the person appointed to attend the trial, and where necessary, to make a report.

SITTINGS OF THE COURT

4. Sittings of the Court shall be held at such places and at such times as may be decided by the Court.
5. The Registrar shall give notice of the place and time of each sitting of the Court to the Chief State Solicitor and to persons to be tried at such sitting. If a person for trial is represented by a solicitor, the Registrar may also give such notice to the solicitor for such person.
6. The members of the Court will take their seats in order of seniority, the senior member present acting as President of the Court.

7. (1) The Court shall be an open Court to which the public generally shall have access so far as the same can conveniently contain them, and subject to such conditions as the Court may from time to time impose.

(2) Where the Court is satisfied, because of the nature or the circumstances of the case or otherwise, in the interests of justice that it is desirable, the Court may exclude the public or any particular person or persons except *bona fide* representatives of the Press from the Court during the hearing.

(3) The Court may permit a witness to give his name in writing to the members of the Court. The Court may further direct that such name, or the evidence or part of the evidence of any witness should not be published.

8. The Court may direct that no witness shall remain in Court while the evidence of another witness is being given and may make provision for the separation of witnesses from each other.

INDICTABLE CASES OTHER THAN CASES BROUGHT UNDER SECTION 47

9. (1) Where a person charged with an indictable offence has been sent forward by a Justice of the District Court for trial to the Central Criminal Court or to the Circuit Court on such charge, and the High Court makes an Order for the transfer of the trial of such person on such charge to the Court, the appropriate County Registrar, within seven days of the making thereof, shall transmit to the Registrar all documents and exhibits in his custody relating to the trial of such person on such charge together with the indictment (if any) which shall have been filed with him relating to such trial.

(2) In any such case the Chief State Solicitor shall file with the Registrar a certified copy of the Order of the High Court within seven days of the making thereof.

10. (1) In the case of an indictable offence the Chief State Solicitor shall file with the Registrar an indictment containing the charges to be preferred against the person charged.

(2) The provisions of the Criminal Justice Administration Act, 1924, and section 18 of the Criminal Procedure Act, 1967, shall, with necessary modifications, apply to every such indictment.

11. (1) Where, in the case of an indictable offence,

(a) a person is sent forward to the Court for trial by a Justice of the District Court, or

(b) the High Court has under the Act transferred the trial of any person to the Court,

such person shall be entitled, on applying therefor to the Registrar, to receive from the Registrar free of charge

(i) a copy of the indictment, and

(ii) copies of the depositions (if any) relating to the offences with which he is charged.

12. In the case of an indictable offence, where a person has been sent forward to the Court for trial the Attorney General shall cause to be served on him a list of any further witnesses whom he proposes to call at the trial, with a statement of the evidence that is to be given by each of them, a list of any further exhibits, a statement of any further evidence that is to be given by any witness whose name apears on the list of witnesses already supplied, and copies of any statement recorded or any deposition taken under section 7 of the Criminal Procedure Act, 1967, and any deposition taken under section 14 of the said Act.

13. Where a person charged with an indictable offence is sent or sent forward by a Justice of the District Court to the Court for trial the Clerk for the Court area where such Order was made shall, within seven days of the making of the Order, transmit to the Registrar such of the following documents as are relevent to the case:—

(a) a statement of the charges upon which the accused was sent or sent forward for trial,

(b) any sworn information in writing upon which the proceedings were initiated,

(c) a list of the witnesses whom it is proposed to call at the trial,

(d) a statement of the evidence that is to be given by each witness,

(e) a list of exhibits (if any),

(f) any deposition or statement taken before any Justice or Peace Commissioner in relation to the charge in respect of which such Order was made,

(g) any exhibit put in evidence and handed in to Court,

(h) the Order of the Justice sending the accused to the Court for trial or sending the accused forward for trial,

(i) the witness order made by the Justice,

(j) any recognisance taken by the Justice in relation to the case.

SUMMARY CASES OTHER THAN SECTION 47 CASES

14. Where a person is brought before a Justice of the District Court charged with an offence which such Justice had jurisdiction to dispose of summarily, and such Justice has sent such person to the Court for trial, the following provisions shall apply —

(a) The Chief State Solicitor, within seven days of the making of such Order by the District Justice, shall furnish to such person a list of the charges to be preferred against him with a summary of the evidence to be given at his trial. Such summary shall not preclude the production of such further evidence as may be adduced by the prosecution at the trial.

(b) The Clerk of the Court Area where such Order was made, within seven days of the making of the Order, shall transmit to the Registrar

(i) a statement of the charges upon which such person was sent for trial,

(ii) the Order of the District Justice sending such person to the Court for trial,

(iii) any recognisance taken by the Justice in the case,

(iv) any exhibit handed in to the District Court,

(v) any sworn information in writing upon which the proceedings were initiated.

CASES UNDER SECTION 47 OF THE ACT

15. (1) Where a person is brought before the Court under section 47 of the Act and charged with an indictable offence, the Chief State Solicitor shall furnish to such person

(a) a list of the charges to be preferred against him,

(b) a list of the witnesses to be called,

(c) a statement of the evidence that is to be given by each of them, and

(d) a list of the exhibits (if any).

(2) Copies of the documents referred to in the preceding sub-paragraph shall also be furnished to the Court.

(3) The accused person shall have the right to inspect all exhibits.

(4) Where on the trial of such a person the Attorney General proposes to call further witnesses, or to adduce further evidence from a witness on the list of witnesses already supplied, he shall furnish such person with

(a) a list of further witnesses with a statement of evidence from each,

(b) a statement of any further evidence from a witness whose name appears on the list of witnesses already supplied.

In either case he shall furnish a list of any further exhibits that are to be produced.

16. (1) Where under section 47 of the Act

(a) the Attorney General directs that a person intended to be charged with a scheduled offence shall be brought before the Court and there charged with the offence, or

(b) the Attorney General certifies that the ordinary Courts, are, in his opinion, inadequate to secure the effective administration of justice and the preservation of public peace and order in relation to the trial of a person whom it is intended to charge with an offence which is not a scheduled offence and the Attorney General then directs that such person whom it is intended to charge with such offence shall be brought before the Court and there charged with such offence;

the Court may on information, or evidence, relating to such offence being given before it, order the issue of a Summons (Form XI or such similar form as the circumstances may require) ordering that such person shall attend before the Court to be tried for such offence at such time and place as the Court shall direct.

(2) The Court may order the issue of a warrant (in such variation of Form V as is applicable) for the arrest of such person and the bringing of him in custody to the Court. Nothing in these Rules shall be construed to prohibit the Court from ordering the issue of a warrant whether or not a Summons has already been issued.

(3) Where under section 47 of the Act, a person has been brought before the Court either in custody or in answer to a Summons, the Court may by Warrant (Form V) commit him to prison or to military custody as the case may be to be there kept until his trial for the offence with which he is charged or admit him to bail in such recognisances and with such sureties as the Court shall direct, conditioned to surrender for his trial by the Court as the Court shall direct, and thereupon the provisions of Rules 17 and 18 shall apply *mutatis mutandis*.

(4) Where a person is brought before the Court under section 47 of the Act by Summons under these Rules, the Chief State Solicitor shall furnish to such person a summary of the evidence to be given at his trial.

ATTENDANCE AT COURT

17. The Governor of the Prison or other place in which a person sent, sent forward or transferred to the Court for trial, is detained, shall on receipt of a body warrant (Form I) produce the said person on the day, at the place and at the hour set out in such warrant.

18. (1) Where a person has been sent, sent forward or transferred to the Court for trial, and is on bail, and has been served with a Notice (Form II) as to the date, time and place of the sitting of the Court for his trial he shall surrender himself accordingly to such persons as the Court shall, from time to time, direct, and thereupon shall be searched by them, and shall be detained in custody or released on bail as the Court shall direct.

(2) Where such person having been duly served with such Notice fails so to surrender himself for his trial as required by this Rule the Court may issue a warrant (Form III) for the apprehension of such person and his detention in prison pending his trial or until further order of the Court, and may estreat his recognisances where the same have been entered into under section 43 (1) (f) or section 48 (v) of the Act.

19. Upon the adjournment by the Court of the trial of any person or the postponement of verdict or sentence the Court may by warrant (Form VI) order the detention of such person in custody pending and until the date of the adjourned hearing of such trial or such postponement.

20. (1) Whenever it shall be made to appear to the Registrar that any person is able to give material evidence either for the prosecution or the defence on any trial the Registrar may issue a summons (Form VII) to such person requiring him to attend at a time and place mentioned in such summons to give evidence on such trial and to produce on such trial such accounts, papers or other documents as shall be in his

possession or powers of procurement and as shall be deemed necessary by the Registrar; but whenever the Court shall be satisfied by evidence on oath that is is probable that such person will not attend to give evidence without being compelled to do so, the Court may issue a warrant (Form VIII) to arrest such person and to bring him to give evidence on such trial and to produce such accounts, papers and documents as may be required.

(2) Where a person to whom such summons has been issued fails to comply with the requirements of such summons, then upon proof of service of the summons or on being satisfied on evidence on oath that such person is evading service thereof the Court may issue the like warrant as is provided for by the preceding subparagraph of this Rule.

MODE OF THE SERVICE OF DOCUMENTS

21. (1) Service of the Notice referred to in Rules 5 and 18 of these Rules may be effected either by serving the same upon the accused person personally, or by sending the same by prepaid ordinary post addressed to the person to be served at his last or usual place of abode, or to his solicitor, and thereupon it shall be deemed to have been served at the time at which it would have been delivered in the ordinary course of post.

(2) In the case of a Summons issued pursuant to Rule 16, or a witness summons issued under Rule 20, either such summons shall be served by a member of the Garda Síochána

(a) by delivering to the person to be served a copy of such summons or by leaving such copy for him at his usual or last place of abode or at his office or place of business with the husband, wife, child, parent, brother, sister, or other relation of such person, or with his agent, clerk, or servant, not being under the age of sixteen years, and such last mentioned service shall be deemed sufficent except where personal service shall be specially required by the Court;

(b) where the person to be charged is a body corporate, by leaving a copy of such summons at, or sending such copy by prepaid ordinary post to, the registered office of the body corporate within the State or any other office or place within the State at which such body corporate trades or carries on business, or by such other form of substituted service as the Court may direct.

22. Proof of service of a summons on a witness may be given by statutory declaration (Form IX) of the person effecting the service, made before a person authorised by law to take and receive statutory declarations. Such declaration shall be endorsed upon the back of the original summons and shall be exempt from stamp duty. Provided always that the Court may require the person who had effected the service of such summons to attend before the Court to give evidence touching such service.

MISCELLANEOUS

23. When a accused person is not defended he shall, at the close of the case for the prosecution be informed by the President of the Court that:—

(a) he may give evidence in his defence on oath and would then be liable to be cross-examined and to be questioned by the Court, or

(b) he may make a statement not on oath and would then not be liable to be cross-examined or to be questioned by the Court, or

(c) he may make no statement.

An accused person shall also be informed that he may address the Court in his defence and may call witnesses in his defence.

24. (1) An official stenographer appointed for the purpose of the Act by the Minister for Justice shall sign the shorthand note taken by him of any trial or proceeding in the Court or of any part of such trial or proceeding and shall certify the same to be a complete and correct shorthand note thereof, and shall lodge the same with the Registrar.

(2) For the purpose of section 44 of the Act the shorthand note of the official stenographer shall consist of the evidence and any objection taken in the course thereof, any statement made by the accused person and the sentence of the Court, but unless otherwise ordered the Court shall not include any part of the speeches of Counsel or solicitor.

25. Every recognisance entered into before the Court shall be in accordance with the Form in the Schedule hereto (Form X) or in such similar form as the circumstances require.

26. (1) The Office of the Registrar shall be at Green Street Courthouse or such other place as shall be fixed by the Court from time to time.

(2) The Registrar shall keep custody of all documents transmitted to or received by him in his capacity as Registrar and all exhibits directed by the Court to be retained by him.

(3) The Registrar shall keep a register containing particulars of all cases for trial by the Court.

27. The Court may abridge or extend the time for doing any act and may adjourn the hearing of any trial or application to the Court or postpone verdict or sentence as it shall think fit.

28. The Court may grant certificates for free legal aid under the Criminal Justice (Legal Aid) Act, 1962, (No. 12 of 1962) and the Regulations made thereunder, as if the Court were the Central Criminal Court, and as if the person sent, sent forward or transferred to the Court for trial, or brought and charged before the Court, has been returned to the Central Criminal Court for trial.

APPENDIX E

RULES OF THE SUPERIOR COURTS – ORDER 86

COURT OF CRIMINAL APPEAL

I. *Preliminary.*

1. In this Order:

"judge of the court of trial" means the judge of any court from the conviction before or the sentence of which, a person desires to appeal;

"proper officer of the court of trial" means the clerk of the court or other person for the time being acting as such in any court from the conviction before or the sentence of which a person desires to appeal;

"official stenographer" means the person appointed to attend the trial and, where necessary, to make a report;

"exhibits" includes all books, papers and documents, and all other property, matters and things whatsoever connected with the proceedings against any person who is entitled or may be authorised to appeal if the same have been forwarded to the court of trial on the person accused being committed for trial, or having been produced and used in evidence during the trial of, or other proceedings in relation to a person entitled or authorised to appeal, and any written statement handed in to the judge of the court of trial by such person, but shall not include the original depositions of witnesses examined before the committing justice nor any indictment against any such person or any plea filed in the court of trial;

"Court" means "Court of Criminal Appeal", and shall, in relation to any interlocutory application, include the Chief Justice or any Judge of the Supreme Court nominated by the Chief Justice to hear and determine such application;

"the Registrar" means the Registrar of the Court of Criminal Appeal.

"appellant" includes an applicant for leave to appeal.

2. The forms set out in Appendix U shall be used in all cases to which such forms are applicable, and the forms of this Order referred to are those set out in such Appendix.

II. *Certificate of the judge of the court of trial.*

3. Every application for a certificate of the judge of the court of trial that the case is a fit case for appeal shall be made at the close of the trial

or within three days thereafter, and the certificate when granted may be in the Form No. 1.

III. *Notice of Appeal.*

4. A person desiring to appeal to the Court shall serve on the Registrar a notice of appeal in the Form No. 2. A person desiring to apply to the Court for leave to appeal shall serve on the Registrar a notice of application for leave to appeal in the Form No. 3. In either case, the notice so served shall answer the questions and comply with the requirements set forth on such forms.

5. Every notice of appeal shall be served within seven days from the date of the grant of the certificate, and every notice of application for leave to appeal shall be served within seven days from the date of the refusal of the certificate.

6. Where the Court has, on a notice of application for leave to appeal duly served, given an appellant leave to appeal, it shall not be necessary for such appellant to give any notice of appeal, but the notice of application for leave to appeal shall in such case be deemed to be a notice of appeal.

7. When the Registrar receives a notice of appeal, or a notice of application for leave to appeal, he shall give notice thereof in the Form No. 4 to the following persons:—

(a) the Chief State Solicitor;

(b) the proper officer of the court of trial;

(c) the Commissioner of the Garda Síochána;

and also, if the appellant is in prison, or has been released on bail —

(d) the Governor of such prison, and

(e) the Secretary of the Department of Justice;

provided that the Registrar shall not be required to give such notice to the Governor of a prison if the appellant's notice of appeal, or notice of application for leave to appeal, shall have been forwarded to the Registrar by such Governor.

IV. *Enlargement of time for appealing.*

8. (1) The Court shall have power to enlarge the time appointed for doing any act or taking any proceeding upon such terms (if any) as the justice of the case may require, and any such enlargement may be ordered although the application for the same is not made until after the expiration of the time appointed.

(2) An application to the Court for an enlargement of time within which notice of appeal or notice of application for leave to appeal may be served shall be in the Form No.5.

(3) The form of application shall, in addition to specifying the

grounds of such application, also specify the grounds on which the applicant proposes to base his appeal or application for leave to appeal.

V. *Appeal where fine only is inflicted.*

9. (1) Where a person has, on his conviction, been sentenced to payment of a fine, and in default of payment to imprisonment, the person lawfully authorised to receive such fine, shall, on receiving the same, retain it until the determination of any appeal in relation thereto.

(2) If such person remains in custody in default of payment of the fine, he shall be deemed to be a person sentenced to imprisonment.

(3) Where any person has been convicted and is thereupon sentenced to the payment of a fine, and in default of such payment, to imprisonment, and he intimates to the judge of the court of trial that he is desirous of appealing against his conviction or sentence to the Court, and applies for a certificate, such judge may, if he gives a certificate, order such person forthwith to enter into recognisances, with or without sureties, to prosecute his appeal, and subject thereto, may order that payment of the said fine shall be made at the final determination of his said appeal, if the same be dismissed, to the Registrar, or as the Court may then order. The recognisances under this rule shall be in the Forms Nos. 6 and 7. A surety becoming duly bound by recognisances under this rule shall be deemed to be, for all purposes and shall have all the powers of a surety under the provisions of rule 20. The proper officer of the Court of trial shall forward the recognisances of the appellant and his surety to the Registrar.

(4) If any convicted person, who has entered upon recognisances in pursuance of sub-rule (3), fails to serve notice of appeal within the time allowed by rule 5 or by any order enlarging time, the Registrar shall certify such failure and shall send his certificate, together with the recognisances forwarded to him in pursuance of sub-rule (3), to the proper officer of the court of trial; and thereupon the judge of the court of trial may notwithstanding the certificate, that the case is a fit case for appeal, make such order for the estreat of the said recognisances, payment of the fine and otherwise as he may think fit.

(5) An appellant who has been sentenced to the payment of a fine, and has paid the same in accordance with such sentence, shall in the event of an appeal by him being successful, be entitled, subject to any order of the Court, to the return of the sum so paid by him.

VI. *Suspension of orders of trial judge pending appeal.*

10. Where the judge of the court of trial is of opinion that the title to any property the subject of an order of restitution made on a conviction of a person before him, or any property to which the provisions of the

Sale of Goods Act, 1893, section 24 (1) apply, is not in dispute, and that such property or a sample or portion or facsimile representation thereof is reasonably necessary to be produced for use at the hearing of any appeal, he shall give such directions to, or impose such terms upon the person in whose favour the order of restitution is made, or in whom such property revests under such sub-section, as he shall think right in order to secure the production of such sample, portion or facsimile representation for use at the hearing of any such appeal.

11. (1) Where, on the conviction of a person, the judge of the court of trial makes an order condemning such person to the payment of the whole or of any part of the costs and expenses of the prosecution for the offence of which he has been convicted out of any moneys taken from such person on his apprehension or otherwise, or where such judge orders a reward to any person who shall appear to have been active in the apprehension of any such convicted person, or where such judge makes any order under the Offences Against the Person Act, 1861, section 74, or where such judge makes any order awarding to any person aggrieved any sum of money to be paid by such convicted person under the Forfeiture Act, 1870, or where such judge makes on the conviction of any person before him any order for the payment of money by such convicted person or by any other person or any order affecting the rights or property of such convicted person, the operation of such orders shall in any of such cases be suspended until the expiration of ten clear days after the day on which any of such orders was made. In cases in relation to which such an order was made, where notice of appeal or notice of application for leave to appeal is served within such ten days, such order shall be further suspended until the determination thereof. The Court may by order annul any order to which this rule refers, or may vary such order, and such order, if annulled, shall not take effect, and, if varied, shall take effect as so varied. The proper officer of the court of trial shall keep a record of any such orders.

(2) Where the judge of the court of trial makes any such order, he shall give such directions as he thinks right as to the retention by any person of any money or valuable securities belonging to the person so convicted and taken from such person on his apprehension, or of any money or valuable securities at the date of his conviction in the possession of the prosecution, for the period of ten clear days, or, in the event of an appeal, or of an application for leave to appeal, until the determination thereof. The proper officer of the court of trial shall keep a record of any such directions.

(3) Where the judge of the court of trial makes any order for the payment of money by a convicted person or by any other person, and by reason of this rule such order would be suspended, he may direct that

the operation of such order shall not be suspended unless the person on whom such order has been made shall, in such manner and within such time as he shall direct, give security by way of undertaking or otherwise for the payment to the person in whose favour such order shall have been made of the amount therein named.

(4) Where on a conviction any property, matters or things the subject of the prosecution or connected therewith are to be or may be ordered to be destroyed or forfeited under the provisions of any statute, the destruction or forfeiture or order for destruction or forfeiture thereof shall be suspended for the period of ten clear days from the close of the trial, and, in the event of an appeal, or of an application for leave to appeal, shall be further suspended until the determination thereof.

(5) Where, upon the conviction of any person, any claim may be made or any proceedings may be taken under any statute against such person or any other person in consequence of such conviction, such proceedings shall not be taken until after the period of ten clear days from the close of the trial, or in the event of an appeal, or of an application for leave to appeal, until the determination thereof.

12. An order of restitution shall be suspended for the period of ten clear days from the day of the close of the trial, and, in cases where notice of appeal or notice of application for leave to appeal is duly given, the period of suspension of such order shall continue until the determination thereof.

13. (1) The clerk of the court of trial, or other officer thereof having the custody of the records of such court, or the deputy of such clerk or other officer, shall not issue, under any statute authorising him so to do, a certificate of conviction of any person convicted on indictment in the court to which he is such clerk, officer, or deputy, for the period of ten clear days after the day of the close of the trial, or, when a notice of appeal or of application for leave to appeal has been duly given, until the determination thereof.

(2) Where an application is made to such clerk, officer, or deputy to issue a certificate of conviction after the expiration of the said period of ten clear days, he shall require, before issuing the same, to be satisfied that there is no appeal or application for leave to appeal, then pending in the Court against such conviction. A person desirous of obtaining a certificate of conviction from such clerk, officer of deputy shall be entitled to obtain from the Registrar a certificate in the Form No. 8 for the purpose of satisfying such clerk, officer or deputy that no appeal or application for leave to appeal against such conviction is then pending. After the expiration of two months from the date of the conviction a certificate thereof may be issued by such clerk, officer, or duputy, except in cases in which he has had notice of an appeal or application for leave to appeal still undetermined. For the purposes of this rule the expression

"conviction" shall mean the verdict or plea of guilty and any final judgment passed thereon.

VII. *Official stenographer and transcript of notes.*

14. (1) The offical stenographer shall at the conclusion of the trial, sign the shorthand note taken by him and certify the same to be complete and correct.

(2) On request by the Registrar, the offical stenographer shall furnish to him a report comprising the original shorthand note and a transcript of the whole of such note or of such part thereof as may be required.

(3) Before furnishing his report to the Registrar, the official stenographer shall submit the transcript to the judge of the court of trial to be certified by him.

(4) A party interested in an appeal or application for leave to appeal may obtain from the Registrar a copy of the transcript of the whole or of any part of such shorthand note as relates to the appeal or application upon payment of the proper charges.

(5) The transcript may be made by the official stenographer who took the shorthand note or other competent person.

(6) The transcript shall be typewritten and certified by the person making the same to be a correct and complete transcript of the whole, or of such part as may be required of the shorthand note taken by the official stenographer.

(7) The report of the official stenographer shall contain the evidence, any objection taken in the course thereof, any statement made by the prisoner, the summing up and the sentence of the judge of the court of trial, but unless otherwise ordered by such judge shall not include any part of the speeches of counsel or solicitor.

VIII. *Exhibits and documents relating to trial.*

15. [Deleted, S.I. No. 224 of 1963].

16. When the Registrar receives a notice of appeal or a notice of application for leave to appeal, he shall forthwith apply to the proper officer of the court of trial for the original depositions of witnesses examined before the committing justice, the indictment or indictments against the appellant, a copy of the record of the trial by the appellant from the Trials Book, any exhibit or exhibits retained by such officer and a list of such exhibits; and such officer shall forthwith furnish the same to the Registrar. Upon the final determination of the appeal or application for leave to appeal, the Registrar shall return the aforesaid documents to such officer.

IX. *Documents for use of the Court and appellants.*

17. (1) The Registrar may, on an application made to him by the appellant or the Attorney General, or shall where he considers the same to be necessary for the proper determination of any appeal or application, or where directed by the Court so to do, obtain and keep available for use by the Court any documents, exhibits or other things relating to the proceedings before the Court, and, pending the determination of the appeal or application for leave to appeal, such documents, exhibits, or other things shall be open, as and when the Registrar may arrange, for the inspection of any party interested.

(2) The Court may, at any stage of an appeal or application for leave to appeal, on the application of an appellant or the Attorney General, order any document, exhibit, or other thing connected with the proceedings to be produced to the Registrar by any person having the custody or control thereof.

(3) Service of any order under this rule shall be personal, unless the Court otherwise orders, and for the purpose of effecting due service thereof the Registrar may require the assistance of the Garda Síochána, and it shall be their duty to carry out any directions of the Registrar under this rule.

18. (1) At any time after notice of appeal or notice of application for leave to appeal has been served, an appellant or the Attorney General, or the solicitor or other person representing either of them may obtain from the Registrar copies of any documents or exhibits in his possession for the purposes of such appeal or application. Such copies shall be supplied by the Registrar at the proper charges.

(2) Where solicitor and counsel, or counsel only, are assigned to an appellant, copies of any documents or exhibits which they or he may request the Registrar to supply shall be supplied free of charge.

(3) A transcript of the shorthand notes taken of the proceedings at the trial of an appellant may be supplied free of charge by order of the Court.

(4) Where an appellant who is not legally represented requires from the Registrar a copy of any document or exhibit in his custody for the purposes of his appeal, he may obtain it free of charge if the Registrar considers it is proper to supply the same.

X. *Report of trial judge.*

19. (1) The Registrar, whenever in relation to any appeal or application for leave to appeal, the Court directs him so to do, shall request the judge of the court of trial to furnish him with a report in writing giving his opinion upon the case generally or upon any point arising thereon, and the judge of the court of trial shall furnish the same in accordance

with such request.

(2) The report of the judge shall be made to the Court, and, except by leave of the Court, the Registrar shall not furnish any part thereof to any person.

XI. *Bail.*

20. (1) An appellant desiring to be admitted to bail, pending the determination of his appeal, or of any re-trial, shall (unless the Court shall dispense therewith) serve upon the Registrar notice in the Forms Nos. 9 or 11 of his application for such bail. The Registrar shall forthwith give notice thereof to the Chief State Solicitor, and as soon as a date shall be fixed by the Court for the hearing of such application shall notify the appellant and the Chief State Solicitor.

(2) The Court when admitting an appellant to bail shall specify the amount in which the appellant and his surety (if any) shall be bound by recognisance.

(3) The Registrar shall notify the Governor of the prison within which the appellant is confined of the terms and conditions on which the Court shall admit the appellant to bail.

(4) Unless otherwise ordered by the Court the recognisances of the appellant and his surety (if any) shall be taken before a justice of the District Court.

(5) The recognisances shall be in the Forms Nos. 10 or 12. The clerk of the District Court area in which the recognisance of a surety shall be taken shall give to such surety a certificate in the Form No. 14 which the surety shall sign and retain.

(6) The clerk of any District Court area before the justice of which any such recognisance shall be taken as aforesaid shall, in the Form No. 13 forthwith notify the Governor of the said prison of the perfection thereof; and the District Court clerk in whose custody such recognisance may be shall forthwith send the same when perfected to the Registrar.

(7) Upon perfection of such recognisances the Governor of the said prison shall release the appellant from custody without further order.

(8) An appellant who has been admitted to bail shall, by the order of the Court under which he was so admitted to bail, be required to be, and shall be, personally present at each and every hearing of his appeal, and at the final determination thereof, and shall, whenever his case is called on before the Court, surrender himself to such persons as the Court shall from time to time direct, and may be searched by them, and shall be deemed to be in their lawful custody until further released on bail or otherwise dealt with as the Court shall direct. The Court may, in the event of such appellant not being present at any hearing of his appeal, dismiss the same and issue a warrant for the apprehension of the

appellant, in the Form No. 15; provided that the Court may consider the appeal in his absence, or make such other order as it thinks fit.

(9) The Court may revoke or vary any bail order or enlarge the recognisance of the appellant or of his sureties or substitute any other surety for a surety previously bound.

(10) Where the surety upon whose recognisance an appellant has been released on bail, suspects that the appellant is about to depart out of the jurisdiction of the Court, or to fail in any manner to observe the conditions of his recognisance, such surety may lay an information before a justice of the District Court acting in and for the district in which the appellant is, or is by such surety believed to be, or in which such surety may then be, in the Form No. 16, and such justice shall thereupon issue a warrant in the Form No. 17 for the apprehension of the appellant.

(11) The appellant shall, on being apprehended, be brought before the District Court specified in the said warrant. The justice shall on verification of the said information by oath of the informant, by warrant of committal in the Form No. 18, commit the appellant to the prison to which persons charged with indictable offences before such District Court are ordinarily committed.

(12) The clerk of the District Court, on the committal of any such appellant, shall forthwith notify the Registrar to that effect, and forward to him the said information and the deposition in verification thereof taken before such District Court together with a copy of the said warrant of committal.

(13) When an appellant has been released on bail and has been apprehended under this rule and is in prison, the Governor thereof shall forthwith notify the Registrar, who shall inform the Court, and the Court may give such directions as to the appeal or otherwise as it thinks fit.

(14) At any time after an appellant has been released on bail the Court may revoke the order admitting him to bail, and issue a warrant in the Form No. 15 for his apprehension and order him to be committed to prison.

(15) Nothing in this rule shall affect the right of a surety to apprehend and surrender into custody the person for whose apearance he has become bound, and thereby to discharge himself of his suretyship.

(16) On breach of the recognisance of an appellant, the Court may order his own recognisance to be estreated and may also, on notice to his surety, order the recognisance of such surety to be estreated. The warrant for such estreat shall be in the Form No. 19.

XII. *Cause list.*

21. (1) The Registrar shall keep a register of all cases in which he shall receive a notice of appeal, or notice of application for leave to appeal which shall be open for public inspection.

(2) The Registrar shall also prepare from time to time a general list of cases to be dealt with by the Court and shall cause such list to be published at such times and in such a manner as shall be convenient for giving due notice to any parties interested of the hearing of such cases by the Court.

22. The Registrar shall obtain and lay before the Court in proper form all documents, exhibits and other things relating to the proceedings in the court of trial which are necessary for the proper determination of the appeal or application.

23. (1) Where an appellant is in custody, the Registrar shall notify the appellant, the Governor of the prison in which the appellant then is, and the Department of Justice, Prisons Section, of the probable day on which his appeal or application will be heard. The said Department shall (where necessary) take steps to transfer the appellant to a prison convenient for this appearance before the Court at such a reasonable time before the hearing as shall enable him to consult his legal adviser.

(2) When the date for the hearing of an appeal or application shall be fixed, the Registrar shall give notice thereof to the appellant and the Chief State Solicitor.

XIII. *Abandonment of appeal.*

24. (1) An appellant at any time after he has duly served notice of appeal or of application for leave to appeal or of application for enlargement of time may abandon his appeal or application by giving notice of abandonment thereof in the Form No. 20.

(2) When the Registrar receives a notice of abandonment of any appeal or application for leave to appeal he shall give notice thereof to all persons to whom he shall have given notice of the receipt by him of notice of such appeal or application for leave to appeal.

XIV. *Examination of witnesses.*

25. (1) An application for the attendance and examination before the Court of any witness shall be in the Form No. 21. There shall be annexed to such form a statement signed by the witness of the evidence which he proposes to give and of the reason why he did not give such evidence at the trial, unless the Court shall dispense with such statement.

(2) Where an order is made for the attendance and examination of a witness, an order in the Form No. 22 shall be served upon him specifying the time and place at which he is to attend.

(3) Where the Court orders the examination of any witness to be conducted otherwise than before the Court, such order shall specify the person appointed as examiner to take, and the place of taking, such examination, and the witness or witnesses to be examined.

(4) The Registrar shall furnish to the person appointed to take such examination any documents or exhibits and any other material relating to the said appeal as and when requested so to do. Such documents and exhibits and other material shall after the examination has been concluded be returned by the examiner, together with any depositions taken by him to the Registrar.

(5) When the examiner has appointed the day and time for the examination he shall request the Registrar to give notice thereof to the appellant and the Attorney General, and their legal representatives (if any) and when the appellant is in prison, the Governor of that prison. The Registrar shall cause to be served on every witness to be so examined notice in the Form No. 23.

(6) Every witness examined before an examiner shall give his evidence upon oath to be administered by such examiner except where any such witness, if giving evidence as a witness on a trial on indictment, need not be sworn.

(7) The examination of every such witness shall be taken in the form of a deposition in the same manner as is prescribed by the Petty Sessions (Ireland) Act, 1851, section 14, and unless otherwise ordered shall be taken in private. The caption in the Form No. 24 shall be attached to any such deposition.

(8) The expenses of any witness attending on the order of the Court, and all expenses of and incidental to any examination of witnesses conducted by any person appointed by the Court shall, if and so far as ordered by the Court, be defrayed up to an amount allowed by the Court as part of the costs of the State in or relating to the appeal.

(9) The provisions of rule 17 (3) shall apply to the service of an order or notice on a witness under this rule.

(10) The appellant and the Attorney General, or counsel or solicitor on their behalf, shall be entitled to be present at and take part in any examination of any witness to which this rule relates.

XV. *Hearing of appeals and other applications.*

26. (1) An appellant who is in custody shall be entitled, if he so desires, to be present in person at the hearing of his appeal or application for leave to appeal and of all interlocutory applications in relation thereto.

(2) The provisions of sub-rule (1) shall apply *mutatis mutandis* to the right of an applicant for enlargement of time to be present at the hearing of such application.

27. If it appears to the Registrar that any notice of application for leave to appeal does not show any substantial ground of appeal the Registrar may list the case for hearing without obtaining for the use of the Court a transcript of the shorthand note taken by the official stenographer at the trial.

28. Where a restitution order has been made by the court of trial, the person in whose favour such order was made, the appellant, and with the leave of the Court any other person, shall be entitled to be heard before any order is made by the Court annulling or varying such order of restitution.

29. (1) When the Court makes an order refusing an application for leave to appeal, or finally determining an appeal, the Registrar shall give notice thereof in the Form No. 25 to the following persons;

(a) the appellant;

(b) the proper officer of the court of trial;

(c) the Commissioner of the Garda Síochána;

and also, if the appellaant is in prison, or has been released on bail —

(d) the Governor of such prison; and

(e) the Secretary of the Department of Justice;

provided that the Registrar shall not be required to give such notice to the appellant if he shall have been present or shall have been legally represented at the hearing.

[rr. 2 and 3 deleted, S.I. No. 219 of 1967.]

(4) The proper officer of the court of trial, on receiving a notice pursuant to sub-rule (1), shall enter the particulars contained therein on the records of the court of trial.

XVI. *Miscellaneous.*

30. Except where otherwise provided by this Order notice of every application to the Court shall be in accordance with the Form No. 26 which shall be served on the Registrar and the Chief State Solicitor or appellant (as the case may be) and such other person, if any, as the Court may direct.

31. In all preliminary and interlocutory proceedings and applications the parties thereto may be represented and appear by a solicitor alone.

32. (1) Every notice of appeal or notice of application for leave to appeal shall be signed by the appellant himself except in the cases mentioned in sub-rules (2), (3) and (4). Any other notice shall be in writing and signed by the person giving the same or his solicitor.

(2) Where an appellant or any other person authorised or required to give or send any notice is unable to write, he may affix his mark thereto in the presence of a witness who shall attest the same and thereupon such notice shall be deemed to be duly signed by him.

(3) Where it is alleged that an appellant is insane at the time when any

notice is required or authorised to be given by him, such notice may be given and signed by a solicitor or other person on his behalf.

(4) In the case of a body corporate, where any notice or other document is required to be signed by the appellant himself, it shall be sufficient compliance therewith if such notice or other document is signed by the secretary, clerk, manager, or solicitor of such body corporate.

(5) Any notice required or authorised to be given to the Court shall be addressed to and served upon the Registrar, The Court of Criminal Appeal, Four Courts, Dublin.

(6) In every case in which an appellant is not in prison or is represented by a solicitor, his notice of appeal or notice of application for leave to appeal shall be served on the Registrar personally or by delivering the same to the proper officer at the Office of the Court at the Four Courts, Dublin. In all other cases not specifically provided for service of any notice or other document may be effected personally or by sending the same by pre-paid post addressed to the person on whom it is to be served.

33. The Registrar shall furnish the necessary forms and instructions in relation to notices of appeal or notices of application to any person who demands the same and to officers of courts, Governors of prisons, and such other officers or persons as he thinks fit and the Governor of a prison shall cause those forms and instructions to be placed at the disposal of the prisoners desiring to make any application, and shall cause any such notice given by a prisoner in his custody to be forwarded on behalf of the prisoner to the Registrar.

34. It shall be the duty of the Garda Síochána of the district in which the appellant shall have resided before his conviction or of the district from which he was committed to enquire as to and report to the Registrar, when required by him, upon the means and circumstances of any appellant where such a question arises.

35. The Department of Justice, Prisons Section, shall on notice from the Registrar, cause from time to time such sufficient number of male and female officers to attend the sittings of the Court, as, having regard to the list of appeals and applications for leave to appeal thereat, the Department shall consider necessary.

36. The performance of any duty imposed upon any person by this Order may be enforced by order of the Court.

37. Any warrant for the apprehension of an appellant issued by the Court shall be deemed to be, for all purposes, a warrant issued by a justice of the District Court for the apprehension of a person charged with any indictable offence under the provisions of the Petty Sessions (Ireland) Act, 1851, or any statute amending the same.

38. In any case where an appeal is taken or an application for leave to

appeal is made by a person who has been sentenced to death, it shall be lawful for the Court to assign to the appellant such legal aid as may appear to be reasonably required, and the costs and expenses of any legal aid so assigned up to an amount allowed by the Court shall be paid as part of the costs of the State in or relating to the appeal.

39. Every order of the Court, when drawn up, shall be dated the day of the week, month and year on which the same was made, unless the Court shall otherwise direct, shall take effect accordingly, and shall be issued out of the Office of the Court.

40. Non-compliance on the part of an appellant with the rules of this Order, or with any rule of practice for the time being in force, shall not prevent the further prosecution of his appeal, or application unless the Court shall so direct, but such appeal or application may be dealt with in such manner and upon such terms as the Court shall think fit.

APPENDIX F

STATE SIDE ORDERS AND FORMS

PART I

Rules of the Superior Courts – Order 84. State Side

1. In this Order:
(a) the expressions –
"order of habeas corpus"
"order of certiorari"
"order of mandamus"
"order of prohibition"
"order of attachment"
means respectively orders of the Court (hereinafter sometimes referred to as State Side orders) witnessed in the name of the Chief Justice or if the office of Chief Justice be vacant in the name of the President of the High Court, sealed with the seal of the High Court and bearing date on the day of issue;
(b) the expression –
"absolute order"
means an order that a State Side order do issue;
(c) the expression –
"conditional order"
means an order that unless cause be shown to the contrary within a specified time, a State Side order do issue pursuant to an absolute order to be obtained under this Order.

I. *Habeas corpus.*

2. An application for an order of habeas corpus *ad subjiciendum* shall be by motion *ex parte* for a conditional order, provided that where the Court may be of opinion that the order should issue forthwith an absolute order may be made in the first instance.
3. Unless the Court shall otherwise direct –
(a) the application for an order of habeas corpus *ad subjiciendum* shall be on affidavit which shall be entitled shortly in the matter in question, and in the matter of the Habeas Corpus Act, 1782, and/or in

the matter of the Constitution as may be appropriate;

(b) no order of habeas corpus *ad subjiciendum* shall be granted where the validity of any warrant, committal order, conviction, or record, shall be questioned unless at the time of moving a copy of such warrant, committal order, conviction or record verified by affidavit be produced to the Court, or the absence thereof accounted for to the satisfaction of the Court.

4. The order of habeas corpus *ad subjiciendum* shall be served personally on the person to whom it is directed, unless the court otherwise directs. If the order is directed to a gaoler or other public official, it shall be served by leaving it with him or his servant or agent at the place of confinement or restraint, or in such manner as the Court may direct. If the order be directed to more than one person the original shall be delivered or left with the person actually detaining or restraining, and copies thereof shall be served on each of the other persons in the same manner as the order.

5. The Court may, on the motion to make absolute notwithstanding cause shown, order either that the body of the person detained be produced before the Court on a named day or that such person be released from such detention.

6. The return to the order of habeas corpus, when the body is not produced, shall be by affidavit to be made by the party to whom the order is directed and shall contain such full answer to the allegation that the person is detained as the circumstances may require.

7. If an order of habeas corpus be disobeyed by the person to whom it is directed, application may be made to the Court, on an affidavit of service and disobedience, for an attachment for contempt. In vacation an application may be made to the Court for a warrant for the apprehension of the person in contempt to be brought before the Court to be bound over to appear at the next ensuing sittings, to answer for his contempt, or to be committed to prison for want of bail.

8. An application to bring up a prisoner to give evidence in any cause or matter, civil or criminal, before any Court, may be made to the Court on affidavit.

II. *Certiorari.*

9. An application for an order of certiorari shall be by motion *ex parte* for a conditional order, provided that where the Court is of opinion that the order should issue forthwith, an absolute order may be made in the first instance.

10. No order of certiorari shall be made to remove any judgment, order, conviction or other proceeding had or made by or before any justice of the District Court or judge of the Circuit Court unless such order of certiorari be applied for within six calendar months next after

such judgment, order, conviction, or other proceedings shall be so had or made.

11. No order of certiorari shall be granted where the validity of any warrant, committal, order, conviction, or record shall be questioned, unless at the time of moving a copy of such warrant, committal, order, conviction, or record, verified by affidavit, be produced to the Court or the absence thereof accounted for to the satisfaction of the Court.

12. The Court may as part of the order absolute, order that the judgment, order, conviction or decision shall be quashed on return without further order.

13. All recognisances to be entered into for the allowance of any order of certiorari shall be certified into the Court with the order of certiorari. In civil causes or matters, the recognisance shall be conditioned, as regards costs, to pay such costs (if any) as the Court shall order.

14. No objection on account of any omission or mistake in the drawing up of any judgment or order of the District Court or the Circuit Court brought up upon a return to an order of certiorari and filed at the Central Office shall be allowed, unless such omission or mistake shall have been specified in the order for issuing such certiorari.

15. The Court may, if necessary, order that the person against whom an order of certiorari is to be directed, do make a record of the judgment, conviction or decision complained of.

III. *Quo warranto.*

IV. *Mandamus.*

25. An application for an order of mandamus shall be made by motion for a conditional order.

26. When a return is made to the first order of mandamus the prosecutor may plead to the return within such time and in like name as if the return were a statement of defence delivered in an action, and all subsequent proceedings may be had and taken as in an action.

27. Unless the Court otherwise directs, when an order of mandamus is directed to companies, or public bodies, service shall be made upon such and so many persons as are competent to do the act required to be done.

28. The Court may order that any order of mandamus shall be peremptory in the first instance.

29. An order of mandamus may be made returnable forthwith or time may be allowed to make the return either with or without terms. The order shall be in the Form No. 8 in Appendix T.

30. Any person by law compellable to make a return to an order of mandamus shall make his return to the first order.

31. When it appears to the Court that the person bound to make a return to an order of mandamus claims no right or interest in the

subject-matter of the application, or that his functions are merely ministerial, the return to the order, and all subsequent proceedings down to judgment, shall still be in the name of such person, and if the Court so orders may be expressed to be made on behalf of the person really interested, in which case such person shall be permitted to frame the return and appear on all subsequent proceedings, and judgment may be given for or against such last mentioned person with, or without costs.

32. Where under rule 31 the return to an order of mandamus is expressed to be made on behalf of some person other than the person to whom the order is directed, the proceedings on the order shall not abate by reason of the death, resignation or removal from office of that person, but they may be continued and carried on in his name, and if a peremptory order is made it shall be directed to the successor in office or right of that person.

33. The procedure and practice provided for in Order 57 shall be applicable in mandamus as far as the nature of the case will admit.

34. No order of mandamus shall be issued unless on the application for the conditional order some person deposes on affidavit that such application is made at his instance as prosecutor. If the order be issued the name of such person shall be endorsed on the order as the person at whose instance it is granted.

35. An application for the costs of a mandamus shall, unless the Court shall otherwise order, be made before the fifth day of the sittings next after that in which the right to make such application accrued, and shall be upon notice of motion.

36. An application for an order of mandamus directed to a judge of the Circuit Court to enter continuances and hear an appeal shall be made within two calendar months from the day on which such judge refused to hear such appeal, unless further time be allowed by the Court, and unless special circumstances appear by affidavit to account for the delay to the satisfaction of the Court.

V. *Prohibition.*

37. An application for the order of prohibition on the State Side shall be made by motion for a conditional order.

38. The order may be made absolute *ex parte* in the first instance on special circumstances being shown, in the discretion of the Court.

VI. *[Attachment for contempt].*

VII. *Bail.*

40. (1) An application for bail by a person in custody charged with a criminal offence shall be by motion on notice to the Chief State Solicitor grounded on the affidavit of the applicant.

(2) Proceedings on an application for bail shall be entitled –

"THE HIGH COURT
STATE SIDE.
In the matter of
The People (at the suit of the Attorney General) v. A.B.
At present pending in the..........................Court
at................................"

or to the like effect.

(3) Where an applicant has no solicitor, the Court may dispense with the necessity for a notice of motion and affidavit, and in lieu thereof shall give all appropriate directions including a direction that the applicant be brought before the Court on a date and at a time to be specified, of which the Chief State Solicitor shall be notified, and for the purpose of giving such directions the Court may hear the applicant.

VIII. *Recognisances.*

41. Every recognisance acknowledged on the removal of an order, or other proceeding, or for the appearing or answering of any party in the Court, or for good behaviour, or for any other purpose shall after the acknowledgement thereof, be transmitted to the Central Office and filed there.

42. No recognisance shall be forfeited, or estreated without an order of the Court, nor unless notice shall have been previously served upon the parties by whom such recognisances shall have been given.

IX. *State Side orders.*

43. Subject to rule 27, every State Side order shall be served personally by delivering the original to the person to whom it is directed unless the Court otherwise directs. In case the order is directed to more than one person the original shall be delivered to the person to to be directed by the Court, and copies thereof shall be served on each of the other persons in the same manner as the order. There shall be indorsed upon the order a memorandum in the form provided for in Order 41, rule 8.

X. *Conditional orders.*

44. (1) Every conditional order shall direct on whom the same shall be served, and to whom notice thereof shall be given.

(2) When the conditional order is directed to a gaoler or other public official, it shall be served by leaving a copy thereof with him or his servant or agent at the place of confinement or restraint, at the same time exhibiting an attested copy thereof, or in such manner as the Court may direct. In any other case the conditional order shall be served personally unless the Court otherwise directs.

45. Every conditional order shall be filed in the Central Office and served together with a copy of the grounding affidavit (if any) within ten days from the day the same shall be pronounced, unless further time be allowed by the Court; and in default thereof such conditional order shall stand discharged.

46. Unless the conditional order shall otherwise direct, cause shall be shown against the same within ten days after service thereof. Any person may by leave of the Court show cause.

47. Cause against a conditional order may be shown by affidavit or, where it is not desired to adduce evidence in support thereof, by notice in the Form No. 12 in Appendix T.

48. (1) Where cause is shown by affidavit, the affidavit shall, in addition to any facts which may be deposed to, state concisely the grounds relied upon as cause. The affidavit shall be filed in the Central Office, and notice of filing shall be served on the prosecutor or his solicitor within the time allowed for showing cause.

(2) Where cause is shown by notice, the notice shall state concisely the grounds relied upon as cause. The notice shall be served on the prosecutor or his solicitor and filed in the Central Office within the time allowed for showing cause.

49. (1) Where cause has been shown in manner aforesaid, the prosecutor shall apply to the Court by motion on notice to make absolute the conditional order or some part thereof notwithstanding such cause and shall move such application according to the course of the Court.

(2) Notice of such motion shall be served on the party showing cause or his solicitor within six days after service by him of a notice in pursuance of rule 48 or where cause is shown by more than one party then within six days after service of the last of such notices, and if such notice of motion shall not be served upon such party within the time aforesaid, he shall be entitled to an order of course allowing the cause shown and directing taxation of his costs of showing cause and payment thereof by the prosecutor.

50. Where cause has not been shown in manner and within the time aforesaid, the prosecutor shall, on filing an affidavit of service of the conditional order and a certificate that no cause has been shown, be entitled to obtain a side bar order making the conditional order absolute (unless the conditional order shall have otherwise directed).

XI. *Pleadings.*

51. At any stage in proceedings in prohibition, or in the nature of a quo warranto, the Court on the application of any party or of its own motion, may direct a plenary hearing with such directions as to pleadings, discovery or otherwise as may be appropriate; and thereupon all further proceedings shall be conducted as in an action originated by plenary summons and the Court may give such judgment and make such order as if the trial were the hearing of an application to make absolute a conditional order to show cause.

XII. *General.*

52. Proceedings on the State Side shall be entitled "THE HIGH COURT: STATE SIDE." In the first affidavit filed on behalf of the prosecutor, and in the first affidavit filed on behalf of any person resisting or showing cause, there shall be stated a registered place of business or an address of service within the meaning of Order 4, rules 14 and 15.

53. Upon motions on the State Side either party may apply to the Court for leave to use additional affidavits upon any new matter arising out of the affidavits of the opposite party; but no additional affidavits shall be used without such leave.

54. In all cases entered for argument on the State Side, the party entering the same or his solicitor, two days before the day appointed for argument, shall deliver at the Central Office books of the proceedings for the use of the Court, unless the Court otherwise directs.

55. Such books shall contain, with a sufficient index, a copy of the conditional order, copies of the affidavits intended to be used, together with copies of all documents referred to or exhibited therein, copies of the pleadings (if any) and of all other documents required for the hearing, including the recognisances (if any).

56. If such books are not delivered, the other party may, on the day following, deliver such books as ought to have been delivered, and the party making default shall not be heard until he shall have paid or deposited at the Central Office a sufficient sum to pay for such books. In default the case may be struck out.

57. If on hearing of a motion or other application, the Court shall be of opinion that any person to whom notice has not been given ought to have or to have had such notice, the Court may either dismiss the motion or application, or adjourn the hearing thereof, in order that such notice may be given, upon such terms, if any, as the Court may think fit to impose.

58. The hearing of any motion or application may from time to time be adjourned upon such terms, if any, as the Court shall think fit.

59. Service of an order or notice pursuant to this Order shall be personal unless the Court shall othewise direct.
60. In this Order, "the prosecutor" means the person who applies for the conditional order, and includes, in the case of proceedings in the nature of a quo warranto, the relator.
61. The forms in Appendix T shall be used in all proceedings on the State Side.

PART II

Rules of the Superior Courts – Appendix T – State Side Forms

No. 1. Order of Habeas Corpus ad Subjiciendum.

[Title]

To/ C.D. of

This is to command you, the said C.D., that you have in the High Court, Four Courts, Dublin, in Court No. on day the day of 19 , at the hour of o'clock in the noon, the body of being taken and detained in your custody as is said, together with the day and cause of his being taken and detained, by whatsoever name he may be called therein, to undergo and receive all and singular such matters and things as the High Court shall then and there consider of concerning him in this behalf and that you have there then this order.

By order Chief Justice of Ireland, the day of 19

(Signed) (Seal)

Master of the High Court.

By order of the Honourable Mr Justice made the day of 19 , at the instance of A.B.,

This order was taken of solicitor for the said A.B.

No. 2. Order of Habeas Corpus ad Testificandum.

[Title]

To/

The gaoler of the prison at

This is to command you that you have before *[description of court]* the day of 19 , at the hour of in the noon, the body of being committed and detained in the prison under your custody, as is said then and there to give evidence *[on behalf of the People against M.N.: or otherwise describe the proceedings as in subpoena]*, and so from day to day until the said shall have given his evidence as aforesaid. And when he shall have given his evidence, then that you take him back without delay to the said prison under your custody, and cause him to be detained there in under safe custody, until he shall be from thence discharged by due course of law.

By order, &c. *[as in Form No. 1]*.

No. 3. Order of Certiorari.

[Title]

To/ C.D.
Judge of the Circuit Court, *(or*
Justice of the District Court,
or as the case may be.)

Whereas it appears that all and singular the order(s) made by you on the day of at whereby *set out shortly the substance of the order(s) or proceedings to be removed]* ought to be sent by you to the High Court.

Now this is to command you, the said C.D. to send forthwith under your hand and seal to the High Court, Four Courts, Dublin, all and singular the said order(s)*[or as the case may be]* with all things touching the same as fully and perfectly as they have been made by you and now remain in your custody or power, together with this order of certiorari, that the same may be quashed.

By order, &c. *[as in Form No. 1]*.

No. 4. Return to Order of Certiorari.

The order of certiorari should be indorsed thus:—

The execution of this order appears by the schedule(s) hereunto annexed.*

The answer of C.D. within mentioned:

(Signed) C. D. (Seal)

*NOTE.—*The schedule(s) comprise the order(s) or proceedings and other documents to be returned.*

[Nos 5-7. *Quo Warranto*.]

No. 8. Order of Mandamus.

[Title]

To/
C.D. and
E.F.

Whereas by *[recite statute or charter, if any, by which the act is required to be done]*.

And whereas it appears that *[set out averments showing failure to perform the act required to be done]* and that you the said C.D. and E.F. were required by on the day of 19 , to *[set out demand]* but that you not regarding your duty in that behalf have wholly neglected and refused to *[set out neglect or refusal]*.

NOW THIS IS TO COMMAND YOU the said A.B. and C.D. that you and each of you according to your duty do *[set out command]* and that you do make known and return forthwith this order to the High Court or that you do show to the High Court cause to the contrary thereof.

By order etc. *[as on Form No. 1]*

No. 9. Return to Order of Mandamus.

(The return may either be indorsed on the back of the original order, or engrossed on a separate schedule.)

When indorsed on the back of the original order.

The answer of *[the parties to whom the order is directed]* to this order.

We, to whom this order is directed, do most humbly certify and return to the High Court at the time and place in this order mentioned, that we have, &c. *[when the return is an obedience to the order, the words of the mandatory part of the order should be recapitulated in the past instead of the future tense]*. As by the said order we are commanded.

[To be signed by the parties making the return, or a sufficient number to form a quorum, unless they be a corporate body, in which case it is sufficient to attach the corporate seal].

When the return is indorsed on a separate schedule, indorse the original order [or as the copy served] thus: The return of to this order *[or is the return is obedience, say,* the execution of this order] appears in the schedule hereunto annexed.

The answer of

[To be signed or sealed as above].

No. 10. Order of Prohibition.

[Title]

To

C.D.

Whereas it appears that you the said C.D. *[set out particulars sufficient to show the nature of the proceedings to be prohibited]*. And that you the said C.D. have no jurisdiction to hear and determine the by reason that *[set out facts showing want of jurisdiction]*. Now THIS IS TO PROHIBIT YOU the said C.D. from further proceeding in the said

By Order, &c. *[as in Form No. 1]*.

[No. 11. Order of Attachment.]

No. 12. Notice showing cause.

[Title]

Take notice that C.D. of doth hereby show cause against the conditional order made herein and dated the day of 19 upon the grounds following:—

[State concisely the grounds relied upon.]

Dated

[To be signed by C.D. or his solicitor.]

To/
A.B. of
the above-named prosecutor.
or, where the prosecutor is represented by a solicitor:
E.F. of
solicitors for the above-named prosecutor.

APPENDIX G

STATUTORY POWERS OF ARREST WITHOUT WARRANT

Provision	Outline of Offence	By whom power exercisable	Restrictions imposed or conditions attached before power may be invoked
Illicit Distillation (Ireland) Act, 1831, s. 19	Person found in place where illegal distillation is in progress	Officer of Excise	—
Id. s. 25	Person carrying or removing stills, etc.	Officer of Excise	—
Id. s. 30	Persons signalling approach of Excise Officer	Any person	—
Licensing (Ireland) Act, 1836, s. 12	Being found drunk in a public place	Garda	—
Vagrancy Act, 1847, s. 4	Begging in public place or causing children so to do	Any person	—
Prevention of Offences Act, 1851, s. 10	Any indictable offence against the Act	Any person	Found committing
Id. s. 11	Any indictable offence by night	Any person	Found committing
Summary Jurisdiction Act, 1851, s. 14 (2)	Miscellaneous offences involving driving of horses, carts, etc.	A Garda or a person assisting a Garda	If name and residence are unknown and cannot be ascertained
Towns Improvement (Ireland) Act, 1854 s. 72 as extended to every town having Commissioners by Local Government (Ireland) Act, 1898, s. 41	*inter alia,* exposing animals for sale or show in unauthorised places, permitting ferocious dogs to go unmuzzled, leading animals on the footpath, loitering for the purpose of prostitution, indecent exposure, offering for sale indecent books, etc., throwing stones, making bonfires,	Garda	Offence must occur within his view

Provision	Outline of Offence	By whom power exercisable	Restrictions imposed or conditions attached before power may be invoked
Towns Improvement (Ireland) Act, 1854 *(cont.)*	wantonly ringing doorbells, beating carpets before 9 a.m., throwing rubbish from houses, hanging a clothes line across a street, etc.		
Coinage Offences Act, 1861, s. 31	An offence under the Act, e.g. counterfeiting, uttering counterfeit coins	Any person	Offender must be found committing
Larceny Act, 1861, s. 103	Any offence punishable on indictment or summarily under the Act (except angling in daytime)	Any person	Id.
Id. s. 104	Person loitering in highway, yard or other place	Garda	Where there is good cause to suspect the person of having committed or being about to commit a felony against the Act
Malicious Damage Act, 1861, s. 61	Any offence under the Act	Garda, owner or agent of owner	Offender must be found committing
Offences against the Person Act, 1861, s.66	Person loitering in highway, yard or other place	Garda	Where there is good cause to suspect the person of having committed or being about to commit a felony against the Act
Penal Servitude Act, 1864, s. 6	Having committed any offence while on licence or breaking any condition of licence	Garda	Reasonable suspicion
Pedlars Act, 1871, s. 18	Refusal to show certificate or having none, or resisting inspection of his pack	Any person authorised by the Act	When committing
Licensing Act, 1872, s. 12	Drunk in charge of a carriage, horse, cattle, steam engine in a public place or drunk in possession of a loaded firearm	Any person	—

Customs Consolidation Act, 1876, s. 186	Importing prohibited goods, carrying goods into warehouse without authority, evading customs duties, etc.	Officer of Customs	—
Indecent Advertisements Act, 1889, s. 6	Exhibiting indecent or obscene pictures or printed material in a shop window or affixing indecent material in any place where it is visible to the public, etc.	Garda	Who finds person committing any offence under the Act
Street Betting Act, 1906, s. 1 (2)	Street betting	Garda	Where person is found committing
Children Act, 1908, s. 19	Causing children to beg, cruelty to children, allowing children to be in brothels, encouraging prostitution of young girls. Also any offence in first Schedule to the Act	Garda	Either where he sees a person committing an offence where the name and address cannot be ascertained or where he has reason to believe an offence has been committed and offender will abscond or if the name and address of the person are unknown and cannot be ascertained
Summary Jurisdiction (Ireland) Act, 1908, s. 8	Employee drunk on employer's premises	Garda	When required to arrest by owner or Manager
Id. s. 9	Drunk in charge of a child under 7 years of age	Any person	—
Protection of Animals Act, 1911, s. 12 (1)	Any offence under the Act, e.g. cruelty to any animal	Garda	Reasonable cause to believe
Criminal Law (Amendment) Act, 1912, s. 1	Any offence under Criminal Law (Amendment) Act, 1885, s. 2, e.g. procuring, attempted procuring	Garda	Good cause to suspect a person of having committed or attempting to commit
Larceny Act, 1916, s. 41 (1)	Any offence under the Act except threatening to publish with intent to extort	Any person	Found committing
Id. s. 41 (2)	Any offence under the Act	Any person to whom property is offered, pawned, etc.	Reasonable cause to suspect

Provision	Outline of Offence	By whom power exercisable	Restrictions imposed or conditions attached before power may be invoked
Id. s. 41 (3)	Loitering in highway, yard or other place at night	Garda	Good cause to suspect of having committed or being about to commit a felony under the Act
Electoral Act, 1923, s. 32	Misconduct in polling station	Garda or person authorised in writing by Presiding Officer	—
Prevention of Electoral Abuses Act, 1923, s. 25	Personation	Garda	Where he receives a direction from Presiding Officer or Returning Officer; or where Garda finds person committing the offence or believes a person to have committed it
Firearms Act, 1925, s. 22 (3)	Failure to produce a firearms certificate	Garda	Where there is a refusal to give name and address or where a name or address is given which is known or suspected to be false
Id. s. 22 (4)	Possession of a firearm or ammunition in contravention of the Act	Garda	Where he believes any person to be in possession
Intoxicating Liquor Act, 1927, s. 22 (2)	Being on licensed premises after hours	Garda	If there is a refusal to give name and address or corroborative evidence thereof
Betting Act, 1931, s. 25 (3)	Failure to produce, or to permit Garda or Customs Officer to read bookmakers licence, failure to give name and address or giving false name and address	Garda	Who observes person engaged in bookmaking
Id. s. 26 (4)	Impeding Customs Officer on non-registered premises where bookmaking is	Garda	When offence is committed in his presence

	carried on, refusing to answer questions put by Customs Officer or Garda or giving false answers, refusing to give name or address or giving a false name or address		
Bourn Vincent Memorial Park Act, 1932, s. 15	Offence in the Park	Park Constable	When offence is committed in his view and (1) there is refusal to give name and address or a false name or address is given, or (2) the person refuses to leave the park
Offences Against the State Act, 1939, s. 29 (3)	Failure to give name and address or giving false name or address when on premises being searched under this section	Garda	—
Id. s. 30 (1)	Having committed or being about to commit any offence under the Act or any offence scheduled under Part V or carrying any document relating to the commission of any such offence or being in possession of information relating thereto	Garda	On suspicion
Id. s. 32	Escaping from detention	Garda	—
Offences Against the State (Amendment) Act, 1940, s. 4	Person at large in respect of whom a Ministerial warrant is in existence	Garda	—
Mental Treatment Act, 1945, s. 165	Person of unsound mind requiring care and control (not involving a criminal offence)	Garda	May 'detain' where of opinion that it is necessary for public safety or for the security of detainee
Air Navigation and Transport Act, 1950, s. 19 (1)	Contravening bye law in State aerodrome	Authorised officer	(a) if there is refusal to give name and address or a name or address is given which is reasonably suspected to be false, or (b) where a person refuses to leave the aerodrome

Provision	Outline of Offence	By whom power exercisable	Restrictions imposed or conditions attached before power may be invoked
Criminal Justice Act, 1951, s. 13 (1)	Conveying in any manner anything stolen or unlawfully obtained	Garda	Reasonable suspicion
Foyle Fisheries Act, 1952, s. 62	Offence against any provision of the Act or the corresponding Northern Ireland Act	Authorised person	If there is a refusal to give name and address
Defence Act, 1954, s. 233 (4)	Failure to comply with conditions of temporary release from military prison	Garda/Member of Defence Forces	—
Id. s. 251 (1)	Desertion and absenteeism	Garda/Member of Defence Forces	Reasonable suspicion
Id. s. 268 (4)	Trespass upon or sketching military installations	Garda/Member of Defence Forces	Reasonable grounds to believe an offence has been committed
Id. s. 284	Contravention of bye law	Authorised officer	If refusal to leave the area to which the bye law relates
Gaming and Lotteries Act, 1956, s. 40	Gaming in a public place	Garda	Where he finds a person conducting or assisting in a game which he reasonably believes contravenes Act
Prisoners of War and Enemy Aliens Act, 1956, s. 8 (3)	Assisting, harbouring, etc. prisoners of war, or interned enemy aliens	Garda/member of Defence Forces	Reasonable ground for believing
Fisheries Consolidation Act, 1959, s. 233 (1) (g)	Contravention of Chapter II or III of Part XIII of the Act	Sea Fisheries Protection Officer	On suspicion
Road Traffic Act, 1961, s. 40 (4)	Refusal to permit Garda to read licence, refusal to give name or address or giving a false name or address	Garda	—
Id. s. 49 (4)	Driving under influence of drink or drugs	Garda	Where he is of opinion that a person is committing or has committed the offence

Id. s. 50 (6)	Being in charge while under influence of drink or drugs	Garda	Id.
Id. s. 51 (4)	Driving animal drawn vehicle or pedal cycle under the influence of drink or drugs	Garda	Id.
Id. s. 53 (6)	Dangerous driving	Garda	When he is of opinion that the person has committed the offence and has caused death or serious bodily harm
Id. s. 55 (4) added by s. 52 of the Road Traffic Act, 1968	Parking in a dangerous position	Garda	Where he is of opinion that a person is committing or has committed the offence
Id. s. 107 (1)	Failure to give name and address or giving false name or address	Garda	Where he suspects a person has committed a specified offence under the Act
Id. s. 107 (2)	Offence committed and no identification mark on vehicle	Garda	May arrest person whom he reasonably believes was using the vehicle when offence was committed
Id. s. 112 (6)	Taking vehicle without consent	Garda	Reasonable ground for believing person is committing offence
Id. s. 113 (3)	Unauthorised interference with vehicle	Garda	Id.
Street and House to House Collections Act, 1962, s. 24 (2)	Any offence under the Act, e.g. unauthorised collections, failure of collector to give Garda name and address, failure to fulfil permit duties, etc.	Garda	Where person is found committing an offence and he refuses to give a name and address or gives a name and address reasonably believed to be false
Official Secrets Act, 1963, s. 15	Contravention of section 9 of the Act, *inter alia* having information on Defence Forces movements, Garda operations or other information prejudicial to the safety of the State	Any person	On reasonable suspicion, as for a person who is found committing a felony

Provision	Outline of Offence	By whom power exercisable	Restrictions imposed or conditions attached before power may be invoked
Id. s. 16 (4)	Refusal to give name and address or giving false name or address while on premises being searched under warrant issued under this section	Garda	—
Pawnbrokers Act, 1964, s. 35	Offering stolen or lost property to pawnbroker	Pawnbroker	Person and property to be delivered to Gardaí
Id. s. 36	Offering, uttering etc. a pawn ticket reasonably suspected to be counterfeit, forged or altered	Pawnbroker	Person and pawn ticket to be delivered to Gardaí
Id. s. 37	Offer of article to pawnbroker in suspicious circumstances or attempt to redeem without right	Pawnbroker	Person, article or pawn ticket to be delivered to Gardaí; if the person refuses to give a satisfactory account or gives false information or if pawnbroker believes the article or ticket has been unlawfully obtained
Diseases of Animals Act, 1966, s. 46 (2)	Any offence contained in s. 49 of the Act	Garda	Person found committing or reasonably suspected of being engaged in committing if person fails to give name and address
Id. s. 46 (3)	Obstructing or impeding or assisting another to obstruct or impede a Garda	Garda	—
Prohibition of Forcible Entry and Occupation Act, 1971, s. 9	Forcible occupation of land or vehicle where serious damage is or may be caused	Garda	If it is necessary to prevent damage and if it is not practicable to obtain a warrant
Air Navigation and Transport Act, 1973, s. 7	Commission of serious offence aboard aircraft	Aircraft Commander	Reason to believe that a person has committed
Id. s. 11 (5)	Hijacking or attempt thereat or aiding and abetting	Garda	Id.

Air Navigation and Transport Act, 1975, s. 4	Any offence under the Act, e.g. placing a device to damage or destroy an aircraft	Garda	Reason to believe a person to have committed or intends to commit
Criminal Law (Jurisdiction) Act, 1976, s. 19	Offences under section 2 of the Act, i.e. offences committed in Northern Ireland and also offences under section 3, i.e. escape from custody in Northern Ireland	Garda	Where there is reasonable cause to suspect a person is committing, has committed or is about to commit an offence under section 2 or has committed an offence under section 3.
Misuse of Drugs Act, 1977, s. 25	Possession under section 15 of controlled drugs for unlawful sale or supply	Garda	On reasonable suspicion
Id.	Any other offence under the Act	Garda	On reasonable suspicion if he believes the person will abscond or evade justice or if he has doubts as to his identity or address or if the person does not ordinarily reside in the State
Road Traffic (Amendment) Act, 1978, s. 15 (3)	Refusal to provide a breath specimen	Garda	Where he is of opinion that the person is committing or has committed an offence
Id. s. 16 (4)	Failure to acknowledge in writing the receipt of written statement indicating concentration of alcohol	Garda	—
Id. s. 17 (3)	Failure of driver under the influence of drink or drugs to comply with requirements to go to Garda station	Garda	Where he is of opinion that a person is committing or has committed an offence
Casual Trading Act, 1980, s. 12	Any offence under the Act, e.g. engaging in casual trading without a valid licence, failing to display licence, etc.	Garda	Reasonable cause to believe a person is contravening the Act
Family Law (Protection of Spouses and Children) Act, 1981, s. 7	Contravening a barring order or a protection order	Garda	On complaint of applicant spouse where there is reasonable cause to believe an offence is being or has been committed

APPENDIX H

TABLE OF INDICTABLE OFFENCES AND PENALTIES

Reference to terms of detention is to imprisonment unless otherwise stated.

The letters "S.C." refer to penalties which may be imposed on summary conviction for indictable offences.

PRELIMINARY NOTES

1. *Penal Servitude*

As to the effect of section 15 of the Criminal Law (Ireland) Act, 1828, section 2 of the Penal Servitude Act, 1857, and section 1 of the Penal Servitude Act, 1891, see p. 396 supra.

2. *Imprisonment*

Section 1 (2) of the Act of 1891 empowers a court to award imprisonment for any term not exceeding two years, in place of a sentence of penal servitude. There is, however, no limit to the term of imprisonment for a *common law* misdemeanour. Imprisonment with hard labour may only be directed if authorised by statute, but since in practice the distinction between imprisonment with or without hard labour no longer exists, reference to such statutes has been omitted.

3. *Alternative Procedures*

A number of Statutes prescribe that an offence may be triable either on indictment or summarily; offences which are *only* triable summarily are not included.

2. *Plea of Guilty in District Court*

If the accused pleads guilty in the District Court to any indictable offence (except for a few very grave offences referred to below) he may by virtue of Section 13 of the Criminal Procedure Act, 1967 or subsequent statutes be sentenced, with the consent of the Director of Public Prosecutions, in that Court. The maximum sentence which may be imposed on such a plea of guilty corresponds to the maximum sentence which may be imposed if the accused is convicted after a summary trial. Offences in respect of which a plea of guilty may not be accepted and bail may not be allowed in the District Court, and in respect of which the Circuit Court has no jurisdiction are marked §.

5. *Minor Offences*

A person charged with an indictable offence may be tried summarily in the District Court if the Justice is satisfied that the offence is of a minor nature, and if the accused, and, in certain cases the Director of Public Prosecutions, consent. In some cases the consent of the Director is only required if the value of the property involved exceeds a certain amount, usually £200. Such cases are covered by section 4 of the Criminal Justice Act, 1951, as amended by section 19 of the Criminal Procedure Act, 1967 or by earlier or later statutes dealing with specific offences. The maximum sentence in such cases is determined by the relevant statute. Such cases are marked,* or (if consent of the Director is required)**, or if such consent is only required where the value exceeds a certain amount (£200 unless otherwise stated)**†.

6. *Alternative Verdicts*

By virtue of section 9 of the Criminal Procedure Act, 1851, a person charged with a complete offence may be convicted of an attempt to commit the offence, if commission of the complete offence is not proved. In addition the accused may in general be convicted at common law of a lesser common law offence the ingredients of which are charged in the indictment, if some further or aggravating ingredient of the offence charged is not established. Only the cases of such lesser verdicts, and various alternative verdicts provided by specific statutes, are indicated in the Table.

Offence	How created	Whether Felony or Misdemeanour	Maximum Sentence [Alternative Verdicts] [See Prelim. Note 6]
ABDUCTION – see also *KIDNAPPING*			
of child under 14	Offences against the Person Act, 1861, s. 56	F	7 yrs P.S. or 2 yrs
of girl under 16	Id. s. 55	M	2 yrs
of girl under 18	Criminal Law Amendment Act, 1885, s. 7	M	Same
of woman on account of her fortune	Offences against the Person Act, 1861, s. 53	F	14 yrs P.S. or 2 yrs
of woman by force with intent, etc.	Id. s. 54	F	Same
ABORTION			
procuring a miscarriage	Offences against the Person Act, 1861, s. 58	M	P.S. life or 2 yrs
supplying poison or instruments	Id. s. 59	M	5 yrs P.S. or 2 yrs
ADMINISTRATION OF JUSTICE – see *COURTS*			
AFFRAY – see *OFFENCES AGAINST THE STATE* etc.			
AIDING AND ABETTING etc (see also specific headings)			
any felony	Accessories and Abettors Act, 1861, s. 1	F	As principal offender
any misdemeanour	Id. s. 8	M	Same
accessory after the fact of felony	Id. ss. 3, 4	F	2 yrs
aiding etc. offence in or escape from Northern Ireland	Criminal Law (Jurisdiction) Act, 1976, ss. 2 (2), (3), 3		As principal offender
AIRCRAFT			
breach of restrictions on air services	Air Navigation and Transport Act, 1965, s. 12 (2)		6m and/or £1000 *S.C. 6m and/or £100*
unlawful seizure of aircraft or committing indictable act of violence against person on board	Air Navigation and Transport Act, 1973, ss. 11, 16		Life[1]
act of violence, damage etc. to aircraft, or communication of false information	Air Navigation and Transport Act, 1975, ss. 3, 6		Life[1]

[1] No probation or suspension.

ANIMALS – see also *LARCENY, MALICIOUS DAMAGE, WILD LIFE*			
killing with intent to steal (if stealing felonious)	Larceny Act, 1916, s. 4	F	14yrs P.S. *S.C. 12m and/or £100***†*
interference etc. with ear-tag	Diseases of Animals Act, 1966, s. 48 as amended by Bovine Diseases (Levies) Act, 1979, s. 23		2 yrs and/or £2,000 *S.C. 6m and/or £500*
falsification of licence, etc.	Id. s. 49 (as so amended)		Same
other breaches of regulations etc. under Diseases of Animals Acts, 1966 and 1979	Id. ss. 48 and 49 (as so amended)		1 yr and/or £1,000 *S.C. 6m and/or £500*
ARSON – see *MALICIOUS DAMAGE*			
ASSAULT – see also *MURDER, SEXUAL OFFENCES*			
common	Common law, and Offences against the Person Act, 1861, s. 42, Criminal Justice Act, 1951, s. 11	M	1 yr *S.C. 6m or £50*
occasioning actual bodily harm	Common law, and Offences against the Person Act, 1861, s. 47	M	5 yrs P.S. or 2yrs *S.C. 12m/or £100** [Common assault (common law)]
with intent to resist arrest etc.	Offences against the Person Act, 1861, s. 38	M	2yrs *S.C. 12m and/or £100*** [same]
upon a peace officer	Id.	M	Same [same]
with intent to rob	Larceny Act, 1916, s. 23; Criminal Law (Jurisdiction) Act, 1976, s. 5	F	Life
wounding or causing grievous bodily harm with intent	Offences against the Person Act, 1861, s. 18	F	P.S. life or 2 yrs [Unlawful wounding if wounding charged (common law)]
by explosives	Id. s. 28	F	Same
malicious wounding, etc.	Id. s. 20	F	5yrs P.S. or 2 yrs [Common assault (common law)]

Offence	How created	Whether Felony or Misdemeanour	Maximum Sentence [Alternative Verdicts] [See Prelim. Note 6]
shooting etc. at customs officer[2]	Customs (Consolidation) Act, 1876, s. 193	F	Same
by poacher at night	Night Poaching Act, 1828, s. 2	M	7 yrs P.S. or 2 yrs
ATTEMPT – see also *SEXUAL OFFENCES* and specific headings			
to commit any crime not otherwise specified	Common law	M	Imp. and/or fine[3] *S.C. 12m and/or £100**
to choke, etc.	Offences against the Person Act, 1861, s. 21	F	P.S. life or 2 yrs
to poison, shoot, drown etc. with intent to murder	Id. s. 14	F	Same
to pervert the course of justice	Common law	M	Imp. and/or fine *S.C. 12m and/or £100***
BANKING			
unlawfully carrying on banking business	Central Bank Act, 1971, s. 7		£5,000+£250 a day if continuing
unlawful use by building and other societies of "bank" etc.	Id. s. 14		Same
failure to keep records	Id. s. 17		Same
to furnish information	Id. s. 18		Same
to publish financial statement	Id. s. 19		Same
to display the like	Id. s. 20		Same
offences relating to collection of cheques etc.	Id. s. 26		Same
unlawful advertising for deposits	Id. s. 27		Same
failure to notify cesser of business	Id. s. 31		Same
offences relating to transfer of licences	Id. s. 33		Same
breach of conditions of licence	Id. s. 58		Same
failure to comply with directions	Id.		Same
contravening regulation	Id.		Same
BANKRUPTCY – see also *COURTS*			
inserting advertisement without authority	Irish Bankrupt and Insolvent Act, 1857, s. 396	M	Imp. and/or fine

[2] Three year limitation on prosecution, s. 257.

[3] Not to exceed penalty for substantive offence.

giving false evidence	Id. s. 383	M	As for perjury
obstructing Court Messenger	Id. 389	M	6m
frauds by bankrupts, etc.	Debtors (Ireland) Act, 1872, s. 11	M	2 yrs
fraudulent transfers, etc. and concealment of property	Id. s. 13 (2) – (4)	M	1 yr *S.C. 12m and/or £100*
absconding with property	Id. s. 12	F	2 yrs
false claim by creditor	Id. s. 14	M	1 yr
acting as company director when bankrupt	Companies Act, 1963, s. 183 (as amended, Companies Act, 1982, s. 15)		2 yrs and/or £2,500 *S.C. 6m and/or £500*
taking part in affairs of Industrial Society when bankrupt	Industrial and Provident Societies (Amendment) Act, 1978, ss. 3, 28		3 yrs and/or £5,000 +£250 a day continuing *S.C. 6m and/or £500*
BARRATRY	Common law	M	Imp. or fine
BIGAMY	Offences against the Person Act, 1861, s. 57	F	7 yrs P.S. or 2 yrs
BLACKMAIL			
demanding with menaces or accusing with intent to extort etc.	Larceny Act, 1916, s. 29	F	P.S. life or 2 yrs *S.C. 12m and/or £100***†
demanding with intent to steal	Id. s. 30	F	5 yrs P.S. or 2 yrs *S.C. as last*
threatening to publish with intent to extort etc.	Id. s. 31	M	2 yrs *S.C. as last*
BLASPHEMY – see also *LIBEL*			
generally	Common law	M	Imp. and/or fine
BRIBERY – see *CORRUPTION*			
BROADCASTING			
unlawful broadcasting from ship	Broadcasting (Offences) Act, 1968, s. 7		2 yrs and/or £500 *S.C. 3m and/or £100*
sending indecent, etc. and false messages	Wireless Telegraphy Act, 1926, s. 11	M	12m *S.C. 1m and/or £10**
BROTHELS – see *PROSTITUTION*			
BUGGERY – see *SEXUAL OFFENCES*			

Offence	How created	Whether Felony or Misdemeanour	Maximum Sentence [Alternative Verdicts] [See Prelim. Note 6]
BUILDING SOCIETIES – see also *BANKING*			
contravention of statutory requirements or regulations	Building Societies Act, 1976, s. 92		£5,000+£250 a day continuing *S.C. £100*
BURGLARY			
entering with intent	Larceny Act, 1916, s. 23A (1) (a) as inserted by Criminal Law (Jurisdiction) Act, 1976, ss. 6, 20 (8)	F	14 yrs *S.C. 12m and/or £100**
stealing or causing bodily harm, having entered as a trespasser	Id. s. 23A (1) (b) as so inserted	F	Same
aggravated burglary	Larceny Act, 1916, s. 23B and Criminal Law (Jurisdiction) Act, 1976, ss. 7, 20 (8)	F	Life *S.C. 12m and/or £100**
CASUAL TRADING			
unauthorised trading	Casual Trading Act, 1980, s. 3 (4), 15 (1)		6m and/or £5,000+ £250 a day continuing *S.C. £500***
CAUSING GRIEVOUS BODILY HARM see – *ASSAULT*			
CHAMPERTY	Common law		Imp. or fine
CHEATING			
at gaming	Gaming and Lotteries Act, 1956, s. 11, Criminal Justice Act, 1951, s. 10	M	5 yrs P.S. or 2 yrs *S.C. 12m and/or £100**
CHILDREN – see also *ABDUCTION, SEXUAL OFFENCES*			
abandonment or exposure of child under 2	Offences against the Person Act, 1861, s. 27	M	5yrs P.S. or 2 yrs† †
allowing child aged 4 and under 17 to be in a brothel	Children Act, 1908, s. 16	M	6m and/or £25 *S.C. same*
cruelty to child by person over 17	Id. s. 12	M	2 yrs and/or £100 *S.C. 6m and/or £25*

the like by person with financial interest	Id. s. 12 (5)	M	5 yrs P.S. or 2 yrs, or £200
COINAGE – see *CURRENCY*			
COMPANIES – see also *BANKRUPTCY*			
false statement on reconstitution of records	Companies (Reconstitution of Records) Act, 1924, s. 8	M	2 yrs and/or £100 *S.C. 6m or £50*
false statement in prospectus	Companies Act, 1963, s. 50 (1) (as amended, Companies Act, 1982, s. 15)		2 yrs and/or £2,500 *S.C. 6m and/or £500*
in statement in lieu of prospectus	Id. s. 35 (5)		Same
issuing shares without delivery of such statement	Id. s. 54 (5)		Same
giving financial assistance for purchase of shares	Id. s. 60 (15)		Same
personation of shareholder	Id. s. 90		Same
acting as director when prohibited by conviction	Id. s. 184 (5)		Same
offences by officer of company in liquidation	Id. s. 293 (1)		5 yrs P.S. or 2 yrs and/or £5,000 *S.C. 6m and/or £500*
falsification of books of such company	Id. s. 294		2 yrs and/or £2,500 *S.C. 6m and/or £500*
fraud by officer of such company	Id. s. 295		Same
failure to keep proper books of account	Id. s. 296		Same
fraudulent trading	Id. s. 297		Same
unlawful issue of prospectus for foreign company	Id. s. 365		Same
false statements in returns etc. required under 10th Schedule to Act	Id. s. 380		3 yrs and/or £2,500 *S.C. 6m and/or £500*
failure to produce books	Id. s. 168 (as amended, Companies Act, 1982, s. 7)		3 yrs and/or £5000 *S.C. 6m and/or £500*
keeping fraudulent accounts	Larceny Act, 1861, s. 82	M	7 yrs P.S. or 2 yrs *S.C. 6m and/or £100**
destruction, etc. of books	Id. s. 83	M	Same
fraudulent statements	Id. s. 84	M	Same
COMPOUNDING FELONY	Common law	M	Imp. and/or fine
CONCEALMENT OF BIRTH	Offences against the Person Act, 1861, s. 60	M	2 yrs *S.C. 12m and/or £100**

Offence	How created	Whether Felony or Misdemeanour	Maximum Sentence [Alternative Verdicts] [See Prelim. Note 6]
CONSPIRACY – see also *SPECIFIC OFFENCES*			
to commit a crime or legal wrong	Common law	M	Imp. and/or fine[4]
CONTEMPT – see *COURTS*			
CONTINENTAL SHELF			
construction etc. of structure in designated area	Continental Shelf Act, 1968, s. 5		Fine *S.C. £100*
unlawful discharge of oil	Id. s. 7		Same
unlawful entry into designated area	Id. s. 6		12m and/or fine *S.C. 3m and/or £100*
CONTRACEPTIVES – see also *FORGERY*			
unauthorised sale or supply[5]	Health (Family Planning) Act, 1979, ss. 4, 14		12m and/or £5,000 – £250 a day continuing *S.C. 6m and/or £500***
unauthorised importation[5]	Id. ss. 5, 14		Same
unauthorised manufacture[5]	Id. ss. 6, 14		Same
unauthorised advertising[5]	Id. ss. 7, 14		Same
breach of family planning regulations[5]	Id. ss. 3, 14		Same
COPYRIGHT			
unauthorised making, etc. of films	Performers' Protection Act, 1968, s. 3 (1)		£2,000 *S.C. £5, per 50 foot of film up to £100*
issue of film without consent	Id. s. 3 (5)		£2,000 *S.C. £100*
unauthorised making, etc. of records	Id. s. 2		£2,000 *S.C. £5 per record up to £100*
CORPSES			
leaving unburied, sale, unauthorised exhumation, etc.	Common law	M	Imp. and/or fine
CORROSIVES			
throwing, etc. with intent to burn, etc.	Offences against the Person Act, 1861, s. 29	F	P.S. life or 2 yrs

[4] Not normally to exceed penalty for substantive offence, supra p. 398. [5] Second or subsequent offence.

CORRUPTION			
by or of agents[6]	Prevention of Corruption Act, 1906, s. 1	M	2 yrs and/or £500 *S.C. 4m and/or £50*
by or of members, etc. of public bodies[6]	Public Bodies Corrupt Practices Act, 1889, ss. 1, 2	M	2 yrs and/or £500
either of above in relation to public contracts	Prevention of Corruption Act, 1916, s. 1		7 yrs P.S. or 2 yrs
bribery of public officials, etc.	Common law	M	Imp. and/or fine
COURTS			
scandalising the Court	Common law	M	Imp. and/or fine
prejudicing fair trial	Id.	M	Same
misconduct by officer of justice	Id.	M	Same
obstructing Court Officers, etc.	Enforcement of Court Orders Act, 1926, s. 24	M	12m and/or £100 *S.C. 6m and/or £50**
obstructing Court Messengers	Irish Bankrupt and Insolvent Act, 1857, s. 389	M	6m
CREDIT – see *FALSE PRETENCES*			
CREDIT UNIONS – see *INDUSTRIAL SOCIETIES*			
CURRENCY – see also *FORGERY*			
colouring, etc. coins	Coinage Act, 1861, s. 3 (as applied by Decimal Currency Act, 1969, s. 22, 2 sch.)	F	P.S. life or 2 yrs
conveying tools out of mint	Id. s. 25	F	Same
counterfeiting Irish silver coins	Id. s. 2	F	Same
copper coins	Id. s. 14	F	7 yrs P.S. or 2 yrs
foreign gold of silver coins	Id. s. 18	F	Same
other foreign coins	Id. s. 22	M	1 yr
second offence		M	7 yrs P.S. or 2 yrs
dealing in Irish silver coins below face value	Id. s. 6	F	P.S. life or 2 yrs
dealing in copper coins below face value	Id. s. 14	F	7 yrs P.S. or 2 yrs
defacing Irish coins	Id. s. 16	M	1 yr
exporting counterfeit Irish coins	Id. s. 8	M	2 yrs
importing counterfeit foreign coins	Id. s. 19	F	7 yrs P.S. or 2 yrs

[6] No prosecution without consent of D.P.P.

Offence	How created	Whether Felony or Misdemeanour	Maximum Sentence [Alternative Verdicts] [See Prelim. Note 6]
impairing Irish silver coins	Id. s. 4	F	14 yrs P.S. or 2 yrs
making, etc. or possession of tools for gold or silver or foreign coins	Id. s. 24	F	P.S. life or 2 yrs
making copper coins	Id. s. 14	F	7 yrs P.S. or 2 yrs
making medals resembling gold or silver coins	Counterfeit Medals Act, 1883, s. 2	M	1 yr
possession of 3 or more Irish silver counterfeit coins	Coinage Act, 1861, s. 11	M	5 yrs P.S. or 2 yrs
possession, second offence	Id. s. 12	F	P.S. life or 2 yrs
possession of filings, etc.	Id. s. 5	F	7 yrs P.S. or 2 yrs
uttering the like	Id. s. 9	M	1 yr
uttering the like, second offence	Id. s. 12	F	P.S. life or 2 yrs
uttering and possession of or uttering like silver coins within 10 days	Id. s. 10	M	2 yrs
uttering or possession, etc. second offence	Id. s. 12	F	P.S. life or 2 yrs
uttering spurious Irish silver coins or medals	Id. s. 13	M	1 yr
uttering copper coins	Id. s. 15	M	1 yr
uttering foreign gold or silver coins	Id. s. 20	M	6m
uttering foreign gold, etc. second offence	Id. s. 21	M	2 yrs
possession of bank-note paper, etc.	Forgery Act, 1913, s. 9	F	7 yrs P.S. or 2 yrs
purchasing, etc. of paper for treasury bills, etc.	Id. s. 10	M	2 yrs
unauthorised making, etc. of decimal coins	Decimal Currency Act, 1969, s. 14		£500 *S.C. £100*
melting down, etc, of decimal coins	Id. s. 15		2 yrs and/or £500 *S.C. 12m and/or £100*
unauthorised dealing with gold and foreign currency	Exchange Control Act, 1954,[7] ss. 4, 20 (5)		2 yrs and/or £5,000+ £50 a day if continuing *S.C. 6m and/or £500+* £10 a day continuing
unauthorised payments etc. to person outside or within scheduled territories	Id. ss. 5, 6, 20 (5)		Same
unauthorised issue etc. of securities	Id. ss. 8-14, 20 (5)		Same

[7] In force until 31st December, 1986, Exchange Control (Continuance) Act, 1982, s. 1.

unlawful import of securities, etc.	Id. ss. 15, 20 (4) (as amended, Exchange Control (Continuance and Amendment) Act, 1978, s. 4		Same
unlawful export of gold, securities, etc.	Id. ss. 16, 20 (5) (as amended, 1978, s. 5)		Same
unlawful export of goods	Id. ss. 17, 20 (5)		Same
CUSTOMS OFFENCES[8] – see also *ASSAULT, EMBEZZLEMENT*			
fraudulent entries, etc.	Customs Consolidation Act, 1876, s. 67, as amended Finance Act, 1963, s. 34 (4), Finance Act, 1976, s. 44		treble value of goods *S.C. the like up to £500*
removal etc. of goods from warehouse, etc.	Id. s. 85	M	2 yrs
claiming drawback unlawfully	Id. s. 106 (as so amended)[9]		treble amount of draw-back, *S.C. the like up to £500*
claiming drawback on tobacco fraudulently	Id. s. 108 as so amended		Same
failure to export, etc.	Id. s. 120 as so amended		treble value of goods *S.C. the like up to £500*
unlawful relanding of stores	Id. s. 126 as so amended		Same
unlawful non-shipment or unshipment	Id. s. 130 as so amended		Same
illegal importation, unshipment, removal from quay, carrying into or removing from warehouse, harbouring etc. or carriage of uncustomed goods, or evasion of duty	Id. s. 186 as so amended		Same
procuring assembly for smuggling	Id. s. 189		12m
the like, when armed	Id.		3 yrs
signalling to smuggling vessel	Id. s. 190	M	1 yr or £100
shooting at revenue vessel or officer	Id. s. 193	F	5 yrs P.S. or 2 yrs
offering pretended smuggled goods for sale	Id. s. 201 as so amended		treble value of goods *S.C. the like, up to £500*
bringing consumer goods into airport	Customs Free Airport Act, 1947, s. 6		Same
DANGEROUS DRIVING			
causing bodily harm by furious driving	Offences against the Person Act, 1861, s. 35	M	2 yrs
dangerous driving causing death or serious bodily harm	Road Traffic Act, 1961, s. 53 (2)		5 yrs P.S. or 2 yrs and/or £500

[8] Time limit for prosecution, three years, Customs (Consolidation) Act, 1876, s. 257. [9] See also Finance Act, 1935, s. 11 (3).

Offence	How created	Whether Felony or Misdemeanour	Maximum Sentence [Alternative Verdicts] [See Prelim. Note 6]
DEFAMATION – see *LIBEL*			
DEFENCE FORCES – see also *ESCAPE*			
members of Reserve joining foreign forces	Defence Act, 1954, s. 241	M	2 yrs
incitement to disaffection, or possession of subversive document	Id. s. 254	M	Same
obstruction of police by officer	Id. s. 109	M	Same
DROWNING – see *ATTEMPT*			
DRUGS – see also *FORGERY*			
Possession of controlled drug other than cannabis[10]	Misuse of Drugs Act, 1977, ss. 3, 27 (1) (b)		7 yrs and/or £1,500 *S.C. 12m and/or £250*
Contravening direction as to prescribing, etc. drugs	Id. ss. 6, 7, 27 (2)		14 yrs and/or £3,000 *S.C. 12m and/or £500*
possession of controlled drug for sale or supply[10]	Id. ss. 15, 27 (2)		Same
smoking opium, etc.[10]	Id. ss. 16, 27 (4)		Same
cultivation of opium, etc.[10]	Id. ss. 17, 27 (5)		Same
permitting unlawful drug activities on premises, etc.	Id. ss. 19, 27 (7)		Same
aiding or abetting commission of a drug offence outside the State	Id. ss. 20 (1), 27 (8)		Same
attempting, etc. to commit drug offence	Id. ss. 21, 27 (9)		As for substantive offence
contravening drug regulations	Id. ss. 21 (2), 27 (10)		14 yrs and/or £3,000 or 2 yrs and/or £500, depending on nature of regulation. *S.C. 12m and/or £250 or 6m and/or £100*
administering with intent to facilitate offence	Offences against the Person Act, 1861, s. 22	F	P.S. life or 2 yrs

[10] As to remand for report, see s. 28.

procuring carnal knowledge by drugs, etc.	Criminal Law Amendment Act, 1885, s. 3 as amended by Criminal Law Amendment Act, 1935, s. 8	M	2 yrs
DUELS			
challenging to a duel	Common law	M	Imp. and/or fine
ELECTIONS			
personation (second offence)[11]	Prevention of Electoral Abuses Act, 1923, s. 6 (2)		3 yrs P.S. or 6m to 12m and £200 *S.C. 6 to 12m and £100*
injuring ballot boxes etc. and papers, etc.[11]	Id. s. 46		5 yrs P.S. or 2 yrs *S.C. 12m*
European Assembly	European Assembly Elections Act, 1981, Sch. rr. 41, 91		2 yrs and/or £1,000
corrupt withdrawal, etc. of petition	Local Elections (Petitions and Disqualifications) Act, 1974, s. 10		3m and/or £300
ELECTRICITY – see also *LARCENY, MALICIOUS DAMAGE*			
abstracting, etc.	Larceny Act, 1916, s. 10	F	As simple larceny
malicious damage to wires, etc.	Electricity Supply Act, 1927, s. 111	F	5 yrs P.S. or 2 yrs
EMBEZZLEMENT			
generally	Larceny Act, 1916, s. 17	F	14 yrs P.S. or 2 yrs *S.C. 12m and/or £100**†*
by officer of Bank of Ireland	Bank of Ireland Act, 1781/82, s. 16		7 yrs P.S. or 2 yrs
of goods in customs warehouse[12]	Customs Consolidation Act, 1876, s. 85	M	Imp or fine
by Post Office official of postal packet containing money	Larceny Act, 1916, s. 18	F	P.S. life or 2 yrs *S.C. 12m and/or £100**†*
the like	Post Office Act, 1908, s. 55	F	P.S. life or 2 yrs
EMBRACERY	Common law	M	Imp. or fine

[11] One or two years limitation on prosecution, s. 52.
[12] Three years limitation on prosecution, s. 257.

Offence	How created	Whether Felony or Misdemeanour	Maximum Sentence [Alternative Verdicts] [See Prelim. Note 6]
EMPLOYMENT			
dismissal for opposing discrimination, etc.	Employment Equality Act, 1981, s. 25		£1,000 and ancillary relief against employers
interference with investigation by Employment Equality Agency	Id. s. 42		£1,000 and order to comply
continued non-compliance with employment agreement	Industrial Relations Act, 1969, s. 10		£100+£10 a day continuing *S.C. £100*
obstruction of equal pay officer	Anti-Discrimination (Pay) Act, 1974, s. 6 (4)		£1,000 *S.C. £100*
wrongful dismissal of woman	Id. s. 9		£1,000 and arrears *S.C. £200 and arrears*
neglecting to provide food, etc. or injuring servant	Offences against the Person Act, 1861, s. 26	M	5 yrs P.S. or 2 yrs *S.C. 12m and/or £20*
the like	Conspiracy and Protection of Property Act, 1875, s. 6	M	6m or £20 *S.C. same*
ESCAPE			
generally	Common law	M	Imp. and/or fine
breaking gaol by force, with intent	Tumultuous Risings (Ireland) Act, 1831, s. 4		P.S. life or 2 yrs
rescuing convict	Id. s. 5		Same
aiding and abetting above	Id. s. 6		7 yrs P.S. or 2 yrs
assisting prisoner in military prison to escape	Defence Act, 1954, s. 234	F	2 yrs imp.
prisoner of war or enemy alien to escape, etc.	Prisoners of War and Enemy Aliens Act, 1956, s. 8		7 yrs P.S. or 2 yrs
aiding, etc. escape from lawful custody	Criminal Law Act, 1976, s. 6 (1)		10 yrs
from lawful custody in Northern Ireland	Criminal Law (Jurisdiction) Act, 1976, s. 3		7 yrs
allowing prisoner to escape	Common law	M	Imp. and/or fine
EXCHANGE CONTROL – see *CURRENCY*			
EXPLOSIVES – see also *POST OFFICE*			
causing explosions likely to endanger life or property[13]	Explosive Substances Act, 1883, s. 2 (as amended by Criminal Law (Jurisdiction) Act, 1976, ss. 4, 20 (8))	F	Life

[13] No prosecution without consent of D.P.P.

doing act with intent, or conspiracy, to cause explosions, making or possessing explosives with intent[13]	Id. s. 3 (as so amended)	F	20 yrs
making or possessing under suspicious circumstances[13]	Explosive Substances Act, 1883, s. 4	F	14 yrs P.S. or 2 yrs
causing bodily injury by	Offences against the Person Act, 1861, s. 28	F	P.S. life or 2 yrs
placing near building, etc. with intent to injure	Id. s. 30	F	14 yrs P.S. or 2 yrs
using, sending, etc. with intent to injure	Id. s. 29	F	P.S. life or 2 yrs
attempting to blow up dwelling-house, etc.	Malicious Damage Act, 1861, s. 9	F	Same
placing near building, etc. with intent to damage	Id. s. 10	F	14 yrs P.S. or 2 yrs
manufacturing, etc.	Id. s. 54	M	2 yrs
placing near ships	Id. s. 45	F	14 yrs P.S. or 2 yrs
EXTORTION – see *BLACKMAIL*			
FALSE IMPRISONMENT	Common law and Criminal Law Act, 1976, s. 11	F	Life
FALSE INFORMATION	Criminal Law Act, 1976, s. 12		5 yrs *S.C. 12m and/or £500*
FALSE PRETENCES			
obtaining money, etc.	Larceny Act, 1916, ss. 32, 37, Criminal Justice Act, 1951, s. 10	M	5 yrs P.S. or 2 yrs *S.C. 12m and/or £100** [No acquittal if larceny proved, Larceny Act, 1916, s. 44 (4)]
obtaining credit by false pretences or fraud	Debtors Act (Ireland), 1872, s. 13 (1)	M	1 yr *S.C. 12m and/or £100**
FALSIFICATION OF ACCOUNTS – see also *COMPANIES, FORGERY*			
by clerk or servant	Falsification of Accounts Act, 1875, s. 1	M	7 yrs P.S. or 2 yrs *S.C. 12m and/or £100**
FAMILY HOMES			
giving false information	Family Home Protection Act, 1976, s. 15		5 yrs *S.C. 12m and/or £200*

[13] No prosecution without consent of D.P.P.

Offence	How created	Whether Felony or Misdemeanour	Maximum Sentence [Alternative Verdicts] [See Prelim. Note 6]
FIRE SERVICES			
offences relating to fire precautions, notices, regulations, etc.	Fire Services Act, 1981, ss. 18 (2), 20, 37		2 yrs and/or £10,000 *S.C. 6m and/or £500***
FIREARMS			
carrying with intent	Firearms Act, 1964, s. 27B and Criminal Law (Jurisdiction) Act, 1976, s. 9		10 yrs
possession without certificate	Firearms Act, 1925, s. 2 (2), Firearms (Amendment) Act, 1971, s. 3		5 yrs and/or £500 *S.C. 1 yr and/or £200*
possession when taking vehicle without authority	Firearms Act, 1964, s. 26, Criminal Law (Jurisdiction) Act, 1976, s. 21 (6)		7 yrs
possession with intent to injure	Firearms Act, 1925, s. 15, Criminal Law (Jurisdiction) Act, 1976, s. 21 (4)		14 yrs
use to resist arrest, etc.	Firearms Act, 1964, s. 27 inserted by Criminal Law (Jurisdiction) Act, 1976, s. 21 (6)		Same
possession in suspicious circumstances	Firearms Act, 1964, s. 27A, inserted by Criminal Law (Jurisdiction) Act, 1976, s. 8		5 yrs
manufacture, etc. of prohibited weapons	Firearms Act, 1925, s. 14	M	5 yrs P.S. or 2 yrs
manufacture and sale	Id. s. 10		2 yrs and/or £100 *S.C. 6m and/or £50*
export	Id. s. 16		Same
FISHERIES			
(For brevity the Fisheries (Consolidation) Act, 1959, Fisheries (Amendment) Act, 1964, Fisheries (Amendment) Act, 1978 and Fisheries Act, 1980, are referred to by the year of enactment. For details of forfeiture, see relevant sections.)			
unlawful entry by foreign sea-fishing boat within exclusive fishery limits[14]	1959, s. 221, 1978, ss. 5, 2		£10,000, discretionary forfeiture *S.C. £500***
failure of like to leave exclusive limits, etc.[14]	1959, s. 222, 1978, ss. 6, 2		Same

[14] Prosecution on indictment by Attorney General instead of D.P.P., 1978, s. 18 (2).

fishing on board the like within exclusive limits[14]	1959, s. 222A, 1978, ss. 7, 2	£10,000 and forfeiture
breach of bye-law as to fishing methods within exclusive limits[14]	1959, s. 223, 1978, ss. 8, 2	£10,000 and forfeiture *S.C. £500 and forfeiture***
breach of conservation order[14]	1959, s. 223A, 1978, ss. 9, 2	Same
breach of order as to carriage of nets[14]	1959, s. 226, 1978, ss. 22, 2	Same
breach of order as to carriage of obstructive devices, etc.[14]	1959, s. 227, 1978, ss. 22, 2	Same
using unlicensed engine for salmon, trout or eels[15]	1959, s. 65, 1980, ss. 46, 50	2 yrs and/or £2,000 *S.C. £500*
fishing for salmon by unlicensed person	1959, s. 66, 1980, ss. 46, 50	Same
unlawful use of non-scheduled engine[15]	1959, s. 69, 1980, ss. 46, 50	2 yrs and/or £2,000 and £100 per day continuing *S.C. £500 and £50 per day continuing up to £600 in all, and forfeiture*
using unlicensed engine for salmon or trout in tidal waters	1959, s. 73, 1980, ss. 46, 50	2 yrs and/or £2,000 *S.C. £500*
use of salmon nets at mouth of river, etc.	1959, s. 94, 1980, ss. 46, 50	2 yrs and/or £2,000 *S.C. £500 and £50 per salmon and £10 other fish caught up to £600 in all*
unlawful use of net in freshwater	1959, s. 95, 1980, ss. 46, 50	2 yrs and/or £2,000 and forfeiture *S.C. 6m and/or £500*
unlawful possession of net	1959, s. 96, 1980, ss. 46, 50	Same
using uncertificated engine for salmon[15]	1959, s. 97, 1980, ss. 46, 50	Same
unlawful fishing for salmon or trout in close season[15]	1959, s. 127, 1980, ss. 46, 50	2 yrs and/or £2,000 and forfeiture *S.C. £500 and £50 per salmon and £10 other fish up to £600 in all*

[15] As to jurisdiction, see Fisheries (Amendment) Act, 1980, s. 47.

Offence	How created	Whether Felony or Misdemeanour	Maximum Sentence [Alternative Verdicts] [See Prelim. Note 6]
failure to dismantle fixed engine in close season	1959, s. 128, 1980, ss. 46, 50		2 yrs and/or £2,000 and £100 per day continuing and forfeiture *S.C. £500 and £50 a day up to £600 in all and forfeiture*
failure to dismantle salmon weir, etc. in close season	1959, s. 129, 1980, ss. 46, 50		Same
failure to remove nets in close season	1959, s. 130, 1980, ss. 46, 50		2 yrs and/or £2,000 and £100 per day continuing and forfeiture *S.C. £500*
use of nets in close season	1959, s. 132, 1980, ss. 46, 50		2 yrs and/or £2,000 and *S.C. 6m and/or £500 and forfeiture*
buying, etc. or possession of salmon or trout in close season	1959, s. 134, 1980, ss. 46, 50		2 yrs and/or £2,000 and forfeiture *S.C. £50 per salmon and £10 other fish up to £600 in all, and forfeiture*
unlawful export of salmon	1959, s. 135, 1980, ss. 46, 50		Same
angling for salmon in close season	1959, s. 137, 1980, ss. 46, 50		Same
unlawful fishing for salmon or trout in weekly close time	1959, s. 140, 1980, ss. 46, 50		2 yrs and/or £2,000 and forfeiture *S.C. £500*
scaring, etc. the like in weekly close time	1959, s. 145, 1980, ss. 46, 50		Same
use of nets in weekly close time	1959, s. 146, 1980, ss. 46, 50		Same
unlawful sale, etc. of salmon or trout	1950, s. 156		2 years and/or £2,000 *S.C. 6m and/or £500 and £50 salmon and £10*

		other fish up to £600 in all
the like Foyle Area	Foyle Fisheries Act, 1952, s. 35, Foyle Fisheries (Amendment) Act, 1983, ss. 2, 3	Same
use or possession of deleterious matters	1959, s. 164, 1962, s. 16, 1980, s. 50	2 yrs and/or £2,000 and forfeiture *S.C. 6m and/or £500 and forfeiture*
taking, etc. unseasonable salmon or trout	1959, s. 176, 1980, ss. 46, 50; cf. Foyle Fisheries Act, 1952, s. 49, Foyle Fisheries (Amendment) Act, 1983, ss. 2, 3	2 yrs and/or £2,000 and forfeiture *S.C. 6m and/or £500 and £50 per salmon and £10 other fish up to £600 in all and forfeiture*
export of unseasonable salmon	1959, s. 177, 1980, ss. 46, 50	Same
purchasing, etc. or possession of unseasonable or unlawfully captured salmon or trout	1959, s. 182, 1980, ss. 46, 50	Same
unlawful use of boat or vehicle	1959, s. 225A, 1962, s. 24, 1980, s. 50	2 yrs and/or £2,000 *S.C. 6m and/or £500*
unlawful purchase of salmon or trout	1962, s. 28, 1980, ss. 46, 50	2 yrs and/or £2,000 and £50 per salmon and £10 per trout and forfeiture *S.C. £200 and £50 per salmon and £10 per trout up to £600 in all and forfeiture*
unlawful fishing for salmon at sea, etc.	1962, s. 29, 1980, ss. 46, 50	2 yrs and/or £2,000 and forfeiture of fish and gear *S.C. 6m and/or £500 and forfeiture*
FORCIBLE ENTRY – see also *AIRCRAFT*		
forcible entry of land or vehicle	Prohibition of Forcible Entry and Occupation Act, 1971, ss. 2, 7	3 yrs and/or £500 *S.C. 6m and/or £50; subs. offence 12m and/or £100*

Offence	How created	Whether Felony or Misdemeanour	Maximum Sentence [Alternative Verdicts] [See Prelim. Note 6]
occupation of the like	Id. s. 3, 7		Same
encouraging either of above	Id. s. 4, 7		Same
forcible entry on land	Forcible Entry Act, 1381	M	Imp. and/or fine
forcible taking, etc. in numbers	Forcible Entry Act, 1786, s. 4	F	7 yrs P.S.
FORGERY – see also *COMPANIES, CURRENCY*			
unspecified documents	Forgery Act, 1913, s. 4	M	2 yrs *S.C. 12m and/or £100**
wills, deeds, etc. or bank notes	Id. s. 2 (1)	F	P.S. life or 2 yrs *S.C. 12m and/or £100**
valuable securities, etc., documents of title, powers of attorney, etc., insurance policies, charter-parties, etc., official certificates	Id. s. 2 (2)	F	14 yrs P.S. or 2 yrs *S.C. as last*
documents stamped with Great Seal, etc.	Id. s. 3 (1)	F	P.S. life or 2 yrs *S.C. as last*
registers of birth, etc.	Id. s. 3 (2)	F	14 yrs P.S. or 2 yrs *S.C. as last*
official documents	Id. s. 3 (3)	F	7 yrs P.S. or 2 yrs *S.C. as last*
the like	Official Secrets Act, 1963, s. 8		7 yrs P.S. or 2 yrs *S.C. 6m and/or £100*
Bank of Ireland Stock entries	Forgery Act, 1861, s. 5	F	P.S. life or 2 yrs
Bank of Ireland Warrants	Id. s. 6	F	7 yrs P.S.
Great Seal	Forgery Act, 1913, s. 5 (1)	F	P.S. life or 2 yrs *S.C. 12m and/or £100**
registry office, etc. seals	Id. s. 5 (2)	F	14 yrs P.S. or 2 yrs *S.C. as last*
court seals	Id. s. 5 (3)	F	7 yrs P.S. or 2 yrs *S.C. as last*

certain dies other than hallmark	Id. s. 5 (4), 5 (5)	F	14 or 7 yrs P.S. or 2 yrs *S.C. as last*
hallmark dies	Id. s. 5 (4) (b), Hallmarking Act, 1981, s. 13 (1)	F	5 yrs and/or £500 *S.C. 12m and/or £500*
entries in registers of birth, etc.	Forgery Act, 1861, ss. 36, 37	F	P.S. life or 2 yrs
prescription of contraceptives (second offence)	Health (Family Planning) Act, 1979, ss. 8, 14		12m and/or £5,000 *S.C. 6m and/or £500*
prescription for drugs[16]	Misuse of Drugs Act, 1977, ss. 18, 27 (6)		3 yrs and/or £750 *S.C. 6m and/or £100*
Vocational Education certificate	Vocational Education Act, 1930, s. 121	M	2 yrs
Housing Act certificate	Housing (Misc. Prov.) Act, 1979, s. 18 (11), (15)		£10,000 *S.C. £500***
mining, etc, certificate	Mines and Quarries Act, 1965, s. 140		2 yrs and/or £200 *S.C. 3m and/or £100*
of money orders	Post Office Act, 1908, s. 59	F	14 yrs P.S. or 2 yrs
of school attendance certificate	School Attendance Act, 1926, s. 22 (1)	M	2 yrs
of ships documents	Mercantile Marine Act, 1955, ss. 88, 98	M	2 yrs and/or £500
demanding money, etc. on forged document	Forgery Act, 1913, s. 7	F	14 yrs P.S. or 2 yrs *S.C. 12m and/or £100**
possession of forged bank note	Id. s. 8 (1)	F	Same
possession of implements of forgery, etc.	Id. s. 9	F	7 yrs or 2 yrs *S.C. 12m and/or £100**
possession of hall-marking and stamp dies, etc.	Id. s. 8 (2) (a), Hallmarking Act, 1981, s. 13 (2)	F	5 yrs and/or £5,000 *S.C. 12m and/or £500*
possession of certain other dies, etc.	Forgery Act, 1913, s. 8 (2) (a)	F	14 yrs P.S. or 2 yrs *S.C. 12m and/or £100**
uttering forged documents	Forgery Act, 1913, s. 6		As for forgery
forgery, etc. of any trade mark[17]	Merchandise Marks Act, 1887, s. 2		2 yrs and/or fine *S.C. 4m or £20 second offence 6m or £50*
FRAUDULENT CONVERSION			
generally	Larceny Act, 1916, ss. 20, 37	M	7 yrs P.S. or 2 yrs and/or fine *S.C. 12m and/or £100***

[16] As to remand for report, see s. 28.

[17] Time limit for prosecution 3 years or 1 year from discovery of offence, whichever is earlier, s. 15.

Offence	How created	Whether Felony or Misdemeanour	Maximum Sentence [Alternative Verdicts] [See Prelim. Note 6]
by trustee[18]	Id. s. 21	M	Same
by factor	Id. s. 22	M	Same
FRAUDULENT TRADING – see *COMPANIES*			
FUEL			
contravention of order relating to supply, etc.	Fuel (Control of Supplies) Act, 1971, s. 4; Fuel (Control of Supplies) Act, 1982, s. 4		10 yrs and/or £100,000 *S.C. 12m and/or £800*
GAMING – see *CHEATING*			
GENEVA CONVENTIONS			
grave breach of Convention for sick and wounded in the field[19]	Geneva Conventions Act, 1962, s. 3 (1) (a)		In case of wilful killing, P.S. life or 2 yrs. Other cases 14 yrs
the like at sea[19]	Id. s. 3 (1) (b)		Same
grave breach of Convention for prisoners of war[19]	Id. s. 3 (1) (c)		Same
grave breach of Convention as to treatment of civilians in time of war[19]	Id. s. 3 (1) (d)		Same
minor breach of any of above Conventions	Id. s. 4		2 yrs and/or £300 *S.C. 6m and/or £50*
GENOCIDE *[See Prelim. Note 6]*			
killing of any person[20]	Genocide Act, 1973, s. 2 (2) (a)		Life
any other case[20]	Id. s. 2 (2) (b)		14 yrs
GRIEVOUS BODILY HARM – see *ASSAULT*			
HALLMARKS – see *FORGERY, PLATE*			
HIGHWAYS			
obstruction	Common law	M	Imp. and/or fine

[18] Sanction of D.P.P. and of Court, if any, in which civil proceedings pending, required, s. 21.
[19] No proceedings, except remand, without consent of Attorney General.
[20] No proceedings, except remand, without consent of Attorney General.

HIJACKING – see *AIRCRAFT, VEHICLES*			
HOUSEBREAKING – see also *BURGLARY*			
implements, possession at night	Larceny Act, 1916, s. 28	M	5 yrs P.S. or 2 yrs *S.C. 12m and/or £100**
after previous conviction or conviction for felony	Id. s. 28	M	10 yrs P.S. or 2 yrs *S.C. 12m and/or £100**
HOUSING – see also *FORGERY*			
offences relating to certificates of reasonable value, etc.	Housing (Miscellaneous Provisions) Act, 1979, s. 18		£10,000 *S.C. £500***
INCITEMENT – see also specific offencs			
to commit crime	Common law	M	Imp. and/or fine
INDUSTRIAL GRANTS			
false statement to obtain grant	Industrial Grants (Amendment) Act, 1964, s. 4		2 yrs and/or £5,000 *S.C. 6m and/or £100*
INDUSTRIAL TRAINING			
obstruction of An Chomhairle Oiliúna	Industrial Training Act, 1967, ss. 41 (3), 45 (12) (a)		£1,000+£100 a day continuing
INDUSTRIAL SOCIETIES and CREDIT UNIONS – see also *BANKING*			
unlawful acceptance etc. of deposits	Industrial and Provident Societies (Amendment) Act, 1978, ss. 5, 28		3 yrs and/or £5,000 +£250 a day continuing *S.C. 6m and/or £500*
unauthorised raising of funds	Id. ss. 6, 28		Same
unauthorised payments from funds	Id. ss. 7, 28		Same
unauthorised advertising	Id. ss. 8, 28		Same
failure to furnish information	Id. ss. 12, 28		Same
failure by officer to answer inspector or assist D.P.P.	Id. ss. 14, 23, 28		Same
failure to arrange for repayment	Id. ss. 17, 27, 28		Same
failure to keep proper accounts	Id. ss. 29, 28		Same
failure to present annual accounts	Id. ss. 30, 28		Same
taking part when bankrupt or after conviction in affairs of Society	Id. ss. 31, 28		Same

Offence	How created	Whether Felony or Misdemeanour	Maximum Sentence [Alternative Verdicts] [See Prelim. Note 6]
unauthorised issue of withdrawable shares	Id. ss. 32, 28		Same
acceptance by investment company of deposits	Id. ss. 36, 28		Same
INFANTICIDE	Infanticide Act, 1949, s. 1	F	P.S. life or 2 yrs and/or fine. [Concealment of Birth, s. 1 (4), Offences against the Person Act, 1968, s. 60]
KIDNAPPING	Common law and Criminal Law Act, 1861, s. 11	F	Life
LARCENY – see also *ANIMALS, EMBEZZLEMENT, FALSE PRETENCES, ROBBERY* *(as to fines and recognisances, see Larceny Act, 1916, s. 37)*			
simple	Larceny Act, 1916, s. 2	F	5 yrs P.S. or 2 yrs *S.C. 12m and/or £100***† [Embezzlement s. 44 (2), false pretences, s. 44 (3)]
after previous conviction for felony and some other offences	Id. s. 37 (1)	F	10 yrs P.S. or 2 yrs *S.C. 12m and/or £100***†
after previous conviction for certain misdemeanours	Id. s. 37 (2)	F	7 yrs P.S. or 2 yrs *S.C. 12m and/or £100***†
in dwellinghouse	Id. s. 13	F	14 yrs P.S. or 2 yrs *S.C. 12m and/or £100***†
from the person (s.v. *ROBBERY*)	Id. s. 14	F	Same
from ships or in ports, etc.	Id. s. 15	F	Same

by clerk or servant	Id. s. 17	F	Same
by tenant or lodger, over £5	Id. s. 16 (a)	F	7 yrs P.S. or 2 yrs *S.C. 12m and/or £100***†
the like, otherwise	Id. s. 16 (b)	F	2 yrs *S.C. 12m and/or £100***†
of cattle	Id. s. 3	F	14 yrs P.S. or 2 yrs *S.C. 12m and/or £100***†
of dogs, or possession of stolen dogs after previous conviction, etc	Larceny Act, 1916, s. 5	M	18m *S.C. 12m and/or £100***†
of electricity	Id. s. 10, Electricity (Supply) (Amendment) Act, 1942, s. 6	F	5 yrs P.S. or 2 yrs *S.C. 6m or £50*
of fish in water near dwellinghouse	Larceny Act, 1861, s. 24	M	Imp. or fine *S.C. 12m and/or £100***†
of fixtures	Larceny Act, 1916, s. 8 (1)	F	5 yrs P.S. or 2 yrs *S.C. 12m and/or £100***†
of hares or rabbits (at night)	Larceny Act, 1861, s. 17	M	2 yrs *S.C. 12m and/or £100***†
of ore	Id. s. 39 and Larceny Act, 1916, s. 11	F	Same
of plants in gardens, etc. after previous conviction	Larceny Act, 1916, s. 8 (3)	F	5 yrs P.S. or 2 yrs *S.C. as last*
of mail bags, etc.	Id. s. 12	F	P.S. life or 2 yrs *S.C. as last*
the like	Post Office Act, 1908, s. 50	F	P.S. life or 2 yrs
of postal packet by officer of Post Office if containing money, etc.	Larceny Act, 1916, s. 18 (a)	F	P.S. life or 2 yrs *S.C. 12m and/or £100***†
the like	Post Office Act, 1908, s. 55	F	P.S. life or 2 yrs
of postal packet if not containing money, etc.	Larceny Act, 1916, s. 18 (a)	F	7 yrs P.S. or 2 yrs *S.C. 12m and/or £100***†

Offence	How created	Whether Felony or Misdemeanour	Maximum Sentence [Alternative Verdicts] [See Prelim. Note 6]
the like	Post Office Act, 1908, s. 55	F	7 yrs P.S. or 2 yrs
of title deeds, etc.	Larceny Act, 1916, s. 7	F	5 yrs P.S. or 2 yrs *S.C. as last*
of trees, depending on previous convictions, value or place	Larceny Act, 1916, s. 8 (2)	F	Same
of wills	Id. s. 6	F	P.S. life or 2 yrs *S.C. as last*
LIBEL			
malicious publication	Defamation Act, 1961, s. 11		1 yr and/or £200 *S.C. £50**[21]
known to be false	Id. s. 12		2 yrs and/or £500
publication of blasphemous, seditious, indecent or obscene matter	Id. s. 13 and Constitution of Ireland, 1937, Article 40.6.1°		7 yrs P.S. or 2 yrs and/or £500
seditious libel (see *OFFENCES AGAINST THE STATE, etc.*)			
LAND ACTS			
False statement as to qualification to purchase land, etc.	Land Act, 1965, s. 45 (6)		3 yrs and/or £10,000 *S.C. 12m and/or £200*
MAINTENANCE	Common law	M	Imp. or fine
MALICIOUS DAMAGE – see also *EXPLOSIVES,* LARCENY, MARITIME OFFENCES			
setting fire to place of worship	Malicious Damage Act, 1861, s. 1	F	P.S. life or 2 yrs
setting fire to dwelling with a person therein	Id. s. 2	F	Same
setting fire to buildings with intent to defraud	Id. s. 3	F	Same
setting fire to railway stations, etc.	Id. s. 4	F	Same
setting fire to public buildings, etc.	Id. s. 5	F	Same
setting fire to unspecified buildings	Id. s. 6	F	14 yrs P.S. or 2 yrs

[21] In case of newspaper propriators, s. 10.

setting fire to things in buildings, etc.	Id. s. 7	F	Same
attempting to set fire to buildings or things therein	Id. s. 8	F	Same
setting fire to coalmines	Id. s. 26	F	P.S. life or 2 yrs
attempting above	Id. s. 27	F	14 yrs P.S. or 2 yrs
setting fire to crops, etc.	Id. s. 16	F	Same
setting fire to stacks of corn, etc.	Id. s. 17	F	P.S. life or 2 yrs
attempting either above	Id. s. 18	F	7 yrs P.S. or 2 yrs
setting fire to, etc. ships	Id. s. 42	F	P.S. life or 2 yrs
setting fire, etc. with intent	Id. s. 43	F	Same
attempting either of above	Id. s. 44	F	14 yrs P.S. or 2 yrs
riotously demolishing buildings	Id. s. 11	F	P.S. life or 2 yrs [Riotous damage, s. 12]
riotously damaging buildings	Id. s. 12	M	7 yrs P.S. or 2 yrs
malicious damage by tenant	Id. s. 13	M	P.S. life or 2 yrs
destroying, etc. machines in course of manufacture	Id. s. 15	F	7 yrs P.S. or 2 yrs
damaging hop-binds	Id. s. 19	F	14 yrs P.S. or 2 yrs
damaging trees, etc. in parks	Id. s. 20	F	5 yrs P.S. or 2 yrs *S.C. 12m and/or £100**
damaging trees elsewhere over £5	Id. s. 21	F	Same
damaging trees, after two convictions	Id. s. 22	M	2 yrs *S.C. 12m and/or £100**
damaging plants in gardens etc., (second offence)	Id. s. 23	F	Same
drowning mines, etc.	Id. s. 28	F	7 yrs P.S. or 2 yrs *S.C. 12m and/or £100**
destroying, etc. engines in mines	Id. s. 29	F	Same
destroying valuable security	Larceny Act, 1861, s. 27	F	5 yrs P.S. or 2 yrs *S.C. 12m and/or £100***†
damaging documents of title	Id. s. 28	F	5 yrs P.S. or 2 yrs *S.C. at last*
damaging wills	Id. s. 29	F	P.S. life or 2 yrs *S.C. as last*
damaging records	Id. s. 30	F	5 yrs P.S. or 2 yrs *S.C. as last*

Offence	How created	Whether Felony or Misdemeanour	Maximum Sentence [Alternative Verdicts] [See Prelim. Note 6]
damaging sea and river banks, etc.	Malicious Damage Act, s. 30	F	P.S. life or 2 yrs
damaging piles in river, etc.	Id. s. 31	F	7 yrs P.S. or 2 yrs
damaging bridges, etc.	Id. s. 33	F	P.S. life or 2 yrs
damaging toll bars, etc.	Id. s. 34	M	Imp. and/or fine
damaging railways, etc.	Id. s. 35	F	P.S. life or 2 yrs
damaging telegraphs	Id. s. 37	M	2 yrs *S.C. 3m or £10*
cutting away buoys, etc.	Id. s. 48	F	7 yrs P.S. or 2 yrs
damaging parts of ships in distress	Id. s. 49	F	14 yrs P.S. or 2 yrs
damaging fish ponds	Id. s. 32	M	7 yrs P.S. or 2 yrs
damaging cattle	Id. s. 40	F	14 yrs P.S. or 2 yrs
damaging works of art, etc.	Id. s. 39	M	6m
damaging electric wires, etc.	Electricity Supply Act, 1927, s. 11	F	5 yrs P.S. or 2 yrs
damage to any property in excess of £50	Malicious Damage Act, 1861, s. 51, Criminal Justice Act, 1951, s. 12	M	2 yrs *S.C. 12m and/or £100**
accessory before the fact etc. to felony under the Malicious Damage Act, 1861	Malicious Damage Act, 1861, s. 56		As for principal offender
accessory after the fact to felony	Id.		2 yrs
aiding and abetting misdemeanour	Id.		As for principal offender
threatening in writing to burn or destroy	Id. s. 50	F	10 yrs P.S. or 2 yrs
MANSLAUGHTER	Common law and Offences against the Person Act, 1861, s. 5	F	P.S. life or 2 yrs and/or fine [Cruelty to child when accused over 17, Children Act, 1908, s. 12 (4)]
MARITIME OFFENCES – see also *FISHERIES, PIRACY, SHIPPING*			
discharge of oil in prohibited zone	Oil Pollution of the Sea Act, 1956, ss. 10, 23, as amended by Oil Pollution of the Sea (Amendment) Act, 1965		£5,000 a day + £500 a continuing *S.C. £500 + £50 a day continuing*

discharge of oil into territorial waters	Id. s. 11		Same
breach of equipment regulations	Id. s. 16		Same
breach of regulations for conservation of resources of the sea	Maritime Jurisdiction Act, 1959, s. 7		£10,000 and forfeiture of boat on second conviction
exhibiting false signals to ships	Malicious Damage Act, 1861, s. 47	F	P.S. life or 2 yrs
unlawful dumping at sea	Dumping at Sea Act, 1981, ss. 2, 8		5 yrs and/or fine *S.C. 12m and/or £500***
MARKETS			
carrying on unlicensed livestock mart, etc.	Livestock Marts Act, 1967, ss. 2, 8 (3)		6m and/or £500+£50 a day continuing *S.C. 3m and/or £100+£10 a day continuing*
MARRIAGE			
celebration by degraded clergyman	Marriage Act, 1725, s. 1	F	7 yrs P.S.
MASTER & SERVANT – see *EMPLOYMENT*			
MENACES – see *BLACKMAIL, THREATS*			
MERCHANT SHIPPING ACTS – see *SHIPPING*			
MERCHANDISE MARKS – see *TRADE MARKS*			
MONEY LENDERS			
false statement, etc. by	Moneylenders Act, 1900, s. 4	M	2 yrs and/or £500
MOTOR VEHICLES – see *DANGEROUS DRIVING, FORCIBLE ENTRY*			
MURDER – see also *SUICIDE*			
capital murder *[See Prelim. Note 6]*	Criminal Justice Act, 1964, s. 5 and Offences against the Person Act, 1861, s. 1	F	Death[22] [Murder or Manslaughter, 1964, s. 3 (2)]
ordinary murder *[See Prelim. Note 6]*	Common law and Criminal Justice Act, 1964, s. 5	F	P.S. life[22] [Manslaughter (common law), concealment of birth of child alleged murdered,

[22] Mandatory.

Offence	How created	Whether Felony or Misdemeanour	Maximum Sentence [Alternative Verdicts] [See Prelim. Note 6]
			Offences against the Person Act, 1861, s. 60, infanticide, Infanticide Act, 1949, s. 1]
wounding, etc. or administering poison with intent *[See Prelim. Note 6]*	Offences against the Person Act, 1861, s. 11	F	P.S. life or 2 yrs
attempting above or to drown	Id. s. 14	F	Same
destroying building with intent	Id. s. 12	F	Same
destroying ships with intent	Id. s. 13	F	Same
other attempts *[See Prelim. Note 6]*	Id. s. 15	F	Same
conspiring to *[See Prelim. Note 6]*	Id. s. 4	M	10 yrs P.S. or 2 yrs
threatening in writing to	Id. s. 16	F	same
NORTHERN IRELAND – see also *AIDING & ABETTING, ESCAPE*			
impeding, etc. apprehension of Northern Ireland offender	Criminal Law (Jurisdiction) Act, 1976, s. 2 (4), (6), (8)		10 yrs if primary offence is murder 7 yrs if primary offence punishable by 14 yrs 5 yrs if primary offence punishable by 10 yrs other cases 3 yrs
committing certain offences in Northern Ireland	Id. s. 2 (1)		As if offence committed in the State [Impeding apprehension s. 2 (5)]
NUCLEAR ENERGY			
breach of fissile fuel order	Nuclear Energy (An Bord Fuinnimh Núicléigh) Act, 1971, s. 6		5 yrs and/or £500 *S.C. 3m and/or £100*
NUISANCE – see *PUBLIC NUISANCE*			

OBSCENE PUBLICATIONS – see *LIBEL*			
OBSTRUCTION – see *OFFENCES AGAINST THE STATE*			
of minister of religion	Offences against the Person Act, 1861, s. 36	M	2 yrs
of officer preserving ship	Id. s. 37	M	7 yrs P.S. or 2 yrs
of person saving life	Id. s. 17	F	P.S. life or 2 yrs
of police officer	Id. s. 38	M	2 yrs *S.C. 12m and/or £100**
OCCASIONAL TRADING			
unauthorised occasional trading	Occasional Trading Act, 1979, ss. 3 (1), 9 (1)		6m and/or £5,000 +£250 a day continuing *S.C. 6m and/or £500***
OFFENCES AGAINST THE STATE AND PUBLIC ORDER			
treason[§]	Constitution of Ireland, 1937, Art. 38, Treason Act, 1939, s. 1		Death
encouraging, harbouring, etc.[§]	Treason Act, 1939, s. 2	F	20 yrs P.S. or 2 yrs and/or £500
misprision of treason[§]	Id. s. 3	F	5 yrs P.S. or 2 yrs
sedition	Common law	M	Imp, and/or fine
usurpation of functions of government[§]	Offences Against the State Act, 1939, s. 6 (1) as amended by Criminal Law Act, 1976, s. 2	F	20 yrs
attempting, aiding and abetting, etc. same[§]	Id. s. 6 (2), as so amended	M	Same
obstruction of government[§]	Id. s. 7 (1) as so amended	F	Same
attempting, aiding and abetting, etc. same[§]	Id. s. 7 (2) as so amended	F	Same
obstruction of President[§]	Id. s. 8 (1)	F	7 yrs P.S. or 2 yrs
attempting, aiding and abetting, etc. same[§]	Id. s. 8 (2)	M	2 yrs
interference, etc. with military or police or inciting same	Id. s. 9 (1) (2)	M	2 yrs
attempt at same	Id. s. 9 (3)	M	6m
unauthorised military exercises, etc	Id. s. 15 (1) as amended by Criminal Law Act, 1976, s. 2	M	15 yrs

Offence	How created	Whether Felony or Misdemeanour	Maximum Sentence [Alternative Verdicts] [See Prelim. Note 6]
formation of secret societies in military or police	Id. s. 16 (1)	M	5 yrs P.S. or 2 yrs
administering, etc. unlawful oath	Id. s. 17 (1)	M	2 yrs
membership of unlawful organisation	Id. s. 21 as amended by Criminal Law Act, 1976, s. 2		7 yrs *S.C. 3m and/or £50*
recruiting for unlawful organisation	Criminal Law Act, 1976, s. 3		10 yrs
statement or meeting, etc. interfering with course of justice	Offences Against the State (Amendment) Act, 1972, s. 4 (2)		5 yrs and/or £1,000 *S.C. 12m and/or £200*
obstruction of Garda in relation to person arrested, in certain circumstances, etc.	Criminal Law Act, 1976, s. 7		5 yrs *S.C. 12m and/or £500*
riot	Common law		Imp. and/or fine *S.C.[20] 12m and/or £100**
failure by 12 or more to disperse after proclamation[23]	Riot Act, 1787, s. 1	F	7 yrs P.S. or 2 yrs
unlawfully administering or taking oath[23]	Id. s. 6	F	7 yrs P.S. or 2 yrs
digging grave, gallows, etc. or otherwise intimidating[23]	Id. s. 8	F	Same
publication to excite riot[23]	Id. s. 9	F	Same
seizing or supplying arms to rioters[23]	Id. s. 10	F	Same
rout	Common law	M	Imp. or fine
unlawful assembly	Common law	M	Imp. or fine *S.C. 12m and/or £100**
affray	Common law	M	Imp. and/or fine
tumultuous assembly	Tumultuous Risings Act, 1775, s. 2	M	Imp. and/or fine
tendering oath by violence	Id. s. 21		Same
compelling to leave house, etc.	Tumultuous Risings (Ireland) Act, 1831, s. 2		P.S. life or 2 yrs
sending threatening notices, etc.	Id. s. 3		7 yrs P.S. or 2 yrs
OFFICIAL DOCUMENTS – see also *FORGERY*			
unauthorised publication	Documentary Evidence Act, 1925, s. 6 (1), (2)	F	7 yrs P.S. or 2 yrs
tendering unauthorised document in evidence	Id. s. 6 (3), (4)	M	5 yrs P.S. or 2 yrs

[23] Prosecution to be commenced within one year.

OFFICIAL SECRETS[24] – see also *OFFICIAL DOCUMENTS*			
obtaining, etc. or possession of information in manner prejudicial to the State[25]	Official Secrets Act, 1963, ss. 9, 13		7 yrs P.S. or 2 yrs *S.C. 6m and/or £100*
disclosure of official information[25]	Id. ss. 4, 13		Same
confidential information[25]	Id. ss. 5, 13		Same
unauthorised retention of official documents[25]	Id. ss. 6, 13		Same
possession of or counterfeiting official dies, etc.[25]	Id. ss. 7, 13		Same
PACKAGING – see *SALE OF GOODS*			
PERJURY, etc.			
in judicial proceedings	Common law, and Perjury Act, 1729, s. 1	M	7 yrs P.S. or 2 yrs *S.C. 12m and/or £100***
subordination of perjury	Common law, and Perjury Act, 1729, s. 1	M	Same
administering oath without jurisdiction	Statutory Declarations Act, 1835, s. 13	M	Imp. and/or fine
swearing false affidavit, etc.	Commissioners for Oaths (Diplomatic and Consular) Act, 1931, s. 4	M	As for perjury
false statement at inquiry	Tribunals of Inquiry (Evidence) Act, 1920, s. 1, Tribunals of Inquiry (Evidence) (Amendment) Act, 1979, s. 3		2 yrs and/or £10,000 *S.C. 12m and/or £500***
false statement before solicitors disciplinary committee	Solicitors (Amendment) Act, 1960, s. 29		As for perjury
false statement before European Court	Court of Justice of the European Communities (Perjury) Act, 1975, s. 1		As for perjury
PERSONATION – see *COMPANIES, ELECTIONS*			
PIRACY *[See Prelim. Note 6]*			
jure gentium	Common law and Piracy Act, 1837, s. 3	F	P.S. life or 2 yrs
with violence	Piracy Act, 1837, s. 2	F	Same
PLATE ASSAY – see also *FORGERY*			
counterfeiting, etc. hallmarks	Plate Assay (Ireland) Act, 1807, s. 16, Hallmarking Act, 1981, s. 13		5 yrs imp. and/or £5,000 *S.C. 12m and/or £500*

[24] Proceedings under the Official Secrets Act, 1963, other than remands up to 8 days, may only be taken with consent of the Attorney General.
[25] No bail in District Court, if prejudicial to State.

Offence	How created	Whether Felony or Misdemeanour	Maximum Sentence [Alternative Verdicts] [See Prelim. Note 6]
POISON – see also *ABORTION, MURDER*			
administering so as to endanger life, etc.	Offences against the Person Act, 1861, s. 23	F	10 yrs P.S. or 2 yrs
administering with intent to injure	Id. s. 24	M	5 yrs P.S. or 2 yrs
POLICE – see *ASSAULT*			
POLLUTION – see *MARITIME OFFENCES*			
POST OFFICE – see also *EMBEZZLEMENT, FORGERY, LARCENY, RECEIVING*			
stopping a mail with intent	Post Office Act, 1908, s. 50 (d)	F	P.S. life or 2 yrs
the like	Larceny Act, 1916, s. 12 (4)	F	P.S. life or 2 yrs *S.C. 12m and/or £100**
opening mail-bag sent by vessel	Post Office Act, 1908, s. 51	F	14 yrs P.S. or 2 yrs
fraudulently retaining, etc. mail	Id. s. 53	M	Imp. and/or fine
opening or diverting mail	Id. s. 54	M	6m or £50
opening or delaying mail by officer of Post Office	Id. s. 56	M	Imp. and/or fine
fraudulently issuing money order	Is. s. 58	F	7 yrs P.S. or 2 yrs
sending dangerous or noxious substances, etc.	Id. s. 63 (a)	M	12m *S.C. £10*
sending indecent print	Id. s. 63 (b)	M	Same
soliciting indictable Post Office offence	Id. s. 69	M	2 yrs
disclosing or intercepting telegraph message	Telegraph Act, 1868, s. 20	M	12m
POUND BREACH	Common law	M	Imp. and/or fine
PRICES – see *SALE OF GOODS*			
PRISONS – see also *ESCAPE*			
conveying, etc. things into prison	Criminal Law Act, 1976, s. 6 (2)		5 yrs *S.C. 12m and/or £500*
possession of photographs, etc.	Id. s. 10		Same
PROSTITUTION – see also *CHILDREN*			
keeping a brothel	Criminal Law (Amendment) Act, 1935, s. 13	M	6m and/or £100 *S.C. 12m and/or £500*

			Subsequent conviction 5 yrs P.S. or 2 yrs and/or £250
procuration of female	Criminal Law Amendment Act, 1885, s. 2, as amended, Criminal Law Amendment Act, 1935, s. 7	M	2 yrs
procuring defilement of female	Id. s. 3, as amended 1935, s. 8	M	Same
detention in brothel, etc.	Criminal Law Amendment Act, 1885, s. 8	M	Same
living on earnings of prostitution	Inebriates Act, 1898, s. 1, Criminal Law Amendment Act, 1912, s. 7	—	2 yrs *S.C. 6m*
PUBLIC INQUIRIES			
failure to attend as witness, etc.	Tribunals of Inquiry (Evidence) Act, 1921, s. 1, Tribunals in Inquiry (Evidence) (Amendment) Act, 1979, s. 3	—	2 yrs and/or £10,000 *S.C. 12m and/or £500***
PUBLIC MISCHIEF			
generally	Common law	M	Imp. and/or fine *S.C. 12m and/or £100***
making false reports	Criminal Law Act, 1976, s. 12	—	5 yrs *S.C. 12m and/or £500***
PUBLIC NUISANCE	Common law	M	Imp. and/or fine
PYRAMID SELLING			
promotion of or participation	Pyramid Selling Act, 1980, s. 6	—	2 yrs and/or £10,000 *S.C. 6m and/or £500***
RAILWAYS			
endangering safety of passengers, etc.	Offences against the Person Act, 1861, ss. 32, 33	F	P.S. life or 2 yrs
endangering safety generally	Id. s. 34	M	2 yrs
maliciously obstructing	Malicious Damage Act, 1861, s. 35	F	P.S. life or 2 yrs
unlawfully obstructing	Id. s. 36	M	2 yrs
RAPE – see *SEXUAL OFFENCES*			
RECEIVING			
property obtained feloniously	Larceny Act, 1916, s. 33 (1) (a)	F	14 yrs P.S. or 2 yrs *S.C. 12m and/or £100***

Offence	How created	Whether Felony or Misdemeanour	Maximum Sentence [Alternative Verdicts] [See Prelim. Note 6]
property obtained by misdemeanour	Id. s. 33 (1) (b)	M	7 yrs P.S. or 2 yrs *S.C. 12m and/or £100***
property stolen etc. abroad	Id. s. 33 (4)	F & M[26]	Same
postal packet stolen, etc.	Id. s. 33 (2)	F	As for primary offence
the like	Post Office Act, 1908, s. 55	F	Same
REGISTRATION OF TITLE			
fraud in relation to Register	Register of Title Act, 1964, s. 119	M	2 yrs and/or £500
RESCUE – *ESCAPE*			
RESTRICTIVE PRACTICES			
breach of restrictive practices order	Restrictive Practices Act, 1972, ss. 20, 23		2 yrs and/or £5,000 +£500 a day continuing *S.C. 6m and/or £200 +£10 a day continuing*
intimidation of witnesses, etc. at restrictive practices inquiry	Id. ss. 21, 23		Same
RIOT – see *OFFENCES AGAINST THE STATE*			
ROAD TRAFFIC OFFENCES – see *DANGEROUS DRIVING, VEHICLES*			
ROBBERY	Larceny Act, 1916, s. 23, Criminal Law (Jurisdiction) Act, 1976, ss. 5, 20 (8)	F	Life *S.C. 12m imp. and or £100***† [Assault with intent to rob, 1916, s. 4 (5)]
SALE OF GOODS, etc. – see also *CASUAL TRADING, OCCASIONAL TRADING*			
breach of duty imposed on packers and importers	Packaged Goods (Quantity Control) Act, 1980, ss. 17 (1), 19		£1,000, second offence £10,000 *S.C. £500***

possession or sale of inadequate package	Id. ss. 17 (5), 19		Same
unlawful promotion of trading stamps scheme	Trading Stamps Act, 1980, s. 2		£5,000 *S.C. £500***
statements, etc. restrictive of buyer's rights	Sale of Goods and Supply of Services Act, 1980, s. 11[26]		2 yrs and/or £10,000 *S.C. 6m and/or £500*
the like as to hire-purchase	Id. s. 30		Same
the like as to supply of services	Id. s. 41		Same
offences as to guarantees	Id. s. 16		Same
offences as to unsolicited goods	Id. s. 47		Same
offences as to directory entries	Id. s. 48		Same
as to invoices	Id. s. 49		Same
failure to state particulars of goods or services	Id. s. 51		Same
failure to give notice of use of standard forms	Id. s. 52		Same
non-compliance with conditions as to size of type in contracts, etc.	Id. s. 53		Same
breach of prices order	Prices Act, 1958, s. 22, as amended by Prices (Amendment) Act, 1972, s. 8		2 yrs and/or £500+£50 a day continuing *S.C. 6m and/or £100 +£10 a day continuing up to £100*
obstruction of authorised officer	Id. s. 24, as so amended		Same
unlawful disclosure of information	Id. s. 25, as so amended		Same
false statement for purposes of trade	Consumer Information Act, 1978,[27], s. 6 (2)		2 yrs and/or £10,000 *S.C. 6m and/or £500*
false or misleading statement as to price, etc.	Id. s. 7		Same
misleading advertisement	Id. s. 8		Same
non-compliance with advertisement order	Id. s. 11		Same
failure to supply name, etc. of advertiser	Id. s. 13		Same
failure to provide proper weighing facilities for food	Id. s. 14		Same
obstructing, etc. reading of retail prices list	Id. s. 15		Same
obstructing authorised officer	Id. s. 16		Same
SAVING BANKS			
frauds by officers	Trustee Savings Bank Act, 1863, s. 9	M	Imp. and/or fine

[26] Depending on quality of primary offence.

[27] Penalties imposed by section 17.

Offence	How created	Whether Felony or Misdemeanour	Maximum Sentence [Alternative Verdicts] [See Prelim. Note 6]
SEAMEN			
forcing on shore	Merchant Shipping Act, 1906, s. 43	M	Imp. and/or fine
leaving on shore	Id. s. 36	M	Same
illegal discharge	Id. s. 30	M	Same
SECRET SOCIETIES – see *OFFENCES AGAINST THE STATE, etc.*			
SEDITION – see *LIBEL, OFFENCES AGAINST THE STATE, etc.*			
SEXUAL OFFENCES – see also *ABDUCTION, ABORTION, PROSTITUTION*			
rape	Common law and Offences against the Person Act, 1861, s 48	F	P.S. life or 2 yrs [Carnal knowledge or attempted carnal knowledge of girl under 15, or between 15 and 17. Procuring carnal knowledge, or Indecent assault, Criminal Law (Amendment) Act, 1935, s. 3. Incest or attempt at same. Punishment of Incest Act, 1908 s. 4 (3) as amended by Criminal Law (Amendment) Act, 1935, s. 12]
indecent assault on a male	Offences against the Person Act, 1861, s. 62	M	10 yrs P.S. or 2 yrs
indecent assault on a female	Common law and Criminal Law (Rape) Act, 1981, ss. 10, 12	M	10 yrs *S.C. 12m and/or £500***

buggery	Common law and Offences against the Person Act, 1861, s. 61	F	P.S. life or 2 yrs
attempting or assault with intent to commit	Id. s. 62	M	10 yrs P.S. or 2 yrs
unlawful carnal knowledge of girl under 15	Criminal Law (Amendment) Act, 1935, s. 1 (1)	F	P.S. life or 2 yrs [Attempted carnal knowledge of girl under 15, carnal knowledge or attempted carnal knowledge of girl under 17; procuring carnal knowledge; indecent assault, Criminal Law (Amendment) Act, 1935, s. 3]
attempting same	Id. s. 1 (2)	M	5 yrs P.S. or 2 yrs Second conviction 10 yrs P.S. or 2 yrs *S.C. 12m and/or £100**
unlawful carnal knowledge of girl between 15 and 17	Id. s. 2 (1)	M	5 yrs P.S. or 2 yrs Second conviction 10 yrs P.S. or 2 yrs
attempting same[28]	Id. s. 2 (2)	M	2 yrs Second conviction 5 yrs P.S. or 2 yrs *S.C. 12m and/or £100**
unlawful carnal knowledge of idiot, etc.[29]	Id. s. 4	M	2 yrs *S.C. 12m and/or £100*
unlawful carnal knowledge by person in charge in mental institution, etc.	Mental Treatment Act, 1945, s. 254	M	5 yrs P.S. or 2 yrs
encouraging seduction of girl under 17	Children Act, 1908, s. 17, as amended by Criminal Law Amendment Act, 1935, s. 11	M	2 yrs
permitting, etc. girl under 15 to be on premises for immoral purposes	Criminal Law Amendment Act, 1885, s. 6 (1) as amended by Criminal Law Amendment Act, 1935, s. 9	F	P.S. life or 2 yrs

[28] No prosecution after 12 months, Criminal Law (Amendment) Act, 1935, s. 2 (3).
[29] No prosecution after 12 months, Criminal Law (Amendment) Act, 1935, s. 2 (3), Id. s. 4 (2).

Offence	How created	Whether Felony or Misdemeanour	Maximum Sentence [Alternative Verdicts] [See Prelim. Note 6]
permitting, etc. between 15 and 17	Id. s. 6 (2), as so amended	M	2 yrs
gross indecency between males	Criminal Law Amendment Act, 1885, s. 11	M	2 yrs
incest by male person[30]	Punishment of Incest Act, 1908, s. 1	M	7 yrs P.S. or 2 yrs [Carnal knowledge or attempted carnal knowledge of girl under 15, or between 15 and 17, Punishment of Incest Act, 1908, s. 4 (3) as amended by Criminal Law (Amendment) Act, 1935, s. 12, or indecent assault]
attempt at above[30]	Id. s. 1 (3)	M	2 yrs [Indecent assault]
incest with girl under 15[30]	Id. (as amended, Criminal Law Amendment Act, 1935, s. 12)	M	P.S. life or 2 yrs
incest by female over 17[30]	Id. s. 2 (as so amended)	M	7 yrs P.S. or 2 yrs
indecent exposure	Common law	M	Imp. and/or fine
unauthorised publication, etc. of identity of complainant or person accused of rape offence	Criminal Law (Rape) Act, 1981, ss. 7 (6), 11, 12		3 yrs and/or £10,000 *S.C. 12m and/or £500*
SHIPPING – see also *FORGERY, MALICIOUS DAMAGE, MARITIME OFFENCES, SEAMEN*			
unlawful seizure of ship, etc.	Criminal Law (Jurisdiction) Act, 1976, s. 10, Criminal Law Act, 1976, s. 11	F	15 yrs
dangerously unfit ships	Merchant Shipping Act, 1981, s. 4		£50,000 *S.C. £500***
breach of deck-cargo regulations	Merchant Shipping (Load lines) Act, 1968, s. 25		£1,000 *S.C. £100*
breach of load-line rules	Id. s. 4		£200 *S.C. 100*
failure, etc. to mark ship	Id. s. 6		Same

[30] No prosecution without consent of D.P.P.

proceeding to sea without load-line certificate	Id. s. 10		Same
submersion of load-line	Id. s. 5 (2)		£400 and up to £400 per inch of excess *S.C. £100*
taking over-loaded ship to sea	Id. s. 5 (4)		Fine *S.C. £100*
sending ship to sea without required personnel	Merchant Shipping (Certification of Seamen) Act, 1979, s. 5 (1)		£5,000 *S.C. £500***
contravention of radio rules	Merchant Shipping (Safety Convention) Act, 1952, s. 15 (6)		£500 *S.C. £100*
failure to assist vessel in distress	Id. s. 37 (5)		Imp. or fine
failure to observe grain cargo precautions	Id. s. 39 (4) as amended Merchant Shipping Act, 1981, s. 2 (5)		£300 *S.C. £100*
concealment of national character of ship	Mercantile Marine Act, 1955, ss. 14, 98	M	2 yrs and/or £500 *S.C. 12m and/or £100*
false declaration as to ownership of ship	Id. ss. 89, 98	M	Same
use of improper certificate of registry	Id. ss. 35, 98	M	Same
false statement as to use, etc. of investment grant	Shipping Investment Grants Act, 1969, s. 8 (1)		2 yrs and/or £1,000 *S.C. 3m and/or £100*
fraudulent application of grant	Id. s. 9		2 yrs and/or £1,000 *S.C. 3m and/or £100*
non-compliance with conditions of investment grant	Id. s. 8 (4)		£1,000 or three times amount repayable *S.C. £100*
SLAVE TRADING	Slave Trade Act, 1824, s. 9	F	P.S. life or 2 yrs
SMELTING			
breach of condition of smelting licence	Smelting Act, 1968, s. 6		£1,000+£500 a day continuing *S.C. £100*
making false statement to obtain licence	Id. s. 7		£1,000 *S.C. £100*
unlawful smelting	Id. s. 2 (2)		£5,000+£500 a day continuing *S.C. £100*
SMUGGLING – see *CUSTOMS*			
SOCIAL WELFARE			
irregularity as to social insurance stamps and cards[31]	Social Welfare (Consolidation) Act, 1981, s. 115 (1) (a)		2 yrs and/or £2,000 *S.C. 1 yr and/or £500*

Offence	How created	Whether Felony or Misdemeanour	Maximum Sentence [Alternative Verdicts] [See Prelim. Note 6]
as to supplementary unemployment cards, etc.[31]	Id. s. 266 (1)		Same
false statement to obtain insurance benefits, etc.[31]	Id. s. 115 (1) (b)		Same
false statement to obtain old age pension[31]	Id. s. 169		Same
false statement to obtain widow's or orphan's pension[32]	Id. s. 188		Same
false statement to obtain children's allowance[31]	Id. s. 231		Same
failure by employer to pay employment contributions, etc.	Id. s. 115 (2)		2 yrs and/or £2,000 or twice amount unpaid *S.C. 1 yr and/or £500*
intermittent employment contribution[31]	Id. s. 266 (2)		Same
breach of regulations[31]	Id. ss. 115 (3), 266 (3)		2 yrs and/or £2,000+ £2,000 a day continuing *S.C. 1 yr and/or £500*
failure by personal representative to furnish information	Id. ss. 174		2 yrs and/or £2,000 *S.C. 1 yr and/or £500*
offences relating to school meals and fuel schemes	Id. s. 294		Same
SOLICITORS – see also *PERJURY*			
acting as solicitor when unqualified	Solicitors Act, 1954, s. 55		2 yrs and/or £200 *S.C. 6m and/or £50*
SPRING GUNS			
setting	Offences against the Person Act, 1861, s. 31	M	5 yrs P.S. or 2 yrs
SPYING – see *OFFICIAL SECRETS*			
SUICIDE			
attempt to commit	Common law and Hard Labour Act, 1822		2 yrs
agreement to commit	Common law		P.S. life

[31] No prosecution without consent of Minister.
[32] Time limit for prosecution 2 years or 3 months from certificate of Minister.

TITLE DEEDS – see also *FORGERY, LARCENY, MALICIOUS DAMAGE*			
concealment etc.[33]	Law of Property Amendment Act, 1859, s. 24	M	2 yrs
THREATS – see *BLACKMAIL, MALICIOUS DAMAGE, MURDER*			
TOWN PLANNING			
development without permission	Local Government (Planning and Development) Act, 1963, s. 24 (3) as amended Local Government (Planning and Development) Act, 1982, s. 8 (3)		2 yrs and/or £10,000 *S.C. 6m and/or £800***
non-compliance, etc. with warning notice	Local Government (Planning and Development) Act, 1976, s. 26 (4), as so amended		Same
continuation of either of above offences after conviction	Local Government (Planning and Development) Act, 1982, s. 8 (4)		2 yrs and/or £1,000 per day *S.C. 6m and/or £150 a day up to £800***
TRADE MARKS & DESIGNS – see also *FORGERY*			
making, etc. false entry in register of designs	Industrial and Commercial Property (Protection) Act, 1927, s. 150	M	2 yrs and/or fine
contravention of Merchandise Marks Order	Merchandise Marks Act, 1970, s. 5		2 yrs and/or £2,000 *S.C. 6m and/or £100*
TRADING STAMPS – see *SALE OF GOODS*			
TRAVEL AGENTS ETC.			
carrying on business without a licence	Transport (Tour Operators and Travel Agents) Act, 1982, s. 20 (1)		5 yrs and/or £100,000 *S.C. 12m and/or £500***
obstruction of authorised person	Id. s. 20 (2)		2 yrs and/or £10,000 *S.C. 12m and/or £500***
making false statement to obtain licence	Id. s. 20 (3)		2 yrs and/or £5,000 *S.C. 12m and/or £500***
UNLAWFUL ASSEMBLY – see *OFFENCES AGAINST THE STATE, etc.*			

Offence	How created	Whether Felony or Misdemeanour	Maximum Sentence [Alternative Verdicts] [See Prelim. Note 6]
UNLAWFUL OATHS – see *OFFENCES AGAINST THE STATE, etc., PERJURY*			
VEHICLES			
unlawful seizure	Criminal Law (Jurisdiction) Act, 1976, s. 10	F	15 yrs
VOCATIONAL EDUCATION – see *FORGERY*			
WATER			
pollution of rivers	Local Government (Water Pollution) Act, 1977, s. 3 (2)		2 yrs and/or £5,000+ £500 a day continuing *S.C. 6m and/or £250+ £100 a day continuing*
discharge of effluents without licence	Id. s. 4 (8)		Same
WHITE BOYS ACTS – *OFFENCES AGAINST THE STATE, etc.*			
WILDLIFE – see also *MARITIME OFFENCES*			
cutting, etc. specially protected flora	Wild Life Act, 1976,[34]		*£500 S.C. £250*
hunting, etc. specially protected wild birds	Id. s. 22 (4)		Same
hunting, etc. the like, wild animals	Id. s. 23 (5)		Same
entering on land, etc, with firearms to hunt specially protected wild birds or animals	Id. s. 44 (1)		Same
unauthorised dealing in specially protected fauna or bodies or birds' eggs	Id. s. 45		Same
unauthorised transport of same	Id. s. 51		Same
failure to re-export fauna or flora illegally imported	Id. s. 52		Same
unlawful export of same	Id. s. 53		Same
non-compliance with regulations as to access	Id. s. 59 (11)		Same
non-compliance with statutory regulations	Id. s. 69 (2)		Same

[34] Penalties prescribed by s. 74, depending on circumstances and species.

any other offence on land the subject matter of an establishment order[35]	Id. s. 74 (2)		Same
hunting deer on enclosed ground after previous conviction	Larceny Act, 1861, s. 13	F	2 yrs *S.C. 12m and/or £100***
hunting deer in open place after previous conviction	Id. s. 12	F	Same
killing hares, etc. in feeding place	Id. s. 17	M	Imp. and/or fine *S.C. 12m and/or £100***†
taking, etc. fish in water near dwelling	Id. s. 24	M	Same
dredging etc. for oysters	Id. s. 26	M	3m *S.C. 12m and/or £100***
WIRELESS TELEGRAPHY –see *BROADCASTING*			
WITNESSES – see also *PERJURY*			
interfering with	Common law	M	Imp. and/or fine
interfering with, at public inquiry	Witness (Public Inquiries) Act, 1892, s. 1	M	3m or £100

[35] Depending on species.

General Index